Give Your CPA Exam Score a Boost
with these Essential Study Tools

Cram Course

Boost your score by 8-10 points!

- Get a final review with this condensed CPA Exam Review supplement – the perfect complement to your full review course

- Reinforce your understanding of the most heavily tested topics on the CPA Exam

- Take the Cram Course leading up to Exam Day to refresh your mind on important topics

Audio Lectures

Maximize every minute leading up to the exam!

- Easy MP3 download – ideal for Apple or Android devices

- Turn any moment into a study opportunity! Listen to lectures on your commute, at the gym, or even as you nod off to sleep

- Immerse yourself in the most important CPA Exam topics

CPA Exam Flashcards

Make studying portable, accessible, and fun!

- Harness overarching CPA Exam concepts

- Create important connections to actual CPA Exam usage and application

- Make studying more exciting by involving family & friends – pull out your flashcards for a quick & interactive study method.

Share Your CPA Story

Would you like to inspire other CPA Candidates to reach their goals like you are? If so, we invite you to create a video to share your story—your successes, your painpoints, and lessons learned.

Email your video to CustomerExperience@rogercpareview.com, and you could be featured on our social channels.

As always, connect with us @RogerCPAreview

REG

Regulation

Written By:

Roger Philipp, CPA, CGMA

Roger CPA Review
2261 Market St. #333
San Francisco, California 94114
www.RogerCPAreview.com
(877) 764-4272
(415) 346-4272

Permissions

The following items are utilized in this volume, and are copyright property of the American Institute of Certified Public Accountants, Inc. (AICPA), all rights reserved:

- Uniform CPA Examination and Questions and Unofficial Answers, Copyright © 1991, 1992, 1993, 1994, 1995, 1996, 1997, 1998, 1999, 2000, 2001, 2002, 2003, 2004, 2005, 2006, 2007, 2008, 2009, 2010, 2011, 2012, 2013, 2014, 2015, 2016 and 2017
- Audit and Accounting Guides, Auditing Procedure Studies, Risk Alerts, Statements of Position, and code of Professional Conduct
- Statements on Auditing Standards, Statements on Standards for Consulting Services, Statements on Responsibilities in Personal Financial Planning Practice, Statements on Standards for Accounting and Review Services, Statements on Quality Control Standards, Statements on Standards for Attestation Engagements, and Statements on Responsibilities in Tax Practice
- Accounting Research Bulletins, APB Opinions, Audit and Accounting Guides, Auditing Procedure Studies, Risk Alerts, Statements of Position, and Code of Professional Conduct
- Uniform CPA Examination Blueprints
- Independent Standard Board (ISB) Standards

Portions of various FASB and GASB documents, copyright property of the Financial Accounting Foundation, 401 Merritt 7, PO Box 5116, Norwalk, CT 06856-5116, are utilized with permission. Complete copies of these documents are available from the Financial Accounting Foundation. These selections include the following:

Financial Accounting Standards Board (FASB)
- *The FASB Accounting Standards Codification* ™ and Statements of Financial Accounting Concepts
- FASB Statements, Interpretations, Technical Bulletins, and Statements of Financial Accounting Concepts

Governmental Accounting Standards Board (GASB)
- GASB Codification of Governmental Accounting and Financial Reporting Standards, GASB Statements, GASB Concepts Statements, and GASB Interpretations
- GASB Statements, Interpretations, and Technical Bulletins

The following items are utilized in this volume, and are copyright property of the International Financial Reporting Standards (IFRS) Foundation and the International Accounting Standards Board (IASB), all rights reserved:
- IASB International Reporting Standards (IFRS), International Accounting Standards (IAS) and Interpretations

Acknowledgement

This book includes contributions by members of the Roger CPA Review Editorial Team.

ABOUT THE AUTHOR

Roger S. Philipp, CPA, CGMA
CEO, Founder, and Instructor, Roger CPA Review

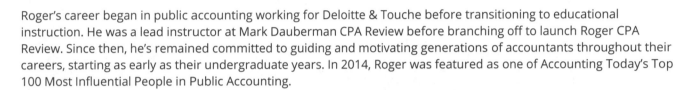

Roger Philipp, CPA, CGMA is one of the most celebrated motivators and instructors in the accounting profession. Known as the dynamic and engaging instructor that makes learning accounting concepts enjoyable, Roger has been helping aspiring accountants across the globe reach career success for almost 30 years.

Roger launched the company in 2001 with the goal to create a CPA review course that would alter the landscape of accounting education. His unique approach to teaching has fueled the company's growth and resulted in the signature teaching methodology, The Roger Method™. Using this approach, Roger breaks down and simplifies complex topics, with support from ingenious memory aids and mnemonic devices to help students retain information. Faculty across the country have been inspired to adopt aspects of The Roger Method™ in their classrooms, which has helped increase students' knowledge of and interest in the CPA designation.

Roger's career began in public accounting working for Deloitte & Touche before transitioning to educational instruction. He was a lead instructor at Mark Dauberman CPA Review before branching off to launch Roger CPA Review. Since then, he's remained committed to guiding and motivating generations of accountants throughout their careers, starting as early as their undergraduate years. In 2014, Roger was featured as one of Accounting Today's Top 100 Most Influential People in Public Accounting.

Roger received a B.A. in accounting from California State University-Northridge. Today, he is a member of the AICPA, CalCPA, and is on the Board of Directors for the American Professional Accounting Certification Providers Association (APACPA). He resides in San Francisco with his wife and co-founder of the company, Louisa, and their three children. He enjoys traveling with his family and the challenges that come with being an entrepreneur.

ABOUT THE EDITOR

Mark E. Dauberman, CPA, EMBA
Senior Editor, Roger CPA Review

Mark Dauberman, CPA, EMBA is known as an expert in helping students take technical knowledge from an academic understanding to a practical understanding. This skillset has proven invaluable to his role at Roger CPA Review in which he ensures educational materials are current and effective with a high level of academic excellence.

Mark has over 50 years of experience in the accounting profession, with a particularly strong background in accounting education, having taught at numerous universities including UCLA, Loyola Marymount University, and California State University-Northridge. In 1975 he launched Mark Dauberman CPA Review, which at one point held the position of the largest CPA Exam preparation course in Southern California.

Throughout his career, Mark has spent several years in both public and private accounting, including serving as a partner and director of the audit practice at NSBN. He has taught continuing professional education (CPE) courses for the AICPA and the CalCPA Education Foundation while also providing staff training for CPA firms and private industry employers. He has furthermore authored several publications, including CPE Course materials, and CCH's "Knowledge Based Preparation, Compilation, and Review Engagements."

Mark earned his Executive MBA in management from Claremont Graduate University. He currently lives in Upland, CA and enjoys an active life of ziplining, skydiving, traveling, and time with his children, grandchildren and great grandchildren.

REGULATION

Table of Contents

Introduction
Table of Contents

INTRODUCTION

Section - Introduction

Corresponding Lectures

Watch the following course lectures with this section:

Lecture 0.01 – Course Introduction
Lecture 0.02 – REG Introduction

Welcome to your Roger CPA Review Course!

Greetings Student,

As you begin your journey with Roger CPA Review, you will quickly learn why our students experience an 88% pass rate. Your motivating and engaging instructor, Roger Philipp, CPA, CGMA, focuses you on the information you need to know to pass the CPA Exam. Our course is structured for a variety of student types. Each topic is broken down from the beginning and taught as if the student has little to no prior knowledge of the particular topic at hand.   Whether you are a first-time review student who has never attempted an exam part, or a seasoned professional returning to the exam after an earlier attempt, you will be prepared. Using the proven *Roger Method*™, you will learn and retain the necessary information rather than simply memorizing terms. Furthermore, all of your course materials and online study tools are part of a fully integrated system to help you reach your goal with as little pain as possible.

Ultimately, you control your destiny. As Roger always says, "The CPA Exam is not an IQ test. It is a test of discipline. If you study, you will pass!" With 300-400 hours of minimum preparation time recommended by the AICPA, the ability to manage your studies is essential. For this reason, your course includes Study Planners and adaptive course diagnostic tools to help you keep your eye on the ball throughout the process. To get the most out of your course, please **read through this Introduction** to understand more about the exam, course content, and study strategies. This book serves as a guide to course lectures; everything covered in the lectures is covered in the book. Within you will find our recommended approach to using your course and its support features, including these following overarching key steps of the *Roger Method*™:

- **Plan** your studies
- **Learn** with your course lectures and textbooks
- **Practice** your skills and understanding
- **Review** for exam day

This course is designed to prepare you to PASS the CPA Exam. The lectures and materials are comprehensive and focus on the most frequently tested topics, saving you time and effort by streamlining your study process. You will learn the topics tested on the exam without wasting time delving into topics not historically emphasized on the exam. All exam question types are taken apart piece-by-piece and presented from scratch to demonstrate the logical progression. Task-Based Simulations (TBSs, including Document Review Simulations or DRSs) and multiple choice questions are also covered during the lecture and reinforced with the Interactive Practice Questions (IPQ) software provided within your course.

Best,

Roger CPA Review Team

FOLLOW ROGER CPA REVIEW ON TWITTER **FOR CPA EXAM TIPS AND TRICKS** AT **@ROGERCPAREVIEW** AND SUBSCRIBE TO OUR BLOG TO GET THE MOST UP-TO-DATE EXAM INFO AS WELL AS PLENTY OF ADVICE ON CAREERS, EDUCATION AND THE CPA EXAM AT **ROGERCPAREVIEW.COM/BLOG**.

USING THE COURSE
A step-by-step guide to successfully studying with your Roger CPA Review course

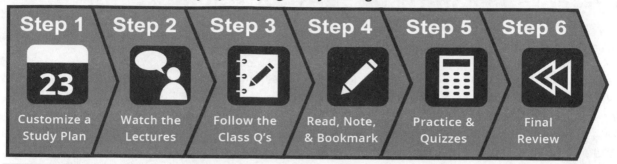

I. PLAN

Step 1.   Start with a plan and stick to it! In your student account, choose between the 3, 6, 9, or 12-month "Study Planner," whichever best suits your projected timeline for exam completion. Then, customize your planner to help build a personalized agenda that meets your individual study needs.

II. LEARN

Courses are broken into sections and topics. Work sequentially through the course and start with the first section. Cover all topics within the first section before moving on to the second section.

Step 2:   Watch one lecture at a time in full, without frequent stops, and simultaneously follow along in your course textbook.

Step 3:   As you proceed through all topics in a section, also watch the *Class Question* lectures and follow along with the Class Questions covered at the end of each section of your course textbook. Make sure to read the solution descriptions in order to understand why each answer option is correct or incorrect.

Step 4:   After watching the lectures for the section, go back to your course textbook and thoroughly read all corresponding pages, making notes as needed. Helpful Note-taking and Video Bookmark functions are available in your course online. You can also follow along, highlight, and take notes in the physical textbooks if you prefer.

III. PRACTICE

Step 5:   Use your Interactive Practice Questions (IPQ) software to reinforce and practice applying the concepts in each section of your course. As you complete every 2-3 sections in your textbooks and lectures, log into the IPQ to quiz yourself on what you've learned. Carefully work through each question, and read answer explanations to understand why you've answered each question correctly or incorrectly. Make sure to flag difficult questions for later review. Keep in mind that repeated exposure to the same questions will help you fully understand the concepts taught.

IV. REVIEW

Step 6:   Revisit any lectures and rework any questions that you have bookmarked or noted for final review. This is also a great time to take a Roger CPA Review Cram Course, which will focus you only on the most heavily tested topics.

Step 7:   To prepare for exam day, take full-length practice exams using the CPA Exam Simulator tool in your IPQ. This will help you hone your test taking strategy, time management and self-discipline under exam-like conditions, while continuing to expose you to the material.

Need help as you study? *Not sure why a question solution is either correct or incorrect, even after double checking in your course textbook and watching the lecture video? Visit the Homework Help Center in your student account for expert support.*

Application, Scheduling, & Taking the Exam

** All information regarding AICPA, NASBA and Prometric rules and regulations in this introduction are up to date as of September 2017. Please see aicpa.org and nasba.org for the most current information.

To ensure that the Uniform CPA Examination keeps pace with the evolution of the accounting and business worlds, the examination is a computer-based test (CBT). The computerized exam:

- Enables testing of higher-level cognitive skills.
- Permits integration of real-world entry-level requirements.
- Provides flexibility and convenience to candidates.
- Offers greater consistency in evaluation.
- Helps save time in administration, grading, and reporting.
- Provides added exam security.

The latest version of the CPA Exam was launched on April 1, 2017.

A tutorial that reviews the examination's format and navigation functions is available at aicpa.org. Choose the "Become a CPA" tab and then pick "CPA Exam" from the options in the list. From there, candidates can find the tutorial and sample tests. All exam candidates are encouraged to review this prior to sitting. The tutorial is intended to familiarize candidates with the functionality and types of questions and responses used in the examination format. The tutorial does not focus on examination content and is not intended as a replacement for study materials.

EXAM APPLICATION

State boards strongly urge candidates to apply online as the processing time is reduced. The applications for the CPA Exam are available online, and the link for the individual states can be found on our website at RogerCPAreview.com. Qualified candidates who have met all of the educational requirements may apply at any time. See individual state boards or NASBA.org for their specific application process. It is the candidate's responsibility to understand their jurisdiction's requirements to sit for the CPA exam and applicants are encouraged to familiarize themselves with licensure requirements prior to applying for the CPA exam.

Depending on the jurisdiction, candidates will apply directly through either their state board of accountancy or CPAES (CPA Examination Services, a division of NASBA). Some states have specific rules regarding coursework, applications and transcripts so candidates should contact their board if they are unsure on or unclear about any requirements. If candidates do not follow instructions and forget to submit required information with their application (fingerprint cards, photographs, etc.), the candidate will be rejected to sit in their state, forfeit application fee(s) and must re-apply.

Candidates in the following states must apply through **NASBA's CPA Examination Services** and may call ***800-CPA-EXAM*** for further information on application requirements and procedures:

Alaska, Colorado, Connecticut, Delaware, Florida, Georgia, Hawaii, Indiana, Iowa, Kansas, Louisiana, Maine, Massachusetts, Michigan, Minnesota, Missouri, Montana, Nebraska, New Hampshire, New Jersey, New Mexico, New York, Ohio, Pennsylvania, Puerto Rico, Rhode Island, South Carolina, Tennessee, Utah, Vermont, Washington, or Wisconsin.

Candidates in the following states must apply with their **Board of Accountancy**: See a full list of boards of accountancy and contact information at the end of this Introduction.

Alabama, Arizona, Arkansas, California, District of Columbia, Guam, Idaho, Illinois, Kentucky, Maryland, Mississippi, Nevada, North Carolina, North Dakota, Oklahoma, Oregon, South Dakota, Texas, U.S. Virgin Islands, Virginia, West Virginia, or Wyoming.

Application Steps

STATE BOARD OF ACCOUNTANCY

1. Meet requirements and submit educational documents to Board
2. Create client account and obtain password from Board
3. Complete application using client account (print Application Remittance Form)
4. Submit signed Application Remittance Form and fee
5. Receive Board approval and select exam section(s)

NASBA

6. Receive Payment Coupon from NASBA
   - If you do not receive the Payment Coupon within 10 business days after section selection, visit NASBA's Web site at *nasba.org* to pay online.
7. Pay NASBA Exam Section Fee(s)
   - NASBA's Online Credit Card Payment Form: Answer only the required fields when paying online. In accordance with the Board's Privacy Policy, NASBA does not collect or require exam applicants to fill in the Mother's Maiden Name field on NASBA's form. Please enter the word UNKNOWN in the Mother's Maiden Name field. This will allow you to continue processing your online payment. For additional payment information, telephone 1-866-696-2722.
8. Receive Notice to Schedule (NTS) from NASBA
   - If you do not receive the NTS within 10 business days after you pay the section fee(s), notify the Board or NASBA. Your NTS is valid in most states for 6 months, in others it can be good for 3, 6, 9, or 12 months.

PROMETRIC

9. Schedule with Prometric
10. Take CPA Exam at a Prometric Testing Center
    - You MUST bring your NTS with you to the testing center. You will be denied entry to the CPA Exam if you do not present the NTS.

BOARD

11. Receive Score Report from Board

Additional Information

For additional information on how to get answers to common questions, consult this table.

For questions about:	Contact:
<ul><li>Eligibility to take the examination</li><li>Special testing accommodations</li><li>Completing application forms</li><li>Name and/or address changes</li><li>Examination scores</li><li>Your Board of Accountancy's fees</li></ul>	Write, call or send an e-mail to the appropriate Board of Accountancy. A complete list of boards of accountancy may be found at the end of this Introduction.
<ul><li>Receiving your Notice to Schedule (NTS)</li><li>Replacing a lost NTS</li><li>Payments to NASBA</li><li>General comments about the test center where you took your examination</li></ul>	Call NASBA at 1-800-CPA-EXAM (1-800-272-3926) or send an e-mail to cbtcpa@nasba.org
For questions about:	**Contact:**
<ul><li>Scheduling, rescheduling or canceling your examination appointment</li><li>Directions to your test center</li></ul>	All information and instant scheduling is available at prometric.com/cpa Additionally, candidates may contact the Prometric Candidate Services Call Center at 1-800-580-9648
<ul><li>Content of the examination</li><li>Specific multiple-choice questions and/or task-based simulations on the examination</li><li>Questions about rescore requests</li></ul>	Visit the AICPA's CPA Page: aicpa.org/BecomeACPA/CPAExam Or send an e-mail to cpaexam@aicpa.org

Test Centers

Test centers move, new ones are opened, and some close from time-to-time. The most current list of test centers may be found on the Prometric website at prometric.com/cpa.

Testing Windows

The Uniform CPA Examination is offered the first two months plus 10 days of each calendar quarter. These months of testing are known as the "testing windows." The examination is given in these testing windows to allow for systems and database maintenance. The exam is not available during the following times: March 11-March 31, June 11-June 30, September 11-September 31, and December 11-December 31. It is important to plan accordingly; it is the candidate's responsibility to schedule the remaining un-passed sections of the examination or the candidate may risk losing credit for previously passed sections. Candidates will be able to take any or all sections of the examination during any testing window and in any order but will not be allowed to take the same section more than once during any testing window. If a section is failed, the candidate must wait for the next available testing window and submit a re-application to receive a new NTS.

Testing is Available	Testing is NOT Available
January, February, March 1-10	March 11 to end of month
April, May, June 1-10	June 11 to end of month
July, August, September 1-10	September 11 to end of month
October, November, December 1-10	December 11 to end of month

EXAM SCHEDULING

Eligibility to Test

In order to make appointments at test centers, candidates must have a valid Notice to Schedule (NTS). Candidates receive an NTS after they apply to take an examination and are deemed eligible by their state boards of accountancy. An NTS is provided for every section a candidate has been approved to take. The NTS is valid only for a specified period of time and cannot be used once it expires. Therefore, **it is important that candidates schedule their test appointments as soon as they receive the NTS.** The NTS is good for **6 months** in most jurisdictions except the following:

- Texas   90 days from date of application
- California   9 months from date NTS is issued
- Hawaii   9 months from date NTS is issued
- Louisiana   9 months from date NTS is issued
- Utah   9 months from date NTS is issued
- North Dakota   12 months from date NTS is issued
- South Dakota   12 months from date NTS is issued
- Virginia   12 months from date NTS is issued

Testing Centers

Prometric will administer the exam at authorized CPA Exam testing sites throughout the United States, Guam, Puerto Rico, the Virgin Islands, and the District of Columbia, as well as at international sites in Japan, Bahrain, Kuwait, Lebanon, the United Arab Emirates, and Brazil. Other international locations are on the horizon. Special citizenship requirements and fees apply to testing internationally.

Candidates are not required to take the CPA Exam at a Prometric site located in the state where they applied and may schedule their exams at any authorized Prometric site regardless of location.

After submitting an application, receiving approval by the State Board of Accountancy (Board), and submitting the required fees to NASBA, the candidate will be authorized to contact Prometric to schedule a specific testing date and time. The test sites are normally open six days each week. Candidates are encouraged to check Prometric's Web site at _prometric.com_ to locate a testing site near them.

Schedule Early

Scheduling is available throughout the year, but candidates should schedule examination appointments as soon as possible after receiving their NTS. Being proactive about scheduling will help to secure the candidate's first choice of date and location of test centers. Tests are scheduled on a first come, first served basis. To ensure that candidates are able to take their examination section(s) on the first desired date and time, candidates should make their appointment(s) at least 65 days before the date they want to take the examination. **The earlier candidates schedule**

appointments, the better their chances are of obtaining the location, date, and time of their choice. Test appointments **cannot** be scheduled fewer than five days in advance of the desired test date. Walk-in testing is **not** allowed. The last two weeks of an exam window tend to fill up early, so candidates should plan ahead and schedule as early as possible.

Candidates may schedule examination sessions at _prometric.com/CPA_ or by calling Prometric's Call Center at 1-800-580-9648. Candidates must have their Notice to Schedule available when making test appointments. Examination section(s) must be taken within the time period for which an NTS is valid (3-12 months depending on jurisdiction) and may not be rescheduled after the NTS has expired. Boards of Accountancy, NASBA and Prometric are not responsible if a candidate cannot schedule an appointment before deadlines in your jurisdiction; it is imperative to plan ahead.

Candidates have three scheduling options:

1. Visit prometric.com/cpa on the Internet

Candidates will find that the easiest and quickest way to schedule an examination appointment (as well as reschedule and cancel an appointment if necessary) is on the Internet. Using the Internet provides 24-hour access to scheduling and avoids any "on hold" waiting time. Because of this, candidates have the quickest and most direct access to preferred dates and test center locations. Additionally, they will quickly receive a detailed confirmation of exam appointments (on screen and via e-mail). Before making any appointments, candidates must have received a valid NTS and should have this available before beginning the scheduling process. Additionally, candidates must be ready to identify the dates, times and locations where they want to take each section. It is not necessary to make all appointments at one time and candidates may schedule one exam at a time even if they have paid for more than one on any particular NTS. During the scheduling process, candidates will be required to provide various pieces of information from the NTS. Online scheduling is done by completing the following easy steps:

1. Go to prometric.com/cpa. Select SCHEDULE APPOINTMENT.
2. Select CPA Exam and Country/State.
3. Read all the information on the Information Review screen, and click NEXT.
4. After viewing welcome screen, click NEXT, read all of the policy information and click "I Agree" to proceed.
5. On the Program Identifier Screen, enter your examination section identification number from your NTS (you have one identification number for each section of the examination— be sure to use the correct examination identification number for the section you are scheduling). Click "Next."
6. Confirm proper section and click NEXT.
7. Follow on-screen instructions to select the date and location you would like to schedule your section.
8. Select COMPLETE REGISTRATION to finalize your scheduling. Print the confirmation number for your appointment and keep it for your records.

2. Call 1-800-580-9648 (Candidate Services Call Center)

Prometric's Candidate Services Call Center is open Monday through Friday from 8:00 a.m. to 8:00 p.m. Eastern time. (Hearing-impaired candidates using teletypewriter (TTY) may call 1-800-529-3590 to schedule appointments.) Candidates must schedule a separate appointment for each section of the examination that they are planning to take. If calling to schedule two or more sections, candidates should be prepared to identify the dates, times and locations they want to take each section. It is not necessary to make all appointments in one call and candidates may make one appointment at a time. Before calling, the candidate must have an NTS and should have access to it during the call as they will be required to provide the customer service representative with various pieces of information from the NTS.

Candidates will NOT receive written confirmation of their appointment so must write down the date, time, location, and confirmation number for each appointment. Candidates may also visit prometric.com/cpa to confirm their appointment(s). If the candidate is not familiar with the test center location they should ask the customer service representative for directions while they are making the appointment over the phone. There are multiple test centers in some metropolitan areas, so it is important for candidates to be certain of the correct test center location where they are scheduled to take their examination(s).

Those interested in a test run of the Prometric system may also use the telephone call center to schedule a 15-minute generic sample test at the facility prior to examination so they can familiarize themselves with the location and Prometric. There is a $30 fee for this *Test Drive* service.

3. Call the Local Test Center

Some candidates prefer to speak to a customer service representative at the local test center; if this is the case, candidates may call the center directly to make an exam appointment. Calls will only be accepted during business hours, which vary for each test center. Leaving a voicemail message at the local test center is NOT an acceptable method of scheduling. If calling to take two or more sections, candidates should be prepared to identify the dates and times they want to take each section. It is not necessary to make all appointments in one call and the candidate may schedule one appointment at a time. Before calling, the candidate must have an NTS and should have access to it during the call as they will be required to provide the customer service representative with various pieces of information from the NTS.

Candidates will NOT receive written confirmation of their appointment so must write down the date, time, location, and confirmation number for each appointment. Candidates may also visit prometric.com/cpa to confirm their appointment(s). If the candidate is not familiar with the test center location they should ask the customer service representative for directions while they are making the appointment over the phone. There are multiple test centers in some metropolitan areas, so it is important for candidates to be certain of the correct test center location where they are scheduled to take their examination(s).

TESTING INTERNATIONALLY

The international testing format follows the same state board licensure process and the current examination structure. The exam is still only offered in English and is available during the same four testing windows per calendar year as offered to US candidates. There are additional fees that applicants must pay if they wish to take the exam internationally.

Who is eligible?

U.S. citizens and permanent residents living abroad, and citizens and long-term residents of the countries in which the exam is being administered are eligible. In some cases, permanent residents or citizens of neighboring countries may test at international testing centers. The only form of identification that an applicant can use to test internationally is a passport.

Non-US Countries Offering CPA Exam Testing

Japan, Brazil, the United Arab Emirates, Lebanon, Kuwait, and Bahrain

Citizenship Status	Eligibility to Test in These Countries						
C = Citizen PR = legal permanent or long term resident	U.S.	Japan	Brazil	UAE	Lebanon	Kuwait	Bahrain
U.S. C/PR	X	X	X	X	X	X	X
Japan C/PR	X	X					
Antigua/Barbuda C/PR			X				
Argentina C/PR	X		X				
Bahamas C/PR			X				
Barbados C/PR			X				
Belize C/PR			X				
Bolivia C/PR	X		X				
Brazil C/PR	X		X				
Cayman Islands C/PR			X				
Chile C/PR	X		X				
Colombia C/PR	X		X				
Costa Rica C/PR			X				
Dominica C/PR			X				
Dominican Republic C/PR			X				
Ecuador C/PR	X		X				
El Salvador C/PR			X				
French Guiana C/PR	X		X				
Grenada C/PR			X				
Guatemala C/PR			X				
Guyana C/PR	X		X				
Haiti C/PR			X				
Honduras C/PR			X				
Jamaica C/PR			X				
Mexico C/PR			X				
Nicaragua C/PR			X				
Panama C/PR			X				
Paraguay C/PR	X		X				
Peru C/PR	X		X				
St. Kitts/Nevis C/PR			X				
St. Lucia C/PR			X				
St. Vincent/Grenadines C/PR			X				
Suriname C/PR	X		X				
Trinidad & Tobago C/PR			X				
Uruguay C/PR	X		X				
Venezuela C/PR	X		X				
Bahrain C/PR	X			X	X	X	X
Egypt C/PR	X			X	X	X	X
Jordan C/PR	X			X	X	X	X
Kuwait C/PR	X			X	X	X	X
Lebanon C/PR	X			X	X	X	X
Oman C/PR	X			X	X	X	X
Qatar C/PR	X			X	X	X	X
Saudi Arabia C/PR	X			X	X	X	X
UAE C/PR	X			X	X	X	X
Yemen C/PR	X			X	X	X	X
India C/PR	X			X	X	X	X
Any other country in the world C/PR	X						

STEPS FOR APPLYING INTERNATIONALLY*

1. Students must first meet eligibility requirements and apply to a US 'State Board' as long as that state board is one that allows international testing. For states that allow this, please see the list on the next page.
2. Applicant receives their Notice to Schedule.
3. Once approved, the student would then need to complete a separate international registration process on the NASBA website.
4. The applicant must make a commitment to seek CPA licensure upon passing the CPA Exam, and thereafter maintain their status as licensees.
5. Meet citizenship/residency requirements in the jurisdiction in which they are sitting for their exams.
6. Pay additional fees (see below).

*For more on how to apply to sit for the CPA Exam in your non-US country please visit nasba.org/international/international-exam/.

Additional Exam Fees for Testing Internationally

Subject	Additional Amount
Auditing and Attestation (AUD)	$ 356.55
Business Environment and Concepts (BEC)	$ 356.55
Financial Accounting and Reporting (FAR)	$ 356.55
Regulation (REG)	$ 356.55

Changes for the International Exam

Scores for international candidates will be released on the same timeline as domestic scores.

You cannot take your test internationally without a passport. This is most relevant for people living within a testing country or area – in which they must STILL have a passport to demonstrate citizenship and nationality.

Students who are not eligible to test within an approved country's jurisdiction, but are still international (non-US applicants), must report to the United States only and cannot go to a different country to test.

US State Boards that Accept International Applicant Test-takers			
Alaska	Indiana	Nevada	South Carolina
Arizona	Iowa	New Hampshire	South Dakota
Arkansas	Kansas	New Mexico	Tennessee
Colorado	Louisiana	New York	Texas
Connecticut	Maine	North Dakota	Utah
District of Columbia	Massachusetts	Ohio	Vermont
Florida	Michigan	Oklahoma	Virginia
Georgia	Minnesota	Oregon	Washington
Guam	Missouri	Pennsylvania	West Virginia
Hawaii	Montana	Puerto Rico	Wisconsin
Illinois	Nebraska	Rhode Island	Wyoming

TAKING THE EXAMINATION IN GUAM

Regardless of which Board of Accountancy has declared a candidate eligible for the examination, if the candidate intends to take their examination in Guam, they must pay an additional $140 surcharge for each examination section. Residents of Guam who are able to pay at the Guam Computer Testing Center, will incur a reduced surcharge fee of $70. All Guam test-takers must schedule their appointments by either of the following two options:

1. Visit nasba.org/exams/cpaexam/guam/ on the Internet

NASBA operates the Guam computer testing center in cooperation with the Guam Board of Accountancy and Prometric. Before visiting this Web site, candidates should have an NTS and credit card readily available. Once at the website, candidates will be asked to provide information from their NTS and will pay the surcharge using a credit card. After paying the additional surcharge for each examination section, the candidate will need to wait at least 24 hours before scheduling an appointment following the instructions described above.

2. Call the Guam Computer Testing Center: 855-CPA-GUAM or 671-300-7441

The Guam computer testing center is open Monday through Friday from 7:00 a.m. to 4:00 p.m. Guam time. Have your NTS and credit card in front of you when you call. Candidates will be asked to provide information from their NTS and will pay the surcharge using a credit card. After paying the additional surcharge for each examination section, the candidate will need to wait at least 24 hours before scheduling an appointment following the instructions described above.

For Pre-approved Special Testing Accommodations, Call 1-800-967-1139

International Locations Accommodations Phone Numbers:
Japan 0120-34-7737
Latin America 1-443-751-4990
Middle East 31-320-239-530

DO NOT CALL ANY OF THESE NUMBER UNLESS YOU HAVE BEEN PRE-APPROVED FOR SPECIAL TESTING ACCOMMODATIONS BY YOUR BOARD OF ACCOUNTANCY.

If the Board of Accountancy has approved a candidate for special testing accommodations, the information regarding the nature of the accommodation will be sent to NASBA. The type of accommodation will be shown on the candidate's NTS and will be sent to Prometric. Neither the candidate nor the customer service representative may make any changes to the accommodations that have been approved. A candidate requiring special testing accommodations should contact their Board of Accountancy before proceeding if they believe there are any errors on the NTS. If you call to take two or more sections, be prepared to identify the dates, times and locations for each section you wish to take. It is not necessary to make all appointments in one call. If you prefer, you may make one appointment at a time.

Before calling, the candidate must have an NTS and should have access to it during the call as they will be required to provide the customer service representative with various pieces of information from the NTS.

Candidates may visit prometric.com/cpa to confirm their appointment(s). If the candidate is not familiar with the test center location they should ask the customer service representative for directions while they are making the appointment over the phone. There are multiple test centers in some metropolitan areas, so it is important for candidates to be certain of the correct test center location where they are scheduled to take their examination(s).

CHANGES TO APPOINTMENTS

After making an appointment for an examination section, the candidate may find it necessary to change or cancel an appointment. Candidates should be aware that they may be required to pay a penalty or forfeit examination fees, depending on when they notify Prometric of the change or cancellation.

Change the Date, Time or Location of an Appointment

There are three methods to reschedule or change an existing exam appointment:

- Use Prometric's Web scheduling tool located at prometric.com/cpa. The system is available 24 hours a day, seven days a week.
- Call the Prometric Candidate Services Call Center at 1-800-580-9648. The Center is open Monday through Friday from 8:00 a.m. to 8:00 p.m. Eastern time.
- Call the local test center where your appointment is scheduled. If you need to reschedule your appointment, review the table below to determine deadlines and associated fees. Please note that Saturday is considered a business day.

If calling to change an exam date, time or location, the candidate must speak with a staff member and cannot leave a message to reschedule. Candidates testing with special testing accommodations should call 1-800-967-1139 to reschedule. Candidates using a teletypewriter (TTY) should call 1-800-529-3590.

Some types of accommodations are only available at a limited number of test centers. A candidate's Board of Accountancy will have already notified the candidate of this before sending an NTS to a candidate who has requested special accommodations.

Ineligibility

If a candidate's Board of Accountancy informs NASBA that they are no longer eligible to take the Uniform CPA Examination for any reason, the NTS will be cancelled. The candidate will receive a copy of a canceled NTS by United States mail, fax or e-mail, depending on the method identified as the candidate's preferred method for receipt of information.

If the candidate has NOT scheduled an appointment, they do not need to take any other action. If they have scheduled an appointment, NASBA will contact Prometric to cancel the appointment and rescind eligibility. In the event that a candidate is determined to be no longer eligible to take the examination by their Board of Accountancy, examination fees will NOT be refunded.

Refunds

Under most circumstances, NASBA **will not** refund section fees. Additional information on payment of section fees can be found on NASBA's Web site at nasba.org.

Test Center Closings

If severe weather or other local emergency requires a test center to be closed, every attempt will be made to contact candidates scheduled to sit for the exam on that day. If a candidate is unsure of whether or not the test center will be open on their exam day due to inclement weather or other unforeseeable circumstance, the candidate may call their test center directly. If the center is open, it is the candidate's responsibility to keep the appointment. If the center is closed, the candidate will be given the opportunity to reschedule without penalty. If unable to contact the local test center, the candidate may check on the Web at prometric.com/cpa, or call the Candidate Services Call Center at 1-800-580-9648, Monday through Friday, from 8:00 a.m. to 8:00 p.m. Eastern time.

Fees

Fees for the 2017 Exam are as follows:

Application/Qualification Fee paid	(Varies by State)
First time Qualifying and Sitting	Approx. $50-$200
Previously Qualified and Sat (Repeat)	Approx. $25-$75
Section Fees to be Paid Directly to NASBA	**(Uniform)**
Auditing and Attestation	$193.45
Financial Accounting and Reporting	$193.45
Regulation	$193.45
Business Environment and Concepts	$193.45
Total fees paid to NASBA for all four sections	**$773.80**

Credit Status

The Exam utilizes a "rolling" 18-month credit status system. This replaced the conditional credit system of the paper-and-pencil exam. Credit status is established by passing one section of the examination. Once a candidate passes a section of the examination, the candidate will be allowed a maximum of 18 months to pass all remaining sections in order to retain credit on the passed section. If the candidate does not pass all four sections within that 18-month period, the candidate will lose credit for the first section of the exam passed. A new 18-month period will commence with a start date of the next section that was passed. There are state boards that offer exceptions to the above-described 18-month credit status period but for the majority of jurisdictions the 18-month rolling period applies and begins from the date the candidate sits for their first passed exam.

TAKE YOUR EXAMINATION

Arrive Early

Candidates must arrive at the test center at least 30 minutes before the scheduled appointment time for their examination. This allows time to sign in, have a digital photograph taken, be fingerprinted, review the security and test center policies and be seated at the workstation. If a candidate arrives for their scheduled testing appointment any time after the scheduled start time, they may be denied permission to test and will not receive a refund. Therefore, candidates should be sure to arrive at least 30 minutes before their scheduled appointment time to avoid forfeiting all fees for the examination section.

YOU MUST BRING YOUR NOTICE TO SCHEDULE (NTS) WITH YOU

The NTS contains an "Examination Password" that will be entered on the computer before starting the exam as a part of the log-in process. It is important to bring the correct NTS to the testing center as it is possible for a candidate to have more than one active NTS at a time. A candidate will not be admitted into the test center without the correct NTS and will forfeit all examination fees for that section if denied entry for this reason.

Personal Identification

The Uniform CPA Examination employs very strict security measures. One level of security involves identification. **The same form of the candidate's name must appear on the candidate's application, NTS, and on the primary identification presented at the test center.** It is important for candidates to spell and present their names correctly during the application process to assure the correct information is reflected on their Notice to Schedule. If the candidate's name is different from identifications presented at check-in, the candidate will not be permitted to test. Candidates must present two forms of identification, one of which must contain a recent photograph, to test center staff before being allowed into the examination. Each form of identification must bear the candidate's signature and must not be expired. Candidates who do not present valid ID will be barred entry to the exam and exam fees will not be refunded.

You must present *one* of the following primary forms of identification:
- A valid (not expired) state- or territory-issued driver's license with photograph and signature
- A valid (not expired) state- or territory-issued identification card with a recent photograph and signature (Candidates who do not drive may have an identification card issued by the agency which also issues driver's licenses.)
- A valid (not expired) government-issued passport with a recent photograph and signature.
- A United States military identification card with a recent photograph and signature

Your secondary form of identification may be one of the following (or another item from the list above):
- An identification card issued by your Board of Accountancy which includes the same name that appears on the NTS (if applicable to your jurisdiction)
- A valid (not expired) credit card
- A bank ATM card
- A debit card

The following are *UNACCEPTABLE* forms of identification:
- A draft classification card
- A Social Security card
- A student identification card
- A United States permanent residency card (green card)

The secondary form of identification **does not** have to match the information on a candidate's NTS exactly. For example, if a candidate's middle name is printed on their driver's license and NTS but not unexpired ATM card, the driver's license may be used as primary identification while the debit card can serve as secondary identification without issue. It is important to keep this in mind when applying to the state board so that the candidate's name is printed correctly on the NTS.

If the test center staff have questions about the identification presented, the candidate may be asked for additional proof of identity and, if staff are unable to verify identity, the candidate may be refused admission to the exam and will forfeit the examination fee for that section. Admittance to the test center and examination does not imply that the identification presented is valid or that the candidate's scores will be reported if subsequent investigations reveal impersonation or forgery.

Fingerprint Requirement

All CPA Exam candidates are required to have a digital fingerprint taken at Prometric that is used as primary identification for subsequent exam appearances as well as for re-admission to the test center after a break.

Digital fingerprint images will be encrypted and stored electronically together with candidate identification information. Fingerprint images will also be used to detect any attempt to impersonate CPA candidates.

Fingerprinting will be required every time a candidate reports to the test center. In addition, candidates returning to test rooms after breaks will be asked to have their fingerprints taken again for comparison with the fingerprints captured at the beginning of the session. Candidates should keep this in mind if they choose to take breaks during the exam.

At the Test Center

The staff at each test center have been trained in the procedures specific to the Uniform CPA Examination. The staff are there to guide candidates through the guidelines that have been developed by the Boards of Accountancy, NASBA and the AICPA.

1. You must arrive at the test center at least 30 minutes before your scheduled appointment. If you arrive after your scheduled appointment time, you may forfeit your appointment and will not be eligible to have your examination fees refunded.

2. Your examination should begin within 30 minutes of the scheduled start time. If circumstances arise that delay your session more than 30 minutes, you will be given the choice of continuing to wait or rescheduling your appointment.

3. You must place personal belongings, such as a purse or cell phone, in the storage lockers provided by the test center. You will be given the key to your locker which must be returned to the test center staff when you leave. The lockers are very small and are not intended to hold large items. Do not bring anything to the test center unless it is absolutely necessary. Test center personnel will not be responsible for lost or stolen items.

4. You will submit a digital fingerprint that will be used for identification purposes for future Prometric visits or to verify your identity if you leave the testing room for any reason during the exam (like a break or to put your sweater in your locker). Keep your photo ID on you at all times as well but expect your fingerprint to be used as your primary identification within the testing center.

5. You will have a digital photograph taken of your face. (If the digital camera equipment is not working, a Polaroid picture will be taken.)

6. You will be required to sign the test center log book. Each time you exit and re-enter the testing room, you will be required to sign the log book and present your identification.

7. You will be escorted to a workstation by test center staff. You must remain in your seat during the examination, except when authorized to get up and leave the testing room. Except for a standard break at the halfway point of the Exam, any breaks taken (e.g. to use the restroom) will count against the clock.

8. Candidates will be provided with two double-sided, laminated, colored sheets called "noteboards," as well as a fine point marker for making notations. This has replaced the paper and pencil scratch paper provided in the past. You will be directed to write your examination Launch Code (from your NTS) on your noteboards. You will be required to return the noteboards to the test center staff when your exam is complete. If more writing space is required, you may request additional noteboards from the test center staff once you have turned in the original noteboards you received. You must not bring any paper or pencils to the workstation in the testing room.

9. Notify the test center staff if:
    a. You experience a problem with your computer
    b. An error message appears on the computer screen (do not clear the message)
    c. You need additional scratch paper or pencils
    d. You need the test center staff for any other reason

10. When you finish the examination, leave the testing room quietly, turn in your noteboard and sign the test center log book. The test center staff will dismiss you after completing all necessary procedures.

Test Center Regulations

A standardized environment is necessary to ensure that candidates take equivalent but different exams. For this reason, all candidates must follow the same regulations.
- Papers, books, food or purses are not allowed in the testing room.
- Eating, drinking or use of tobacco is not allowed in the testing room.
- Talking or communicating with other candidates is not allowed in the testing room
- Calculators, personal digital assistants or other computer devices are not allowed in the testing room.
- Communication devices (e.g., cell phones, pagers, two-way radios, wireless internet connections to personal digital assistants or devices) are not allowed in the testing room.
- Recording devices (audio and video) are not allowed in the testing room.
- You must not leave the testing room without the permission of the test center staff.
- You must be fingerprinted to re-enter the room after any breaks.

A complete list of prohibited items can be found on the AICPA website.

Breaks

Each examination section contains units known as testlets. Each testlet is comprised of either a group of multiple-choice questions or several task-based problems known as simulations. After each testlet, the candidate will be asked if he or she would like to take a non-standardized break (see below for information about the new standardized break). Those who do choose a break must indicate in the software that they will take an optional break and will be asked to leave the testing room quietly and sign the test center log book. Test center staff will confirm that the candidate has completed a testlet before allowing a break. Remember: you do not have to take a break and the clock will keep running if you do (for a non-standardized break)! Therefore, it is recommended that you use break time wisely. Leaving the testing room at any time without exiting the testlet and selecting the break option will result in the candidate being barred from reentry into the testing room and information regarding the candidate's absence will be reported to their Board of Accountancy.

Beginning April 1, 2017, Exam candidates are given a standardized break after the third (of five) testlets. This standardized break is up to 15 minutes and will NOT count against the candidate's time in the Exam. **We recommend that you take this break** to refresh before continuing with the exam.

The standardized break will not count against a candidate's time on the exam, but any other break will count against the time on the exam.

Examination Confidentiality and Break Policy

All candidates must accept the terms of the confidentiality and break policy statement before beginning their examination. The statement must be accepted or the test will be terminated and any exam fees will be forfeited.

Candidate Misconduct, Cheating, Copyright Infringement

The Boards of Accountancy, NASBA and the AICPA take candidate misconduct, including cheating on the Uniform CPA Examination, very seriously. If a Board of Accountancy determines that a candidate is culpable of misconduct or has cheated, the candidate will be subject to a variety of penalties including, but not limited to: invalidation of grades, disqualification from subsequent examination administrations, and civil and criminal penalties. In cases where candidate misconduct or cheating is discovered after a candidate has obtained a CPA license or certificate, a Board of Accountancy may rescind the license or certificate. If the test center staff suspects misconduct, a warning will be given to the candidate for any of the following situations:

- Communicating, orally or otherwise, with another candidate or person
- Copying from or looking at another candidate's materials or workstation
- Allowing another candidate to copy from or look at materials or workstation
- Giving or receiving assistance in answering examination questions or problems
- Reading examination questions or simulations aloud
- Engaging in conduct that interferes with the administration of the examination or unnecessarily disturbing staff or other candidates
- Grounds for confiscation of a prohibited item and warning the candidate include: Possession of any prohibited item (whether or not in use) inside, or while entering or exiting the testing room. This includes use of any prohibited item during a break in a manner that could result in cheating or the removal of examination questions or simulations

Prohibited items include, but are not limited to:

- Books
- Briefcase
- Calculator/Portable Computer
- Calculator Watch
- Camera, Photographic or Scanning Device (still or video)
- Cellular Phone
- Cigarette/Tobacco Product
- Container of any kind
- Dictionary
- Earphone
- Eraser
- Eyeglass Case
- Food or Beverage
- Handbag/Backpack/Hip Pack
- Hat or Visor (except head coverings worn for religious reasons)
- Headset or Audio Earmuffs (if not provided by Testing Center). You may bring soft, foam earplugs with no strings attached for your use. TCAs will inspect the earplugs
- Jewelry – Pendant Necklace or Large Earrings
- Newspaper or Magazine
- Non-Prescription Sunglasses
- Notebook
- Notes in any written form
- Organizer / Day Planner
- Outline
- Pager / Beeper
- Paper (if not provided by Test Center)
- Pen / Pencil (if not provided by Test Center)
- Pencil Sharpener
- Personal Digital Assistant or Other Electronic Device
- Plastic Bag
- Purse/Wallet
- Radio/Transmitter/Receiver
- Ruler/Slide Ruler
- Study Material
- Tape/Disk Recorder or Player
- Umbrella
- Watch
- Weapon of any kind

In addition, jackets, coats, and sweaters are also prohibited; however, if you require a separate sweater or a jacket due to room temperature, it must be worn at all times.

The Boards of Accountancy, NASBA, the AICPA and Prometric use a variety of procedures to prevent candidate misconduct and cheating on the examination. Test center staff are trained to watch for unusual behavior and incidents during the examination. In addition, all examination sessions are audio/videotaped to document the occurrence of any unusual activity and candidate misconduct is reported to Boards of Accountancy on a daily basis.

All examination materials are owned and copyrighted by the AICPA. Any reproduction and/or distribution of examination materials, including memorization, without the express written authorization of the AICPA, is prohibited. This behavior infringes on the legal rights of the AICPA and, in addition to the penalties listed above, the AICPA will take appropriate legal action when any copyright infringements have occurred.

Please see the AICPA's website at *aicpa.org* for a complete list of prohibited items and current information on examination policies.

Grounds for Dismissal

Test center staff may dismiss candidates from the examination or may have scores canceled by the candidate's Board of Accountancy for engaging in misconduct or not following the test center regulations. The following are examples of behavior that will not be tolerated during the examination:

- Repeating acts of misconduct after receiving prior warning(s)
- Attempting to remove or removing examination questions from the testing room by any means
- Copying, writing or summarizing examination questions on any material other than the scratch paper issued to you
- Tampering with computer software or hardware, or attempting to use a computer for any reason other than completing the examination session
- Intentional refusal or failure to comply with instructions of the test center staff
- Attempting to have an impersonator gain admission to the testing room or to substitute for you after a break
- Conduct that may threaten bodily harm or damage to property

RECEIVE YOUR SCORE(S)

Generally, Boards of Accountancy will report scores on a numeric scale of 0-99, with 75 as a passing score. This scale does NOT represent "percent correct." A score of 75 reflects examination performance that represents the knowledge and skills needed to protect the public. A few Boards of Accountancy have elected to report a pass or fail status instead of numeric scores. All questions contained in the examination, including BEC written communication task-based simulations, are formatted to allow responses to be scored electronically. Human graders score selected written communication responses. Candidates receive points for each correct answer to a multiple-choice question.

Similarly, responses to the questions asked in the simulations receive points based on correct answers or correct completion of the presented task. Points are not subtracted for incorrect responses. The points are accumulated according to the relative contributions of each question, which are weighted (see the Uniform CPA Examination Blueprints and skills definition documents for specific content areas and weights, or go to aicpa.org). Overall scores are then adjusted to ensure scores for all candidates (even those who test in different administrations with different examinations) are comparable and equivalent.

When You Should Expect Your Scores

The AICPA sends candidate scores to NASBA. The AICPA will release scores for the exams taken in a window on a specific target date according to the schedule on the following page. However, distribution of scores to the exam takers is the responsibility of the Boards of Accountancy. Each Board of Accountancy sets its own schedule regarding the frequency with which it will approve and release scores.

The AICPA target dates are not guaranteed and may be pushed back due to unforeseen issues. Additionally, BEC scores may be subject to longer delays due to the scoring of Written Communication. Candidates who do not receive their scores should call NASBA at 866-MY-NASBA.

Day of Exam in Testing Window*	Target Release Date Timeline
Day 1-20	11 business days following day 20 of the testing window
Day 21-45	6 business days following day 45 of the testing window
Day 46-Close of Window	6 business days following the close of the testing window
After Close of Window	6 business days after receiving all scoring data for the window

*date the records are received by the AICPA

The Score Review and Appeal Processes

Score Review

Score Review is an independent verification of a candidate's Uniform CPA Examination score, and NOT a re-grading or reconsideration of the candidate's responses on the examination. Because all scores undergo several quality control checks before they are reported, the likelihood of a score change following score review is exceedingly small, **or less than 1%** of all requested score reviews since the inception of the computer-based test. However, the score review option is available to candidates who would like to have their scores checked one more time. Fees apply.

Appeals

If allowed in a candidate's jurisdiction, an option to appeal a failing score may exist. This option enables the candidate to view the questions that he or she answered incorrectly as well as their responses. Such viewing takes place only in an authorized location, under secure conditions, and in the presence of a representative of the candidate's Board of Accountancy. In order to qualify for a score appeal, the candidate must submit a formal request to their Board of Accountancy within 30 days of the date printed on the score report, obtain the Board of Accountancy's approval, and pay the required fee. Contact your Board of Accountancy for specific instructions on the score appeal process. If a candidate is allowed a score appeal, they will be given the opportunity to view the questions they answered incorrectly as well as their responses to those questions. The AICPA will respond to any comments made by the candidate, rescore appealed responses and forward the results to NASBA. NASBA will then forward the scores to the candidate's Board of Accountancy.

RETAKING THE EXAMINATION

Candidates who fail any section of the CPA Exam may retake that section in a future testing window but are not allowed to repeat a failed section within the same two-month testing window. Information on how to retake a failed examination section will be sent to the candidate from their Board of Accountancy with a score report detailing the candidate's performance in each area of that particular exam section. This information may be helpful when preparing to retake any examination sections or in planning for near-term continuing professional education needs. For any questions on retake policies and fees, contact your Board of Accountancy.

ETHICS EXAM

Some jurisdictions require CPA Exam candidates to successfully complete an ethics examination as a requirement of CPA licensure, generally after the candidate has passed all four sections of the exam. The ethics portion is either administered through the AICPA or through continuing education (CPE) provided by your state society of CPAs. Check with your state board for more information on ethics requirements for your jurisdiction.

The CPA Exam
STRUCTURE
The Uniform CPA Examination spans 16 hours and consists of four separate exam parts.

The Uniform CPA Exam
Auditing & Attestation (AUD - 4 hours)
Financial Accounting & Reporting (FAR - 4 hours)
Regulation (REG - 4 hours)
Business Environment & Concepts (BEC - 4 hours)

Examination Content

The content areas for each exam part, along with skills tested, are outlined in the Uniform CPA Examination Blueprints published by the AICPA. For more information about the examination blueprints, visit aicpa.org and choose the "Become a CPA" tab.

Uniform CPA Examination Blueprints

With the 2017 exam the AICPA introduced a set of Uniform CPA Examination Blueprints, which document the minimum level of knowledge and skills needed for initial licensure in content areas and in representative tasks. The blueprints are organized by content AREA, content GROUP, and content TOPIC. Each topic includes one or more representative TASK(s) that a newly licensed CPA may be expected to complete. Each representative task is linked to a SKILL tested in the exam.

Skills are based on Bloom's Taxonomy of Educational Objectives. Critical thinking skills range from the lowest level (Remembering and Understanding) to the highest level (Evaluation), as summarized in the following table.

Skill Levels (beginning with the highest)	
Evaluation	The examination or assessment of problems and use of judgment to draw conclusions.
Analysis	The examination and study of the interrelationships of separate areas in order to identify causes and find evidence to support inferences.
Application	The use or demonstration of knowledge, concepts or techniques.
Remembering and Understanding	The perception and comprehension of the significance of an area utilizing knowledge gained.

The AICPA conducted a Practice Analysis from 2014-2015 in which one main finding was clear: firms expect newly licensed CPAs on their staff to perform at a higher level. The AICPA raised the bar with the revamped 2017 CPA Exam that more authentically tests candidates on the tasks and skill levels that will be required of them as newly licensed CPAs.

Types of Questions

Your score on each exam part is determined by the sum of points assigned to individual questions and simulation parts. Thus, you must attempt to maximize your points on each individual item. To familiarize yourself with the examination's format, functions, and question and response types, review the examination tutorial at aicpa.org. A sample test that contains a few sample multiple-choice questions and simulations for each applicable section is currently available. Neither the tutorial nor the sample test will be available at the test centers and candidates are encouraged to familiarize themselves with the test format prior to taking their first examination.

Multiple Choice Questions

A format is considered objective when it can be graded without subjectivity. Grading objective examinations is a mechanical process that requires little judgment. Any format that can be graded by machine is generally considered objective. Objective formats result in very consistent scores because the acceptability of particular responses is determined before grading begins. The most widely used objective format is multiple-choice (i.e., 4-option questions) because it has a restricted set of alternatives from which the correct answer must be selected. Multiple-choice questions (MCQs) make up 50% of FAR, AUD, REG and BEC.

The multiple-choice questions within each exam part are organized into two groups which are referred to as testlets. The first two testlets of each exam section will contain 31-38 multiple-choice questions per testlet, which are together worth up 50 percent of the exam part. The multiple-choice testlets vary in overall difficulty. A testlet is labeled either 'moderate' or 'difficult' based on its makeup. The questions in a 'difficult' testlet have a higher average level of difficulty than those in a 'moderate' testlet; however, questions of higher difficulty carry a higher point percentage rate therefore fewer must be answered correctly to pass. Every candidate's first multiple-choice testlet in each section will be a 'moderate' testlet. If a candidate scores well on the first testlet, he or she will receive a 'difficult' second testlet. Candidates that do not perform well on the first testlet receive a second 'moderate' testlet. Because the scoring procedure takes the difficulty of the testlet into account, candidates are scored fairly regardless of the type of testlets they receive.

Each multiple-choice testlet contains "operational" and "pretest" questions. The operational questions are the only ones that are used to determine your score. Pretest questions are not scored; they are being tested for future use as operational questions. However, you have no way of knowing which questions are operational and which questions are pretest questions. Therefore, you must approach each question as if it will be used to determine your grade. Of the multiple-choice questions, there are 72 operational and 12 pretest questions in the AUD exam, 66 operational and 11 pretest questions in the FAR exam, 76 operational and 12 pretest questions in the REG exam, and 62 operational and 10 pretest questions in the BEC exam.

Task-Based Simulations

Task-based simulations (TBSs) make up 50% of the FAR, AUD, and REG exams, but only 35% of the BEC exam (with written communications problems taking up the remaining 15%). Each operational TBS in the FAR, AUD and REG exams is worth approximately 7.1% of the exam score. Each operational TBS in the BEC exam is worth approximately 11.7% of the exam score. The FAR, AUD, and REG sections of the exam each contain 8 task-based simulations. The BEC section includes 4 simulation problems as well as 3 written communication problems, of which 2 are graded. Each of these 2 graded written communications problems is worth approximately 7.5% of the exam score. The actual percentage of total score assigned to each requirement will vary according to its difficulty. Each TBS should be allotted about 10 to 20 minutes to complete, depending on difficulty. Candidates will be required to demonstrate their ability to apply certain skills (application, analysis, or evaluation) in each part of the CPA Exam using task-based simulations. These skills will be tested in a variety of methods such as simulation, or relational case studies, which will test candidates' knowledge and skills using work-related situations. Simulations will require candidates to have basic computer skills, knowledge of common spreadsheet and word processing functions, the ability to use a financial calculator or a spreadsheet to perform standard financial calculations, and the ability to use electronic tools such as databases for research. Therefore, you need to become proficient in the use of these tools to maximize your score on the task-based simulation component of each applicable exam section.

Each TBS contains at least two tabs: the work tab, labeled according to the exhibits used in the TBS (Research, Journal Entry, or Form 1065) and the help tab, labeled Help. The work tab (identified by a pencil icon) is the part of the question that will be graded and contains directions for completion of the task. Some task-based simulations may contain more than one information tab while others may not have any information tabs at all. The help tab provides assistance with the exam software such as instructions on using the provided word processor for written communication problems. While the exam environment closely mirrors common software programs that candidates are likely familiar with, it is recommended that candidates view the help tab for specific instructions on using the exam's provided software.

Document Review Simulations

A new type of simulation was introduced in the July 2016 exam and is known as the Document Review Simulation, or DRS. DRSs are designed to simulate tasks that the candidate will be required to perform as a newly licensed CPA (based on up to two years' experience as a CPA). Each DRS presents a document that has a series of highlighted phrases or sentences that the candidate will need to determine are correct or incorrect. To help make these conclusions, numerous supporting documents, or resources, such as legal letters, phone transcripts, financial statements, trial balances and authoritative literature will be included. The candidate will need to sort through these documents to determine what is, and what is not important to solving the problem. Please see the Appendix at the end of this book for more information about DRSs.

Written Communication – BEC

Written communication will be assessed through the use of responses to essay questions, which will be based upon the content topics as outlined in the Blueprints. Candidates will have access to a word processor, which includes a spell check feature. Candidates are encouraged to use the "Help" tab for more information on the word processor functionality as it is similar to but not exactly like popular word processor programs the candidate may already be familiar with.

Research Task Format

FAR, AUD and REG will each contain at least one research problem. If a candidate's exam contains two research problems, it is likely that one of them is a problem being pre-tested.

Candidates will be asked to search through the database to find an appropriate reference that addresses the issue presented in the research problem. A scenario is presented in which the candidate must find his or her answer in the authoritative literature using a pre-determined list of codes (such as Professional Standards or federal taxation code). The candidate will choose the appropriate code title from the drop-down list and then enter a specific reference number applicable to their given scenario.

Authoritative literature for each section appears as follows:

FAR: Candidates will search the FASB ASC (Accounting Standards Codification) for their responses; this section does not have a dropdown menu to select from.

REG: IRC - Internal Revenue Code

AUD: AU-C - Clarified U.S. Auditing Standards
PCAOB – AS - PCAOB Auditing Standards
AT-C - Attestation Services
AR-C - Statements on Standards for Accounting and Review Services
ET - Code of Professional Conduct
BL - Bylaws
VS - Statements on Standards for Valuation Services
CS - Statement on Standards for Consulting Services
PFP - Personal Financial Planning
CPE - Continuing Professional Education
TS – Tax Services
PR – Peer Review Standards
QC - Quality Control

For example, a candidate may be asked the following question:

> A client has entered into an interest rate swap and just learned that it is considered a derivative. The cost was negligible and the entity is trying to determine at what amount to report it on its balance sheet. Identify the location in professional standards that indicates how derivatives should initially be measured.

Using the Authoritative Literature icon at the top of the screen, the candidate will search for keywords associated with the question using the search box, which will pull up all references within the literature to those keywords. From there, the candidate should use the "search within" function to find specific instances of keywords within each subsection. Keywords will be highlighted in the text and the candidate can go through them to find the relevant text that answers the research problem.

In this case, a search for "derivative" and a more detailed search within all references to that topic using the *search within* button would likely bring up FASB ASC 815-10-30-1, which reads:

> All derivative instruments shall be measured initially at fair value.

Using the provided drop-down menu, the candidate would then select the appropriate literature reference from the list (in this case, FASB codification) and enter the codification numbers in the blank boxes. It will look something like this:

> A client has entered into an interest rate swap and just learned that it is considered a derivative. The cost was negligible and the entity is trying to determine at what amount to report it on its balance sheet. Identify the location in professional standards that indicates how derivatives should initially be measured.

Enter your response in the answer fields below.

FASB ASC	815	10	30	1

Research questions will also alert the candidate if they have correctly formatted their answer by displaying a message like "Examples of correctly formatted sections are shown below" or "A correctly formatted IRC subsection is a lower case letter" in a box above the candidate response.

To master research type questions, you can either practice at the below NASBA website, or you can use the Interactive Practice Questions software included in your course.

CPA Exam Candidates: Free Online Access to Professional Literature Package

CPA Exam candidates can get a free six-month subscription to professional literature used in the CPA Examination. This online package includes AICPA Professional Standards, FASB Current Text and FASB Original Pronouncements. Only candidates who have applied to take the CPA Exam and have been deemed eligible by state boards of accountancy will receive access to this package of professional literature. NASBA will verify that a candidate has a valid NTS (Notice to Schedule). A candidate must be in receipt of a valid NTS prior to receiving authorization to the professional literature.

To subscribe visit: https://nasba.org/proflit/

Another good source for Researching Tax Codes for the **Regulation Exam**:
https://www.irs.gov/tax-professionals/tax-code-regulations-and-official-guidance

Testlets

Each section of the exam is presented in 5 testlets. The first 2 testlets contain multiple-choice questions (MCQs) and the last 3 testlets contain task-based simulations. (In the BEC exam, 2 of the last 3 testlets contain task-based simulations and 1 contains written communication problems.) Candidates can go back and forth between different questions within a testlet but cannot go back to previous testlets or review their questions once they have submitted their exam as complete.

Additional facts about the Exam
- You may take 1 part at a time.
- Results are released at various times throughout the exam window.
- In most jurisdictions, candidates must pass all four parts of the Uniform CPA Examination within a "rolling" eighteen-month period, which begins on the date that the first section(s) passed is taken.
- Generally, any credit for any exam part(s) passed outside the eighteen-month period will expire and that section(s) must be retaken.
- Candidates will not be allowed to retake a failed exam part(s) within the same quarter (examination window)
- Candidates will take different, equivalent exams.

Effective Date of Pronouncements (AICPA, 11/12/2015)

Accounting and auditing pronouncements are eligible to be tested on the Uniform CPA Examination in the later of: (1) the first testing window beginning after the pronouncement's earliest mandatory effective date or (2) the first testing window beginning six (6) months after the pronouncement's issuance date. In either case, there is a simultaneous introduction of content related to the new pronouncement and removal of content related to the previous pronouncement.

For the federal taxation area, the Internal Revenue Code and federal tax regulations in effect six months after the enactment date or the change's effective date, whichever is later, are eligible for testing.

For all other subjects covered in the Regulation (REG) and Business Environment and Concepts (BEC) sections, materials eligible to be tested include federal laws in the window beginning six months after their effective date, and uniform acts in the window beginning one year after their adoption by a simple majority of the jurisdictions.

Lecture 0.02

Regulation – 4 Hours

Content Allocation

The content areas tested in the REG exam, as well as the weight given to each content area, are summarized in the following table.

Content Area		Weight
Area I	Ethics, Professional Responsibilities and Federal Tax Procedures	10-20%
Area II	Business Law	10-20%
Area III	Federal Taxation of Property Transactions	12-22%
Area IV	Federal Taxation of Individuals	15-25%
Area V	Federal Taxation of Entities	28-38%

Skill Allocation

The skills tested in the REG exam, as well as the weight given to each skill, are summarized in the following table.

Skill	Weight
Evaluation	-
Analysis	25-35%
Application	35-45%
Remembering and Understanding	25-35%

REG Exam	
Testlet 1 *38 MCQ*	48 min
Testlet 2 *38 MCQ*	48 min
Testlet 3 *2 TBS*	30 min
Testlet 4 *3 TBS*	57 min
Testlet 5 *3 TBS*	57 min
Total Time:	4 hours

Things to consider:
- o **Allocate 75 seconds per multiple choice question**
- o **Allocate 15-20 minutes per simulation, depending on complexity**
- o **Plan to use no more than 10 minutes per research question**
- o **Take the standard 15-minute break after the 3rd testlet – it doesn't count against your time**

Uniform CPA Examination Blueprints
<u>Effective January 1, 2018</u>

REGULATION (REG)

The AICPA gives candidates clear guidelines for the knowledge and skills that are tested on the CPA Exam. In the following excerpt we point to the most important information published by the AICPA describing the Exam sections.

The Regulation (REG) exam tests the knowledge and skills that a newly licensed CPA must demonstrate with respect to:
- Federal taxation
- Ethics and professional responsibilities related to tax practice
- Business law

Area I of the REG exam blueprint covers several topics, including the following:
- Ethics and Responsibilities in Tax Practice – Requirements based on Treasury Department Circular 230 and the rules and regulations for tax return preparers
- Licensing and Disciplinary Systems – Requirements of state boards of accountancy to obtain and maintain the CPA license
- Federal Tax Procedures – Understanding federal tax processes and procedures, including appropriate disclosures, substantiation, penalties and authoritative hierarchy
- Legal Duties and Responsibilities – Understanding legal issues that affect the CPA and his or her practice

Area II of the REG exam blueprint covers several topics of Business Law, including the following:
- Knowledge and understanding of the legal implications of business transactions, particularly as they relate to accounting, auditing and financial reporting
- Areas of agency, contracts, debtor-creditor relationships, government regulation of business, and business structure
  - The Uniform Commercial Code under the topics of contracts and debtor- creditor relationships
  - Nontax-related business structure content. Area V of the REG section blueprint covers the tax-related issues of the various business structures
- Federal and widely adopted uniform state laws and references as identified in References below.

Area III, Area IV and Area V of the REG exam blueprint cover various topics of federal income taxation and gift and estate tax. Accounting methods and periods, and tax elections are included in the Areas listed below:
- Area III covers the federal income taxation of property transactions. Area III also covers topics related to federal estate and gift taxation
- Area IV covers the federal income taxation of individuals from both a tax preparation and tax planning perspective
- Area V covers the federal income taxation of entities including sole proprietorships, partnerships, limited liability companies, C corporations, S corporations, joint ventures, trusts, estates and tax-exempt organizations, from both a tax preparation and tax planning perspective

References – Regulation

Revised Model Business Corporation Act
Revised Uniform Limited Partnership Act
Revised Uniform Partnership Act
Securities Act of 1933
Securities Exchange Act of 1934
Uniform Accountancy Act
Uniform Commercial Code
Internal Revenue Code of 1986, as amended
Treasury Department Circular 230
Treasury Regulations
Other administrative pronouncements regarding federal taxation
Case law on federal taxation
Public Law 86-272
Uniform Division of Income for Tax Purposes Act (UDITPA)
Current textbooks covering business law, federal taxation, auditing, accounting and ethics

REGULATION

Area I — Ethics, Professional Responsibilities and Federal Tax Procedures (10–20%)

Content Group/Topic	Remembering and Understanding	Application	Analysis	Evaluation	Representative Task
A. ETHICS AND RESPONSIBILITIES IN TAX PRACTICE					
1. Regulations governing practice before the Internal Revenue Service	✓				Recall the regulations governing practice before the Internal Revenue Service.
		✓			Apply the regulations governing practice before the Internal Revenue Service given a specific scenario.
2. Internal Revenue Code and Regulations related to tax return preparers	✓				Recall who is a tax return preparer.
	✓				Recall situations that would result in federal tax return preparer penalties.
		✓			Apply potential federal tax return preparer penalties given a specific scenario.
B. LICENSING AND DISCIPLINARY SYSTEMS					
	✓				Understand and explain the role and authority of state boards of accountancy.
C. FEDERAL TAX PROCEDURES					
1. Audits, appeals and judicial process	✓				Explain the audit and appeals process as it relates to federal tax matters.
	✓				Explain the different levels of the judicial process as they relate to federal tax matters.
		✓			Identify options available to a taxpayer within the audit and appeals process given a specific scenario.
		✓			Identify options available to a taxpayer within the judicial process given a specific scenario.

Uniform CPA Examination Section Blueprints: Regulation (REG) | REG 6

REGULATION

Area I — Ethics, Professional Responsibilities and Federal Tax Procedures (10–20%) Continued

Content Group/Topic	Remembering and Understanding	Skill			Representative Task
		Application	Analysis	Evaluation	
C. FEDERAL TAX PROCEDURES, continued					
2. Substantiation and disclosure of tax positions	✓				Summarize the requirements for the appropriate disclosure of a federal tax return position.
		✓			Identify situations in which disclosure of federal tax return positions is required.
		✓			Identify whether substantiation is sufficient given a specific scenario.
3. Taxpayer penalties	✓				Recall situations that would result in taxpayer penalties relating to federal tax returns.
		✓			Calculate taxpayer penalties relating to federal tax returns.
4. Authoritative hierarchy	✓				Recall the appropriate hierarchy of authority for federal tax purposes.
D. LEGAL DUTIES AND RESPONSIBILITIES					
1. Common law duties and liabilities to clients and third parties	✓				Summarize the tax return preparer's common law duties and liabilities to clients and third parties.
		✓			Identify situations which result in violations of the tax return preparer's common law duties and liabilities to clients and third parties.
2. Privileged communications, confidentiality and privacy acts	✓				Summarize the rules regarding privileged communications as they relate to tax practice.
		✓			Identify situations in which communications regarding tax practice are considered privileged.

Uniform CPA Examination Section Blueprints: Regulation (REG) | REG 7

REGULATION

Area II — Business Law (10–20%)

Content Group/Topic	Remembering and Understanding	Skill			Representative Task
		Application	Analysis	Evaluation	
A. AGENCY					
1. Authority of agents and principals	✓				Recall the types of agent authority.
		✓			Identify whether an agency relationship exists given a specific scenario.
2. Duties and liabilities of agents and principals	✓				Explain the various duties and liabilities of agents and principals.
		✓			Identify the duty or liability of an agent or principal given a specific scenario.
B. CONTRACTS					
1. Formation	✓				Summarize the elements of contract formation between parties.
		✓			Identify whether a valid contract was formed given a specific scenario.
		✓			Identify different types of contracts (e.g., written, verbal, unilateral, express, implied, etc.) given a specific scenario.
2. Performance	✓				Explain the rules related to the fulfillment of performance obligations necessary for an executed contract.
		✓			Identify whether both parties to a contract have fulfilled their performance obligation given a specific scenario.

Uniform CPA Examination Section Blueprints: Regulation (REG) | REG 8

REGULATION

Area II — Business Law (10–20%) Continued

Content Group/Topic	Skill				Representative Task
	Remembering and Understanding	Application	Analysis	Evaluation	
B. CONTRACTS, continued					
3. Discharge, breach and remedies	✓				Explain the different ways in which a contract can be discharged (e.g., performance, agreement, operation of the law, etc.)
	✓				Summarize the different remedies available to a party for breach of contract.
		✓			Identify situations involving breach of contract.
		✓			Identify whether a contract has been discharged given a specific scenario.
		✓			Identify the remedy available to a party for breach of contract given a specific scenario.
C. DEBTOR-CREDITOR RELATIONSHIPS					
1. Rights, duties, and liabilities of debtors, creditors and guarantors	✓				Explain the rights, duties and liabilities of debtors, creditors and guarantors.
		✓			Identify the rights, duties or liabilities of a debtors, creditors or guarantors given a specific scenario.
2. Bankruptcy and insolvency	✓				Explain the rights of the debtors and the creditors in bankruptcy and insolvency.
	✓				Summarize the rules related to the different types of bankruptcy.
	✓				Explain discharge of indebtedness in bankruptcy.
		✓			Identify the rights of the debtors and the creditors in bankruptcy and insolvency given a specific scenario.
		✓			Identify the type of bankruptcy described in a specific scenario.

Uniform CPA Examination Section Blueprints: Regulation (REG) | REG 9

REGULATION

Area II — Business Law (10–20%) Continued

Content Group/Topic	Skill				Representative Task
	Remembering and Understanding	Application	Analysis	Evaluation	
C. DEBTOR-CREDITOR RELATIONSHIPS, continued					
3. Secured transactions	✓				Explain how property can serve as collateral in secured transactions.
	✓				Summarize the priority rules of secured transactions.
	✓				Explain the requirements needed to create and perfect a security interest.
		✓			Identify the prioritized ordering of perfected security interests given a specific scenario.
		✓			Identify whether a creditor has created and perfected a security interest given a specific scenario.
D. GOVERNMENT REGULATION OF BUSINESS					
1. Federal securities regulation	✓				Summarize the various securities laws and regulations that affect corporate governance with respect to the Federal Securities Act of 1933 and the Federal Securities and Exchange Act of 1934.
		✓			Identify violations of the various securities laws and regulations that affect corporate governance with respect to the Federal Securities Act of 1933 and the Federal Securities and Exchange Act of 1934.
2. Other federal laws and regulations (e.g., employment tax, Affordable Care Act and worker classification)	✓				Summarize federal laws and regulations, for example, employment tax, Affordable Care Act and worker classification federal laws and regulations.
		✓			Identify violations of federal laws and regulations, for example, employment tax, Affordable Care Act and worker classification federal laws and regulations.

Uniform CPA Examination Section Blueprints: Regulation (REG) | REG 10

REGULATION

Area II — Business Law (10–20%) Continued

Content Group/Topic	Remembering and Understanding	Skill			Representative Task
		Application	Analysis	Evaluation	
E. BUSINESS STRUCTURE					
1. Selection and formation of business entity and related operation and termination	✓				Summarize the processes for formation and termination of various business entities.
	✓				Summarize the nontax operational features for various business entities.
		✓			Identify the type of business entity that is best described by a given set of nontax-related characteristics.
2. Rights, duties, legal obligations and authority of owners and management	✓				Summarize the rights, duties, legal obligations and authority of owners and management.
		✓			Identify the rights, duties, legal obligations or authorities of owners or management given a specific scenario.

REGULATION

Area III — Federal Taxation of Property Transactions (12–22%)

Content Group/Topic	Remembering and Understanding	Skill			Representative Task
		Application	Analysis	Evaluation	
A. ACQUISITION AND DISPOSITION OF ASSETS					
1. Basis and holding period of assets		✓			Calculate the tax basis of an asset.
		✓			Determine the holding period of a disposed asset for classification of tax gain or loss.
2. Taxable and nontaxable dispositions		✓			Calculate the realized and recognized gain or loss on the disposition of assets for federal income tax purposes.
		✓			Calculate the realized gain, recognized gain and deferred gain on like-kind property exchange transactions for federal income tax purposes.
			✓		Analyze asset sale and exchange transactions to determine whether they are taxable or nontaxable.
3. Amount and character of gains and losses, and netting process (including installment sales)		✓			Calculate the amount of capital gains and losses for federal income tax purposes.
		✓			Calculate the amount of ordinary income and loss for federal income tax purposes.
		✓			Calculate the amount of gain on an installment sale for federal income tax purposes.
			✓		Review asset transactions to determine the character (capital vs. ordinary) of the gain or loss for federal income tax purposes.
			✓		Analyze an agreement of sale of an asset to determine whether it qualifies for installment sale treatment for federal income tax purposes.

REGULATION

Area III — Federal Taxation of Property Transactions (12–22%) Continued

Content Group/Topic	Remembering and Understanding	Skill			Representative Task
		Application	Analysis	Evaluation	
A. ACQUISITION AND DISPOSITION OF ASSETS, continued					
4. Related party transactions (including imputed interest)	✓				Recall related parties for federal income tax purposes.
	✓				Recall the impact of related party ownership percentages on acquisition and disposition transactions of property for federal income tax purposes.
		✓			Calculate the direct and indirect ownership percentages of corporation stock to determine whether there are related parties for federal income tax purposes.
		✓			Calculate a taxpayer's basis in an asset that was disposed of at a loss to the taxpayer by a related party.
		✓			Calculate a taxpayer's gain or loss on a subsequent disposition of an asset to an unrelated third party that was previously disposed of at a loss to the taxpayer by a related party.
		✓			Calculate the impact of imputed interest on related party transactions for federal tax purposes.
B. COST RECOVERY (DEPRECIATION, DEPLETION AND AMORTIZATION)					
		✓			Calculate tax depreciation for tangible business property and tax amortization of intangible assets.
		✓			Calculate depletion for federal income tax purposes.
			✓		Compare the tax benefits of the Section 179 expense deduction vs. the regular tax depreciation deduction.
			✓		Reconcile the activity in the beginning and ending accumulated tax depreciation account.

REGULATION

Area III — Federal Taxation of Property Transactions (12–22%) Continued

Content Group/Topic	Remembering and Understanding	Skill			Representative Task
		Application	Analysis	Evaluation	
C. ESTATE AND GIFT TAXATION					
1. Transfers subject to gift tax	✓				Recall transfers of property subject to federal gift tax.
	✓				Recall whether federal Form 709 — *United States Gift (and Generation-Skipping Transfer) Tax Return* is required to be filed.
		✓			Calculate the amount and classification of a gift for federal gift tax purposes.
		✓			Calculate the amount of a gift subject to federal gift tax.
2. Gift tax annual exclusion and gift tax deductions	✓				Recall allowable gift tax deductions and exclusions for federal gift tax purposes.
	✓				Recall situations involving the gift tax annual exclusion, gift-splitting and the impact on the use of the lifetime exclusion amount for federal gift tax purposes.
		✓			Compute the amount of taxable gifts for federal gift tax purposes.
3. Determination of taxable estate	✓				Recall assets includible in a decedent's estate for federal estate tax purposes.
	✓				Recall allowable estate tax deductions in a decedent's estate.
		✓			Calculate the taxable estate for federal estate tax purposes.
		✓			Calculate the gross estate for federal estate tax purposes.
		✓			Calculate the allowable estate tax deductions for federal estate tax purposes.

REGULATION

Area IV — Federal Taxation of Individuals (including tax preparation and planning strategies) (15–25%)

| Content Group/Topic | Remembering and Understanding | Skill | | | Representative Task |
		Application	Analysis	Evaluation	
A. GROSS INCOME (INCLUSIONS AND EXCLUSIONS) (INCLUDES TAXATION OF RETIREMENT PLAN BENEFITS)					
		✓			Calculate the amounts that should be included in or excluded from an individual's gross income (including retirement plan distributions) as reported on federal Form 1040 — *U.S. Individual Income Tax Return.*
			✓		Analyze projected income for use in tax planning in future years.
			✓		Analyze client-provided documentation to determine the appropriate amount of gross income to be reported on federal Form 1040 — *U.S. Individual Income Tax Return.*
B. REPORTING OF ITEMS FROM PASS-THROUGH ENTITIES					
		✓			Prepare federal Form 1040 — *U.S. Individual Income Tax Return* based on the information provided on Schedule K-1.
C. ADJUSTMENTS AND DEDUCTIONS TO ARRIVE AT ADJUSTED GROSS INCOME AND TAXABLE INCOME					
		✓			Calculate the amount of adjustments and deductions to arrive at adjusted gross income and taxable income on federal Form 1040 — *U.S. Individual Income Tax Return.*
			✓		Analyze client-provided documentation to determine the validity of the deductions taken to arrive at adjusted gross income or taxable income on federal Form 1040 — *U.S. Individual Income Tax Return.*
D. PASSIVE ACTIVITY LOSSES (EXCLUDING FOREIGN TAX CREDIT IMPLICATIONS)					
	✓				Recall passive activities for federal income tax purposes.
		✓			Calculate net passive activity gains and losses for federal income tax purposes.
		✓			Prepare a loss carryforward schedule for passive activities for federal income tax purposes.
		✓			Calculate utilization of suspended losses on the disposition of a passive activity for federal income tax purposes.

Uniform CPA Examination Section Blueprints: Regulation (REG) | REG 15

REGULATION

Area IV — Federal Taxation of Individuals (including tax preparation and planning strategies) (15–25%) Continued

| Content Group/Topic | Remembering and Understanding | Skill | | | Representative Task |
		Application	Analysis	Evaluation	
E. LOSS LIMITATIONS					
		✓			Calculate loss limitations for federal income tax purposes for an individual taxpayer.
			✓		Analyze projections to effectively minimize loss limitations for federal income tax purposes for an individual taxpayer.
			✓		Determine the basis and the potential application of at-risk rules that can apply to activities for federal income tax purposes.
F. FILING STATUS AND EXEMPTIONS					
	✓				Recall taxpayer filing status for federal income tax purposes.
	✓				Recall relationships qualifying for personal exemptions reported on federal Form 1040 — *U.S. Individual Income Tax Return.*
		✓			Identify taxpayer filing status for federal income tax purposes given a specific scenario.
		✓			Identify the number of personal exemptions reported on federal Form 1040 — *U.S. Individual Income Tax Return* given a specific scenario.
G. COMPUTATION OF TAX AND CREDITS					
	✓				Recall and define the minimum requirements for individual federal estimated tax payments to avoid penalties.
		✓			Calculate the tax liability based on an individual's taxable income for federal income tax purposes.
		✓			Calculate the impact of tax deductions and tax credits and their effect on federal Form 1040 — *U.S. Individual Income Tax Return.*

Uniform CPA Examination Section Blueprints: Regulation (REG) | REG 16

REGULATION

Area IV — Federal Taxation of Individuals (including tax preparation and planning strategies) (15–25%) Continued

| Content Group/Topic | Remembering and Understanding | Skill | | | Representative Task |
		Application	Analysis	Evaluation	
H. ALTERNATIVE MINIMUM TAX					
	✓				Recall income and expense items includible in the computation of an individual taxpayer's alternative minimum taxable income (AMTI).
		✓			Calculate alternative minimum tax (AMT) for an individual taxpayer.

REGULATION

Area V — Federal Taxation of Entities (including tax preparation and planning strategies) (28–38%)

| Content Group/Topic | Remembering and Understanding | Skill | | | Representative Task |
		Application	Analysis	Evaluation	
A. TAX TREATMENT OF FORMATION AND LIQUIDATION OF BUSINESS ENTITIES					
		✓			Calculate the realized and recognized gain for the owner and entity upon the formation and liquidation of business entities for federal income tax purposes.
			✓		Compare the tax implications of liquidating distributions from different business entities.
			✓		Analyze the tax advantages and disadvantages in the formation of a new business entity.
B. DIFFERENCES BETWEEN BOOK AND TAX INCOME(LOSS)					
		✓			Identify permanent vs. temporary differences to be reported on Schedule M-1 and/or M-3.
		✓			Calculate the book/tax differences to be reported on a Schedule M-1 or M-3.
		✓			Prepare a Schedule M-1 or M-3 for a business entity.
			✓		Reconcile the differences between book and taxable income (loss) of a business entity.
C. C CORPORATIONS					
1. Computations of taxable income (including alternative minimum taxable income), tax liability and allowable credits		✓			Calculate alternative minimum taxable income and alternative minimum tax for a C corporation.
		✓			Calculate taxable income and tax liability for a C corporation.
		✓			Calculate credits allowable as a reduction to regular and alternative minimum tax for a C corporation.

REGULATION

Area V — Federal Taxation of Entities (including tax preparation and planning strategies) (28–38%) Continued

Content Group/Topic	Remembering and Understanding	Application	Analysis	Evaluation	Representative Task
C. C CORPORATIONS, continued					
2. Net operating losses and capital loss limitations		✓			Calculate the current-year net operating or capital loss of a C corporation.
		✓			Prepare a net operating and/or capital loss carryforward schedule for a C corporation.
			✓		Analyze the impact of the charitable contribution and/or dividends received deductions on the net operating loss calculation of a C corporation.
			✓		Analyze the impact of potentially expiring net operating and/or capital losses during tax planning for a C corporation.
3. Entity/owner transactions, including contributions, loans and distributions		✓			Calculate an entity owner's basis in C corporation stock for federal income tax purposes.
		✓			Calculate the tax gain (loss) realized and recognized by both the shareholders and the corporation on a contribution or on a distribution in complete liquidation of a C corporation for federal income tax purposes.
		✓			Calculate the tax gain (loss) realized and recognized on a nonliquidating distribution by both a C corporation and its shareholders for federal income tax purposes.
		✓			Calculate the amount of the cash distributions to shareholders of a C corporation that represents a dividend, return of capital or capital gain for federal income tax purposes.
			✓		Reconcile an owner's beginning and ending basis in C corporation stock for federal income tax purposes.
4. Consolidated tax returns	✓				Recall the requirements for filing a consolidated federal Form 1120 — *U.S. Corporation Income Tax Return.*
		✓			Prepare a consolidated federal Form 1120 — *U.S. Corporation Income Tax Return.*
		✓			Calculate federal taxable income for a consolidated federal Form 1120 — *U.S. Corporation Income Tax Return.*

Uniform CPA Examination Section Blueprints: Regulation (REG) | REG 19

REGULATION

Area V — Federal Taxation of Entities (including tax preparation and planning strategies) (28–38%) Continued

Content Group / Topic	Remembering and Understanding	Application	Analysis	Evaluation	Representative Task
C. C CORPORATIONS, continued					
5. Multijurisdictional tax issues (including consideration of local, state and international tax issues)	✓				Define the general concept and rationale of nexus with respect to multijurisdictional transactions.
	✓				Define the general concept and rationale of apportionment and allocation with respect to state and local taxation.
	✓				Explain the difference between a foreign branch and foreign subsidiary with respect to federal income taxation to a U.S. company.
	✓				Explain how different types of foreign income are sourced in calculating the foreign tax credit for federal income tax purposes.
	✓				Recall payment sources to determine federal tax withholding requirements.
		✓			Identify situations that would create nexus for multijurisdictional transactions.
		✓			Identify the federal filing requirements of cross border business investments.
		✓			Calculate the apportionment percentage used in determining state taxable income.
D. S CORPORATIONS					
1. Eligibility and election	✓				Recall eligible shareholders for an S corporation for federal income tax purposes.
	✓				Recall S corporation eligibility requirements for federal income tax purposes.
	✓				Explain the procedures to make a valid S corporation election for federal income tax purposes.
		✓			Identify situations in which S corporation status would be revoked or terminated for federal income tax purposes.

Uniform CPA Examination Section Blueprints: Regulation (REG) | REG 20

REGULATION

Area V — Federal Taxation of Entities (including tax preparation and planning strategies) (28–38%) Continued

Content Group/Topic	Remembering and Understanding	Application	Analysis	Evaluation	Representative Task
D. S CORPORATIONS, continued					
2. Determination of ordinary business income (loss) and separately stated items		✓			Calculate ordinary business income (loss) for an S corporation for federal income tax purposes.
		✓			Calculate separately stated items for an S corporation for federal income tax purposes.
			✓		Analyze both the accumulated adjustment account and the other adjustments account of an S corporation for federal income tax purposes.
			✓		Analyze the accumulated earnings and profits account of an S corporation that has been converted from a C corporation.
			✓		Analyze components of S corporation income/deductions to determine classification as ordinary business income (loss) or separately stated items on federal Form 1120S — U.S Income Tax Return for an S Corporation.
3. Basis of shareholder's interest		✓			Calculate the shareholder's basis in S corporation stock for federal income tax purposes.
			✓		Analyze shareholder transactions with an S corporation to determine the impact on the shareholder's basis for federal income tax purposes.
4. Entity/owner transactions (including contributions, loans and distributions)		✓			Calculate the realized and recognized gain or loss to the shareholder of property contribution to an S corporation.
		✓			Calculate the allocation of S corporation income (loss) after the sale of a shareholder's share in the S corporation for federal income tax purposes.
			✓		Analyze the shareholder's impact of an S corporation's loss in excess of the shareholder's basis for federal income tax purposes.
			✓		Analyze the federal income tax implication to the shareholders and the S corporation resulting from shareholder contributions and loans as well as S corporation distributions and loans to shareholders.
5. Built-in gains tax	✓				Recall factors that cause a built-in gains tax to apply for federal income tax purposes.

Uniform CPA Examination Section Blueprints: Regulation (REG) | REG 21

REGULATION

Area V — Federal Taxation of Entities (including tax preparation and planning strategies) (28–38%) Continued

Content Group/Topic	Remembering and Understanding	Application	Analysis	Evaluation	Representative Task
E. PARTNERSHIPS					
1. Determination of ordinary business income (loss) and separately stated items		✓			Calculate ordinary business income (loss) for a partnership for federal income tax purposes.
		✓			Calculate separately stated items for a partnership for federal income tax purposes.
			✓		Analyze components of partnership income/deductions to determine classification as ordinary business income (loss) or separately stated items on federal Form 1065 — U.S Return of Partnership Income.
2. Basis of partner's interest and basis of assets contributed to the partnership		✓			Calculate the partner's basis in the partnership for federal income tax purposes.
		✓			Calculate the partnership's basis in assets contributed by the partner for federal income tax purposes.
			✓		Analyze partner contributions to the partnership to determine the impact on the partner's basis for federal income tax purposes.
3. Partnership and partner elections	✓				Recall partner elections applicable to a partnership for federal income tax purposes.
4. Transactions between a partner and the partnership (including services performed by a partner and loans)		✓			Calculate the tax implications of certain transactions between a partner and partnership (such as services performed by a partner or loans) for federal income tax purposes.
			✓		Analyze the tax implications of a partner transaction with the partnership (such as services performed by a partner or loans) to determine the impact on the partner's tax basis for federal income tax purposes.
5. Impact of partnership liabilities on a partner's interest in a partnership		✓			Calculate the impact of increases and decreases of partnership liabilities on a partner's basis for federal income tax purposes.
			✓		Analyze the impact of partnership liabilities as they relate to the general partners and limited partners for federal income tax purposes.

Uniform CPA Examination Section Blueprints: Regulation (REG) | REG 22

REGULATION

Area V — Federal Taxation of Entities (including tax preparation and planning strategies) (28–38%) Continued

Content Group/Topic	Remembering and Understanding	Application	Analysis	Evaluation	Representative Task
E. PARTNERSHIPS, continued					
6. Distribution of partnership assets		✓			Calculate the realized and recognized gains (losses) by the partnership and partners of liquidating distributions from the partnership for federal income tax purposes.
		✓			Calculate the realized and recognized gains (losses) by the partnership and partners of nonliquidating distributions from the partnership for federal income tax purposes.
		✓			Calculate the partner's basis of partnership assets received in a liquidating distribution for federal income tax purposes.
		✓			Calculate the partner's basis of partnership assets received in a nonliquidating distribution for federal income tax purposes.
7. Ownership changes	✓				Recall the situations in which a partnership would be terminated for federal income tax purposes.
		✓			Calculate the allocation of partnership income (loss) after the sale of a partner's share in the partnership for federal income tax purposes.
		✓			Calculate the revised basis of partnership assets when making a Section 754 election due to a transfer of a partnership interest for federal income tax purposes.
F. LIMITED LIABILITY COMPANIES					
	✓				Recall the tax classification options for a limited liability company for federal income tax purposes.
G. TRUSTS AND ESTATES					
1. Types of trusts	✓				Recall and explain the differences between simple and complex trusts for federal income tax purposes.

REGULATION

Area V — Federal Taxation of Entities (including tax preparation and planning strategies) (28–38%) Continued

Content Group/Topic	Remembering and Understanding	Application	Analysis	Evaluation	Representative Task
G. TRUSTS AND ESTATES, continued					
2. Income and deductions		✓			Calculate the total amount of income items reportable on a federal Form 1041 — *U.S. Income Tax Return for Estates and Trusts.*
		✓			Calculate the total amount of deductible expenses reportable on a federal Form 1041 — *U.S. Income Tax Return for Estates and Trusts.*
3. Determination of beneficiary's share of taxable income		✓			Calculate the beneficiary's share of taxable income from a trust for federal income tax purposes.
H. TAX EXEMPT ORGANIZATIONS					
1. Types of organizations	✓				Recall the different types of tax-exempt organizations for federal tax purposes.
2. Obtaining and maintaining tax exempt status	✓				Recall the requirements to qualify as an IRC Section 501(c)(3) tax-exempt organization.
	✓				Summarize the federal filing and disclosure requirements to obtain tax-exempt status for an organization.
	✓				Summarize the annual federal filing and disclosure requirements for a tax-exempt organization.
	✓				Explain the requirements necessary for retaining tax-exempt status.
	✓				Explain the procedures and recall the time period required to obtain tax-exempt status once the status has been revoked.
3. Unrelated business income		✓			Calculate the unrelated business income for a tax-exempt organization for federal income tax purposes.

State	State Board Web Address	Telephone #
AK	commerce.state.ak.us/occ/pcpa.htm	(907) 465-3811
AL	asbpa.alabama.gov	(334) 242-5700
AR	state.ar.us/asbpa	(501) 682-1520
AZ	azaccountancy.gov	(602) 364-0804
CA	dca.ca.gov/cba	(916) 263-3680
CO	dora.state.co.us/accountants	(303) 894-7800
CT	ct.gov/sboa	(860) 509-6179
DC	pearsonvue.com/dc/accountancy/	(202) 442-4320
DE	dpr.delaware.gov/boards/accountancy/index.shtml	(302) 744-4500
FL	myfloridalicense.com/dbpr/cpa/	(850) 487-1395
GA	sos.state.ga.us/plb/accountancy/	(478) 207-1400
GU	guamboa.org	(671) 647-0813
HI	hawaii.gov/dcca/areas/pvl/boards/accountancy	(808) 586-2696
IA	state.ia.us/iacc	(515) 281-5910
ID	isba.idaho.gov	(208) 334-2490
IL	ilboa.org	(217) 531-0950
IN	in.gov/pla/accountancy.htm	(317) 234-3040
KS	ksboa.org	(785) 296-2162
KY	cpa.ky.gov	(502) 595-3037
LA	cpaboard.state.la.us	(504) 566-1244
MA	mass.gov/reg/boards/pa	(617) 727-1806
MD	dllr.state.md.us/license/occprof/account.html	(410) 230-6322
ME	maine.gov/pfr/professionallicensing/professions/accountants/index.htm	(207) 624-8603
MI	michigan.gov/accountancy	(517) 241-9249
MN	boa.state.mn.us	(651) 296-7938
MO	pr.mo.gov/accountancy.asp	(573) 751-0012
MS	msbpa.state.ms.us	(601) 354-7320
MT	publicaccountant.mt.gov	(406) 841-2389
NC	nccpaboard.gov	(919) 733-4222
ND	state.nd.us/ndsba	(800) 532-5904
NE	nol.org/home/BPA	(402) 471-3595
NH	nh.gov/accountancy	(603) 271-3286
NJ	state.nj.us/lps/ca/accountancy/	(973) 504-6380
NM	rld.state.nm.us/accountancy/index.html	(505) 841-9108
NV	nvaccountancy.com/	(775) 786-0231
NY	op.nysed.gov/cpa.htm	(518) 474-3817
OH	acc.ohio.gov/	(614) 466-4135
OK	oab.state.ok.us	(405) 521-2397
OR	egov.oregon.gov/BOA/	(503) 378-4181
PA	dos.state.pa.us/account	(717) 783-1404
PR	estado.gobierno.pr/	(787) 722-4816
RI	dbr.ri.gov/divisions/accountancy/	(401) 222-3185
SC	llr.state.sc.us/POL/Accountancy	(803) 896-4770
SD	state.sd.us/dol/Boards/accountancy/acc-home.htm	(605) 367-5770
TN	tn.gov/commerce/boards/tnsba/index.shtml	(615) 741-2550
TX	tsbpa.state.tx.us	(512) 305-7800
UT	dopl.utah.gov	(801) 530-6396
VA	boa.virginia.gov	(804) 367-8505
VI	dlca.gov.vi	(340) 773-4305
VT	vtprofessionals.org/opr1/accountants	(802) 828-2837
WA	cpaboard.wa.gov	(360) 753-2585
WI	drl.wi.gov/profession.asp?profid=60&locid=0	(608) 266-5511
WV	boa.wv.gov/Pages/default.aspx	(304) 558-3557
WY	cpaboard.state.wy.us	(307) 777-7551

Taxation

(55% - 80%)

Section 1 – Individual Taxation
Corresponding Lectures

Watch the following course lectures with this section:

Lecture 1.01 – Individual Income Tax Return
Lecture 1.02 – Filing Requirements
Lecture 1.03 – Individual Income Tax Return – Class Questions
Lecture 1.04 – Gross Income
Lecture 1.05 – Gross Income Continued
Lecture 1.06 – Tax Schedules
Lecture 1.07 – Adjustments for (to) AGI
Lecture 1.08 – Adjustments for (to) AGI Continued
Lecture 1.09 – Adjustments for (to) AGI – Class Questions
Lecture 1.10 – Standard and Itemized Deductions
Lecture 1.11 – Itemized Deductions – Class Questions
Lecture 1.12 – Exemptions and Filing Status
Lecture 1.13 – Tax Credits and Tax Procedures
Lecture 1.14 – Tax Credits and Tax Procedures – Class Questions
Lecture 1.15 – Alternative Minimum Tax
Lecture 1.16 – Alternative Minimum Tax – Class Questions
Lecture 1.17 – Individual Taxation – Class Questions - TBS
Lecture 1.18 – Individual Taxation – Class Questions - TBS Continued
Lecture 1.19 – Research Task Format

EXAM NOTE: *Please refer to the AICPA REG Blueprint in the Introduction to find a listing of the representative tasks (and their associated skill levels—i.e., Remembering and Understanding, Application, and Analysis) that the candidate should be able to perform based on the knowledge obtained in this section.*

Individual Taxation

INDIVIDUAL INCOME TAX RETURN

The AICPA has historically only tested amounts applicable to the calendar year previous to the year of the exam (e.g., 2017 tax numbers for the first half of 2018 and then 2018 numbers for the second half of 2018 and the first half of 2019); however, the examiners tend not to focus on inflation-adjusted numbers in exam questions. The Internal Revenue Code (IRC) is the basic foundation of federal tax laws and represents a codification of the federal tax laws of the United States.

Form 1040

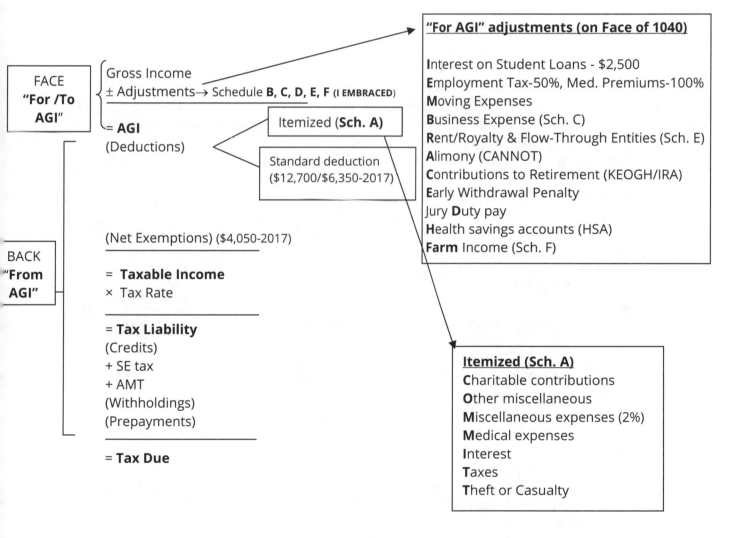

Caution: At the time of this writing, President Trump had introduced his broad plan for tax reform. Some information in the preceding section, such as standard deduction amounts, may be subject to change soon. Please refer to the Course Textbook Updates section of the Roger CPA Review website for legislation updates: https://www.rogercpareview.com/dashboard/my-courses/course-textbook-updates.

Lecture 1.02

FILING REQUIREMENTS

An Individual **must file** a tax return if their income is greater than the sum of their personal exemption plus their standard deduction, or if they:
- Have net self-employment earnings of $400 or more
- Are claimed as a dependent on another taxpayer's return, and have gross income greater than the dependent's standard deduction—
  - $1,050 (2017) or,
  - If larger, earned income plus $350 (total not to exceed $6,350-2017)
    (e.g., Suzie, who is claimed on her parents' return, has no unearned income but works at the corner store and makes $1,300 in 2017. She does not have to file a return because her standard deduction as a dependent is $1,300 plus $350, or $1,650. If Suzie had unearned income from dividends of $500 on top of her $1,300 earned income, she would have to file a return because her gross income is $1,800 and her filing threshold is still $1,650.)
- Are receiving advanced payments of the Earned Income Credit (EIC) or Premium Tax Credit (PTC)
- Are subject to the **Kiddie Tax**

The Kiddie tax was established to prevent the "wealthy" from avoiding taxes on their investment income by transferring the investments into the names of their children, who might not be subject to tax or, if so, would be taxed at lower rates. Thus, a child's unearned income above the following thresholds in 2017 is subject to tax at the parent's higher rate:
- $2,100, or
- If greater, $1,050 plus itemized deductions related to the production of the unearned income.

The Kiddie tax applies to children meeting the following conditions:
- The child has unearned income in excess of $2,100 (2017);
- Either parent is alive as of the end of the taxable year;
- The child does not file a joint tax return for the year; and
- The child is:
  1. Under 18 years old as of the end of the tax year, or
  2. 18 years old with earned income that does not exceed 50% of the child's support, or
  3. A student between the ages of 19 and 24 with earned income that does not exceed 50% of the child's support.

In calculating the Kiddie tax, the child's unearned income can generally be broken down into three increments:
- Up to the amount of the dependent's standard deduction (i.e., $0 - $1,050, 2017) – not taxed.
- Above the dependent's standard deduction up to 2 times that amount (i.e., $1,051 - $2,100, 2017) – taxed at child's rate.
- Any remainder (i.e., >$2,100, 2017) – taxed at the parent's tax rate; this is the Kiddie tax.

For **example**, Richie Rich, age 11, has $25,000 in unearned income and no earned income. The amount of Richie Rich's unearned income subject to the Kiddie tax is $25,000 – $2,100 (i.e., 2 × his $1,050 standard deduction for 2017), or $22,900, meaning $22,900 of Richie's unearned income will be taxed at his parents' tax rate.

Cash Basis and Accrual Basis of Accounting

Most individuals use the cash basis of accounting; however, the accrual method is generally required if purchases and sales of inventory are necessary for the determination of income.
- Service-type businesses whose gross receipts do not exceed $10M may use the cash basis. This generally includes:
  - Most individuals, S corps, Partnerships owned by individuals, and personal service corporations (PSCs). **Note:** $10M limit does not apply to *qualified PSCs* where 95% of stock is owned by owner-employees (i.e., ownership test) and 95% of activities are in certain fields, such as health, law, accounting, etc. (i.e., function test).

Some entities that are **prohibited** from using the cash basis include:
- C corporations with gross receipts exceeding $5M
- Partnerships that have a C corporation as a partner exceeding $5M
- Tax shelters
- Certain trusts

Cash Basis
- **Recognize Income**
  - Cash or property received, at FMV
    - Even if "unearned" (prepaid rent), still income when received.

  - **Actually or constructively received** (i.e., made available – earlier of two)
    - Postdated check

- **Report Deductions**
  - Cash or check is disbursed
  - Expense charged on a credit card
    - Prepaid interest is not deductible. Amortize over the period to which it applies.

Accrual Basis
- Recognize income when "earned"
  - Right to receive and amount can be determined
- Book expenses as "incurred"
  - Liability exists and amount is determinable (property and services have been provided)
- If inventories are necessary to clearly determine income, then the accrual method must be used.
- An accrual basis taxpayer that receives rents or royalties in advance is required to include them in taxable income in the period received.

Lecture 1.03

CLASS QUESTIONS

Please see the Class Questions and Class Solutions for this Lecture at the end of this Section.

Lecture 1.04

GROSS INCOME

GENERALLY INCOME	NOT INCOME
Compensation for services including: • Wages and salaries (W-2) • Tips • Fees for jury duty service • Bonuses and commissions • Unemployment compensation • Most fringe benefits, such as the rental value of using a company car on weekends for personal purposes • Bargain purchases of employer merchandise/services	• Health insurance coverage • Group term life insurance coverage, up to a $50,000 policy • Fringe benefits that primarily are incurred for the employer's benefit, such as free housing given to an on-site hotel manager • Immaterial fringe benefits, such as free photocopies made on the company machine • Employer-provided educational assistance • Up to employer's gross profit percentage of regular merchandise price • Up to 20% of FMV of employer services obtained at discount
• Prizes and awards • Gambling winnings • Illegal drug income (net of COGS) • Treasure trove (i.e., if you find money or something of value and you keep it; it's taxable)	A prize or award that is both: • Tangible personal property up to certain dollar values • Received by an employee for his years of company employment or safety achievement OR a prize or award where: • No services required of recipient; • Selected without action on recipient's part; *and* • Payment assigned by recipient to a governmental unit or charitable organization.
• Scholarships and fellowships	A scholarship or fellowship that is both: • Not compensation for required services • Spent by a degree candidate for tuition
• Interest accrued each year on a zero-coupon bond or bond purchased at a discount • Interest on U.S. Treasury obligations • Interest on Series HH U.S. savings bonds (paid semi-annually)	• Interest on state or municipal bonds • Interest earned on qualified higher education bonds • Interest on a Series EE U.S. savings bond is not reported as income until the time that the bond is redeemed.
• Dividends	• Stock dividends • Dividends received from an S corporation • Dividends received on a life insurance policy • Dividends received from a mutual fund that invests in tax-exempt bonds
Rents and royalties, including: • Rent collected in advance by a landlord • Nonrefundable deposits collected from tenants	Refundable security deposits

GENERALLY INCOME	NOT INCOME
The **bargain discount** from exercising a stock option to buy an employer's stock for a price below market value	A special type of stock option, called an incentive stock option (ISO)
Proceeds withdrawn from a traditional IRA or pension plan if the original contributions to the plan were excluded or deducted from income	The portion, if any, of a traditional IRA or pension withdrawal that represents the recovery of prior nondeductible contributions and all Roth IRA withdrawals.
Injury awards, if they are for: • Punitive damages • Lost business profits • Non-physical injuries, such as age or race discrimination • Emotional distress (in excess of associated medical bills)	• Damages for bodily injury, pain and suffering, and lost wages • Emotional distress attributable to physical injury or sickness • Workers' compensation benefits
Up to 85% of Social Security benefits if the taxpayer has substantial income in addition to the benefits	Up to 100% of Social Security benefits, if the taxpayer does not have much income in addition to benefits
State tax refunds, if the state taxes paid were originally claimed as a deduction in an earlier year	Federal tax refunds
• The interest component of an annuity. For example, assume that a person spends $400 to buy an annuity of $100 for each of 5 years, or $500 proceeds in total. Since a $100 interest profit is part of the $500 proceeds, the portion of each payment that is reported as income is: Profit/Total Proceeds=$100/$500=20% • Income generated by gifts and inheritances (e.g., rent received on inherited rental property)	• Gifts • Inheritances • Life insurance proceeds paid upon the death of the insured
Alimony (**CANNOT**) • **C**ash Only or its equivalent • **A**part when payments made • **N**ot child support • **N**ot a property settlement • **O**wn return for payer and payee • **T**erminates on death of recipient	• Child Support • Property Settlement
Cancellation of Debt	• Debt forgiven as gift, bequest, or inheritance • Certain qualified student loans • Debt that would have provided a tax deduction • Debt cancelled in Chapter 11 bankruptcy • Debt cancelled when debtor is insolvent • Qualified farm indebtedness • Qualified real property business indebtedness
Capital gains	• Up to $250,000 gain on personal residence ($500,000 MFJ)
Note: This is not meant to be an all-inclusive list. IRC Section 61 provides that all income from whatever source derived is includible in gross income unless specifically excluded by law.	

Gross Income

An item must be included in the gross income of an individual in the year it is **constructively received.** This refers to when the cash becomes available to the taxpayer. Thus, a dividend that is credited to the shareholder's brokerage account but automatically reinvested in the purchase of additional shares is considered received by the taxpayer. The receipt of property or services is treated as the receipt of the cash that normally would have been required to pay for them.

Earned Income

- *Salaries and wages* (**W-2**) are reported when cash or other consideration is received. **For example**, an expensive watch or stock in the corporation that is given to an employee is treated as compensation at the fair market value of the property.
- *Tips* are normally reported by the employee to their employer, and are included in the reported wages of that employee**.** Tips not reported to the employer must be directly reported on the tax return by the employee based on when the tips are **received**.
- Jury duty fees
- Unemployment compensation
- Payment in non-money form reported at FMV when received (stock, property)
- Premiums on group term life insurance over $50,000 are taxable (fringe benefits), but the death benefits received are tax free.
- Life insurance proceeds are generally tax free, unless purchased from a person other than the insurance co (as an investment) or if paid out in installments; then a pro rata part of the receipts is taxable as interest.
  - A qualified cafeteria plan (menu of benefits) is an employer-sponsored benefit plan where the employee can choose either cash (taxable) or benefits (accident insurance, life insurance, legal services – not taxable). With the exception of 401(k) plans, deferred compensation plans are excluded from qualifying cafeteria plans.
- Gambling winnings – Gross winnings must be included in gross income. Gambling losses may be claimed as itemized deductions to the extent of winnings.
- Prizes and awards are taxable, unless received for years of service or safety achievement and such prizes and awards do not exceed $400 (reported at FMV).
- Health and medical insurance coverage is not taxable.
- Immaterial fringe benefits not taxable (e.g., Xeroxing resume)
- Illegal drug income (net of COGS, not any other expenses)

Scholarships, taxable unless both (no strings):

- Not compensation for services *and*
- Money spent for tuition, books, or class supplies for degree-seeking student

Interest (Schedule B)

- State and local municipal bond interest is not taxable.
- All other government interest is taxable (e.g., Federal bonds, T-bills).
- Accrual basis taxpayers are taxed on interest on U.S. savings bonds in the period it accrues, regardless of when received.
- **Series HH** bonds, the last of which mature in 2024, were issued at face value.
  - Interest is payable twice per year.
  - Cash basis taxpayers are taxed on interest in the period received.
- **Series EE** savings bonds
  - Taxable interest is equal to the difference between the redemption value and the purchase price.
  - May be paper or electronic

- Paper issued at discount and redeemed at face value
- Electronic issued at face and redeemed at face plus accrued interest
  - o Exempt if used for *higher education* for self, spouse, or dependent
    - Bought by taxpayer (or spouse)
    - Buyer at least 24 years of age
    - Redeem directly – need not transfer to school
    - Tuition and fees qualify, but room and board do not qualify
- **Series E** savings bonds, which were issued prior to Series EE savings bonds, were issued at a discount and redeemed at face value.
- **Series I** savings bonds, which are inflation-indexed bonds, are issued at face and redeemed at maturity at face value plus accrued interest.
- A **cash basis** taxpayer can choose either of the following methods for reporting interest income on Series E, EE, or I bonds:
  - o Report all interest when bonds are redeemed or sold
  - o Report interest as the increase in the redemption value of the bond each year

Dividends (Schedule B)
- Taxable when received ***unless:***
  - o Life insurance dividend - return of premium
    - But interest on the dividend is taxable
  - o Received from an S corporation
  - o Stock dividends or stock splits on common stock
    - Stock dividends from Preferred stock are taxable at FMV.
    - Cash and property dividends from common stock are taxable.
  - o Liquidating dividend - return of capital
- Qualified dividends are taxed at special 0%, 15% or 20%, *similar to long-term capital gains*.
  - o **0%** tax rate if in the 10% or 15% tax brackets
  - o **15%** tax rate if in the 25%, 28%, 33%, 35% tax bracket
  - o **20%** tax rate if in the 39.6% tax bracket ("**high income**" taxpayers with AGI over $450,000 (MFJ), $400,000 (Single)—$470,700, $418,400 for 2017)
  - o Applies to *qualified dividends* from a domestic corporation and certain qualified foreign corporations. Must hold 60+ days during 121-day period beginning 60 days prior to ex-dividend date.
  - o **Note:** Special rate doesn't apply to dividends from nontaxable entities such as REITs or dividends that are deductible by the payer organization. Treatment of mutual fund distributions is based on source of income being distributed (e.g., dividends representing distribution of interest earned by bond-oriented mutual fund doesn't qualify).

  Caution: At the time of this writing, President Trump had introduced his broad plan for tax reform. Some information in the preceding section may be subject to change soon. Please refer to the Course Textbook Updates section of the Roger CPA Review website for legislation updates: https://www.rogercpareview.com/dashboard/my-courses/course-textbook-updates.

- **Surtax on Unearned Income** - A surtax called the ***Unearned Income Medicare Contribution Tax*** is imposed on the *unearned income* of individuals, estates, and trusts. This is part of the Patient Protection and Affordable Care Act (PPACA). For individuals, the surtax is **3.8%** of the **lesser** of:

1. The taxpayer's **net** investment income
   o "Net" investment income is investment income reduced by allowable investment expenses. Investment income includes interest income, dividends, annuities, royalties, rents (other than those derived from a trade or business), capital gains (other than those derived from a trade or business), trade or business income that is a passive activity with respect to the taxpayer, and trade or business income with respect to the trading of financial instruments or commodities. Retirement plan distributions are excluded. **OR**

2. The excess of modified adjusted gross income (MAGI), which is AGI before any foreign earned income exclusion, over the threshold amount **($250,000 for a joint return or surviving spouse**, $125,000 for a married individual filing a separate return, and **$200,000** for all others)
   o This effectively makes the tax rate on L/T capital gains and qualified dividends 23.8% (20% + 3.8%) for high-income taxpayers ($450k MFJ, $400k single). Still applies if income under $450k but over $250k, but rate would be 15% + 3.8% = 18.8%.
   o **Example**: Roger and Louisa have investment income of $40,000 and Modified AGI of $300,000. The net investment income of $40,000 is lower than the excess of MAGI over the threshold ($300,000 - $250,000 = $50,000). Therefore, they will be taxed on the lower amount of $40,000 vs $50,000, which is $40,000 x 3.8% = $1,520. If investment income had been $75,000, then they would be taxed on the lower of $50,000 vs $75,000, or $50,000 x 3.8% = $1,900.

Stock Options
- *Non-qualified* – taxed when **exercised**; excess of fair market value over exercise price treated as compensation.
- *Qualified* (incentive stock option **– ISO**) – taxed when **sell** stock; difference between sales price and exercise price treated as capital gain or loss.
  o For AMT purposes, however, ISOs are taxed when exercised.
  o ISO must be held 2 years from grant date and 1 year from exercise date.

Injury awards
- Non-physical – **Taxable**
  o Age, race discrimination
  o Punitive damages
  o Lost business profits
- Bodily injury – **tax free (blood)**
  o Pain & suffering for physical injury
  o Workers' compensation
  o Reimbursement of medical expenses paid and not itemized on Schedule A

Prizes and awards – Taxable at FMV unless *all* conditions satisfied:
- No services required of recipient.
- Selected without any action on recipient's part.
- Payment assigned by recipient to a governmental unit or charitable organization so that recipient *never actually receives* the prize or award.

Lecture 1.05

GROSS INCOME (Continued)

Social Security Benefits

- **Social security benefits** may or may not be taxable based on a complicated calculation using **provisional income** (adjusted gross income before social security + tax-exempt income + one-half of social security benefits). As a result of the calculation, anywhere from 0 to 85% of benefits may be taxable. In general, a person collecting social security who has **less than $25,000** of provisional income can *exclude all* social security benefits, while taxpayers with provisional income **exceeding $60,000** usually are subject to the maximum **85%** inclusion.

Debt Forgiveness

- In general, when a debtor's debts are cancelled, forgiven, or discharged, such as through relief in bankruptcy, the amount forgiven is *taxable to the debtor*.
- There are certain debts that are *not taxable* when forgiven. These include:
  - Amounts excludable from income such as gifts, bequests, or inheritances
  - Cancellation of certain qualified student loans
  - Debt that, upon payment, would provide a tax deduction to the taxpayer
- In addition, cancellation of debt is *not taxable* to the debtor in certain circumstances. These include:
  - Debt that is cancelled in a Chapter 11 bankruptcy case
  - Debt that is cancelled when the debtor is insolvent, which is when debts exceed the market value of the debtor's assets
  - Qualified farm indebtedness
  - Qualified real property business indebtedness

Pensions and Annuities

- *Pension benefits and annuities* (other than excluded recovery of capital), including distributions from IRAs (other than Roth IRA accounts), may be taxable. The amount considered a return of capital will NOT be taxable. If the taxpayer did not pay any portion of the cost of the pension plan, such as one in which all costs were incurred by an employer, all benefits are taxable.

  $$\frac{\text{Cost of annuity}}{\text{Expected total annuity payments}} = \text{percentage of each payment that is excluded from taxes}$$

- *Lump-sum distributions* from qualified pension, profit-sharing, stock bonus, and Keogh plans (but not IRAs) may be eligible for special tax treatment. Certain distributions may be rolled-over tax-free (within 60 days) to a traditional IRA account.

Foreign Earned Income Exclusion

- An individual meeting either a *bona fide residence test* or a *physical presence test* may elect to exclude up to $102,100 for 2017) of income earned in a foreign country. Qualifying taxpayers also may elect to exclude additional amounts based on foreign housing costs.
  - To qualify, an individual must be a (1) U.S. citizen who is a foreign resident for an uninterrupted period that includes an entire taxable year (bona fide residence test), or (2) U.S. citizen or resident present in a foreign country for at least 330 full days in any 12-month period (physical presence test).

Tax Refunds

- *Federal*
  - Refund – Not taxable (a return of YOUR money)
  - Interest – YES, taxable
- *State*
  - Interest – YES, taxable
  - Refund – Generally, if itemized in the prior year, got deduction on Schedule A, taxable in current year (Form 1099G). If didn't itemize in prior year, not taxable in current year. **Note:** A refund is taxable to the extent the taxpayer received a *tax benefit* in the prior year. For example, if the taxpayer itemizes their deductions because $500 in state taxes allowed their deductions to exceed the standard deduction by $100, then only the $100 tax benefit is taxable in the current year since the taxpayer would have otherwise claimed the standard deduction.

Inheritances, Gifts and Life Insurance Proceeds

- Not taxable to recipient
  - However, any income received from the property is taxable.
  - Discussed in more detail in the Estate, Trust and Gift Tax section

Capital Assets (Sch. D)

- Long-term **capital gains** special tax rates if held over 1 year
  - Now taxed at special 0%, 15% or 20% long-term capital gain rate
    - **0%** tax rate if in the 10% or 15% tax bracket
    - **15%** tax rate if in the 25% - 35% tax bracket
    - **20%** tax rate if in the 39.6% tax bracket ("**high income**" taxpayers with AGI over $450,000 (MFJ), $400,000 (Single)—$470,700, $418,400 for 2017)
  - $\leq$ 1 year, ordinary tax rate
- Net **capital loss** up to *$3,000* against ordinary income ($1,500 for MFS)
  - Unused amount carried forward *indefinitely*
  - **Corporations** get $0 net capital loss. Can carry back 3 years and forward 5 years. No special tax rate.
- In most cases, one must report capital gains and losses on Form 8949 and then report the totals on Schedule D.
- Personal assets, such as the family home or automobile, are also considered capital assets.
  - Gains from the sales of personal assets are taxed as capital gains.
    - Gain on personal residence excludable up to $250,000, or $500,000 if MFJ
  - Losses on the sale or abandonment of personal use assets are not deductible.
    - **Note:** IRC §165(c) generally limits the deduction of losses by an individual to (1) losses incurred in a trade or business; (2) losses incurred in a transaction entered into for profit; and (3) losses of property arising by casualty or theft.
  - Discussed in more detail in the Property Tax section

Net Operating Losses (NOL) Carryback 2 and Carryforward 20 Years

- Generally, a business loss, but could also result from a personal casualty loss.
- Include in calculation: Trade or business income (Sch. C, K-1), wages, casualty or theft loss, moving expenses, rental property (Sch. E).
  - Do not include in calculation: personal exemption, interest, dividends, or capital losses in excess of capital gains, nonbusiness deductions (e.g., standard deduction) in excess of nonbusiness income
- **Corporations**, similar rules

Example: Sammy is in the comic book business. He is single and has the following income and deductions on his Form 1040 for year 1:

- **Income**
  - ○ Wages from part-time job $1,500
  - ○ Interest on savings $500
  - ○ Net long-term capital gain on sale of real estate used in business $2,500

  Sammy's total income *$4,500*

- **Deductions**
  - ○ Net loss from business $8,000 ($42,000 income – $50,000 expenses)
  - ○ Net short-term capital loss—sale of stock $1,000
  - ○ Standard deduction $6,350
  - ○ Personal exemption $4,050

  Sammy's total deductions *$19,400*

    - ▪ Sammy's deductions exceed his income by $14,900 ($19,400 – $4,500). However, to figure whether he has an NOL, the following deductions are *not allowed*:
      - ▫ Nonbusiness net short-term capital loss $1,000
      - ▫ Nonbusiness deductions (standard deduction, $6,350) – nonbusiness income (interest, $500) $5,850
      - ▫ Deduction for personal exemption $4,050

      Total deductions not allowed in NOL calculation $10,900

  Thus, total deductions allowed is *$8,500* ($19,400 total deductions – $10,900 disallowed deductions).

- Therefore, Sammy's NOL for year 1 is $4,000 ($4,500 total income – $8,500 deductions allowed).

Lecture 1.06

TAX SCHEDULES

A   Itemized Deductions (Personal & Employ**ee** expenses)
B   Interest and dividend income
C   Profit and loss from a business (Employ**er** expenses / **1099** Income)
D   Capital gains and losses (S/T and L/T investments)
E   Supplementary income or loss (**RRF-COP**)
  - **R**ental Income
  - **R**oyalties
    - ○ **C**opyrights
    - ○ **O**il/Gas leases
    - ○ **P**atents
  - **F**low-through entities (Schedule K-1 income)
    - ○ S corps, Partnerships, Estates & Trusts
F   Profit and Loss from Farming
Form 1040X–Amended return (3 years)
Form 1116–Foreign Tax Credit
Form 4562–Depreciation and Amortization
Form 4797–Sale of L/T business property (not inventory or receivables – Schedule C)

Lecture 1.07

ADJUSTMENTS *"FOR* (TO) AGI" (I-EMBRACED)

Student loan *I*nterest for higher education

- $2,500, phase out applies
- Applies to entire repayment period

Self-*E*mployment tax – pays both employer and employee's share (15.3%)

- 50% of SE tax (7.65%) is deductible on return
    - 6.2% Social Security - on wages up to $127,200 – 2017
    - 1.45% Medicare – unlimited
- 100% of medical insurance premiums paid by a self-employed taxpayer for self and family are deductible (no member of the family may have coverage through an employer).

*M*oving expenses

- New work must be at least 50 miles further from old home, each way (i.e.,100-mile round trip).
- Includes direct costs of moving you and your stuff
- Does not include meals, house hunting costs or temporary living expenses
- Must work full-time at least 39 weeks (9 months) during 1st year following move (or 78 weeks during first 2 years if self-employed).
    - If moving expenses were paid by employee and then reimbursed by employer, income shouldn't be included as long as no moving expense deduction was taken.

*B*usiness expenses (Schedule C – Sole Proprietorship/1099 Income)

- All costs of running a business
- All taxes paid by the business
- Bad debts recognized under direct write-off method
- The Uniform Capitalization Rules (UNiCAP – Section 263A) requires that certain costs be capitalized to inventory produced or held for sale.
- Interest paid in advance is not deductible when paid, even by a cash basis taxpayer.
- Rent paid in advance is not deductible when paid, even by a cash basis taxpayer. Only the amount that applies to use of rented property during the tax year can be deducted. The rest can be deducted over the period to which it applies.
- Gifts to customers up to $25 per recipient per year
- $4 per promotional item
- 50% meals and entertainment
- 100% travel
- Similar to a small corporation
- If no profit in 3 of 5 years, loss generally not deductible – **Hobby Loss**
    - *Net Income (Other income) line 21*
    - *Expenses on Schedule A (Misc. 2%)*

*R*ental, Royalty, & Flow-through entities (Schedule E)

In general, rents and royalties are taxable when earned by an accrual basis taxpayer and in the period received by a taxpayer on the cash basis. When rents or royalties are received in advance, however, even an accrual basis taxpayer will include them in taxable income in the period received.

- Passive activity?

- o Any business venture in which the taxpayer doesn't materially participate (see 7 tests below)
  - All limited partnership interests
  - All rental activity (unless taxpayer is real estate professional, Schedule C)
  - 7 Tests for **Material Participation** determined on annual basis:
    - More than *500 hours* of participation by individual.
    - Individual's participation is *substantially all* of participation by all owners/nonowners.
    - More than 100 hours and not less than any other's participation.
    - Activity is a "significant participation activity" (i.e., >100 hours) and all significant participation activities > 500 hours.
    - Material participation for 5 of last 10 years.
    - Material participation for any 3 prior years for personal service activities.
    - Depending on facts and circumstances, participation occurs on a *regular, continuous, and substantial* basis.
- o Losses deductible only to extent of passive gains
  - Unused losses carried forward until disposal of activity
  - Active rental losses partially deductible up to **$25,000**
    - **Reduced by 50% of AGI over $100,000**
    - No deduction if AGI over $150,000
- o Allocation required when various passive activities involve both gains and losses.
  - Excess loss allocated among activities involving losses
  - Allocation in proportion of activity's loss to total of losses

    For example, if an entity has 3 passive activities with losses: Activity 1 - $20,000 loss; Activity 2 - $30,000 loss; and Activity 3 - $50,000 loss; and 1 passive activity with a gain of $25,000.
    - Total losses amount to $100,000
    - The excess loss is $100,000 – $25,000 = $75,000
    - It will be allocated as follows:
      - Activity 1 - $20,000/$100,000 x $75,000 = $15,000
      - Activity 2 - $30,000/$100,000 x $75,000 = $22,500
      - Activity 3 - $50,000/$100,000 x $75,000 = $37,500

- In general, **passive activity losses** may only be offset against passive income, with any unused loss carried forward **indefinitely** or until the activity is disposed of. Tax credits from passive activities can only offset taxes arising from passive activities, with similar carryforward rules. Limitations on the deductibility of passive activity losses apply to individuals, estates, trusts (other than grantor trusts), closely held or nonpublicly traded C corporations, and personal service corporations (provides personal services by owner-employees, such as an architecture and engineering firm). There is no limit on the credits or passive activity losses that may be deducted by grantor trusts, partnerships, and S corporations, since they are flow-through entities and these items are passed through to the individual shareholders and partners.

- Rental activities in which the taxpayer **materially participates** may, however, be used to offset ordinary income in certain circumstances:
  - o **Real estate person** – If the taxpayer meets the technical requirements to be classified as a "real estate person," losses from real estate rental activities may be treated as ordinary business losses.

- **Active Participation Exception**– Even if the taxpayer doesn't qualify as a real estate person, if they actively participate in the rental activity (at least a 10% interest in the activity to be considered active), they may deduct up to $25,000 of losses against ordinary income each year (with the remainder carried forward the same as other unused passive losses). The **$25,000 limit** is reduced, however, by **50%** of the excess of the taxpayer's modified AGI **over $100,000. For example**, if the taxpayer's modified AGI is $110,000, the maximum amount of net losses from rental activities in which the taxpayer actively participates that can be deducted is $25,000 – 50% (110,000 – 100,000) = $20,000. A taxpayer with modified AGI exceeding $150,000 will not be allowed to claim any rental losses against ordinary income based on this limitation, but the losses may be carried forward until the taxpayer disposes of the property.

- The treatment of rental income and expenses for a dwelling unit that is also used for personal purposes (**Vacation home**) depends on whether the taxpayer uses it as a *home*. A dwelling unit is used as a home if personal use exceeds the greater of 14 days or 10% of the number of days rented.
    - If a dwelling unit is used as a home and it is *rented for **less than 15 days*** during the tax year, rental income is *excluded* from gross income and expenses are not deductible as rental expenses. Can deduct on Schedule A.
    - If it is rented for **more than 14 days:**
        - And *personal use* is **more than** the greater of 14 days or 10% of the number of days rented (considered a *home*), rental income is *included* and deductions are limited to gross rental income. Unused deductions may be *carried forward* to future years.
        - And *personal use* is **not more than** the greater of 14 days or 10% of the number of day's rented (considered a *real rental*), rental income is *included* and all expenses allocated to the rental portion are allowed. Expenses in excess of income are subject to *passive activity loss limits.*
- ***Depreciation*** is discussed in detail in another section.

- Income from **flow-through entities** (e.g., partnerships, S corporations – discussed in another section) is taxable to the individual in the period in which it is reported (Schedule K-1) by the flow-through entity.
    - Losses from a partnership are only deductible to the extent that the taxpayer is **at risk**.
    - A partner is at risk for:
        - Money and the adjusted basis of property contributed to the partnership.
        - Debts of the partnership if the partner is personally liable or has pledged personal (not partnership) property as collateral, up to the net fair value of the partner's interest in the property.

*A*limony paid (**CANNOT**)

- Payments for **child support** and **property settlements** are exempt from taxation (and not deductible by the payer). However, alimony is both *taxable to the recipient and deductible by the payer*. To be considered alimony, payment must satisfy **all** of the following conditions:
    - **C**ash only or its equivalent (not property)
    - **A**part when payments made (do not live together)
    - **N**ot child support (child support must be fully paid)
        - Child support not taxable/not deductible
        - Payments first applied to child support, then alimony

- o **N**ot designated as property settlement (not taxable/not deductible)
- o **O**wn return for payer and payee
- o **T**erminates on death of recipient

- If pay for college as part of divorce agreement, considered Alimony.
- If an agreement to pay alimony **and** child support is not fully honored by the payer, payments are applied to the **child support first**. **For example**, if the payer agrees to make $15,000 in alimony payments and $10,000 in child support payments during 20X1, but only $12,000 is paid in total that year, the payee only has to report $2,000 in taxable alimony, since the first $10,000 is treated as child support. The payer can deduct only $2,000 on their return. The purpose is to minimize the benefit to the payer when they do not fully honor their agreement, and to provide the custodial parent some relief from taxation when they do not receive all expected funds.
- Alimony recapture rule is to prevent property settlements from being treated as Alimony.

Lecture 1.08

Contributions to Retirement plan

Any taxpayer with earned income is generally entitled to establish and make contributions to an **Individual Retirement Account** (IRA). They can do so even if they are actively participating in other pension or profit-sharing plans. For purposes of eligibility for the IRA, earned income includes:
- Salaries and wages
- Net self-employment income
- Alimony received

Contributions are limited for 2017 to $5,500 ($11,000 MFJ) per year, per individual (+$1,000 for individuals 50+). A married couple filing a joint return can establish and contribute $5,500 ($6,500 50+) each to separate IRAs as long as the earned income of the couple is at least $11,000 ($13,000 if both 50+). IRAs come in **two basic varieties:**
- **Traditional**
- **Roth**

The contribution limit per individual applies to the total contributed to both varieties of IRA. The full contribution limit for Roth IRAs applies to taxpayers with modified AGI below $118,000 ($186,000 MFJ) for 2017. The allowed contribution amount is reduced above these thresholds, and taxpayers with MAGI of $133,000 or more for 2017 ($196,000 MFJ) cannot contribute to a Roth IRA. Traditional IRAs generally can be used by all taxpayers regardless of AGI (unless they also actively participated in an employer's retirement plan during the year).

Contributions to a traditional IRA are **deductible** in arriving at AGI unless **both** of the following conditions apply:
- The individual is actively participating in another pension or profit-sharing plan *AND*
- AGI on the tax return exceeds a threshold amount ($72,000 single, $119,000 MFJ for 2017).

For a married couple, if the individual is not actively participating in another plan but the individual's spouse **is** a participant, contributions for the non-participating spouse cannot be deducted if the joint AGI exceeds $196,000 for 2017.

Contributions to a *Roth IRA* are **not** deductible. The benefit of a Roth IRA is that all withdrawals after the age of 59 ½ are exempt from taxation (as long as the Roth IRA has been in effect for at least 5 years), including both contributions and earnings. Withdrawals of contributions are exempt from taxation in all cases. Withdrawals from a traditional IRA are fully taxable (except to recover nondeductible contributions made earlier).

Contributions may still be made even after the taxpayer reaches age 70 ½. Roth IRA is not available if the taxpayer's modified AGI exceeds, for 2017, $133,000 ($196,000 MFJ).

Withdrawals from either type of IRA prior to the **age of 59½** may result in a tax **penalty of 10%** of the amount withdrawn (in addition to the inclusion in gross income). The **penalty** does **not** apply (but amounts withdrawn from a traditional IRA are still included in gross income) when the withdrawal is the result of:

- Payment of **medical expenses** exceeding 10% of AGI
- Payment of qualified higher **education** costs
- **Death** or disability of the participant
- First time purchase of a **home** (up to $10,000 may be withdrawn)

	Traditional IRA	**Roth IRA**
Age Limit?	< 70 ½ years old	No
Income Limit?	No	< $133,000 ($196,000 MFJ) - 2017
Contributions Deductible?	Yes	No
Contribution Limit?	$5,500 (+$1,000 catch-up contribution for > age 50 (limited to taxable compensation)	
Contribution Deadline?	Filing deadline (no extensions) – e.g., April 15	
Required Minimum Distributions (RMDs)?	Yes, after age 70 ½	No
Withdrawals Generally Taxable?	Yes	No
	10% penalty for distributions prior to age 59 ½	

Contributions of up to **$2,000 per year** can be made on behalf of any beneficiary (even someone unrelated to the contributor) under the age of 18 to **Coverdell Education Savings Accounts (ESA)** (formerly known as *education IRAs*). Contributions are *not deductible*, but amounts may be withdrawn free of taxation to pay elementary, middle, high school and college expenses (including tuition, fees, books, room and board) of the beneficiary. Amounts not spent by the time the beneficiary reaches the age of 30 are distributed to the beneficiary and subject to taxation and penalties. However, unspent amounts may be transferred to the education savings account of another family member of the same generation without taxation or penalties. Contributions can be made up to the due date of the return (not including extensions).

Qualified Tuition Programs (QTP – 529 plans) are set up to allow a taxpayer to make *nondeductible* contributions to be used for qualified higher education (undergraduate and graduate level). The earnings from investment in the plans accumulate free of federal tax as long as the money stays in the plan and is used for educational purposes. Educational purposes include tuition, room and board, books, supplies, and fees; expanded by December 2015 PATH Act to include computer hardware, software, peripherals and internet access. There is a federal *penalty of 10%* if the funds are withdrawn for non-educational purposes. Two types of plans include either a *Prepaid program* (paid to the school) or a *Savings account plan*. Can contribute up to annual gift tax exclusion ($14,000 for 2017) or file an election that allows contributions larger than the exclusion amount to be taken into account ratably over 5 years (e.g., $70,000, as long as no further gifts to the same person for the next 5 years - $14,000 per year).   No AGI phase-out limitation exists, and can contribute to Coverdell ESA and QTP for the same beneficiary during the same year.

An **ABLE account** is a tax-advantaged savings account available to the disabled made possible by the **A**chieving a **B**etter **L**ife **E**xperience Act passed by Congress in December 2014. Similar to a 529 plan, funds up to the annual gift tax exclusion may be contributed to an ABLE account on behalf of a disabled beneficiary, and the earnings in the account accumulate tax free as long as the money is spent on qualifying expenses for the beneficiary. (Note: Contributions are not deductible.) Qualifying expenses include education, housing, transportation, and assistive technology. Funds held in an ABLE account do not count for the purposes of means testing for the receipt of various government disability benefits.

Other retirement contributions that may be deducted from gross income include:
- **Keogh plans**
- **Simplified employee pensions (SEPs)**
    - Up to lesser of 25% of compensation or $54,000 (2017)
- **SIMPLE plans**

These plans are established by business owners. On an individual return, contributions on behalf of the owner are deducted from gross income in arriving at AGI, while contributions on behalf of employees of the owner are claimed as ordinary business deductions in the computation of net business profit or loss.

Contributions to a **Keogh** plan are limited to **25% of net** self-employment income after the Keogh deduction and 50% of self-employment tax is claimed (this works out to 20% of self-employment income before the Keogh deduction). For instance, if the client has $100,000 self-employment income before making a Keogh contribution, the maximum allowable contribution is $20,000, and net self-employment income is $80,000. The maximum contribution allowed (as opposed to the deduction allowed for tax purposes) to a Keogh plan is the lesser of $54,000 (2017), or 100% of earned income.

SIMPLE plans (**S**avings **I**ncentive **M**atch **Pl**an for **E**mployees) allow voluntary contributions up to $12,500 (2017) per year by each employee and by the individual employer, up to 100% of income. Withdrawals within 2 years are subject to a 25% tax penalty instead of the usual 10%.

***E*arly Withdrawal penalty** – premature interest withdrawal penalty (e.g., from a C.D.) is deductible.

Jury *D*uty fee if remitted to employer
- Fee received always included in gross income.
- If remit fee to employer, deduct in arriving at AGI.

Contributions to *H*ealth *S*avings *A*ccount (HSA)

Contributions to Health Savings Account (HSA) may be deducted by a self-employed taxpayer or employee (Form 8889 must be filed).

- Taxpayer must have high-deductible health plan (HDHP). Deductible must be at least $1,300 (2017) for self-only coverage and $2,600 (2017) for family coverage.
- Contribution is limited to lesser of deductible or limit of $3,400 in 2017 for self-only and $6,750 in 2017 for family.
- Taxpayers 55 or older may increase limit by $1,000.
- Amounts contributed by employer are excluded from W-2 gross income but reduce amount that employee can contribute.
- Distributions from HSA tax free if used for qualified medical expenses (those that would have normally been deductible on Schedule A for itemizers, excluding premiums on the HDHP itself).
- Schedule A deduction cannot be claimed for expenses paid from the HSA.
- Distributions that are not used for medical expenses are subject to taxation and 20% penalty. No penalty if distributions are made after the account beneficiary dies, becomes disabled, or turns 65.

*F*arm Income (Schedule F – similar to Schedule C)

- Accounting methods include:
  - Cash, Accrual, Crop method (Cost of producing the crop is deducted in the year the crop income is realized) or the Hybrid/combination method may be used if show income and is used consistently.
    - If cash method is used for figuring income, must be used for reporting expenses.
    - If accrual method is used for reporting expenses, must be used for figuring income.

- Income Items (farmers may elect to average farm income over 3 years)
  - Schedule F Income (subject to SE tax):
    - Raised livestock, produce, and grains held for sale
    - Livestock and other items bought for resale
  - Form 4797 Income (Not subject to SE tax):
    - Animals not held primarily for sale
    - Livestock held for draft, breeding, dairy or sporting purposes
    - Gains from sales of farmland or depreciable farm equipment
- Expense Items
  - Car and truck expense, chemicals and pesticides, depreciation and Section 179 deductions, feed purchased, fertilizers, mortgage interest, seeds and plants. Reasonable wages paid to children, meals to feed workers.

- Depreciation (Discussed in another section)
  - Section 179 deduction (immediate expense) would include tangible personal property, such as machinery and equipment, milk tanks, livestock (horses, cattle, hogs, sheep, goats, mink and other fur-bearing animals). Also includes single-purpose agricultural and horticultural structures.
  - 10-year assets would include single-purpose agricultural (constructed to house, raise and feed livestock) and horticultural structures (greenhouse).

Lecture 1.09

CLASS QUESTIONS

Please see the Class Questions and Class Solutions for this Lecture at the end of this Section.

Lecture 1.10

STANDARD DEDUCTION

The IRS automatically gives every taxpayer a standard deduction based on filing status.

- If being *claimed as a dependent* of another, standard deduction is the greater of $1,050 (2017) or earned income + $350, never to exceed the regular standard deduction.
- If elderly *65 or older* and/or blind, additional deductions of $1,250 to $1,550 (2017).
- A taxpayer may claim a standard deduction where the amount depends on filing status. This is an **alternative** to claiming itemized deductions. The amount of the standard deduction based on filing status may be increased if the taxpayer (and/or spouse, for a married joint return) reached their 65th birthday during the tax year, and may be increased if the taxpayer (and/or spouse) is legally blind. The highest standard deduction would result from a married couple filing jointly if both taxpayer and spouse are at least 65 and both are legally blind. The dollar amounts of the standard deductions are indexed for inflation and change on an annual basis. **The CPA exam consistently avoids testing amounts that change each year.**

Caution: At the time of this writing, President Trump had introduced his broad plan for tax reform. Some information in the preceding section, such as standard deduction amounts, may be subject to change soon. Please refer to the Course Textbook Updates section of the Roger CPA Review website for legislation updates: https://www.rogercpareview.com/dashboard/my-courses/course-textbook-updates.

ITEMIZED DEDUCTIONS *"FROM* AGI" (*SCHEDULE A*) (COMMITT)

Charitable contributions

- **Charitable contributions to qualified organizations** are deductible to the extent the taxpayer has provided cash or property that exceeds any value received from the charity. **For example**, if the taxpayer makes a contribution to their local public television station for $240 and receives books and videos worth $60 as thanks, the actual charitable contribution is only $180.
  - If donations of *$250 or more* are given, written substantiation from the donee organization is required.
  - Donations are deductible in the year the charity receives the funds. (Contributions made by credit card are deductible when they are charged.)
  - Ordinary payments to charitable organizations for services rendered (e.g., school tuition paid to a parochial school) are not contributions.
  - Donations to qualified organizations only (i.e., donations to needy individuals are not deductible.)
  - *Volunteer services* to a charitable organization may not be deducted except for out-of-pocket costs incurred in the performance of the volunteer work (such as *transportation expenses* between home and the site of the work – **Mileage & Parking**).

- Contributions of **property** are normally subject to **two rules**:
  - ○ **Ordinary Income Rule** - Property is ordinary income property if its sale at fair market value (FMV) on the date it was contributed would have resulted in ordinary income or in short-term capital gain. This includes inventory, self-created works of art, and capital assets held for ≤ 1 year. The amount you can deduct is its FMV minus the amount that would be ordinary income or short-term capital gain if you sold the property for its FMV. Generally, this rule limits the deduction to the **lower** of the **tax basis** in the property or the **FMV** on the date of the contribution.
  - ○ **Long-Term Capital Gain Rule** - Property is capital gain property if its sale at fair market value on the date of the contribution would have resulted in a long-term capital gain. Long-term capital gain property includes non-business capital assets held more than 1 year and inherited assets (considered long-term regardless of holding period) that have increased in value, such as stocks, bonds, personal items (clothes, furniture, autos). This allows the taxpayer to claim the **higher FMV** of long-term capital gains property. The deduction of such property is limited to **30% of AGI** in a tax year.

    For example, assume a taxpayer with AGI of $100,000 donates stock to a qualified charity. The stock was purchased 10 years ago for $10,000, and was worth $40,000 on the date of the contribution. Since it qualifies as long-term capital gain property, the taxpayer may claim the FMV of $40,000, except that this exceeds 30% of AGI, so the deduction in the tax year is limited to $30,000.

- Overall contributions are generally limited to **50% of AGI.** Contributions exceeding this amount may be **carried forward up to 5 years**.
- **Corporations** are limited to **10% of adjusted taxable income (ATI)** and also have a **5-year** carryforward.

Other Miscellaneous Expenses

- Not subject to 2% of AGI minimum.
  - ○ Gambling losses – to extent of winnings – no carryover.
  - ○ Gambling winnings on face of 1040.
  - ○ Professional gamblers can now deduct non-wagering business expenses on Schedule C.
- Estate taxes on income in respect of a decedent (IRD).

Miscellaneous Expenses (BIT) ⟶
| **B**usiness Expenses of Employee (2106) |
| **I**nvestment Costs |
| **T**ax Preparation/legal advice relating to TAXABLE income |

- Deductible to extent total exceeds **2% of AGI**.
- **B**usiness expense of an Employee (Form *2106, Schedule A*)
  - ○ Business mileage
  - ○ Job travel
  - ○ AICPA and Union dues
  - ○ Uniforms (pizza boy)
    - ▪ Not a tuxedo for a waiter
  - ○ Laptop
  - ○ CPE/Job education
    - ▪ NOT CPA review – new profession
  - ○ Business Use of Home (home office for convenience of the employer)
    - ▪ Schedule C if self-employed
  - ○ Appraisal fees for charitable donations or casualty losses

- o   When an employee incurs meals and entertainment expenses that, when reimbursed by the employer, are characterized as compensation and wages, the reimbursement is included in the employee's taxable income and the meals and entertainment cost is included as a business expense.
- *Investment* expenses (Safety deposit box)
  - o   Does not include fees to buy or sell stock (included in calculation of gain/loss on sale)
  - o   Includes investment advisory fees and newsletters (and IRA custodial fees if paid separately and contributions do not cover the fees)
  - o   **Note:** Be careful to differentiate investment *expenses* from investment *interest,* which is fully deductible on a different line of Schedule A.
- *T*ax preparation and Attorney fees (with respect to *taxable* income)
  - o   Tax preparation and advice
  - o   Costs incurred to collect money owed by others (for example, the hiring of an attorney to collect alimony or the hiring of an appraiser to collect on an insurance claim)

*M*edical expenses – paid and not reimbursed

- Medical services – not cosmetic
- Most medical goods/devices
- Health insurance premiums
- Long-term care insurance premiums on qualified policies
- Mileage to Doctor and transportation costs for medical and dental
- Must be for specific injury, illness or birth defect
- Drugs must be prescriptions
  - o   Minus insurance reimbursement in year received
- Deductible for amounts that exceed **10% of AGI**

Qualified expenses include most obvious items, such as hospitals, doctors, dentists, nurses, labs, hearing aid and batteries, eye exam and prescription glasses, and x-rays. Health insurance premiums may be deducted (except to the extent they've already been claimed for self-employed taxpayers in arriving at AGI or were paid out of health savings accounts with tax-free funds). Travel costs associated with obtaining medical care also may be deducted. **Prescription** drugs and insulin qualify. Costs to install **medically prescribed** facilities in a home, such as a swimming pool for physical therapy to treat a specific medical condition or an elevator, are deductible to the extent the costs exceed the increase in the value of the home resulting from the addition.

Examples of **nondeductible expenses** tested on previous exams include:
- Non-prescription drugs and medicines.
- Costs for general health improvement that are not treatments for specific medical conditions.
- Premiums on life insurance and policies to cover loss of earnings from injuries and illnesses.
- Plastic surgery, except to cure disfiguring illnesses, injuries, or birth defects.
- Medicare portion of social security and self-employment taxes.

Costs must be paid by the taxpayer (or spouse) during the tax year, but may be payments on behalf of the taxpayer, spouse, a dependent, or **other people for whom the taxpayer provides over 50% of support,** even if they do not qualify as dependents because the *income or joint return* tests are not satisfied. Reimbursements by insurance must be subtracted from deductible expenses. Payments made by credit card are considered to have been made in the period they are charged to the credit card, not in the period in which the taxpayer pays the credit card balance.

Medical expenses paid for a deceased spouse or dependent are deductible as medical expenses in the year paid, regardless of whether they were paid before or after the decedent's death, provided the individual qualified as the taxpayer's spouse or dependent either at the time the expenses were incurred or at the time payment was made.

*I*nterest paid

- *Investment interest expense*
  - o Deductible to extent of net investment income (*Schedule B*)
  - o Unused carried forward indefinitely
- *Mortgage loan interest* ⟶
  - o Acquisition indebtedness up to $1,000,000
  - o Home equity loans up to $100,000
    - ▪ Only up to 100% of net equity in home

Home Mortgage = $1,000,000 (2 houses) Equity = $100,000

Interest on **investments** or **personal residences** may be claimed as itemized deductions. Interest related to a business is claimed as a business deduction in arriving at net business profit or loss on Schedule C, and is part of the reported gross income.

Investment interest refers to borrowings that are used to make personal investments, such as margin loans in the purchase of stock. Such interest is only deductible to the extent of reported **net investment income** on the tax return. Investment interest that exceeds net investment income is carried forward indefinitely and may be claimed to the extent of net investment income in future tax years.

Interest paid in advance is not deductible in the period paid, even by a cash basis taxpayer. Interest paid in advance is required to be allocated over the tax years to which it applies.

Personal residence interest (which may be claimed on both a primary and secondary residence) includes:

- **Points** paid on a loan to acquire the residence (deductible immediately) or points paid on other qualified personal residence loans (deductible by amortization over the life of the loan).
- Periodic interest payments on **acquisition indebtedness up to $1 million**. This refers to loans used to acquire or construct the home (or an addition to the home) as well as to loans that replace previous acquisition indebtedness.
- Periodic interest payments on **home equity loans up to $100,000** are also fully deductible. This refers to loans that provided the taxpayer with money that was secured by equity in the home, regardless of how the funds are used. The combination of acquisition indebtedness and home equity loans may not exceed the fair market value of the home.

For example, if the taxpayer buys a home for $150,000, making a down payment of $30,000 and taking out a loan from the bank for $120,000 to finance the balance, the $120,000 loan is acquisition indebtedness. A few years later, the payments on the loan have reduced the balance to $110,000, while the home has increased in value to $200,000. The taxpayer refinances with a loan company that agrees to lend 125% of the value of the home, or $250,000, using $110,000 to repay the bank loan and providing $140,000 in cash. The refinanced loan is considered to be acquisition indebtedness of $110,000, a home equity loan of $90,000 (up to the FMV of the home), and a personal loan of $50,000. Interest on personal loans is not deductible.

*T*axes paid

- Personal Property taxes and real estate taxes
- State and local sales taxes (in lieu of state and local income taxes)
- State, local, or foreign taxes—
  - o Foreign taxes paid may be claimed as a credit or deduction.
  - o Credit limited to portion of U.S. tax on foreign income.
- Fees, Fines, Federal, FICA**, FORGET IT!!**
- **Taxes** paid to **state**, **local**, or **foreign** governments based on **income** or **property** may be deducted if a taxpayer itemizes and is the owner of the property (joint tenancy – ok). Delinquent taxes are apportioned between buyer and seller on a daily basis within the real property tax year.   Assessments for improvements (streets, sewers) are added to the basis. Foreign income taxes that are used to claim the foreign tax credit may **not** also be claimed as deductions. There is no deduction for taxes paid to the federal government or for gas or excise taxes. Fees charged by state and local governments may not be deducted unless they are based specifically on income or property values.
- **State and local *sales taxes* (based on actual amount paid or an IRS table) may be deducted INSTEAD of state and local income taxes.** Useful for people who live in one of 9 states with no state taxes. This provision was made permanent by the 2015 PATH Act.

*T*heft and Casualty losses

Casualty losses that exceed 10% of AGI may be deducted. A casualty loss is a *sudden event* (theft or destruction) that causes the taxpayer to lose an asset or for its value to seriously drop over the course of a time period not exceeding 30 days. Accidental breakage of items in the home by family members is not considered a casualty event. Progressive deterioration is also not included (e.g., *termite, moth, or drought damage)*.

The loss is measured by the **drop in fair market value** caused by the event, but is limited to the **tax basis** of the asset. Costs incurred by the taxpayer to repair damaged property increase the tax basis of the property, but do not affect the drop in FMV loss measurement.

For example, assume the taxpayer purchased their home for $100,000, it was worth $300,000 prior to a fire, and the fire reduced the property's value to $220,000. The taxpayer spent $60,000 to partially repair the damage resulting from the fire. The drop in FMV from the event was $300,000 - $220,000 = $80,000. The tax basis of the property is $100,000 + $60,000 = $160,000. The loss that may be claimed is $80,000, the lower of the two.

Once the loss is determined, it must be reduced by **all** of the following:
  - o Insurance and government **reimbursements** that the taxpayer is entitled to receive (if reimbursements exceed the loss, an involuntary conversion gain has occurred).
  - o **$100 per event**
  - o **10% of AGI per year**

- **Phase out of itemized deductions** were eliminated but returned for 2013 and beyond.
  - o The total of all itemized deductions is reduced by the **smaller of**:
    - ▪ 3% of the amount by which AGI exceeds the annual limit, or
    - ▪ 80% of the itemized deductions that are affected by the limit. (not counting **G**ambling losses, **I**nvestment interest, **M**edical expenses and **C**asualty losses - **GIMC**)

Caution: At the time of this writing, President Trump had introduced his broad plan for tax reform. Some information in the preceding section may be subject to change soon (e.g., many itemized deductions currently available may disappear). Please refer to the Course Textbook Updates section of the Roger CPA Review website for legislation updates: **https://www.rogercpareview.com/dashboard/my-courses/course-textbook-updates**.

Lecture 1.11

CLASS QUESTIONS

Please see the Class Questions and Class Solutions for this Lecture at the end of this Section.

Lecture 1.12

EXEMPTIONS AND FILING STATUS

Personal Exemptions

- Two for married filing jointly (Spouse is not considered a dependency exemption; it is still a personal exemption.)
- If a parent supports a dependent child, the child may not claim a personal exemption on their own return.
- The amount one can claim for personal exemptions starts to *phase out* once you reach certain income thresholds.

Dependency Exemptions

- **Dependent** if **all** requirements met for "Qualifying Relative" or "Qualifying Child"
  - *Qualifying Child* – [taxpayer's child, stepchild, foster child, sibling, step sibling, half sibling, or a descendant of any such individual (e.g., nephew or grandchild)] Note: A qualifying child, unless disabled, must be younger than either the taxpayer or the taxpayer's spouse.
    - **J**oint return-no, **A**ge, **R**esidency, **R**elationship and **S**upport tests (JARRS)
  - *Qualifying Relative* - (**C-IRS-J**ack you)

- **C**itizenship or Resident
  - U.S. citizen or
  - Resident of U.S., Mexico, or Canada.
- **I**ncome – limited to exemption amount ($4,050 for 2017)
  - Social security ignored
  - Unless *"qualifying child"* who is:
    - Under 19 years old,
    - A full-time (5 months) student under 24 years old, or
    - Any age and permanently and totally disabled.

- **R**elationship, or unrelated and a **Household member** for entire year
  - Lineal descendant
    - Parent, grandparent, brother, sister, step-brother, uncle, aunt, in-laws, brother-in-law
  - Doesn't include cousins
  - Test met if dependent lives the entire year with taxpayer.

- o Note: A "qualifying child" (e.g., child, stepchild, grandchild) must live with taxpayer for more than ½ of year.

- **S**upport – over 50% of total annual support
  - o Includes tax exempt items like Social Security, AFDC
  - o Multiple support agreement
    - If more than 1 person supports individual, but no one person pays >50%, can give exemption to any person who paid at least 10%.
  - o "Qualifying child" must NOT have provided more than ½ of their own support, scholarships not included. (So, you DON'T need to support over 50%; they just can't provide over 50% of their own support.)

- No **J**oint Return with spouse
  - o Unless dependent and spouse are filing only to get a total refund of taxes withheld or paid, and weren't actually required to file.

- **Phase out of Personal and Dependency Exemptions** was eliminated but returned for 2013 and beyond.

Filing Status (Tax Rates)

On every return, the taxpayer(s) must select the filing status, which is used to determine the tax rates on income and the value of various deductions, thresholds, and limitations. In selecting the status, the following choices should be considered in order, using the first one for which all requirements are satisfied:

- **Married filing Jointly (MFJ)**
  - o Determined on last day of year or at time of death.
  - o If divorced during year, not MFJ.
  - o Taxpayers are considered unmarried for the whole year if, on the last day of the year, they are divorced or are legally separated under a divorce or legal separate maintenance decree.
  - o Includes *same-sex married couples*, not registered domestic partnerships or civil unions (*Obergefell v. Hodges*); thus, any rules that apply to MFJ/MFS also apply to same-sex married individuals.
- **Married filing Separately (MFS)**
  - o Each files own return.
  - o In community property state, everything is split 50/50.
- **Qualifying widow (surviving spouse)** *with a dependent child*
  - o Spouse died in prior 2 years and qualified to file a joint return in year of death
  - o Provided over 50% of cost of maintaining principal residence of dependent child (or stepchild)
  - o Not remarried as of end of current year
  - o Same rate as MFJ
- **Head of household (HOH)**
  - o To quality – **Both:**
    - Taxpayer *not* married at year end - **and**
    - Taxpayer must maintain a home as the principal place of residence for over 50% of the year and provide more than 50% of costs of maintaining a household for:

- Dependent **"Qualifying Relative" living with the taxpayer,** including uncle, aunt, nephew, niece or certain step-relatives and in-laws. Other relatives and unrelated persons may be dependents if they live with taxpayer for the entire year, but NOT qualify them as HOH.
- **"Qualifying Child,"** stepchild, or grandchild living with the taxpayer (Must be a dependent. Note: Custodial parent who releases the right to claim the dependency exemption to the noncustodial parent by filing Form 8332 may still qualify for HOH status. Form 8332 does not qualify noncustodial parent for HOH status.)
- **Parent** must be a dependent, but need not live with the taxpayer.
  - Note: A child must be a qualifying dependent child or a qualifying relative in order to qualify a taxpayer for HOH status.

- **Single** - all others
  - Married, but legally separated under a decree of separate maintenance.

Note: Your ***marginal tax rate*** is the rate at which your *last and your next* dollar of taxable income are taxed. Your **effective rate** is the average rate of taxation for *all* your dollars (total tax / total taxable income).

Lecture 1.13

TAX CREDITS (DOLLAR-FOR-DOLLAR REDUCTION OF TAXES PAYABLE)

There are a few different credits related to having children.

Child tax credits

- **$1,000** < 17 years old at year-end. The child tax credit is also a **refundable credit** (known as the "additional child tax credit") for certain low-income taxpayers with one or more qualifying children when the taxpayer is not able to claim the full child tax credit for each child (because tax liability is less than the available credit). This provision has been made permanent by the 2015 PATH Act.

Child & Dependent Care credit

- A child and **dependent care credit** is available if the taxpayer requires care for a child or disabled dependent in order to be gainfully employed. The credit is based on the smallest of three amounts:
  - Actual dependent care expenses
  - Earned income
  - $3,000 (for care of one dependent) or $6,000 (for care of multiple dependents)

For married couples, the earned income limit is based on the income of the lower-paid spouse. If, however, one of the couple is gainfully employed and the other is a full-time student, the limit is based on the earned income of the spouse who is gainfully employed.

The credit percentage is between 20% and 35% depending on the AGI of the taxpayer. For taxpayer with AGI over $45,000, the credit is the minimum of 20%.

Up to $5,000 of benefits under an employer dependent care assistance plan can be excluded from an employee's taxable wage.

A taxpayer may claim the child and dependent care credit (if all other applicable requirements are met) for a child who lives with the taxpayer for more than half the year, even if the taxpayer does not provide more than half the cost of maintaining the household.

Adoption credits

- The **adoption credit** is available for costs incurred in adopting a child under the age of 18. The credit is limited for 2017 to the first $13,570 of costs. Credits exceeding the tax liability may be carried forward up to 5 years. Phaseout exists.

Education credits (phases-out)

- There are **two different credits** associated with the payment of **tuition and fees** to qualified educational institutions.
  - The **Hope scholarship credit** (renamed the "**American Opportunity Tax Credit**"— AOTC) applies to the first 4 years of post-secondary school (i.e., post-high school) education. The credit is equal to 100% of the first $2,000 and 25% of the next $2,000 in payments, for a maximum credit of **$2,500 *per student***. The credit may be claimed by a taxpayer for tuition, textbooks and fees of the taxpayer, spouse, or dependent, and may be claimed for payments on behalf of each student in the family. 40% of the credit is also refundable ($1,000). The AOTC has been made permanent by the 2015 PATH Act.
  - The **lifetime learning credit** applies to any year of education, and can include tuition paid to a qualified institution for education to improve job skills. The credit is equal to 20% of the first $10,000 paid on behalf of all family members, for a maximum credit of **$2,000 *per family***.
- There are several restrictions placed on both credits, including:
  - The credits generally apply only to **tuition and fees** paid to qualified institutions, and not other costs. Taxpayer must have valid Form 1098-T from the institution.
  - The credits are not available to individual taxpayers with modified AGI exceeding certain amounts.
  - The credit cannot be claimed on the tax return of the dependent.
  - Cannot claim both AOTC and a Lifetime learning credit for the same student in the same year.
  - Cannot be MFS.

Savers Credit

- The **savers credit** is available for low to moderate income workers to enable and encourage them to make voluntary contributions to IRAs and 401(k) plans. The amount of the credit is up to $1,000 ($2,000 MFJ) for making contributions to an IRA or an employer-sponsored retirement plan.
- The credit may be claimed by:
  - MFJ with income up to $62,000 in 2017.
  - HOH with income up to $46,500 in 2017.
  - Single and MFS with income up to $31,000 in 2017.
- The amount of the credit can range from 10% to 50% of the amount of IRA contribution made based on income and filing status (Form 8880).

Foreign Tax credit

- The **foreign tax credit** is available for payments of foreign income taxes that are not being claimed as itemized deductions. The calculation of the credit is identical to that for corporations. One special exception for individuals, however, allows the taxpayer to claim a credit for up to $300 ($600 on a joint return) for foreign income taxes paid on investment income without being subject to any other limits. This enables a taxpayer whose mutual fund had withholdings on foreign dividends to claim a credit for the taxes paid by the mutual fund without the need for complicated computations.

Credit for the elderly and disabled

- The credit for the elderly and disabled is available only to those over 65 or permanently disabled with nontaxable Social Security (or equivalent) of less than $7,500 for MFJ.

Earned Income Credit (EIC)

- If a taxpayer has some form of earned income, they may qualify for this **Refundable credit.** Earned income for purposes of calculating EIC only includes taxable income.
- A qualifying child does not have to meet the support test. Also, a qualifying child must have lived with the taxpayer in the United States for more than half the year and have a social security number that is valid for employment in the United States. If investment income is greater than $3,450 for 2017, the credit is denied.

In general, tax credits may be offset, dollar for dollar, against a tax liability in the period to which the credit applies. When the amount of the credit exceeds the amount of applicable tax due, unused credits can be carried back or forward, depending on the provisions of the credit. They may only be used, however, to reduce taxes and, with the exception of refundable credits such as the Earned Income Credit, cannot result in a refund to the taxpayer.

Since the EIC is a refundable credit, the excess of the credit over the tax liability is payable to the taxpayer in the form of a tax refund. In essence, a refundable credit is treated similarly to a payment of estimated tax or taxes withheld.

OTHER TAXES AND TAX PROCEDURES

Self-Employment Taxes (Schedule SE)

- Tax rate double FICA rate
  - 6.2% OASDI (i.e., Social Security) tax on amounts up to $127,200 for 2017
  - 1.45% Medicare (i.e., Hospital Insurance—HI) tax—no maximum
    - Total 7.65% × 2 = 15.3%
  - 50% claimed as deduction for AGI.
- Individuals are subject to self-employment taxes on **net self-employment income**. This includes all business revenue reduced by all ordinary and necessary business expenses (except retirement plan contributions on behalf of the taxpayer). One of the business expenses that is deducted is one-half of the self-employment tax itself; this is claimed as a deduction from gross income in arriving at AGI.

Increased *Medicare tax rate* (HI rate) for high-income earners:

The 1.45% rate is increased by 0.9% for individual taxpayers earning in excess of the threshold levels ($250,000 MFJ and $200,000 all others). The new rate is 2.35% (1.45% + 0.9%) on amounts in excess of the thresholds.

- This increases the Medicare tax rate for self-employed individuals from 2.9% to 3.8% on amounts in excess of the thresholds.

Universal Healthcare Coverage Mandate

The Patient Protection and Affordable Care Act imposes a penalty on those individuals who do not have health insurance.

Caution: At the time of this writing, President Trump had introduced his broad plan for tax reform, which included repealing much of the Affordable Care Act. Please refer to the Course Textbook Updates section of the Roger CPA Review website for legislation updates: https://www.rogercpareview.com/dashboard/my-courses/course-textbook-updates.

Underpayment penalty

Individual taxpayers who have withholding on salaries and wages may not need to make estimated tax payments to the IRS during the year. If **estimated tax payments** are required, they are due on Form 1040ES by the *4th, 6th & 9th* months of the taxable year and by the *15th of January*. An individual is only subject to an underpayment penalty if the balance due on the tax return is greater than **$1,000.**

- Must have balance due under **$1,000** at due date of April 15.
- **No penalty if** withholding & estimated taxes paid exceed lower of either:
  - 100% of prior year liability
    - Must be 110% of prior year liability if taxable income is over $150,000 in prior year.
  - 90% of current year tax liability

The **late *filing* penalty** is based on the net amount of unpaid tax by the tax return filing due date (April 15th). The penalty is 5% per month, or part of a month, that the return is late, up to a total of 25% of the unpaid tax.

The **late *payment* penalty** is ½ of 1% (0.5%) for each month, or part of a month, after the due date that the tax is not paid. If both penalties apply for any month, the late filing penalty is reduced by the late payment penalty so that the maximum penalty is 5% per month, or part of a month.

Any balance due must be paid by April 15, the normal due date for the individual return. An individual can obtain an **automatic 6-month extension** of the due date for the return until October 15, but the extension is only for the filing, not the payment of the entire tax. Interest is charged from April 15 to the date of actual payment. In addition, as discussed above, there are penalties of 0.5% per month for late payment, and 5% per month for late filing or not filing. Both penalties have a maximum of 25% of the net tax owed. There are additional civil penalties related to negligence and substantial understatement of tax liability on the return, and civil and criminal penalties for fraud on the return. Both penalties are based on the amount of Net tax due.

An **accuracy-related penalty of 20%** of the underpayment applies if the underpayment of tax is attributable to negligence or disregard of rules and regulations, any substantial understatement of income tax, any substantial valuation overstatement, any substantial overstatement of pension liabilities, or any substantial gift or estate tax valuation understatement. Note: This penalty is increased to 40% for certain egregious misstatements (a.k.a., gross valuation misstatements).

Unlike corporations, an individual is **not required to file** a tax return if the gross income during the year is clearly insufficient for any tax liability to result. This is the case if the gross income of the taxpayer for the year does not **exceed the sum of:**
- **Personal exemptions** for the taxpayer and spouse
- The basic **standard deduction** based on filing status
- The additional standard deductions based on **age**

For purposes of determining whether a return has to be filed, the taxpayer cannot consider *dependency exemptions* nor the additional standard deductions based on *blindness*, since these are not automatically available without supporting evidence.

Even if the taxpayer does not have gross income exceeding the calculated limit, a return must be filed if the taxpayer's net income from **self-employment exceeds $400**, since self-employment taxes may be owed even though income taxes are not. The self-employment tax is 15.3%.

When an examination results in a proposed tax deficiency, the taxpayer will be issued a **30-day letter,** including a report of the examination that indicates the proposed deficiency and the reasons for it. The letter also will advise the taxpayer of the right to appeal the proposed action if the taxpayer does not agree with it. The taxpayer may, within 30 days of the date of the letter, ask the Appeals Office to consider the case.

Lecture 1.14

CLASS QUESTIONS

Please see the Class Questions and Class Solutions for this Lecture at the end of this Section.

Lecture 1.15

ALTERNATIVE MINIMUM TAX

Caution: At the time of this writing, President Trump had introduced his broad plan for tax reform, which included repealing the Alternative Minimum Tax (AMT). Please refer to the Course Textbook Updates section of the Roger CPA Review website for legislation updates: https://www.rogercpareview.com/dashboard/my-courses/course-textbook-updates.

Individuals benefiting from large itemized deductions or special tax benefits may be subject to the alternative minimum tax (AMT). This is based on a calculation of alternative minimum taxable income (AMTI), which denies certain deductions and benefits available in the computation of regular taxable income. To calculate the AMT, the individual performs the following calculation:

AMT - Individuals

Regular taxable income
+/- **Adjustments** and **preferences**
= AMTI before exemption
- Exemption
= **AMTI**
× Tax rate (26%/28%)
= Tentative minimum tax
- Regular tax
= **AMT**

The **Adjustments** are income or expense items computed differently for AMT and regular tax. They can increase or decrease AMTI. The adjustments made by an individual include: (**SIMPLE-PIE**)

- The **Standard deduction** may not be claimed.
- **Interest on My home equity loans** is not deducted (unless to buy, build or improve main or second home. Interest on acquisition indebtedness and investments may still be claimed).
- **Personal and dependency exemptions** are not allowed (there is a much larger exemption available against AMTI).
- **Local and state income taxes, all property taxes, and sales taxes** are not deductible.
- **Employee business expenses, tax preparation expenses, and investment expenses subject to the 2% (BIT) threshold** are not deductible. Other miscellaneous deductions not subject to the 2% of AGI rule are still allowed.

In addition, the individual is required to adjust income for certain tax preferences, which can only increase AMTI. **Tax Preferences (PIE):**

- **Private activity bond interest** is fully taxable (private activity interest). Private activity bonds are used to finance nongovernmental activities, such as industrial development, student loans and low-income housing. Interest is not a preference item if bonds were issued in 2009 or 2010.
- **Incentive stock options** are taxed when exercised for the difference between the exercise price and market price of the stock.
- **Excess depreciation on personal property** over 150% declining balance when double-declining balance was used for regular tax purposes.

Note that the following items are still allowed to be deducted for AMT purposes: charitable contributions, other miscellaneous itemized deductions (not 2%), medical expenses, mortgage interest, and theft or casualty losses.

Note: Corporations have an additional **ACE adjustment** that does not apply to individuals.

In calculating the amount of the AMT, AMTI is reduced by an exemption amount. The result is the AMT base. The amount of the exemption depends on the filing status of the tax return, and is phased out for taxpayers with AMTI (before exemption) exceeding certain amounts.

The Individual AMT Exemptions are:

	2017
Married filing joint	$84,500
Married filing separately	$42,250
Single and Head of Household	$54,300

Phaseout of exemptions:

Married filing Joint (MFJ)	= $84,500 – 25% (AMTI before exemption - $160,900)
Married filing Separate (MFS)	= $42,250 – 25% (AMTI before exemption - $80,450)
All Others (Single, HOH)	= $54,300 – 25% (AMTI before exemption - $120,700)

The **Tentative minimum tax** equals the total of:
- 26% of the first $187,800 ($93,900 for MFS) of AMT Base for 2017
- 28% of the AMT Base above $187,800 ($93,900 for MFS) for 2017

The CPA exam has tested the calculation of the exemption for corporate taxpayers (discussed in another section), and AMT has also shown up as a TBS problem recently for individuals. When the AMT is paid, the portion of the tax associated with timing preferences (primarily those involving incentive stock options) may be **carried forward indefinitely** and **credited** against regular income taxes in future years. **For example**, assume an incentive stock option to purchase shares at $10 is exercised when the stock is worth $50. The $40 difference is not reported for regular tax purposes, but is included as a preference in determining AMTI. Assume this preference causes the taxpayer to be subject to the AMT in the year of exercise. If the stock is sold years later for $75, a $65 gain on sale is reported for regular tax purposes, but $40 of that gain had already been taxed due to the AMT in the year of exercise. The alternative minimum tax paid as a result of the exercise of the ISO several years ago is now claimed as a credit against the regular tax liability, to avoid unfairly taxing the same gain twice.

Note that the AMT is only credited against **regular taxes** arising in later years as a result of the reversal of income differences. There is no AMT credit for taxes paid that are the result of exclusion preferences and adjustments (differences between AMTI and regular taxable income that do not reverse), such as private activity bond interest and the various itemized deductions that are not allowed for AMTI purposes.

The nonrefundable personal credits (e.g., child and dependent care credit, credit for the elderly and disabled, the adoption credit, the nonrefundable portions of the child tax credit and the AOTC, lifetime learning credit, etc.) are allowed to offset both regular tax liability and the alternative minimum tax.

Carryover Rules

	Carryback	**Carryforward**
Charitable contributions	No	5 years
Net Operating Losses (NOL)	2 years	20 years
Net Capital Losses: **Corporations (0 net Cap. loss)**	3 years	5 years
Net Capital Losses: **Individuals ($3,000)**	No	Indefinitely
Investment interest	No	Indefinitely
Net Passive Losses	No	Indefinitely, or may be claimed when the investment is sold
Net gambling losses	No	No

Lecture 1.16

CLASS QUESTIONS

Please see the Class Questions and Class Solutions for this Lecture at the end of this Section.

Lecture 1.17

CLASS QUESTIONS

Please see the Class Questions and Class Solutions for this Lecture at the end of this Section.

Lecture 1.18

CLASS QUESTIONS (Continued)

Please see the Class Questions and Class Solutions for this Lecture at the end of this Section.

Lecture 1.19

RESEARCH TASK FORMAT

Research is tested in its own independent task-based simulation problem. Each REG exam will include at least 1 Research-type TBS. The Candidates will be asked to search through the database to find the appropriate reference to the Internal Revenue Code (IRC) that addresses the issue presented in the research problem.

Using the Authoritative Literature, the candidate will search for keywords associated with the question using the search box, which will pull up all references to those keywords within the literature. From there, the candidate should use the "search within" function to find specific instances of keywords within each subsection. Keywords will be highlighted in the text, and the candidate can skim through them to find the relevant text that answers the research problem.

Research questions will also alert the candidate if they have correctly formatted their answer by displaying "Your response is correctly formatted" in a box below the candidate response if the candidate has entered reference numbers correctly.

Don't forget that you can use the Authoritative Literature to look up answers to other TBSs in the exam!

IRC-Internal Revenue Code

Officially Title 26 of the United States Code, the IRC is comprised of eleven subtitles, A through K. The subtitles are each divided into chapters as follows (repealed chapters omitted):

Subtitle A – Income Taxes
1 – Normal taxes and surtaxes
2 – Tax on self-employment income
2A – Unearned income Medicare contribution
3 – Withholding of tax on nonresident aliens and foreign corporations
4 – Taxes to enforce reporting on certain foreign accounts
6 – Consolidated returns

Subtitle B – Estate and Gift Taxes
11 – Estate tax
12 – Gift tax
13 – Tax on generation-skipping transfers
14 – Special valuation rules
15 – Gifts and bequests from expatriates

Subtitle C – Employment Taxes
21 – Federal Insurance Contributions Act
22 – Railroad Retirement Tax Act
23 – Federal Unemployment Tax Act
23A – Railroad Unemployment Repayment Tax
24 – Collection of income tax at source on wages
25 – General provisions relating to employment taxes

Subtitle D – Miscellaneous Excise Taxes
31 – Retail excise taxes
32 – Manufacturers excise taxes
33 – Facilities and services
34 – Taxes on certain insurance policies
35 – Taxes on wagering
36 – Certain other excise taxes
38 – Environmental taxes
39 – Registration-required obligations
40 – General provisions relating to occupational taxes
41 – Public charities
42 – Private foundations; and certain other tax-exempt organizations
43 – Qualified pension, etc., plans
44 – Qualified investment entities
45 – Provisions relating to expatriated entities
46 – Golden parachute payments

47 – Certain group health plans
48 – Maintenance of minimum essential coverage
49 – Cosmetic services
50 – Foreign procurement

Subtitle E – Alcohol, Tobacco, and Certain Other Excise Taxes
51 – Distilled spirits, wines, and beer
52 – Tobacco products and cigarette papers and tubes
53 – Machine guns, destructive devices, and certain other firearms
54 – Greenmail
55 – Structured settlement factoring transactions

Subtitle F – Procedure and Administration
61 – Information and returns
62 – Time and place for paying tax
63 – Assessment
64 – Collection
65 – Abatements, credits, and refunds
66 – Limitations
67 – Interest
68 – Additions to the tax, additional amounts, and assessable penalties
69 – General provisions relating to stamps
70 – Jeopardy, receiverships, etc.
71 – Transferees and fiduciaries
72 – Licensing and registration
73 – Bonds
74 – Closing agreements and compromises
75 – Crimes, other offenses, and forfeitures
76 – Judicial proceedings
77 – Miscellaneous provisions
78 – Discover of liability and enforcement of title
79 – Definitions
80 – General rules

Subtitle G – The Joint Committee on Taxation
91 – Organization and membership of the Joint Committee
92 – Powers and duties of the Joint Committee

Subtitle H – Financing of Presidential Election Campaigns
95 – Presidential election campaign fund
96 – Presidential primary matching payment account

Subtitle I – Trust Fund Code
98 –Trust fund code

Subtitle J – Coal Industry Health Benefits
99 – Coal industry health benefits

Subtitle K – Group Health Plan Requirements
100 – Group health plan requirements

Each chapter is further divided into subchapters. Some chapters are too specific to require subchapters, in which case the individual tax code sections are identified. Most research questions are derived from Subtitle A, *Income Taxes*, and Subtitle B, *Estate and Gift Taxes*. The subchapters for these are as follows:

Subtitle A – Income Taxes

>   CHAPTER 1 - NORMAL TAXES AND SURTAXES
>> Subchapter A - Determination of Tax Liability (Sections 1-59)
>> Subchapter B - Computation of Taxable Income (Sections 61-291)
>> Subchapter C - Corporate Distributions and Adjustments (Sections 301-385)
>> Subchapter D - Deferred Compensation, Etc. (Sections 401-436)
>> Subchapter E - Accounting Periods and Methods of Accounting (Sections 441-483)
>> Subchapter F - Exempt Organizations (Sections 501-530)
>> Subchapter G - Corporations Used to Avoid Income Tax on Shareholders (Sections 531-565)
>> Subchapter H - Banking Institutions (Sections 581-601)
>> Subchapter I - Natural Resources (Sections 611-638)
>> Subchapter J - Estates, Trusts, Beneficiaries, and Decedents (Sections 641-692)
>> Subchapter K - Partners and Partnerships (Sections 701-777)
>> Subchapter L - Insurance Companies (Sections 801-848)
>> Subchapter M - Regulated Investment Companies and Real Estate Investment Trusts (Sections 851-860)
>> Subchapter N - Tax Based on Income From Sources Within or Without the United States (Sections 861-1000)
>> Subchapter O - Gain or Loss on Disposition of Property (Sections 1001-1111)
>> Subchapter P - Capital Gains and Losses (Sections 1201-1298)
>> Subchapter Q - Readjustment of Tax Between Years and Special Limitations (Sections 1301-1351)
>> Subchapter R - Election to Determine Corporate Tax on Certain International Shipping Activities Using Per Ton Rate (Sections 1352-1359)
>> Subchapter S - Tax Treatment of S Corporations and Their Shareholders (Sections 1361-1379)
>> Subchapter T - Cooperatives and Their Patrons (Section 1381-1388)
>> Subchapter U - Designation and Treatment of Empowerment Zones, Enterprise Communities, and Rural Development Investment Areas (Sections 1391-1397)
>> Subchapter V - Title 11 Cases (Sections 1398-1399)
>> Subchapter W - District of Columbia Enterprise Zone (Sections 1400-1400C)
>> Subchapter X - Renewal Communities (Sections 1400E-1400J)
>> Subchapter Y - Short-Term Regional Benefits (Sections 1400L-1400U3)
>   CHAPTER 2 - TAX ON SELF-EMPLOYMENT INCOME (Sections 1401-1403)
>> Section 1401 – Rate of tax
>> Section 1402 – Definitions
>> Section 1403 – Miscellaneous provisions
>   CHAPTER 2A – UNEARNED INCOME MEDICARE CONTRIBUTION (Section 1411)
>> Section 1411 – Imposition of tax
>   CHAPTER 3 - WITHHOLDING OF TAX ON NONRESIDENT ALIENS AND FOREIGN CORPORATIONS (Sections 1441-1465)
>> Subchapter A – Nonresident Aliens and Foreign Corporations (Sections 1441-1446)
>> Subchapter B – Application of Withholding Provisions (Sections 1451-1465)
>   CHAPTER 4 - TAXES TO ENFORCE REPORTING ON CERTAIN FOREIGN ACCOUNTS (Sections 1471-1474)
>> Section 1471 – Withholdable payments to foreign financial institutions
>> Section 1472 – Withholdable payments to other foreign entities
>> Section 1473 – Definitions
>> Section 1474 – Special rules
>   CHAPTER 5 - REPEALED
>   CHAPTER 6 - CONSOLIDATED RETURNS (Sections 1501-1564)
>> Subchapter A – Returns and Payment of Tax (Sections 1501-1505)
>> Subchapter B – Related Rules (Sections 1551-1564)

Subtitle B – Estate and Gift Taxes

Sample Research Question:

Mr. Philipp received a distribution from a qualified tuition program that was not used to pay qualified higher education expenses and is trying to determine what portion, if any, should be included in gross income. To what section of the Internal Revenue Code will Mr. Philipp refer to determine the amount?

Solution: Since a *qualified tuition program* is considered an exempt organization, the information will be found in Subchapter F, Exempt Organizations, of Chapter 1, Normal Taxes and Surtaxes, from Subtitle A, Income Taxes.

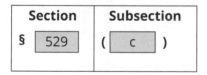

Section	Subsection
§ 529	(c)

Note: The 2016 forms are provided since 2017 forms were unavailable at the time of publication.

Form 1040 Department of the Treasury—Internal Revenue Service (99)

U.S. Individual Income Tax Return **2016** OMB No. 1545-0074 | IRS Use Only—Do not write or staple in this space.

For the year Jan. 1–Dec. 31, 2016, or other tax year beginning _____ , 2016, ending _____ , 20 ___   See separate instructions.

Your first name and initial	Last name		Your social security number

If a joint return, spouse's first name and initial	Last name		Spouse's social security number

Home address (number and street). If you have a P.O. box, see instructions. | Apt. no.

▲ Make sure the SSN(s) above and on line 6c are correct.

City, town or post office, state, and ZIP code. If you have a foreign address, also complete spaces below (see instructions).

Presidential Election Campaign
Check here if you, or your spouse if filing jointly, want $3 to go to this fund. Checking a box below will not change your tax or refund. ☐ You ☐ Spouse

Foreign country name	Foreign province/state/county	Foreign postal code

Filing Status

Check only one box.

1 ☐ Single
2 ☐ Married filing jointly (even if only one had income)
3 ☐ Married filing separately. Enter spouse's SSN above and full name here. ▶
4 ☐ Head of household (with qualifying person). (See instructions.) If the qualifying person is a child but not your dependent, enter this child's name here. ▶ _____
5 ☐ Qualifying widow(er) with dependent child

Exemptions

6a ☐ **Yourself.** If someone can claim you as a dependent, **do not** check box 6a . . . . .
b ☐ **Spouse** . . . .

c **Dependents:**

(1) First name Last name	(2) Dependent's social security number	(3) Dependent's relationship to you	(4) ✓ if child under age 17 qualifying for child tax credit (see instructions)
			☐
			☐
			☐
			☐

If more than four dependents, see instructions and check here ▶☐

Boxes checked on 6a and 6b ___
No. of children on 6c who:
• lived with you
• did not live with you due to divorce or separation (see instructions)
Dependents on 6c not entered above
Add numbers on lines above ▶

d   Total number of exemptions claimed . . . .

Income

Attach Form(s) W-2 here. Also attach Forms W-2G and 1099-R if tax was withheld.

If you did not get a W-2, see instructions.

7	Wages, salaries, tips, etc. Attach Form(s) W-2	7
8a	**Taxable** interest. Attach Schedule B if required	8a
b	**Tax-exempt** interest. **Do not** include on line 8a . . .	8b
9a	Ordinary dividends. Attach Schedule B if required	9a
b	Qualified dividends	9b
10	Taxable refunds, credits, or offsets of state and local income taxes	10
11	Alimony received	11
12	Business income or (loss). Attach Schedule C or C-EZ	12
13	Capital gain or (loss). Attach Schedule D if required. If not required, check here ▶☐	13
14	Other gains or (losses). Attach Form 4797	14
15a	IRA distributions . [15a]	b Taxable amount . .	15b
16a	Pensions and annuities [16a]	b Taxable amount . . .	16b
17	Rental real estate, royalties, partnerships, S corporations, trusts, etc. Attach Schedule E	17
18	Farm income or (loss). Attach Schedule F	18
19	Unemployment compensation	19
20a	Social security benefits [20a]	b Taxable amount . . .	20b
21	Other income. List type and amount _____	21
22	Combine the amounts in the far right column for lines 7 through 21. This is your **total income** ▶	22

Adjusted Gross Income

23	Educator expenses	23
24	Certain business expenses of reservists, performing artists, and fee-basis government officials. Attach Form 2106 or 2106-EZ	24
25	Health savings account deduction. Attach Form 8889 .	25
26	Moving expenses. Attach Form 3903	26
27	Deductible part of self-employment tax. Attach Schedule SE .	27
28	Self-employed SEP, SIMPLE, and qualified plans . .	28
29	Self-employed health insurance deduction . . .	29
30	Penalty on early withdrawal of savings	30
31a	Alimony paid b Recipient's SSN ▶ _____	31a
32	IRA deduction	32
33	Student loan interest deduction	33
34	Tuition and fees. Attach Form 8917	34
35	Domestic production activities deduction. Attach Form 8903	35
36	Add lines 23 through 35 . . . . ▶	36
37	Subtract line 36 from line 22. This is your **adjusted gross income** . . . . ▶	37

For Disclosure, Privacy Act, and Paperwork Reduction Act Notice, see separate instructions.   Cat. No. 11320B   Form **1040** (2016)

Form 1040 (2016)   Page **2**

Tax and Credits	38	Amount from line 37 (adjusted gross income)		38	
	39a	Check if: ☐ **You** were born before January 2, 1952, ☐ Blind. } **Total boxes** ☐ **Spouse** was born before January 2, 1952, ☐ Blind. } checked ▶ 39a			
	b	If your spouse itemizes on a separate return or you were a dual-status alien, check here▶ 39b☐			

Standard Deduction for—
- People who check any box on line 39a or 39b **or** who can be claimed as a dependent, see instructions.
- All others:
Single or Married filing separately, $6,300
Married filing jointly or Qualifying widow(er), $12,600
Head of household, $9,300

40	**Itemized deductions** (from Schedule A) **or** your **standard deduction** (see left margin)		40	
41	Subtract line 40 from line 38		41	
42	**Exemptions.** If line 38 is $155,650 or less, multiply $4,050 by the number on line 6d. Otherwise, see instructions		42	
43	**Taxable income.** Subtract line 42 from line 41. If line 42 is more than line 41, enter -0- . . .		43	
44	**Tax** (see instructions). Check if any from: **a** ☐ Form(s) 8814 **b** ☐ Form 4972 **c** ☐ _____		44	
45	**Alternative minimum tax** (see instructions). Attach Form 6251		45	
46	Excess advance premium tax credit repayment. Attach Form 8962		46	
47	Add lines 44, 45, and 46 . . . . ▶		47	
48	Foreign tax credit. Attach Form 1116 if required	48		
49	Credit for child and dependent care expenses. Attach Form 2441	49		
50	Education credits from Form 8863, line 19	50		
51	Retirement savings contributions credit. Attach Form 8880	51		
52	Child tax credit. Attach Schedule 8812, if required . . .	52		
53	Residential energy credits. Attach Form 5695	53		
54	Other credits from Form: **a** ☐ 3800 **b** ☐ 8801 **c** ☐ _____	54		
55	Add lines 48 through 54. These are your **total credits**		55	
56	Subtract line 55 from line 47. If line 55 is more than line 47, enter -0- . . . . . ▶		56	

Other Taxes	57	Self-employment tax. Attach Schedule SE	57	
	58	Unreported social security and Medicare tax from Form: **a** ☐ 4137 **b** ☐ 8919	58	
	59	Additional tax on IRAs, other qualified retirement plans, etc. Attach Form 5329 if required . .	59	
	60a	Household employment taxes from Schedule H	60a	
	b	First-time homebuyer credit repayment. Attach Form 5405 if required	60b	
	61	Health care: individual responsibility (see instructions) Full-year coverage ☐ . . .	61	
	62	Taxes from: **a** ☐ Form 8959 **b** ☐ Form 8960 **c** ☐ Instructions; enter code(s) _____	62	
	63	Add lines 56 through 62. This is your **total tax** . . . . ▶	63	

Payments	64	Federal income tax withheld from Forms W-2 and 1099 . .	64	
	65	2016 estimated tax payments and amount applied from 2015 return	65	
If you have a qualifying child, attach Schedule EIC.	66a	**Earned income credit (EIC)**	66a	
	b	Nontaxable combat pay election	66b	
	67	Additional child tax credit. Attach Schedule 8812	67	
	68	American opportunity credit from Form 8863, line 8 . . .	68	
	69	Net premium tax credit. Attach Form 8962	69	
	70	Amount paid with request for extension to file	70	
	71	Excess social security and tier 1 RRTA tax withheld . . .	71	
	72	Credit for federal tax on fuels. Attach Form 4136 . . .	72	
	73	Credits from Form: **a** ☐ 2439 **b** ☐ Reserved **c** ☐ 8885 **d** ☐	73	
	74	Add lines 64, 65, 66a, and 67 through 73. These are your **total payments** . . . . . ▶	74	

Refund	75	If line 74 is more than line 63, subtract line 63 from line 74. This is the amount you **overpaid**	75	
	76a	Amount of line 75 you want **refunded to you.** If Form 8888 is attached, check here ▶ ☐	76a	
Direct deposit? See instructions.	▶ b	Routing number _____ ▶ c Type: ☐ Checking ☐ Savings		
	▶ d	Account number _____		
	77	Amount of line 75 you want **applied to your 2017 estimated tax** ▶ 77		
Amount You Owe	78	**Amount you owe.** Subtract line 74 from line 63. For details on how to pay, see instructions ▶	78	
	79	Estimated tax penalty (see instructions) 79		

Third Party Designee

Do you want to allow another person to discuss this return with the IRS (see instructions)?   ☐ **Yes.** Complete below.   ☐ **No**

Designee's name ▶ _____   Phone no. ▶ _____   Personal identification number (PIN) ▶ _____

Sign Here

Joint return? See instructions.
Keep a copy for your records.

Under penalties of perjury, I declare that I have examined this return and accompanying schedules and statements, and to the best of my knowledge and belief, they are true, correct, and accurately list all amounts and sources of income I received during the tax year. Declaration of preparer (other than taxpayer) is based on all information of which preparer has any knowledge.

Your signature	Date	Your occupation	Daytime phone number
Spouse's signature. If a joint return, **both** must sign.	Date	Spouse's occupation	If the IRS sent you an Identity Protection PIN, enter it here (see inst.)

Paid Preparer Use Only

Print/Type preparer's name	Preparer's signature	Date	Check ☐ if self-employed	PTIN
Firm's name ▶			Firm's EIN ▶	
Firm's address ▶			Phone no.	

www.irs.gov/form1040   Form **1040** (2016)

SCHEDULE A
(Form 1040)

Department of the Treasury
Internal Revenue Service (99)

Itemized Deductions

▶ Information about Schedule A and its separate instructions is at *www.irs.gov/schedulea*.
▶ **Attach to Form 1040.**

OMB No. 1545-0074

2016

Attachment
Sequence No. **07**

Name(s) shown on Form 1040   **Your social security number**

Medical and Dental Expenses

Caution: Do not include expenses reimbursed or paid by others.

1 Medical and dental expenses (see instructions) . . . . . | **1**
2 Enter amount from Form 1040, line 38 | **2**
3 Multiply line 2 by 10% (0.10). But if either you or your spouse was born before January 2, 1952, multiply line 2 by 7.5% (0.075) instead | **3**
4 Subtract line 3 from line 1. If line 3 is more than line 1, enter -0- . . . . | **4**

Taxes You Paid

5 State and local **(check only one box):**
  a ☐ Income taxes, **or**
  b ☐ General sales taxes . . . . | **5**
6 Real estate taxes (see instructions) . . . . | **6**
7 Personal property taxes . . . . | **7**
8 Other taxes. List type and amount ▶ _____ | **8**
9 Add lines 5 through 8 . . . . | **9**

Interest You Paid

Note:
Your mortgage interest deduction may be limited (see instructions).

10 Home mortgage interest and points reported to you on Form 1098 | **10**
11 Home mortgage interest not reported to you on Form 1098. If paid to the person from whom you bought the home, see instructions and show that person's name, identifying no., and address ▶ _____ | **11**
12 Points not reported to you on Form 1098. See instructions for special rules . . . . | **12**
13 Mortgage insurance premiums (see instructions) . . . . . | **13**
14 Investment interest. Attach Form 4952 if required. (See instructions.) | **14**
15 Add lines 10 through 14 . . . . | **15**

Gifts to Charity

If you made a gift and got a benefit for it, see instructions.

16 Gifts by cash or check. If you made any gift of $250 or more, see instructions . . . . | **16**
17 Other than by cash or check. If any gift of $250 or more, see instructions. You **must** attach Form 8283 if over $500 . . . | **17**
18 Carryover from prior year . . . . | **18**
19 Add lines 16 through 18 . . . . | **19**

Casualty and Theft Losses

20 Casualty or theft loss(es). Attach Form 4684. (See instructions.) . . . . | **20**

Job Expenses and Certain Miscellaneous Deductions

21 Unreimbursed employee expenses—job travel, union dues, job education, etc. Attach Form 2106 or 2106-EZ if required. (See instructions.) ▶ _____ | **21**
22 Tax preparation fees . . . . | **22**
23 Other expenses—investment, safe deposit box, etc. List type and amount ▶ _____ | **23**
24 Add lines 21 through 23 . . . . | **24**
25 Enter amount from Form 1040, line 38 | **25**
26 Multiply line 25 by 2% (0.02) . . . . | **26**
27 Subtract line 26 from line 24. If line 26 is more than line 24, enter -0- . . . . . | **27**

Other Miscellaneous Deductions

28 Other—from list in instructions. List type and amount ▶ _____ | **28**

Total Itemized Deductions

29 Is Form 1040, line 38, over $155,650?
☐ **No.** Your deduction is not limited. Add the amounts in the far right column for lines 4 through 28. Also, enter this amount on Form 1040, line 40.
☐ **Yes.** Your deduction may be limited. See the Itemized Deductions Worksheet in the instructions to figure the amount to enter. | **29**
30 If you elect to itemize deductions even though they are less than your standard deduction, check here . . . . ▶ ☐

For Paperwork Reduction Act Notice, see Form 1040 instructions.   Cat. No. 17145C   **Schedule A (Form 1040) 2016**

SCHEDULE B	Interest and Ordinary Dividends	OMB No. 1545-0074
(Form 1040A or 1040) (Rev. January 2017) Department of the Treasury Internal Revenue Service (99)	▶ Attach to Form 1040A or 1040. ▶ Information about Schedule B and its instructions is at *www.irs.gov/scheduleb*.	20**16** Attachment Sequence No. **08**

Name(s) shown on return | Your social security number

			Amount
Part I **Interest** (See instructions on back and the instructions for Form 1040A, or Form 1040, line 8a.) **Note:** If you received a Form 1099-INT, Form 1099-OID, or substitute statement from a brokerage firm, list the firm's name as the payer and enter the total interest shown on that form.	**1**	List name of payer. If any interest is from a seller-financed mortgage and the buyer used the property as a personal residence, see instructions on back and list this interest first. Also, show that buyer's social security number and address ▶	**1**
	2	Add the amounts on line 1	**2**
	3	Excludable interest on series EE and I U.S. savings bonds issued after 1989. Attach Form 8815	**3**
	4	Subtract line 3 from line 2. Enter the result here and on Form 1040A, or Form 1040, line 8a . . . . ▶	**4**

Note: If line 4 is over $1,500, you must complete Part III.

			Amount
Part II **Ordinary Dividends** (See instructions on back and the instructions for Form 1040A, or Form 1040, line 9a.) **Note:** If you received a Form 1099-DIV or substitute statement from a brokerage firm, list the firm's name as the payer and enter the ordinary dividends shown on that form.	**5**	List name of payer ▶	**5**
	6	Add the amounts on line 5. Enter the total here and on Form 1040A, or Form 1040, line 9a . . . . ▶	**6**

Note: If line 6 is over $1,500, you must complete Part III.

		You must complete this part if you **(a)** had over $1,500 of taxable interest or ordinary dividends; **(b)** had a foreign account; or **(c)** received a distribution from, or were a grantor of, or a transferor to, a foreign trust.	Yes	No
Part III **Foreign Accounts and Trusts** (See instructions on back.)	**7a**	At any time during 2016, did you have a financial interest in or signature authority over a financial account (such as a bank account, securities account, or brokerage account) located in a foreign country? See instructions		
		If "Yes," are you required to file FinCEN Form 114, Report of Foreign Bank and Financial Accounts (FBAR), to report that financial interest or signature authority? See FinCEN Form 114 and its instructions for filing requirements and exceptions to those requirements		
	b	If you are required to file FinCEN Form 114, enter the name of the foreign country where the financial account is located ▶		
	8	During 2016, did you receive a distribution from, or were you the grantor of, or transferor to, a foreign trust? If "Yes," you may have to file Form 3520. See instructions on back		

For Paperwork Reduction Act Notice, see your tax return instructions.   Cat. No. 17146N   Schedule B (Form 1040A or 1040) 2016

SCHEDULE C
(Form 1040)

Department of the Treasury
Internal Revenue Service (99)

Profit or Loss From Business
(Sole Proprietorship)

▶ Information about Schedule C and its separate instructions is at *www.irs.gov/schedulec.*
▶ Attach to Form 1040, 1040NR, or 1041; partnerships generally must file Form 1065.

OMB No. 1545-0074

2016

Attachment
Sequence No. **09**

Name of proprietor | Social security number (SSN)

A Principal business or profession, including product or service (see instructions)

B Enter code from instructions ▶

C Business name. If no separate business name, leave blank.

D Employer ID number (EIN), (see instr.)

E Business address (including suite or room no.) ▶
City, town or post office, state, and ZIP code

F Accounting method: **(1)** ☐ Cash **(2)** ☐ Accrual **(3)** ☐ Other (specify) ▶

G Did you "materially participate" in the operation of this business during 2016? If "No," see instructions for limit on losses . ☐ Yes ☐ No

H If you started or acquired this business during 2016, check here . . . . ▶ ☐

I Did you make any payments in 2016 that would require you to file Form(s) 1099? (see instructions) . . . . ☐ Yes ☐ No

J If "Yes," did you or will you file required Forms 1099? . . . . ☐ Yes ☐ No

Part I   Income

1	Gross receipts or sales. See instructions for line 1 and check the box if this income was reported to you on Form W-2 and the "Statutory employee" box on that form was checked . . . . ▶ ☐	1	
2	Returns and allowances	2	
3	Subtract line 2 from line 1	3	
4	Cost of goods sold (from line 42)	4	
5	**Gross profit.** Subtract line 4 from line 3	5	
6	Other income, including federal and state gasoline or fuel tax credit or refund (see instructions)	6	
7	**Gross income.** Add lines 5 and 6 . . . . ▶	7	

Part II   Expenses. Enter expenses for business use of your home **only** on line 30.

8	Advertising	8		18	Office expense (see instructions)	18	
9	Car and truck expenses (see instructions).	9		19	Pension and profit-sharing plans .	19	
				20	Rent or lease (see instructions):		
10	Commissions and fees .	10		a	Vehicles, machinery, and equipment	20a	
11	Contract labor (see instructions)	11		b	Other business property . . .	20b	
12	Depletion	12		21	Repairs and maintenance . . .	21	
13	Depreciation and section 179 expense deduction (not included in Part III) (see instructions).	13		22	Supplies (not included in Part III) .	22	
				23	Taxes and licenses	23	
				24	Travel, meals, and entertainment:		
14	Employee benefit programs (other than on line 19). .	14		a	Travel	24a	
15	Insurance (other than health)	15		b	Deductible meals and entertainment (see instructions) .	24b	
16	Interest:			25	Utilities	25	
a	Mortgage (paid to banks, etc.)	16a		26	Wages (less employment credits) .	26	
b	Other	16b		27a	Other expenses (from line 48) . .	27a	
17	Legal and professional services	17		b	**Reserved for future use** . . .	27b	

28	**Total expenses** before expenses for business use of home. Add lines 8 through 27a . . . . . . ▶	28	
29	Tentative profit or (loss). Subtract line 28 from line 7	29	
30	Expenses for business use of your home. Do not report these expenses elsewhere. Attach Form 8829 unless using the simplified method (see instructions). Simplified method filers only: enter the total square footage of: (a) your home: _____ and (b) the part of your home used for business: _____ . Use the Simplified Method Worksheet in the instructions to figure the amount to enter on line 30	30	
31	**Net profit or (loss).** Subtract line 30 from line 29. • If a profit, enter on both **Form 1040, line 12** (or **Form 1040NR, line 13**) and on **Schedule SE, line 2.** (If you checked the box on line 1, see instructions). Estates and trusts, enter on **Form 1041, line 3.** • If a loss, you **must** go to line 32.	31	
32	If you have a loss, check the box that describes your investment in this activity (see instructions). • If you checked 32a, enter the loss on both **Form 1040, line 12,** (or **Form 1040NR, line 13**) and on **Schedule SE, line 2.** (If you checked the box on line 1, see the line 31 instructions). Estates and trusts, enter on **Form 1041, line 3.** • If you checked 32b, you **must** attach **Form 6198.** Your loss may be limited.	32a ☐ All investment is at risk. 32b ☐ Some investment is not at risk.	

For Paperwork Reduction Act Notice, see the separate instructions.   Cat. No. 11334P   Schedule C (Form 1040) 2016

| **Part III** | **Cost of Goods Sold** (see instructions) |

33 Method(s) used to
value closing inventory: **a** ☐ Cost **b** ☐ Lower of cost or market **c** ☐ Other (attach explanation)

34 Was there any change in determining quantities, costs, or valuations between opening and closing inventory?
If "Yes," attach explanation . . . . ☐ **Yes**   ☐ **No**

35	Inventory at beginning of year. If different from last year's closing inventory, attach explanation . . .	**35**
36	Purchases less cost of items withdrawn for personal use	**36**
37	Cost of labor. Do not include any amounts paid to yourself	**37**
38	Materials and supplies	**38**
39	Other costs	**39**
40	Add lines 35 through 39	**40**
41	Inventory at end of year	**41**
42	**Cost of goods sold.** Subtract line 41 from line 40. Enter the result here and on line 4	**42**

| **Part IV** | **Information on Your Vehicle.** Complete this part **only** if you are claiming car or truck expenses on line 9 and are not required to file Form 4562 for this business. See the instructions for line 13 to find out if you must file Form 4562. |

43 When did you place your vehicle in service for business purposes? (month, day, year) ▶ ____ / ____ / ____

44 Of the total number of miles you drove your vehicle during 2016, enter the number of miles you used your vehicle for:

a Business _____ **b** Commuting (see instructions) _____ **c** Other _____

45 Was your vehicle available for personal use during off-duty hours? . . . . ☐ **Yes** ☐ **No**

46 Do you (or your spouse) have another vehicle available for personal use?. . . . . ☐ **Yes** ☐ **No**

47a Do you have evidence to support your deduction? . . . . ☐ **Yes** ☐ **No**

b If "Yes," is the evidence written? . . . . ☐ **Yes** ☐ **No**

| **Part V** | **Other Expenses.** List below business expenses not included on lines 8–26 or line 30. |

--------------------	
48 **Total other expenses.** Enter here and on line 27a	**48**

Schedule C (Form 1040) 2016

SCHEDULE D
(Form 1040)

Department of the Treasury
Internal Revenue Service (99)

Capital Gains and Losses

▶ Attach to Form 1040 or Form 1040NR.
▶ Information about Schedule D and its separate instructions is at *www.irs.gov/scheduled*.
▶ Use Form 8949 to list your transactions for lines 1b, 2, 3, 8b, 9, and 10.

OMB No. 1545-0074

2016

Attachment
Sequence No. **12**

Name(s) shown on return

Your social security number

Part I   Short-Term Capital Gains and Losses—Assets Held One Year or Less

See instructions for how to figure the amounts to enter on the lines below. This form may be easier to complete if you round off cents to whole dollars.	(d) Proceeds (sales price)	(e) Cost (or other basis)	(g) Adjustments to gain or loss from Form(s) 8949, Part I, line 2, column (g)	(h) Gain or (loss) Subtract column (e) from column (d) and combine the result with column (g)
1a Totals for all short-term transactions reported on Form 1099-B for which basis was reported to the IRS and for which you have no adjustments (see instructions). However, if you choose to report all these transactions on Form 8949, leave this line blank and go to line 1b .				
1b Totals for all transactions reported on Form(s) 8949 with **Box A** checked				
2 Totals for all transactions reported on Form(s) 8949 with **Box B** checked				
3 Totals for all transactions reported on Form(s) 8949 with **Box C** checked				

4 Short-term gain from Form 6252 and short-term gain or (loss) from Forms 4684, 6781, and 8824 .	**4**	
5 Net short-term gain or (loss) from partnerships, S corporations, estates, and trusts from Schedule(s) K-1	**5**	
6 Short-term capital loss carryover. Enter the amount, if any, from line 8 of your **Capital Loss Carryover Worksheet** in the instructions	**6** ( )
7 **Net short-term capital gain or (loss).** Combine lines 1a through 6 in column (h). If you have any long-term capital gains or losses, go to Part II below. Otherwise, go to Part III on the back	**7**	

Part II   Long-Term Capital Gains and Losses—Assets Held More Than One Year

See instructions for how to figure the amounts to enter on the lines below. This form may be easier to complete if you round off cents to whole dollars.	(d) Proceeds (sales price)	(e) Cost (or other basis)	(g) Adjustments to gain or loss from Form(s) 8949, Part II, line 2, column (g)	(h) Gain or (loss) Subtract column (e) from column (d) and combine the result with column (g)
8a Totals for all long-term transactions reported on Form 1099-B for which basis was reported to the IRS and for which you have no adjustments (see instructions). However, if you choose to report all these transactions on Form 8949, leave this line blank and go to line 8b .				
8b Totals for all transactions reported on Form(s) 8949 with **Box D** checked				
9 Totals for all transactions reported on Form(s) 8949 with **Box E** checked				
10 Totals for all transactions reported on Form(s) 8949 with **Box F** checked.				

11 Gain from Form 4797, Part I; long-term gain from Forms 2439 and 6252; and long-term gain or (loss) from Forms 4684, 6781, and 8824	**11**	
12 Net long-term gain or (loss) from partnerships, S corporations, estates, and trusts from Schedule(s) K-1	**12**	
13 Capital gain distributions. See the instructions	**13**	
14 Long-term capital loss carryover. Enter the amount, if any, from line 13 of your **Capital Loss Carryover Worksheet** in the instructions	**14** ( )
15 **Net long-term capital gain or (loss).** Combine lines 8a through 14 in column (h). Then go to Part III on the back	**15**	

For Paperwork Reduction Act Notice, see your tax return instructions.   Cat. No. 11338H   Schedule D (Form 1040) 2016

Part III	Summary

16 Combine lines 7 and 15 and enter the result . . . . | **16** |

- If line 16 is a **gain,** enter the amount from line 16 on Form 1040, line 13, or Form 1040NR, line 14. Then go to line 17 below.
- If line 16 is a **loss,** skip lines 17 through 20 below. Then go to line 21. Also be sure to complete line 22.
- If line 16 is **zero,** skip lines 17 through 21 below and enter -0- on Form 1040, line 13, or Form 1040NR, line 14. Then go to line 22.

17 Are lines 15 and 16 **both** gains?
☐ **Yes.** Go to line 18.
☐ **No.** Skip lines 18 through 21, and go to line 22.

18 Enter the amount, if any, from line 7 of the **28% Rate Gain Worksheet** in the instructions . . ▶ | **18** |

19 Enter the amount, if any, from line 18 of the **Unrecaptured Section 1250 Gain Worksheet** in the instructions . . . . ▶ | **19** |

20 Are lines 18 and 19 **both** zero or blank?
☐ **Yes.** Complete the **Qualified Dividends and Capital Gain Tax Worksheet** in the instructions for Form 1040, line 44 (or in the instructions for Form 1040NR, line 42). **Don't** complete lines 21 and 22 below.

☐ **No.** Complete the **Schedule D Tax Worksheet** in the instructions. **Don't** complete lines 21 and 22 below.

21 If line 16 is a loss, enter here and on Form 1040, line 13, or Form 1040NR, line 14, the **smaller** of:

- The loss on line 16 or
- ($3,000), or if married filing separately, ($1,500) . . . . | **21** ( )

Note: When figuring which amount is smaller, treat both amounts as positive numbers.

22 Do you have qualified dividends on Form 1040, line 9b, or Form 1040NR, line 10b?

☐ **Yes.** Complete the **Qualified Dividends and Capital Gain Tax Worksheet** in the instructions for Form 1040, line 44 (or in the instructions for Form 1040NR, line 42).

☐ **No.** Complete the rest of Form 1040 or Form 1040NR.

Schedule D (Form 1040) 2016

SCHEDULE E
(Form 1040)

Department of the Treasury
Internal Revenue Service (99)

Supplemental Income and Loss

(From rental real estate, royalties, partnerships, S corporations, estates, trusts, REMICs, etc.)

▶ Attach to Form 1040, 1040NR, or Form 1041.

▶ Information about Schedule E and its separate instructions is at *www.irs.gov/schedulee.*

OMB No. 1545-0074

20**16**

Attachment
Sequence No. **13**

Name(s) shown on return

Your social security number

Part I   **Income or Loss From Rental Real Estate and Royalties**   **Note:** If you are in the business of renting personal property, use **Schedule C** or **C-EZ** (see instructions). If you are an individual, report farm rental income or loss from **Form 4835** on page 2, line 40.

A Did you make any payments in 2016 that would require you to file Form(s) 1099? (see instructions)   ☐ Yes ☐ No

B If "Yes," did you or will you file required Forms 1099?   ☐ Yes ☐ No

1a Physical address of each property (street, city, state, ZIP code)

A _____

B _____

C _____

1b	Type of Property (from list below)	2	For each rental real estate property listed above, report the number of fair rental and personal use days. Check the **QJV** box only if you meet the requirements to file as a qualified joint venture. See instructions.		Fair Rental Days	Personal Use Days	QJV
A				A			☐
B				B			☐
C				C			☐

Type of Property:

1 Single Family Residence   3 Vacation/Short-Term Rental   5 Land   7 Self-Rental
2 Multi-Family Residence   4 Commercial   6 Royalties 8 Other (describe)

Income:	Properties:		A	B	C
3	Rents received	3			
4	Royalties received	4			
Expenses:					
5	Advertising	5			
6	Auto and travel (see instructions)	6			
7	Cleaning and maintenance	7			
8	Commissions.	8			
9	Insurance	9			
10	Legal and other professional fees	10			
11	Management fees	11			
12	Mortgage interest paid to banks, etc. (see instructions)	12			
13	Other interest.	13			
14	Repairs.	14			
15	Supplies	15			
16	Taxes	16			
17	Utilities.	17			
18	Depreciation expense or depletion	18			
19	Other (list) ▶ _____	19			
20	Total expenses. Add lines 5 through 19	20			
21	Subtract line 20 from line 3 (rents) and/or 4 (royalties). If result is a (loss), see instructions to find out if you must file **Form 6198**	21			
22	Deductible rental real estate loss after limitation, if any, on **Form 8582** (see instructions)	22	(	)(	)(	)

23a	Total of all amounts reported on line 3 for all rental properties . . .	23a	
b	Total of all amounts reported on line 4 for all royalty properties . . .	23b	
c	Total of all amounts reported on line 12 for all properties	23c	
d	Total of all amounts reported on line 18 for all properties	23d	
e	Total of all amounts reported on line 20 for all properties	23e	

24	**Income.** Add positive amounts shown on line 21. **Do not** include any losses	24	
25	**Losses.** Add royalty losses from line 21 and rental real estate losses from line 22. Enter total losses here	25	( )
26	**Total rental real estate and royalty income or (loss).** Combine lines 24 and 25. Enter the result here. If Parts II, III, IV, and line 40 on page 2 do not apply to you, also enter this amount on Form 1040, line 17, or Form 1040NR, line 18. Otherwise, include this amount in the total on line 41 on page 2 . . .	26	

For Paperwork Reduction Act Notice, see the separate instructions.   Cat. No. 11344L   Schedule E (Form 1040) 2016

Schedule E (Form 1040) 2016   Attachment Sequence No. **13**   Page **2**

Name(s) shown on return. Do not enter name and social security number if shown on other side. | Your social security number

Caution: The IRS compares amounts reported on your tax return with amounts shown on Schedule(s) K-1.

| **Part II** | **Income or Loss From Partnerships and S Corporations** **Note:** If you report a loss from an at-risk activity for which **any** amount is **not** at risk, you **must** check the box in column **(e)** on line 28 and attach **Form 6198.** See instructions. |

27 Are you reporting any loss not allowed in a prior year due to the at-risk, excess farm loss, or basis limitations, a prior year unallowed loss from a passive activity (if that loss was not reported on Form 8582), or unreimbursed partnership expenses? If you answered "Yes," see instructions before completing this section.   ☐ **Yes**   ☐ **No**

28

	(a) Name	**(b)** Enter P for partnership; **S** for S corporation	**(c)** Check if foreign partnership	**(d)** Employer identification number	**(e)** Check if any amount is not at risk
A			☐		☐
B			☐		☐
C			☐		☐
D			☐		☐

	Passive Income and Loss		Nonpassive Income and Loss		
	(f) Passive loss allowed (attach **Form 8582** if required)	**(g)** Passive income from **Schedule K-1**	**(h)** Nonpassive loss from **Schedule K-1**	**(i)** Section 179 expense deduction from **Form 4562**	**(j)** Nonpassive income from **Schedule K-1**
A					
B					
C					
D					
29a Totals					
b Totals					

30	Add columns (g) and (j) of line 29a	**30**	
31	Add columns (f), (h), and (i) of line 29b	**31**	( )
32	**Total partnership and S corporation income or (loss).** Combine lines 30 and 31. Enter the result here and include in the total on line 41 below	**32**	

| **Part III** | **Income or Loss From Estates and Trusts** |

33

	(a) Name	**(b)** Employer identification number
A		
B		

	Passive Income and Loss		Nonpassive Income and Loss	
	(c) Passive deduction or loss allowed (attach **Form 8582** if required)	**(d)** Passive income from **Schedule K-1**	**(e)** Deduction or loss from **Schedule K-1**	**(f)** Other income from **Schedule K-1**
A				
B				
34a Totals				
b Totals				

35	Add columns (d) and (f) of line 34a	**35**	
36	Add columns (c) and (e) of line 34b	**36**	( )
37	**Total estate and trust income or (loss).** Combine lines 35 and 36. Enter the result here and include in the total on line 41 below	**37**	

| **Part IV** | **Income or Loss From Real Estate Mortgage Investment Conduits (REMICs)—Residual Holder** |

38

	(a) Name	**(b)** Employer identification number	**(c)** Excess inclusion from **Schedules Q,** line 2c (see instructions)	**(d)** Taxable income (net loss) from **Schedules Q,** line 1b	**(e)** Income from **Schedules Q,** line 3b

39	Combine columns (d) and (e) only. Enter the result here and include in the total on line 41 below	**39**	

| **Part V** | **Summary** |

40	Net farm rental income or (loss) from **Form 4835.** Also, complete line 42 below	**40**	
41	**Total income or (loss).** Combine lines 26, 32, 37, 39, and 40. Enter the result here and on Form 1040, line 17, or Form 1040NR, line 18 ▶	**41**	
42	**Reconciliation of farming and fishing income.** Enter your **gross** farming and fishing income reported on Form 4835, line 7; Schedule K-1 (Form 1065), box 14, code B; Schedule K-1 (Form 1120S), box 17, code V; and Schedule K-1 (Form 1041), box 14, code F (see instructions) . .	**42**	
43	**Reconciliation for real estate professionals.** If you were a real estate professional (see instructions), enter the net income or (loss) you reported anywhere on Form 1040 or Form 1040NR from all rental real estate activities in which you materially participated under the passive activity loss rules . .	**43**	

Schedule E (Form 1040) 2016

SCHEDULE F
(Form 1040)

Department of the Treasury
Internal Revenue Service (99)

Profit or Loss From Farming

▶ Attach to Form 1040, Form 1040NR, Form 1041, Form 1065, or Form 1065-B.
▶ Information about Schedule F and its separate instructions is at *www.irs.gov/schedulef.*

OMB No. 1545-0074

20**16**

Attachment
Sequence No. **14**

Name of proprietor

Social security number (SSN)

A Principal crop or activity	B Enter code from Part IV ▶	C Accounting method: ☐ Cash ☐ Accrual	D Employer ID number (EIN), (see instr)

E Did you "materially participate" in the operation of this business during 2016? If "No," see instructions for limit on passive losses ☐ Yes ☐ No

F Did you make any payments in 2016 that would require you to file Form(s) 1099 (see instructions)? . . . . ☐ Yes ☐ No

G If "Yes," did you or will you file required Forms 1099? . . . . ☐ Yes ☐ No

Part I   **Farm Income—Cash Method.** Complete Parts I and II (Accrual method. Complete Parts II and III, and Part I, line 9.)

1a	Sales of livestock and other resale items (see instructions)	**1a**		
b	Cost or other basis of livestock or other items reported on line 1a . . .	**1b**		
c	Subtract line 1b from line 1a		**1c**	
2	Sales of livestock, produce, grains, and other products you raised		**2**	
3a	Cooperative distributions (Form(s) 1099-PATR) . **3a**	**3b** Taxable amount	**3b**	
4a	Agricultural program payments (see instructions) . **4a**	**4b** Taxable amount	**4b**	
5a	Commodity Credit Corporation (CCC) loans reported under election		**5a**	
b	CCC loans forfeited **5b**	**5c** Taxable amount	**5c**	
6	Crop insurance proceeds and federal crop disaster payments (see instructions)			
a	Amount received in 2016 . . . . . . **6a**	**6b** Taxable amount	**6b**	
c	If election to defer to 2017 is attached, check here ▶ ☐	**6d** Amount deferred from 2015	**6d**	
7	Custom hire (machine work) income		**7**	
8	Other income, including federal and state gasoline or fuel tax credit or refund (see instructions)		**8**	
9	**Gross income.** Add amounts in the right column (lines 1c, 2, 3b, 4b, 5a, 5c, 6b, 6d, 7, and 8). If you use the accrual method, enter the amount from Part III, line 50 (see instructions) . . . . ▶		**9**	

Part II   **Farm Expenses—Cash and Accrual Method.** Do not include personal or living expenses (see instructions).

10	Car and truck expenses (see instructions). Also attach **Form 4562**	**10**		**23**	Pension and profit-sharing plans	**23**	
11	Chemicals	**11**		**24**	Rent or lease (see instructions):		
12	Conservation expenses (see instructions)	**12**		**a**	Vehicles, machinery, equipment	**24a**	
13	Custom hire (machine work) .	**13**		**b**	Other (land, animals, etc.) . .	**24b**	
14	Depreciation and section 179 expense (see instructions) .	**14**		**25**	Repairs and maintenance . .	**25**	
				26	Seeds and plants	**26**	
15	Employee benefit programs other than on line 23 . . .	**15**		**27**	Storage and warehousing . .	**27**	
16	Feed	**16**		**28**	Supplies	**28**	
17	Fertilizers and lime . . .	**17**		**29**	Taxes	**29**	
18	Freight and trucking . . .	**18**		**30**	Utilities	**30**	
19	Gasoline, fuel, and oil . . .	**19**		**31**	Veterinary, breeding, and medicine	**31**	
20	Insurance (other than health)	**20**		**32**	Other expenses (specify):		
21	Interest:			**a**	_____	**32a**	
a	Mortgage (paid to banks, etc.)	**21a**		**b**	_____	**32b**	
b	Other	**21b**		**c**	_____	**32c**	
22	Labor hired (less employment credits)	**22**		**d**	_____	**32d**	
				e	_____	**32e**	
				f	_____	**32f**	

33	**Total expenses.** Add lines 10 through 32f. If line 32f is negative, see instructions . . . . ▶	**33**	
34	**Net farm profit or (loss).** Subtract line 33 from line 9	**34**	

If a profit, stop here and see instructions for where to report. If a loss, complete lines 35 and 36.

35 Did you receive an applicable subsidy in 2016? (see instructions) . . . . ☐ Yes ☐ No

36 Check the box that describes your investment in this activity and see instructions for where to report your loss.

a ☐ All investment is at risk.   **b** ☐ Some investment is not at risk.

For Paperwork Reduction Act Notice, see the separate instructions.   Cat. No. 11346H   **Schedule F (Form 1040) 2016**

Schedule F (Form 1040) 2016   Page **2**

Part III   Farm Income—Accrual Method   (see instructions).

37	Sales of livestock, produce, grains, and other products (see instructions)		**37**	
38a	Cooperative distributions (Form(s) 1099-PATR) .	**38a**	**38b** Taxable amount	**38b**	
39a	Agricultural program payments	**39a**	**39b** Taxable amount	**39b**	
40	Commodity Credit Corporation (CCC) loans:			
a	CCC loans reported under election			**40a**	
b	CCC loans forfeited	**40b**	**40c** Taxable amount	**40c**	
41	Crop insurance proceeds			**41**	
42	Custom hire (machine work) income			**42**	
43	Other income (see instructions)			**43**	
44	Add amounts in the right column for lines 37 through 43 (lines 37, 38b, 39b, 40a, 40c, 41, 42, and 43) . .			**44**	
45	Inventory of livestock, produce, grains, and other products at beginning of the year. Do not include sales reported on Form 4797	**45**			
46	Cost of livestock, produce, grains, and other products purchased during the year	**46**			
47	Add lines 45 and 46	**47**			
48	Inventory of livestock, produce, grains, and other products at end of year .	**48**			
49	Cost of livestock, produce, grains, and other products sold. Subtract line 48 from line 47*			**49**	
50	**Gross income.** Subtract line 49 from line 44. Enter the result here and on Part I, line 9 . . . . . . ▶			**50**	

*If you use the unit-livestock-price method or the farm-price method of valuing inventory and the amount on line 48 is larger than the amount on line 47, subtract line 47 from line 48. Enter the result on line 49. Add lines 44 and 49. Enter the total on line 50 and on Part I, line 9.

Part IV   Principal Agricultural Activity Codes

⚠ **CAUTION**   *Do not file Schedule F (Form 1040) to report the following.*

• *Income from providing agricultural services such as soil preparation, veterinary, farm labor, horticultural, or management for a fee or on a contract basis. Instead file Schedule C (Form 1040) or Schedule C-EZ (Form 1040).*

• *Income from breeding, raising, or caring for dogs, cats, or other pet animals. Instead file Schedule C (Form 1040) or Schedule C-EZ (Form 1040).*

• *Sales of livestock held for draft, breeding, sport, or dairy purposes. Instead file Form 4797.*

These codes for the Principal Agricultural Activity classify farms by their primary activity to facilitate the administration of the Internal Revenue Code. These six-digit codes are based on the North American Industry Classification System (NAICS).

Select the code that best identifies your primary farming activity and enter the six-digit number on line B.

Crop Production
111100   Oilseed and grain farming
111210   Vegetable and melon farming
111300   Fruit and tree nut farming
111400   Greenhouse, nursery, and floriculture production
111900   Other crop farming

Animal Production
112111   Beef cattle ranching and farming
112112   Cattle feedlots
112120   Dairy cattle and milk production
112210   Hog and pig farming
112300   Poultry and egg production
112400   Sheep and goat farming
112510   Aquaculture
112900   Other animal production

Forestry and Logging
113000   Forestry and logging (including forest nurseries and timber tracts)

Schedule F (Form 1040) 2016

SCHEDULE SE
(Form 1040)

Department of the Treasury
Internal Revenue Service (99)

Self-Employment Tax

▶ Information about Schedule SE and its separate instructions is at *www.irs.gov/schedulese.*
▶ **Attach to Form 1040 or Form 1040NR.**

OMB No. 1545-0074

20**16**

Attachment
Sequence No. **17**

Name of person with **self-employment** income (as shown on Form 1040 or Form 1040NR)

Social security number of person
with **self-employment** income ▶

Before you begin: To determine if you must file Schedule SE, see the instructions.

May I Use Short Schedule SE or Must I Use Long Schedule SE?

Note. Use this flowchart **only if** you must file Schedule SE. If unsure, see *Who Must File Schedule SE* in the instructions.

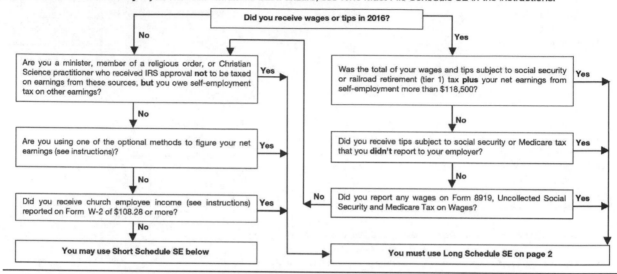

Section A—Short Schedule SE. Caution. Read above to see if you can use Short Schedule SE.

1a	Net farm profit or (loss) from Schedule F, line 34, and farm partnerships, Schedule K-1 (Form 1065), box 14, code A	**1a**	
b	If you received social security retirement or disability benefits, enter the amount of Conservation Reserve Program payments included on Schedule F, line 4b, or listed on Schedule K-1 (Form 1065), box 20, code Z	**1b**	( )
2	Net profit or (loss) from Schedule C, line 31; Schedule C-EZ, line 3; Schedule K-1 (Form 1065), box 14, code A (other than farming); and Schedule K-1 (Form 1065-B), box 9, code J1. Ministers and members of religious orders, see instructions for types of income to report on this line. See instructions for other income to report	**2**	
3	Combine lines 1a, 1b, and 2	**3**	
4	Multiply line 3 by 92.35% (0.9235). If less than $400, you don't owe self-employment tax; **don't** file this schedule unless you have an amount on line 1b. . . . . ▶	**4**	
	Note. If line 4 is less than $400 due to Conservation Reserve Program payments on line 1b, see instructions.		
5	**Self-employment tax.** If the amount on line 4 is:		
	• $118,500 or less, multiply line 4 by 15.3% (0.153). Enter the result here and on **Form 1040, line 57,** or **Form 1040NR, line 55**		
	• More than $118,500, multiply line 4 by 2.9% (0.029). Then, add $14,694 to the result. Enter the total here and on **Form 1040, line 57,** or **Form 1040NR, line 55**	**5**	
6	**Deduction for one-half of self-employment tax.** Multiply line 5 by 50% (0.50). Enter the result here and on **Form 1040, line 27,** or **Form 1040NR, line 27**	**6**	

For Paperwork Reduction Act Notice, see your tax return instructions.   Cat. No. 11358Z   **Schedule SE (Form 1040) 2016**

Schedule SE (Form 1040) 2016   Attachment Sequence No. **17**   Page **2**

Name of person with **self-employment** income (as shown on Form 1040 or Form 1040NR)	Social security number of person with **self-employment** income ▶

Section B—Long Schedule SE

Part I Self-Employment Tax

Note. If your only income subject to self-employment tax is **church employee income,** see instructions. Also see instructions for the definition of church employee income.

A If you are a minister, member of a religious order, or Christian Science practitioner **and** you filed Form 4361, but you had $400 or more of **other** net earnings from self-employment, check here and continue with Part I . . . . ▶ ☐

1a Net farm profit or (loss) from Schedule F, line 34, and farm partnerships, Schedule K-1 (Form 1065), box 14, code A. **Note.** Skip lines 1a and 1b if you use the farm optional method (see instructions) | **1a** |

b If you received social security retirement or disability benefits, enter the amount of Conservation Reserve Program payments included on Schedule F, line 4b, or listed on Schedule K-1 (Form 1065), box 20, code Z | **1b** | (|) |

2 Net profit or (loss) from Schedule C, line 31; Schedule C-EZ, line 3; Schedule K-1 (Form 1065), box 14, code A (other than farming); and Schedule K-1 (Form 1065-B), box 9, code J1. Ministers and members of religious orders, see instructions for types of income to report on this line. See instructions for other income to report. **Note.** Skip this line if you use the nonfarm optional method (see instructions) . . . . | **2** |

3 Combine lines 1a, 1b, and 2 . . . . | **3** |

4a If line 3 is more than zero, multiply line 3 by 92.35% (0.9235). Otherwise, enter amount from line 3 | **4a** |
   Note. If line 4a is less than $400 due to Conservation Reserve Program payments on line 1b, see instructions.

b If you elect one or both of the optional methods, enter the total of lines 15 and 17 here . . | **4b** |

c Combine lines 4a and 4b. If less than $400, **stop;** you do not owe self-employment tax. **Exception.** If less than $400 and you had **church employee income,** enter -0- and continue ▶ | **4c** |

5a Enter your **church employee income** from Form W-2. See instructions for definition of church employee income . . . | **5a** |

b Multiply line 5a by 92.35% (0.9235). If less than $100, enter -0- . . . . | **5b** |

6 Add lines 4c and 5b . . . . | **6** |

7 Maximum amount of combined wages and self-employment earnings subject to social security tax or the 6.2% portion of the 7.65% railroad retirement (tier 1) tax for 2016 . . . . . . | **7** | 118,500 | 00 |

8a Total social security wages and tips (total of boxes 3 and 7 on Form(s) W-2) and railroad retirement (tier 1) compensation. If $118,500 or more, skip lines 8b through 10, and go to line 11 | **8a** |

b Unreported tips subject to social security tax (from Form 4137, line 10) | **8b** |

c Wages subject to social security tax (from Form 8919, line 10) | **8c** |

d Add lines 8a, 8b, and 8c . . . . | **8d** |

9 Subtract line 8d from line 7. If zero or less, enter -0- here and on line 10 and go to line 11 . ▶ | **9** |

10 Multiply the **smaller** of line 6 or line 9 by 12.4% (0.124) . . . . | **10** |

11 Multiply line 6 by 2.9% (0.029) . . . . | **11** |

12 **Self-employment tax.** Add lines 10 and 11. Enter here and on **Form 1040, line 57,** or **Form 1040NR, line 55** | **12** |

13 **Deduction for one-half of self-employment tax.**
   Multiply line 12 by 50% (0.50). Enter the result here and on
   Form 1040, line 27, or **Form 1040NR, line 27** . . . . . . | **13** |

Part II Optional Methods To Figure Net Earnings (see instructions)

Farm Optional Method. You may use this method **only** if (a) your gross farm income[1] was not more than $7,560, **or** (b) your net farm profits[2] were less than $5,457.

14 Maximum income for optional methods . . . . | **14** | 5,040 | 00 |

15 Enter the **smaller** of: two-thirds (²/₃) of gross farm income[1] (not less than zero) **or** $5,040. Also include this amount on line 4b above . . . . | **15** |

Nonfarm Optional Method. You may use this method **only** if (a) your net nonfarm profits[3] were less than $5,457 and also less than 72.189% of your gross nonfarm income,[4] **and** (b) you had net earnings from self-employment of at least $400 in 2 of the prior 3 years. **Caution.** You may use this method no more than five times.

16 Subtract line 15 from line 14 . . . . | **16** |

17 Enter the **smaller** of: two-thirds (²/₃) of gross nonfarm income[4] (not less than zero) **or** the amount on line 16. Also include this amount on line 4b above . . . . | **17** |

[1] From Sch. F, line 9, and Sch. K-1 (Form 1065), box 14, code B.
[2] From Sch. F, line 34, and Sch. K-1 (Form 1065), box 14, code A—minus the amount you would have entered on line 1b had you not used the optional method.
[3] From Sch. C, line 31; Sch. C-EZ, line 3; Sch. K-1 (Form 1065), box 14, code A; and Sch. K-1 (Form 1065-B), box 9, code J1.
[4] From Sch. C, line 7; Sch. C-EZ, line 1; Sch. K-1 (Form 1065), box 14, code C; and Sch. K-1 (Form 1065-B), box 9, code J2.

Schedule SE (Form 1040) 2016

CLASS QUESTIONS

Work through the below Class Questions while following along with the respective lectures. Once this is complete, you can begin independently practicing what you've learned by quizzing yourself on this course section in your Interactive Practice Questions (IPQ), which can be found in your online Student Dashboard. Your IPQ simulates the computer-based testing experience, and will also help you understand how concepts are applied to the exam. Each question includes answer explanations from expert CPAs that will help you determine why you answered a question correctly or incorrectly. This is key to your success on the CPA Exam.

Lecture 1.03

1. Perle, a dentist, billed Wood $600 for dental services. Wood paid Perle $200 cash and built a bookcase for Perle's office in full settlement of the bill. Wood sells comparable bookcases for $350. What amount should Perle include in taxable income as a result of this transaction?

   a. $0
   b. $200
   c. $550
   d. $600

2. A cash-basis taxpayer should report gross income

   a. Only for the year in which income is actually received in cash.
   b. Only for the year in which income is actually received whether in cash or in property.
   c. For the year in which income is either actually or constructively received in cash only.
   d. For the year in which income is either actually or constructively received, whether in cash or in property.

3. Nan, a cash basis taxpayer, borrowed money from a bank and signed a 10-year interest-bearing note on business property on January 1 of the current year. The cash flow from Nan's business enabled Nan to prepay the first three years of interest attributable to the note on December 31 of the current year. How should Nan treat the prepayment of interest for tax purposes?

   a. Deduct the entire amount as a current expense.
   b. Deduct the current year's interest and amortize the balance over the next two years.
   c. Capitalize the interest and amortize the balance over the 10-year loan period.
   d. Capitalize the interest as part of the basis of the business property.

Lecture 1.09

4. Which of the following conditions must be present in a divorce agreement for a payment to qualify as deductible alimony?

   I.   Payments must be in cash.
   II. The payment must end at the recipient's death.

   a. I only.
   b. II only.
   c. Both I and II.
   d. Neither I nor II.

5. Bill and Hillary were divorced in year 1. The divorce decree provides that Hillary pay alimony of $10,000 per year, to be reduced by 20% on their child's 18th birthday. During year 5, Hillary paid $7,000 directly to Bill and $3,000 to UCLA for Bill's tuition. What amount of these payments should be reported as income in Bill's year 5 income tax return?

   a. $ 5,600
   b. $ 8,000
   c. $ 8,600
   d. $ 10,000

6. Which allowable deduction can be claimed in arriving at the individual's adjusted gross income?

   a. Alimony payment
   b. Charitable contribution
   c. Personal casualty loss
   d. Unreimbursed business expense of an outside salesperson

7. With regard to the inclusion of social security benefits in gross income for the 20X3 tax year, which of the following statements is correct?

   a. The social security benefits in excess of modified adjusted gross income are included in gross income.
   b. The social security benefits in excess of one half the modified adjusted gross income are included in gross income.
   c. Eighty-five percent of the social security benefits is the maximum amount of benefits to be included in gross income.
   d. The social security benefits in excess of the modified adjusted gross income over $32,000 are included in gross income.

Lecture 1.11

8. Clark filed Form 1040EZ for the 20X2 taxable year. In July 20X3, Clark received a state income tax refund of $900, plus interest of $10, for overpayment of 20X2 state income tax. What amount of the state tax refund and interest is taxable in Clark's 20X3 federal income tax return?

    a. $0
    b. $10
    c. $900
    d. $910

9. During 20X3, Scott charged $4,000 on his credit card for his dependent son's medical expenses. Payment to the credit card company had not been made by the time Scott filed his income tax return in 20X4. However, in 20X3, Scott paid a physician $2,800 for the medical expenses of his wife, who died in 20X2. Disregarding the adjusted gross income percentage threshold, what amount could Scott claim in his 20X3 income tax return for medical expenses?

    a. $0
    b. $2,800
    c. $4,000
    d. $6,800

10. Which of the following is a miscellaneous itemized deduction subject to the 2% of adjusted gross income floor?

    a. Gambling losses up to the amount of gambling winnings
    b. Medical expenses
    c. Real estate tax
    d. Employee business expense

11. The Browns borrowed $20,000, secured by their home, to purchase a new automobile. At the time of the loan, the fair market value of their home was $400,000, and it was unencumbered by other debt. The interest on the loan qualifies as

    a. Deductible personal interest.
    b. Deductible qualified residence interest.
    c. Nondeductible interest.
    d. Investment interest expense.

Lecture 1.14

12. Which of the following tax credits can result in a refund even if the individual had no income tax liability?

    a. Credit for prior year alternative minimum tax
    b. Elderly and permanently and totally disabled credit
    c. Earned income credit
    d. Child and dependent care credit

13. An accuracy-related penalty applies to the portion of tax underpayment attributable to

    I.   Negligence or a disregard of the tax rules or regulations
    II.   Any substantial understatement of income tax

      a.   I only.
      b.   II only.
      c.   Both I and II.
      d.   Neither I nor II.

Lecture 1.16

14. In 20X3, Don Mills, a single taxpayer, had $70,000 in taxable income before personal exemptions. Mills had no tax preferences. His itemized deductions were as follows:

State and local income taxes	$ 5,000
Home mortgage interest on loan to acquire residence	6,000
Miscellaneous deductions that exceed 2% of adjusted gross income	2,000

What amount did Mills report as alternative minimum taxable income before the AMT exemption?

      a. $72,000
      b. $75,000
      c. $77,000
      d. $83,000

15. Alternative minimum tax preferences include:

	Tax exempt interest from private activity bonds issued during the year	Charitable contributions of appreciated capital gain property
a.	Yes	Yes
b.	Yes	No
c.	No	Yes
d.	No	No

CLASS SOLUTIONS

1. (c) When services are exchanged for cash and property, income will be measured at the amount of cash plus the fair value of property received. Perle received cash of $200 and a bookcase with a fair value of $350, for a total taxable amount of $550.

2. (d) The requirement is to determine the correct statement regarding the reporting of income by a cash-basis taxpayer. A cash-basis taxpayer should report gross income for the year in which income is either actually or constructively received, whether in cash or in property. Constructive receipt means that an item of income is unqualifiedly available to the taxpayer without restriction (e.g., interest on bank deposit is income when credited to account).

3. (b) In general, under the cash basis of accounting, individuals are allowed to deduct expenses in the year they are paid. However, interest on a loan that has been prepaid for a time beyond the end of the current taxable year cannot be deducted in the year the prepayment is made. In this case, Nan paid the current year interest and prepaid years 2 and 3. Nan is allowed to deduct only the interest attributable to the current year on her current year tax return and will be entitled to a tax deduction on her years 2 and 3 tax returns for the prepaid interest for years 2 and 3, respectively, that Nan paid in the current tax year.

4. (c) In order for alimony to be deductible, we remember the mnemonic CANNOT (i.e., Cash only, Apart, Not child support, Not a property settlement, Own returns, Terminates on death). Payments must be in cash or their equivalent (cash paid as tuition would count). The payments must end at the recipient's death.

5. (b) The fact that the payment is reduced by 20% when the child reaches 18 indicates that 20% of the payments is for child support and 80%, or $8,000, is for alimony. Although it is normally required to be paid in cash to be deductible by the payer and taxable to the payee, payment of tuition on behalf of the recipient is deductible and taxable as alimony if the other conditions are met.

6. (a) Alimony is taxable and included in the AGI of the recipient; it is an adjustment for AGI and, thus, is deducted in the calculation of the AGI of the payer. Answer (b) is incorrect because charitable contributions are allowed as itemized deductions and are deductible from AGI. Answer (c) is incorrect because personal casualty losses, in excess of certain thresholds, are allowed as itemized deductions and are deductible from AGI. Answer (d) is incorrect because the unreimbursed business expenses of an outside salesperson in excess of a certain amount are allowed as itemized deductions and are deductible from AGI.

7. (c) Social security benefits become partially taxable to a recipient with adjusted income in excess of a certain amount. The higher the recipient's income, above that amount, the greater the portion of social security benefits that will be taxable, up to a maximum of 85%. Answer (a) is incorrect because the taxable amount is based on a percentage, not the total of benefits in excess of an amount such as modified AGI. Answer (b) is incorrect because the taxable amount is based on a percentage, not the total of benefits in excess of an amount such as one-half of modified AGI. Answer (d) is incorrect because the taxable amount is based on a percentage, not the total of benefits in excess of an amount, such as the excess of modified AGI that is in excess of $32,000.

8. (b) Since Clark filed a Form 1040EZ for 20X2, Clark could not have itemized deductions for that year, which is not allowed on a 1040EZ. A refund of state income taxes is only taxable in the year received if the recipient had itemized deductions in the year to which the refund applied. As a result, Clark would not be taxed on the state income tax refund. The interest received is not tax exempt and would be taxable, regardless of whether or not Clark itemized deductions.

9. (d) A taxpayer may deduct as medical expenses, subject to limitations, expenses paid on behalf of a dependent or spouse, including one that is deceased, as long as the individual qualified as a dependent or spouse either at the time the services were provided or at the time the payment was made. Payment of medical expenses by credit card are considered to be paid by the taxpayer in the period in which they are charged to the credit card, not the period in which the credit card balance is paid.

10. (d) An employee's unreimbursed business expenses are deductible as miscellaneous itemized deductions, which are combined and reduced by 2% of AGI. Answer (a) is incorrect because gambling losses, to the extent of winnings, are deductible as a miscellaneous itemized deduction that is not subject to the 2% reduction. Answer (b) is incorrect because medical expenses are deductible after reducing them by 10%, not 2%, of AGI. Answer (c) is incorrect because real estate taxes are deductible in their entirety and are not reduced by 2% of AGI.

11. (b) Interest on qualified residence indebtedness is fully deductible. The amount deductible is 100% of the interest on debt incurred to acquire the home plus interest on an amount up to the 1st $100,000 of equity indebtedness, regardless of what the proceeds are used for. Interest on equity indebtedness is deductible, however, only to the extent that total debt does not exceed the fair value of the residence. With a market value of $400,000 and total residential indebtedness of $20,000, Brown would be able to deduct all of the interest paid on the $20,000 debt.

12. (c) The Earned Income Credit (EIC) is referred to as a refundable tax credit. When the amount of a refundable credit exceeds a taxpayer's tax liability, the excess is refunded to the taxpayer, similarly to an overpayment of taxes through estimated payments or withholding. Answer (a) is incorrect because a credit for a prior period's alternative minimum tax is not a refundable credit. Answer (b) is incorrect because the credit for the elderly and disabled is not a refundable credit. Answer (d) is incorrect because the child and dependent care credit is not a refundable credit.

13. (c) A 20% accuracy-related penalty for underpayment of tax will apply for underpayment of tax due to negligence or disregard of rules and regulations as well as for any substantial underpayment of income tax.

14. (c) Alternative minimum taxable income (AMTI) is calculated by adjusting taxable income for certain tax preferences and by adding back the personal exemption and certain deductions. These include interest on home equity loans, local and state income taxes, property taxes, and sales taxes, and the miscellaneous itemized deductions that are subject to the 2% of AGI reduction. As a result, Mills would not be required to add back interest on the residential acquisition indebtedness, and Mills' AMTI would be $70,000 + $5,000 + $2,000, or $77,000.

15. (b) Interest on specified private activity bonds issued after 1986 is considered a tax preference for AMT purposes. Charitable contributions are not included in the list of tax preferences. Alternative minimum taxable income (AMTI) is calculated by adjusting taxable income for certain tax preferences and adding back the personal exemption and certain deductions. Tax-exempt interest on private activity bonds is considered a tax preference and would be added to taxable income to determine AMTI. There is no tax preference for charitable contributions, nor is it an itemized deduction that is required to be added back, regardless of whether the contribution is made in cash or property.

TASK-BASED SIMULATIONS

Task-Based Simulation 1

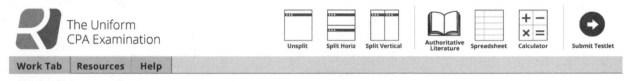

Work Tab | **Resources** | **Help**

Note: Situation applies to TBS 1 and 2.

Required:

Situation

Mrs. Vick, a forty-year-old cash-basis taxpayer, earned $45,000 as a teacher and $5,000 as a part-time real estate agent in 20X1. Mr. Vick, who died on July 1, 20X1, had been permanently disabled on his job and collected state disability benefits until his death. For all of 20X1 and 20X2, the Vicks' residence was the principal home of both their eleven-year-old daughter, Joan, and Mrs. Vick's unmarried cousin, Fran Phillips, who had no income in either year. During 20X1, Joan received $200 a month in survivor social security benefits that began on August 1, 20X1, and will continue at least until her eighteenth birthday. In 20X1 and 20X2, Mrs. Vick provided over one-half the support for Joan and Fran, both of whom were U.S. citizens. Mrs. Vick did not remarry. Mr. and Mrs. Vick received the following in 20X1:

Earned income	$50,000
State disability benefits	1,500
Interest on:	
Refund from amended tax return	50
Savings account and certificates of deposit	350
Municipal bonds	100
Gift	3,000
Pension benefits	900
Jury duty pay	200
Gambling winnings	450
Life insurance proceeds	5,000

Additional information:

- Mrs. Vick received the $3,000 cash gift from her uncle.
- Mrs. Vick received the pension distributions from a qualified pension plan, paid for exclusively by her husband's employer.
- Mrs. Vick had $100 in gambling losses in 20X1.
- Mrs. Vick was the beneficiary of the life insurance policy on her husband's life. She received a lump-sum distribution. The Vicks had paid $500 in premiums.
- Mrs. Vick received Mr. Vick's accrued vacation pay of $500 in 20X2.

Items to be answered:

For **items 1 and 2,** determine and select from the choices below, **BOTH** the filing status and the number of exemptions for each item.

	Filing Status	**Exemptions**
S.	Single	1
M.	Married filing joint	2
H.	Head of household	3
Q.	Qualifying widow with dependent child	4

	Filing Status	**Exemptions**
	(S) (M) (H) (Q)	(1) (2) (3) (4)
1. Determine the filing status and the number of exemptions that Mrs. Vick can claim on the 20X1 federal income tax return, to get the most favorable tax results.	○ ○ ○ ○	○ ○ ○ ○
2. Determine the filing status and the number of exemptions that Mrs. Vick can claim on the 20X2 federal income tax return to get the most favorable tax results, if she solely maintains the costs of her home.	○ ○ ○ ○	○ ○ ○ ○

For **items 3 through 9,** determine the amount, if any, that is taxable and should be included in Adjusted Gross Income (AGI) on the 20X1 federal income tax return filed by Mrs. Vick.

3. State disability benefits

4. Interest income

5. Pension benefits

6. Gift

7. Life insurance proceeds

8. Jury duty pay

9. Gambling winnings

Task-Based Simulation 2

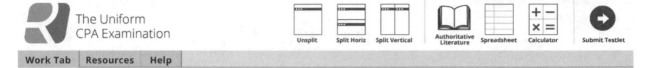

| Work Tab | Resources | Help |

Items to be answered:

During 20X1 the following payments were made or losses were incurred. For **items 1 through 14,** select the appropriate tax treatment. A tax treatment may be selected once, more than once, or not at all.

Tax treatment

A. Not deductible.

B. Deductible in Schedule A—Itemized Deductions, subject to threshold of 10% of adjusted gross income.

C. Deductible in Schedule A—Itemized Deductions, subject to threshold of 2% of adjusted gross income.

D. Deductible on page 1 of Form 1040 to arrive at adjusted gross income.

E. Deductible in full in Schedule A— Itemized Deductions.

F. Deductible in Schedule A—Itemized Deductions, subject to maximum of 50% of adjusted gross income.

	(A)	(B)	(C)	(D)	(E)	(F)
1. Premiums on Mr. Vick's personal life insurance policy.	○	○	○	○	○	○
2. Penalty on Mrs. Vick's early withdrawal of funds from a certificate of deposit.	○	○	○	○	○	○
3. Mrs. Vick's substantiated cash donation to the American Red Cross.	○	○	○	○	○	○
4. Payment of estimated state income taxes.	○	○	○	○	○	○
5. Payment of real estate taxes on the Vick home.	○	○	○	○	○	○
6. Loss on the sale of the family car.	○	○	○	○	○	○
7. Cost in excess of the increase in value of residence, for the installation of a stairlift in January 20X2, related directly to the medical care of Mr. Vick.	○	○	○	○	○	○
8. The Vicks' health insurance premiums for hospitalization coverage.	○	○	○	○	○	○
9. CPA fees to prepare the 20X1 tax return.	○	○	○	○	○	○
10. Amortization over the life of the loan of points paid to refinance the mortgage at a lower rate on the Vick home.	○	○	○	○	○	○
11. One-half the self-employment tax paid by Mrs. Vick.	○	○	○	○	○	○
12. Mrs. Vick's $100 in gambling losses.	○	○	○	○	○	○
13. Mrs. Vick's union dues.	○	○	○	○	○	○
14. 20X1 federal income tax paid with the Vicks' tax return on April 15, 20X2.	○	○	○	○	○	○

Lecture 1.18

Task-Based Simulation 3

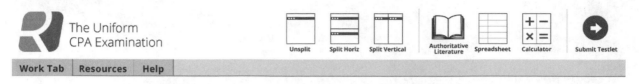

The Uniform CPA Examination

| Unsplit | Split Horiz | Split Vertical | Authoritative Literature | Spreadsheet | Calculator | Submit Testlet |

Work Tab   Resources   Help

Alima Xanders has provided you with several documents to be used in determining her deductions. In addition, she prepared the following note attached to her documents.

A Note from Alima

In addition to the documents enclosed, here is a list of other items that you may need for my tax return.

I started a new job in January at North Cityview Hospital. It is an administrative position, similar to my old position but with more responsibilities. I moved in February to be closer to work and bought a house. The costs are listed below.

Let me know if you need anything else.

Thanks!

Alimony paid to Jim Johnson	$26,000	SSN# 123-XX-XXXX
Safe deposit box fee	100	
Union dues	600	
Bank charges (for checking account)	125	
Nursing Journal subscriptions	165	
Cityview Daily Press (local newspaper)	105	
Work Clothes	525	Required to wear a jacket and nice slacks.
Job hunting for current position	1,350	
Moving costs	965	Cross-town move (30 miles).

Charity gifts:

Local Church cash donations	200	
Nairobi National Museum	500	See gift letter.
Humane Society	75	
Independent Political Party	150	

Interest & Taxes are reported on forms:
- Commerce Mortgage is my home mortgage.
- GMC Mortgage is for a loan on a vacant lot I own for recreational purposes.
- State Mortgage is on a vacation home I have in Colorado.

Review the documents Alima has provided. Complete the Adjusted Gross Income section, Lines 23 through 37, on Form 1040 and Schedule A for Alima Xanders. Round to the nearest dollar.
Note: Line 38 of Form 1040 (not shown) is AGI, which is carried over from Line 37 of Form 1040.

Resources

22222	a Employee's social security number XXX-XX-3698	OMB No. 1545-0008		
b Employer identification number (EIN) 91-XXXXXX			1 Wages, tips, other compensation 105,000	2 Federal income tax withheld 15,750
c Employer's name, address, and ZIP code NORTH CITIVIEW HOSPITAL			3 Social security wages 105,000	4 Social security tax withheld 6,510
			5 Medicare wages and tips 105,000	6 Medicare tax withheld 1,522.50
			7 Social security tips	8 Allocated tips
d Control number			9	10 Dependent care benefits
e Employee's first name and initial Last name Suff. ALIMA XANDERS 8899 VISTA LANE CITYVIEW, VA			11 Nonqualified plans	12a
			13 Statutory employee Retirement plan Third-party sick pay	12b
			14 Other	12c
				12d
f Employee's address and ZIP code				

15 State VA	Employer's state ID number 64-XXXXXX	16 State wages, tips, etc. 105,000	17 State income tax 5,985	18 Local wages, tips, etc.	19 Local income tax	20 Locality name

Form **W-2** Wage and Tax Statement   20XX   Department of the Treasury—Internal Revenue Service

Copy 1—For State, City, or Local Tax Department

☐ CORRECTED (if checked)

TRUSTEE'S or ISSUER'S name, street address, city or town, state or province, country, and ZIP or foreign postal code		1 IRA contributions (other than amounts in boxes 2–4, 8–10, 13a, and 14a) $ 5,000	OMB No. 1545-0747 20XX Form 5498	IRA Contribution Information
SAFEGUARD INVESTMENTS		2 Rollover contributions $		
		3 Roth IRA conversion amount $	4 Recharacterized contributions $	Copy B
TRUSTEE'S or ISSUER'S federal identification no.	PARTICIPANT'S social security number XXX-XX-3698	5 Fair market value of account $	6 Life insurance cost included in box 1 $	For Participant
PARTICIPANT'S name ALIMA XANDERS		7 IRA ☑ SEP ☐	SIMPLE ☐ Roth IRA ☐	This information is being furnished to the Internal Revenue Service.
		8 SEP contributions $	9 SIMPLE contributions $	
Street address (including apt. no.) 8899 VISTA LANE		10 Roth IRA contributions $	11 If checked, required minimum distribution for 2018 ☐	
		12a RMD date	12b RMD amount $	
City or town, state or province, country, and ZIP or foreign postal code CITYVIEW, VA		13a Postponed contribution $	13b Year 13c Code	
		14a Repayments $	14b Code	
Account number (see instructions)		15a FMV of certain specified assets $	15b Code(s)	

Form **5498**   (keep for your records)   www.irs.gov/form5498   Department of the Treasury - Internal Revenue Service

INVOICE

ACE CPAS, LLP
123 4ᵀᴴ STREET
CITYVIEW, VA

CLIENT: .
Alima Xanders
8899 Vista Lane
Cityview, VA

TAX RETURN PREPARATION	1040	$365

Nairobi National Museum
PO Box 40658
723 Museum Hill
Nairobi, City, Kenya

July 2, 20XX

Alima Xanders
8899 Vista Lane
Cityview, VA

Dear Alima Xanders:

Thank you for your generous gift of $500 to the Nairobi National Museum. Generous support from people like you make it possible for us to collect and preserve Kenya's past and present. If you should be in Kenya and want to visit the museum, a free pass will be made available for you.

Sincerely,

Betty Karanja,
Chair, Patrons Association
Nairobi National Museum

☐ CORRECTED (if checked)

RECIPIENT'S/LENDER'S name, street address, city or town, state or province, country, ZIP or foreign postal code, and telephone number	* **Caution:** *The amount shown may not be fully deductible by you. Limits based on the loan amount and the cost and value of the secured property may apply. Also, you may only deduct interest to the extent it was incurred by you, actually paid by you, and not reimbursed by another person.*	OMB No. 1545-0901 20XX Form **1098**	**Mortgage Interest Statement**
COMMERCE MORTGAGE CO			

RECIPIENT'S federal identification no.	PAYER'S social security number **XXX-XX-3698**	1 Mortgage interest received from payer(s)/borrower(s)* $ **11,634**	**Copy B** **For Payer/Borrower**
PAYER'S/BORROWER'S name **ALIMA XANDERS**		2 Points paid on purchase of principal residence $	The information in boxes 1, 2, and 3 is important tax information and is being furnished to the Internal Revenue Service. If you are required to file a return, a negligence penalty or other sanction may be imposed on you if the IRS determines that an underpayment of tax results because you overstated a deduction for this mortgage interest or for these points or because you did not report this refund of interest on your return.
Street address (including apt. no.) **8899 VISTA LANE**		3 Refund of overpaid interest $	
City or town, state or province, country, and ZIP or foreign postal code **CITYVIEW, VA**		4 LAND PROPERTY TAX: $2,852.48	
Account number (see instructions)		5 LOAN BALANCE: $258,533	

Form **1098**   (keep for your records)   www.irs.gov/form1098   Department of the Treasury - Internal Revenue Service

☐ CORRECTED (if checked)

RECIPIENT'S/LENDER'S name, street address, city or town, state or province, country, ZIP or foreign postal code, and telephone number	* Caution: The amount shown may not be fully deductible by you. Limits based on the loan amount and the cost and value of the secured property may apply. Also, you may only deduct interest to the extent it was incurred by you, actually paid by you, and not reimbursed by another person.	OMB No. 1545-0901 20XX Form 1098	Mortgage Interest Statement
GMC MORTGAGE CO			

RECIPIENT'S federal identification no.	PAYER'S social security number XXX-XX-3698	1 Mortgage interest received from payer(s)/borrower(s)* $ 3,850	**Copy B** For Payer/Borrower
PAYER'S/BORROWER'S name ALIMA XANDERS		2 Points paid on purchase of principal residence $	The information in boxes 1, 2, and 3 is important tax information and is being furnished to the Internal Revenue Service. If you are required to file a return, a negligence penalty or other sanction may be imposed on you if the IRS determines that an underpayment of tax results because you overstated a deduction for this mortgage interest or for these points or because you did not report this refund of interest on your return.
Street address (including apt. no.) 8899 VISTA LANE		3 Refund of overpaid interest $	
City or town, state or province, country, and ZIP or foreign postal code CITYVIEW, VA		4 LAND PROPERTY TAX: $569.04	
Account number (see instructions)		5 LOAN BALANCE: $75,691	

Form **1098**   (keep for your records)   www.irs.gov/form1098   Department of the Treasury - Internal Revenue Service

☐ CORRECTED (if checked)

RECIPIENT'S/LENDER'S name, street address, city or town, state or province, country, ZIP or foreign postal code, and telephone number	* Caution: The amount shown may not be fully deductible by you. Limits based on the loan amount and the cost and value of the secured property may apply. Also, you may only deduct interest to the extent it was incurred by you, actually paid by you, and not reimbursed by another person.	OMB No. 1545-0901 20XX Form 1098	Mortgage Interest Statement
STATE MORTGAGE CO			

RECIPIENT'S federal Identification no.	PAYER'S social security number XXX-XX-3698	1 Mortgage interest received from payer(s)/borrower(s)* $ 6,850	**Copy B** For Payer/Borrower
PAYER'S/BORROWER'S name ALIMA XANDERS		2 Points paid on purchase of principal residence $	The information in boxes 1, 2, and 3 is important tax information and is being furnished to the Internal Revenue Service. If you are required to file a return, a negligence penalty or other sanction may be imposed on you if the IRS determines that an underpayment of tax results because you overstated a deduction for this mortgage interest or for these points or because you did not report this refund of interest on your return.
Street address (including apt. no.) 8899 VISTA LANE		3 Refund of overpaid interest $	
City or town, state or province, country, and ZIP or foreign postal code CITYVIEW, VA		4 LAND PROPERTY TAX: $1,153	
Account number (see instructions)		5 LOAN BALANCE: $135,874	

Form **1098**   (keep for your records)   www.irs.gov/form1098   Department of the Treasury - Internal Revenue Service

Excerpt from Page 1 of Form 1040

Income	7	Wages, salaries, tips, etc. Attach Form(s) W-2	7	105,000
	8a	Taxable interest. Attach Schedule B if required	8a	
Attach Form(s) W-2 here. Also attach Forms W-2G and 1099-R if tax was withheld.	b	Tax-exempt interest. **Do not** include on line 8a . . .	8b	90,000		
	9a	Ordinary dividends. Attach Schedule B if required	9a	
	b	Qualified dividends	9b		
	10	Taxable refunds, credits, or offsets of state and local income taxes	10	
	11	Alimony received	11	
If you did not get a W-2, see instructions.	12	Business income or (loss). Attach Schedule C or C-EZ	12	
	13	Capital gain or (loss). Attach Schedule D if required. If not required, check here ▶ ☐	13	
	14	Other gains or (losses). Attach Form 4797	14	
	15a	IRA distributions .	15a		b Taxable amount . . .	15b	
	16a	Pensions and annuities	16a		b Taxable amount . . .	16b	
	17	Rental real estate, royalties, partnerships, S corporations, trusts, etc. Attach Schedule E	17	
	18	Farm income or (loss). Attach Schedule F	18	
	19	Unemployment compensation	19	
	20a	Social security benefits	20a		b Taxable amount . . .	20b	
	21	Other income. List type and amount			21	
	22	Combine the amounts in the far right column for lines 7 through 21. This is your **total income** ▶	22	105,000
Adjusted Gross Income	23	Educator expenses	23		
	24	Certain business expenses of reservists, performing artists, and fee-basis government officials. Attach Form 2106 or 2106-EZ	24		
	25	Health savings account deduction. Attach Form 8889 .	25		
	26	Moving expenses. Attach Form 3903	26		
	27	Deductible part of self-employment tax. Attach Schedule SE .	27		
	28	Self-employed SEP, SIMPLE, and qualified plans . .	28		
	29	Self-employed health insurance deduction	29		
	30	Penalty on early withdrawal of savings	30		
	31a	Alimony paid b Recipient's SSN ▶	31a		
	32	IRA deduction	32		
	33	Student loan interest deduction	33		
	34	Tuition and fees. Attach Form 8917	34		
	35	Domestic production activities deduction. Attach Form 8903	35		
	36	Add lines 23 through 35	36	
	37	Subtract line 36 from line 22. This is your **adjusted gross income** . . . . . ▶	37	

Excerpt from Schedule A

Medical and Dental Expenses

Caution: Do not include expenses reimbursed or paid by others.

1. Medical and dental expenses (see instructions) . . . . . **[1]**
2. Enter amount from Form 1040, line 38 **[2]**
3. Multiply line 2 by 10% (0.10). But if either you or your spouse was born before January 2, 1952, multiply line 2 by 7.5% (0.075) instead **[3]**
4. Subtract line 3 from line 1. If line 3 is more than line 1, enter -0- . . . . **[4]**

Taxes You Paid

5. State and local **(check only one box):**
   a. ☐ Income taxes, **or**
   b. ☐ General sales taxes . . . . **[5]**
6. Real estate taxes (see instructions) . . . . **[6]**
7. Personal property taxes . . . . **[7]**
8. Other taxes. List type and amount ▶ **[8]**
9. Add lines 5 through 8 . . . . **[9]**

Interest You Paid

Note: Your mortgage interest deduction may be limited (see instructions).

10. Home mortgage interest and points reported to you on Form 1098 **[10]**
11. Home mortgage interest not reported to you on Form 1098. If paid to the person from whom you bought the home, see instructions and show that person's name, identifying no., and address ▶ **[11]**
12. Points not reported to you on Form 1098. See instructions for special rules . . . . **[12]**
13. Mortgage insurance premiums (see instructions) . . . . . **[13]**
14. Investment interest. Attach Form 4952 if required. (See instructions.) **[14]**
15. Add lines 10 through 14 . . . . **[15]**

Gifts to Charity

If you made a gift and got a benefit for it, see instructions.

16. Gifts by cash or check. If you made any gift of $250 or more, see instructions . . . . **[16]**
17. Other than by cash or check. If any gift of $250 or more, see instructions. You **must** attach Form 8283 if over $500 . . . **[17]**
18. Carryover from prior year **[18]**
19. Add lines 16 through 18 . . . . **[19]**

Casualty and Theft Losses

20. Casualty or theft loss(es). Attach Form 4684. (See instructions.) . . . . **[20]**

Job Expenses and Certain Miscellaneous Deductions

21. Unreimbursed employee expenses—job travel, union dues, job education, etc. Attach Form 2106 or 2106-EZ if required. (See instructions.) ▶ **[21]**
22. Tax preparation fees . . . . **[22]**
23. Other expenses—investment, safe deposit box, etc. List type and amount ▶ **[23]**
24. Add lines 21 through 23 . . . . **[24]**
25. Enter amount from Form 1040, line 38 **[25]**
26. Multiply line 25 by 2% (0.02) . . . . **[26]**
27. Subtract line 26 from line 24. If line 26 is more than line 24, enter -0- . . . . . **[27]**

Other Miscellaneous Deductions

28. Other—from list in instructions. List type and amount ▶ **[28]**

Total Itemized Deductions

29. Is Form 1040, line 38, over $155,650?

   ☐ **No.** Your deduction is not limited. Add the amounts in the far right column for lines 4 through 28. Also, enter this amount on Form 1040, line 40.

   ☐ **Yes.** Your deduction may be limited. See the Itemized Deductions Worksheet in the instructions to figure the amount to enter. **[29]**

30. If you elect to itemize deductions even though they are less than your standard deduction, check here . . . . ▶ ☐

Task-Based Simulation 4

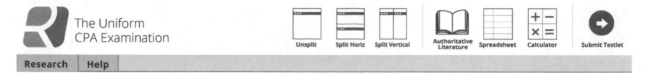

A taxpayer is trying to determine whether or not unemployment compensation received during the year is taxable.

Which code section and subsection indicate whether unemployment compensation is taxable?

Task-Based Simulation 5

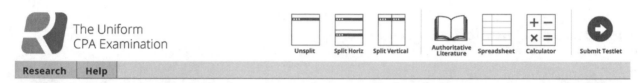

A taxpayer is required under a divorce decree to make certain payments that consist of alimony of $12,000 per year and child support of $15,000. Due to financial difficulties, however, the taxpayer made equal monthly payments totaling $9,000. The taxpayer is trying to determine what portion of the amount paid will be considered child support.

Which code section, subsection, and paragraph indicate if the payments made will be considered child support?

Task-Based Simulation 6

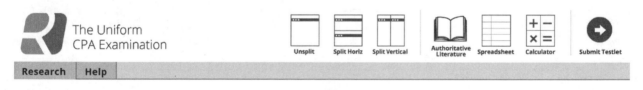

A taxpayer was recently widowed and has a dependent child living in his home. He is trying to determine if he qualifies as a surviving spouse for tax purposes.

Which code section, subsection, and paragraph will provide him with the general definition of a surviving spouse?

Task-Based Simulation 7

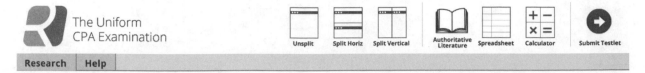

A taxpayer received a scholarship to a university in a state other than her state of residence. In order to qualify for the scholarship, the taxpayer is required to teach basic classes and perform various research projects. She is trying to determine the extent to which, if any, the scholarship will be taxable to her.

Which code section, subsection and paragraph indicate whether or not the scholarship will be taxable to her?

Task-Based Simulation 8

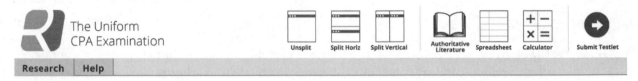

A taxpayer is being relocated by her employer and has incurred various moving expenses. She is trying to determine whether or not they are deductible.

Which code section and subsection will provide her with information about the conditions under which moving expenses may be deducted?

Task-Based Simulation 9

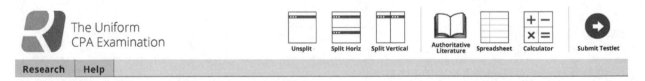

A taxpayer is providing 100% of the support for a niece, who resided with him for the entire year. He is trying to determine if he may deduct an exemption for her as a qualifying relative.

Which code section, subsection, and paragraph will provide him with information about what constitutes a qualifying relationship for the purpose of deducting a personal exemption?

TASK-BASED SIMULATION SOLUTIONS
Task-Based Simulation Solution 1

For **items 1 and 2,** candidates were asked to determine the filing status and number of exemptions for Mrs. Vick.

1. (M, 4) A taxpayer may file as married, filing jointly, which provides the most favorable rates if they are married as of the last day of the year, or at the time of death if the spouse died during the year. Mrs. Vick would qualify for MFJ. A joint return entitles Mrs. Vick to 2 exemptions, one for her and one for Mr. Vick. She is also entitled to an exemption for each qualifying child and qualifying relation. To be a qualifying child or qualifying relation, the individual must be a citizen; have income, excluding social security, below a certain amount; be a direct relative, such as the daughter, or, if not, have lived with the taxpayer for the entire year; have over one-half of their annual support provided by the taxpayer; and not be filing a joint tax return with a spouse. Both Mrs. Vick's daughter and cousin qualify and, as a result, Mrs. Vick will be entitled to 4 exemptions.

2. (Q, 3) While Mrs. Vick will not qualify to file as married filing jointly, which provides the most favorable rates and exemptions for both husband and wife, she will qualify for the next most favorable, which is qualifying widow or surviving spouse. This provides her with the same rates as MFJ, but only one exemption for herself. She qualifies because her spouse died within the last 2 years, she is providing over 50% of the cost of maintaining a household that is the principal residence of a child or stepchild, she was eligible to file a joint return in the year of death, and she has not remarried. In addition to one exemption for herself, she will be entitled to an exemption for each qualifying child and qualifying relation. To be a qualifying child or qualifying relation, the individual must be a citizen; have income, excluding social security, below a certain amount; be a direct relative, such as the daughter, or, if not, have lived with the taxpayer for the entire year; have over one-half of their annual support provided by the taxpayer; and not be filing a joint tax return with a spouse. Both Mrs. Vick's daughter and cousin qualify and, as a result, Mrs. Vick will be entitled to 3 exemptions.

3. ($0) State disability benefits received as a result of an injury on the job are excluded from gross income under IRC §104(a)(3), which applies to "amounts received through accident or health insurance." IRC §105(e)(2) provides that "amounts received from a sickness and disability fund for employees maintained under the law of a State or the District of Columbia, shall be treated as amounts received through accident or health insurance" for purposes of IRC §104.

4. ($400) Interest on tax refunds is fully taxable, as is interest on savings accounts and certificates of deposit. Interest on municipal bonds is tax exempt. As a result, Mrs. Vick will be taxed on $400 ($50 + $350) in interest income.

5. ($900) Pension benefits are taxable except to the extent that they are considered a return of capital. Since the entire cost of the pension plan was incurred by the employer, the Vicks had no cost and the $900 in benefits would be entirely taxable.

6. ($0) Gifts received are generally excluded from gross income under IRC §102(a). Note: Gifts from employers are generally included.

7. ($0) Life insurance proceeds are generally excluded from gross income under IRC §101, unless purchased from a person other than the insurance company (e.g., as an investment). Note: If the proceeds are paid out in installments, then part of the receipts will be taxable as interest.

8. ($200) Jury duty pay is considered earned compensation and is fully taxable. Note: Even if jury duty pay is remitted to the taxpayer's employer, the amount is still included in gross income, but the taxpayer may deduct the amount remitted to their employer as an adjustment to income.

9. ($450) Winnings from gambling activities are fully taxable. Gambling losses are not netted against winnings but may be deducted (to the extent of gambling winnings) as a miscellaneous itemized deduction not subject to the 2% of AGI limitation.

Task-Based Simulation Solution 2

For **items 1 through 14,** candidates were asked to select the appropriate tax treatment for the payments made or losses incurred by Mrs. Vick for 20X1.

	(A)	(B)	(C)	(D)	(E)	(F)
1. Premiums on Mr. Vick's personal life insurance policy.	●	○	○	○	○	○
2. Penalty on Mrs. Vick's early withdrawal of funds from a certificate of deposit.	○	○	○	●	○	○
3. Mrs. Vick's substantiated cash donation to the American Red Cross.	○	○	○	○	○	●
4. Payment of estimated state income taxes.	○	○	○	○	●	○
5. Payment of real estate taxes on the Vick home.	○	○	○	○	●	○
6. Loss on the sale of the family car.	●	○	○	○	○	○
7. Cost in excess of the increase in value of residence, for the installation of a stair lift in January 20X1, related directly to the medical care of Mr. Vick.	○	●	○	○	○	○
8. The Vicks' health insurance premiums for hospitalization coverage.	○	●	○	○	○	○
9. CPA fees to prepare the 20X0 tax return.	○	○	●	○	○	○
10. Amortization over the life of the loan of points paid to refinance the mortgage at a lower rate on the Vick home.	○	○	○	○	●	○
11. One-half the self-employment tax paid by Mrs. Vick.	○	○	○	●	○	○
12. Mrs. Vick's $100 in gambling losses.	○	○	○	○	●	○
13. Mrs. Vick's union dues.	○	○	●	○	○	○
14. 20X1 federal income tax paid with the Vicks' tax return on April 15, 20X2.	●	○	○	○	○	○

Explanations:

1. (A) Premiums on life insurance are not deductible, which is fair since the death benefits are not taxable.

2. (D) A penalty for early withdrawal of funds from a certificate of deposit is actually a reduction in the interest earned. As a result, it is a deduction for AGI deducted on page 1 of Form 1040.

3. (F) Charitable contributions are itemized deductions on Schedule A. They are allowed up to a maximum of 50% of AGI, and any unused portion may be carried forward up to 5 years.

4. (E) State and local income taxes are deductible in the year paid, regardless of the year to which they apply. As a result, estimated state income taxes are fully deductible as itemized deductions on Schedule A.

5. (E) Real estate taxes on the taxpayer's principal residence are deductible in the year paid. They are fully deductible as itemized deductions on Schedule A.

6. (A) Gains from the sale of personal assets, including the family automobile, are taxable as capital gains. Losses on the sale of personal assets, however, are not deductible.

7. (B) Costs of home improvements that are directly related to a medical condition of a taxpayer, the taxpayer's spouse, or a dependent, are deductible as medical expenses to the extent that they exceed the increase in the value of the home resulting from the improvement. As a medical expense, the costs are deductible on Schedule A as an itemized deduction and are reduced by 10% of AGI.

8. (B) Health insurance premiums are deductible as a medical expense. As a result, they are deductible as itemized deductions on Schedule A and are reduced by 10% of AGI.

9. (C) Tax return preparation fees may be claimed as a miscellaneous itemized deduction subject to the 2% of AGI limitation on Schedule A. Note: Tax return preparation fees incurred with respect to certain types of income should be deducted on the corresponding schedule (e.g., Schedule C for a business income).

10. (E) Loan points paid upon refinancing a mortgage are amortized over the life of the loan and the amortization is treated as an adjustment to the mortgage interest expense, which is fully deductible on Schedule A as an itemized deduction.

11. (D) One half of the self-employment tax paid by a self-employed taxpayer is allowed as an adjustment for AGI, deductible on page 1 of Form 1040.

12. (E) Gambling losses are deductible to the extent of gambling winnings. While the winnings are included in AGI, losses, to the extent deductible, are treated as a miscellaneous itemized deduction. Unlike some, such as unreimbursed employee expenses, it is not reduced by 2% of AGI and is fully deductible on Schedule A.

13. (C) Union dues are considered an employee expense and, to the extent that they are not reimbursed, they are deductible as a miscellaneous itemized deduction subject to the 2% of AGI limitation on Schedule A.

14. (A) Federal income tax payments are not deductible.

Task-Based Simulation Solution 3

Excerpt from Page 1 of Form 1040

Income	7	Wages, salaries, tips, etc. Attach Form(s) W-2	7	105,000
Attach Form(s) W-2 here. Also attach Forms W-2G and 1099-R if tax was withheld.	8a	Taxable interest. Attach Schedule B if required	8a	
	b	Tax-exempt interest. **Do not** include on line 8a . . .	8b	90,000		
	9a	Ordinary dividends. Attach Schedule B if required	9a	
	b	Qualified dividends	9b			
	10	Taxable refunds, credits, or offsets of state and local income taxes	10	
	11	Alimony received	11	
	12	Business income or (loss). Attach Schedule C or C-EZ	12	
If you did not get a W-2, see instructions.	13	Capital gain or (loss). Attach Schedule D if required. If not required, check here ▶ ☐	13	
	14	Other gains or (losses). Attach Form 4797	14	
	15a	IRA distributions .	15a		**b** Taxable amount . . .	15b	
	16a	Pensions and annuities	16a		**b** Taxable amount . . .	16b	
	17	Rental real estate, royalties, partnerships, S corporations, trusts, etc. Attach Schedule E	17	
	18	Farm income or (loss). Attach Schedule F	18	
	19	Unemployment compensation	19	
	20a	Social security benefits	20a		**b** Taxable amount . . .	20b	
	21	Other income. List type and amount		21	
	22	Combine the amounts in the far right column for lines 7 through 21. This is your **total income** ▶	22	105,000
Adjusted Gross Income	23	Educator expenses	23		
	24	Certain business expenses of reservists, performing artists, and fee-basis government officials. Attach Form 2106 or 2106-EZ	24		
	25	Health savings account deduction. Attach Form 8889 .	25		
	26	Moving expenses. Attach Form 3903	26		
	27	Deductible part of self-employment tax. Attach Schedule SE .	27		
	28	Self-employed SEP, SIMPLE, and qualified plans . .	28		
	29	Self-employed health insurance deduction	29		
	30	Penalty on early withdrawal of savings	30		
	31a	Alimony paid **b** Recipient's SSN ▶	31a	26,000	
	32	IRA deduction	32	5,000	
	33	Student loan interest deduction	33		
	34	Tuition and fees. Attach Form 8917	34		
	35	Domestic production activities deduction. Attach Form 8903	35		
	36	Add lines 23 through 35	36	31,000
	37	Subtract line 36 from line 22. This is your **adjusted gross income** . . . . . ▶	37	74,000

Excerpt from Schedule A

Medical and Dental Expenses	**Caution:** Do not include expenses reimbursed or paid by others.			
	1 Medical and dental expenses (see instructions)	**1**		
	2 Enter amount from Form 1040, line 38 ⬚ **2**			
	3 Multiply line 2 by 10% (0.10). But if either you or your spouse was born before January 2, 1952, multiply line 2 by 7.5% (0.075) instead	**3**		
	4 Subtract line 3 from line 1. If line 3 is more than line 1, enter -0-		**4**	
Taxes You Paid	**5** State and local (check only one box):			
	a ⬚ Income taxes, **or**	**5**	5,985	
	b ⬚ General sales taxes			
	6 Real estate taxes (see instructions)	**6**	4,575	
	7 Personal property taxes	**7**		
	8 Other taxes. List type and amount ▶	**8**		
	9 Add lines 5 through 8		**9**	10,560
Interest You Paid	**10** Home mortgage interest and points reported to you on Form 1098	**10**	18,484	
Note: Your mortgage interest deduction may be limited (see instructions).	**11** Home mortgage interest not reported to you on Form 1098. If paid to the person from whom you bought the home, see instructions and show that person's name, identifying no., and address ▶	**11**		
	12 Points not reported to you on Form 1098. See instructions for special rules .	**12**		
	13 Mortgage insurance premiums (see instructions)	**13**		
	14 Investment interest. Attach Form 4952 if required. (See instructions.)	**14**		
	15 Add lines 10 through 14		**15**	18,484
Gifts to Charity	**16** Gifts by cash or check. If you made any gift of $250 or more, see instructions	**16**	275	
If you made a gift and got a benefit for it, see instructions.	**17** Other than by cash or check. If any gift of $250 or more, see instructions. You **must** attach Form 8283 if over $500 . . .	**17**		
	18 Carryover from prior year	**18**		
	19 Add lines 16 through 18		**19**	275
Casualty and Theft Losses	**20** Casualty or theft loss(es). Attach Form 4684. (See instructions.)		**20**	
Job Expenses and Certain Miscellaneous Deductions	**21** Unreimbursed employee expenses—job travel, union dues, job education, etc. Attach Form 2106 or 2106-EZ if required. (See instructions.) ▶	**21**	2,115	
	22 Tax preparation fees	**22**	365	
	23 Other expenses—investment, safe deposit box, etc. List type and amount ▶ SAFE DEPOSIT BOX $100	**23**	100	
	24 Add lines 21 through 23	**24**	2,580	
	25 Enter amount from Form 1040, line 38 ⬚ **25** 74,000			
	26 Multiply line 25 by 2% (0.02)	**26**	1,480	
	27 Subtract line 26 from line 24. If line 26 is more than line 24, enter -0-		**27**	1,100
Other Miscellaneous Deductions	**28** Other—from list in instructions. List type and amount ▶		**28**	
Total Itemized Deductions	**29** Is Form 1040, line 38, over $155,650?			
	⬚ **No.** Your deduction is not limited. Add the amounts in the far right column for lines 4 through 28. Also, enter this amount on Form 1040, line 40. } . .		**29**	30,419
	⬚ **Yes.** Your deduction may be limited. See the Itemized Deductions Worksheet in the instructions to figure the amount to enter.			
	30 If you elect to itemize deductions even though they are less than your standard deduction, check here . . . . ▶ ⬚			

Explanation of solutions

Form 1040

Lines 23 through 30: **null**

These lines do not apply to Alima. She cannot deduct the $965 of moving expenses on Line 26 because the distance she moved was less than 50 miles.

Line 31a/31b: **$26,000/123-XX-XXXX**

Alima paid $26,000 in alimony to Jim Johnson. So long as she provides his Social Security number, she may deduct that amount in arriving at her adjusted gross income, and Jim must include it in his income on his return.

Line 32: **$5,000**

Alima contributed $5,000 to her traditional IRA. It is fully deductible in arriving at AGI because she did not actively participate in another pension or profit-sharing plan and it does not exceed the annual limit of $5,500.

Lines 33 through 35: **null**

These lines do not apply to Alima.

Line 36: **$31,000**

Line 36 is the total of all deductions in arriving at AGI—$31,000 ($26,000 alimony + $5,000 IRA).

Line 37: **$74,000**

Line 37 calculates AGI by subtracting Line 36 (total deductions for AGI—$31,000) from the total income on Line 22 ($105,000).

Schedule A

Lines 1 through 4: **null**
These lines do not apply to Alima.

Line 5: **$5,985**
Box 17 on Alima's W-2 shows that $5,985 in state income tax was withheld from her pay. She can deduct this amount from her AGI as an itemized deduction on her Schedule A, Line 5.

Line 6: **$4,575**
All of the real estate taxes Alima paid (shown in Box 4 on her three Forms 1098) are deductible from AGI as an itemized deduction on her Schedule A, Line 6. There is no limit on the number of properties for real estate taxes ($2,852.48 + $569.04 + $1,153 = $4,575 rounded to the nearest dollar).

Lines 7 and 8: **null**
These lines do not apply to Alima.

Line 9: **$10,560**
Line 9 is the total of all taxes paid by Alima—$10,560 ($5,985 + $4,575).

Line 10: **$18,484**
Home mortgage interest is deductible for a primary and secondary residence; therefore, Alima may deduct the $11,634 mortgage interest for her home (Commerce Mortgage) and the $6,850 interest on the Colorado vacation home (State Mortgage), for a total of $18,484. The GMC Mortgage interest on the vacant lot is not deductible.

Lines 11 through 14: **null**
These lines do not apply to Alima.

Line 15: **$18,484**
Line 15 is the total of deductible interest paid, which includes only $18,484 in mortgage interest.

Line 16: **$275**
The church and Humane Society charitable contributions are deductible without receipts as they are less than $250. The Independent political party contribution is not deductible because it is political, and the Nairobi National Museum contribution is not deductible because it is a foreign charity.

Lines 17 and 18: **null**
These lines do not apply to Alima.

Line 19: **$275**
Line 19 is the total amount of deductible charitable contributions, Lines 16 through 18.

Line 20: **null**
This line does not apply to Alima.

Line 21: **$2,115**
Line 21 includes the following unreimbursed, job-related expenses: $600 union dues + $165 Nursing Journal subscriptions + $1,350 job-hunting expenses. The $105 for the local newspaper and the $525 for work clothes are not deductible. The newspaper is not specific to her career, and the clothes can be worn for other occasions. If she had to wear hospital scrubs, then they would be deductible.

Line 22: **$365**
According to the Invoice provided, Alima paid $365 to have her Form 1040 prepared. It is deductible on Line 22 as a miscellaneous itemized deduction, subject to a 2% of AGI floor.

Line 23: **Safe deposit box/$100**
The $100 safe deposit box fee is deductible on Line 23. The type of expense and the amount must be listed on the blank line.

Line 24: **$2,580**
Line 24 is the total of the deductible miscellaneous expenses, subject to a 2% of AGI floor:

Safe deposit box	100
Union dues	600
Nursing journals	165
Tax return prep	365
Job hunting	1,350
Total	$2,580

Note: The bank charges and the Cityview Daily Press are not deductible because they are not employee or investment expenses. The work clothes are not deductible because they are not uniforms and can be worn outside of work.

Line 25: **$74,000**
Line 25 is asking for Alima's AGI from Line 38 (not shown, but Line 37 is the same amount) of Form 1040, which is $74,000.

Line 26: **$1,480**
Line 26 calculates the 2% of AGI floor ($74,000 × 2% = $1,480).

Line 27: **$1,100**
Line 27 is the amount of miscellaneous expenses in excess of the 2% of AGI floor ($1,480) that may be deducted ($2,580 − $1,480 = $1,100).

Line 28: **null**
This line does not apply to Alima.

Line 29: **$30,419**
Line 29 calculates the total itemized deductions that may be carried to Form 1040 and deducted from AGI ($10,560 + $18,484 + $275 + $1,100 = $30,419).

Task-Based Simulation Solution 4

85	(a)

Task-Based Simulation Solution 5

71	(c)	(3)

Task-Based Simulation Solution 6

2	(a)	(1)

Task-Based Simulation Solution 7

117	(c)	(1)

Task-Based Simulation Solution 8

217	(c)

Task-Based Simulation Solution 9

152	(d)	(2)

Section 2 – Corporate Tax

Corresponding Lectures

Watch the following course lectures with this section:

Lecture 2.01 – C Corporation
Lecture 2.02 – Formation of a C Corporation
Lecture 2.03 – Corporate Tax Formation – Class Questions
Lecture 2.04 – Revenues
Lecture 2.05 – Charitable Contributions, Capital Gains/Losses
Lecture 2.06 – Charity and Capital Loss – Class Questions
Lecture 2.07 – Penalty Taxes, AET and PHC Tax
Lecture 2.08 – Penalty Taxes – Class Questions
Lecture 2.09 – Supplementary Schedules, M-1, M-2, M-3
Lecture 2.10 – Supplementary Schedules – Class Questions
Lecture 2.11 – Corporate Distributions
Lecture 2.12 – Corporate Distributions – Class Questions
Lecture 2.13 – Alternative Minimum Tax
Lecture 2.14 – Corporate Tax – Class Questions – TBS
Lecture 2.15 – Corporate Tax – Class Questions – TBS (Continued)

Exam Note: Please refer to the AICPA REG Blueprint in the Introduction of this book to find a listing of the representative tasks (and their associated skill levels—i.e., Remembering and Understanding, Application, and Analysis) that the candidate should be able to perform based on the knowledge obtained in this section.

Corporate Tax

C CORPORATION OVERVIEW

C Corporations are legal entities that are separate and distinct from its owners. They are formally created by filing its Articles of incorporation. A corporation is taxed as a separate entity, and shareholders are generally taxed on corporate earnings that are distributed to them (i.e., earnings are taxed twice).

- **C Corporation**
  - Created formally – Articles of incorporation
  - Limited Liability
  - Taxpaying entity (Form 1120)
  - Amended corporate return – 1120X
- 90% is GAAP which uses Accrual - rest are exceptions
  - **Calendar year** or **fiscal year**, which is chosen when the first tax return is filed. A **52-53-week** tax year is a fiscal tax year that varies from 52 to 53 weeks and ends on the same day (but does not have to end on the last day of a month).
- For years beginning after 2015, the return is due 4/15 (3 ½ months after year-end), with an automatic 5-month extension available for calendar-year corporations. Corporations with fiscal years get a 6-month extension, except for those with a June 30 year-end, which get a 7-month extension. Note, however, that return due dates and extensions are no longer tested on the CPA Exam.

FORMATION OF A C CORPORATION

Formation – Formal (Articles of Incorporation)

No gain or loss is recognized if property is transferred to a corporation solely in exchange for stock and, immediately after the transfer, the transferors are in **control** of the corporation.

Tax-free exchange if contributors of cash and property gain 80% or more of the stock – control
- **Cash or property 80%** or more (control)
  - Tax free
  - Carryover basis
    - If property subject to debt, C.V. 40 –10 debt = 30 basis in stock
  - Carryover holding period

- **Services** (excluded from the definition of property) or **< 80% of stock**
  - Taxable income at FMV of stock
  - Wage expense for corporation

- **If no control**
  - Taxable to all parties, similar to services

- **Reorganizations** of corporation generally also tax free
  - Carryover basis

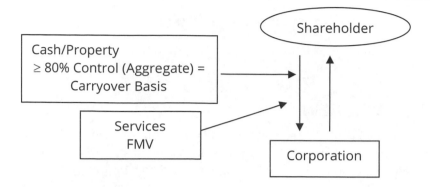

Shares issued for **cash** are handled in a straightforward manner: the shareholder's basis in the corporation is equal to the amount of cash paid.

Shares issued in exchange for the rendering of **services** to the corporation result in ordinary income to the service provider, since the shares are treated as compensation for the services. The service provider reports income equal to the estimated FMV of the shares. **For example**, if Saul Server is given 10% of the total outstanding shares of a company valued at $100,000 in exchange for Saul's services to the company, he will report $10,000 of ordinary income. This income is also subject to FICA or self-employment taxes, depending on whether Saul is considered an employee or independent contractor. His basis in the corporate stock is the same $10,000.

When a shareholder has contributed **property** to obtain stock, there are two possibilities as to the valuation of the investment:
- **Tax basis** of the property to the shareholder (80% or more—Control)
- **Fair market value** (FMV) at the date of contribution (less than 80%)

In most circumstances, Section 351 allows the *basis* of the property to be used, and FMV is ignored. **For example**, if land with an original cost to the shareholder of $100 and FMV of $300 is contributed, the shareholder will have a basis in the stock received of $100, and the corporation's basis in the land will be $100. As a result of this treatment, the transfer of the property is a *nontaxable* event to the shareholder as long as **80% or more** of the corporate stock is in the hands of shareholders that provided either cash or property to obtain their shares.

For example, assume that a corporation is formed and 100 shares in total are issued to three different shareholders. Carlos Cash paid $600 in cash to obtain 60 shares. Paulette Property contributed land costing her $100 and valued at $300 for 30 shares. Sadie Service received 10 shares in exchange for services. The total corporation was valued at $1,000 immediately after these actions.

Carlos' 60 shares have a basis of $600, equal to the cash contributed. Sadie's 10 shares represent 10% of the total corporation, so Sadie's shares have a basis of $1,000 x 10% = $100, and Sadie must report ordinary income of $100 on her individual return. Since Carlos and Paulette (the shareholders contributing cash or property) received a combined 90% of the total shares, Paulette's 30 shares have a basis of $100, equal to the basis of the land she contributed, and the corporation has a tax basis of $100 in the land.

Although the tax basis of property is generally carried over from the shareholder to the corporation, a special rule applies to property contributions when **less than 80% (no Control)** of the total voting stock is in the hands of shareholders that contributed cash or property (meaning that more than 20% of the stock is in the hands of shareholders that received them in exchange for services). In such cases, the property contribution is reported at the *FMV* of the property on the date of contribution, and is reported as a sale by the contributor.

For example, assume again that a corporation is formed and 100 shares in total are issued to three different shareholders. Carlos Cash paid $450 in cash to obtain 45 shares. Paulette Property contributed land costing her $100 and valued at $300 for 30 shares. Sadie Service received 25 shares in exchange for services. The total corporation was valued at $1,000 immediately after these actions.

Carlos' 45 shares have a basis of $450, equal to the cash contributed. Sadie's 25 shares represent 25% of the total corporation, so Sadie's shares have a basis of $1,000 x 25% = $250, and Sadie must report ordinary income of $250 on her individual return. Since Carlos and Paulette (the shareholders contributing cash or property) received a combined 75% of the total shares, Paulette's 30 shares have a basis of $300, equal to the FMV of the land she contributed, and the corporation has a tax basis of $300 in the land. Paulette must report a gain on sale of land of $200 on her individual tax return.

A corporation can be formed from an existing business operating in the form of a proprietorship or partnership. In such cases, the business interests transferred by the proprietor or partners are considered property, so the incorporation is nontaxable, and the assets and liabilities of the business are carried over to the corporation, as long as the owners of the previous business are given at least 80% of the voting stock of the corporation.

Nonrecognition of gain applies only to amounts transferred solely in exchange for stock. If the *shareholder receives cash or other property* (i.e., boot) in addition to stock, gain is recognized up to the amount of cash or FMV of other property received. Securities are considered property for this purpose.

For example, Charlotte transfers property with FMV of $20,000 and adjusted basis of $12,000 to Roberts Corporation in exchange for 80% of its stock. In addition to stock, she receives $3,000 in cash. Although the transfer qualifies under Section 351, Charlotte recognizes a gain of $3,000. Her basis in the stock is $12,000 (adjusted basis of property transferred, plus gain, less cash received). The corporation's basis in the property is $15,000 (transferor's basis plus gain recognized by transferor).

If a shareholder contributes *property subject to liabilities*, the shareholder's basis in the stock received is reduced by the amount of liability relief. If liabilities exceed the shareholder's adjusted basis in the property, gain is recognized on the excess, and the shareholder's basis in the stock is zero.

Basis of Property Exchanged for Corporate Stock	
Tax-free exchanges under Section 351 **Transferors have at least 80% control after the exchange**	
Shareholder's basis in stock received equals:	*Corporation's basis* in property received equals:
+ Adjusted basis of property transferred + Recognized gain + Cash Paid + Liabilities assumed + Transaction costs and fees - Cash received - FMV of property received - Liabilities transferred	+ Adjusted basis of the property in the hands of the transferor + Gain recognized by the transferor

For Sec. 351 transactions, if the aggregate adjusted basis of transferred property (e.g., C/O basis = $10,000) exceeds its aggregate FMV (e.g., $7,000), the corporate transferee's aggregate basis for the property is generally limited to its aggregate FMV immediately after the transaction ($7,000). Any required basis reduction is allocated among the transferred properties in proportion to their built-in loss immediately before the transaction. (The Transferor's basis in the stock would still be the carryover basis of the property of $10,000).

Alternatively, the transferor and the corporate transferee are allowed to make an irrevocable election to limit the basis in the stock received by the transferor to the aggregate FMV of the transferred property. (The Transferor would then have a basis of $7,000, but the corporation would have a basis in the property of $10,000).

A corporation can also be created as the result of **reorganization** of an existing corporation. Corporate reorganizations are affected by the transfer of virtually all the assets and liabilities of one corporation to another in exchange for stock in the new corporation, and are generally nontaxable, with the shareholders having the same basis in the stock of the new corporation as they did in the old. Some examples of reorganizations that qualify for such **tax-free status** include:
- Changes in the place of organization (e.g., the assets of a New York corporation are all transferred into a corporation with a Florida charter.)
- Mergers and consolidations of businesses
- Absorption of subsidiaries (i.e., the assets and liabilities of a controlled subsidiary are transferred to the parent.)

In all of the examples cited, nontaxable status required that a standard of 80% ownership be met for parties providing consideration other than services for their stock. This 80% level is the standard of **control** for tax purposes, and is the minimum ownership level required to identify an investee company as a controlled subsidiary and allow the preparation of *consolidated tax returns*. The preparation of consolidated tax returns with controlled subsidiaries is *optional*.

In contrast, generally accepted accounting principles consider control to take place when a majority of the voting stock is owned, or when other acceptable standards are met, and require the preparation of consolidated financial statements when such circumstances arise. Be certain not to confuse the 80% standard of control for tax purposes with the majority rule (50%) for accounting purposes.

Once a corporation is formed, shareholders may subsequently transfer additional property to the corporation. In some cases, it will be in exchange for additional stock but, in others, no stock may be issued in exchange. When that is the case:
- The shareholder will recognize no gain or loss on the transfer and will increase the tax basis in the stock by the tax basis of the property transferred.
- The shareholder's tax basis in the transferred property will carry over to the corporation and become its tax basis in the property.

Corporate Income Tax Return (1120)

Gross Income (worldwide)
(Ordinary deductions)
Income before "special deductions"
(Charitable Contribution)
(Div. Received Deduction) (DRD)
 Taxable Income
 × tax rate
 Gross Tax Liability
(Foreign Tax Credit)
 Net Regular Tax Liability
+ Personal Holding Company Tax **(PHC)**
+ Accumulated Earnings Tax
+ Alternative Minimum Tax **(AMT)**
Total Tax Liability

Lecture 2.03

CLASS QUESTIONS

Please see the Class Questions and Class Solutions for this Lecture at the end of this Section.

Lecture 2.04

COMPUTING TAXABLE INCOME

Revenues (same as individual tax with some exceptions)
- Revenue recognized at the *earlier of when earned or collected*.
  - Rental income received in advance
  - Interest income received in advance (not municipal bond interest)
  - Royalty income received in advance

- Life insurance proceeds on key employee

- o If the corporation is the beneficiary, the premiums paid on such policies are not deductible, since the proceeds are not taxable.
- o Premiums on life insurance to benefit employee's family are deductible.
- o Company-Owned Life Insurance (COLI) - The beneficiary may exclude from gross income benefits received only up to the total amount of premiums and other amounts paid by the policyholder for the contract; any excess would be taxable. Certain exceptions do apply (e.g., director or highly compensated employee).

Deductions (all reasonable operating expenses)

- In general, deductions on a corporate tax return are claimed in accordance with the same matching principle used for GAAP purposes. As a result, expenses can be deducted in the period that they are accrued for financial reporting purposes. An accrual basis taxpayer can accrue an expense if the transaction meets *both* an **all-events test** *and* an **economic performance test**. The all-events test is met when the existence of a liability is established and the amount of liability can be determined with reasonable accuracy. In the event that another person is to provide the taxpayer with property or services, the economic performance test is satisfied when the property or services are actually provided. Certain accrued items are expected to be paid within a short period of time after accrual, however. These may only be deducted when accrued if they are paid within **2 ½ months** of the tax year-end. The items subject to this requirement include:
  - o Wages
  - o Bonuses
  - o Vacation pay

- **Organizational expenses**
  - o State incorporation fees (including legal and accounting fees related to the incorporation)
    - ▪ The corporation may elect to deduct up to **$5,000 of organizational expenditures and start-up costs**. The $5,000 amount ($5,000 for each organizational and start-up costs) is reduced by the amount by which the organizational expenditures or start-up costs exceeds **$50,000**, respectively. Any costs not currently deductible are amortized over 180 months (15 years), beginning with the month in which the active trade or business begins.
      - ▫ The entity must elect to amortize the organization costs in the period of organization.
      - ▫ If no election is made, the costs are capitalized and remain until the entity is liquidated.
  - o Costs of issuing, printing, and selling stock (including legal and accounting fees related to the offering of securities) are NOT organizational expenses (reduction of APIC).

- **Salaries and wages**, payroll taxes, fringe benefits
  - o Can only deduct up to $1M of compensation expense for each of the highest paid executive officers of a public corporation (1125-E) ($500k if under TARP).
  - o Entertainment expenses for officers, directors, and 10%-or-greater owners may be deducted only to the extent that they are included in the individual's gross income.

- **Bonuses and vacation pay**, if paid within **2 ½ months** of year-end (3/15 for calendar year-end)

- **Estimated losses are not deductible.**
  - Bad debts not claimed until actual **direct write-offs**.
  - Warranty costs not claimed until actual repairs.
    - For book, both accrued
    - For tax, direct write-off method

- **Interest expense**
  - Not deductible if loan proceeds used for tax-exempt investments.

- **Reimbursed employee expenses**
  - 50% of meals and entertainment
    - When reimbursed meals and entertainment are treated by the employer as compensation and wages, they are fully deductible to the entity.
    - The payee will be taxed on the amount of the reimbursement and will be allowed to deduct 50% of the meals and entertainment as an unreimbursed business expense.
  - All travel costs
  - The cost of a luxury skybox is disallowed to the extent that the cost exceeds the cost of the most expensive non-luxury seat in the venue.
    - The limit does not apply if the skybox is rented for one event only.
    - Rental of a skybox for more than one event in the same sports arena, such as a series of playoff tickets, is subject to the limitation.
  - *Lodging expenses* for non-away-from-home travel (i.e., Local lodging)
    - If incurred for the convenience or personal benefit of the employee, such as additional employee compensation, to enable employees to avoid long commutes, to accommodate overtime, to provide temporary housing to a relocated employee, or for an employee's use indefinitely, it is deductible to the employer and taxable to the employee.
    - Safe Harbor Test: Deductible to employer and not taxable to employee as tax-free working condition fringe benefit if *4 conditions* are met:
      - Necessary for full participation in bona fide business meeting, conference, training activity, or other business function.
      - Does not exceed 5 calendar days nor once per calendar quarter.
      - Required by employer to remain at activity or function overnight.
      - Lodging is not lavish or extravagant.
    - Facts and Circumstances Test: Even if such expenses do not meet the requirements above, they may still qualify as deductible if they are considered ordinary and necessary business expenses based on the facts and circumstances. For example, the expenses may still be deductible if they are required by the employer for a bona fide business purpose; they are not for social or personal benefit to the employee; and the lodging is not lavish or extravagant.

- **Casualty losses**
  - Business property—Lesser of adjusted basis immediately before the casualty, or decline in value.
  - Note that "$100 floor" and "10% of adjusted gross income" limitations do not apply.

- **Goodwill, franchises & trademarks** amortized over 15 years.
  - For book, tested annually for impairment.

- Some expenditures are **never deductible** (forget it!!)
  - Government fines, fees, and penalties, including interest on penalties
  - Federal income taxes
    - Can deduct state and local taxes on the federal return

- **Research and development costs**
  - Immediately or over a minimum of 60 months

- **Dividends** from other taxable domestic corporations:
  - Reported fully in gross income
  - Dividends Received Deduction (DRD)
    - To avoid triple taxation on dividends

Percentage of ownership by corporate shareholder	Allowed DRD
< 20%	70% - **Unaffiliated Co.**
≥ 20% to 80%	80%
≥ 80%	100% - **Control**

    - If own at least 80%, may file consolidated tax returns and eliminate intercompany dividends – same effect.

    - Investor **doesn't qualify for DRD if:**
      - Dividends are from a foreign corporation (since IRS didn't tax investee)
      - Borrowed the money to buy the investment (Interest expense)
      - Received from a tax-exempt organization (muni-bond interest, not taxable)
      - Owned for less than 46 days (minimum holding period)

    - **Exception** if DRD < TI before DRD < Dividend
      There is a **rare limitation** on the amount of the DRD applicable to investments that qualify for the 70% or 80% DRD. This limitation applies when the taxable income (TI) before DRD is less than the amount of the dividend itself, but not lower than the dividend multiplied by the applicable percentage. In these cases, the DRD percentage is applied to TI before DRD instead of to the dividend itself. **For example**, if:
      - Dividend = $100
      - DRD = $70 (70% x $100)
      - TI before DRD = $80
      Then, DRD is limited to $56 ($80 TI x 70%) because:
      - *$70 DRD < $80 TI before DRD < $100 Dividend*

For example, assume the corporation's gross revenue consists of sales and $100 in dividend income, and deductions other than the DRD total $490. Also assume the dividend was received from another taxable domestic corporation in which the investor holds a tiny 2% interest, so that the appropriate DRD is 70%. Let's look at five examples in which sales are (a) $530, (b) $500, (c) $470, (d) $440, and (e) $410. The calculation of taxable income is as follows:

	(a)	(b)	(c)	(d)	(e)
Sales	530	500	470	440	410
Dividend income	100	100	100	100	100
Gross income	630	600	570	540	510
Ordinary deductions	(490)	(490)	(490)	(490)	(490)
Income before DRD	140	110	80	50	20
DRD (70%)	(70)	(70)	**(56)**	(70)	(70)
Taxable income	70	40	24	(20)	(50)

Notice that the DRD is based on the dividend income ($100 x 70% = $70) in most of the examples. Only in example (c), in which income before DRD is lower than $100 but not lower than $70, is the exception applicable, and the DRD is calculated on TI before DRD ($80 x 70% = $56). Because of the narrow range of income before DRD (between 70% and 100% of dividend income) in which the exception applies, this is a rarely-tested item. In general, the percentage will simply be applied to the dividend income. Note that the limitation does not apply when there is a net operating loss after subtracting the full DRD amount—examples (d) and (e).

Lecture 2.05

Deductions (Continued)

- **Charitable Contributions**
    - o   Claimed after all others, except "special deductions."
    - o   Limited to 10% of income before claiming deduction (**10% ATI**).
    - o   Adjusted Taxable Income (**ATI**) is Net Income adjusted for:
        - ▪   Charity
        - ▪   DRD
        - ▪   NOL carryback
        - ▪   Capital loss carryback
    - o   Unused amount carried forward **5 years**.
    - o   Pledge may be accrued if paid within 3 ½ months of year-end.
    - o   Individuals
        - ▪   Max per year is 50% of AGI.
        - ▪   Unused portion carried forward 5 years.

Gross income	$200
(Ordinary deductions)	-40
Income before special deductions (ATI)	**160**
(Charity)	-10
(DRD)	-50
Taxable Income	$100
(max deduction is 10% of $160 = $16)	

- **Capital Gains and Losses**
    When a corporation sells assets that are held for investment, the difference between the tax bases and proceeds from sale are recognized as capital gains and losses. Noncurrent

assets used in a trade or business, however, are subject to special rules (discussed in more detail in the Property Tax Section):
- o   If they are held for one year or less, gains and losses are treated as ordinary income or losses (i.e., ordinary assets).
- o   If they are held for more than one year, losses are treated as ordinary losses and gains are treated as long-term capital gains (i.e., Section 1231 assets).

Capital losses are not deductible to a corporation.
- o   **Capital losses for corporations** may only offset capital gains per IRC Section 1211. (No <u>net</u> Cap. loss)
  - ▪ Unused carried back *3 years* and forward *5 years.*
  - ▪ All loss carrybacks and carryforwards are considered Short Term (S/T).
  - ▪ Individuals—Net loss of $3,000 per year, rest carried forward indefinitely.

- • **Net Operating Losses (NOL)** carried back 2 years and forward 20 years.
  - o   Individuals, same rules

Nondeductible Items

There are certain expenses that are *not deductible* for income tax purposes:
- • **Federal income taxes** – These are treated as offsets against the federal tax owed, and not as deductions. State and local income taxes are fully deductible on a normal accrual accounting basis.
- • **Government fines and penalties** – Since the intention of these is punishment, no deduction is allowed, even though such penalties may appear to be in the form of interest.
- • **Costs of issuing stock** – These are treated as adjustments to the proceeds from sale.
- • **Lobbying costs** – Corporations are discouraged from political involvement, and may claim no costs associated with influencing candidates and legislation.
- • **Compensation over $1 million** to the top executive officers of a public corporation – Pay to other employees is not limited.
- • **Club dues** – These are considered too personal in nature to qualify as business expenses.

In addition, only **50% of meals and entertainment** costs are deductible since they are considered to have personal as well as business elements. Other reimbursed employee expenses are fully deductible.

The federal tax code does not permit the deduction of estimated **costs until they are paid**. As a result:
- • **Bad debts** – These are only deductible at the time individual debts are written off. Allowance approaches are not permitted.
- • **Warranties** – The cost of repairs and replacements of products under warranty are deductible when costs are incurred. No deduction may be claimed for estimated warranty liabilities.
- • **Lawsuits** – Losses may not be deducted until paid. Unlike GAAP, the tax code does not permit the deduction of losses just because they are probable and estimable.
- • **Marketable securities** – Changes in market value are not reported on the tax return. Gains and losses are only recognized at the time of sale.
- • **Inventory** – Declines in market value are not deductible until disposal of the inventory takes place.

Foreign Tax Credit

U.S. tax liability × $\dfrac{\text{Foreign income}}{\text{Worldwide income}}$ = Foreign tax credit (never to exceed actual foreign taxes paid)

Once the tax is determined from the tax table, it is reduced by available tax credits. The most frequently tested is the **foreign tax credit**. This credit is available to U.S. corporations for income taxes paid to foreign countries on income that is also reported on the U.S. return. The credit is limited to the portion of the U.S. gross tax that applies to the income on which the foreign tax was assessed. **For example**, assume that the following facts apply:

Worldwide income	$100,000
Foreign income included in above	$30,000
U.S. gross tax before foreign credit	$20,000
Foreign income tax	$8,000

Since 30% ($30,000 / $100,000) of the total income is from a foreign country, 30% of the gross tax of $20,000, or $6,000, is the portion of the U.S. gross tax applicable to the foreign income, and is the amount of the credit (the remaining $2,000 can be carried back 1 year or forward 10 years). A corporation may elect to claim the entire amount of foreign taxes as a deduction from taxable income instead of claiming the credit.

General Business Credit

There is a general business credit that consists of numerous individual tax credits. Two of these include:
- Work opportunity credit
- Research credit

Work Opportunity Credit
Equal to 40% of qualified first-year wages for the year.
- Qualified first-year wages are:
  - Paid to members of a targeted group, including veterans, ex-felons, and summer youth employees, among others.
  - Generally limited to $6,000 per individual, but may be $12,000, $14,000, or $24,000 for certain qualified veterans.

- The work opportunity tax credit was retroactively extended through 2019 by the 2015 PATH Act.

Research Credit
Equal to 20% of qualified research expenses over base amount.
- Qualified research expenses include in-house costs incurred directly by the entity and contract research expenses.
  - In-house costs include wages, supplies, and the right to use computers to the extent that they are associated with the conduct of research.
  - Contract expenses are 25% of amounts paid to nonemployees for qualified research.

- The base amount is calculated by multiplying a percentage by the gross receipts for the taxable year.

  o The percentage is equal to the total of aggregate research expenses incurred
    between December 31, 1983 and January 1, 1989, divided by the total aggregate
    revenues for those tax years.
  o Base amount is at least 50% of qualified research expenses for the year for which
    the credit is sought.

- The research credit was permanently extended by the 2015 PATH Act.

Lecture 2.06

CLASS QUESTIONS

Please see the Class Questions and Class Solutions for this Lecture at the end of this Section.

Lecture 2.07

PENALTY TAXES

Accumulated Earnings Tax (AET)

To penalize corporations that accumulate earnings beyond the reasonable needs for expansion,
retirement of debt and working capital needs.
- Excessive retained earnings in judgment of IRS
- Not self-assessed (by audit)
- Tax on undistributed income only **(20% rate)**
  o Reduce or eliminate if pay any of the following:
    - Actual dividend
    - Consent dividend – *hypothetical dividends* you pay taxes on, even though no
      money was actually received.
    - If already paid PHC tax (Below)

- **Safe harbor** allows certain amounts to be retained:
  o $250,000 for a manufacturing co.   **OR**
  o $150,000 for personal service corporations—provides personal services by owner-
    employees, e.g., health, law, accounting, consulting;   **PLUS**
  o Additional sums retained for the purpose of paying federal income taxes owed.
  The sum of these two amounts is known as the minimum accumulated earnings credit.

- **For example**, assume a manufacturing corporation in its first year of existence reports
  taxable income of $500,000 and has a federal income tax liability of $100,000. It is allowed
  to accumulate $250,000 + $100,000 = $350,000, so the maximum amount that might be
  subject to the penalty tax is $500,000 - $350,000 = $150,000. As long as dividend
  distributions of at least $150,000 are made, this corporation cannot be liable for the
  accumulated earnings tax.

Personal Holding Company (PHC) Tax

To discourage the sheltering of certain types of passive income in corporations.
- **If Both:**
  o **5 or fewer** individuals own *more than 50%* of stock
  o **60% or more** of revenue from *passive sources* (taxable interest, dividends, rental &
    royalty income)

- Tax on undistributed personal holding company income (**UPHCI**) only (**20% rate**)
- Self-assessed by filing form (Sch. PH) with return (Form 1120)
  - Can avoid if pay:
    - Actual dividend
    - Consent dividend – Hypothetical dividend
- This tax was created to prevent individuals in high individual tax brackets from establishing corporations to hold their personal investments and benefit from lower corporate tax rates on income. As a result, the tax only applies to **undistributed income** of the corporation, after deducting corporate taxes and net long-term capital gains to arrive at UPHCI, and the tax can be reduced or eliminated by sufficient dividend distributions (of course, this results in the individual shareholders paying taxes on the dividends received).

Personal Service Corporations (PSC)

A PSC is one that performs professional services and is predominantly owned by the parties providing those services. Qualified PSCs are taxed at a flat rate of 35%. To qualify as a PSC, two criteria must be met:

- Substantially all activities involve the performance of health, law, engineering, architecture, accounting, actuarial science, performing arts, or consulting services; and
- 95% or more of the stock is owned by employees performing those services. Includes:
  - Retired employees who had performed such services;
  - Estates of employees or retirees who performed such services; and
  - Persons who acquired stock as a result of the death of such an employee or retiree for the 2-year period beginning on the date of the employee's or retiree's death.

Note: Owner-employees of a PSC are considered related parties for purposes of IRC §267(a)(2), which requires a deduction to be matched with the related payee's recognition of income; thus, payments made to owner-employees may be deducted by a PSC only in the period in which they are taxable to the owner-employees.

Lecture 2.08

CLASS QUESTIONS

Please see the Class Questions and Class Solutions for this Lecture at the end of this Section.

Lecture 2.09

Supplementary Schedules M-1, M-2, M-3

- **M-1 Reconciliation of book income to taxable income**
  The corporation must prepare a reconciliation of book income to taxable income (*before special deductions – DRD & NOL Deduction*) on the **Schedule M-1**. The purpose of this schedule is to identify to the IRS amounts that are reported differently for GAAP and tax purposes. The calculation begins with book income. It is then increased/decreased by items that cause taxable income to be higher/lower than book income.
  - **Temporary** differences – bad debt expense, warranty expense, depreciation differences, etc.
  - **Permanent** differences – municipal bond interest, 50% of meals and entertainment, fines, penalties, premiums paid on key person life insurance, etc.

Schedule M-1 **Reconciliation of Income (Loss) per Books With Income per Return**

Note: The corporation may be required to file Schedule M-3 (see instructions).

1	Net income (loss) per books		7	Income recorded on books this year not included on this return (itemize):	
2	Federal income tax per books			Tax-exempt interest $ ____	
3	Excess of capital losses over capital gains .				
4	Income subject to tax not recorded on books this year (itemize):____				
			8	Deductions on this return not charged against book income this year (itemize):	
5	Expenses recorded on books this year not deducted on this return (itemize):		a	Depreciation . . $ ____	
a	Depreciation . . . . $ ____		b	Charitable contributions $ ____	
b	Charitable contributions . $ ____				
c	Travel and entertainment . $ ____				
			9	Add lines 7 and 8	
6	Add lines 1 through 5		10	Income (page 1, line 28)—line 6 less line 9	

- **M-2 Reconciliation of Unappropriated Beg. RE to End RE**

  The corporation must also prepare a **Schedule M-2**, which is a statement of retained earnings (RE). The IRS examines this schedule to determine if any prior period adjustments might require amending returns of earlier years.

Schedule M-2 **Analysis of Unappropriated Retained Earnings per Books (Line 25, Schedule L)**

1	Balance at beginning of year		5	Distributions: a Cash	
2	Net income (loss) per books			b Stock	
3	Other increases (itemize): ____			c Property . . .	
			6	Other decreases (itemize):____	
			7	Add lines 5 and 6	
4	Add lines 1, 2, and 3		8	Balance at end of year (line 4 less line 7)	

- **M-3 Reconciliation of Financial Accounting Income With Taxable Income**

  For corporations with total assets of $10 million or more, this schedule is prepared in lieu of Schedule M-1 and is, in essence, simply a more detailed form of that schedule. Unlike Schedule M-1, the Schedule M-3 income and expense differences are separately reported as *temporary or permanent differences*. Schedule M-3 also reconciles worldwide consolidated net income (loss) per the income statement to the net income (loss) per income statement of includible corporations. Income/Loss reconciliation Items are shown as single line items.

Lecture 2.10

CLASS QUESTIONS

Please see the Class Questions and Class Solutions for this Lecture at the end of this Section.

Lecture 2.11

CORPORATE DISTRIBUTIONS

Is the distribution taxable, or is it a return of capital? Distributions made by the corporation to its shareholders generally are taxable as dividends to the extent of Earnings & Profits (E&P), and remaining dividends reduce the investor's basis in their shares.

- More specifically, dividends are treated as dividend income up to the greater of:
  - Current earnings & profits (CEP), or
  - The Sum of Current & Accumulated E&P before distribution.
    - **Current Earnings & Profits (CEP)** – Similar to current year Net Income (NI).

- **Accumulated E&P (AEP)** – The sum of all previous years' E&P, similar to retained earnings (RE) at the beginning of the year.

Note: Calculation of CEP/AEP is no longer testable on the CPA Exam. If CEP or AEP is relevant to a problem (e.g., a problem where the candidate must determine the taxability of corporate distributions), the CEP and/or AEP will simply be provided.

Current E&P – (NI)	+	-	+	-
Accumulated E&P – (RE)	-	+	+	-
Dividend (Taxable portion)	+	NET	++	0

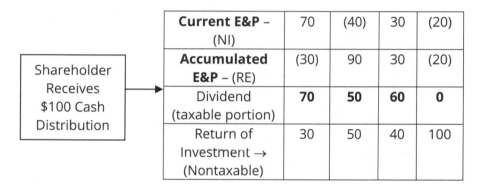

Current E&P – (NI)	70	(40)	30	(20)
Accumulated E&P – (RE)	(30)	90	30	(20)
Dividend (taxable portion)	**70**	**50**	**60**	**0**
Return of Investment → (Nontaxable)	30	50	40	100

Shareholder Receives $100 Cash Distribution

- In each case, the taxable dividend represents the higher of current E&P or total E&P. When both are negative, as in the last example, none of the distribution is treated as a taxable dividend.
- If total distributions during the year exceed current earnings and profits (CEP), the corporation's CEP must be prorated proportionately to each distribution. The ratio would be CEP/total distributions and would be applied to each distribution received throughout the year.

- **Property Distributions** as Dividend
  - Appreciated property dividends result in gain on sale.
  - Losses not deductible except in liquidation of company.
  - No gain or loss when subsidiary liquidates into parent.

  $ 100 FMV
  $ – 75 Basis
  $ 25 Gain → Increase E&P and usually already included in current E&P

Stock Redemptions

Redemptions (repurchase of shares from a shareholder) are treated as exchanges, generally resulting in capital gain or loss treatment to the shareholder if at least *one* of the following tests is met (constructive stock ownership rules generally apply in each case):
- Redemption is not essentially equivalent to a dividend;
- Redemption is substantially disproportionate (i.e., after redemption, shareholder owns less than 50% voting stock and is reduced to less than 80% of previous ownership in voting stock and total FMV of stock);

- All of the shareholder's stock is redeemed;
- Redemption is from a non-corporate shareholder in a partial liquidation; or
- Distribution is a redemption of stock to pay death taxes under Sec. 303.

Terminating the Corporation

Corporation discontinues operations and distributes all its assets—i.e., Liquidating distribution.
- Corporation recognizes BOTH gains and losses—usually ordinary (capital if related to the distribution of investments in stock).
- Shareholder's get capital gain/loss (proceeds – basis = gain/loss).

		Non-Liquidating (dividend/return of capital)	Liquidating (treated as sale/exchange for stock)
Corporation		Taxed on Gain (Capital Gain)	Ordinary Gain (capital if stock)
		Cannot deduct Loss	Ordinary Loss (as if sold)
Shareholder		Ordinary/Dividend Income (Up to E&P)	Capital Gain
			Capital Loss

When a corporation **distributes property to a shareholder** (sometimes referred to as a dividend-in-kind), it is recognized by the individual shareholder at the fair market value (FMV) of the property received. The distributing corporation also must **recognize a gain** as if the property had been sold if the FMV of the property exceeded its tax basis on the date of declaration. If the FMV of the property is lower than the tax basis, the corporation is not allowed a loss deduction (unless the distribution is in connection with a complete liquidation of the business).

For example, assume a corporation is carrying land with a tax basis of $100 and FMV of $500, and distributes it to its sole shareholder as a dividend-in-kind. The shareholder will report the distribution at $500, and the corporation will report a gain on sale of land of $400.

Keep in mind that the shareholder's tax treatment of the distribution depends on the same earnings and profits rules applicable to cash distributions, and that the gain (if any) on the property distribution is included in the determination of current earnings and profits.

If an asset is **subject to a liability**, and the corporation distributes the liability to the shareholder along with the asset, the liability reduces the amount of the distribution. Furthermore, if the basis of the liability exceeds the FMV of the asset, the corporation must report a gain on the excess in addition to the gain on sale discussed earlier.

For example, a corporation has land with a tax basis of $100 and a FMV of $500, and an outstanding note payable secured by the land of $200. If the land is distributed and the shareholder assumes the note, the shareholder reports a distribution of $500 - $200 = $300, and the corporation reports a gain of $400 as if the land had been sold.

If the facts are the same, except that the note payable assumed by the shareholder is for $800 instead of $200, then the corporation has been relieved of a liability of $800 that exceeds the FMV of the land of $500, and the excess of $300 is an additional gain to the corporation. It reports a total gain from the distribution of $700, including the $400 for the excess of the FMV of the asset over the tax basis and $300 for the excess of the liability over the FMV of the asset. The total gain of $700 can also be computed directly as the excess of the liability ($800) over the tax basis of the asset ($100); that is, IRC Sec. 336 treats the excess liability as the true FMV of the asset.

When a corporation distributes all of its assets and liabilities in a **complete liquidation** of the corporation, it reports gains *and* losses in full as if all of the assets had been sold, and may deduct all expenses associated with the corporation.

The only exception is if the assets and liabilities are being transferred pursuant to a corporate **reorganization**, in which case, all the assets and liabilities retain their tax bases in the new corporation.

When a non-corporate shareholder receives a distribution in exchange for their stock in a partial or total liquidation of the corporation, this is treated as a sale of the stock, and the gain or loss on redemption is reported as a capital gain or loss.

Exception to liquidating distribution
- When subsidiary is liquidated into the parent:
    - Tax-free reorganization
    - No gain/loss for either parent or subsidiary
    - Carryover basis

Corporate Reorganizations

Two corporations join together to form one corporation.
- **Mergers & acquisitions**
    - Stock for stock and must end up with control.
    - New shares at Carryover basis of old shares.
    - No gain or loss except to extent that cash/boot is received.
    - Reorganizations generally receive non-recognition treatment under IRC Sec. 368.

- **Types of Reorganizations**
    - Type A: mergers or consolidations
    - Type B: Use of voting stock of the acquiring corporation to acquire at least 80% of the voting power and 80% of each class of nonvoting stock of the target corporation
    - Type C: Use of voting stock to acquire substantially all of the target's net assets
    - Type D: Transfer of assets by an acquiring corporation to acquire controlling interest in a target corporation
    - Type E: Recapitalization to change the capital structure of a single corporation
    - Type F: Mere change of identity, form, or state of incorporation
    - Type G: Transfer of assets of an insolvent corporation, including as part of bankruptcy proceedings, to former creditors

Consolidated Returns

An affiliated group of corporations may elect to file a consolidated tax return instead of filing separately. An affiliated group is one or more chains of includible corporations connected through stock ownership, with a common parent corporation owning at least 80% of the voting power and total value of stock in at least one other includible corporation. C corps and S corps may not consolidate together.

- If one corporation has control (80%+), consolidated returns may be prepared. Need to eliminate intercompany profits, interest and dividends.

Section 1244 Stock

Since most startups fail, Section 1244 of the tax code allows losses from the sale of small, domestic corporation stock that was sold directly to individual shareholders, to be deducted as ordinary losses up to $50,000 (MFJ $100,000), as opposed to treating the loss as a capital loss. The remaining loss will be treated as a capital loss subject to the $3,000 per year limit. If a gain is realized, that gain would be taxed as a Capital gain. To qualify, the aggregate capital must not exceed $1 million when the stock was issued, and the corporation must not derive more than 50% of its income from passive investments.

- If appreciates, gain is considered a Capital Gain (Schedule D).
- If value declines, loss is considered an Ordinary Loss (Form 4797, L/T business property).
- Up to $50,000 ordinary loss ($100,000 MFJ), rest is a capital loss.
- Only applies to the first $1 million of stock.
- Must be sold by original purchaser.
- To qualify under Sec. 1244, the stock must be issued by a domestic (U.S.) corporation to an individual or partnership in exchange for money or property (other than stock or securities), and not for services. In addition, for the 5 most recent tax years ending before the date of the loss, the entity earned less than 50% of its revenues from royalties, rents, dividends, interest, annuities, and sales or exchanges of stocks and securities. Any type of stock can qualify, whether common or preferred; voting or nonvoting.

Section 1202 Stock

A similar provision, which was made permanent by the 2015 PATH Act, is Section 1202 Qualified Small Business Stock (QSBS). If certain requirements are met, gain on the sale of Section 1202 stock acquired after September 27, 2010, and held for more than 5 years, is 100% excludable from income, up to $10 million ($5 million if MFS) or, if greater, 10 times the total basis of such stock sold during the year. This exclusion also applies for purposes of AMT, and the gain is not subject to the 3.8% surtax on unearned income either.

- If acquired prior to February 18, 2009 – 50% exclusion
- If acquired after February 17, 2009, and before September 28, 2010 – 75% exclusion

Lecture 2.12

CLASS QUESTIONS

Please see the Class Questions and Class Solutions for this Lecture at the end of this Section.

Lecture 2.13

ALTERNATIVE MINIMUM TAX (AMT)

Caution: At the time of this writing, President Trump had introduced his broad plan for tax reform, which included repealing the Alternative Minimum Tax (AMT). Please refer to the Course Textbook Updates section of the Roger CPA Review website for legislation updates: https://www.rogercpareview.com/dashboard/my-courses/course-textbook-updates.

Once the regular tax is calculated, the corporation must then determine if it is subject to the **Alternative Minimum Tax (AMT)**. This tax may apply if the corporation benefits from certain items that have preferential tax treatment in determining regular taxable income. It requires the calculation of **Alternative Minimum Taxable Income (AMTI)**, which differs from regular taxable income in its handling of these items.

Corporate AMT

Regular taxable income
<u>+/- **Adjustments and preferences**</u>
= AMTI before ACE adjustment
<u>+/- Adjusted Current Earnings (**ACE**) adjustment</u>
= AMTI before exemption
<u>- Exemption</u>
= **AMTI**
<u>× Tax rate (20%)</u>
= Tentative minimum tax
<u>- Regular tax</u>
= **AMT**

The **adjustments and preferences** for a corporation include: (**PILE**)

- Interest income on certain forms of municipal bonds known as **Private activity bonds,** however, if the bonds were issued in 2009 or 2010, they are not a tax preference. Private activity bonds are used to finance nongovernmental activities, such as industrial development, student loans, and low-income housing.
- The difference between accrual accounting and the installment method for **Installment sales of inventory** when the installment method was used for regular tax purposes.
- **Long-term contract income** must be calculated using the *percentage-of-completion* method.
- **Excess depreciation on personal property** over 150% declining balance when double-declining balance was used for regular tax purposes.

To compute the **ACE (adjusted current earnings)** adjustment, the corporation begins with AMTI before the ACE adjustment, then adds certain items, including: (**SLIM**)

- **S**eventy-percent dividends-received deduction on dividends from unrelated corporations (80% and 100% DRDs do not have to be added back).
- **L**ife **I**nsurance proceeds on the death of a key employee.
- **M**unicipal bond interest from all such bonds (except private activity bonds, which were already included in AMTI before the ACE adjustment).

ACE is compared to the AMTI before the ACE adjustment, and the difference is then multiplied by 75% to determine the ACE adjustment. In effect, the actual adjustment is equal to **75%** of each of the items included in the determination of ACE.

The ACE adjustment may be a negative amount. A negative ACE adjustment may reduce AMTI to the extent that the cumulative increases to AMTI in prior years due to ACE adjustments exceeds decreases in AMTI in prior years due to ACE adjustments. In other words, the cumulative amount cannot be a negative amount.

For example, assume a corporation has regular taxable income of $500,000, and the only items it has that are relevant to the computation of AMTI are interest on general obligation municipal

---

bonds of $100,000 and interest on private activity municipal bonds of $200,000. To determine AMTI, the following calculation is made:

Regular taxable income	500,000
Private activity bond interest	200,000
AMTI before ACE adjustment	700,000
Other municipal bond interest (75%)	75,000
AMTI	775,000

In order to minimize the impact of the AMT on corporations with relatively low amounts of income, an exemption of up to $40,000 may be claimed against the AMTI. This exemption is reduced, however, by 25% of the amount by which the AMTI before exemption exceeds $150,000. Once AMTI exceeds $310,000, no exemption is available. Summarizing it as an equation:

Exemption = $40,000 – 25% (AMTI before exemption – $150,000)

Let's look at a few examples:

AMTI before exemption	100,000	200,000	300,000	400,000
Exemption	40,000	27,500	2,500	0
Taxable AMTI	60,000	172,500	297,500	400,000

In the first example, with AMTI below $150,000, the full exemption is available. In the second and third examples, it is reduced. In the final example, with AMTI above $310,000, no exemption is available.

The tax rates for computation of the tentative minimum tax based on AMTI appear to be beyond the scope of exam testing. When the tentative minimum tax exceeds the regular tax, the excess is the alternative minimum tax and is owed in addition to the regular tax. If the tentative minimum tax is less than the regular tax, there is no AMT for that year.

A corporation is exempt from the corporate AMT for its first tax year, regardless of income. It will also be exempt in the second year if its first year's gross receipts do not exceed $5 million.

Lecture 2.14

CLASS QUESTIONS

Please see the Class Questions and Class Solutions for this Lecture at the end of this Section.

Lecture 2.15

CLASS QUESTIONS

Please see the Class Questions and Class Solutions for this Lecture at the end of this Section.

Note: The 2016 forms are provided since 2017 forms were unavailable at the time of publication.

Form 1120

Department of the Treasury
Internal Revenue Service

U.S. Corporation Income Tax Return

For calendar year 2016 or tax year beginning _____, 2016, ending _____, 20 _____

▶ Information about Form 1120 and its separate instructions is at *www.irs.gov/form1120.*

OMB No. 1545-0123

2016

A Check if:				
1a Consolidated return (attach Form 851) ☐		**TYPE OR PRINT**	Name	**B Employer identification number**
b Life/nonlife consolidated return ☐			Number, street, and room or suite no. If a P.O. box, see instructions.	**C Date incorporated**
2 Personal holding co. (attach Sch. PH) ☐				
3 Personal service corp. (see instructions) ☐			City or town, state, or province, country, and ZIP or foreign postal code	**D Total assets (see instructions)** $
4 Schedule M-3 attached ☐				

E Check if: (1) ☐ Initial return　(2) ☐ Final return　(3) ☐ Name change　(4) ☐ Address change

Income					
	1a	Gross receipts or sales	1a		
	b	Returns and allowances	1b		
	c	Balance. Subtract line 1b from line 1a		1c	
	2	Cost of goods sold (attach Form 1125-A)		2	
	3	Gross profit. Subtract line 2 from line 1c		3	
	4	Dividends (Schedule C, line 19)		4	
	5	Interest		5	
	6	Gross rents		6	
	7	Gross royalties		7	
	8	Capital gain net income (attach Schedule D (Form 1120))		8	
	9	Net gain or (loss) from Form 4797, Part II, line 17 (attach Form 4797)		9	
	10	Other income (see instructions—attach statement)		10	
	11	**Total income.** Add lines 3 through 10 . . . . ▶		11	

Deductions (See instructions for limitations on deductions.)					
	12	Compensation of officers (see instructions—attach Form 1125-E) . . . . . ▶		12	
	13	Salaries and wages (less employment credits)		13	
	14	Repairs and maintenance		14	
	15	Bad debts		15	
	16	Rents		16	
	17	Taxes and licenses		17	
	18	Interest		18	
	19	Charitable contributions		19	
	20	Depreciation from Form 4562 not claimed on Form 1125-A or elsewhere on return (attach Form 4562) .		20	
	21	Depletion		21	
	22	Advertising		22	
	23	Pension, profit-sharing, etc., plans		23	
	24	Employee benefit programs		24	
	25	Domestic production activities deduction (attach Form 8903)		25	
	26	Other deductions (attach statement)		26	
	27	**Total deductions.** Add lines 12 through 26 . . . . ▶		27	
	28	Taxable income before net operating loss deduction and special deductions. Subtract line 27 from line 11.		28	
	29a	Net operating loss deduction (see instructions)	29a		
	b	Special deductions (Schedule C, line 20)	29b		
	c	Add lines 29a and 29b		29c	

Tax, Refundable Credits, and Payments					
	30	**Taxable income.** Subtract line 29c from line 28. See instructions		30	
	31	Total tax (Schedule J, Part I, line 11)		31	
	32	Total payments and refundable credits (Schedule J, Part II, line 21)		32	
	33	Estimated tax penalty. See instructions. Check if Form 2220 is attached . . . . ▶ ☐		33	
	34	**Amount owed.** If line 32 is smaller than the total of lines 31 and 33, enter amount owed		34	
	35	**Overpayment.** If line 32 is larger than the total of lines 31 and 33, enter amount overpaid		35	
	36	Enter amount from line 35 you want: **Credited to 2017 estimated tax** ▶ _____ Refunded ▶		36	

Sign Here

Under penalties of perjury, I declare that I have examined this return, including accompanying schedules and statements, and to the best of my knowledge and belief, it is true, correct, and complete. Declaration of preparer (other than taxpayer) is based on all information of which preparer has any knowledge.

▶ _____　_____　▶ _____
Signature of officer　Date　Title

May the IRS discuss this return with the preparer shown below? See instructions. ☐ Yes ☐ No

Paid Preparer Use Only

Print/Type preparer's name	Preparer's signature	Date	Check ☐ if self-employed	PTIN
Firm's name ▶			Firm's EIN ▶	
Firm's address ▶			Phone no.	

For Paperwork Reduction Act Notice, see separate instructions.　　Cat. No. 11450Q　　Form **1120** (2016)

Form 1120 (2016)   Page **2**

Schedule C	Dividends and Special Deductions (see instructions)	(a) Dividends received	(b) %	(c) Special deductions (a) × (b)
1	Dividends from less-than-20%-owned domestic corporations (other than debt-financed stock)		70	
2	Dividends from 20%-or-more-owned domestic corporations (other than debt-financed stock)		80	
3	Dividends on debt-financed stock of domestic and foreign corporations		see instructions	
4	Dividends on certain preferred stock of less-than-20%-owned public utilities . . .		42	
5	Dividends on certain preferred stock of 20%-or-more-owned public utilities		48	
6	Dividends from less-than-20%-owned foreign corporations and certain FSCs . . .		70	
7	Dividends from 20%-or-more-owned foreign corporations and certain FSCs . . .		80	
8	Dividends from wholly owned foreign subsidiaries		100	
9	**Total.** Add lines 1 through 8. See instructions for limitation			
10	Dividends from domestic corporations received by a small business investment company operating under the Small Business Investment Act of 1958		100	
11	Dividends from affiliated group members		100	
12	Dividends from certain FSCs		100	
13	Dividends from foreign corporations not included on line 3, 6, 7, 8, 11, or 12 . . .			
14	Income from controlled foreign corporations under subpart F (attach Form(s) 5471) .			
15	Foreign dividend gross-up			
16	IC-DISC and former DISC dividends not included on line 1, 2, or 3			
17	Other dividends			
18	Deduction for dividends paid on certain preferred stock of public utilities			
19	**Total dividends.** Add lines 1 through 17. Enter here and on page 1, line 4 . . . ▶			
20	**Total special deductions.** Add lines 9, 10, 11, 12, and 18. Enter here and on page 1, line 29b . . . . ▶			

Form **1120** (2016)

Form 1120 (2016)

Page **3**

| Schedule J | Tax Computation and Payment (see instructions) |

Part I–Tax Computation

1	Check if the corporation is a member of a controlled group (attach Schedule O (Form 1120)). See instructions ▶ ☐			
2	Income tax. Check if a qualified personal service corporation. See instructions . . . . ▶ ☐	2		
3	Alternative minimum tax (attach Form 4626)	3		
4	Add lines 2 and 3	4		
5a	Foreign tax credit (attach Form 1118)	5a		
b	Credit from Form 8834 (see instructions)	5b		
c	General business credit (attach Form 3800)	5c		
d	Credit for prior year minimum tax (attach Form 8827) . . .	5d		
e	Bond credits from Form 8912	5e		
6	**Total credits.** Add lines 5a through 5e	6		
7	Subtract line 6 from line 4	7		
8	Personal holding company tax (attach Schedule PH (Form 1120))	8		
9a	Recapture of investment credit (attach Form 4255)	9a		
b	Recapture of low-income housing credit (attach Form 8611)	9b		
c	Interest due under the look-back method—completed long-term contracts (attach Form 8697)	9c		
d	Interest due under the look-back method—income forecast method (attach Form 8866) . . .	9d		
e	Alternative tax on qualifying shipping activities (attach Form 8902)	9e		
f	Other (see instructions—attach statement)	9f		
10	**Total.** Add lines 9a through 9f	10		
11	**Total tax.** Add lines 7, 8, and 10. Enter here and on page 1, line 31	11		

Part II–Payments and Refundable Credits

12	2015 overpayment credited to 2016	12		
13	2016 estimated tax payments	13		
14	2016 refund applied for on Form 4466	14	(	)
15	Combine lines 12, 13, and 14	15		
16	Tax deposited with Form 7004	16		
17	Withholding (see instructions)	17		
18	**Total payments.** Add lines 15, 16, and 17	18		
19	Refundable credits from:			
a	Form 2439	19a		
b	Form 4136	19b		
c	Form 8827, line 8c	19c		
d	Other (attach statement—see instructions). . . .	19d		
20	**Total credits.** Add lines 19a through 19d	20		
21	**Total payments and credits.** Add lines 18 and 20. Enter here and on page 1, line 32 . . .	21		

Schedule K	Other Information (see instructions)		Yes	No
1	Check accounting method: **a** ☐ Cash **b** ☐ Accrual **c** ☐ Other (specify) ▶ _____			
2	See the instructions and enter the:			
a	Business activity code no. ▶ _____			
b	Business activity ▶ _____			
c	Product or service ▶ _____			
3	Is the corporation a subsidiary in an affiliated group or a parent-subsidiary controlled group?			
	If "Yes," enter name and EIN of the parent corporation ▶ _____			
4	At the end of the tax year:			
a	Did any foreign or domestic corporation, partnership (including any entity treated as a partnership), trust, or tax-exempt organization own directly 20% or more, or own, directly or indirectly, 50% or more of the total voting power of all classes of the corporation's stock entitled to vote? If "Yes," complete Part I of Schedule G (Form 1120) (attach Schedule G)			
b	Did any individual or estate own directly 20% or more, or own, directly or indirectly, 50% or more of the total voting power of all classes of the corporation's stock entitled to vote? If "Yes," complete Part II of Schedule G (Form 1120) (attach Schedule G) .			

Form **1120** (2016)

Form 1120 (2016)   Page **4**

Schedule K	Other Information *(continued from page 3)*			Yes	No

5 At the end of the tax year, did the corporation:

  a Own directly 20% or more, or own, directly or indirectly, 50% or more of the total voting power of all classes of stock entitled to vote of any foreign or domestic corporation not included on **Form 851,** Affiliations Schedule? For rules of constructive ownership, see instructions. If "Yes," complete (i) through (iv) below.

(i) Name of Corporation	(ii) Employer Identification Number (if any)	(iii) Country of Incorporation	(iv) Percentage Owned in Voting Stock

  b Own directly an interest of 20% or more, or own, directly or indirectly, an interest of 50% or more in any foreign or domestic partnership (including an entity treated as a partnership) or in the beneficial interest of a trust? For rules of constructive ownership, see instructions. If "Yes," complete (i) through (iv) below.

(i) Name of Entity	(ii) Employer Identification Number (if any)	(iii) Country of Organization	(iv) Maximum Percentage Owned in Profit, Loss, or Capital

6 During this tax year, did the corporation pay dividends (other than stock dividends and distributions in exchange for stock) in excess of the corporation's current and accumulated earnings and profits? See sections 301 and 316 . . . .

  If "Yes," file **Form 5452,** Corporate Report of Nondividend Distributions.

  If this is a consolidated return, answer here for the parent corporation and on Form 851 for each subsidiary.

7 At any time during the tax year, did one foreign person own, directly or indirectly, at least 25% of **(a)** the total voting power of all classes of the corporation's stock entitled to vote or **(b)** the total value of all classes of the corporation's stock? . . . .

  For rules of attribution, see section 318. If "Yes," enter:

  (i) Percentage owned ▶ _____ and **(ii)** Owner's country ▶ _____

  (c) The corporation may have to file **Form 5472,** Information Return of a 25% Foreign-Owned U.S. Corporation or a Foreign Corporation Engaged in a U.S. Trade or Business. Enter the number of Forms 5472 attached ▶ _____

8 Check this box if the corporation issued publicly offered debt instruments with original issue discount . . . . ▶ ☐

  If checked, the corporation may have to file **Form 8281,** Information Return for Publicly Offered Original Issue Discount Instruments.

9 Enter the amount of tax-exempt interest received or accrued during the tax year ▶ $ _____

10 Enter the number of shareholders at the end of the tax year (if 100 or fewer) ▶ _____

11 If the corporation has an NOL for the tax year and is electing to forego the carryback period, check here . . . . . ▶ ☐

  If the corporation is filing a consolidated return, the statement required by Regulations section 1.1502-21(b)(3) must be attached or the election won't be valid.

12 Enter the available NOL carryover from prior tax years (don't reduce it by any deduction on line 29a.) ▶ $ _____

13 Are the corporation's total receipts (page 1, line 1a, plus lines 4 through 10) for the tax year **and** its total assets at the end of the tax year less than $250,000? . . . .

  If "Yes," the corporation isn't required to complete Schedules L, M-1, and M-2. Instead, enter the total amount of cash distributions and the book value of property distributions (other than cash) made during the tax year ▶ $ _____

14 Is the corporation required to file Schedule UTP (Form 1120), Uncertain Tax Position Statement? See instructions . . . .

  If "Yes," complete and attach Schedule UTP.

15a Did the corporation make any payments in 2016 that would require it to file Form(s) 1099? . . . .

  b If "Yes," did or will the corporation file required Forms 1099? . . . .

16 During this tax year, did the corporation have an 80% or more change in ownership, including a change due to redemption of its own stock? . . . .

17 During or subsequent to this tax year, but before the filing of this return, did the corporation dispose of more than 65% (by value) of its assets in a taxable, non-taxable, or tax deferred transaction? . . . .

18 Did the corporation receive assets in a section 351 transfer in which any of the transferred assets had a fair market basis or fair market value of more than $1 million? . . . .

19 During the corporation's tax year, did the corporation make any payments that would require it to file Forms 1042 and 1042-S under chapter 3 (sections 1441 through 1464) or chapter 4 (sections 1471 through 1474) of the Code? . . . .

Form **1120** (2016)

Form 1120 (2016)

Page **5**

Schedule L	Balance Sheets per Books	Beginning of tax year		End of tax year	
	Assets	(a)	(b)	(c)	(d)
1	Cash				
2a	Trade notes and accounts receivable				
b	Less allowance for bad debts	( )		( )	
3	Inventories				
4	U.S. government obligations				
5	Tax-exempt securities (see instructions)				
6	Other current assets (attach statement)				
7	Loans to shareholders				
8	Mortgage and real estate loans				
9	Other investments (attach statement)				
10a	Buildings and other depreciable assets				
b	Less accumulated depreciation	( )		( )	
11a	Depletable assets				
b	Less accumulated depletion	( )		( )	
12	Land (net of any amortization)				
13a	Intangible assets (amortizable only)				
b	Less accumulated amortization	( )		( )	
14	Other assets (attach statement)				
15	Total assets				
	Liabilities and Shareholders' Equity				
16	Accounts payable				
17	Mortgages, notes, bonds payable in less than 1 year				
18	Other current liabilities (attach statement)				
19	Loans from shareholders				
20	Mortgages, notes, bonds payable in 1 year or more				
21	Other liabilities (attach statement)				
22	Capital stock: a Preferred stock				
	b Common stock				
23	Additional paid-in capital				
24	Retained earnings—Appropriated (attach statement)				
25	Retained earnings—Unappropriated				
26	Adjustments to shareholders' equity (attach statement)				
27	Less cost of treasury stock		( )		( )
28	Total liabilities and shareholders' equity				

Schedule M-1 Reconciliation of Income (Loss) per Books With Income per Return

Note: The corporation may be required to file Schedule M-3. See instructions.

1	Net income (loss) per books		7	Income recorded on books this year not included on this return (itemize):	
2	Federal income tax per books				
3	Excess of capital losses over capital gains			Tax-exempt interest $ _____	
4	Income subject to tax not recorded on books this year (itemize): _____		8	Deductions on this return not charged against book income this year (itemize):	
	_____			a Depreciation $ _____	
5	Expenses recorded on books this year not deducted on this return (itemize):			b Charitable contributions $ _____	
a	Depreciation $ _____				
b	Charitable contributions $ _____			_____	
c	Travel and entertainment $ _____		9	Add lines 7 and 8	
	_____		10	Income (page 1, line 28)—line 6 less line 9	
6	Add lines 1 through 5				

Schedule M-2 Analysis of Unappropriated Retained Earnings per Books (Line 25, Schedule L)

1	Balance at beginning of year		5	Distributions: a Cash	
2	Net income (loss) per books			b Stock	
3	Other increases (itemize): _____			c Property	
	_____		6	Other decreases (itemize): _____	
	_____		7	Add lines 5 and 6	
4	Add lines 1, 2, and 3		8	Balance at end of year (line 4 less line 7)	

Form **1120** (2016)

SCHEDULE M-3 (Form 1120)	Net Income (Loss) Reconciliation for Corporations With Total Assets of $10 Million or More	OMB No. 1545-0123
Department of the Treasury Internal Revenue Service	▶ Attach to Form 1120 or 1120-C. ▶ Information about Schedule M-3 (Form 1120) and its separate instructions is available at *www.irs.gov/form1120*.	2016

Name of corporation (common parent, if consolidated return)	Employer identification number

Check applicable box(es):   (1) ☐ Non-consolidated return   (2) ☐ Consolidated return (Form 1120 only)

(3) ☐ Mixed 1120/L/PC group   (4) ☐ Dormant subsidiaries schedule attached

Part I   Financial Information and Net Income (Loss) Reconciliation (see instructions)

1a Did the corporation file SEC Form 10-K for its income statement period ending with or within this tax year?
  ☐ **Yes.** Skip lines 1b and 1c and complete lines 2a through 11 with respect to that SEC Form 10-K.
  ☐ **No.** Go to line 1b. See instructions if multiple non-tax-basis income statements are prepared.
 b Did the corporation prepare a certified audited non-tax-basis income statement for that period?
  ☐ **Yes.** Skip line 1c and complete lines 2a through 11 with respect to that income statement.
  ☐ **No.** Go to line 1c.
 c Did the corporation prepare a non-tax-basis income statement for that period?
  ☐ **Yes.** Complete lines 2a through 11 with respect to that income statement.
  ☐ **No.** Skip lines 2a through 3c and enter the corporation's net income (loss) per its books and records on line 4a.
2a Enter the income statement period: Beginning ___MM/DD/YYYY___ Ending ___MM/DD/YYYY___
 b Has the corporation's income statement been restated for the income statement period on line 2a?
  ☐ **Yes.** (If "Yes," attach an explanation and the amount of each item restated.)
  ☐ **No.**
 c Has the corporation's income statement been restated for any of the five income statement periods immediately preceding the period on line 2a?
  ☐ **Yes.** (If "Yes," attach an explanation and the amount of each item restated.)
  ☐ **No.**
3a Is any of the corporation's voting common stock publicly traded?
  ☐ **Yes.**
  ☐ **No.** If "No," go to line 4a.
 b Enter the symbol of the corporation's primary U.S. publicly traded voting common stock . . . .
 c Enter the nine-digit CUSIP number of the corporation's primary publicly traded voting common stock . . . .

4a	Worldwide consolidated net income (loss) from income statement source identified in Part I, line 1 .	**4a**
b	Indicate accounting standard used for line 4a (see instructions): (1) ☐ GAAP (2) ☐ IFRS (3) ☐ Statutory (4) ☐ Tax-basis (5) ☐ Other (specify) _____	
5a	Net income from nonincludible foreign entities (attach statement)	**5a** ( )
b	Net loss from nonincludible foreign entities (attach statement and enter as a positive amount) . . .	**5b**
6a	Net income from nonincludible U.S. entities (attach statement)	**6a** ( )
b	Net loss from nonincludible U.S. entities (attach statement and enter as a positive amount)	**6b**
7a	Net income (loss) of other includible foreign disregarded entities (attach statement)	**7a**
b	Net income (loss) of other includible U.S. disregarded entities (attach statement)	**7b**
c	Net income (loss) of other includible entities (attach statement)	**7c**
8	Adjustment to eliminations of transactions between includible entities and nonincludible entities (attach statement)	**8**
9	Adjustment to reconcile income statement period to tax year (attach statement)	**9**
10a	Intercompany dividend adjustments to reconcile to line 11 (attach statement)	**10a**
b	Other statutory accounting adjustments to reconcile to line 11 (attach statement)	**10b**
c	Other adjustments to reconcile to amount on line 11 (attach statement)	**10c**
11	**Net income (loss) per income statement of includible corporations.** Combine lines 4 through 10 .	**11**
	Note: Part I, line 11, must equal Part II, line 30, column (a) or Schedule M-1, line 1 (see instructions).	

12 Enter the total amount (not just the corporation's share) of the assets and liabilities of all entities included or removed on the following lines.

	Total Assets	Total Liabilities
a Included on Part I, line 4 . . . . ▶		
b Removed on Part I, line 5 . . . . ▶		
c Removed on Part I, line 6 . . . . ▶		
d Included on Part I, line 7 . . . . ▶		

For Paperwork Reduction Act Notice, see the Instructions for Form 1120.   Cat. No. 37961C   **Schedule M-3 (Form 1120) 2016**

Schedule M-3 (Form 1120) 2016   Page **2**

Name of corporation (common parent, if consolidated return)	Employer identification number

Check applicable box(es): **(1)** ☐ Consolidated group   **(2)** ☐ Parent corp   **(3)** ☐ Consolidated eliminations   **(4)** ☐ Subsidiary corp   **(5)** ☐ Mixed 1120/L/PC group

Check if a sub-consolidated: **(6)** ☐ 1120 group   **(7)** ☐ 1120 eliminations

Name of subsidiary (if consolidated return)	Employer identification number

Part II   **Reconciliation of Net Income (Loss) per Income Statement of Includible Corporations With Taxable Income per Return** (see instructions)

Income (Loss) Items (Attach statements for lines 1 through 12)	(a) Income (Loss) per Income Statement	(b) Temporary Difference	(c) Permanent Difference	(d) Income (Loss) per Tax Return
1 Income (loss) from equity method foreign corporations				
2 Gross foreign dividends not previously taxed . . .				
3 Subpart F, QEF, and similar income inclusions . .				
4 Section 78 gross-up				
5 Gross foreign distributions previously taxed . . .				
6 Income (loss) from equity method U.S. corporations				
7 U.S. dividends not eliminated in tax consolidation .				
8 Minority interest for includible corporations . . .				
9 Income (loss) from U.S. partnerships				
10 Income (loss) from foreign partnerships				
11 Income (loss) from other pass-through entities . .				
12 Items relating to reportable transactions				
13 Interest income (see instructions)				
14 Total accrual to cash adjustment				
15 Hedging transactions				
16 Mark-to-market income (loss)				
17 Cost of goods sold (see instructions)	( )			( )
18 Sale versus lease (for sellers and/or lessors) . . .				
19 Section 481(a) adjustments				
20 Unearned/deferred revenue				
21 Income recognition from long-term contracts . .				
22 Original issue discount and other imputed interest .				
23a Income statement gain/loss on sale, exchange, abandonment, worthlessness, or other disposition of assets other than inventory and pass-through entities				
b Gross capital gains from Schedule D, excluding amounts from pass-through entities				
c Gross capital losses from Schedule D, excluding amounts from pass-through entities, abandonment losses, and worthless stock losses				
d Net gain/loss reported on Form 4797, line 17, excluding amounts from pass-through entities, abandonment losses, and worthless stock losses				
e Abandonment losses				
f Worthless stock losses (attach statement)				
g Other gain/loss on disposition of assets other than inventory				
24 Capital loss limitation and carryforward used . . .				
25 Other income (loss) items with differences (attach statement)				
26 **Total income (loss) items.** Combine lines 1 through 25				
27 **Total expense/deduction items** (from Part III, line 38)				
28 Other items with no differences				
29a Mixed groups, see instructions. All others, combine lines 26 through 28				
b PC insurance subgroup reconciliation totals . . .				
c Life insurance subgroup reconciliation totals . . .				
30 **Reconciliation totals.** Combine lines 29a through 29c				

Note: Line 30, column (a), must equal Part I, line 11, and column (d) must equal Form 1120, page 1, line 28.

Schedule M-3 (Form 1120) 2016

Schedule M-3 (Form 1120) 2016   **Page 3**

Name of corporation (common parent, if consolidated return)	Employer identification number

Check applicable box(es): **(1)** ☐ Consolidated group   **(2)** ☐ Parent corp   **(3)** ☐ Consolidated eliminations   **(4)** ☐ Subsidiary corp   **(5)** ☐ Mixed 1120/L/PC group

Check if a sub-consolidated: **(6)** ☐ 1120 group   **(7)** ☐ 1120 eliminations

Name of subsidiary (if consolidated return)	Employer identification number

Part III   **Reconciliation of Net Income (Loss) per Income Statement of Includible Corporations With Taxable Income per Return—Expense/Deduction Items** (see instructions)

Expense/Deduction Items	(a) Expense per Income Statement	(b) Temporary Difference	(c) Permanent Difference	(d) Deduction per Tax Return
1 U.S. current income tax expense				▓
2 U.S. deferred income tax expense				▓
3 State and local current income tax expense				
4 State and local deferred income tax expense				▓
5 Foreign current income tax expense (other than foreign withholding taxes)				
6 Foreign deferred income tax expense				▓
7 Foreign withholding taxes				
8 Interest expense (see instructions)				
9 Stock option expense				
10 Other equity-based compensation				
11 Meals and entertainment				
12 Fines and penalties				
13 Judgments, damages, awards, and similar costs				
14 Parachute payments				
15 Compensation with section 162(m) limitation				
16 Pension and profit-sharing				
17 Other post-retirement benefits				
18 Deferred compensation				
19 Charitable contribution of cash and tangible property				
20 Charitable contribution of intangible property				
21 Charitable contribution limitation/carryforward	▓			
22 Domestic production activities deduction	▓			
23 Current year acquisition or reorganization investment banking fees				
24 Current year acquisition or reorganization legal and accounting fees				
25 Current year acquisition/reorganization other costs				
26 Amortization/impairment of goodwill				
27 Amortization of acquisition, reorganization, and start-up costs				
28 Other amortization or impairment write-offs				
29 Reserved	▓	▓	▓	▓
30 Depletion				
31 Depreciation				
32 Bad debt expense				
33 Corporate owned life insurance premiums				
34 Purchase versus lease (for purchasers and/or lessees)				
35 Research and development costs				
36 Section 118 exclusion (attach statement)				
37 Other expense/deduction items with differences (attach statement)				
38 **Total expense/deduction items.** Combine lines 1 through 37. Enter here and on Part II, line 27, reporting positive amounts as negative and negative amounts as positive				

Schedule M-3 (Form 1120) 2016

CLASS QUESTIONS

Work through the below Class Questions while following along with the respective lectures. Once this is complete, you can begin independently practicing what you've learned by quizzing yourself on this course section in your Interactive Practice Questions (IPQ), which can be found in your online Student Dashboard. Your IPQ simulates the computer-based testing experience, and will also help you understand how concepts are applied to the exam. Each question includes answer explanations from expert CPAs that will help you determine why you answered a question correctly or incorrectly. This is key to your success on the CPA Exam.

Lecture 2.03

1. Feld, the sole stockholder of Maki Corp., paid $50,000 for Maki's stock in 20X1. In 20X8, Feld contributed a parcel of land to Maki but was not given any additional stock for this contribution. Feld's basis for the land was $10,000, and its fair market value was $18,000 on the date of the transfer of title. What is Feld's adjusted basis for the Maki stock?

    a. $50,000
    b. $52,000
    c. $60,000
    d. $68,000

2. Adams, Beck, and Carr organized Flexo Corp. with authorized voting common stock of $100,000. Adams received 10% of the capital stock in payment for the organizational services that he rendered for the benefit of the newly-formed corporation. Adams did not contribute property to Flexo and was under no obligation to be paid by Beck or Carr. Beck and Carr transferred property in exchange for stock as follows:

	Adjusted Basis	Fair Market value	Percentage of Flexo stock acquired
Beck	$ 5,000	$20,000	20%
Carr	60,000	70,000	70%

    What amount of gain did Carr recognize from this transaction?

    a. $40,000
    b. $15,000
    c. $10,000
    d. $0

Lecture 2.06

3. Tapper Corp., an accrual-basis calendar-year corporation, was organized on January 2, 20X3. During 20X3, revenue was exclusively from sales proceeds and interest income. The following information pertains to Tapper:

Taxable income before charitable contributions for the year ended December 31, 20X3	$ 500,000
Tapper's matching contribution to employee designated qualified universities made during 20X3	10,000
Board of Directors' authorized contribution to a qualified charity (authorized December 1, 20X3, made February 1, 20X4)	30,000

What is the maximum allowable deduction that Tapper may take as a charitable contribution on its tax return for the year ended December 31, 20X3?

    a. $0
    b. $10,000
    c. $30,000
    d. $40,000

4.   In 20X3, Cable Corp., a calendar-year C corporation, contributed $80,000 to a qualified charitable organization. Cable's 20X3 taxable income before the deduction for charitable contributions was $820,000 after a $40,000 dividends received deduction. Cable also had carryover contributions of $10,000 from the prior year. In 20X3, what amount can Cable deduct as charitable contributions?

    a. $90,000
    b. $86,000
    c. $82,000
    d. $80,000

5.   A C corporation's net capital losses are

    a.   Carried forward indefinitely until fully utilized.
    b.   Carried back three years and forward five years.
    c.   Deductible in full from the corporation's ordinary income.
    d.   Deductible from the corporation's ordinary income only to the extent of $3,000.

6.   When a corporation has an unused net capital loss that is carried back or carried forward to another tax year,

    a.   It retains its original identity as short-term or long-term.
    b.   It is treated as a short-term capital loss whether or not it was short-term when sustained.
    c.   It is treated as a long-term capital loss whether or not it was long-term when sustained.
    d.   It can be used to offset ordinary income up to the amount of the carryback or carryover.

Lecture 2.08

7.   Edge Corp. met the stock ownership requirements of a personal holding company. What sources of income must Edge consider to determine if the income requirements for a personal holding company have been met?

    I.   Interest earned on tax-exempt obligations.
    II.   Dividends received from an unrelated domestic corporation.

    a.   I only.
    b.   II only.
    c.   Both I and II.
    d.   Neither I nor II.

8. Kari Corp., a manufacturing company, was organized on January 2, 20X3. Its 20X3 federal taxable income was $400,000 and its federal income tax was $100,000. What is the maximum amount of accumulated taxable income that may be subject to the accumulated earnings tax for 20X3 if Kari takes only the minimum accumulated earnings credit?

    a. $300,000
    b. $150,000
    c. $50,000
    d. $0

9. The following information pertains to Hull, Inc., a personal holding company, for the year ended December 31, 20X3:

Undistributed personal holding company income	$100,000
Dividends paid during 20X3	20,000
Consent dividends reported in the 20X3 individual income tax returns of the holders of Hull's common stock, but **not** paid by Hull to its stockholders	10,000

    In computing its 20X3 personal holding company tax, what amount should Hull deduct for dividends paid?

    a. $0
    b. $10,000
    c. $20,000
    d. $30,000

Lecture 2.10

10. For its taxable year 20X6, Asher Corp. had net income per books of $80,000, which included municipal bond interest of $5,000, dividend income of $10,000, a deduction for a net capital loss of $6,000, a deduction for business meals of $4,000, and a deduction for federal income taxes of $18,000. What is the amount of income that would be shown on the last line of Schedule M-1 (Reconciliation of Income [Loss] Per Books with Income [Loss] Per Return) of Asher Corp.'s corporate income tax return for 20X6?

    a. $90,000
    b. $93,000
    c. $99,000
    d. $101,000

Lecture 2.12

11. Dahl Corp. was organized and commenced operations in 20X1. At December 31, 20X6, Dahl had accumulated earnings and profits of $9,000 before dividend declaration and distribution. On December 31, 20X6, Dahl distributed cash of $9,000 and a vacant parcel of land to Green, Dahl's only stockholder. At the date of distribution, the land had a basis of $5,000 and a fair market value of $40,000. What was Green's taxable dividend income in 20X6 from these distributions?

    a. $9,000
    b. $14,000
    c. $44,000
    d. $49,000

12. On January 1, 20X9, Kee Corp., a C corporation, had a $50,000 deficit in earnings and profits. For 20X9, Kee had current earnings and profits of $10,000 and made a $30,000 cash distribution to its stockholders. What amount of the distribution is taxable as dividend income to Kee's stockholders?

    a. $30,000
    b. $20,000
    c. $10,000
    d. $0

CLASS SOLUTIONS

1. (c) When a shareholder contributes appreciated property to a corporation without receiving additional stock, the transfer is nontaxable. The shareholder will increase the tax basis in the stock by the tax basis of the transferred property, which will also become the corporation's tax basis in the property. Thus, Feld will not recognize a gain on the transfer of the land but will increase the tax basis in Maki's stock from $50,000 to $60,000 by adding the $10,000 tax basis in the land transferred.

2. (d) When shareholders contribute cash or property to a corporation in exchange for stock and control at least 80% of the stock immediately thereafter, the transaction is a nontaxable exchange. The shareholder's basis in the stock will be cash paid plus the tax basis of property transferred. Since Beck and Carr transferred property to Flexo in exchange for a combined 90% ownership, the transfers would be nontaxable and neither would recognize a gain.

3. (d) The requirement is to determine the **maximum** charitable contribution deduction that Tapper Corp. may take on its 20X3 return. Since Tapper is an accrual method calendar-year corporation, it can deduct contributions actually made during 20X3, plus Tapper can elect to deduct any contribution authorized by its board of directors during 20X3, so long as the contribution is subsequently made no later than 3 1/2 months after the end of the tax year. Thus, to maximize its deduction for 20X3, Tapper can deduct both the $10,000 contribution made during 20X3 as well as the $30,000 contribution authorized during 20X3 and paid on February 1, 20X4. The total ($40,000) is deductible for 20X3, since it is less than the limitation amount ($500,000 × 10% = $50,000).

4. (b) A corporation may deduct charitable contributions in an amount up to 10% of its taxable income before deducting charitable contributions and special deductions. Cable had $820,000 of taxable income before charitable contributions but after deducting the special dividends received deduction of $40,000. As a result, Cable may deduct up to 10% × $860,000, or $86,000. The $80,000 contributed during the current year would qualify as would the $10,000 carryforward. Cable will therefore deduct the maximum allowable $86,000 and carryforward the remaining $4,000.

5. (b) A corporation may not deduct capital losses but may offset them against capital gains. Capital losses in excess of capital gains are carried back 3 years and offset against capital gains that had been taxed 3 periods earlier, then 2 periods earlier, then the previous period. Any remainder is carried forward for up to 5 years.

6. (b) Net capital losses that are carried back or forward by a corporation to offset against capital gains in those periods are always considered short-term capital losses, regardless of their nature at the time they were incurred.

7. (b) A personal holding company is one that derives at least 60% of its revenue from passive sources that include taxable interest, dividends, rentals, and royalty income. Thus, Edge would consider dividends earned from an unrelated domestic corporation but not tax-exempt interest.

8. (c) The minimum accumulated earnings credit is a reasonable amount for working capital ($250,000 for a manufacturing company), plus an amount to cover its income taxes ($100,000 for Kari). As a result, Kari's minimum accumulated earnings credit would be $350,000 and Kari would have $50,000 in income potentially subject to the accumulated earnings tax.

9. (d) To avoid personal holding company tax, a company may either pay dividends or issue consent dividends. Consent dividends do not involve an actual distribution to shareholders, but the shareholders include the amounts on their tax returns as if the dividends had been distributed. Hull would be able to reduce personal holding company income by the $20,000 in dividends paid and the $10,000 in consent dividends, for a total of $30,000.

10. (d) Schedule M-1 reconciles book income to taxable income before taking the dividends received deduction. Book income of $80,000 would be reduced by $5,000 of municipal bond interest, which is not taxable. It will be increased by the $6,000 capital loss, which is not deductible but will be carried back or forward to offset against capital gains. It will also be increased by ½ of the $4,000 meals and entertainment expense, or $2,000, which is not deductible, and $18,000 in federal income taxes, which are also not deductible. The resulting amount is $80,000 – $5,000 + $6,000 + $2,000 + $18,000 = $101,000.

11. (c) Green would recognize taxable dividend income in an amount equal to Dahl's accumulated earnings and profits. Dahl had accumulated earnings and profits of $9,000, which was distributed in cash. Dahl also distributed land with a tax basis of $5,000 and a fair value of $40,000 to Green, which would result in a gain on the disposal of $35,000, increasing Dahl's accumulated earnings and profits. As a result, $35,000 of the distribution of land with a fair value of $40,000 would also be taxable dividend income, and the remaining $5,000 of the distribution would decrease Green's basis in Dahl's stock. The total taxable dividends to Green would be $9,000 + $35,000, or $44,000.

12. (c) When a corporation makes a distribution to shareholders, it is taxable as dividend income to the shareholders to the extent of the corporation's earnings and profits. The amount that is taxable will be the current period's earnings and profits plus accumulated earnings and profits, if any. When the accumulated amount is a loss, a distribution up to the current period's earnings and profits is still taxable—$10,000 in this case.

Lecture 2.14

TASK-BASED SIMULATIONS

Task-Based Simulation 1

 The Uniform
CPA Examination

 Unsplit   Split Horiz   Split Vertical   Authoritative Literature   Spreadsheet   Calculator   Submit Testlet

Work Tab | **Resources** | **Help**

Required:

Situation

Kimberly Corp. is a calendar-year accrual-basis corporation that commenced operations on January 1, 20X1. The following adjusted accounts appear on Kimberly's records for the year ended December 31, 20X3. Kimberly is not subject to the uniform capitalization rules.

Revenues and gains	
Gross sales	$2,000,000
Dividends:	
30%-owned domestic corporation	10,000
XYZ Corp.	10,000
Interest:	
U.S. treasury bonds	26,000
Municipal bonds	25,000
Insurance proceeds	40,000
Gain on sale:	
Unimproved lot (1)	20,000
XYZ stock (2)	5,000
State franchise tax refund	14,000
Total	2,150,000

Costs and expenses	
Cost of goods sold	350,000
Salaries and wages	470,000
Depreciation:	
Real property	50,000
Personal property (3)	100,000
Bad debt (4)	10,000
State franchise tax	25,000
Vacation expense	10,000
Interest expense (5)	16,000
Life insurance premiums	20,000
Federal income taxes	200,000
Entertainment expense	20,000
Other expenses	29,000
Total	1,300,000
Net income	$ 850,000

Additional information

1. Gain on the sale of unimproved lot: Purchased in 20X1 for use in business for $50,000. Sold in 20X3 for $70,000. Kimberly has never had any Sec. 1231 losses.

2. Gain on sale of XYZ Stock: Purchased in 20X1.

3. Personal Property: The book depreciation is the same as tax depreciation for all the property that was placed in service before January 1, 20X3. The book depreciation is straight-line over the useful life, which is the same as class life. Company policy is to use the half-year convention per books for personal property. Furniture and fixtures costing $56,000 were placed in service on January 2, 20X3.

4. Bad Debt: Represents the increase in the allowance for doubtful accounts based on an aging of accounts receivable. Actual bad debts written off were $7,000.

5. Interest expense on

Mortgage loan	$10,000
Loan obtained to purchase municipal bonds	4,000
Line of credit loan	2,000

For **items 1 through 5,** determine the amount that should be reported on Kimberly Corporation's 20X3 Federal income tax return.

Items to be answered:

1. What amount of interest income is taxable from the U.S. Treasury bonds?

2. Determine the tax depreciation expense under the Modified Accelerated Cost Recovery System (MACRS), for the furniture and fixtures that were placed in service on January 2, 20X3. Round the answer to the nearest thousand. Kimberly did not use the alternative depreciation system (ADS) or a straight-line method of depreciation. No election was made to expense part of the cost of the property, and Kimberly elected not to use bonus depreciation.

3. Determine the amount of bad debt to be included as an expense item.

4. Determine Kimberly's net long-term capital gain.

5. What amount of interest expense is deductible?

Task-Based Simulation 2

Items to be answered:

For **items 1 through 5,** select whether the following expenses are fully deductible, partially deductible, or nondeductible, for regular tax purposes, on Kimberly's 20X3 federal income tax return.

Selections

F.   Fully deductible for regular tax purposes on Kimberly Corp's 20X3 federal income tax return.

P.   Partially deductible for regular tax purposes on Kimberly Corp's 20X3 federal income tax return.

N.   Nondeductible for regular tax purposes on Kimberly Corp's 20X3 federal income tax return.

		(F)	(P)	(N)
1.	Organization expense incurred at corporate inception in 20X1 to draft the corporate charter. No deduction was taken for the organization expense in 20X1.	○	○	○
2.	Life insurance premiums paid by the corporation for its executives as part of their compensation for services rendered. The corporation is neither the direct nor the indirect beneficiary of the policy, and the amount of compensation is reasonable.	○	○	○
3.	Vacation pay earned by employees which vested under a plan by December 31, 20X3, and was paid February 1, 20X4.	○	○	○
4.	State franchise tax liability that has accrued during the year and was paid on March 15, 20X4.	○	○	○
5.	Entertainment expense to lease a luxury skybox during football season to entertain clients. A bona fide business discussion precedes each game. The cost of regular seats would have been one-half the amount paid.	○	○	○

Task-Based Simulation 3

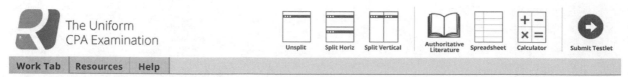

Required:

Items 1 through 10 refer to Kimberly Corp's need to determine if it will be subject to the alternative minimum tax for corporate purposes. Determine whether the statement is True or False.

Items to be answered:

		True	False
1.	The method of depreciation for commercial real property to arrive at alternative minimum taxable income before the adjusted current earnings (ACE) adjustment, is the straight-line method.	○	○
2.	The corporate exemption amount reduces the alternative minimum taxable income.	○	○
3.	The ACE adjustment can be a positive or negative amount.	○	○
4.	Depreciation on personal property to arrive at alternative minimum taxable income before the ACE adjustment is straight-line over the MACRS recovery period.	○	○
5.	The alternative minimum tax is the excess of the tentative minimum tax over the regular tax liability.	○	○
6.	Municipal bond interest, other than from private activity bonds, is includible income to arrive at alternative minimum taxable income before the ACE adjustment.	○	○
7.	The maximum corporate exemption amount for minimum tax purposes is $150,000.	○	○
8.	The 70% dividends received deduction is available to determine ACE.	○	○
9.	Municipal bond interest is includible income to determine ACE.	○	○
10.	The method of depreciation for personal property for determining ACE is the sum-of-the-years' digits method.	○	○

Lecture 2.15

Task-Based Simulation 4

 The Uniform CPA Examination

 Unsplit   Split Horiz   Split Vertical   Authoritative Literature   Spreadsheet   Calculator   Submit Testlet

| Work Tab | Resources | Help |

Required:

Situation

Jasper Junction Corporation (JJC) is an accrual basis, calendar-year entity that was created by Chao, Iris, and Nolan in 20X1. JJC furnishes the original incorporation agreement. The shareholders' bases in the assets contributed are as follows:

- Cash $150,000
- Equipment $245,000
- Inventory $380,000
- Land and Building $375,000

The first five years of business have been lean years. Nolan had to loan the corporation $75,000 to ensure that JJC had enough cash to pay its bills and its Accumulated Earnings and Profits only amounts to $23,000 at the end of 20X5. JJC has its first year of substantial income in 20X6. It also sells some of its land for $100,000 cash, but the sale results in an $18,000 capital loss. The Board of Directors decides to pay $250,000 in dividends to its shareholders. This is in addition to the $3,500 of interest it pays on the bonds and the $1,500 it pays to Nolan on the money he loaned JJC. The income and expenses of JJC for 20X6, taxable income, and current E&P are provided in the Table below.

Income	Amount	Taxable Income	Current E&P
Taxable Income			176,500
Sales	450,000	450,000	
COGS	150,000	(150,000)	
Dividends (own 5%)	95,000	95,000	
Muni Bond Interest	1,000		1,000
Expenses			
Capital loss	18,000		(18,000)
Interest Expense	5,000	(5,000)	
Operating Expenses	120,000	(120,000)	
Key Life Insurance Premiums	6,000	_____	(6,000)
Taxable income before Special Deductions		270,000	
Charitable Contributions	30,000	(27,000)	(3,000)
Dividends Received Deduction		66,500	66,500
Taxable Income		176,500	
Federal Income Tax		52,000	(52,000)
Current E&P			165,000

Resources

CORPORATE AGREEMENT
Jasper Junction Corporation

This corporation agreement (the "Agreement") made and entered into this 6 day of January, 20X1 (the "Execution Date"),

AMONGST:

- Chao of 693 Feather Street, Crane, North Dakota, 58585
- Iris of 459 Wing Street, Crane, North Dakota, 58585
- Nolan of 4455 Nest Street, Crane, North Dakota, 58585

Individually the "Shareholder" and collectively the "Shareholders"

BACKGROUND:

- The Shareholders wish to associate themselves as owners in the business.
- The terms and conditions of this Agreement set out the terms and conditions as to how they will be Shareholders.
- The firm name of the Corporation will be: JASPER JUNCTION CORPORATION. It will also be known as JJC and referred to in the remainder of this document as JJC.

Purpose

- The purpose of JJC will be: MANUFACTURING.

Place of Business

- The principal location of the business of JJC will be at 9322 Flight Avenue, Crane, North Dakota, 58585 until such time that the corporation Board of Directors designates a different location.

IN CONSIDERATION OF and as a condition of the Shareholders entering into this Agreement and other valuable consideration, the receipt and sufficiency of which consideration is acknowledged, the parties to this Agreement agree as follows:

Formation

- By this Agreement the Shareholders enter into a corporation in accordance with the laws of the State of North Dakota. The rights and obligations of the Shareholders will be as stated in the applicable legislation of the State of North Dakota (the "Act"), except as otherwise provided here.
- Authorized common shares of JJC are 1 million. The par value of each share of common stock will be $100.00 and its fair value will vary based on the value of JJC. Each share of common stock will have the rights of one vote at shareholder meetings. Nonvoting stock is authorized to be issued with not more than 500,000 shares permissible.
- Common stock will be issued to the shareholders based on the net fair value contributed to the corporation.
- Authorized preferred shares are 5,000 with a par value of $1,000.00 per share.
- No preferred shares will be issued at the time of incorporation.
- Bonds in valuation units of $10,000 may be issued.

Governance

- The first shareholder meeting shall take place the first day of February, 20X1 and thereafter annually on the first day of February. Written minutes of the meetings must be available for shareholder review.
- A Board of Directors shall be established by a vote of the shareholders.
- The Board of Directors will appoint the officers and review their performance annually.
- Changes to the incorporation agreement must be approved by a 60% shareholder vote based on common stock voting rights.

Distributions

- Subject to state law, the Board of Directors will declare dividends based on ownership as of a date the Board selects, and payment of the dividends must be within 30 days of such date.
- Distributions that would impair the manufacturing operations are not permitted.
- Dividends on common stock are not cumulative.
- Shareholders can force distributions by a 60% vote when there are excess liquid assets that have no valid business purpose for their accumulation.

Capitalization

- Initial capitalization is provided by the initial Shareholders of Nolan, Chao and Iris.
- Each of the Shareholders has contributed to the capital of JJC in the form of cash or property in agreed-upon value for the stated shares of stock, as follows:

Shareholder	Contribution Description	Common Stock
Chao	$150,000 CASH and EQUIPMENT valued at $320,000. There is a $120,000 recourse loan on the equipment.	350
Iris	INVENTORY valued at $500,000. No loans are attached to this asset.	400*
Nolan	LAND and BUILDING valued at $650,000 with a $400,000 nonrecourse mortgage.	250

*   At time of incorporation, Iris will receive 10 bonds ($100,000) as partial consideration for her inventory contribution.

Required:

Analyze the information provided to reconcile the shareholders' beginning and ending bases in their stock to determine the federal tax consequences of JJC's corporate distributions in 20X6.

Shareholder	Ownership Percentage	Beginning Basis in Stock	Increases or (Decreases)	Ending Basis in Stock	Taxable Distributions
Chao	1.	2.	3.	4.	5. Dividend 6. Capital Gain
Iris	7.	8.	9.	10.	11. Dividend 12. Capital Gain
Nolan	13.	14.	15.	16.	17. Dividend 18. Capital Gain

Task-Based Simulation 5

Research | Help

A corporation has received dividends from an unaffiliated corporation in which it owns stock. It is trying to determine what percentage of the dividends, if any, may be deducted in calculating the corporation's taxable income.

Which code section and subsection indicates the percentage of dividends received that a corporation may deduct?

Task-Based Simulation 6

Research | Help

A newly formed corporation incurred organization expenses that exceeded the amount that could be deducted in the period incurred and is trying to determine over what period the remainder should be amortized.

Which code section, subsection, and paragraph indicates the period over which these excess organizational expenses will be amortized?

Task-Based Simulation 7

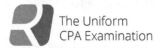

Research | Help

A corporate taxpayer has numerous uncollectible accounts, for which an allowance for doubtful accounts was established. Several accounts were written off as wholly worthless during the tax year. The corporation is trying to determine the amount of bad debts that may be deducted.

Which code section and subsection will provide the corporation with information as to the deductibility of these accounts?

Task-Based Simulation 8

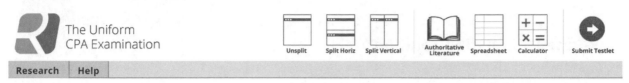

A corporation is trying to determine if it is exempt from the accumulated earnings tax.

Which code section and subsection indicates what types of entities are exempt from the accumulated earnings tax?

Task-Based Simulation 9

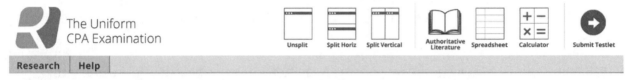

A corporation is trying to determine if it is exempt from the personal holding company tax.

Which code section and subsection indicates what types of entities are not considered personal holding companies?

Task-Based Simulation 10

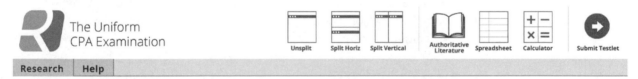

A corporation has used the most aggressive accelerated deprecation allowed and is calculating its alternative minimum tax. It wishes to determine what adjustments are necessary related to depreciation in calculating its alternative minimum taxable income.

Which code section, subsection, and paragraph will provide information about adjustments for depreciation when calculating alternative minimum taxable income?

TASK-BASED SIMULATION SOLUTIONS

Task-Based Simulation Solution 1

1. ($26,000) Interest on U.S. Treasury bonds is fully taxable.

2. ($8,000) Furniture and fixtures are considered 7-year recovery property. Under MACRS, it will be depreciated over a 7-year period using the double-declining balance approach. As a result, depreciation will be 2 times the straight-line rate multiplied by the carrying value of the property. The straight-line rate is 1/7, making double the straight-line rate 2/7. It is multiplied by the carrying value, which will be the cost of $56,000 in the first year, resulting in annual depreciation of $56,000 × 2/7, or $16,000. Since Kimberly's policy is to use the half-year convention, depreciation in the first year will be $16,000/2, or $8,000.

3. ($7,000) For tax purposes, bad debts may only be deducted in the period in which they are written off. Kimberly wrote off $7,000 of bad debts in 20X1, which will be its deductible bad debts expense.

4. ($25,000) The sale of investment property held for more than one year results in long-term capital gains and losses, indicating that the gain on the sale of XYZ stock will result in a long-term capital gain of $5,000. The unimproved lot was being held for use in the business and is considered Section 1231 property. Since it was held for more than one year, losses are treated as ordinary, but gains are treated as long-term capital gains. The sale resulted in a long-term capital gain of $20,000, which is added to the gain on the stock for a total of $25,000 in long-term capital gains.

5. ($12,000) In general, interest on a corporation's indebtedness is deductible. When debts are incurred to acquire investments that provide tax-exempt income, however, the interest on those obligations is not deductible. As a result, Kimberly will be able to deduct the interest on the mortgage and on the line of credit, but not on the loan obtained to acquire municipal bonds because interest income on municipal bonds is tax exempt.

Task-Based Simulation Solution 2

		(F)	(P)	(N)
1.	Organization expense incurred at corporate inception in 20X1 to draft the corporate charter. No deduction was taken for the organization expense in 20X1.	○	○	●
2.	Life insurance premiums paid by the corporation for its executives as part of their compensation for services rendered. The corporation is neither the direct nor the indirect beneficiary of the policy and the amount of compensation is reasonable.	●	○	○
3.	Vacation pay earned by employees which vested under a plan by December 31, 20X3, and was paid February 1, 20X4.	●	○	○
4.	State franchise tax liability that has accrued during the year and was paid on March 15, 20X4.	●	○	○
5.	Entertainment expense to lease a luxury skybox during football season to entertain clients. A bona fide business discussion precedes each game. The cost of regular seats would have been one-half the amount paid.	○	●	○

Explanation of solutions

1. (N) A corporation may amortize organizational costs over 180 months but, in order to do so, it must make an election in the year of inception and begin amortization in the month in which the entity commences operations. If a proper election is not made, they remain capitalized until the corporation is liquidated. Since Kimberly did not deduct organization costs in 20X1, it apparently did not make an election to do so and would not be able to deduct amortization in 20X3.

2. (F) When a corporation provides life insurance to its employees and the employee has the option of determining the beneficiary of the policy, other than the corporation, the insurance is considered an employee benefit, and the premiums are deductible to the corporation. If the corporation is the direct or indirect beneficiary of the policy, it is a key person policy and the premiums would not be deductible.

3. (F) An accrual basis taxpayer may deduct certain expenses for accrued vacation pay and bonuses, provided they are paid within 2 ½ months after the end of the entity's tax year. Since the vacation pay is vested and meets the criteria for accrual, and since it was paid on February 1, 20X4, within 2 ½ months of the year-end, it will be deductible in full in 20X3.

4. (F) State franchise tax is an ordinary cost of doing business that is deductible by an accrual basis taxpayer in the year to which it applies, regardless of when paid. The state franchise tax would be deductible in 20X3.

5. (P) When a company rents a seat in a luxury skybox for more than one event in the same sports arena, as would be the case with football season tickets, the deductible amount is limited to the cost of the most expensive non-luxury seat in the same arena. In this case, since regular seats cost one-half as much as luxury skyboxes, Kimberly would be able to deduct 50% of the nonluxury seat cost.

Task-Based Simulation Solution 3

		True	**False**
1.	The method of depreciation for commercial real property to arrive at alternative minimum taxable income before the adjusted current earnings (ACE) adjustment, is the straight-line method.	●	○
2.	The corporate exemption amount reduces the alternative minimum taxable income.	●	○
3.	The ACE adjustment can be a positive or negative amount.	●	○
4.	Depreciation on personal property to arrive at alternative minimum taxable income before the ACE adjustment is straight-line over the MACRS recovery period.	○	●
5.	The alternative minimum tax is the excess of the tentative minimum tax over the regular tax liability.	●	○
6.	Municipal bond interest, other than from private activity bonds, is includible income to arrive at alternative minimum taxable income before the ACE adjustment.	○	●
7.	The maximum corporate exemption amount for minimum tax purposes is $150,000.	○	●
8.	The 70% dividends received deduction is available to determine ACE.	○	●
9.	Municipal bond interest is includible income to determine ACE.	●	○
10.	The method of depreciation for personal property for determining ACE is the sum-of-the-years' digits method.	○	●

Explanation of solutions

1. (T)   Real property is depreciated using the straight-line method for both regular tax and AMT purposes.

2. (T)   A corporation is allowed an exemption of $40,000, which reduces the AMT. It phases out, beginning when a corporation's AMTI exceeds $150,000 and is eliminated in its entirety when AMTI reaches $310,000.

3. (T)   An ACE adjustment may be a negative amount, and it can reduce AMTI to the extent that cumulative positive ACE adjustments in prior years exceed cumulative negative ACE adjustments in prior years.

4. (F)   For regular tax purposes, depreciable personal property may be depreciated using the double-declining balance method. The excess over depreciation calculated under the 150% DB method (using 1 ½ times the straight-line rate instead of double the rate), is an adjustment that increases regular taxable income to calculate AMTI.

5. (T)   AMTI, after any ACE adjustment and net of any exemption, is multiplied by the AMT rate to establish a tentative minimum tax. The excess of this amount over regular tax is the AMT liability.

6. (F)   Interest income on a certain form of municipal obligations referred to as private activity bonds is a tax preference that is added back to corporate income in calculating AMTI. Interest on other municipal bonds is not.

7. (F)   Corporations are entitled to a maximum exemption from AMT of $40,000, which is phased out when AMTI before the exemption exceeds $150,000.

8. (F)   While the 80% and 100% DRD deductions are available to determine adjusted current earnings (ACE), the 70% DRD deduction must be added back to alternative minimum taxable income to determine adjusted current earnings (ACE).

9. (T)   Although only interest on private activity bonds is added back to taxable income as a tax preference in computing alternative minimum taxable income (AMTI) before the ACE adjustment, interest on any remaining municipal bonds is added to AMTI to determine adjusted current earnings (ACE).

10. (F) Depreciation on personal property is calculated using the 150% declining balance method for AMT purposes; there is no difference when calculating adjusted current earnings (ACE). To compute ACE, the corporation begins with AMTI and adds certain items (SLIM): *S*eventy (70%) DRD, *L*ife *I*nsurance proceeds, and *M*unicipal bond interest.

Task-Based Simulation Solution 4

Shareholder	Ownership Percentage	Beginning Basis in Stock	Increases or (Decreases)	Ending Basis in Stock	Taxable Distributions	
Chao	1. 35%	2. $275,000	3. $(21,700)	4. $253,300	5. Dividend 6. Capital gain	$65,800 -0-
Iris	7. 40%	8. $380,000	9. $(24,800)	10. $355,200	11. Dividend 12. Capital gain	$75,200 -0-
Nolan	13. 25%	14. -0-	15. -0-	16. -0-	17. Dividend 18. Capital gain	$47,000 $15,500

Explanation of solutions

1. Chao receives 350 shares of the total 1,000 shares of common stock in exchange for his contribution of equipment and $150,000; thus, his ownership percentage is 35% (350/1,000).

2. Chao's beginning basis in his stock is $275,000 ($150,000 cash + $245,000 equip. basis – $120,000 loan).

3. To determine whether a shareholder's basis increases or decreases, one must determine the taxability of the distributions. Remember that, to the extent dividends paid are from current and accumulated earnings and profits ($165,000 CEP + $23,000 AEP = $188,000), they are considered taxable dividends; amounts paid in excess of E&P are a return of capital, which is not taxable and reduces the bases of the shareholders. So, of the $250,000 distributed, only $188,000 are dividends, and the other $62,000 ($250,000 – $188,000) is return of capital, which reduces the shareholders' bases; thus, Chao's basis decreases by $21,700 ($62,000 × 35%).

4. Chao's ending basis in his stock is $253,300 ($275,000 beginning basis – $21,700 return of capital).

5. To the extent dividends paid are from current and accumulated earnings and profits ($165,000 CEP + $23,000 AEP = $188,000), they are considered taxable dividends; amounts paid in excess of E&P are a return of capital, which is not taxable. So, of the $250,000 distributed, only $188,000 are dividends, and the other $62,000 ($250,000 – $188,000) is return of capital; thus, Chao receives $87,500 ($250,000 × 35%), but only $65,800 ($188,000 × 35%) of the distribution is considered a taxable dividend.

6. Chao does not recognize a capital gain as a result of the distributions. Chao receives $87,500 ($250,000 × 35%), but only $65,800 ($188,000 × 35%) of the distribution is considered a taxable dividend; the rest ($87,500 total distribution – $65,800 dividend = $21,700) is a return of capital, which reduces his basis.

7. Iris receives 400 shares of the total 1,000 shares of common stock (and $100,000 in bonds) in exchange for her contribution of inventory; thus, her ownership percentage is 40% (400/1,000).

8. Iris's beginning basis in her stock is equal to the $380,000 basis she had in the contributed inventory. Since Iris received something other than stock in exchange for the inventory, she would have decreased her basis by the $100,000 in bonds received, but she would have also had to recognize a gain on the $100,000 in the year of formation; thus, her beginning basis is still $380,000 (i.e., $380,000 basis in inventory – $100,000 bonds + $100,000 gain recognized).

9. To determine whether a shareholder's basis increases or decreases, one must determine the taxability of the distributions. Remember that, to the extent dividends paid are from current and accumulated earnings and profits ($165,000 CEP + $23,000 AEP = $188,000), they are considered taxable dividends; amounts paid in excess of E&P are a return of capital, which is not taxable and reduces the bases of the shareholders. So, of the $250,000 distributed, only $188,000 are dividends, and the other $62,000 ($250,000 – $188,000) is return of capital, which reduces the shareholders' bases; thus, Iris's basis decreases by $24,800 ($62,000 × 40%).

10. Iris's ending basis in her stock is $355,200 ($380,000 beginning basis – $24,800 return of capital).

11. To the extent dividends paid are from current and accumulated earnings and profits ($165,000 CEP + $23,000 AEP = $188,000), they are considered taxable dividends; amounts paid in excess of E&P are a return of capital, which is not taxable. So, of the $250,000 distributed, only $188,000 are dividends, and the other $62,000 ($250,000 – $188,000) is return of capital; thus, Iris receives $100,000 ($250,000 × 40%), but only $75,200 ($188,000 × 40%) of the distribution is considered a taxable dividend.

12. Iris does not recognize a capital gain as a result of the distributions. Iris receives $100,000 ($250,000 × 40%), but only $75,200 ($188,000 × 40%) of the distribution is considered a taxable dividend; the rest ($100,000 total distribution – $75,200 dividend = $24,800) is a return of capital, which reduces her basis.

13. Nolan receives 250 shares of the total 1,000 shares of common stock in exchange for his contribution of equipment and $150,000; thus, his ownership percentage is 25% (250/1,000).

14. Nolan contributed land and a building with an adjusted basis of $375,000, for which the corporation assumed the mortgage of $400,000. Because the $400,000 amount of the mortgage exceeded his basis of $375,000 by $25,000, Nolan would have had to recognize a gain of $25,000 in the year of formation. Thus, Nolan's beginning basis in his stock is $0 ($375,000 basis in property – $400,000 loan + $25,000 gain recognized).

15. To determine whether a shareholder's basis increases or decreases, one must determine the taxability of the distributions. Remember that, to the extent dividends paid are from current and accumulated earnings and profits ($165,000 CEP + $23,000 AEP = $188,000), they are considered taxable dividends; amounts paid in excess of E&P are a return of capital, which is not taxable and reduces the bases of the shareholders. So, of the $250,000 distributed, only $188,000 are dividends, and the other $62,000 ($250,000 – $188,000) is return of capital, which reduces the shareholders' bases; however, in Nolan's case, his basis is already $0, so he must recognize a capital gain for the amount received in excess of dividends, or $15,500 ($62,000 × 25%). The change in his basis is a net $0 ($0 basis – $15,500 return of capital + $15,500 capital gain recognized). Note: The loan made to the corporation by Nolan does not increase his basis in his stock. Loans only increase basis in flow-through entities.

16. Nolan's ending basis in his stock is $0 ($0 beginning basis – $15,500 return of capital + $15,500 capital gain recognized).

17. To the extent dividends paid are from current and accumulated earnings and profits ($165,000 CEP + $23,000 AEP = $188,000), they are considered taxable dividends; amounts paid in excess of E&P are a return of capital, which is not taxable. So, of the $250,000 distributed, only $188,000 are dividends, and the other $62,000 ($250,000 – $188,000) is return of capital; thus, Nolan receives $62,500 ($250,000 × 25%), but only $47,000 ($188,000 × 25%) of the distribution is considered a taxable dividend.

18. Nolan must recognize a capital gain of $15,500 as a result of the distribution. Nolan receives $62,500 ($250,000 × 25%), but only $47,000 ($188,000 × 25%) of the distribution is considered a taxable dividend; the rest ($62,500 total distribution – $47,000 dividend = $15,500) is a return of capital, which normally reduces the shareholder's basis, but in Nolan's case, his basis is already $0, so he must recognize a capital gain for the amount received in excess of dividends, or $15,500 ($62,000 × 25%).

Task-Based Simulation Solution 5

243	(a)

Task-Based Simulation Solution 6

248	(a)	(2)

Task-Based Simulation Solution 7

166	(a)

Task-Based Simulation Solution 8

532	(b)

Task-Based Simulation Solution 9

542	(c)

Task-Based Simulation Solution 10

56	(a)	(1)

Section 3 – S Corporations

Corresponding Lectures

Watch the following course lectures with this section:

Lecture 3.01 – S Corporations: Formation and Operation
Lecture 3.02 – Separately Stated Items
Lecture 3.03 – Distributions to Shareholders
Lecture 3.04 – S Corporations – Class Questions
Lecture 3.05 – S Corporations – Class Questions – TBS

Exam Note: *Please refer to the AICPA REG Blueprint in the Introduction of this book to find a listing of the representative tasks (and their associated skill levels—i.e., Remembering and Understanding, Application, and Analysis) that the candidate should be able to perform based on the knowledge obtained in this section.*

S Corporations

S CORPORATIONS: FORMATION AND OPERATION

Some corporations elect to be treated in a manner similar to partnerships, filing a tax return (**1120-S**) but not paying taxes directly. Instead, the income reported by an **S corporation** is allocated to the shareholders (**K-1**), who must report their shares of the S corporation's income on their personal tax returns (flow-through entity). Corporations that pay income taxes directly are known as C corporations.

In order to make an election to be an S corporation, certain conditions must be satisfied: (**Simple & Small**)

- There can be no more than **100 shareholders** (family members with a common ancestor no more than six generations above and their spouses may be treated as a single shareholder for purposes of this rule).
- All shareholders must be **individuals** (or certain estates or trusts for the benefit of individuals).
  - No corporations, partnerships or big trusts as shareholders.
    - But S corp can own stock in a C corp, S corp, or be a partner in a P/S.
  - Grantor & Testamentary trusts are Ok.
  - Husband and Wife count as one until Divorce is Final.
- All shareholders must be either **residents or citizens** of the United States.
- The corporation must be a **domestic** corporation.
- There can be only **one class** of stock (no preferred stock).
- Tax return is due on March 15th, if calendar year, but may file a 6-month extension. Note, however, that tax return due dates and extensions are no longer tested on the CPA Exam.

The last requirement needs to be carefully understood. The requirement of one class of stock means only that each share must be allocated an equal amount of the income of the corporation. It is acceptable for some of the shares to have voting rights and others to be non-voting, so long as the income allocation requirement is satisfied.

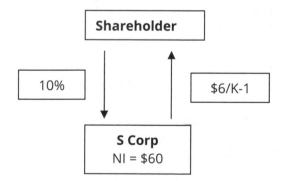

- **Formation – Similar to a C corporation - Formal**
  - **Cash or property 80%** or more (control)
    - Tax free to both
    - Carryover basis
    - Carryover holding period

- ○ **Services or < 80%**
  - ▪ Taxable at FMV of stock

S Election

The election to become an S corporation must be made **unanimously (100%)** by the shareholders (including those with non-voting shares), since they are agreeing to be personally liable for the income taxes resulting from the election. The election can be made at any time on Form 2553, but it must be made by the 15th day of the 3rd month of the tax year (March 15 for calendar corporations, **2 ½ Months**) in order to be effective for that year. Any election made after that cannot become effective until the start of the following tax year. The tax year may be a calendar year or a fiscal year if it has an established business purpose.

Operation of S Corp

	+/- % Income/loss*			
	Muni bond interest	-	Distributions	
Initial Basis	**Separately stated items**		**Received**	**= Net Basis**

*Note: The following order applies in *calculating stock basis* to determine whether a distribution is taxable or whether a loss is deductible:

1. + Income items, including gains
2. – Distributions (does not include dividend distributions from C corp years)
3. – Nondeductible, noncapital expenses (e.g., nondeductible portion of meals and entertainment expense) and depletion
4. – Items of loss and deduction (if amounts are greater than remaining basis, allocate them proportionally until basis is reduced to 0, and remainder is suspended until enough basis exists to absorb it)

For example, Roger, the sole shareholder of an S corporation, has $10,000 of stock basis (and no debt basis) on January 1, year 1. Roger received a Schedule K-1 for year 1 with the following items:

Ordinary business income (loss)	(15,000)
Net §1231 gain	5,000
Nondeductible expenses	2,000
Charitable contribution	1,000
Distributions	9,000

1. Using the ordering rule, stock basis is first increased by items of income, so our initial stock basis of $10,000 is increased by the $5,000 net §1231 gain, for a stock basis before distributions of $15,000.

2. Then we reduce the $15,000 stock basis by distributions of $9,000, for a remaining basis amount of $6,000. Since the shareholder has adequate stock basis before distributions, the $9,000 distribution is not taxable.

3. Next, Roger's $6,000 stock basis is reduced by the $2,000 of nondeductible expenses, bringing stock basis to $4,000.

4. Finally, Roger has an ordinary loss of $15,000 and a $1,000 charitable deduction. Since Roger's loss and deduction items exceed his stock basis, we would look to see if he had any

debt basis (money loaned to company). Since there is no debt basis, the loss and deduction items must be pro-rated to determine the amount currently allowable:

- o $15,000 loss/$16,000 total loss and deduction items × $4,000 remaining basis = $3,750 loss allowable in year 1
- o $1,000 deduction/$16,000 total loss and deduction items × $4,000 remaining basis = $250 allowable charitable deduction in year 1

Roger's remaining $11,250 ordinary loss and $750 charitable deduction are suspended until Roger has enough basis to absorb it.

Types of Income

Net Business Income (Ordinary Business Income)

- **Income** = Ordinary income/Loss + Muni-bond interest + Separately stated income items
  - o   Income computed on an *Average daily basis.*
    - ▪   **For example,** Assume an S corporation with 100 shares outstanding reported $365,000 of income in 20X1 (a 365-day year). One particular shareholder purchased 5 shares on 11/30/X1, and held them through the end of the year. The income averages $365,000 / 365 days = $1,000 per day. With 100 shares outstanding, this comes to $1,000 / 100 shares = $10 per share per day. The individual shareholder making the purchase on 11/30/X1 held the shares for the last 31 days of the year, and is allocated $10 x 5 shares x 31 days = $1,550.

- **Losses**
  - o   *Basis Limitation*—Losses are limited to amount invested (i.e., **stock basis**) + amount loaned to company (i.e., **debt basis**). Basis cannot go below zero; losses are suspended until the shareholder has sufficient basis to absorb the loss. Note: For S corporations, basis is often equal to the amount "at-risk."
  - o   *At-Risk Rules*—Losses are further limited by the investor's amount "at risk" under IRC Sec. 465 (similar to basis rules but amounts at-risk do not include amounts for which the investor bears no economic risk of loss—e.g., certain nonrecourse loans and loans from certain related parties).
  - o   *Passive Activity Loss Limitation*—IRC §469 provides that passive losses are limited to passive income.

    Note: For CPA exam purposes, you should be aware of the impact of the at-risk and passive activity loss limitations, but you are unlikely to be asked to calculate anything beyond the basis limitation.

- **Municipal bond interest**
  - o   Increases basis
  - o   Not taxable

- **Distribution received by the shareholder**
  - o   Reduces basis
  - o   Not taxed

Lecture 3.02

Types of Income (Continued)

- **Separately Stated Items**
  - o Any amount that can hit a limit on the Individual tax return:
    - Capital gains/losses
    - Section 1231 gains/losses
    - Section 179 depreciation deduction
    - Rent & Royalty income (i.e., passive income)
    - Charitable contributions
    - Interest income/expense on Investments

Items are passed through according to their percentage of ownership based on a ***per-share/per-day method***. If there is no change in ownership during the year, then simply use the percentage of stock owned to determine the amount passed though. If a change in ownership occurred, then each shareholder's percentage is weighted for the number of days the stock was held (Like Weighted Average).

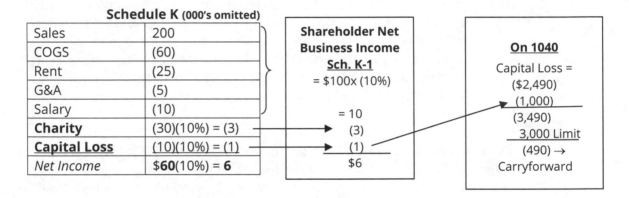

Reporting Operating & Separately Stated Items

S corporations do not pay income taxes, but are required to file annual information returns (Form 1120-S) reporting income and the allocation of that income to the various shareholders.

Since the items will be reported on the tax returns of the shareholders, the shareholders must segregate items that have special treatment on individual tax returns. The S corporation prepares a **Schedule K** that summarizes the ordinary income and then separately lists all items that are not ordinary. Additionally, a Schedule K-1 is prepared for each shareholder, showing that owner's allocated share of all of the items on the Schedule K.

You should try and remember the list of items that are reported separately, as this has been tested. Also, keep in mind that the purpose of separately stating items is to allow any special treatment on individual returns to be applied. As a result, any item which is always included in the gross income of an individual without restrictions or limitations need not be separately stated. A few examples of separately stated items are:

Separately stated item	Reason not included in ordinary income
Capital gains and losses	Limit on deductibility of net capital losses
Section 1231 gains and losses	Classification of net gain as capital gain
Investment Income (e.g., Dividends and interest)	Needed for investment interest limitation
Passive activities	Passive activity loss limitations
Charitable contributions	Must itemize to deduct/ Up to 50% of AGI
Section 179 depreciation election	Dollar limit on use of election per year
Tax credits	Limited to tax liability

Note: The calculation of income and identification of special items that need to be passed through to the shareholders separately are handled in the same way for S corporations as they are for partnerships, and are normally addressed on the CPA exam in the partnership questions.

Lecture 3.03

DISTRIBUTIONS TO SHAREHOLDERS

Distributions to Shareholders are nontaxable to the extent of the Accumulated Adjustment Account (AAA) and are applied to reduce the AAA and shareholder's stock basis.

- AAA represents the cumulative total of undistributed net income items for S corporation taxable years beginning after 1982. (Pre-1983, Previously Taxed Income (PTI)—beyond scope of exam.)
- Accumulated Earnings and Profits (AEP) represent earnings and profits that were accumulated (and never taxed to shareholders) during C corporation taxable years.
    1. Distributions to the extent of the AAA are *not taxable*.
    2. Distributions in excess of the AAA are treated as *Ordinary Dividends* to the extent of the corporation's AEP.
    3. Distributions are next *nontaxable* to the extent of remaining stock basis, as a tax-free return of capital.
    4. Distributions in excess of stock basis are treated as *gain* from the sale of stock.

Note: The tax treatment for liquidating distributions is the same for S corporations as it is for C corporations (i.e., recognize gain/loss on the distribution of property to a shareholder as if the property were sold at its FMV in exchange for the shareholder's stock), except that gains/losses recognized by an S corporation are ultimately passed through to the shareholders.

Accumulated Adjustment Account (AAA)

The AAA generally represents the cumulative balance of all items of the undistributed net income and deductions for S corporations. The AAA is generally increased by all income items and is decreased by distributions and all loss and deduction items; however, adjustments for tax-exempt income and related expenses, as well as adjustments for federal income taxes attributable to a taxable year in which the corporation was a C corporation are made to the Other Adjustments Account (OAA), rather than the AAA.

Note that the amounts represented in the AAA differ from AEP. A positive AEP balance represents earning's and profits accumulated in C corporation years that have never been taxed to shareholders. A positive AAA balance represents income from S corporation years that has already been taxed to shareholders but not yet distributed.

Distributions from an S corporation are generally treated as first coming from its accumulated adjustment account (AAA), and then are treated as coming from its accumulated earnings and profits (AEP); however, note that an S corporation may *elect* to distribute AEP before AAA. A positive balance in an S corporation's AAA is generally nontaxable when distributed because it represents amounts that have already been taxed to shareholders during S years. In contrast, an S corporation's AEP represents earnings accumulated during C years that have never been taxed to shareholders, and must be reported as dividend income when received.

S Status Termination

An election to **terminate** a corporation's status as an S corporation only requires shareholders holding a **majority** of the shares (again, including those that normally are non-voting shares) to agree (**50% - Voluntary**). An S corporation's status will be revoked automatically (**Involuntary**) if an event occurs that causes it to violate one of the requirements (**for example**, if shares are sold to a non-resident alien). Once an S corporation's status has been revoked, it cannot reelect such status for **5 years**.

Per Sec. 1362, termination will occur if the S corporation has passive investment income exceeding *25% of its gross receipts* for each of 3 consecutive years and, if during these 3 years, the corporation was a corporation with accumulated earning and profits attributable to prior C corporation status. Passive investment income includes receipts from rents, royalties, dividends, interest, annuities, and the gain from sales or exchanges of stock or securities.

An S election termination can be effective at any time during a tax year, resulting in the need to allocate income between the resulting S short year and C corporation short year. If no special election is made, the income must be allocated on a daily basis between the two based on a 365-day year.

Advantages and Disadvantages of S Status

When the shareholders of a C corporation decide to elect S corporation status, there may be advantages and disadvantages. Shareholders will be taxed on all income of the S corporation, whether distributed or not. Since an S corporation is a pass-through entity, however, any capital losses pass through to the shareholders, instead of being carried back or forward to offset against corporate capital gains. Any net capital loss or net operating loss (NOL) carryforwards from an S corporation's time as a C corporation are not immediately deductible by shareholders; however, they may be used to offset any built-in gains tax that arises from the sale of appreciated assets during the recognition period.

Built-in Gains Tax (**BIG**) applies if a C corporation elects S corporation status and the FMV of its assets exceeds their bases. The difference is a net unrealized built-in gain. If the assets are sold within 5 years, a special built-in gains tax at the highest corporate rate applies. This is the tax that would be due if the assets were sold prior to the election of the S status. This would not apply if FMV is less than basis, because in this case no built-in gain is present in the transaction. Prior to 2010, the holding period during which this special S corporation tax on built-in gains would be assessed was 10 years, and then in 2010, the period was reduced to 7 years. For dispositions in 2011, 2012 and 2013, the holding period was shortened to **5 years**. With the December 2015 passage of the PATH Act, the **5-year holding period** is made permanent for the 2015 tax year and all future tax years.

Health insurance premiums and other ***fringe benefits*** paid by an S corporation on behalf of a more than **2%** shareholder-employee are deductible by the S corporation as compensation and includible in the shareholder-employee's gross income on Form W-2.

Lecture 3.04

CLASS QUESTIONS

Please see the Class Questions and Class Solutions for this Lecture at the end of this Section.

Lecture 3.05

CLASS QUESTIONS

Please see the Class Questions and Class Solutions for this Lecture at the end of this Section.

Note: The 2016 forms are provided since 2017 forms were unavailable at the time of publication.

Form **1120S**

Department of the Treasury
Internal Revenue Service

U.S. Income Tax Return for an S Corporation

▶ **Do not file this form unless the corporation has filed or is attaching Form 2553 to elect to be an S corporation.**
▶ **Information about Form 1120S and its separate instructions is at** *www.irs.gov/form1120s.*

OMB No. 1545-0123

2016

For calendar year 2016 or tax year beginning _____ , 2016, ending _____ , 20 ____

A S election effective date		Name	D Employer identification number
	TYPE OR PRINT		
B Business activity code number (see instructions)		Number, street, and room or suite no. If a P.O. box, see instructions.	E Date incorporated
		City or town, state or province, country, and ZIP or foreign postal code	F Total assets (see instructions) $
C Check if Sch. M-3 attached ☐			

G Is the corporation electing to be an S corporation beginning with this tax year? ☐ Yes ☐ No   If "Yes," attach Form 2553 if not already filed
H Check if: **(1)** ☐ Final return **(2)** ☐ Name change **(3)** ☐ Address change **(4)** ☐ Amended return **(5)** ☐ S election termination or revocation
I Enter the number of shareholders who were shareholders during any part of the tax year . . . . ▶

Caution: Include **only** trade or business income and expenses on lines 1a through 21. See the instructions for more information.

Income

1a	Gross receipts or sales	**1a**		
b	Returns and allowances	**1b**		
c	Balance. Subtract line 1b from line 1a		**1c**	
2	Cost of goods sold (attach Form 1125-A)		**2**	
3	Gross profit. Subtract line 2 from line 1c		**3**	
4	Net gain (loss) from Form 4797, line 17 (attach Form 4797)		**4**	
5	Other income (loss) (see instructions—attach statement)		**5**	
6	**Total income (loss).** Add lines 3 through 5 . . . . ▶		**6**	

Deductions (see instructions for limitations)

7	Compensation of officers (see instructions—attach Form 1125-E)	**7**	
8	Salaries and wages (less employment credits)	**8**	
9	Repairs and maintenance	**9**	
10	Bad debts	**10**	
11	Rents	**11**	
12	Taxes and licenses	**12**	
13	Interest	**13**	
14	Depreciation not claimed on Form 1125-A or elsewhere on return (attach Form 4562)	**14**	
15	Depletion **(Do not deduct oil and gas depletion.)**	**15**	
16	Advertising	**16**	
17	Pension, profit-sharing, etc., plans	**17**	
18	Employee benefit programs	**18**	
19	Other deductions (attach statement)	**19**	
20	**Total deductions.** Add lines 7 through 19 . . . . ▶	**20**	
21	**Ordinary business income (loss).** Subtract line 20 from line 6	**21**	

Tax and Payments

22a	Excess net passive income or LIFO recapture tax (see instructions) . .	**22a**		
b	Tax from Schedule D (Form 1120S)	**22b**		
c	Add lines 22a and 22b (see instructions for additional taxes) . . .		**22c**	
23a	2016 estimated tax payments and 2015 overpayment credited to 2016	**23a**		
b	Tax deposited with Form 7004	**23b**		
c	Credit for federal tax paid on fuels (attach Form 4136)	**23c**		
d	Add lines 23a through 23c		**23d**	
24	Estimated tax penalty (see instructions). Check if Form 2220 is attached . . . . . ▶ ☐		**24**	
25	**Amount owed.** If line 23d is smaller than the total of lines 22c and 24, enter amount owed . .		**25**	
26	**Overpayment.** If line 23d is larger than the total of lines 22c and 24, enter amount overpaid . .		**26**	
27	Enter amount from line 26 **Credited to 2017 estimated tax** ▶ _____ **Refunded** ▶		**27**	

Sign Here

Under penalties of perjury, I declare that I have examined this return, including accompanying schedules and statements, and to the best of my knowledge and belief, it is true, correct, and complete. Declaration of preparer (other than taxpayer) is based on all information of which preparer has any knowledge.

▶ _____   ▶ _____
Signature of officer   Date   Title

May the IRS discuss this return with the preparer shown below (see instructions)? ☐ Yes ☐ No

Paid Preparer Use Only

Print/Type preparer's name	Preparer's signature	Date	Check ☐ if self-employed	PTIN
Firm's name ▶			Firm's EIN ▶	
Firm's address ▶			Phone no.	

For Paperwork Reduction Act Notice, see separate instructions.   Cat. No. 11510H   Form **1120S** (2016)

Schedule B	**Other Information** (see instructions)				Yes	No

1 Check accounting method: **a** ☐ Cash **b** ☐ Accrual
 c ☐ Other (specify) ▶ ....

2 See the instructions and enter the:
 a Business activity ▶ .... **b** Product or service ▶ ....

3 At any time during the tax year, was any shareholder of the corporation a disregarded entity, a trust, an estate, or a nominee or similar person? If "Yes," attach Schedule B-1, Information on Certain Shareholders of an S Corporation . .

4 At the end of the tax year, did the corporation:

 a Own directly 20% or more, or own, directly or indirectly, 50% or more of the total stock issued and outstanding of any foreign or domestic corporation? For rules of constructive ownership, see instructions. If "Yes," complete (i) through (v) below . . . .

(i) Name of Corporation	**(ii)** Employer Identification Number (if any)	**(iii)** Country of Incorporation	**(iv)** Percentage of Stock Owned	**(v)** If Percentage in (iv) is 100%, Enter the Date (if any) a Qualified Subchapter S Subsidiary Election Was Made

 b Own directly an interest of 20% or more, or own, directly or indirectly, an interest of 50% or more in the profit, loss, or capital in any foreign or domestic partnership (including an entity treated as a partnership) or in the beneficial interest of a trust? For rules of constructive ownership, see instructions. If "Yes," complete (i) through (v) below . . . .

(i) Name of Entity	**(ii)** Employer Identification Number (if any)	**(iii)** Type of Entity	**(iv)** Country of Organization	**(v)** Maximum Percentage Owned in Profit, Loss, or Capital

5 a At the end of the tax year, did the corporation have any outstanding shares of restricted stock? . . . .

 If "Yes," complete lines (i) and (ii) below.
 (i) Total shares of restricted stock. . . . . ▶ ....
 (ii) Total shares of non-restricted stock . . . . ▶ ....

 b At the end of the tax year, did the corporation have any outstanding stock options, warrants, or similar instruments? .

 If "Yes," complete lines (i) and (ii) below.
 (i) Total shares of stock outstanding at the end of the tax year ▶ ....
 (ii) Total shares of stock outstanding if all instruments were executed ▶ ....

6 Has this corporation filed, or is it required to file, **Form 8918,** Material Advisor Disclosure Statement, to provide information on any reportable transaction?

7 Check this box if the corporation issued publicly offered debt instruments with original issue discount . . . . ▶ ☐

 If checked, the corporation may have to file **Form 8281,** Information Return for Publicly Offered Original Issue Discount Instruments.

8 If the corporation: **(a)** was a C corporation before it elected to be an S corporation **or** the corporation acquired an asset with a basis determined by reference to the basis of the asset (or the basis of any other property) in the hands of a C corporation **and (b)** has net unrealized built-in gain in excess of the net recognized built-in gain from prior years, enter the net unrealized built-in gain reduced by net recognized built-in gain from prior years (see instructions) . . . . ▶ $ ....

9 Enter the accumulated earnings and profits of the corporation at the end of the tax year. $ ....

10 Does the corporation satisfy **both** of the following conditions?
 a The corporation's total receipts (see instructions) for the tax year were less than $250,000 . . . .
 b The corporation's total assets at the end of the tax year were less than $250,000 . . . .

 If "Yes," the corporation is not required to complete Schedules L and M-1.

11 During the tax year, did the corporation have any non-shareholder debt that was canceled, was forgiven, or had the terms modified so as to reduce the principal amount of the debt? . . . .
 If "Yes," enter the amount of principal reduction $ ....

12 During the tax year, was a qualified subchapter S subsidiary election terminated or revoked? If "Yes," see instructions .

13a Did the corporation make any payments in 2016 that would require it to file Form(s) 1099? . . . .
 b If "Yes," did the corporation file or will it file required Forms 1099? . . . .

Form **1120S** (2016)

Form 1120S (2016)

Page **3**

Schedule K		Shareholders' Pro Rata Share Items		Total amount	
Income (Loss)	**1**	Ordinary business income (loss) (page 1, line 21)	**1**		
	2	Net rental real estate income (loss) (attach Form 8825)	**2**		
	3a	Other gross rental income (loss) **3a**			
	b	Expenses from other rental activities (attach statement) . . **3b**			
	c	Other net rental income (loss). Subtract line 3b from line 3a	**3c**		
	4	Interest income	**4**		
	5	Dividends: **a** Ordinary dividends	**5a**		
		b Qualified dividends **5b**			
	6	Royalties	**6**		
	7	Net short-term capital gain (loss) (attach Schedule D (Form 1120S))	**7**		
	8a	Net long-term capital gain (loss) (attach Schedule D (Form 1120S))	**8a**		
	b	Collectibles (28%) gain (loss) **8b**			
	c	Unrecaptured section 1250 gain (attach statement) **8c**			
	9	Net section 1231 gain (loss) (attach Form 4797)	**9**		
	10	Other income (loss) (see instructions) . . Type ▶	**10**		
Deductions	**11**	Section 179 deduction (attach Form 4562)	**11**		
	12a	Charitable contributions	**12a**		
	b	Investment interest expense	**12b**		
	c	Section 59(e)(2) expenditures **(1)** Type ▶ _____ **(2)** Amount ▶	**12c(2)**		
	d	Other deductions (see instructions) Type ▶	**12d**		
Credits	**13a**	Low-income housing credit (section 42(j)(5))	**13a**		
	b	Low-income housing credit (other)	**13b**		
	c	Qualified rehabilitation expenditures (rental real estate) (attach Form 3468, if applicable) . .	**13c**		
	d	Other rental real estate credits (see instructions) Type ▶	**13d**		
	e	Other rental credits (see instructions) . . . Type ▶	**13e**		
	f	Biofuel producer credit (attach Form 6478)	**13f**		
	g	Other credits (see instructions) . . . . . Type ▶	**13g**		
Foreign Transactions	**14a**	Name of country or U.S. possession ▶			
	b	Gross income from all sources	**14b**		
	c	Gross income sourced at shareholder level	**14c**		
		Foreign gross income sourced at corporate level			
	d	Passive category	**14d**		
	e	General category	**14e**		
	f	Other (attach statement)	**14f**		
		Deductions allocated and apportioned at shareholder level			
	g	Interest expense	**14g**		
	h	Other	**14h**		
		Deductions allocated and apportioned at corporate level to foreign source income			
	i	Passive category	**14i**		
	j	General category	**14j**		
	k	Other (attach statement)	**14k**		
		Other information			
	l	Total foreign taxes (check one): ▶ ☐ Paid ☐ Accrued	**14l**		
	m	Reduction in taxes available for credit (attach statement)	**14m**		
	n	Other foreign tax information (attach statement)			
Alternative Minimum Tax (AMT) Items	**15a**	Post-1986 depreciation adjustment	**15a**		
	b	Adjusted gain or loss	**15b**		
	c	Depletion (other than oil and gas)	**15c**		
	d	Oil, gas, and geothermal properties—gross income	**15d**		
	e	Oil, gas, and geothermal properties—deductions	**15e**		
	f	Other AMT items (attach statement)	**15f**		
Items Affecting Shareholder Basis	**16a**	Tax-exempt interest income	**16a**		
	b	Other tax-exempt income	**16b**		
	c	Nondeductible expenses	**16c**		
	d	Distributions (attach statement if required) (see instructions)	**16d**		
	e	Repayment of loans from shareholders	**16e**		

Form **1120S** (2016)

Schedule K		Shareholders' Pro Rata Share Items (continued)		Total amount	
Other Information	17a	Investment income	17a		
	b	Investment expenses	17b		
	c	Dividend distributions paid from accumulated earnings and profits	17c		
	d	Other items and amounts (attach statement)			
Recon- ciliation	18	**Income/loss reconciliation.** Combine the amounts on lines 1 through 10 in the far right column. From the result, subtract the sum of the amounts on lines 11 through 12d and 14l	18		

Schedule L		Balance Sheets per Books	Beginning of tax year		End of tax year	
		Assets	(a)	(b)	(c)	(d)
1		Cash				
2a		Trade notes and accounts receivable				
	b	Less allowance for bad debts	( )		( )	
3		Inventories				
4		U.S. government obligations				
5		Tax-exempt securities (see instructions)				
6		Other current assets (attach statement)				
7		Loans to shareholders				
8		Mortgage and real estate loans				
9		Other investments (attach statement)				
10a		Buildings and other depreciable assets				
	b	Less accumulated depreciation	( )		( )	
11a		Depletable assets				
	b	Less accumulated depletion	( )		( )	
12		Land (net of any amortization)				
13a		Intangible assets (amortizable only)				
	b	Less accumulated amortization	( )		( )	
14		Other assets (attach statement)				
15		Total assets				
		Liabilities and Shareholders' Equity				
16		Accounts payable				
17		Mortgages, notes, bonds payable in less than 1 year				
18		Other current liabilities (attach statement)				
19		Loans from shareholders				
20		Mortgages, notes, bonds payable in 1 year or more				
21		Other liabilities (attach statement)				
22		Capital stock				
23		Additional paid-in capital				
24		Retained earnings				
25		Adjustments to shareholders' equity (attach statement)				
26		Less cost of treasury stock		( )		( )
27		Total liabilities and shareholders' equity				

Form **1120S** (2016)

Form 1120S (2016)   Page **5**

	Schedule M-1	Reconciliation of Income (Loss) per Books With Income (Loss) per Return		

Note: The corporation may be required to file Schedule M-3 (see instructions)

1	Net income (loss) per books		5	Income recorded on books this year not included on Schedule K, lines 1 through 10 (itemize):	
2	Income included on Schedule K, lines 1, 2, 3c, 4, 5a, 6, 7, 8a, 9, and 10, not recorded on books this year (itemize)_____		a	Tax-exempt interest $ _____	
3	Expenses recorded on books this year not included on Schedule K, lines 1 through 12 and 14l (itemize):		6	Deductions included on Schedule K, lines 1 through 12 and 14l, not charged against book income this year (itemize):	
a	Depreciation $ _____		a	Depreciation $ _____	
b	Travel and entertainment $ _____			_____	
	_____		7	Add lines 5 and 6	
4	Add lines 1 through 3		8	Income (loss) (Schedule K, line 18). Line 4 less line 7	

	Schedule M-2	Analysis of Accumulated Adjustments Account, Other Adjustments Account, and Shareholders' Undistributed Taxable Income Previously Taxed (see instructions)

		(a) Accumulated adjustments account	(b) Other adjustments account	(c) Shareholders' undistributed taxable income previously taxed
1	Balance at beginning of tax year			
2	Ordinary income from page 1, line 21 . . .			
3	Other additions			
4	Loss from page 1, line 21	( )		
5	Other reductions	( )	( )	
6	Combine lines 1 through 5			
7	Distributions other than dividend distributions			
8	Balance at end of tax year. Subtract line 7 from line 6			

Form **1120S** (2016)

671113

Schedule K-1
(Form 1120S)
Department of the Treasury
Internal Revenue Service

2016

For calendar year 2016, or tax
year beginning _____ , 2016
ending _____ , 20 _____

Shareholder's Share of Income, Deductions, Credits, etc.
▶ See back of form and separate instructions.

Part I	Information About the Corporation

A Corporation's employer identification number

B Corporation's name, address, city, state, and ZIP code

C IRS Center where corporation filed return

Part II	Information About the Shareholder

D Shareholder's identifying number

E Shareholder's name, address, city, state, and ZIP code

F Shareholder's percentage of stock
ownership for tax year .   .   .   . _____ %

For IRS Use Only

Part III	Shareholder's Share of Current Year Income, Deductions, Credits, and Other Items

#	Item	#	Item
1	Ordinary business income (loss)	13	Credits
2	Net rental real estate income (loss)		
3	Other net rental income (loss)		
4	Interest income		
5a	Ordinary dividends		
5b	Qualified dividends	14	Foreign transactions
6	Royalties		
7	Net short-term capital gain (loss)		
8a	Net long-term capital gain (loss)		
8b	Collectibles (28%) gain (loss)		
8c	Unrecaptured section 1250 gain		
9	Net section 1231 gain (loss)		
10	Other income (loss)	15	Alternative minimum tax (AMT) items
11	Section 179 deduction	16	Items affecting shareholder basis
12	Other deductions		
		17	Other information

* See attached statement for additional information.

For Paperwork Reduction Act Notice, see Instructions for Form 1120S.   IRS.gov/form1120s   Cat. No. 11520D   **Schedule K-1 (Form 1120S) 2016**

This list identifies the codes used on Schedule K-1 for all shareholders and provides summarized reporting information for shareholders who file Form 1040. For detailed reporting and filing information, see the separate Shareholder's Instructions for Schedule K-1 and the instructions for your income tax return.

1. **Ordinary business income (loss).** Determine whether the income (loss) is passive or nonpassive and enter on your return as follows:

	Report on
Passive loss	See the Shareholder's Instructions
Passive income	Schedule E, line 28, column (g)
Nonpassive loss	Schedule E, line 28, column (h)
Nonpassive income	Schedule E, line 28, column (j)

2. **Net rental real estate income (loss)** — See the Shareholder's Instructions

3. **Other net rental income (loss)**

Net income	Schedule E, line 28, column (g)
Net loss	See the Shareholder's Instructions

4. **Interest income** — Form 1040, line 8a
5a. **Ordinary dividends** — Form 1040, line 9a
5b. **Qualified dividends** — Form 1040, line 9b
6. **Royalties** — Schedule E, line 4
7. **Net short-term capital gain (loss)** — Schedule D, line 5
8a. **Net long-term capital gain (loss)** — Schedule D, line 12
8b. **Collectibles (28%) gain (loss)** — 28% Rate Gain Worksheet, line 4 (Schedule D instructions)
8c. **Unrecaptured section 1250 gain** — See the Shareholder's Instructions
9. **Net section 1231 gain (loss)** — See the Shareholder's Instructions
10. **Other income (loss)**
   Code
   A   Other portfolio income (loss) — See the Shareholder's Instructions
   B   Involuntary conversions — See the Shareholder's Instructions
   C   Sec. 1256 contracts & straddles — Form 6781, line 1
   D   Mining exploration costs recapture — See Pub. 535
   E   Other income (loss) — See the Shareholder's Instructions
11. **Section 179 deduction** — See the Shareholder's Instructions
12. **Other deductions**
   A   Cash contributions (50%)
   B   Cash contributions (30%)
   C   Noncash contributions (50%)
   D   Noncash contributions (30%)
   E   Capital gain property to a 50% organization (30%)   } See the Shareholder's Instructions
   F   Capital gain property (20%)
   G   Contributions (100%)
   H   Investment interest expense — Form 4952, line 1
   I   Deductions—royalty income — Schedule E, line 19
   J   Section 59(e)(2) expenditures — See the Shareholder's Instructions
   K   Deductions—portfolio (2% floor) — Schedule A, line 23
   L   Deductions—portfolio (other) — Schedule A, line 28
   M   Preproductive period expenses — See the Shareholder's Instructions
   N   Commercial revitalization deduction from rental real estate activities — See Form 8582 instructions
   O   Reforestation expense deduction — See the Shareholder's Instructions
   P   Domestic production activities information — See Form 8903 instructions
   Q   Qualified production activities income — Form 8903, line 7b
   R   Employer's Form W-2 wages — Form 8903, line 17
   S   Other deductions — See the Shareholder's Instructions
13. **Credits**
   A   Low-income housing credit (section 42(j)(5)) from pre-2008 buildings
   B   Low-income housing credit (other) from pre-2008 buildings
   C   Low-income housing credit (section 42(j)(5)) from post-2007 buildings
   D   Low-income housing credit (other) from post-2007 buildings   } See the Shareholder's Instructions
   E   Qualified rehabilitation expenditures (rental real estate)
   F   Other rental real estate credits
   G   Other rental credits
   H   Undistributed capital gains credit — Form 1040, line 73, box a
   I   Biofuel producer credit
   J   Work opportunity credit
   K   Disabled access credit
   L   Empowerment zone employment credit   } See the Shareholder's Instructions
   M   Credit for increasing research activities

Code		Report on
N	Credit for employer social security and Medicare taxes	
O	Backup withholding	See the Shareholder's Instructions
P	Other credits	

14. **Foreign transactions**
   A   Name of country or U.S. possession
   B   Gross income from all sources   } Form 1116, Part I
   C   Gross income sourced at shareholder level

   Foreign gross income sourced at corporate level
   D   Passive category
   E   General category   } Form 1116, Part I
   F   Other

   Deductions allocated and apportioned at shareholder level
   G   Interest expense — Form 1116, Part I
   H   Other — Form 1116, Part I

   Deductions allocated and apportioned at corporate level to foreign source income
   I   Passive category
   J   General category   } Form 1116, Part I
   K   Other

   Other information
   L   Total foreign taxes paid — Form 1116, Part II
   M   Total foreign taxes accrued — Form 1116, Part II
   N   Reduction in taxes available for credit — Form 1116, line 12
   O   Foreign trading gross receipts — Form 8873
   P   Extraterritorial income exclusion — Form 8873
   Q   Other foreign transactions — See the Shareholder's Instructions

15. **Alternative minimum tax (AMT) items**
   A   Post-1986 depreciation adjustment
   B   Adjusted gain or loss
   C   Depletion (other than oil & gas)   See the Shareholder's Instructions and the Instructions for Form 6251
   D   Oil, gas, & geothermal—gross income
   E   Oil, gas, & geothermal—deductions
   F   Other AMT items

16. **Items affecting shareholder basis**
   A   Tax-exempt interest income — Form 1040, line 8b
   B   Other tax-exempt income
   C   Nondeductible expenses
   D   Distributions   } See the Shareholder's Instructions
   E   Repayment of loans from shareholders

17. **Other information**
   A   Investment income — Form 4952, line 4a
   B   Investment expenses — Form 4952, line 5
   C   Qualified rehabilitation expenditures (other than rental real estate) — See the Shareholder's Instructions
   D   Basis of energy property — See the Shareholder's Instructions
   E   Recapture of low-income housing credit (section 42(j)(5)) — Form 8611, line 8
   F   Recapture of low-income housing credit (other) — Form 8611, line 8
   G   Recapture of investment credit — See Form 4255
   H   Recapture of other credits — See the Shareholder's Instructions
   I   Look-back interest—completed long-term contracts — See Form 8697
   J   Look-back interest—income forecast method — See Form 8866
   K   Dispositions of property with section 179 deductions
   L   Recapture of section 179 deduction
   M   Section 453(l)(3) information
   N   Section 453A(c) information
   O   Section 1260(b) information
   P   Interest allocable to production expenditures   } See the Shareholder's Instructions
   Q   CCF nonqualified withdrawals
   R   Depletion information—oil and gas
   S   Reserved
   T   Section 108(i) information
   U   Net investment income
   V   Other information

CLASS QUESTIONS

Work through the below Class Questions while following along with the respective lectures. Once this is complete, you can begin independently practicing what you've learned by quizzing yourself on this course section in your Interactive Practice Questions (IPQ), which can be found in your online Student Dashboard. Your IPQ simulates the computer-based testing experience, and will also help you understand how concepts are applied to the exam. Each question includes answer explanations from expert CPAs that will help you determine why you answered a question correctly or incorrectly. This is key to your success on the CPA Exam.

Lecture 3.04

1. Village Corp., a calendar-year corporation, began business in 20X1. Village made a valid S corporation election on September 5, 20X7, with the unanimous consent of its shareholders. The eligibility requirements for S status continued to be met throughout 20X7. On what date did Village's S status become effective?

   a. January 1, 20X7
   b. January 1, 20X8
   c. September 5, 20X7
   d. September 5, 20X8

2. A shareholder's basis in the stock of an S corporation is increased by the shareholder's pro rata share of income from

	Tax-exempt Interest	Taxable Interest
a.	No	No
b.	No	Yes
c.	Yes	No
d.	Yes	Yes

3. An S corporation has 30,000 shares of voting common stock and 20,000 shares of nonvoting common stock issued and outstanding. The S election can be revoked voluntarily with the consent of the shareholders holding, on the day of the revocation,

	Shares of voting stock	Shares of nonvoting stock
a.	0	20,000
b.	7,500	5,000
c.	10,000	16,000
d.	20,000	0

4. Beck Corp. has been a calendar-year S corporation since its inception on January 2, 20X1. On January 1, 20X4, Lazur and Lyle each owned 50% of the Beck stock, in which their respective tax bases were $12,000 and $9,000. For the year ended December 31, 20X4, Beck had $81,000 in ordinary business income and $10,000 in tax-exempt income. Beck made a $51,000 cash distribution to each shareholder on December 31, 20X4. What was Lazur's tax basis in Beck after the distribution?

   a. $ 1,500
   b. $ 6,500
   c. $52,500
   d. $57,500

5. An S corporation is **not** permitted to take a deduction for

    a. Compensation of officers.

    b. Interest paid to individuals who are not stockholders of the S corporation.

    c. Charitable contributions.

    d. Employee benefit programs established for individuals who are not stockholders of the S corporation.

6. Smart Corp., a calendar-year corporation, was formed in 20X3 and made an S corporation election in 20X6 that is still in effect. Its books and records for 20X13 reflect the following information:

Accumulated earnings and profits at 1/1/X13	$90,000
Accumulated adjustments account at 1/1/X13	50,000
Ordinary income for 20X13	200,000

Smart Corp. is solely owned by Roger, whose basis in Smart's stock was $100,000 on January 1, 20X13. During 20X13, Smart distributed $310,000 to Roger. What is the amount of the $310,000 distribution that Roger must report as dividend income for 20X13, assuming no special elections were made with regard to the distribution?

    a. $0

    b. $ 60,000

    c. $ 90,000

    d. $140,000

CLASS SOLUTIONS

1. (b) An S corporation election must be made within 2 ½ months of the beginning of a fiscal period, by March 15 for a calendar year company, to be effective for that period. If it is filed after that date, it becomes effective at the beginning of the next fiscal period. Village did not make the election by March 15 and, as a result, it will go into effect at the beginning of the next year.

2. (d) An S corporation is a flow-through entity, which means that the transactions of the entity basically flow through to its shareholders. As the entity earns income, it is treated as income to the shareholder, increasing the shareholder's basis. Its status as being taxable or nontaxable also flows through. As a result, tax-exempt interest increases the shareholder's basis but is not taxable to the shareholder, while taxable interest increases the shareholder's basis and is taxable to the shareholder.

3. (c) Voluntarily revoking an S corporation election requires the consent of a majority of the shares, regardless of whether they are voting or nonvoting shares. With 30,000 voting shares and 20,000 nonvoting shares, there are a total of 50,000 shares outstanding. It will require at least 25,001 shares in total, including voting and nonvoting shares, to revoke the election. That might include 10,000 shares of voting stock and 16,000 shares of nonvoting stock for a total of 26,000 shares.

4. (b) Lazur had a beginning tax basis of $12,000, which would be increased by Lazur's 50% share of Beck's $81,000 ordinary business income and $10,000 tax-exempt income. As a result, Lazur's tax basis in the S corp would be $12,000 + $40,500 + $5,000 = $57,500. A distribution of $51,000 to Lazur reduces the tax basis to $57,500 - $51,000 = $6,500.

5. (c) An S corporation is not allowed to take a deduction for charitable contributions when calculating its ordinary business income. Since an S Corporation is a pass-through entity, any items of income or expense that require special tax treatment (such as long-term capital gains) or have limitations (such as on the deductibility of charitable contributions) are reported separately and pass through directly to shareholders.

6. (b) Assuming no special elections are made, distributions from an S corporation are first assumed to come from the current period's earnings and profits, $200,000 for Smart. Any remainder is next assumed to come from earnings and profits accumulated since the entity elected S corporation status, referred to as the accumulated adjustments account, which is $50,000 for Smart. Since these distributions represent amounts that are already taxed to the shareholder, Roger, due to the flow-through nature of an S corp. The remaining $60,000 is assumed to be distributed from earnings and profits accumulated prior to the S corporation election. These earnings had not previously been taxable to Roger and would be treated as taxable dividends when distributed.

Lecture 3.05

TASK-BASED SIMULATIONS

Task-Based Simulation 1

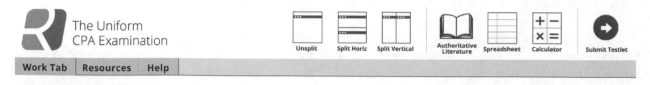

| Work Tab | Resources | Help |

Required:

Lan Corp., an accrual-basis calendar-year repair service corporation, was formed and began business on January 6, 20X9. Lan's valid S corporation election took effect retroactively on January 6, 20X9. Since the question requires a numeric answer, a list of numeric amounts would be provided for the candidate to select from.

Items to be answered:

For **items 1 through 4,** determine the amount, if any, using the fact pattern for each item.

1. Assume the following facts:

    Lan's 20X9 books recorded the following items:

Gross receipts	$7,260
Interest income on investments	50
Charitable contributions	1,000
Supplies	1,120

    What amount of net business income should Lan report on its 20X9 Form 1120S, U.S. Income Tax Return for an S corporation, Schedule K?

2. Assume the following facts:

    As of January 6, 20X9, Taylor and Barr each owned 100 shares of the 200 issued shares of Lan stock. On January 31, 20X9, Taylor and Barr each sold 20 shares to Pike. No election was made to terminate the tax year. Lan had net business income of $14,400 for the year ended December 31, 20X9, and made no distributions to its shareholders. Lan's 20X9 calendar year had 360 days.

    What amount of net business income should have been reported on Pike's 20X9 Schedule K-1 from Lan? (20X9 is a 360-day tax year.) Round the answer to the nearest hundred.

3. Assume the following facts:

    Pike purchased 40 Lan shares on January 31, 20X9, for $4,000. Lan made no distributions to shareholders, and Pike's 20X9 Schedule K-1 from Lan reported

Ordinary business loss	$(1,000)
Municipal bond income	150

    What was Pike's basis in his Lan stock at December 31, 20X9?

4. Assume the following facts:

    On January 6, 20X9, Taylor and Barr each owned 100 shares of the 200 issued shares of Lan stock. Taylor's basis in Lan shares on that date was $10,000. Taylor sold all of his Lan shares to Pike on January 31, 20X9, and Lan made a valid election to terminate its tax year. Taylor's share of ordinary income from Lan prior to the sale was $2,000. Lan made a cash distribution of $3,000 to Taylor on January 30, 20X9.

    What was Taylor's basis in Lan shares for determining gain or loss from the sale to Pike?

Task-Based Simulation 2

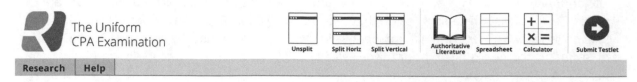

A group of investors is planning to establish an S corporation. They wish to determine how many investors they may have and still qualify for S corporation status.

Which code section, subsection, paragraph, and subparagraph will provide information about the maximum number of shareholders a corporation may have and still qualify for S corporation status?

Task-Based Simulation 3

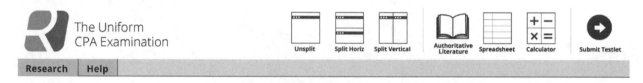

A C corporation elected S corporation status during the current year. On the date that the election became effective, the entity had various assets with fair values that exceeded their adjusted bases. The entity is trying to determine the amount of its net unrealized built-in gain.

Which code section, subsection, and paragraph defines the term net unrealized built-in gain?

TASK-BASED SIMULATION SOLUTIONS

Task-Based Simulation Solution 1

For **items 1 through 4,** candidates were asked to determine the amount for Lan Corp. (an accrual-basis calendar-year S corporation), using the fact pattern for each item.

1. ($6,140) Business income, often referred to as ordinary business income, includes those revenue and expenses that are not flow-through items because they neither require special tax treatment, like capital gains, nor are they subject to limitations, such as the limit on the deductibility of charitable contributions. Interest income on investments is a flow-through item because of limitations on the deductibility of investment interest expense. Charitable contributions also flow through because of the limit on their deductibility. As a result, business income would consist of gross receipts of $7,260, reduced by supplies of $1,120, for a net of $6,140.

2. ($2,700) Pike acquired a 20% interest (a total of 40 shares out of 200) on January 31, 25 days after the corporation had been formed. Since there were only 360 days in the corporation's initial year, from January 6 through December 31, Pike held the shares for 335 of the 360 days. Pike's share of the income can be calculated as $14,400 × 20% × 335/360 = $2,680, which, when rounded to the nearest $100, is approximately $2,700.

3. ($3,150) The tax basis of the shares held in an S corporation are increased by the shareholder's share of the corporation's income, whether taxable or not, and decreased by the shareholder's share of losses and distributions. Pike's initial basis is the cost of $4,000. It will be decreased by Pike's $1,000 share of ordinary losses and increased by Pike's $150 share of the municipal bond interest, resulting in an ending balance of $4,000 - $1,000 + $150 = $3,150.

4. ($9,000) A shareholder's basis in the stock of an S corporation is increased by the shareholder's share of the corporation's income, whether taxable or not, and decreased by the shareholder's share of losses and distributions. Taylor had a beginning basis of $10,000, which will be increased by Taylor's share of January earnings of $2,000 and reduced by the $3,000 in cash distributed to Taylor. As a result, Taylor's basis is $10,000 + $2,000 - $3,000 = $9,000.

Task-Based Simulation Solution 2

1361	(b)	(1)	(A)

Task-Based Simulation Solution 3

1374	(d)	(1)

Section 4 – Partnership Taxation

Corresponding Lectures

Watch the following course lectures with this section:

Lecture 4.01 – Partnership Taxation
Lecture 4.02 – Partnership Taxation: Basis
Lecture 4.03 – Operation of Partnership
Lecture 4.04 – Partnership Taxation: Basis – Class Questions
Lecture 4.05 – Partnership Distributions
Lecture 4.06 – Partnership Termination
Lecture 4.07 – Partnership Distributions – Class Questions
Lecture 4.08 – Partnership Taxation – Class Questions – TBS
Lecture 4.09 – Partnership Taxation – Class Questions – DRS

EXAM NOTE: *Please refer to the AICPA REG Blueprint in the Introduction to find a listing of the representative tasks (and their associated skill levels—i.e., Remembering and Understanding, Application, and Analysis) that the candidate should be able to perform based on the knowledge obtained in this section.*

Partnership Taxation

PARTNERSHIP TAXATION

A partnership (P/S) is an association between two or more persons to operate a business as co-owners for profit.

- File an Information tax return, since a P/S is a flow-through entity (**Form 1065).**
- For tax years beginning after 2015, the due date is 3/15 for calendar-year partnerships (2 ½ months after year-end), and the extension period is six months. Note, however, that tax return due dates and extensions are no longer tested on the CPA Exam.
- Tax year generally must be the same as the partners, or a majority of partners.
- Accounting is similar to S corporations.
- **Informal** creation since all partners have unlimited liability (i.e., everything is **"at risk"** in a general partnership).
  - **Cash or Property**
    - Tax-free exchange (No 80%/control rule!)
    - Carryover basis
    - Carryover holding period
  - **Services**
    - Taxable at FMV of capital interest received (i.e., generally the FMV of Services provided).

The **holding period** of a partnership interest acquired in exchange for a contributed property:
- For capital assets or Sec. 1231 (non-current business) assets: includes period held by the partner
- All other property—when partnership interest acquired.

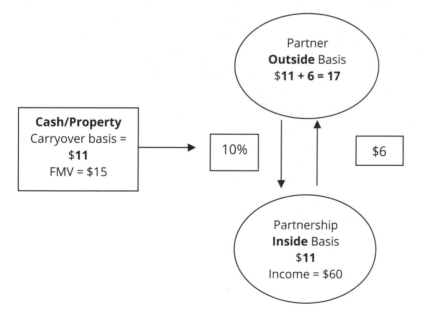

Terms

The following terms appear frequently in exam questions related to partnership taxation:
- **Outside** Basis – Partner basis in the P/S
- **Inside** Basis – Partnership basis in its assets
- Basis in **Asset received** from P/S distribution
- **Guaranteed payment** – like a salary in an S Corp
    - Taxable as ordinary income to partner receiving payment and subject to self-employment tax
    - Deductible to P/S as ordinary expense
        - Not a separately stated item to the P/S, but is separately reported to the partner receiving the payment.
    - Not based on Income—should be for services or use of capital.
    - Does not directly reduce partner's basis.

Lecture 4.02

PARTNERSHIP TAXATION: BASIS

Operation of P/S

Initial	+/-	% Income/Loss*	- Distributions	+ **Your % of**	- **Liabilities**	= Ending
Outside		Muni bond int.	Received	**P/S**	**contributed**	**Outside**
Basis		Sep. stated items	from P/S	**Liabilities**	**to P/S**	Basis

Basis

The most important concept in partnership tax law is that of a partner's **basis**, which generally equals the amount the partner has "at risk" in the partnership. A partner's basis is **not** identical to the partner's Equity/Capital in the business, since a partner's basis includes the partner's share of partnership liabilities to creditors and the partner's capital account does not. Note: Basis is generally equal the amount at-risk unless a particular reason is given as to why the partner is not at-risk for such amount (e.g., a partner is not personally liable for repayment of a liability).
- A partner's basis **increases** for:
    - Contributions of assets by the partner to the partnership
    - Borrowings and other debts incurred by the partnership
    - Allocation of partnership income (distributive share) to the partner
- A partner's basis **decreases** for:
    - Distributions of assets from the partnership to the partner
    - Allocation of partnership losses (distributive share) to the partner
    - Repayments and other reductions of debts of the partnership

*Note: In determining whether a partner's distributive share of loss is deductible, *distributions are required to be taken into account before losses* due to the IRC Sec. 704(d) basis limitation. Any excess of such loss over basis is allowed as a deduction when the excess is repaid to the partnership (i.e., there is sufficient basis to absorb the loss). Similarly, losses are also limited by the *at-risk rules* under IRC Sec. 465 and the *passive activity loss rules* under IRC Sec. 469, as previously discussed.

When a partnership is created, the partners normally make contributions of **cash or property**. When a partner contributes cash, their basis is increased by the amount paid. When a partner contributes property, their basis in their partnership interest is increased by the partner's tax basis in the contributed asset (fair market value is ignored). If the asset being **contributed is subject to a liability**, the partner's net contribution is reduced because of the contributed liability, but then each partner's basis is increased by their individual shares of the liability the partnership has assumed.

For example, assume that the ABC Partnership is formed with three equal partners: Andy, Billie, and Cindy. Andy and Billie each contribute $100 of cash. Cindy contributes land with a tax basis of $80 and a fair market value of $130, subject to an unpaid mortgage of $30 that is being assumed by the partnership. In terms of fair value, each partner has contributed an equal $100, but the tax determination of basis is as follows:

Initial Contribution	± Income/Loss	- Distribution Received	+ % Partnership Liabilities	- Contributed Liabilities	= Net Basis (outside)
AA $100			+$10		=$110
BB $100			+$10		=$110
CC $80			+$10	- $30	= $60

Partners	A	B	C
Contributed Asset	100	100	80
Contributed Liability	—	—	(30)
Net Contribution	100	100	50
Share of Liability	10	10	10
Basis (At Risk)	110	110	60

Notice that the $30 liability contributed by Cindy first decreases her basis due to the contributed debt but then increases it by $30 / 3 = $10, which is her share of the new partnership liability.

When a partner renders **services** to the partnership in exchange for an interest in the business, the partner reports ordinary income equal to the fair market value of the partnership interest being granted, and the partner's basis is increased by the same amount.

Under no circumstances can a partner's basis ever be reduced below $0. If a loss would have reduced the partner's basis below zero, that portion of the loss is not deductible. If a distribution would have reduced the partner's basis below zero, the partner will either adjust the basis of the distributed asset or, in the case of cash distributions, report a gain from the distribution.
- Basis never declines below $0
    - Loss reducing basis below $0 not deductible.
    - Cash distribution exceeding basis results in gain.
    - Contributed asset subject to higher liability results in gain.
        - **Example:** Get a 20% interest by contributing an asset with a FMV of $10,000, a carryover basis of $4,000 and subject to a mortgage of $6,000, which P/S assumes.

Initial Outside Basis	+/- % Income/Loss Muni bond int. Sep stated items	- Distributions Received from P/S	+ **Your % of P/S Liabilities**	- Liabilities contributed to P/S	Ending = **Outside** Basis
4,000			+1,200 (6,000 × 20%)	- (6,000)	= (800)

(Since basis cannot be negative, the partner has an $800 gain and basis is $0.)

Recourse Vs. Nonrecourse Liabilities
- Recourse Liabilities – Debtor bears an economic risk of loss.
  - Partners generally share in recourse liabilities to the extent they are personally liable for repayment.
  - Since limited partners in a limited partnership are not generally liable for the repayment of debt, *recourse liabilities are allocated only to general partners*, unless otherwise specified.
- Nonrecourse liabilities – Debtor does NOT bear an economic risk of loss.
  - Partners (general and limited) generally share in nonrecourse liabilities in relation to their profits interest in the partnership. If a profits interest is not stated, it is the same as the capital interest.
    - Profits interest – Partner's share of future profits/losses.
    - Capital interest – Partner's share of net assets if partnership liquidates.

Capital (Equity) accounts represent the partners' shares of partnership equity (partnership assets minus liabilities). A separate capital account for each partner is maintained. The partnership keeps track of each partner's capital account and presents an analysis of the capital account on Schedule K-1. **Note**, the capital account is different than the partner's adjusted basis. **For example**, the capital account does not include a partner's share of partnership liabilities, whereas basis does.

Organizational and Start-up Costs

A partnership may deduct up to $5,000 of organizational expenditures and up to $5,000 of start-up costs for the tax year in which the partnership begins business, with any remaining expenditures deducted ratably over the **180-month period** beginning with the month in which the partnership begins business. The $5,000 amount ($5,000 for each organizational and start-up costs) is reduced by the amount by which the organizational expenditures or start-up costs exceed $50,000, respectively. Organizational costs include partnership filing fees as well as legal and accounting fees incident to the organization of the partnership. Note: Syndication fees incurred to sell the interests are not organizational expenses and must be capitalized. Start-up costs include training, advertising and testing incurred before the start of active trade or business.

Lecture 4.03

OPERATION OF A PARTNERSHIP

Partnerships do not pay income taxes, but are required to file annual information returns (Form 1065), reporting partnership income and the allocation of that income to the various partners.

Since the items will be reported on the tax returns of the partners, the partnership must segregate items that have special treatment on individual tax returns. The partnership prepares a Schedule K that summarizes the partnership ordinary income and then separately lists all items that are not ordinary. Additionally, a Schedule K-1 is prepared for each partner showing that partner's allocated share of all items on the Schedule K.

You should try and remember the list of the items that are reported separately as this has been tested. Also, keep in mind that the purpose of separately stating items is to allow any special treatment on individual returns to be applied. As a result, any item which is always included in the gross income of an individual without restrictions or limitations need not be separately stated. A few examples of separately stated items are:

Separately stated item	Reason not included in ordinary income
Capital gains and losses	Limit on deductibility of net capital losses
Section 1231 gains and losses	Classification of net gain as capital gain
Dividends and investment interest	Investment interest expense limitation
Passive activities	Passive activity loss limitations
Charitable contributions	Must itemize to deduct/ Up to 50% of AGI
Section 179 depreciation election	Dollar limit on use of election per year
Tax credits	Limited to tax liability

Examples of items that are included in partnership ordinary income are sales, depreciation, supplies, and salaries.

One item that is unusual and unique to partnerships is **guaranteed payments to partners**, referring to payments that are not based on the amount of partnership income or loss but on separate contractual relationships between the partnership and a partner, such as for services rendered or for the use of capital. The most common example of a guaranteed payment is a salary allocated to a partner who works actively in the conduct of the business, as long as the salary is to be paid regardless of partnership income.

Because such payments represent ordinary business expenses of the partnership, they are included in the determination of the ordinary income of the partnership. They must also, however, be separately stated on the Schedule K-1 of each partner receiving such payments, so that the partner will include the income received on their individual tax return.

Partnership Tax Year

Per IRC Sec. 706(a), generally a partnership is required to adopt the same tax year as that of the partners (or a *majority* of partnership interests). Thus, if the partners are all individuals that report income using calendar years, the partnership itself should have a December 31 year-end. If there is no majority interest tax year, the tax year of the *principal* partners (i.e., those owning 5%+) is used. If there are no principal partners or their tax years are not the same, the year with the *least aggregate deferral* is used. Least aggregate deferral means the year that defers the least amount of the partners' income for the least amount of time, which is determined by adding together for each year: deferral period per partner × partner's % ownership.

For example, Partner A (50% interest) reports income on the fiscal year ending 6/30 and Partner B (50% interest) reports income on the fiscal year ending 7/31.

Year-end 6/30

Partner	Year-end	% Interest in partnership	Months of deferral	Interest × deferral
A	6/30	.5	0	0
B	7/31	.5	1	.5
Aggregate deferral				.5*

Year-end 7/31

A	6/30	.5	11	5.5
B	7/31	.5	0	0
Aggregate deferral				5.5

*A 6/30 year-end must be used since it results in the least aggregate deferral of income.

A partnership is allowed to use a tax year other than the normally required year if it **either:**
- Provides a valid *business purpose* for the alternate tax year
  - A retail store with a natural business year ending on January 31.
  - Ski resort with a natural business year ending May 31.
  - Income deferral can exceed 3 months; business reason is the only criterion.

- Makes a *Section 444 election* – no business reason needed, but no more than 3 months' income deferral allowed. For example, a partnership that is normally required to use December 31 can, upon making a Section 444 election, choose November 30, October 31, or September 30. The result is to make it possible for up to 3 months of partnership income to be deferred into the following year before being taxed on the returns of the partners.

When the tax year of the partnership doesn't coincide with the tax year of a partner to whom the partnership is making guaranteed payments, the reporting of the payment received will be based on the tax year of the partnership.

For example, assume the ABC partnership paid a regular $2,000 monthly salary to one of its partners, Andy Anderson, during calendar 20X1, and increased it to $3,000 monthly in calendar year 20X2. Andy's individual tax return is filed using a calendar year, but ABC is using the valid business reason exception and has a September 30 fiscal year.

The salary that will be reported by Andy on his individual tax return for 20X2 is **not** the $36,000 ($3,000 per month × 12 months) that he received in 20X2. He will be getting his 20X2 salary from the partnership K-1 for the year ended September 30, 20X2, and the partnership only paid $33,000 during the 12 months ended September 30, 20X2 ($2,000 per month x 3 months in 20X1, plus $3,000 per month for 9 months in 20X2).

Transactions Between Partner and Partnership

Transactions between a partner and the partnership generally are considered as occurring between two completely independent entities. The exception is if the partner owns over a majority interest in the partnership. *Losses* from sales of property between the controlling partner and the partnership are not allowed (related party transactions). *Gains* from the sale of property are characterized as *ordinary* income. This is the case whether the interest is owned directly or indirectly. If, for example, partner A has a 40% ownership and related partner B has a 20% ownership, partner A would be considered to have a 60% controlling interest, thus, losses on transactions between partner A and the partnership would not be deductible.

Lecture 4.04

CLASS QUESTIONS

Please see the Class Questions and Class Solutions for this Lecture at the end of this Section.

PARTNERSHIP DISTRIBUTIONS

A distribution of assets from the partnership to a partner reduces that partner's basis in the partnership. The amount by which the partner's basis is reduced depends on several different factors. First, it must be determined if the distribution is:

- **Nonliquidating (Current or Operating Distributions)** – The partner continues in the business after the distribution.
- **Liquidating** – The distribution is in settlement of the partner's entire interest in the business.

Distributions to a retiring partner are generally treated as received in exchange for that partner's interest in partnership property, and as such are generally treated under the rules that apply to liquidating distributions. Payments made by a personal service partnership to a retired partner that are determined by partnership income are treated as income by the retired partner for tax purposes.

Normally, a **nonliquidating distribution** reduces the partner's basis in the partnership by the tax basis of the distributed asset in the partnership (the fair market value of distributed property is ignored, just as it is for contributed property). Since a partner's basis cannot be reduced below zero, however, a distribution in which the asset's basis exceeds the partner's basis must be handled specially:

- Cash distributions – The excess of the cash distribution over the partner's basis is reported as a gain on the partner's individual tax return.
- Property distributions – The basis of the distributed asset in the hands of the partner is reduced to equal the partner's basis in the partnership prior to the distribution.

For example, assume a partnership makes a **nonliquidating distribution** of $10 to a partner. If the partner's basis in the partnership was $17 before the distribution, the effect of cash distributions and property distributions is the same:

Type of asset	Cash	Property
Partner's basis before distribution	17	17
Distribution	(10)	(10)
Partner's basis after distribution	7	7
Gain or loss	0	0

If the partner's basis before the distribution was $8, the treatment varies:

Type of asset	Cash	Property
Partner's basis before distribution	8	8
Distribution	(10)	(8)
Partner's basis after distribution	0	0
Gain or loss	2	0

Notice that the basis of the property is simply reduced to $8 so that it will not exceed the partner's basis. Since cash cannot be adjusted, a gain must be reported.

A **liquidating distribution** is in some ways simpler, since the partner's basis in the partnership must be reduced to $0 in all cases. The difference between cash and property distributions is as follows:

- **Cash, inventory and unrealized receivable distributions –**
  - The total of cash, unrealized receivables, and inventory distributed to a partner is compared to the partner's basis in the partnership before the distribution and any excess basis is reported as a *loss* on the partner's individual tax return.
  - Only cash (and marketable securities) is used to determine a *gain*.
- **Property distributions** – The basis of the distributed asset is always equal to the partner's basis in the partnership before the distribution, so *no gain or loss* is recognized.

For example, if a $10 **liquidating distribution** is made to a partner with a $17 basis in the business, the treatment is as follows:

Type of asset	Cash	Property
Partner's basis before distribution	17	17
Distribution	(10)	(17)
Partner's basis after distribution	0	0
Gain or loss	(7)	0

If the partner's basis in the partnership before the distribution was $8, the treatment is as follows:

Type of asset	Cash	Property
Partner's basis before distribution	8	8
Distribution	(10)	(8)
Partner's basis after distribution	0	0
Gain or loss	2	0

Note: If receive both cash and property, do cash first, the remainder is allocated to property.

To summarize the amount used for distributed property other than cash when the basis to the partnership of the distributed asset is different from the partner's basis in the partnership.

	Nonliquidating Distribution (Lower of inside or outside basis)	Liquidating Distribution (Outside basis)
Partner's basis > Asset's basis	Asset	Partner
Partner's basis < Asset's basis	Partner	Partner

Lecture 4.06

PARTNERSHIP TERMINATION

Sale of Partnership Interest

When a partner wishes to sell their interest to another party (either another partner or an outsider), the *amount realized is the sum of*:

- Cash and property received
- + Relief from debt

For example, assume that Ronnie Remainder and Sammy Seller are equal partners in the R&S Partnership, and that the partnership, which reports on a cash basis for income tax purposes, has the following balance sheet:

	Tax Basis	Fair Market Value
Cash	150	150
Accounts receivable	---	300
Goodwill	---	400
Total assets	150	850
Liabilities	100	100
RR, capital	25	375
SS, capital	25	375
Total liabilities & capital	150	850

Bobby Buyer purchases Sammy's 50% interest in the partnership, paying Sammy $375 cash (based on the fair value of the partnership) and assuming Sammy's share of partnership liabilities.

In this transaction, the sales proceeds to Sammy are $425, including the cash received of $375 and the debt relief of $100 × 50% = $50. Sammy's basis in the partnership before the sale was $75, including the capital account's tax basis of $25 and Sammy's share of liabilities of $100 × 50% = $50. The gain on sale reported on Sammy's individual tax return is $425 - $75 = $350.

Actual Cash Proceeds	375
+ Debt Relief	+50
= Amount Realized	**425**
- Partner's Basis (Outside)	-75
= Gain/Loss	**350**

Normally, the gain on sale reported by a partner is a capital gain, since it results from the sale of an investment asset (the interest in the business) rather than a business asset itself.

There is, however, one possible complication. When a partner sells their interest, the amount the buyer is willing to pay is based on the fair market value of the assets and liabilities (including goodwill), and not on the tax bases of these assets and liabilities. If the partnership has **unrealized ordinary income assets (inventories and accounts receivable – "Hot Assets")** at the time of sale, the partner has effectively converted income that would have been ordinary (once the partnership realized the assets) to capital gains (since the partner sold the interest before the assets were realized). To prevent this, the gain on sale of a partnership must be reported as ordinary income to the extent of unrealized **ordinary income** assets at the time of sale. The rest is considered a capital gain.

Ordinary Gain/Loss for inventory and receivables → **Capital** Gain/Loss for everything else.

Again, assume Bobby Buyer purchases Sammy's 50% interest in the partnership so that Sammy realizes a gain of $350. In this example, the tax basis fails to reflect accounts receivable of $300 that result in ordinary income once the receivables are collected. Since Sammy's share of that receivable is $300 × 50% = $150, the first $150 of the gain on sale to Bobby is reported as **ordinary income**, and only the remaining $350 - $150 = $200 qualifies as a **capital gain.**

Termination for Tax Purposes

Other than for electing termination for large partnerships (over 100 partners), a partnership terminates for tax purposes when any of the following occurs:

- The business and financial operations are discontinued.
- The business is reduced to one owner.
- 50% or more of partnership interests change hands within a 12-month period.

A terminated partnership must file a final return that covers the period up to the date of termination. If the business continues, the new business must obtain a different tax identification number and file an initial return that begins from the date of the termination of the previous partnership. The end of the previous partnership and start of the new business are treated as distributions of all assets from the terminated partnership, followed by contributions of all the assets to the new business.

If a partnership divides into two or more separate partnerships, the partnership into which a majority of the interests of the old partnership are transferred is considered a continuation of that partnership, and the other partnerships are treated as brand-new businesses with new contributions of the transferred assets. If none of the separate partnerships holds a majority of previous interests, all are treated as new partnerships and the previous partnership is terminated.

If two or more partnerships merge and the partners in one of the businesses are given a majority of the interests of the merged entity, then the merged entity is considered a continuation of that previous partnership and the other previous partnerships are terminated. If no one former partnership gets a majority of interests in the new merged partnership, then all previous partnerships dissolve and the merged partnership is a new partnership with new contributions of the transferred assets.

Partnership Elections

A partnership may elect to change its tax status to that of a **Large Partnership** by filing Form 1065-B. To qualify as a large partnership, the partnership must have had 100 or more partners in the preceding tax year. A large partnership may be required to pay certain taxes, such as a recapture of investment tax credit, but generally all other items of profit and loss pass through to the partners.

A partnership may file a Sec. 754 election to adjust the basis of partnership property whenever there is a transfer of a partnership interest (i.e., sale/exchange or when a partner dies). When this election is in effect, the partnership must increase/decrease its inside basis in partnership assets to make the new partner's outside basis equal to their share of inside basis in partnership property. The election applies to all such transfers until the election is revoked by the partnership with IRS consent. (Note that the Sec. 754 election also covers basis adjustments in the event of a distribution of property, but this is likely beyond the scope of the exam).

SIMILARITIES AND DIFFERENCES BETWEEN LLPS AND LLCS

Limited Liability Company (LLC)

Some states allow for a type of business entity referred to as a Limited Liability Company (LLC). Owners of LLCs, which generally can be individuals, corporations, other LLCs, or foreign entities, are referred to as **members**. In most cases, all members have the right to participate in the management of the LLC and are treated as agents. Certain types of companies, such as banks and insurance companies, may not be structured as LLCs.

Unless the members elect otherwise, an LLC is **taxed** as a **flow-through entity**.

- If there is one member, it is considered a "disregarded entity" and the activities of the LLC are reported on the individual's tax return, using Schedule C to report income from a business or profession.
- If there are multiple members, the entity is usually treated as a partnership and is required to file an information return (1065). Profits, losses, and other pass-through items, however, may be allocated as the members see fit and not necessarily on the basis of ownership percentages.
- The entity may choose to be taxed as a corporation by filing an election (Form 8832). It may then elect to be taxed as a C corporation or an S corporation.

In addition to being able to elect how it is taxed, LLCs provide several other ***advantages***. An LLC is considered an entity that is separate from its owners. It may sue or be sued. In addition, it provides the members with liability that is limited to the amount of their investments, although a distribution to members that renders the LLC insolvent will cause the members to be personally liable.

One ***disadvantage*** of the LLC is that, in most states, if a member leaves the LLC, the business is required to be dissolved. The remaining members must fulfill any business obligations and close the business, although they may start a new LLC if they so desire. Another disadvantage is that members of an LLC are considered self-employed and are subject to self-employment tax on their share of the entire earnings of the LLC.

Limited Liability Partnership (LLP)

Another form of entity is the Limited Liability Partnership (LLP), in which some or all partners, depending on the state of jurisdiction, have limited liability. It is like a general partnership in that all partners have the right to participate in management of the partnership. Unlike general partnerships, partners in an LLP are not liable for the misconduct or negligence of other partners. In addition, an obligation of a partnership that is incurred while it is an LLP is generally the sole obligation of the partnership and the partners are not personally liable. [RUPA §306(c); adopted by a majority of states]

LLPs are popular among professionals, such as lawyers, accountants, and architects, to provide protection to partners from liability for ill advice that may be given by other partners within the firm.

Although an LLP provides its partners limited liability, it is **taxed** similarly to a general partnership.

- Taxed as a Partnership (Form 1065), unless elect to be taxed as a Corporation.
- If taxed as a Partnership:
  - A general partner, if there are any, is subject to both income tax and self-employment tax.
  - A limited partner's share of an LLP's income or loss is reported as passive income or loss, subject to the passive activity loss limitations.

Similarities and differences between LLPs and LLCs

Formation:

- Both require an enabling statute in the state of formation.
- Both are easier to form than a corporation.
- Both require filing a certificate with an appropriate state authority, such as the secretary of state.

- An LLC may be formed with one or more owners, referred to as members, while an LLP requires 2 or more partners.

Taxation:
- Both are pass-through entities.
- Both may report their operations by filing information returns (Form 1065) and distributing K-1s to its members or partners.
  - An LLP is, by default, treated as a partnership.
  - An LLC with more than one member is treated as a partnership, and those with one member are treated as sole proprietorships (Schedule C).

Liability:
- Both provide owners with some degree of protection.
  - LLCs generally limit the liability of members to their investments, plus the costs resulting from their own negligence or malpractice.
  - Partners of LLPs are generally not liable for the actions of copartners but are liable for the obligations and debts of the LLP in some states.

LLC	LLP (Accounting Firms)
Formal creation	Formal
≥ 1 Person	≥ 2 people
• Limited Liability for Contracts and debts • Unlimited Liability for Malpractice or Negligence	• Limited Liability for Malpractice or Negligence • Unlimited Liability for Contracts/Debts in some states
Agents/Member	Agents
Taxed as a P/S (or Corp or Sch. C)	Taxed as a P/S (or Corp)

Lecture 4.07

CLASS QUESTIONS

Please see the Class Questions and Class Solutions for this Lecture at the end of this Section.

Lecture 4.08

CLASS QUESTIONS

Please see the Class Questions and Class Solutions for this Lecture at the end of this Section.

Lecture 4.09

CLASS QUESTIONS

Please see the Class Questions and Class Solutions for this Lecture at the end of this Section.

Note: The 2016 forms are provided since 2017 forms were unavailable at the time of publication.

Form **1065**

Department of the Treasury
Internal Revenue Service

U.S. Return of Partnership Income

For calendar year 2016, or tax year beginning _____ , 2016, ending _____ , 20_____ .

▶ Information about Form 1065 and its separate instructions is at *www.irs.gov/form1065.*

OMB No. 1545-0123

20**16**

A Principal business activity		Name of partnership	D Employer identification number
B Principal product or service	**Type or Print**	Number, street, and room or suite no. If a P.O. box, see the instructions.	E Date business started
C Business code number		City or town, state or province, country, and ZIP or foreign postal code	F Total assets (see the instructions) $

G Check applicable boxes: **(1)** ☐ Initial return **(2)** ☐ Final return **(3)** ☐ Name change **(4)** ☐ Address change **(5)** ☐ Amended return
  (6) ☐ Technical termination - also check (1) or (2)

H Check accounting method: **(1)** ☐ Cash **(2)** ☐ Accrual **(3)** ☐ Other (specify) ▶ _____

I Number of Schedules K-1. Attach one for each person who was a partner at any time during the tax year ▶ _____

J Check if Schedules C and M-3 are attached . . . . ☐

Caution. *Include **only** trade or business income and expenses on lines 1a through 22 below. See the instructions for more information.*

Income

1a	Gross receipts or sales	1a		
b	Returns and allowances	1b		
c	Balance. Subtract line 1b from line 1a	1c		
2	Cost of goods sold (attach Form 1125-A)	2		
3	Gross profit. Subtract line 2 from line 1c	3		
4	Ordinary income (loss) from other partnerships, estates, and trusts (attach statement) . .	4		
5	Net farm profit (loss) (attach Schedule F (Form 1040))	5		
6	Net gain (loss) from Form 4797, Part II, line 17 (attach Form 4797)	6		
7	Other income (loss) (attach statement)	7		
8	**Total income (loss).** Combine lines 3 through 7	8		

Deductions (see the instructions for limitations)

9	Salaries and wages (other than to partners) (less employment credits)	9		
10	Guaranteed payments to partners	10		
11	Repairs and maintenance	11		
12	Bad debts	12		
13	Rent	13		
14	Taxes and licenses	14		
15	Interest	15		
16a	Depreciation (if required, attach Form 4562)	16a		
b	Less depreciation reported on Form 1125-A and elsewhere on return	16b	16c	
17	Depletion **(Do not deduct oil and gas depletion.)**	17		
18	Retirement plans, etc.	18		
19	Employee benefit programs	19		
20	Other deductions (attach statement)	20		
21	**Total deductions.** Add the amounts shown in the far right column for lines 9 through 20 .	21		
22	**Ordinary business income (loss).** Subtract line 21 from line 8	22		

Sign Here

Under penalties of perjury, I declare that I have examined this return, including accompanying schedules and statements, and to the best of my knowledge and belief, it is true, correct, and complete. Declaration of preparer (other than general partner or limited liability company member manager) is based on all information of which preparer has any knowledge.

▶ _____
Signature of general partner or limited liability company member manager

▶ _____
Date

May the IRS discuss this return with the preparer shown below (see instructions)? ☐ **Yes** ☐ **No**

Paid Preparer Use Only

Print/Type preparer's name	Preparer's signature	Date	Check ☐ if self-employed	PTIN
Firm's name ▶			Firm's EIN ▶	
Firm's address ▶			Phone no.	

For Paperwork Reduction Act Notice, see separate instructions. Cat. No. 11390Z Form **1065** (2016)

Form 1065 (2016) Page **2**

Schedule B	Other Information			

			Yes	No
1	What type of entity is filing this return? Check the applicable box:			

a	☐ Domestic general partnership	b	☐ Domestic limited partnership	
c	☐ Domestic limited liability company	d	☐ Domestic limited liability partnership	
e	☐ Foreign partnership	f	☐ Other ▶	

		Yes	No
2	At any time during the tax year, was any partner in the partnership a disregarded entity, a partnership (including an entity treated as a partnership), a trust, an S corporation, an estate (other than an estate of a deceased partner), or a nominee or similar person?		
3	At the end of the tax year:		
a	Did any foreign or domestic corporation, partnership (including any entity treated as a partnership), trust, or tax-exempt organization, or any foreign government own, directly or indirectly, an interest of 50% or more in the profit, loss, or capital of the partnership? For rules of constructive ownership, see instructions. If "Yes," attach Schedule B-1, Information on Partners Owning 50% or More of the Partnership		
b	Did any individual or estate own, directly or indirectly, an interest of 50% or more in the profit, loss, or capital of the partnership? For rules of constructive ownership, see instructions. If "Yes," attach Schedule B-1, Information on Partners Owning 50% or More of the Partnership		
4	At the end of the tax year, did the partnership:		
a	Own directly 20% or more, or own, directly or indirectly, 50% or more of the total voting power of all classes of stock entitled to vote of any foreign or domestic corporation? For rules of constructive ownership, see instructions. If "Yes," complete (i) through (iv) below		

(i) Name of Corporation	(ii) Employer Identification Number (if any)	(iii) Country of Incorporation	(iv) Percentage Owned in Voting Stock

		Yes	No
b	Own directly an interest of 20% or more, or own, directly or indirectly, an interest of 50% or more in the profit, loss, or capital in any foreign or domestic partnership (including an entity treated as a partnership) or in the beneficial interest of a trust? For rules of constructive ownership, see instructions. If "Yes," complete (i) through (v) below . .		

(i) Name of Entity	(ii) Employer Identification Number (if any)	(iii) Type of Entity	(iv) Country of Organization	(v) Maximum Percentage Owned in Profit, Loss, or Capital

		Yes	No
5	Did the partnership file Form 8893, Election of Partnership Level Tax Treatment, or an election statement under section 6231(a)(1)(B)(ii) for partnership-level tax treatment, that is in effect for this tax year? See Form 8893 for more details		
6	Does the partnership satisfy **all four** of the following conditions?		
a	The partnership's total receipts for the tax year were less than $250,000.		
b	The partnership's total assets at the end of the tax year were less than $1 million.		
c	Schedules K-1 are filed with the return and furnished to the partners on or before the due date (including extensions) for the partnership return.		
d	The partnership is not filing and is not required to file Schedule M-3		
	If "Yes," the partnership is not required to complete Schedules L, M-1, and M-2; Item F on page 1 of Form 1065; or Item L on Schedule K-1.		
7	Is this partnership a publicly traded partnership as defined in section 469(k)(2)?		
8	During the tax year, did the partnership have any debt that was cancelled, was forgiven, or had the terms modified so as to reduce the principal amount of the debt?		
9	Has this partnership filed, or is it required to file, Form 8918, Material Advisor Disclosure Statement, to provide information on any reportable transaction?		
10	At any time during calendar year 2016, did the partnership have an interest in or a signature or other authority over a financial account in a foreign country (such as a bank account, securities account, or other financial account)? See the instructions for exceptions and filing requirements for FinCEN Form 114, Report of Foreign Bank and Financial Accounts (FBAR). If "Yes," enter the name of the foreign country. ▶		

Form **1065** (2016)

Schedule B	**Other Information** *(continued)*	Yes	No

11 At any time during the tax year, did the partnership receive a distribution from, or was it the grantor of, or transferor to, a foreign trust? If "Yes," the partnership may have to file Form 3520, Annual Return To Report Transactions With Foreign Trusts and Receipt of Certain Foreign Gifts. See instructions . . . .

12a Is the partnership making, or had it previously made (and not revoked), a section 754 election? . . . .
See instructions for details regarding a section 754 election.

  b Did the partnership make for this tax year an optional basis adjustment under section 743(b) or 734(b)? If "Yes," attach a statement showing the computation and allocation of the basis adjustment. See instructions . . . .

  c Is the partnership required to adjust the basis of partnership assets under section 743(b) or 734(b) because of a substantial built-in loss (as defined under section 743(d)) or substantial basis reduction (as defined under section 734(d))? If "Yes," attach a statement showing the computation and allocation of the basis adjustment. See instructions

13 Check this box if, during the current or prior tax year, the partnership distributed any property received in a like-kind exchange or contributed such property to another entity (other than disregarded entities wholly owned by the partnership throughout the tax year) . . . . ▶ ☐

14 At any time during the tax year, did the partnership distribute to any partner a tenancy-in-common or other undivided interest in partnership property? . . . .

15 If the partnership is required to file Form 8858, Information Return of U.S. Persons With Respect To Foreign Disregarded Entities, enter the number of Forms 8858 attached. See instructions ▶

16 Does the partnership have any foreign partners? If "Yes," enter the number of Forms 8805, Foreign Partner's Information Statement of Section 1446 Withholding Tax, filed for this partnership. ▶

17 Enter the number of Forms 8865, Return of U.S. Persons With Respect to Certain Foreign Partnerships, attached to this return. ▶

18a Did you make any payments in 2016 that would require you to file Form(s) 1099? See instructions . . . . . .
  b If "Yes," did you or will you file required Form(s) 1099? . . . .

19 Enter the number of Form(s) 5471, Information Return of U.S. Persons With Respect To Certain Foreign Corporations, attached to this return. ▶

20 Enter the number of partners that are foreign governments under section 892. ▶

21 During the partnership's tax year, did the partnership make any payments that would require it to file Form 1042 and 1042-S under chapter 3 (sections 1441 through 1464) or chapter 4 (sections 1471 through 1474)? . . . .

22 Was the partnership a specified domestic entity required to file Form 8938 for the tax year (See the Instructions for Form 8938)? . . . .

Designation of Tax Matters Partner (see instructions)
Enter below the general partner or member-manager designated as the tax matters partner (TMP) for the tax year of this return:

Name of
designated ▶
TMP

Identifying ▶
number of TMP

If the TMP is an
entity, name ▶
of TMP representative

Phone number ▶
of TMP

Address of
designated ▶
TMP

Form **1065** (2016)

Form 1065 (2016)   Page **4**

Schedule K	Partners' Distributive Share Items		Total amount	

Income (Loss)	**1**	Ordinary business income (loss) (page 1, line 22)		**1**	
	2	Net rental real estate income (loss) (attach Form 8825)		**2**	
	3a	Other gross rental income (loss)	**3a**		
	b	Expenses from other rental activities (attach statement)	**3b**		
	c	Other net rental income (loss). Subtract line 3b from line 3a		**3c**	
	4	Guaranteed payments		**4**	
	5	Interest income		**5**	
	6	Dividends: **a** Ordinary dividends		**6a**	
		b Qualified dividends	**6b**		
	7	Royalties		**7**	
	8	Net short-term capital gain (loss) (attach Schedule D (Form 1065)) . . .		**8**	
	9a	Net long-term capital gain (loss) (attach Schedule D (Form 1065)) . . .		**9a**	
	b	Collectibles (28%) gain (loss)	**9b**		
	c	Unrecaptured section 1250 gain (attach statement) . .	**9c**		
	10	Net section 1231 gain (loss) (attach Form 4797)		**10**	
	11	Other income (loss) (see instructions) Type ▶		**11**	
Deductions	**12**	Section 179 deduction (attach Form 4562)		**12**	
	13a	Contributions		**13a**	
	b	Investment interest expense		**13b**	
	c	Section 59(e)(2) expenditures: **(1)** Type ▶_____ **(2)** Amount ▶		**13c(2)**	
	d	Other deductions (see instructions) Type ▶		**13d**	
Self-Employ-ment	**14a**	Net earnings (loss) from self-employment		**14a**	
	b	Gross farming or fishing income		**14b**	
	c	Gross nonfarm income		**14c**	
Credits	**15a**	Low-income housing credit (section 42(j)(5))		**15a**	
	b	Low-income housing credit (other)		**15b**	
	c	Qualified rehabilitation expenditures (rental real estate) (attach Form 3468, if applicable)		**15c**	
	d	Other rental real estate credits (see instructions) Type ▶		**15d**	
	e	Other rental credits (see instructions) Type ▶		**15e**	
	f	Other credits (see instructions) Type ▶		**15f**	
Foreign Transactions	**16a**	Name of country or U.S. possession ▶			
	b	Gross income from all sources		**16b**	
	c	Gross income sourced at partner level		**16c**	
		Foreign gross income sourced at partnership level			
	d	Passive category ▶_____ **e** General category ▶_____ **f** Other ▶		**16f**	
		Deductions allocated and apportioned at partner level			
	g	Interest expense ▶_____ **h** Other . . . . ▶		**16h**	
		Deductions allocated and apportioned at partnership level to foreign source income			
	i	Passive category ▶_____ **j** General category ▶_____ **k** Other ▶		**16k**	
	l	Total foreign taxes (check one): ▶ Paid ☐ Accrued ☐		**16l**	
	m	Reduction in taxes available for credit (attach statement)		**16m**	
	n	Other foreign tax information (attach statement)			
Alternative Minimum Tax (AMT) Items	**17a**	Post-1986 depreciation adjustment		**17a**	
	b	Adjusted gain or loss		**17b**	
	c	Depletion (other than oil and gas)		**17c**	
	d	Oil, gas, and geothermal properties—gross income		**17d**	
	e	Oil, gas, and geothermal properties—deductions		**17e**	
	f	Other AMT items (attach statement)		**17f**	
Other Information	**18a**	Tax-exempt interest income		**18a**	
	b	Other tax-exempt income		**18b**	
	c	Nondeductible expenses		**18c**	
	19a	Distributions of cash and marketable securities		**19a**	
	b	Distributions of other property		**19b**	
	20a	Investment income		**20a**	
	b	Investment expenses		**20b**	
	c	Other items and amounts (attach statement)			

Form **1065** (2016)

Analysis of Net Income (Loss)

1	Net income (loss). Combine Schedule K, lines 1 through 11. From the result, subtract the sum of Schedule K, lines 12 through 13d, and 16l					**1**		

2	Analysis by partner type:	**(i)** Corporate	**(ii)** Individual (active)	**(iii)** Individual (passive)	**(iv)** Partnership	**(v)** Exempt Organization	**(vi)** Nominee/Other
a	General partners						
b	Limited partners						

Schedule L — Balance Sheets per Books

	Assets	Beginning of tax year (a)	(b)	End of tax year (c)	(d)
1	Cash				
2a	Trade notes and accounts receivable . . .				
b	Less allowance for bad debts				
3	Inventories				
4	U.S. government obligations				
5	Tax-exempt securities				
6	Other current assets (attach statement) . .				
7a	Loans to partners (or persons related to partners)				
b	Mortgage and real estate loans				
8	Other investments (attach statement) . . .				
9a	Buildings and other depreciable assets . .				
b	Less accumulated depreciation				
10a	Depletable assets				
b	Less accumulated depletion				
11	Land (net of any amortization)				
12a	Intangible assets (amortizable only) . . .				
b	Less accumulated amortization . . .				
13	Other assets (attach statement) . . .				
14	Total assets				
	Liabilities and Capital				
15	Accounts payable				
16	Mortgages, notes, bonds payable in less than 1 year				
17	Other current liabilities (attach statement) .				
18	All nonrecourse loans				
19a	Loans from partners (or persons related to partners)				
b	Mortgages, notes, bonds payable in 1 year or more				
20	Other liabilities (attach statement) . . .				
21	Partners' capital accounts				
22	Total liabilities and capital				

Schedule M-1 — Reconciliation of Income (Loss) per Books With Income (Loss) per Return
Note. The partnership may be required to file Schedule M-3 (see instructions).

1	Net income (loss) per books . . .		6	Income recorded on books this year not included on Schedule K, lines 1 through 11 (itemize):	
2	Income included on Schedule K, lines 1, 2, 3c, 5, 6a, 7, 8, 9a, 10, and 11, not recorded on books this year (itemize): _____		a	Tax-exempt interest $ _____	
3	Guaranteed payments (other than health insurance)		7	Deductions included on Schedule K, lines 1 through 13d, and 16l, not charged against book income this year (itemize):	
4	Expenses recorded on books this year not included on Schedule K, lines 1 through 13d, and 16l (itemize):		a	Depreciation $ _____	
a	Depreciation $ _____		8	Add lines 6 and 7	
b	Travel and entertainment $ _____		9	Income (loss) (Analysis of Net Income (Loss), line 1). Subtract line 8 from line 5 .	
5	Add lines 1 through 4				

Schedule M-2 — Analysis of Partners' Capital Accounts

1	Balance at beginning of year . . .		6	Distributions: a Cash	
2	Capital contributed: a Cash . . .			b Property	
	b Property . .		7	Other decreases (itemize): _____	
3	Net income (loss) per books				
4	Other increases (itemize): _____		8	Add lines 6 and 7	
5	Add lines 1 through 4		9	Balance at end of year. Subtract line 8 from line 5	

Form **1065** (2016)

651113

| | Final K-1 | | Amended K-1 | OMB No. 1545-0123 |

Schedule K-1
(Form 1065)

Department of the Treasury
Internal Revenue Service

20**16**

For calendar year 2016, or tax
year beginning _____ , 2016
ending _____ , 20 ___

Partner's Share of Income, Deductions, Credits, etc.
▶ See back of form and separate instructions.

| Part I | Information About the Partnership |

A Partnership's employer identification number

B Partnership's name, address, city, state, and ZIP code

C IRS Center where partnership filed return

D ☐ Check if this is a publicly traded partnership (PTP)

| Part II | Information About the Partner |

E Partner's identifying number

F Partner's name, address, city, state, and ZIP code

G ☐ General partner or LLC member-manager ☐ Limited partner or other LLC member

H ☐ Domestic partner ☐ Foreign partner

I1 What type of entity is this partner? _____

I2 If this partner is a retirement plan (IRA/SEP/Keogh/etc.), check here
. . . . ☐

J Partner's share of profit, loss, and capital (see instructions):

	Beginning	Ending
Profit	%	%
Loss	%	%
Capital	%	%

K Partner's share of liabilities at year end:

Nonrecourse	$ _____
Qualified nonrecourse financing .	$ _____
Recourse	$ _____

L Partner's capital account analysis:

Beginning capital account . . .	$ _____
Capital contributed during the year	$ _____
Current year increase (decrease) .	$ _____
Withdrawals & distributions . .	$ (_____)
Ending capital account	$ _____

☐ Tax basis ☐ GAAP ☐ Section 704(b) book
☐ Other (explain)

M Did the partner contribute property with a built-in gain or loss?
☐ Yes ☐ No
If "Yes," attach statement (see instructions)

| Part III | Partner's Share of Current Year Income, Deductions, Credits, and Other Items |

1	Ordinary business income (loss)	15	Credits
2	Net rental real estate income (loss)		
3	Other net rental income (loss)	16	Foreign transactions
4	Guaranteed payments		
5	Interest income		
6a	Ordinary dividends		
6b	Qualified dividends		
7	Royalties		
8	Net short-term capital gain (loss)		
9a	Net long-term capital gain (loss)	17	Alternative minimum tax (AMT) items
9b	Collectibles (28%) gain (loss)		
9c	Unrecaptured section 1250 gain		
10	Net section 1231 gain (loss)	18	Tax-exempt income and nondeductible expenses
11	Other income (loss)		
		19	Distributions
12	Section 179 deduction		
13	Other deductions	20	Other information
14	Self-employment earnings (loss)		

*See attached statement for additional information.

For IRS Use Only

For Paperwork Reduction Act Notice, see Instructions for Form 1065.   IRS.gov/form1065   Cat. No. 11394R   Schedule K-1 (Form 1065) 2016

This list identifies the codes used on Schedule K-1 for all partners and provides summarized reporting information for partners who file Form 1040. For detailed reporting and filing information, see the separate Partner's Instructions for Schedule K-1 and the instructions for your income tax return.

1. Ordinary business income (loss). Determine whether the income (loss) is passive or nonpassive and enter on your return as follows.

	Report on
Passive loss	See the Partner's Instructions
Passive income	Schedule E, line 28, column (g)
Nonpassive loss	Schedule E, line 28, column (h)
Nonpassive income	Schedule E, line 28, column (j)

2. Net rental real estate income (loss)   See the Partner's Instructions

3. Other net rental income (loss)

Net income	Schedule E, line 28, column (g)
Net loss	See the Partner's Instructions

4. Guaranteed payments   Schedule E, line 28, column (j)
5. Interest income   Form 1040, line 8a
6a. Ordinary dividends   Form 1040, line 9a
6b. Qualified dividends   Form 1040, line 9b
7. Royalties   Schedule E, line 4
8. Net short-term capital gain (loss)   Schedule D, line 5
9a. Net long-term capital gain (loss)   Schedule D, line 12
9b. Collectibles (28%) gain (loss)   28% Rate Gain Worksheet, line 4 (Schedule D instructions)
9c. Unrecaptured section 1250 gain   See the Partner's Instructions
10. Net section 1231 gain (loss)   See the Partner's Instructions
11. Other income (loss)

Code
A	Other portfolio income (loss)	See the Partner's Instructions
B	Involuntary conversions	See the Partner's Instructions
C	Sec. 1256 contracts & straddles	Form 6781, line 1
D	Mining exploration costs recapture	See Pub. 535
E	Cancellation of debt	Form 1040, line 21 or Form 982
F	Other income (loss)	See the Partner's Instructions

12. Section 179 deduction   See the Partner's Instructions
13. Other deductions

A	Cash contributions (50%)	
B	Cash contributions (30%)	
C	Noncash contributions (50%)	
D	Noncash contributions (30%)	See the Partner's
E	Capital gain property to a 50% organization (30%)	Instructions
F	Capital gain property (20%)	
G	Contributions (100%)	
H	Investment interest expense	Form 4952, line 1
I	Deductions—royalty income	Schedule E, line 19
J	Section 59(e)(2) expenditures	See the Partner's Instructions
K	Deductions—portfolio (2% floor)	Schedule A, line 23
L	Deductions—portfolio (other)	Schedule A, line 28
M	Amounts paid for medical insurance	Schedule A, line 1 or Form 1040, line 29
N	Educational assistance benefits	See the Partner's Instructions
O	Dependent care benefits	Form 2441, line 12
P	Preproductive period expenses	See the Partner's Instructions
Q	Commercial revitalization deduction from rental real estate activities	See Form 8582 instructions
R	Pensions and IRAs	See the Partner's Instructions
S	Reforestation expense deduction	See the Partner's Instructions
T	Domestic production activities information	See Form 8903 instructions
U	Qualified production activities income	Form 8903, line 7b
V	Employer's Form W-2 wages	Form 8903, line 17
W	Other deductions	See the Partner's Instructions

14. Self-employment earnings (loss)

Note: If you have a section 179 deduction or any partner-level deductions, see the Partner's Instructions before completing Schedule SE.

A	Net earnings (loss) from self-employment	Schedule SE, Section A or B
B	Gross farming or fishing income	See the Partner's Instructions
C	Gross non-farm income	See the Partner's Instructions

15. Credits

A	Low-income housing credit (section 42(j)(5)) from pre-2008 buildings	
B	Low-income housing credit (other) from pre-2008 buildings	
C	Low-income housing credit (section 42(j)(5)) from post-2007 buildings	
D	Low-income housing credit (other) from post-2007 buildings	See the Partner's Instructions
E	Qualified rehabilitation expenditures (rental real estate)	
F	Other rental real estate credits	
G	Other rental credits	
H	Undistributed capital gains credit	Form 1040, line 73; check box a
I	Biofuel producer credit	
J	Work opportunity credit	See the Partner's Instructions
K	Disabled access credit	

Code
		Report on
L	Empowerment zone employment credit	
M	Credit for increasing research activities	
N	Credit for employer social security and Medicare taxes	See the Partner's Instructions
O	Backup withholding	
P	Other credits	

16. Foreign transactions

A	Name of country or U.S. possession	
B	Gross income from all sources	Form 1116, Part I
C	Gross income sourced at partner level	

Foreign gross income sourced at partnership level
D	Passive category	
E	General category	Form 1116, Part I
F	Other	

Deductions allocated and apportioned at partner level
G	Interest expense	Form 1116, Part I
H	Other	Form 1116, Part I

Deductions allocated and apportioned at partnership level to foreign source income
I	Passive category	
J	General category	Form 1116, Part I
K	Other	

Other information
L	Total foreign taxes paid	Form 1116, Part II
M	Total foreign taxes accrued	Form 1116, Part II
N	Reduction in taxes available for credit	Form 1116, line 12
O	Foreign trading gross receipts	Form 8873
P	Extraterritorial income exclusion	Form 8873
Q	Other foreign transactions	See the Partner's Instructions

17. Alternative minimum tax (AMT) items

A	Post-1986 depreciation adjustment	
B	Adjusted gain or loss	See the Partner's
C	Depletion (other than oil & gas)	Instructions and
D	Oil, gas, & geothermal—gross income	the Instructions for
E	Oil, gas, & geothermal—deductions	Form 6251
F	Other AMT items	

18. Tax-exempt income and nondeductible expenses

A	Tax-exempt interest income	Form 1040, line 8b
B	Other tax-exempt income	See the Partner's Instructions
C	Nondeductible expenses	See the Partner's Instructions

19. Distributions

A	Cash and marketable securities	
B	Distribution subject to section 737	See the Partner's Instructions
C	Other property	

20. Other information

A	Investment income	Form 4952, line 4a
B	Investment expenses	Form 4952, line 5
C	Fuel tax credit information	Form 4136
D	Qualified rehabilitation expenditures (other than rental real estate)	See the Partner's Instructions
E	Basis of energy property	See the Partner's Instructions
F	Recapture of low-income housing credit (section 42(j)(5))	Form 8611, line 8
G	Recapture of low-income housing credit (other)	Form 8611, line 8
H	Recapture of investment credit	See Form 4255
I	Recapture of other credits	See the Partner's Instructions
J	Look-back interest—completed long-term contracts	See Form 8697
K	Look-back interest—income forecast method	See Form 8866
L	Dispositions of property with section 179 deductions	
M	Recapture of section 179 deduction	
N	Interest expense for corporate partners	
O	Section 453(l)(3) information	
P	Section 453A(c) information	
Q	Section 1260(b) information	
R	Interest allocable to production expenditures	See the Partner's Instructions
S	CCF nonqualified withdrawals	
T	Depletion information—oil and gas	
U	Reserved	
V	Unrelated business taxable income	
W	Precontribution gain (loss)	
X	Section 108(i) information	
Y	Net investment income	
Z	Other information	

CLASS QUESTIONS

Work through the below Class Questions while following along with the respective lectures. Once this is complete, you can begin independently practicing what you've learned by quizzing yourself on this course section in your Interactive Practice Questions (IPQ), which can be found in your online Student Dashboard. Your IPQ simulates the computer-based testing experience, and will also help you understand how concepts are applied to the exam. Each question includes answer explanations from expert CPAs that will help you determine why you answered a question correctly or incorrectly. This is key to your success on the CPA Exam.

Lecture 4.04

1. At partnership inception, Black acquires a 50% interest in Decorators Partnership by contributing property with an adjusted basis of $250,000. Black recognizes a gain if

   I.   The fair market value of the contributed property exceeds its adjusted basis.
   II. The property is encumbered by a mortgage with a balance of $100,000.

   a. I only.
   b. II only.
   c. Both I and II.
   d. Neither I nor II.

2. In computing the ordinary income of a partnership, a deduction is allowed for

   a. Contributions to recognized charities.
   b. The first $100 of dividends received from qualifying domestic corporations.
   c. Short-term capital losses.
   d. Guaranteed payments to partners.

Items 3 and 4 are based on the following:
Jones and Curry formed Major Partnership as equal partners by contributing the assets below.

	Asset	Adjusted basis	Fair market value
Jones	Cash	$45,000	$45,000
Curry	Land	30,000	57,000

The land was held by Curry as a capital asset, subject to a $12,000 mortgage, that was assumed by Major.

3. What was Curry's initial basis in the partnership interest?

   a. $45,000
   b. $30,000
   c. $24,000
   d. $18,000

4. What was Jones' initial basis in the partnership interest?

   a. $51,000
   b. $45,000
   c. $39,000
   d. $33,000

5. The holding period of a partnership interest acquired in exchange for a contributed capital asset begins on the date

    a. The partner is admitted to the partnership
    b. The partner transfers the asset to the partnership
    c. The partner's holding period of the capital asset began
    d. The partner is first credited with the proportionate share of partnership capital

6. A $100,000 increase in partnership liabilities is treated in which of the following ways?

    a. Increases each partner's basis in the partnership by $100,000
    b. Increases the partners' bases only if the liability is nonrecourse
    c. Increases each partner's basis in proportion to their ownership
    d. Does not change any partner's basis in the partnership regardless of whether the liabilities are recourse or nonrecourse.

Lecture 4.07

Items 7 and 8 are based on the following:
The adjusted basis of Jody's partnership interest was $50,000 immediately before Jody received a current distribution of $20,000 cash and property with an adjusted basis to the partnership of $40,000 and a fair market value of $35,000.

7. What amount of taxable gain must Jody report as a result of this distribution?

    a. $0
    b. $ 5,000
    c. $10,000
    d. $20,000

8. What is Jody's basis in the distributed property?

    a. $0
    b. $30,000
    c. $35,000
    d. $40,000

9. Under which of the following circumstances is a partnership that is not an electing large partnership considered terminated for income tax purposes?

    I.   55% of the total interest in partnership capital and profits is sold within a 12-month period.
    II. The partnership's business and financial operations are discontinued.

    a. I only.
    b. II only.
    c. Both I and II.
    d. Neither I nor II.

CLASS SOLUTIONS

1. (d) Black would recognize a gain on the transfer of property to a partnership in exchange for a partnership interest only if the property was subject to a liability that exceeds the tax basis of the property. Black's basis in the partnership will be the basis in the property of $250,000 less any encumbrance assumed by the partnership.

2. (d) Guaranteed payments to partners are generally in the form of salary due to a partner's involvement in the operations of the partnership, or a return on capital invested. They are treated as ordinary expenses of the partnership and reduce the partnership's ordinary income. Answer (a) is incorrect because contributions to recognized charities are not deducted by the partnership but are reported as pass-through items to be reported on each partner's tax return. This is due to the limitation on the deductibility of charitable contributions. Answer (b) is incorrect because dividend income is a separately stated item and the amount of any dividends-received deduction allowed would be determined on a corporate partner's return. Answer (c) is incorrect because short-term capital losses pass through to shareholders because there is a limit on their deductibility.

3. (c) When a partner contributes property to a partnership in exchange for a partnership interest, it is a nontaxable transaction and the partner's basis in the partnership is the same as the basis in the property, $30,000. That is reduced by any related liabilities that are assumed by the partnership, $12,000, but increased by that partner's proportionate share of those liabilities, in the amount of $6,000, or 50%. As a result, Curry's initial basis will be $30,000 - $12,000 + $6,000 = $24,000.

4. (a) When a partner contributes cash to a partnership in exchange for a partnership interest, the partner's basis in the partnership will be equal to the amount of cash contributed plus that partner's proportionate share of any liabilities being assumed by the partnership. Since the partnership is assuming Curry's $12,000 obligation, $6,000 (50%) will increase Jones' basis, making it $45,000 + $6,000, or $51,000.

5. (c) When a partner transfers a capital asset to a partnership in exchange for a partnership interest, it is a nontaxable exchange. As a result, the partner's basis in the asset is the same as the partner's tax basis and the holding period begins at the beginning of the partner's holding period in order for any gains or losses on disposal to retain their character.

6. (c) Since partners are jointly and severally liable for the obligations of the partnership, an increase in the partnerships liabilities results in an increase in each partner's basis for their proportionate share of the increase in liabilities.

7. (a) In a nonliquidating distribution of cash and property, the cash will first reduce the partner's basis dollar for dollar. The partner will then recognize the property at its tax basis in a nontaxable transaction, reducing the basis in the partnership for that amount. The partnership basis, however, cannot be reduced below zero. When the tax basis of property distributed exceeds the partner's basis in the partnership, the basis in the property will be equal to the remaining basis in the partnership and the partner's basis is reduced to zero; thus, no gain or loss is recognized.

8. (b) In a nonliquidating distribution of cash and property, the cash will first reduce the partner's basis dollar for dollar. The partner will then recognize the property at its tax basis in a nontaxable transaction, reducing the basis in the partnership for that amount. The partnership basis, however, cannot be reduced below zero. When the tax basis of property distributed exceeds the partner's basis in the partnership, the basis in the property will be equal to the remaining basis in the partnership and the partner's basis is reduced to zero; thus, no gain or loss is recognized. In this case, the $20,000 in cash distributed reduces Jody's basis in the partnership from $50,000 to $30,000. Since the partnership's basis in the distributed property exceeded that amount, Jody's basis in the partnership is reduced to zero and Jody's basis in the property is $30,000.

9. (c) In general, a partnership is considered to be terminated if either 50% or more of the total interests in the partnership are sold or if the partnership's business and financial operations are discontinued. This is not true of an electing large partnership. Since it is taxed on items such as investment credit recapture, these may continue despite a discontinuation of business and financial operations.

Lecture 4.08

TASK-BASED SIMULATIONS

Task-Based Simulation 1

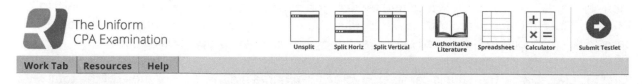

Work Tab	Resources	Help

Required:

During 20X1, Adams, a general contractor, Brinks, an architect, and Carson, an interior decorator, formed the Dex Home Improvement General Partnership by contributing the assets below.

	Asset	Adjusted basis	Fair market value	% of partner share in capital, profits & losses
Adams	Cash	$40,000	$40,000	50%
Brinks	Land	$12,000	$21,000	20%
Carson	Inventory	$24,000	$24,000	30%

The land was a capital asset to Brinks, subject to a $5,000 mortgage, which was assumed by the partnership.

Items to be answered:

For items 1 and 2, determine and select the initial basis of the partner's interest in Dex.

(A) (B) (C)
○ ○ ○

1. Brinks' initial basis in Dex is
   A. $21,000
   B. $12,000
   C. $ 8,000

(A) (B) (C)
○ ○ ○

2. Carson's initial basis in Dex is
   A. $25,500
   B. $24,000
   C. $19,000

Task-Based Simulation 2

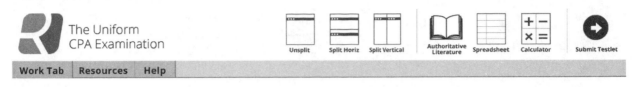

| Work Tab | Resources | Help |

Required:

During 20X1, the Dex Partnership breaks even but decides to make distributions to each partner.

Items to be answered:

For items 1 through 6, determine whether the statement is True or False.

		True	False
1.	A nonliquidating cash distribution may reduce the recipient partner's basis in his partnership interest below zero.	○	○
2.	A nonliquidating distribution of unappreciated inventory reduces the recipient partner's basis in his partnership interest.	○	○
3.	In a liquidating distribution of property other than money, where the partnership's basis of the distributed property exceeds the basis of the partner's interest, the partner's basis in the distributed property is limited to his predistribution basis in the partnership interest.	○	○
4.	Gain is recognized by the partner who receives a nonliquidating distribution of property, where the adjusted basis of the property exceeds his basis in the partnership interest before the distribution.	○	○
5.	In a nonliquidating distribution of inventory, where the partnership has no unrealized receivables or appreciated inventory, the basis of inventory that is distributed to a partner cannot exceed the inventory's adjusted basis to the partnership.	○	○
6.	The partnership's nonliquidating distribution of encumbered property to a partner who assumes the mortgage, does not affect the other partners' bases in their partnership interests.	○	○

Task-Based Simulation 3

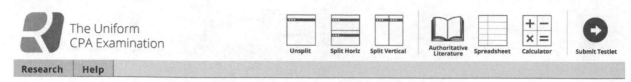

A partner is trying to determine the effect of losses of the partnership on the basis of her interest in the partnership.

Which section, subsection, paragraph, and subparagraph will she refer to determine the effect of partnership losses on the basis of her interest in the partnership?

Task-Based Simulation 4

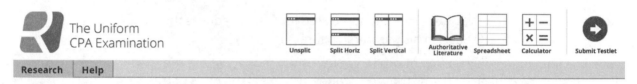

A partner, who is a construction subcontractor, is performing services for the partnership as a subcontractor and not in his capacity as a partner. He is trying to determine if the transaction requires special treatment by the partnership because he is a partner.

Which code section, subsection, and paragraph indicates how a transaction with a partner other than in his capacity as a member of the partnership should be considered?

Task-Based Simulation 5

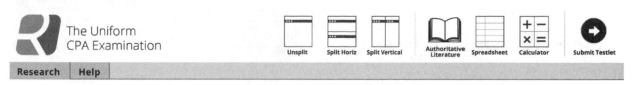

You are preparing a partnership tax return and trying to determine which items of income, expense, gain, or loss should be taken into account separately when figuring each partner's distributive share of the partnership's income.

Which code section and subsection will provide you with the information necessary to determine what items should be taken into account separately?

Task-Based Simulation 6

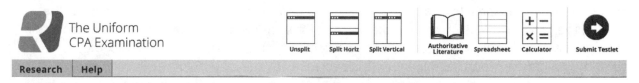

A partnership is being formed in which the various partners have differing tax years. You are trying to determine what would be an appropriate tax year for the partnership.

Which code section, subsection, paragraph, and subparagraph indicates how the partnership's taxable year will be determined?

TASK-BASED SIMULATION SOLUTIONS

Task-Based Simulation Solution 1

1. Brinks' initial basis in Dex is
    A. $21,000
    B. $12,000
    C. $ 8,000

(A) (B) (C)
  ○   ○   ●

2. Carson's initial basis in Dex is
    A. $25,500
    B. $24,000
    C. $19,000

(A) (B) (C)
  ●   ○   ○

Explanation of solutions

1. (C) When a partner contributes property to a partnership in exchange for a partnership interest, it is a nontaxable transaction, the partner's basis in the partnership is the same as the basis in the property transferred, and the partnership's basis in the property is the same as that of the partner. When that property is subject to a liability assumed by the partnership, the contributing partner's partnership interest is decreased by the amount of the liability and increased by that partner's proportionate share of it. As a result, Brink's basis in the partnership will be the basis in the land, minus the mortgage, plus 20% of the mortgage, or $12,000 - $5,000 + $1,000 = $8,000.

2. (A) When a partner contributes an asset, such as inventory, to a partnership in exchange for a partnership interest, the partner's basis in the asset becomes the partnership's basis in it and that becomes the partner's basis in the partnership. If the partnership assumes any liabilities of the partner, they reduce the partner's basis in his partnership interest, but it is increased by that partner's share of that and any other liabilities assumed by the partnership. Carson's partnership interest will equal Carson's basis in the inventory contributed plus a proportionate amount of the mortgage assumed by the partnership, or $24,000 + (30% × $5,000) = $25,500.

Task-Based Simulation Solution 2

		True	**False**
1.	A nonliquidating cash distribution may reduce the recipient partner's basis in his partnership interest below zero.	○	●
2.	A nonliquidating distribution of unappreciated inventory reduces the recipient partner's basis in his partnership interest.	●	○
3.	In a liquidating distribution of property other than money, where the partnership's basis of the distributed property exceeds the basis of the partner's interest, the partner's basis in the distributed property is limited to his predistribution basis in the partnership interest.	●	○
4.	Gain is recognized by the partner who receives a nonliquidating distribution of property, where the adjusted basis of the property exceeds his basis in the partnership interest before the distribution.	○	●
5.	In a nonliquidating distribution of inventory, where the partnership has no unrealized receivables or appreciated inventory, the basis of inventory that is distributed to a partner cannot exceed the inventory's adjusted basis to the partnership.	●	○
6.	The partnership's nonliquidating distribution of encumbered property to a partner who assumes the mortgage, does not affect the other partners' bases in their partnership interests.	○	●

Explanation of solutions

1. (**F**) A partner's basis in a partnership interest can never go below zero. A nonliquidating cash distribution in excess of a partner's partnership interest will be recognized as a gain and the interest will be reduced to zero.

2. (**T**) A nonliquidating distribution of unappreciated inventory will be recognized by the partnership as a reduction to inventory at its carrying value and will reduce the receiving partner's basis in his partnership interest by the same amount. The partner's basis in the inventory will be the same as the partnership's basis.

3. (**T**) A liquidating distribution of property with a carrying value that exceeds the receiving partner's basis in his partnership interest does not result in a gain to the partner. The partner will first reduce his basis in the partnership interest for any cash received and any property distributed will have a basis to the partner equal to the remaining basis of the partnership interest.

4. (**F**) A partner does not recognize a gain when property with a carrying value that exceeds the partner's basis in the partnership is distributed. Instead, his basis in the partnership interest is reduced to zero and the basis of the property becomes the same as the basis in the partnership interest before the distribution. Only a nonliquidating distribution of cash in excess of the partner's basis in his partnership interest will result in a gain.

5. (**T**) In a nonliquidating distribution, only distributions of cash will result in a gain to the partner. In all other cases, if the partnership's basis in distributed property is the same as or lower than the partner's basis in the partnership interest, the property will have the same basis to the partner as the partnership. If the partnership's basis in the property is higher than the partner's basis in the partnership interest, the partner's basis in the partnership interest will be reduced to zero and the partner's basis in the distributed property will be equal to the partner's basis in the partnership interest before the distribution.

6. **(F)** When a partner assumes a mortgage that was the obligation of the partnership as part of a nonliquidating distribution, all the partners' bases, including the one assuming the mortgage, are decreased by a proportionate share of the mortgage for which the partnership is no longer responsible.

Task-Based Simulation Solution 3

705	(a)	(2)	(A)

Task-Based Simulation Solution 4

707	(a)	(1)

Task-Based Simulation Solution 5

702	(a)

Task-Based Simulation Solution 6

706	(b)	(1)	(B)

Lecture 4.09

DOCUMENT REVIEW SIMULATION

Document Review Simulation 1

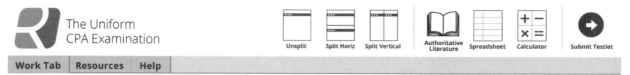

| Work Tab | Resources | Help |

Earl Jackson, the owner of a computer sales business, has contacted your firm to help him determine which type of entity would be most advantageous as he merges with another company to grow his business. Supporting documents are provided in the Resources tab for your analysis. Your coworker, a staff accountant at your firm, Beach & Seas CPAs, has prepared a letter explaining the advantages and disadvantages of each type of entity. Juan Orlando, the managing partner, has asked you to review the letter and the supporting documents to make any necessary corrections before he signs and sends it to the client.

To revise the document, click on each segment of <u>underlined</u> text below and select the needed correction, if any, from the list provided. If the underlined text is already correct in the context of the document, select [Original text] from the list.

Beach & Sea CPAs, LLP
2300 Ocean Drive
Flipperville, FL 33999

January 10, 20X1

Earl Jackson
48684 Clermont Avenue
Flipperville, FL 33999

Dear Earl:

Based on our meeting last month, it is our understanding that you are planning to combine your business with AA Computer Service, Inc. (AACS), owned by Kathleen Hamilton, and are seeking an entity with more flexibility than your current sole proprietorship. 1.) <u>The new business, E&K ComputerLand (E&K), will be an accrual basis, calendar-year entity.</u> Both you and Kathleen will continue to be calendar-year taxpayers. Three of the options available to the new combined computer sales and service business are a regular C corporation (C Corp), an S corporation (S Corp) and a general partnership (Pship). 2.) <u>However, to be a Pship, AACS must liquidate, as it cannot be a partner of E&K; only individuals can be owners in a Pship.</u>

When determining which entity form to choose for your new business, there are several factors to be considered. An important factor is the taxation of the business. 3.) <u>S Corps are separate taxable entities, so double taxation can occur when the entity has taxable income.</u> 4.) <u>Pships and S Corps are tax reporting entities, meaning the entity level income flows through to the owners and is taxed only once on the owners' personal returns.</u> 5.) <u>With C Corps and S Corps, income and losses are allocated according to the capital interest accounts.</u> 6.) <u>This provides more flexibility than with Pships, which requires an allocation based on capital interest accounts.</u>

The possible loss due to a lawsuit or upon liquidation should be considered when selecting the entity form. 7.) <u>S Corps and Pships have the least protection because owners include all liabilities in their basis; whereas a C Corp has the ability to limit liability since owners are liable only to the extent of their investment.</u> When you decide to expand the ownership of E&K, limited liability may be of great importance to new investors. Speaking of investors, in C Corps and Pships, there can be multiple classes of ownership. 8.) <u>However, in S Corps there can only be one class of ownership, and at least one of the owners must be a C Corp.</u>

I hope this information helps you with your decision as to which entity form is best for E&K ComputerLand. Let us know what decision you make, and we will be happy to help you with the accounting and tax aspects of combining your business with AACS to create E&K.

Sincerely,
Juan Orlando, CPA
Managing Partner

Resources

ENTITY AGREEMENT
DRAFT
Incomplete
(Not for legal use; planning purposes only)

THIS AGREEMENT (the "Agreement") made and entered into this _____ day of _____, in the year _____ (the "Execution Date"), among

- **Earl Jackson** of 48684 Clermont Ave, Flipperville, FL 33999, owner of **Jackson Computer Sales** AND

- **AA Computer Services, Inc.** of 2400 Ocean Drive, Flipperville, FL 33999, whose sole shareholder is **Kathleen Hamilton** of 6203 Front Street, Flipperville, FL 33999

Thereby set forth their desire to combine **Jackson Computer Sales** and **AA Computer Services, Inc.** to create a new entity of **E&K ComputerLand** to be located at 2400 Ocean Drive, Flipperville, FL 33999.

The ownership percentages will be based on the net fair value of the assets contributed to **E&K ComputerLand.**

Legal Entity
The parties agree that the combination of **Jackson Computer Sales** and **AA Computer Services**, Inc. will result in **E&K ComputerLand**, carrying on business in the form of a _____ legal entity with all the rights, privileges and obligations prescribed by the state law of Florida. All documents, licenses, and registrations necessary to create the legal entity will be filed with the State of Florida.

Tax Entity
In accordance with the law of the Internal Revenue Code (IRC), **E&K ComputerLand** will elect to be taxed as a(n) _____ entity and file a Form _____ tax return.

Accounting Method: As required by the IRC, the entity will use the accrual method for determining its gross profit from sales of inventory and the cash method for all other aspects of the business, where possible. Valuing inventory will use the lower of cost or market and first-in, first-out methods.

Tax Year: The ending date of the tax year will be determined based on the tax law requirements. If there are options, March 31 is preferred, followed by June 30 and October 31. A calendar year is the least desired.

Notes for Completing Draft
Income: If the entity created is –
- C Corporation: Earl and Kathleen will receive salaries. Any net income in excess of reasonable business needs being retained will be paid as dividends based on common share ownership.
- S Corporation: Earl and Kathleen will receive salaries. All income and expenses will be allocated based on tax law with only common stock issued to owners.

- Partnership: Earl and Kathleen will receive guaranteed payments. All income and expenses will be allocated based on this agreement. Profit and loss allocations to be based on ownership percentages with rights to adjust as partners deem necessary. In addition, all of the depreciation on the building located at 2400 Ocean Drive, Flipperville, FL 33999, will be allocated to Kathleen, and income from initial inventory will be allocated to Earl.

EMAIL
From: Kathleen Hamilton [KH@AACS.com]
Sent: Thursday, January 5, 20X1 7:50 PM
To: Juan Orlando
Subject: Re: Combination of Businesses

Hello Juan,

Here is the information you requested about AA Computer Services (AACS).
- Set up as a regular corporation within Florida.
- Files an 1120 tax return with a March 31 year-end with about $300,000 of gross income.
- Uses cash basis of accounting primarily because it is a service business.
- For the few sales of products, accrual basis is used.
- AACS has a $300,000 mortgage on its building. Earl will move in his business here and our new company will be at this location. No other liabilities.

I'm not expecting to have to liquidate to combine with Earl's business. Please let me know if this is not the case.

As requested by the lawyers, I had AACS appraised by Jefferson & Sons. The appraisal came in at $700,000. The formal write-up with all the details was sent directly to the lawyers, and I had another copy sent to you.

As for tax information for me, I just have a salary from AACS, which is basically whatever net income AACS has for the year after all other expenses. I have some investment income and that is it.

Let me know if you need anything else.

Kathy

EMAIL

From:	Earl Jackson [EJIII@flipperville.com]
Sent:	Friday, January 6, 20X1 4:31 PM
To:	Juan Orlando
Subject:	Re: Combination of Businesses

Dear Juan,

I just got the appraisal from Jefferson & Sons and they valued my business at $500,000. Of course, this does not take into consideration that I owe $200,000 on my business loan. They said that Kathy Hamilton told them to send a copy of her appraisal and mine to Beach & Sea and Davis, Garcia & Brown, so you should receive a copy of both at the same time.

You asked about my taxes for Jackson Computer Sales. Most of the $400,000 gross revenue comes from sales of computers, monitors, peripherals, and accessories. I also sell tablets. All of its income and expenses have been reported on my personal return on my Schedule C. I pay self-employment taxes on the net amount, which has been about $100,000.

If there is anything else you need, just let me know.

Have a great weekend,

Earl

Items for Analysis

The new business, E&K ComputerLand (E&K), will be an accrual basis, calendar-year entity.

1. Choose an option below:
   - [Original text] The new business, E&K ComputerLand (E&K), will be an accrual basis, calendar-year entity.
   - The new business, E&K ComputerLand (E&K), will be an accrual basis, fiscal-year entity.
   - The new business, E&K ComputerLand (E&K), will be a cash basis, calendar-year entity.
   - The new business, E&K ComputerLand (E&K), will be a cash basis, fiscal-year entity.
   - The new business, E&K ComputerLand (E&K), will be a hybrid basis, calendar-year entity.
   - The new business, E&K ComputerLand (E&K), will be a hybrid basis, fiscal-year entity.

However, to be a Pship, AACS must liquidate, as it cannot be a partner of E&K; only individuals can be owners in a Pship.

2. Choose an option below:

    - [Original text] However, to be a Pship, AACS must liquidate, as it cannot be a partner of E&K; only individuals can be owners in a Pship.

    - However, to be a C Corp, AACS must liquidate as it cannot be a shareholder of E&K; only individuals can be owners in a small C Corp.

    - However, to be a C Corp, you must incorporate your business because AACS, which is a C Corp, cannot combine with a sole proprietorship.

    - However, to be an S Corp, AACS must liquidate as it cannot be an owner of E&K; C Corps cannot be owners in an S Corp.

    - However, to be an S Corp, you must incorporate your business because AACS, which is a C Corp, cannot combine with a sole proprietorship.

S Corps are separate taxable entities, so double taxation can occur when the entity has taxable income and distributions are made.

3. Choose an option below:

    - [Original text] S Corps are separate taxable entities, so double taxation can occur when the entity has taxable income and distributions are made.

    - C Corps are separate taxable entities, so double taxation can occur when the entity has taxable income and distributions are made.

    - Pships are separate taxable entities, so double taxation can occur when the entity has taxable income and distributions are made.

    - C Corps and S Corps are separate taxable entities, so double taxation can occur when the entity has taxable income and distributions are made.

    - S Corps and Pships are separate taxable entities, so double taxation can occur when the entity has taxable income and distributions are made.

    - C Corps and Pships are separate taxable entities, so double taxation can occur when the entity has taxable income and distributions are made.

Pships and S Corps are tax reporting entities, meaning the entity level income flows through to the owners and is taxed only once on the owners' personal returns.

4. Choose an option below:

    - [Original text] Pships and S Corps are tax reporting entities, meaning the entity level income flows through to the owners and is taxed only once on the owners' personal returns.

    - C Corps are tax reporting entities, meaning the entity level income flows through to the owners and is taxed only once on the owners' personal returns.

    - S Corps are tax reporting entities, meaning the entity level income flows through to the owners and is taxed only once on the owners' personal returns.

- Pships are tax reporting entities, meaning the entity level income flows through to the owners and is taxed only once on the owners' personal returns.

- C Corps and S Corps are tax reporting entities, meaning the entity level income flows through to the owners and is taxed only once on the owners' personal returns.

- C Corps and Pships are tax reporting entities, meaning the entity level income flows through to the owners and is taxed only once on the owners' personal returns.

With C Corps and S Corps, income and losses are allocated according to the capital interest accounts.

5. Choose an option below:

- [Original text] With C Corps and S Corps, income and losses are allocated according to the capital interest accounts.

- With S Corps and Pships, income and losses are allocated on a per-share, per-day ownership basis.

- With C Corps and Pships, income and losses are allocated based on the initial investments in the entity.

- With S Corps, income and losses are allocated based on the balances in the ownership accounts.

- With Pships, income and losses are allocated based on the ownership agreement, and special allocations are permitted.

- With C Corps, income and losses are allocated by the board of directors.

This provides more flexibility than with Pships, which requires an allocation based on capital interest accounts.

6. Choose an option below:

- [Original text] This provides more flexibility than with Pships, which requires an allocation based on capital interest accounts.

- This provides more flexibility than with C Corps, which requires an allocation based on the board of director's declarations.

- This provides more flexibility than with S Corps, which requires an allocation based on per-share, per-day ownership.

- This provides more flexibility than with Pships, which requires an allocation based on the ownership accounts.

- This provides more flexibility than with S Corps, which requires an allocation based on the ownership agreement.

- This provides more flexibility than with C Corps, which requires an allocation based on initial investments in the entity.

S Corps and Pships have the least protection because owners include all liabilities in their basis; whereas a C Corp has the ability to limit liability since owners are liable only to the extent of their investments.

7. Choose an option below:

- [Original text] S Corps and Pships have the least protection because owners include all liabilities in their basis; whereas a C Corp has the ability to limit liability since owners are liable only to the extent of their investment.

- C Corps have the least protection because upon liquidation, owners must contribute to the entity to the extent of any losses; whereas S Corps and Pships are only liable to the extent of recourse debt.

- General Pships have the least protection because there is unlimited liability for the owners; whereas C Corps and S Corps have the ability to limit liability since the owners are liable only to the extent of their investments.

- S Corps have the least protection because upon liquidation, owners are liable to the extent of recourse debt; whereas C Corps have the most protection due to the owners being liable only to the extent of their investment.

- S Corps and Pships have the least protection because owners include all liabilities in their basis; whereas C Corps owners are only liable to the extent of their investment plus short-term debts (accounts payables).

- C Corps and S Corps have the least protection because to the extent of recourse debt, the owners are liable; whereas Pships owners increase their protection by including all liabilities in their basis.

However, in S Corps there can only be one class of ownership, and at least one of the owners must be a C Corp.

8. Choose an option below:

- [Original text] However, in S Corps there can only be one class of ownership, and at least one of the owners must be a C Corp.

- However, in S Corps there can only be one class of ownership, and the owners must be within the same family or limited extended group.

- However, in S Corps there can only be one class of ownership, and this class must all have the same voting rights.

- However, in S Corps there can only be one class of ownership, and revenue cannot be of a passive nature.

- However, in S Corps there can only be one class of ownership, and not more than 75 owners of which none are C Corps.

- However, in S Corps there can only be one class of ownership, and not more than 100 owners of which none are nonresident aliens.

DOCUMENT REVIEW SIMULATION SOLUTION

Document Review Simulation Solution 1

Beach & Sea CPAs, LLP

2300 Ocean Drive

Flipperville, FL

Earl Jackson
48684 Clermont Avenue
Flipperville, FL

Dear Earl:

Based on our meeting last month, it is our understanding that you are planning to combine your business with AA Computer Service, Inc. (AACS), owned by Kathleen Hamilton, and are seeking an entity with more flexibility than your current sole proprietorship. 1.) <u>The new business, E&K ComputerLand (E&K), will be a hybrid basis, fiscal-year entity.</u> Both you and Kathleen will continue to be calendar-year taxpayers. Three of the options available to the new combined computer sales and service business are a regular C corporation (C Corp), an S corporation (S Corp) and a general partnership (Pship). 2.) <u>However, to be an S Corp, AACS must liquidate, as it cannot be an owner of E&K; C Corps cannot be owners in an S Corp.</u>

When determining which entity form to choose for your new business, there are several factors to be considered. An important factor is the taxation of the business. 3.) <u>C Corps are separate taxable entities, so double taxation can occur when the entity has taxable income and distributions are made.</u> 4.) <u>Pships and S Corps are tax reporting entities, meaning the entity level income flows through to the owners and is taxed only once on the owners' personal returns.</u> 5.) <u>With Pships, income and losses are allocated based on the ownership agreement, and special allocations are permitted.</u> 6.) <u>This provides more flexibility than with S Corps, which requires an allocation based on per-share, per-day ownership.</u>

The possible loss due to a lawsuit or upon liquidation should be considered when selecting the entity form. 7.) <u>General Pships have the least protection because there is unlimited liability for the owners; whereas C Corps and S Corps have the ability to limit liability since the owners are liable only to the extent of their investments.</u> When you decide to expand the ownership of E&K, limited liability may be of great importance to new investors. Speaking of investors, in C Corps and Pships, there can be multiple classes of ownership. 8.) <u>However, in S Corps there can only be one class of ownership, and not more than 100 owners of which none are nonresident aliens.</u>

I hope this information helps you with your decision as to which entity form is best for E&K ComputerLand. Let us know what decision you make, and we will be happy to help you with the accounting and tax aspects of combining your business with AACS to create E&K.

Sincerely,
Juan Orlando, CPA
Managing Partner

Explanation of solutions

1. **The new business, E&K ComputerLand (E&K), will be a hybrid basis, fiscal-year entity.**

    The Entity Agreement Draft states that, "As required by the IRC, the entity will use the accrual method for determining its gross profit from sales of inventory and the cash method for all other aspects of the business, where possible." It also provides that neither of the owners desire a calendar year. Regardless of the entity form chosen, E&K will qualify for a fiscal year. It will meet the Partnership and S corporation majority interest rule for a March 31 year-end, because AASC will be the majority owner and its year-end is March 31. If a corporation is chosen for the entity structure, corporations may choose to use a fiscal year. Therefore, the sentence should be revised to read, "The new business, E&K ComputerLand (E&K), will be a hybrid basis, fiscal-year entity."

2. **However, to be an S Corp, AACS must liquidate, as it cannot be an owner of E&K; C Corps cannot be owners in an S Corp.**

    Of the three types of entities being considered, only an S corporation has restrictions as to who can be an owner. A corporation may not be a shareholder in an S corporation. You know AACS is a C corporation because it says so in the email from Kathleen. Thus, the sentence should be revised to read, "However, to be an S Corp, AACS must liquidate, as it cannot be an owner of E&K; C Corps cannot be owners in an S Corp."

3. **C Corps are separate taxable entities, so double taxation can occur when the entity has taxable income and distributions are made.**

    Of the three types of entities being considered, only C corporations are separate taxable entities. Thus, the sentence should be revised to read, "C Corps are separate taxable entities, so double taxation can occur when the entity has taxable income and distributions are made."

4. **[Original text] Pships and S Corps are tax reporting entities, meaning the entity level income flows through to the owners and is taxed only once on the owners' personal returns.**

    Of the three types of entities being considered, only partnerships and S corporations are considered tax *reporting* entities, meaning the entity level income flows through to the owners and is taxed only once on the owners' personal returns. C corporations are tax *paying* entities, so double taxation can occur when the entity has taxable income and distributions are made. Therefore, the original text is correct and does not need to be revised.

5. **With Pships, income and losses are allocated based on the ownership agreement, and special allocations are permitted.**

    Of the three types of entities being considered, only partnerships generally have the ability to allocate income in any way the partners choose in the ownership agreement. The income of C corporations is distributed in the form of dividends based on a per-share basis as of the date of declaration. S corporation income is allocated on a per-share, per-day ownership basis. Therefore, the sentence should be revised to read, "With Pships, income and losses are allocated based on the ownership agreement, and special allocations are permitted."

6. **This provides more flexibility than with S Corps, which requires an allocation based on per-share, per-day ownership.**

   Of the three types of entities being considered, only partnerships generally have the ability to allocate income in any way the partners choose in the ownership agreement. S corporation income is allocated on a per-share, per-day ownership basis. The income of C corporations is distributed in the form of dividends based on a per-share basis as of the date of declaration. Therefore, the sentence should be revised to read, "This provides more flexibility than with S Corps, which requires an allocation based on per-share, per-day ownership."

7. **General Pships have the least protection because there is unlimited liability for the owners; whereas C Corps and S Corps have the ability to limit liability since the owners are liable only to the extent of their investments.**

   If a general partnership is sued or liquidates with liabilities in excess of assets, the general partners would be personally liable (usually jointly and severally). If a corporation is sued or liquidates, only the assets of the corporation are at stake; that is, C corporation and S corporation shareholders have limited liability only to the extent of their respective capital contributions. Therefore, the sentence should be revised to read, "General Pships have the least protection because there is unlimited liability for the owners; whereas C Corps and S Corps have the ability to limit liability since the owners are liable only to the extent of their investments."

8. **However, in S Corps there can only be one class of ownership, and not more than 100 owners of which none are nonresident aliens.**

   S corporations are limited to 100 owners/shareholders. Corporations and nonresident aliens cannot be owners in an S corporation. Therefore, the sentence should be revised to read, "However, in S Corps there can only be one class of ownership, and not more than 100 owners of which none are nonresident aliens." While owners within the same family are treated as a single shareholder for purposes of the limit on shareholders, there is no rule that the owners must be within the same family or limited extended group. Although S corporations can have only one class of stock, different voting rights are allowed. The nature of revenue does not matter.

Section 5 – Estates, Trusts & Gift Taxes
Corresponding Lectures

Watch the following course lectures with this section:

Lecture 5.01 – Estates and Trusts Overview
Lecture 5.02 – Trusts and Operation
Lecture 5.03 – Creation of a Trust
Lecture 5.04 – Estates
Lecture 5.05 – Fiduciary Income Tax Return
Lecture 5.06 – Estates and Trusts – Class Questions
Lecture 5.07 – Gift Tax
Lecture 5.08 – Estate Tax
Lecture 5.09 – Gift and Estate Tax – Class Questions
Lecture 5.10 – Gift and Estate Tax – Class Questions – TBS

EXAM NOTE: Please refer to the AICPA REG Blueprint in the Introduction to find a listing of the representative tasks (and their associated skill levels—i.e., Remembering and Understanding, Application, and Analysis) that the candidate should be able to perform based on the knowledge obtained in this section.

Estates, Trusts & Gift Taxes

Lecture 5.01

ESTATES AND TRUSTS OVERVIEW

Individuals and corporations file tax returns. There are two artificial entities that also file tax returns; they are Trusts and Estates. The **Fiduciary Income Tax Return** (**Form 1041**) must be filed on an annual basis for both entities. The beneficiaries must also pay taxes when the income is distributed to them.

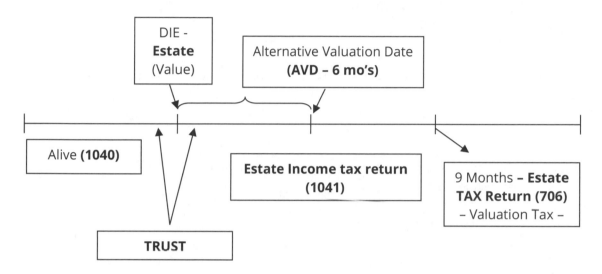

Lecture 5.02

TRUSTS

Trusts are typically established for the purpose of benefiting specific individuals or charities without giving them current control of the principal (corpus) of the trust.

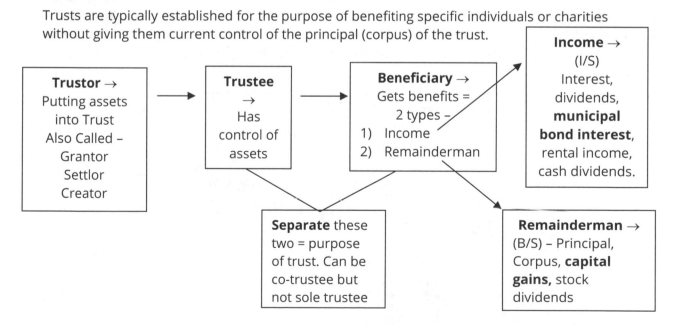

OPERATION OF TRUSTS & ESTATES

The allocation between the income and remainder beneficiaries can be tricky. The corpus of the trust will eventually go to the remainder beneficiaries, and the income will go to the income beneficiaries.

- **Remainder** – Receives **principal** of trust (including capital gains allocable to corpus).
  - o All assets contributed to the trust (Trust property)
  - o Property acquired in exchange for trust corpus
  - o Proceeds from the sale of the corpus
  - o Capital gains
  - o Stock dividends
  - o Mortgage premium payments
  - o Capital improvements
  - o Insurance proceeds

Income includes most of the items that are reported as income on accrual financial statements (regardless of whether it is reported for tax purposes). Notice, however, that the proceeds from the sale of corpus are allocated entirely to corpus, so that gains and losses on asset sales are **not** income to the income beneficiary.

- **Income** – Receives **earnings** of trust (but not net capital gains)
  - o Cash dividends
  - o Interest income
  - o Rental income, expense
  - o Property taxes
  - o Insurance premiums
  - o Depreciation
  - o Municipal bond Interest

For example, if a trust is formed with a contribution of $100,000 cash, the cash is classified as corpus. When the cash is used to purchase common stock, the stock is corpus. A cash dividend paid on the common stock is income (a stock dividend or split remains in corpus, though, since it is not reported on an accrual basis income statement). If the stock is subsequently sold for $350,000 cash, all of the cash is corpus, since it represents the proceeds from the sale of corpus.

Income (Income Statement Items)	Principal (Balance Sheet Items)
Rental Income/Expense	Original Property
Interest/Dividend Income	Bonds (accrued interest)
Cash Dividend	Capital Gains
Mortgage Interest Payments	Mortgage Principal Payments
Property Taxes	Stock Dividends/Splits
Royalty Income	

CREATION OF A TRUST

One legal arrangement that is often used is known as a trust. Assets transferred into a trust by a living person will not be part of the estate of that person upon their death. These living trusts are known as *inter vivos* trusts. A trust can also be established at the time of someone's death, usually to provide for minor children of the deceased. These trusts set up from the assets of a decedent are known as **testamentary** trusts.

In order for a trust to be a **Valid Express Trust**, it must satisfy **five conditions (BRATS):**
- **B**eneficiary – The trust must identify who will receive the benefits deriving from the trust. A trust often identifies an income beneficiary to receive the earnings of the trust, and a remainder beneficiary to receive the principal of the trust when it terminates.

- **R**easonable intent – There must be a valid purpose (tax savings do not qualify) for the existence of the trust. This is usually the separation of control of the assets from benefits, so a trust with a single individual serving as both trustee and sole beneficiary will usually fail. A trust will also fail when its purpose is impossible to fulfill.

- **A**ssets – The trust must contain some **corpus** or property. A trust without corpus has no earnings for the income beneficiaries or principal for the remainder beneficiaries.

- **T**rustee – A trustee must be in place to exercise control over the assets in the trust. This person does not need to be named in any legal document; however, they can be selected by the court or personal representative of the estate in the case of a testamentary trust. A successor trustee is not needed, and can simply be selected in the event the trustee can no longer serve.

- **S**pecified life – A trust must have an identifiable termination point, expressed in years or in the length of a life in being at the time the trust is created, plus a maximum of 21 years.
  - Private Trust = cannot live forever – lives until purpose is satisfied (e.g., if established for college, after graduation → trust ends)
  - Charitable Trust = lives forever (**perpetuity**)

There are some special *types of trust* arrangements occasionally discussed on the exam:
- *Inter vivos* **trust** – Created between living people
- **Testamentary trust** – Created through the execution of a will
- **Spendthrift trust** – A trust that prohibits assets from being pledged to pay the debts of a beneficiary. This arrangement is designed to prevent an irresponsible beneficiary from borrowing money from others and promising to use trust assets to repay the debt, thereby defeating the purpose of the trust.
- **Resulting trust** – A trust that is created by the courts due to the failure of an express trust and is intended to achieve a purpose that the creator of the express trust might have chosen had they known of the failure. **For example**, if a testamentary trust is established to put the decedent's daughter through college, and the daughter dies before completing college, the assets might be placed in a resulting trust that is to benefit the infant son of the daughter.
- *Cy pres* **trust** – A trust that is established due to the failure of a charitable trust, and that is designed to achieve a similar goal. **For example**, if a trust is established to find a cure for a particular disease, and a cure is found, the remaining assets might be placed in a trust to find a cure for a similar disease.

- **Totten or Tentative Trust** – A trust created when the settlor opens a bank account in his own name "as trustee" for another. The trust may be revoked by the settlor by withdrawing the funds from the account. Once the settlor dies, the trust becomes irrevocable. If the beneficiary dies before the settlor, the trust terminates.
- **Constructive Trusts** – A court will impose a constructive trust when there has been abuse of a confidential relation or where actual fraud or duress is considered an equitable ground for creating the trust. **For example**, if an agent acquired title to property, he is obligated to transfer it back to the principal because the acquisition was by breach of a fiduciary duty.
- **Real Estate Investment Trust (REIT)** – A trust created by a transfer of the legal title to real estate to a trustee. The trustee manages the trust property for the benefit of specified beneficiaries. The trust doesn't pay corporate taxes; the beneficiaries do. The major portion of the trust's income must be derived from real estate (rent, interest on mortgages, and gains on sale of real property). The certificates of ownership must be freely transferable. Must have a minimum of 100 certificate holders during each year and no fewer than 6 may own 50% or all outstanding certificates.

Trusts are irrevocable, unless:
- Reserve rights
- End of term
- Occurrence of an event (death)
- Purpose accomplished
- Consent of trustor & all beneficiaries, remainderman & courts

The grantor of a *revocable trust* has full control over the funds in the trust during the grantor's lifetime, unless control is voluntarily relinquished. Transfers to a revocable trust are not subject to gift tax since, being revocable, they are considered incomplete transfers. Upon the death of the grantor, a revocable trust becomes irrevocable. It is included in the gross estate of the grantor, bypassing probate.

When a trust allocates income and/or remainder to offspring, the creator must decide if the allocation will be *per capita* or *per stirpes*.
- A **per capita** allocation is equal to each person (**each beneficiary**). If there are three children, each is allocated 1/3. If one of the children dies during the term of the trust, and the decedent had two children (grandchildren of the trustor), the allocation is now 1/4 to each of the surviving children and each of the offspring of the deceased child.

- A **per stirpes** allocation is equal at the level of the first generation (**each group**). If there are three children, each is allocated 1/3. If one child dies with two offspring, the allocation to each surviving child remains 1/3, and each of the offspring of the deceased child is allocated 1/6.

    If Die without a Will (i.e., Intestate), the assets will be distributed in the following order:
    - Spouse
    - Descendants (Children/Grandchildren)
    - Ascendants (Parent/Grandparents)
    - Collaterals (Brothers/Sisters)

Lecture 5.04

ESTATES

Estates are created at the time of a person's death to temporarily hold the property of the decedent until it can be distributed to the heirs (An estate kicks in when a person kicks OUT!!) Since the deceased person's investments still generate interest, dividends and rental income, the estate must pay income taxes on the earnings. The **Executor** is responsible for filing the income tax return. Can die with a Will, or without a Will.

- **Intestate** – When someone dies *without* a written Will.
- **Testate** – When someone dies *with a Will.*

Do not confuse the fiduciary income tax return of an estate (Form 1041) with the estate tax return (Form 706). The former is to report income of the estate received **after** the decedent's date of death, while the latter is a form of property tax on the value of the decedent's estate **at the time of death**. Estate taxes are discussed later.

At the time a person dies, their property generally is transferred to a successor legal entity known as the **estate of the decedent**. This doesn't apply to property that is held in joint tenancy or some other form of ownership that provides right of survivorship, however. Such property automatically goes to the survivors and bypasses the estate.

The process of settling an estate is called **probate**. The personal representative in charge of the estate is known as the **executor** (if named by the decedent's will - **Testate**) or **administrator** (if named by the courts). The responsibilities of the personal representative include:

- Paying the debts of the decedent out of estate assets.
- Filing all necessary tax returns.
- Distributing remaining assets to the appropriate beneficiaries.

The personal representative has a **fiduciary duty** to the estate, its creditors, and beneficiaries. This means the representative must act in a loyal manner in the best interests of these parties. They may not engage in **self-dealing**, which includes personally borrowing money from the estate or entering joint business ventures with it. They are expected to carry out the wishes of the decedent as expressed in the will to the extent possible, subject to the legitimate claims of creditors (including government tax authorities). If the decedent died **intestate** (without a will), the administrator will distribute assets based on applicable state law in the jurisdiction the decedent resided at the time of death.

A trustee has the same **fiduciary responsibility** to the trust that the personal representative has to the estate. Additionally, the trustee is responsible for ensuring that the income and principal of the trust are properly assigned to the income and remainder beneficiaries, respectively.

Trustee – fiduciary duty
- Act loyally
- Due care
- Distribute income and principal according to the trust terms
- Keep accurate records

FIDUCIARY INCOME TAX RETURN (1041)

Estates and trusts are required to file an annual fiduciary income tax return, Form 1041.

- Filed annually by estates and trusts to report the income earned by the entity.
    - Estates – Required when gross income is $600 or more, or there is a nonresident alien beneficiary
    - Trusts – Required for *any* taxable income, gross income of $600 or more, or there is a nonresident alien beneficiary
    - Similar to Form 1040, but no standard deduction is given and different exemptions exist.

- **Trusts** are normally planned in advance, so federal law requires that they adopt a calendar year for the reporting of taxable income.
    - **Calendar year** taxpayer due **4/15**. Trusts must pay **quarterly estimated taxes.**

- **Estates** result from the death of a person and are not as controllable, so federal law permits the personal representative of the estate to adopt any tax year, with the return due by the 15th day of the 4th month following the end of the tax year (3 ½ months after the close of the reporting year). Since most estates are settled in less than a year, the executor of the estate typically chooses a year-end once the processing of the estate assets has been virtually completed. **For example**, if the decedent's death occurs on 7/22/X1, and the executor completes the distribution of assets on 1/17/X2, a tax year ending in January is typically chosen. This way, only a single fiduciary income tax return needs to be filed to report estate income from 7/22/X1 through 1/17/X2. The 4th month following the end of the tax year (January) is May, so the return is due 5/15/X2.
    - A **fiscal or Calendar year** is acceptable for an Estate, usually starting on the deceased's date of death. The tax return is due 3 ½ months after the close of the reporting year. **Estimated quarterly tax payments** are *not required during the first two years*, but are required thereafter.

Types of Trusts

- **Grantor (revocable) trust** – This is a trust whose creator (grantor) reserves the right to withdraw assets at any time.
    - Tax code ignores this trust. The income is taxed on the Grantor's Form 1040 as if the trust did not exist.

- **Simple trust** – One that makes annual distributions exactly equal to DNI (Distributable Net Income) to taxpaying beneficiaries each year.
    - Form 1041 must be prepared every year.
    - Taxable income normally reduced to $0 by distributions.
        - Net capital gains can result in retained income.
        - Personal exemption is $300.
    - Distributions may exceed DNI.
        - Only amount up to DNI is included in beneficiary's gross income.
        - Multiple beneficiaries share in DNI proportionately when distribution exceeds DNI.

- **Complex trust** – Any trust that fails to meet the criteria for a simple trust and:
  - Satisfies one of three conditions during the tax year:
    - Less than Distributable Net Income (DNI) is distributed and some of current income is retained within the trust;
    - Amounts are permanently set aside for charitable gifts; or
    - A distribution was made from amounts allocated to trust principal.
  - Personal exemption is only $100.
  - Often pays taxes on undistributed income.

- Trusts and estates cannot claim standard deductions or dependency exemptions. **Personal exemptions** available are:
  - **Complex trusts – $100**
  - **Simple trusts – $300**
  - **Estates – $600**

- The IRS has reduced the extension period for Form 1041 from 6 months to **5 1/2** months (no longer tested). The purpose of the change is to help individuals better meet their filing obligations who must report information from *Schedules K-1* and similar documents on their individual tax returns.

Income Taxation of Trusts and Estates (1041)

Trusts/Estates	DNI
Income Tax Return	= Max amount that can be taxed to beneficiaries as income. Rest considered a distribution of principal. (**Payoutable profits**)
Gross Income (same as Indiv.) Interest Dividends Rental income Capital Gains All income rules SAME between individuals and trust	**Gross Income** + Municipal Bond Interest (no Capital Gains) - Everything else the same as Trust/Estate
Deductions = Same, except 3 rules (in addition to no standard deduction)	
1. **Trustee Management Fees (Fiduciary Fees)** – Accountants, attorneys, income tax preparation (only deduct % based on taxable income)	*Same*
2. **Charity** – Can give 100% away; individuals only up to 50% of AGI	*Same*
3. **Income Distribution Deduction** – Taxed once and only once! No double taxation. Either stays or gets distributed to K-1 → Sch. E → 1040	**None**
Exemptions - Simple = $300 - Complex = $100 - Estates = $600	**None**
= Taxable Income	= **DNI** (Maximum amount that's taxable)

Income Taxation of Trusts and Estates

Calculate **distributable net income (DNI)** – Maximum amount that can be taxed to the beneficiary; the rest is a tax-free distribution of principal (**Payoutable Profits**).

- Different from taxable income in certain ways:
    - Includes tax-exempt income (Municipal bond interest).
    - Excludes net capital gains (unless they are to be distributed to the beneficiary).
    - Actual distributions of DNI reduce taxable income (100% deductible, except for any tax-exempt income included).
        - Such distributions reported on recipients' returns.
    - No income distributions deduction.
    - No personal exemption allowed.

Distributable net income identifies the income that is available to distribute to the income beneficiaries of the trust each year. It is based on the income and expenses reported on the income tax return of the trust, with two adjustments:

- **Tax-exempt income** (e.g., municipal bond interest) is included in DNI since it is available to distribute, even though it is not subject to taxation.
- **Net capital gains** are **not** included in DNI since, under trust law, they are treated as adjustments to the corpus (unless they are to be distributed to the beneficiary).

The calculation of income on a **fiduciary income tax return** is almost identical to the determination of income on an individual return. The most significant **differences** that apply are:

- There is no limit on **charitable deductions** (they must be authorized in the trust instrument or will of the decedent). Can give an unlimited amount to charity.
- Income paid to an estate that was earned by the decedent prior to death (such as the final paycheck of the taxpayer from their employer or installment payments paid to a decedent's estate) must be included in the fiduciary income tax return (Form 1041) and also reported as a receivable on the estate tax return of the decedent (Form 706). This is known as **income in respect of a decedent (IRD)**. Note: Estate taxes paid on IRD are deductible on the Form 1041.
- Fees paid to the **trustee (fiduciary fees)** and other costs of administering the trust are generally deductible. Fees paid to administer an estate can be deducted on the fiduciary income tax return if the executor waives the right to deduct these costs on the estate tax return.
- A deduction is claimed for all **distributions of DNI** to beneficiaries of the trust or estate. The beneficiaries report the income on their personal tax returns. The amounts flow through on a 1041 Schedule K-1, then to the Schedule E on their individual 1040 tax returns. Distributions of corpus are not deductible and not taxable to the beneficiaries.

Certain costs incurred by estates and non-grantor trusts are deductible only to the extent that they exceed 2% of adjusted income. The expenses included in this category are predominantly those related to property of the estate or trust that would not have been incurred if the property was not held in a trust. They are largely associated with trustee and investment fee arrangements.

- Examples include costs related to the ownership of property, such as insurance premiums or maintenance costs; tax preparation fees other than for estate tax returns, generation-skipping transfer tax returns, fiduciary income tax returns, and a decedent's final individual income tax return; investment advisory fees; and appraisal fees.
- In applying this threshold, adjusted income does not include deductions for those expenses that are subject to the 2% threshold.

As a result of the Patient Protection and Affordable Care Act (PPACA), there is a **surtax on unearned income** that may have to be paid by estates and trusts. The surtax, which is added to any other taxes the estate or trust is liable for, is computed at 3.8% of the lesser of two amounts:

- Undistributed taxable income for the taxable year, or
- The excess, if any, of AGI for the taxable year over the dollar amount at which the highest tax bracket begins for that taxable year.

Caution: At the time of this writing, President Trump had introduced his broad plan for tax reform, which included repealing the 3.8% Net Investment Income Tax. Please refer to the Course Textbook Updates section of the Roger CPA Review website for legislation updates: https://www.rogercpareview.com/dashboard/my-courses/course-textbook-updates.

Lecture 5.06

CLASS QUESTIONS

Please see the Class Questions and Class Solutions for this Lecture at the end of this Section.

Lecture 5.07

GIFT TAX

Taxes may be owed by those who transfer large amounts of their wealth to others during their lifetime and upon their death, based on the **unified transfer tax**. Transfers made during their lifetime are reported on **gift tax returns (Form 709)**, and the **estate tax return (Form 706)** combines all reported gifts and the value of the estate at death to determine if any additional taxes are due. The estate tax is discussed later.

Gross Gifts – Form 709	Gross Estate – Like a personal B/S (706)
+ Cash ⎧ Life insurance + Property ⎪ charity + Loan interest **Not** ⎨ political contrib's + Bargain sale ⎪ joint account + Irrevocable Trust (P.V.) ⎩ Revocable trust = Gross Gifts	+ All Assets (+IRD → Money coming in later) + Life Insurance Proceeds + Revocable Trust **+ ½ of property with spouse** = **Gross Estate** → (Value @ Death or AVD-6 mo's)
EXCLUSIONS	**DEDUCTIONS**

− Support Minors
− Marital Deduction
− Education & Medical Bills → (Paid directly
    to school/hospital)
− **$14,000** Gift Exclusion
    (start enjoyment <u>now</u>)
	− Charity
	− Marital Deduction
	− Liabilities/Expenses (e.g., Medical,
	Mortgages, Administrative Exp., Funeral)

= **Taxable Gifts (709)** + T.G.s over the years + Taxable **Estate** ◄ = **Total Taxable Transfer** × tax rate = tentative tax liability − Unified credit − Other credits − Prepayments = **Tax due** (**706** due **9 mo's after death**)	= **Taxable Estate**

There are **three types of transfers** that may take place during a person's lifetime:
- Gift of a ***present interest*** – An immediate transfer of wealth that can be accessed by the recipient immediately.
- Gift of a ***future interest*** – An irrevocable transfer of the right to access wealth at a future time.
- ***Uncompleted gift*** (***no interest***) – A revocable transfer of the right to access wealth at a future time.

A **gift of a present interest** ("start enjoyment NOW") normally must be reported in years in which the taxpayer transfers more than **$14,000** in wealth to a single individual ($28,000 for MFJ with gift-splitting election).

- Right to immediately use and enjoy the property. A present interest exists if:
    - Annuity starting now
    - Outright ownership of the property
    - The guaranteed right to immediately receive the periodic dividends, rents or other income stream the property generates.
- A delayed right to property does not qualify.
- Depositing cash into a *joint bank account* with an intended beneficiary (noncontributing tenant) only becomes a gift when the beneficiary withdraws funds from that account for his own benefit.
- **Exclusions**:
    - Gifts to spouses. Gifts given in contemplation of marriage (engagement rings) are not exempt.
    - Support minors
    - Payments directly to schools for tuition for another.
    - Payments directly to health care providers for another.
    - **$14,000 annual exclusion**

A **gift of a future interest** must be reported, regardless of size, at the present value of the future interest.
- Any gift in which amount is not immediately available to gift beneficiary (cannot enjoy now).
- Does not qualify for the $14,000 annual exclusion.

An **uncompleted gift (no interest)** is not reported, and the wealth is still considered a part of the taxpayer's estate as long as they retain their right to revoke the transfer.
- When donor retains right to revoke gift (e.g., revocable trust)

Gifts may involve:
- Transfers of cash or property
- Sales of property at a bargain price to another family member
- Loans to family members on which a fair rate of interest is not charged (i.e., imputed interest)
- Trusts established for others in which income and/or corpus will eventually go to someone other than the taxpayer

It is possible for the interests in a trust to be split. If the income of the trust each year goes immediately to *one beneficiary*, and the corpus will go to another at the time the trust terminates, then the grantor of the trust is making a gift of a present interest to the *income beneficiary* each year and a gift of a future interest (assuming it is irrevocable) to the *remainder beneficiary*.

The following are automatically **excluded** from the definition of taxable gifts:
- Transfers to **spouses** (must be married at the time of transfer)
- Transfers to qualified **charitable** organizations
- **Political** contributions to organizations
- Payment of medical expenses or tuition of another (must be made **directly to** the health care or education provider)

Gift tax returns (Form 709) are due by April 15 of the year following the calendar year in which the reportable gifts occur. The fact that a gift must be reported on a gift tax return does not, however, automatically mean that any tax liability will be owed. Each individual is permitted to make taxable gifts up to their lifetime limit before owing any tax. The lifetime exclusion amount is **$5,490,000 for 2017**.

Since gift taxes are applied to each individual donor, a husband and wife may each use the annual and lifetime exclusions mentioned. They can also agree to split large gifts made by one of them and treat each as having given half of the amount. Each gift tax return represents one individual donor. **Portability** between spouses permits the surviving spouse to apply the decedent's unused exclusion amount to the surviving spouse's own transfers during life (gift) and at death (Estate).

For example, assume that Gerald Generous, a single individual, files a gift tax return on 4/15/X2 for the first time, reporting gifts made to three different persons in 20X1:
- Fran Friend – Gerald gave $1,000,000 cash to Fran.
- Pat Parent – Gerald sold Pat his condo in Florida for $500,000 (its appraised value was $2,000,000 at the time of sale).
- Nellie Niece – Gerald established an irrevocable trust that paid all income to Gerald for 10 years, then transferred the trust corpus to Nellie at the end of that period. The value of the corpus was $4,500,000 when the trust was established, and the present value of the gift was determined to be $2,000,000.

The gift to Fran is $1,000,000, of which $986,000 must be reported after the annual exclusion. The gift to Pat is $1,500,000, of which $1,486,000 must be reported after the annual exclusion. The gift to Nellie is $2,000,000, and doesn't qualify for an annual exclusion since the corpus is not immediately available to Nellie.

The total gifts reported on the return are $986,000 + $1,486,000 + $2,000,000 = $4,472,000. This uses $4,472,000 of the lifetime exclusion, but no tax is owed at this time. If Gerald makes reportable gifts of $2,000,000 in 20X2, however, (assuming the lifetime exclusion of $5,490,000) he will have to pay gift taxes, since he will now have exceeded the cumulative lifetime exclusion.

The Top tax bracket for the estate and gift tax is **40%** for 2013 **- 2017**.

Lecture 5.08

ESTATE TAX

Caution: At the time of this writing, President Trump had introduced his broad plan for tax reform, which included repealing the estate tax. Please refer to the Course Textbook Updates section of the Roger CPA Review website for legislation updates:
https://www.rogercpareview.com/dashboard/my-courses/course-textbook-updates.

An **estate tax return (Form 706)** must be filed on behalf of anyone who, at the time of death, had a gross estate exceeding the lifetime exclusion. For someone dying in 2017, the Estate Tax Exclusion is $5,490,000 with a maximum tax rate of 40% (MFJ is $10,980,000). The due date of the return is exactly **9 months** after the date of death.

The **gross estate includes** all of the following:
- Cash and property owned by the decedent at the time of death.
- All gifts reported on gift tax returns during the lifetime of the decedent made after 1976 (gift and estate taxes are unified in this manner).

- Receivables, including **income in respect of a decedent** representing amounts earned by the decedent but not paid until after their death (e.g., company bonus).
- Trusts in which the decedent had an interest or a right to revoke at the time of death.
- Life insurance proceeds on policies that the decedent controlled for purposes of naming the beneficiary (incident of ownership), **even if the proceeds are not being paid to the decedent's estate.**
- One-half of all property jointly held with a spouse.
- **All** property jointly held with anyone other than a spouse, reduced only by the percentage of the cost of the property that the other can prove they paid.

With regard to property jointly held with a non-spouse, the purpose of including all of it unless the other party can prove they contributed to the cost is to prevent taxpayers from bypassing estate taxes through the use of joint accounts.

For example, assume Edie Elder puts $1,000,000 into a savings account with ownership in the form of joint tenancy with right of survivorship with her son, Less Elder. The value of the account increases due to interest income to $1,200,000 by the time of Edie's death. The entire account balance is included in Edie's estate at the time of her death (the right of survivorship only means Less gets immediate control of the account without the legal process of probate; it doesn't eliminate estate taxes). On the other hand, if Less dies first, the entire account can be excluded from Less' estate once Edie shows she contributed 100% of the money that funded the account.

The valuation of the assets in the gross estate is normally based on fair market values at the **time of death**. If, however, the executor elects the **alternate valuation date (AVD)**, assets are valued at the time of distribution or sale from the estate. Items not distributed within six months of death have an alternative valuation of the fair market value exactly **6 months** after the date of death. The alternate valuation may be elected for an estate only if it will reduce both the value of the gross estate and the amount of estate tax liability.

An exception to the fair market value at time of death (or AVD) applies to appreciated property received by the decedent within one year of death. In such cases, the property retains the *original donor's basis*.

Effective for estate tax returns filed after July 31, 2015, there are new requirements for reporting the basis of estate assets. In a nutshell, *basis must be consistently reported between the estate and the heirs*; more specifically, IRC Sec. 1014(f)(1) provides that the basis of any property to which this provision applies cannot exceed the final valuation of the property determined for estate tax purposes.
- Only applies to property that increased the tax liability of the estate.
- An information statement (Form 8971, *Information Regarding Beneficiaries Acquiring Property From a Decedent*, and Schedules A) must be filed with the IRS and furnished to each beneficiary stating such valuation/basis within 30 days of the earlier of the due date of the estate tax return or the date the return was filed.

Portability allows spouses to combine their estate tax exemptions, so they can give away or leave more than $10,980,000 (2017) without owing taxes. So, if the first spouse to die doesn't use up their individual gift/estate tax exemption, the surviving spouse gets to use what is left. It does require the living spouse to file an estate tax return, even though no tax is due at that time. When the second spouse dies, their heirs can use some of the first spouse's unused exemption plus the current spouse's exemption, so no estate tax may be due, even though the estate is over the exemption amount.

An estate is liable for estate taxes only if the **taxable estate** exceeds the lifetime exclusion. The taxable estate is the gross estate reduced by **allowable deductions**. The most important deductions are:

- **State Death tax deduction** includes only taxes actually paid and claimed as a deduction. This replaces the State death tax Credit.
- **Marital deduction** – Anything transferred to the decedent's surviving spouse.
- **Charitable deduction** – All contributions authorized by the decedent in their will (no deduction is available if the decedent died intestate—that is, without a will).
- **Funeral expenses**
- **Casualty and theft loss** during the estate administration
- **Administrative expenses** – Costs incurred in the settlement of the estate, unless the executor waives the right to deduct these amounts in order to claim them on the fiduciary income tax return of the estate (Form 1041).
- **Liabilities of the estate** – All debts existing at the time of death with the exception of the estate tax liability itself. Medical expenses owed at the time of death may be included unless the executor waives the right to deduct these amounts in order to claim them on the final **individual income tax return of the decedent** (Form 1040).

	Individual Tax Return (1040)	Estate Income Tax Return (I/S) (1041)		Estate tax Return (B/S) (706)
Medical Bills	X	OR	X	Normally goes here but if sign a waiver, can go on individual tax return
Fees to Executor (Deductions)		X	OR	X
IRD (Income)		X	**AND**	X

Once the taxable estate is determined, the **tentative tax** is computed based on the appropriate tax tables. This tentative tax is then reduced by **various credits**:

- **Foreign tax credit** – Taxes paid on property in other countries to the extent the property has been taxed twice.
- **Unified credit** (a.k.a., applicable credit) – A credit that is large enough to eliminate the tax on an estate equal to the lifetime exclusion (i.e., about 40% × $5,490,000 lifetime exclusion for 2017).
- The former *State Death Tax credit* has been replaced by the **State Death Tax deduction**.

Once these credits are claimed, the resulting net tax is reduced by gift taxes that were paid by the decedent over the course of their lifetime. Due to the unified nature of gift and estate taxes, gift taxes are not considered credits against the estate tax. Instead, they are reported as **prior payments** on the overall **unified transfer tax**, reducing the balance due on the estate tax return.

Generation-Skipping Tax

There is one additional component to the unified transfer tax that is reported on the estate tax return known as the **generation-skipping tax**. This tax is imposed when the decedent's estate is transferring substantial property to beneficiaries at least two generations below the decedent.

The generation-skipping tax applies when amounts exceeding the lifetime exclusion are transferred. The lifetime exclusion is **$5,490,000 for 2016.** This exclusion is unrelated to the lifetime exclusion on gift and estate taxes, and any tax resulting from transfers exceeding this amount is owed in addition to those taxes.

The intent of the generation-skipping tax is to prevent taxpayers from avoiding the estate taxes on a generation by giving, **for example**, to grandchildren instead of children. The amount of the generation-skipping tax is usually reasonably close to the additional estate taxes that would have been paid to the government if the taxpayer had transferred the property to their children and then the children had transferred the property to the grandchildren. The generation-skipping tax does **not** apply to transfers to a grandchild if the taxpayer's child who is the parent of the grandchild is already deceased, since the grandchild is actually the first generation in that line below the taxpayer.

Surtax on Unearned Income

As mentioned in Individual tax, estates and trusts are also now subject to **the Surtax on Unearned Income.** This surtax, called the ***Unearned Income Medicare Contribution Tax,*** is imposed on the *unearned income* of individuals, estates, and trusts. For trusts and estates, the surtax is **3.8%** of the **lesser** of:

1. An estate or trust's undistributed net investment income (UNII), **OR**
2. The excess of an estate or trust's Adjusted Gross Income (AGI) reduced by a fixed threshold amount ($12,500 for 2017). The threshold is adjusted each year based on the dollar amount that starts the highest tax bracket.

Caution: At the time of this writing, President Trump had introduced his broad plan for tax reform, which included repealing the 3.8% Net Investment Income Tax. Please refer to the Course Textbook Updates section of the Roger CPA Review website for legislation updates: https://www.rogercpareview.com/dashboard/my-courses/course-textbook-updates.

Lecture 5.09

CLASS QUESTIONS

Please see the Class Questions and Class Solutions for this Lecture at the end of this Section.

Lecture 5.10

CLASS QUESTIONS

Please see the Class Questions and Class Solutions for this Lecture at the end of this Section.

Note: The 2016 forms are provided since 2017 forms were unavailable at the time of publication.

Form **1041** Department of the Treasury—Internal Revenue Service
U.S. Income Tax Return for Estates and Trusts 20**16** OMB No. 1545-0092

▶ Information about Form 1041 and its separate instructions is at *www.irs.gov/form1041.*

A Check all that apply:	For calendar year 2016 or fiscal year beginning	, 2016, and ending	, 20

A Check all that apply:
- ☐ Decedent's estate
- ☐ Simple trust
- ☐ Complex trust
- ☐ Qualified disability trust
- ☐ ESBT (S portion only)
- ☐ Grantor type trust
- ☐ Bankruptcy estate-Ch. 7
- ☐ Bankruptcy estate-Ch. 11
- ☐ Pooled income fund

Name of estate or trust (If a grantor type trust, see the instructions.)

Name and title of fiduciary

Number, street, and room or suite no. (If a P.O. box, see the instructions.)

City or town, state or province, country, and ZIP or foreign postal code

C Employer identification number

D Date entity created

E Nonexempt charitable and split-interest trusts, check applicable box(es), see instructions.
- ☐ Described in sec. 4947(a)(1). Check here if not a private foundation . . . ▶ ☐
- ☐ Described in sec. 4947(a)(2)

B Number of Schedules K-1 attached (see instructions) ▶

F Check applicable boxes:
- ☐ Initial return
- ☐ Change in trust's name
- ☐ Final return
- ☐ Change in fiduciary
- ☐ Amended return
- ☐ Change in fiduciary's name
- ☐ Net operating loss carryback
- ☐ Change in fiduciary's address

G Check here if the estate or filing trust made a section 645 election . . . . ▶ ☐ Trust TIN ▶

Income

1	Interest income	1	
2a	Total ordinary dividends	2a	
b	Qualified dividends allocable to: **(1)** Beneficiaries _____ **(2)** Estate or trust _____		
3	Business income or (loss). Attach Schedule C or C-EZ (Form 1040)	3	
4	Capital gain or (loss). Attach Schedule D (Form 1041)	4	
5	Rents, royalties, partnerships, other estates and trusts, etc. Attach Schedule E (Form 1040)	5	
6	Farm income or (loss). Attach Schedule F (Form 1040)	6	
7	Ordinary gain or (loss). Attach Form 4797	7	
8	Other income. List type and amount _____	8	
9	**Total income.** Combine lines 1, 2a, and 3 through 8 . . . . . ▶	9	

Deductions

10	Interest. Check if Form 4952 is attached ▶ ☐	10	
11	Taxes	11	
12	Fiduciary fees	12	
13	Charitable deduction (from Schedule A, line 7)	13	
14	Attorney, accountant, and return preparer fees	14	
15a	Other deductions **not** subject to the 2% floor (attach schedule) . .	15a	
b	Net operating loss deduction. See instructions	15b	
c	Allowable miscellaneous itemized deductions subject to the 2% floor .	15c	
16	Add lines 10 through 15c . . . . ▶	16	
17	Adjusted total income or (loss). Subtract line 16 from line 9 . . .	17	
18	Income distribution deduction (from Schedule B, line 15). Attach Schedules K-1 (Form 1041)	18	
19	Estate tax deduction including certain generation-skipping taxes (attach computation) . . .	19	
20	Exemption	20	
21	Add lines 18 through 20 . . . . ▶	21	

Tax and Payments

22	Taxable income. Subtract line 21 from line 17. If a loss, see instructions	22	
23	**Total tax** (from Schedule G, line 7)	23	
24	**Payments: a** 2016 estimated tax payments and amount applied from 2015 return	24a	
b	Estimated tax payments allocated to beneficiaries (from Form 1041-T) . . .	24b	
c	Subtract line 24b from line 24a	24c	
d	Tax paid with Form 7004. See instructions	24d	
e	Federal income tax withheld. If any is from Form(s) 1099, check ▶ ☐	24e	
	Other payments: **f** Form 2439 _____ ; **g** Form 4136 _____ ; Total ▶	24h	
25	**Total payments.** Add lines 24c through 24e, and 24h . . . . . ▶	25	
26	Estimated tax penalty. See instructions	26	
27	**Tax due.** If line 25 is smaller than the total of lines 23 and 26, enter amount owed	27	
28	**Overpayment.** If line 25 is larger than the total of lines 23 and 26, enter amount overpaid . .	28	
29	Amount of line 28 to be: **a** Credited to 2017 estimated tax ▶ ; **b** Refunded ▶	29	

Sign Here

Under penalties of perjury, I declare that I have examined this return, including accompanying schedules and statements, and to the best of my knowledge and belief, it is true, correct, and complete. Declaration of preparer (other than taxpayer) is based on all information of which preparer has any knowledge.

▶ _____ ▶ _____
Signature of fiduciary or officer representing fiduciary   Date   EIN of fiduciary if a financial institution

May the IRS discuss this return with the preparer shown below (see instr.)? ☐ Yes ☐ No

Paid Preparer Use Only

Print/Type preparer's name	Preparer's signature	Date	Check ☐ if self-employed	PTIN
Firm's name ▶			Firm's EIN ▶	
Firm's address ▶			Phone no.	

For Paperwork Reduction Act Notice, see the separate instructions.   Cat. No. 11370H   Form **1041** (2016)

Form 1041 (2016)   Page **2**

Schedule A — Charitable Deduction. Don't complete for a simple trust or a pooled income fund.

1	Amounts paid or permanently set aside for charitable purposes from gross income. See instructions	1	
2	Tax-exempt income allocable to charitable contributions. See instructions	2	
3	Subtract line 2 from line 1	3	
4	Capital gains for the tax year allocated to corpus and paid or permanently set aside for charitable purposes	4	
5	Add lines 3 and 4	5	
6	Section 1202 exclusion allocable to capital gains paid or permanently set aside for charitable purposes. See instructions	6	
7	**Charitable deduction.** Subtract line 6 from line 5. Enter here and on page 1, line 13	7	

Schedule B — Income Distribution Deduction

1	Adjusted total income. See instructions	1	
2	Adjusted tax-exempt interest	2	
3	Total net gain from Schedule D (Form 1041), line 19, column (1). See instructions	3	
4	Enter amount from Schedule A, line 4 (minus any allocable section 1202 exclusion)	4	
5	Capital gains for the tax year included on Schedule A, line 1. See instructions	5	
6	Enter any gain from page 1, line 4, as a negative number. If page 1, line 4, is a loss, enter the loss as a positive number	6	
7	**Distributable net income.** Combine lines 1 through 6. If zero or less, enter -0-	7	
8	If a complex trust, enter accounting income for the tax year as determined under the governing instrument and applicable local law ·	8	
9	Income required to be distributed currently	9	
10	Other amounts paid, credited, or otherwise required to be distributed	10	
11	Total distributions. Add lines 9 and 10. If greater than line 8, see instructions	11	
12	Enter the amount of tax-exempt income included on line 11	12	
13	Tentative income distribution deduction. Subtract line 12 from line 11	13	
14	Tentative income distribution deduction. Subtract line 2 from line 7. If zero or less, enter -0-	14	
15	**Income distribution deduction.** Enter the smaller of line 13 or line 14 here and on page 1, line 18	15	

Schedule G — Tax Computation (see instructions)

1	**Tax: a** Tax on taxable income. See instructions	1a		
	b Tax on lump-sum distributions. Attach Form 4972	1b		
	c Alternative minimum tax (from Schedule I (Form 1041), line 56)	1c		
	d **Total.** Add lines 1a through 1c ▶		1d	
2a	Foreign tax credit. Attach Form 1116	2a		
b	General business credit. Attach Form 3800	2b		
c	Credit for prior year minimum tax. Attach Form 8801	2c		
d	Bond credits. Attach Form 8912	2d		
e	**Total credits.** Add lines 2a through 2d ▶		2e	
3	Subtract line 2e from line 1d. If zero or less, enter -0-		3	
4	Net investment income tax from Form 8960, line 21		4	
5	Recapture taxes. Check if from: ☐ Form 4255 ☐ Form 8611		5	
6	Household employment taxes. Attach Schedule H (Form 1040)		6	
7	**Total tax.** Add lines 3 through 6. Enter here and on page 1, line 23 ▶		7	

Other Information

		Yes	No
1	Did the estate or trust receive tax-exempt income? If "Yes," attach a computation of the allocation of expenses. Enter the amount of tax-exempt interest income and exempt-interest dividends ▶ $		
2	Did the estate or trust receive all or any part of the earnings (salary, wages, and other compensation) of any individual by reason of a contract assignment or similar arrangement?		
3	At any time during calendar year 2016, did the estate or trust have an interest in or a signature or other authority over a bank, securities, or other financial account in a foreign country?		
	See the instructions for exceptions and filing requirements for FinCEN Form 114. If "Yes," enter the name of the foreign country ▶		
4	During the tax year, did the estate or trust receive a distribution from, or was it the grantor of, or transferor to, a foreign trust? If "Yes," the estate or trust may have to file Form 3520. See instructions		
5	Did the estate or trust receive, or pay, any qualified residence interest on seller-provided financing? If "Yes," see the instructions for required attachment		
6	If this is an estate or a complex trust making the section 663(b) election, check here. See instructions ▶ ☐		
7	To make a section 643(e)(3) election, attach Schedule D (Form 1041), and check here. See instructions ▶ ☐		
8	If the decedent's estate has been open for more than 2 years, attach an explanation for the delay in closing the estate, and check here ▶ ☐		
9	Are any present or future trust beneficiaries skip persons? See instructions		
10	Was the trust a specified domestic entity required to file Form 8938 for the tax year (see the Instructions for Form 8938)?		

Form **1041** (2016)

661113

☐ Final K-1   ☐ Amended K-1   OMB No. 1545-0092

Schedule K-1
(Form 1041)
Department of the Treasury
Internal Revenue Service

20**16**

For calendar year 2016,
or tax year beginning _____, 2016,
and ending _____, 20 _____

Beneficiary's Share of Income, Deductions, Credits, etc.

▶ See back of form and instructions.

Part I	Information About the Estate or Trust
A	Estate's or trust's employer identification number
B	Estate's or trust's name
C	Fiduciary's name, address, city, state, and ZIP code

D ☐ Check if Form 1041-T was filed and enter the date it was filed
_____

E ☐ Check if this is the final Form 1041 for the estate or trust

Part II	Information About the Beneficiary
F	Beneficiary's identifying number
G	Beneficiary's name, address, city, state, and ZIP code

H ☐ Domestic beneficiary   ☐ Foreign beneficiary

Part III	Beneficiary's Share of Current Year Income, Deductions, Credits, and Other Items
1 Interest income	
2a Ordinary dividends	
2b Qualified dividends	
3 Net short-term capital gain	
4a Net long-term capital gain	
4b 28% rate gain	
4c Unrecaptured section 1250 gain	
5 Other portfolio and nonbusiness income	
6 Ordinary business income	
7 Net rental real estate income	
8 Other rental income	
9 Directly apportioned deductions	
10 Estate tax deduction	

| **11** Final year deductions |
| **12** Alternative minimum tax adjustment |
| **13** Credits and credit recapture |
| **14** Other information |

*See attached statement for additional information.

Note. A statement must be attached showing the beneficiary's share of income and directly apportioned deductions from each business, rental real estate, and other rental activity.

For IRS Use Only

For Paperwork Reduction Act Notice, see the Instructions for Form 1041.   IRS.gov/form1041   Cat. No. 11380D   **Schedule K-1 (Form 1041) 2016**

This list identifies the codes used on Schedule K-1 for beneficiaries and provides summarized reporting information for beneficiaries who file Form 1040. For detailed reporting and filing information, see the Instructions for Schedule K-1 (Form 1041) for a Beneficiary Filing Form 1040 and the instructions for your income tax return.

	Report on
1. Interest income	Form 1040, line 8a
2a. Ordinary dividends	Form 1040, line 9a
2b. Qualified dividends	Form 1040, line 9b
3. Net short-term capital gain	Schedule D, line 5
4a. Net long-term capital gain	Schedule D, line 12
4b. 28% rate gain	28% Rate Gain Worksheet, line 4 (Schedule D Instructions)
4c. Unrecaptured section 1250 gain	Unrecaptured Section 1250 Gain Worksheet, line 11 (Schedule D Instructions)
5. Other portfolio and nonbusiness income	Schedule E, line 33, column (f)
6. Ordinary business income	Schedule E, line 33, column (d) or (f)
7. Net rental real estate income	Schedule E, line 33, column (d) or (f)
8. Other rental income	Schedule E, line 33, column (d) or (f)
9. Directly apportioned deductions	
Code	
A Depreciation	Form 8582 or Schedule E, line 33, column (c) or (e)
B Depletion	Form 8582 or Schedule E, line 33, column (c) or (e)
C Amortization	Form 8582 or Schedule E, line 33, column (c) or (e)
10. Estate tax deduction	Schedule A, line 28
11. Final year deductions	
A Excess deductions	Schedule A, line 23
B Short-term capital loss carryover	Schedule D, line 5
C Long-term capital loss carryover	Schedule D, line 12; line 5 of the wksht. for Sch. D, line 18; and line 16 of the wksht. for Sch. D, line 19
D Net operating loss carryover — regular tax	Form 1040, line 21
E Net operating loss carryover — minimum tax	Form 6251, line 11
12. Alternative minimum tax (AMT) items	
A Adjustment for minimum tax purposes	Form 6251, line 15
B AMT adjustment attributable to qualified dividends	
C AMT adjustment attributable to net short-term capital gain	
D AMT adjustment attributable to net long-term capital gain	
E AMT adjustment attributable to unrecaptured section 1250 gain	See the beneficiary's instructions and the Instructions for Form 6251
F AMT adjustment attributable to 28% rate gain	
G Accelerated depreciation	
H Depletion	
I Amortization	
J Exclusion items	2017 Form 8801

13. Credits and credit recapture	
Code	*Report on*
A Credit for estimated taxes	Form 1040, line 65
B Credit for backup withholding	Form 1040, line 64
C Low-income housing credit	
D Rehabilitation credit and energy credit	
E Other qualifying investment credit	
F Work opportunity credit	
G Credit for small employer health insurance premiums	
H Biofuel producer credit	
I Credit for increasing research activities	
J Renewable electricity, refined coal, and Indian coal production credit	
K Empowerment zone employment credit	See the beneficiary's instructions
L Indian employment credit	
M Orphan drug credit	
N Credit for employer-provided child care and facilities	
O Biodiesel and renewable diesel fuels credit	
P Credit to holders of tax credit bonds	
Q Credit for employer differential wage payments	
R Recapture of credits	
14. Other information	
A Tax-exempt interest	Form 1040, line 8b
B Foreign taxes	Form 1040, line 48 or Sch. A, line 8
C Qualified production activities income	Form 8903, line 7, col. (b) (also see the beneficiary's instructions)
D Form W-2 wages	Form 8903, line 17
E Net investment income	Form 4952, line 4a
F Gross farm and fishing income	Schedule E, line 42
G Foreign trading gross receipts (IRC 942(a))	See the Instructions for Form 8873
H Adjustment for section 1411 net investment income or deductions	Form 8960, line 7 (also see the beneficiary's instructions)
I Other information	See the beneficiary's instructions

Note. If you are a beneficiary who does not file a Form 1040, see instructions for the type of income tax return you are filing.

Form 709

Department of the Treasury
Internal Revenue Service

United States Gift (and Generation-Skipping Transfer) Tax Return

▶ Information about Form 709 and its separate instructions is at *www.irs.gov/form709.*

(For gifts made during calendar year 2016)
▶ See instructions.

OMB No. 1545-0020

2016

1 Donor's first name and middle initial	2 Donor's last name	3 Donor's social security number
4 Address (number, street, and apartment number)		5 Legal residence (domicile)
6 City or town, state or province, country, and ZIP or foreign postal code		7 Citizenship (see instructions)

Part 1—General Information

		Yes	No
8	If the donor died during the year, check here ▶ ☐ and enter date of death _____, _____		
9	If you extended the time to file this Form 709, check here ▶ ☐		
10	Enter the total number of donees listed on Schedule A. Count each person only once ▶		
11a	Have you (the donor) previously filed a Form 709 (or 709-A) for any other year? If "No," skip line 11b		
b	Has your address changed since you last filed Form 709 (or 709-A)?		
12	**Gifts by husband or wife to third parties.** Do you consent to have the gifts (including generation-skipping transfers) made by you and by your spouse to third parties during the calendar year considered as made one-half by each of you? (see instructions.) (If the answer is "Yes," the following information must be furnished and your spouse must sign the consent shown below. **If the answer is "No," skip lines 13–18.**)		
13	Name of consenting spouse		
14	SSN		
15	Were you married to one another during the entire calendar year? (see instructions)		
16	If 15 is "No," check whether ☐ married ☐ divorced or ☐ widowed/deceased, and give date (see instructions) ▶		
17	Will a gift tax return for this year be filed by your spouse? (If "Yes," mail both returns in the same envelope.)		
18	**Consent of Spouse.** I consent to have the gifts (and generation-skipping transfers) made by me and by my spouse to third parties during the calendar year considered as made one-half by each of us. We are both aware of the joint and several liability for tax created by the execution of this consent.		

Consenting spouse's signature ▶   Date ▶

| 19 | Have you applied a DSUE amount received from a predeceased spouse to a gift or gifts reported on this or a previous Form 709? If "Yes," complete Schedule C . . . . | | |

Part 2—Tax Computation

1	Enter the amount from Schedule A, Part 4, line 11	1	
2	Enter the amount from Schedule B, line 3	2	
3	Total taxable gifts. Add lines 1 and 2	3	
4	Tax computed on amount on line 3 (see *Table for Computing Gift Tax* in instructions)	4	
5	Tax computed on amount on line 2 (see *Table for Computing Gift Tax* in instructions)	5	
6	Balance. Subtract line 5 from line 4	6	
7	Applicable credit amount. If donor has DSUE amount from predeceased spouse(s), enter amount from Schedule C, line 4; otherwise, see instructions	7	
8	Enter the applicable credit against tax allowable for all prior periods (from Sch. B, line 1, col. C) .	8	
9	Balance. Subtract line 8 from line 7. Do not enter less than zero	9	
10	Enter 20% (.20) of the amount allowed as a specific exemption for gifts made after September 8, 1976, and before January 1, 1977 (see instructions)	10	
11	Balance. Subtract line 10 from line 9. Do not enter less than zero	11	
12	Applicable credit. Enter the smaller of line 6 or line 11	12	
13	Credit for foreign gift taxes (see instructions)	13	
14	Total credits. Add lines 12 and 13	14	
15	Balance. Subtract line 14 from line 6. Do not enter less than zero	15	
16	Generation-skipping transfer taxes (from Schedule D, Part 3, col. H, Total)	16	
17	Total tax. Add lines 15 and 16	17	
18	Gift and generation-skipping transfer taxes prepaid with extension of time to file	18	
19	If line 18 is less than line 17, enter **balance due** (see instructions)	19	
20	If line 18 is greater than line 17, enter **amount to be refunded**	20	

Attach check or money order here.

Sign Here

Under penalties of perjury, I declare that I have examined this return, including any accompanying schedules and statements, and to the best of my knowledge and belief, it is true, correct, and complete. Declaration of preparer (other than donor) is based on all information of which preparer has any knowledge.

May the IRS discuss this return with the preparer shown below (see instructions)? ☐ Yes ☐ No

▶ Signature of donor   Date

Paid Preparer Use Only

Print/Type preparer's name	Preparer's signature	Date	Check ☐ if self-employed	PTIN
Firm's name ▶			Firm's EIN ▶	
Firm's address ▶			Phone no.	

For Disclosure, Privacy Act, and Paperwork Reduction Act Notice, see the instructions for this form.   Cat. No. 16783M   Form **709** (2016)

Form 706
(Rev. August 2013)

Department of the Treasury
Internal Revenue Service

United States Estate (and Generation-Skipping Transfer) Tax Return

▶ Estate of a citizen or resident of the United States (see instructions). To be filed for decedents dying after December 31, 2012.
▶ Information about Form 706 and its separate instructions is at *www.irs.gov/form706*.

OMB No. 1545-0015

Part 1—Decedent and Executor

1a Decedent's first name and middle initial (and maiden name, if any)	**1b** Decedent's last name	**2** Decedent's social security no.

3a City, town, or post office; county; state or province; country; and ZIP or foreign postal code.	**3b** Year domicile established	**4** Date of birth	**5** Date of death

6b Executor's address (number and street including apartment or suite no.; city, town, or post office; state or province; country; and ZIP or foreign postal code) and phone no.

6a Name of executor (see instructions)

6c Executor's social security number (see instructions)

Phone no.

6d If there are multiple executors, check here ☐ and attach a list showing the names, addresses, telephone numbers, and SSNs of the additional executors.

7a Name and location of court where will was probated or estate administered

7b Case number

8 If decedent died testate, check here ▶ ☐ and attach a certified copy of the will. **9** If you extended the time to file this Form 706, check here ▶ ☐

10 If Schedule R-1 is attached, check here ▶ ☐ **11** If you are estimating the value of assets included in the gross estate on line 1 pursuant to the special rule of Reg. section 20.2010-2T(a) (7)(ii), check here ▶ ☐

Part 2—Tax Computation

1	Total gross estate less exclusion (from Part 5—Recapitulation, item 13)	**1**
2	Tentative total allowable deductions (from Part 5—Recapitulation, item 24)	**2**
3a	Tentative taxable estate (subtract line 2 from line 1)	**3a**
b	State death tax deduction	**3b**
c	Taxable estate (subtract line 3b from line 3a)	**3c**
4	Adjusted taxable gifts (see instructions)	**4**
5	Add lines 3c and 4	**5**
6	Tentative tax on the amount on line 5 from Table A in the instructions	**6**
7	Total gift tax paid or payable (see instructions)	**7**
8	Gross estate tax (subtract line 7 from line 6)	**8**
9a	Basic exclusion amount	**9a**	
9b	Deceased spousal unused exclusion (DSUE) amount from predeceased spouse(s), if any (from Section D, Part 6—Portability of Deceased Spousal Unused Exclusion). .	**9b**	
9c	Applicable exclusion amount (add lines 9a and 9b)	**9c**	
9d	Applicable credit amount (tentative tax on the amount in 9c from Table A in the instructions)	**9d**	
10	Adjustment to applicable credit amount (May not exceed $6,000. See instructions.)	**10**	
11	Allowable applicable credit amount (subtract line 10 from line 9d)	**11**
12	Subtract line 11 from line 8 (but do not enter less than zero)	**12**
13	Credit for foreign death taxes (from Schedule P). (Attach Form(s) 706-CE.)	**13**	
14	Credit for tax on prior transfers (from Schedule Q)	**14**	
15	Total credits (add lines 13 and 14)	**15**
16	Net estate tax (subtract line 15 from line 12)	**16**
17	Generation-skipping transfer (GST) taxes payable (from Schedule R, Part 2, line 10)	**17**
18	Total transfer taxes (add lines 16 and 17)	**18**
19	Prior payments (explain in an attached statement)	**19**
20	Balance due (or overpayment) (subtract line 19 from line 18)	**20**

Under penalties of perjury, I declare that I have examined this return, including accompanying schedules and statements, and to the best of my knowledge and belief, it is true, correct, and complete. Declaration of preparer other than the executor is based on all information of which preparer has any knowledge.

Sign Here

▶ Signature of executor   ▶ Date

▶ Signature of executor   ▶ Date

Paid Preparer Use Only

Print/Type preparer's name	Preparer's signature	Date	Check ☐ if self-employed	PTIN
Firm's name ▶			Firm's EIN ▶	
Firm's address ▶			Phone no.	

For Privacy Act and Paperwork Reduction Act Notice, see instructions. | Cat. No. 20548R | Form **706** (Rev. 8-2013)

CLASS QUESTIONS

Work through the below Class Questions while following along with the respective lectures. Once this is complete, you can begin independently practicing what you've learned by quizzing yourself on this course section in your Interactive Practice Questions (IPQ), which can be found in your online Student Dashboard. Your IPQ simulates the computer-based testing experience, and will also help you understand how concepts are applied to the exam. Each question includes answer explanations from expert CPAs that will help you determine why you answered a question correctly or incorrectly. This is key to your success on the CPA Exam.

Lecture 5.06

1. The standard deduction for an estate in the fiduciary income tax return is

   a. $0
   b. $100
   c. $300
   d. $600

2. An executor of a decedent's estate that has only U.S. citizens as beneficiaries is required to file a fiduciary income tax return, if the estate's gross income for the year is at least

   a. $ 400
   b. $ 500
   c. $ 600
   d. $1,000

3. For income tax purposes, the estate's initial taxable period for a decedent who died on October 24th

   a. May be either a calendar year, or a fiscal year beginning on the date of the decedent's death.
   b. Must be a fiscal year beginning on the date of the decedent's death.
   c. May be either a calendar year, or a fiscal year beginning on October 1 of the year of the decedent's death.
   d. Must be a calendar year beginning on January 1 of the year of the decedent's death.

4. Astor, a cash-basis taxpayer, died on February 3. During the year, the estate's executor made a distribution of $12,000 from estate income to Astor's sole heir and adopted a calendar year to determine the estate's taxable income. The following additional information pertains to the estate's income and disbursements for the year:

Estate income	
Taxable interest	$65,000
Net long-term capital gains allocable to corpus	5,000
Municipal Bond interest	1,000

Estate disbursements	
Administrative expenses attributable to taxable income	14,000
Charitable contributions from gross income to a public charity, made under the terms of the will	9,000

For the calendar year, what was the estate's distributable net income (DNI)?

    a. $39,000
    b. $43,000
    c. $58,000
    d. $65,000

5. A distribution to an estate's sole beneficiary for the 20X3 calendar year equaled $15,000, the amount currently required to be distributed by the will. The estate's 20X3 records were as follows:

    Estate income
    $40,000 Taxable interest

    Estate disbursements
    $34,000 Expenses attributable to taxable interest

    What amount of the distribution was taxable to the beneficiary?

    a. $40,000
    b. $15,000
    c. $ 6,000
    d. $0

Lecture 5.09

6. Which of the following credits may be offset against the gross estate tax to determine the net estate tax of a U.S. citizen dying during 20X3?

	Applicable (Unified) Credit	**Credit for gift taxes paid on gifts made after 1976**
a.	Yes	Yes
b.	No	No
c.	No	Yes
d.	Yes	No

7. If the executor of a decedent's estate elects the alternate valuation date and none of the property included in the gross estate has been sold or distributed, the estate assets must be valued as of how many months after the decedent's death?

    a. 12
    b. 9
    c. 6
    d. 3

8. During 20X3, Blake transferred a corporate bond with a face amount and fair market value of $20,000 to a trust for the benefit of her sixteen-year old child. Annual interest on this bond is $2,000, which is to be accumulated in the trust and distributed to the child on reaching the age of twenty-one. The bond is then to be distributed to the donor or her successor-in-interest in liquidation of the trust. Present value of the total interest to be received by the child is $8,710. The amount of the gift that is excludable from taxable gifts is

    a. $20,000
    b. $11,000
    c. $ 8,710
    d. $0

9. Don and Linda Grant, U.S. citizens, were married for the entire 20X1 calendar year. In 20X1, Don gave a $60,000 cash gift to his sister. The Grants made no other gifts in 20X1. They each signed a timely election to treat the $60,000 gift as one made by each spouse. Disregarding the unified credit and estate tax consequences, what amount of the 20X1 gift is taxable to the Grants for gift tax purposes?

    a. $0
    b. $32,000
    c. $46,000
    d. $60,000

10. Under the unified rate schedule,

    a. Lifetime taxable gifts are taxed on a noncumulative basis.
    b. Transfers at death are taxed on a noncumulative basis.
    c. Lifetime taxable gifts and transfers at death are taxed on a cumulative basis.
    d. The gift tax rates are 5% higher than the estate tax rates.

CLASS SOLUTIONS

1. (a) There is no standard deduction on a fiduciary income tax return for an estate or a trust. There is, however, a personal exemption. Answer (b) is incorrect because the personal exemption is $100 for a complex trust. Answer (c) is incorrect because the personal exemption is $300 for a simple trust. Answer (d) is incorrect because the personal exemption is $600 for an estate.

2. (c) A trust or estate is required to file a fiduciary income tax return, Form 1041, if it has gross income of $600 or more.

3. (a) For income tax purposes, an estate may select a calendar year or any fiscal year that begins with the decedent's date of death.

4. (b) Distributable net income (DNI) is equal to the gross income of the estate, including tax-exempt income, but excluding capital gains because they are allocated to corpus, the principal of the estate. Gross income is reduced by administrative expenses and charitable contributions. As a result, DNI is $65,000 + $1,000 - $14,000 - $9,000 = $43,000.

5. (c) The estate's distributable net income (DNI) is equal to its taxable interest less attributable expenses, for a net of $6,000. When distributions exceed DNI, the beneficiary includes an amount up to DNI in gross income and the remainder is considered a distribution of corpus.

6. (d) The net estate tax is equal to the gross estate tax minus the applicable unified gift and estate tax credit. Payments of gift taxes made after 1976 are treated as prepayments of the tax, not reductions of it.

7. (c) The executor of a decedent's estate has the option of valuing the estate's assets as of the date of death or may select an alternate valuation date (AVD). The AVD is 6 months from the date of death, which will be applied to all assets remaining in the estate at that time. Any assets disposed of before that date will be valued as of the date of sale or distribution.

8. (d) Although gifts of a present interest are only taxed to the extent that they exceed a certain amount per year, there is no exemption when it comes to future interests. The future interest will be valued at $8,710 and will be subject to gift tax in its entirety.

9. (b) A taxpayer may give gifts up to $14,000 to an individual without being subject to gift tax. When a gift is made by a married individual, the husband and wife may elect to treat the gift as given equally by each, in which case each would be entitled to the $14,000 exemption. A total of $28,000 of the $60,000 gift would be exempt, making the remaining $32,000 taxable.

10. (c) Under the uniform rate schedule, gift and estate tax is calculated on the basis of the transfers at death plus the cumulative total of all taxable gifts made over the taxpayer's lifetime. The total is reduced by the unified gift and estate tax credit to calculate the tax amount, which is reduced by the cumulative amount of gift taxes paid.

Lecture 5.10

TASK-BASED SIMULATIONS

Task-Based Simulation 1

 The Uniform CPA Examination

 Unsplit   Split Horiz   Split Vertical   Authoritative Literature   Spreadsheet   Calculator   Submit Testlet

| Work Tab | Resources | Help |

Required:

During 20X1, various clients went to Rowe, CPA, for tax advice concerning possible gift tax liability on transfers they made throughout 20X1. For each client, indicate whether the transfer of cash, the income interest, or the remainder interest is a gift of a present interest, a gift of a future interest, or not a completed gift.

Answer List

P   Present Interest
F.   Future Interest
N   Not Completed

Items to be answered:

Assume the following facts:

Cobb created a $500,000 trust that provided his mother with an income interest for her life and the remainder interest to go to his sister at the death of his mother. Cobb expressly retained the power to revoke both the income interest and the remainder interest at any time.

	(P)	(F)	(N)
1. The income interest at the trust's creation.	○	○	○
2. The remainder interest at the trust's creation.	○	○	○

Kane created a $100,000 trust that provided her nephew with the income interest until he reached forty-five years of age. When the trust was created, Kane's nephew was twenty-five. The income distribution is to start when Kane's nephew is twenty-nine. After Kane's nephew reaches the age of forty-five, the remainder interest is to go to Kane's niece.

	(P)	(F)	(N)
3. The income interest.	○	○	○

During 20X1, Hall, an unmarried taxpayer, made a $10,000 cash gift to his son in May and a further $12,000 cash gift to him in August.

	(P)	(F)	(N)
4. The cash transfers.	○	○	○

During 20X1, Yeats transferred property worth $20,000 to a trust with the income to be paid to her twenty-two-year-old niece Jane. After Jane reaches the age of thirty, the remainder interest is to be distributed to Yeats' brother. The income interest is valued at $9,700 and the remainder interest at $10,300.

	(P)	(F)	(N)
5. The income interest.	○	○	○
6. The remainder interest.	○	○	○

Tom and Ann Curry, U.S. citizens, were married for the entire 20X1 calendar year. Tom gave a $40,000 cash gift to his uncle, Grant. The Currys made no other gifts to Grant in 20X1. Tom and Ann each signed a timely election stating that each made one-half of the $40,000 gift.

	(P)	(F)	(N)
7. The cash transfers.	○	○	○

Murry created a $1,000,000 trust that provided his brother with an income interest for ten years, after which the remainder interest passes to Murry's sister. Murry retained the power to revoke the remainder interest at any time. The income interest was valued at $600,000.

	(P)	(F)	(N)
8. The income interest.	○	○	○
9. The remainder interest.	○	○	○

Determine whether the transfer is subject to the generation-skipping tax, the gift tax, or both taxes. Disregard the use of any exclusions and the unified credit.

Answer List

A   Generation-Skipping Tax
B   Gift Tax
C   Both Taxes

	(A)	(B)	(C)
10. Martin's daughter, Kim, has one child, Dale. During 20X1, Martin made an outright $6,000,000 gift to Dale.	○	○	○

Task-Based Simulation 2

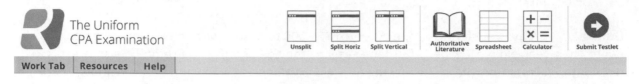

| Work Tab | Resources | Help |

Required:

Situation

Scott Lane, an unmarried U.S. citizen, made no lifetime transfers prior to 20X1. During 20X1, Lane made the following transfers:

- Gave a $13,000 cash gift to Kamp, a close friend.
- Made two separate $10,000 cash gifts to his only child.
- Created an **irrevocable** trust beginning in 20X1 that provided his aunt with an income interest to be paid for the next five years. The remainder interest is to pass to Lane's sole cousin. The income interest is valued at $26,000 and the remainder interest is valued at $74,000.
- Paid $25,000 tuition directly to his grandchild's university on his grandchild's behalf.
- Created an **irrevocable** trust that provided his brother with a lifetime income interest beginning in 20X3, after which a remainder interest passes to their sister.
- Created a **revocable** trust with his niece as the sole beneficiary. During 20X1, the niece received $15,000 interest income from the trust.

Items to be answered:

For **items 1 through 7,** determine whether the tax transactions are fully taxable, partially taxable, or not taxable to Lane in 20X1 for gift tax purposes after considering the gift tax annual exclusion. Ignore the transfer tax credit when answering the items. An answer may be selected once, more than once, or not at all.

Gift Tax Treatments

F. Fully taxable to Lane in 20X1 for gift tax purposes.
P. Partially taxable to Lane in 20X1 for gift tax purposes.
N. Not taxable to Lane in 20X1 for gift tax purposes.

	(F)	(P)	(N)
1. What is the gift tax treatment of Lane's gift to Kamp?	○	○	○
2. What is the gift tax treatment of Lane's cash gifts to his child?	○	○	○
3. What is the gift tax treatment of the trust's income interest to Lane's aunt?	○	○	○
4. What is the gift tax treatment of the trust's remainder interest to Lane's cousin?	○	○	○
5. What is the gift tax treatment of the tuition payment to Lane's grandchild's university?	○	○	○
6. What is the gift tax treatment of the trust's income interest to Lane's brother?	○	○	○
7. What is the gift tax treatment of the $15,000 interest income that Lane's niece received from the revocable trust?	○	○	○

Task-Based Simulation 3

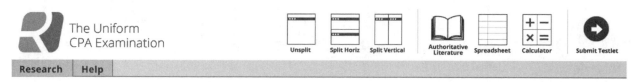

A CPA is preparing tax returns for a variety of trusts and is trying to determine the amount that may be deducted as a personal exemption.

Which code section, subsection, and paragraph will provide information about a trust's deduction for a personal exemption?

Task-Based Simulation 4

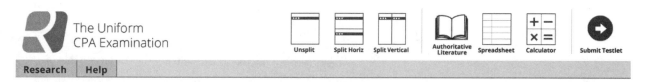

The terms of a trust require that all income be distributed currently and do not provide for amounts to be paid, set aside, or used for charitable or other purposes. The amount of income required to be distributed exceeds the distributable net income of the trust and the trust is trying to determine the amount of distributable net income that may be deducted in computing the trust's taxable income.

Which code section and subsection indicates the limitation on the deduction for distributable net income?

Task-Based Simulation 5

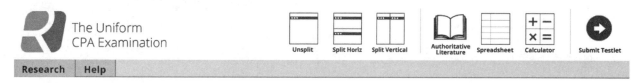

A trust that is required to distribute all income currently is not making a distribution in the current taxable year. The beneficiaries of the trust are uncertain as to whether or not the amount required to be distributed should be included in their gross income if it is not distributed.

Which code section and subsection indicates whether or not the undistributed amounts will be taxable to the beneficiaries?

Task-Based Simulation 6

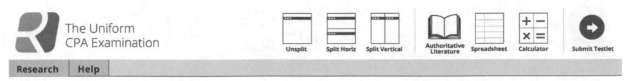

The executor of an estate elected the alternative valuation date. Certain property was sold 4 months after the date of death and the trustee is trying to determine the amount to be included for the property in the gross estate.

Which code section, subsection, and paragraph indicates what amount should be included in a gross estate for property that has been sold shortly after death when the alternate valuation date is elected?

Task-Based Simulation 7

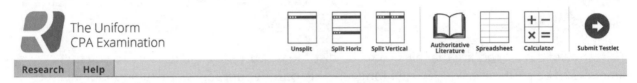

A CPA preparing an estate tax return is trying to determine the value of the taxable estate. He is not certain what amounts may be deducted from the gross estate.

Which code section and subsection indicates what amounts may be deducted from the gross estate in calculating the taxable estate?

Task-Based Simulation 8

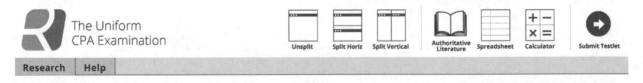

A taxpayer has made numerous gifts of various amounts ranging in value from $1,000 to $15,000. The taxpayer is curious as to the amount given to each recipient that is not included in the total amounts of gifts made during the year.

Which code section, subsection, and paragraph indicates the amount of each gift given that may be excluded from the amount of gifts made during the year?

Task-Based Simulation 9

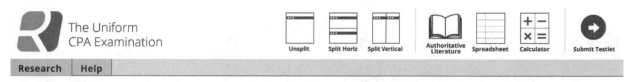

A taxpayer has decided to distribute property to his children, grandchildren, and great grandchildren. He is concerned about the generation-skipping tax, which he understands applies if he makes a gift to certain individuals referred to as "skip persons". He is not certain what that term means.

Which code section and subsection defines what a "skip person" is for purposes of applying the generation-skipping tax?

TASK-BASED SIMULATION SOLUTIONS

Task-Based Simulation Solution 1

For items 1 through 9, candidates were asked to determine whether the transfer of cash, an income interest, or a remainder interest represents a gift of a present interest (P), a gift of a future interest (F), or not a completed gift (N).

		(P)	(F)	(N)
1.	The income interest at the trust's creation.	○	○	●
2.	The remainder interest at the trust's creation.	○	○	●
3.	The income interest.	○	●	○
4.	The cash transfers.	●	○	○
5.	The income interest.	●	○	○
6.	The remainder interest.	○	●	○
7.	The cash transfers.	●	○	○
8.	The income interest.	●	○	○
9.	The remainder interest.	○	○	●

Explanation of solutions

1.   **(N)** When a Trustor creates a trust and retains the power to revoke the trust at any time, neither the income beneficiary nor the remainder beneficiary is receiving a complete gift.

2.   **(N)** When a Trustor creates a trust and retains the power to revoke the trust at any time, neither the income beneficiary nor the remainder beneficiary is receiving a complete gift.

3.   **(F)** Since Kane's nephew, the income beneficiary, will not begin receiving distributions of income until reaching the age of 29, which is 4 years after the creation of the trust, the nephew's interest is considered a future interest.

4.   **(P)** Gifts involving cash transfers provide the beneficiary with an immediate benefit and are considered present interests.

5.   **(P)** Since Jane, the income beneficiary, will begin receiving distributions of income immediately, her interest is considered a present interest.

6.   **(F)** Since Yeats' brother, the remainder beneficiary, will not receive a distribution until Jane reaches 30, after 8 years, he has a future interest.

7.   **(P)** A gift of cash provides an immediate benefit to the beneficiary and is considered a present interest. The fact that Tom and Ann signed a timely election to split the gift, they will each be able to apply the gift tax exemption to their half, reducing the amount of the gift that is taxable.

8.   **(P)** Since Murry's brother begins receiving income distributions immediately, and there is no provision making that revocable, Murry's brother has a present interest.

9.   **(N)** Although an interest to be received by a remainder beneficiary is generally a future interest, when the Trustor has the right to revoke the remainder interest, it is not a completed gift.

(A) (B) (C)

10. Martin's daughter, Kim, has one child, Dale. During 20X1, Martin made an
outright $6,000,000 gift to Dale.

Explanation of solution

(C) An outright gift of $6,000,000 exceeds the $14,000 exemption and would be subject to gift tax.
In addition, it will be subject to the generation-skipping tax, which was established for
circumstances like this. If a gift is made to a child that is subject to gift tax, and the child then
makes the same gift to their child, it too will be subject to gift tax. Without the generation-skipping
tax, one of those taxes could be avoided by making the gift directly to the grandchild. As a result, a
gift of that nature is subject to both the gift tax and the generation-skipping tax.

Task-Based Simulation Solution 2

For **items 1 through 7,** candidates were asked to identify the federal gift tax treatment for each item by indicating whether the item is fully taxable (F), partially taxable (P), or not taxable (N) to Lane in 20X1 for gift tax purposes after considering the gift tax annual exclusion.

		(F)	(P)	(N)
1.	What is the gift tax treatment of Lane's gift to Kamp?	○	○	●
2.	What is the gift tax treatment of Lane's cash gifts to his child?	○	●	○
3.	What is the gift tax treatment of the trust's income interest to Lane's aunt?	○	●	○
4.	What is the gift tax treatment of the trust's remainder interest to Lane's cousin?	●	○	○
5.	What is the gift tax treatment of the tuition payment to Lane's grandchild's university?	○	○	●
6.	What is the gift tax treatment of the trust's income interest to Lane's brother?	●	○	○
7.	What is the gift tax treatment of the $15,000 interest income that Lane's niece received from the revocable trust?	○	●	○

Explanation of solutions

1.   **(N)** The gift to Kamp is less than the annual exclusion and, as a result, would not be taxable.

2.   **(P)** The gift totaling $20,000 would be subject to the annual $14,000 exclusion. As a result, it would be partially taxable to the extent of $6,000.

3.   **(P)** Since Lane's aunt begins receiving distributions of the income immediately, she has a present interest. As a result, it will be subject to the $14,000 exclusion and will be partially taxable to the extent of $12,000.

4.   **(F)** The remainder interest will not be distributed to Lane's cousin until the end of 5 years and, as a result, is a future interest, which is not subject to an exclusion and is fully taxable.

5.   **(N)** There is an unlimited exclusion from gift tax for payments that are made for another party's tuition or medical expenses as long as they are made directly to the university or health care facility. As a result, payments for the grandchild's tuition would not be subject to gift tax.

6.   **(F)** Since Lane's brother will not begin receiving distributions until 2 years after the establishment of the trust, Lane's brother has a future interest, which is not subject to any exclusion. As a result, the entire amount would be subject to gift tax.

7.   **(P)** The beneficiary of a revocable trust is not receiving a completed gift. As a result, the income of the trust would revert to Lane, the Trustor, and would be considered a gift when given to his daughter. The $15,000 cash gift is a present interest and would be subject to the $14,000 exclusion, resulting in it being partially taxable to the extent of $1,000.

Task-Based Simulation Solution 3

642	(b)	(2)

Task-Based Simulation Solution 4

651	(b)

Task-Based Simulation Solution 5

652	(a)

Task-Based Simulation Solution 6

2032	(a)	(1)

Task-Based Simulation Solution 7

2053	(a)

Task-Based Simulation Solution 8

2503	(b)	(1)

Task-Based Simulation Solution 9

2613	(a)

Section 6 – Depreciation

Corresponding Lectures

Watch the following course lectures with this section:

Lecture 6.01 – Depreciation: Real vs. Tangible Personal Property
Lecture 6.02 – Section 179 Depreciation Deduction
Lecture 6.03 – Depreciation – Class Questions

EXAM NOTE: *Please refer to the AICPA REG Blueprint in the Introduction to find a listing of the representative tasks (and their associated skill levels—i.e., Remembering and Understanding, Application, and Analysis) that the candidate should be able to perform based on the knowledge obtained in this section.*

Depreciation

DEPRECIATION

Federal tax law uses a method of depreciation called Modified Accelerated Cost Recovery System (**MACRS**) for property placed in service after 1986. This system **differs** from GAAP depreciation in three significant ways:

1. The cost of the asset is deducted over a stated recovery period that is shorter than the estimated useful life of the asset in most cases.
2. The recovery period for **new and used** property is identical.
3. Salvage values are **ignored.**

Real property (Section **1250**)

The recovery period is:

- **27.5 years** – Residential rental property
- **39 years –** Most other buildings, a.k.a, Nonresidential real property (business and investment realty)
    - Land is not depreciated.
    - Salvage value of building is ignored.
    - *Straight-line* method is used (MACRS).
    - *Mid-month convention*
        - Only depreciate the real property for ½ the month when placed into service and ½ in the month of disposal.

The method of depreciation that must be used is **straight-line**, and the business must use the **mid-month** convention, which means that all real estate bought and sold during a particular month are treated as having been bought and sold in the middle of the month.

> **For example**: Assume that the client purchases an office building on 11/1/X1 for $500,000, which includes land with a value of $32,000. The cost of the building itself is $500,000 − $32,000 = $468,000, and this is recovered over a 39-year period, resulting in MACRS deductions of $468,000 / 39 years = $12,000 per year. In 20X1, the year of acquisition, the property is treated as having been purchased in the middle of November, so that only 1 ½ months of depreciation are claimed that year. Depreciation of $12,000 / 12 months = $1,000 per month is multiplied by 1 ½ months, resulting in a $1,500 MACRS deduction in 20X1.

Tangible personal property (non-realty) (Section **1245**) varies:

- **3 years** – Small tools, off-the-shelf (OTS) software*
- **5 years** – Automobiles, light trucks, copiers, computers & printers
- **7 years** – Most other personal property, equipment, office furniture, desks
- **10 years** – Barges, tugs, vessels, water transportation equipment
- **15 years** – Municipal wastewater treatment plants and assets used in cement production
- **20 years** – Municipal sewer and farm buildings

- o **MACRS**
  - ▪ *Double Declining Balance* (200% DB — 3, 5, 7,10-year property)
    - □ Switch to straight line (S/L) when it results in a greater deduction.
    - □ Straight line may be elected instead of DDB.
    - *Note: DDB does not apply to OTS software—S/L depreciation only.
  - ▪ 150% Declining Balance (15, 20-year property)
- o Salvage value is ignored.
- o Half-year convention
- o *Mid-quarter convention*
  - ▪ If acquired at least 40% of its assets in the final 3 months of the year, it is assumed that every asset purchased occurred at the mid-point of that particular quarter in which it was purchased.

Unless the business makes a specific election to use straight-line depreciation, the method of depreciation used for personal property is **double-declining balance**. In addition, purchases and sales are normally handled using the **half-year** convention, so that all transactions are treated as taking place in the middle of the year.

> **For example**: Assume the client purchases office furniture for $490 on 2/1/X1. Furniture, like most personal property, has a 7-year recovery period. Assuming straight-line depreciation of 1/7 of cost per year is not elected, the client will use double-declining balance, and claim 2/7 of the remaining basis each year. In the year of acquisition, 20X1, the half-year convention is applied, so the MACRS deduction is $490 x 2/7 x ½ = $70. In 20X2, the remaining basis of $490 - $70 = $420 is used, and the MACRS deduction is $420 x 2/7 = $120.

The half-year convention may not be used in all cases. In order to prevent businesses from getting a half-year of depreciation on an excessive number of assets acquired late in the year, businesses acquiring 40% or more of their personal property in the final quarter of the year are required to use a **mid-quarter** convention, meaning that items are treated as having been purchased in the middle of the quarter in which they were purchased, instead of the middle of the year.

> **For example**: Assume the client purchased small tools for $300 on 12/29/X1, and that this was the **only** purchase of tangible personal property that took place during 20X1. Small tools have a 3-year recovery period, and the MACRS deduction using double-declining balance and the half-year convention would have been $300 × 2/3 × ½ = $100. This is not allowed, however, since more than 40% (actually, 100%) of personal property was acquired in the last quarter of the year. As a result, the small tools are treated as having been acquired in the middle of November (the middle of the last quarter), and only 1 ½ months of depreciation may be claimed in 20X1. Since 1 ½ months is equal to 1/8 of a year, the MACRS deduction using the mid-quarter convention in 20X1 is $300 × 2/3 × 1/8 = $25.

A depreciation table may be used in order to calculate depreciation expense for MACRS Personal Property. This table is assuming 200% declining balance (Double Declining Balance), switching to straight-line when it is beneficial to do so. Remember that we are assuming half-year convention and salvage value is ignored.

For example: If a computer (5-year property) is purchased for $100, depreciation expense for the first 2 years would be calculated as follows:
- *Year 1* = $100 × 1/5 yrs × 200% = $40 × 1/2 (half-year convention) = $20 dep exp in the 1st year
- *Year 2* = $100 – $20 yr 1 dep = $80 x 1/5 yrs x 200% = $32 dep exp in the 2nd year

You could also simply use the factors from the table (20% and 32%) to calculate the same results.

This table is set up for 3, 5 and 7-year property.

MACRS Depreciation 200% DDB Table Half-Year Convention for Personal Property			
Year	3 Year	5 Year	7 Year
1	33.33%	20.00%	14.29%
2	44.45%	32.00%	24.49%
3	14.81%	19.20%	17.49%
4	7.41%	11.52%	12.49%
5		11.52%	8.93%
6		5.76%	8.92%
7			8.93%
8			4.46%
			100%

Lecture 6.02

Section 179 Depreciation Deduction

Since the recovery period for tangible personal property is relatively short, the federal tax code permits some businesses to make a Section 179 **election** to immediately expense certain *New and Used* depreciable property, instead of capitalizing and depreciating it.

- Can immediately expense depreciable business property rather than capitalize it.
- Not allowed if a net loss exists or if taking the depreciation expense would create a net loss.
- The property must be acquired by purchase from an unrelated party for use in an active trade or business.
- With the passage of the PATH Act in December 2015, the Section 179 amount is permanently enacted into law at $500,000 for the 2015 tax year and will be indexed for inflation in $10,000 increments in future tax years. The phase out begins at $2,000,000; that is, the $500,000 limit is reduced $1 for every $1 spent over $2,000,000. Thus, the Section 179 election is not available if total purchases exceed $2,500,000. Note: On the CPA Exam, tax threshold amounts subject to frequent change will often be provided within the related problems.
  - **Based on an amount of $500,000:**
    - If the maximum expense amount is $500,000 and the phase out begins at $2,000,000 (Section 179 is not available if total purchases are over $2,500,000).
    - Expense maximum up to **$500,000** ($510,000 – 2017).
    - Reduced dollar for dollar by excess of purchases over **$2,000,000** ($2,030,000 – 2017).
    - Not available if purchases exceed **$2,500,000** ($2,540,000 – 2017).

  For example, if the maximum election permitted for the tax year is **$500,000**, this maximum is phased out on a dollar-for-dollar basis if the purchases of qualified property during the tax year **exceed $2,000,000**. As a result, a business that purchases $2,500,000 or more in tangible personal property may not use this election. A few examples of the maximum election follow:

Qualified purchases	30,000	580,000	2,300,000	2,700,000
Maximum election	30,000	500,000	200,000	0
Remaining basis	0	80,000	2,100,000	2,700,000

Notice in the case of qualified purchases of $2,300,000, the purchases exceed the threshold of $2,000,000 by $300,000, so the maximum election is reduced from $500,000 to $200,000 ($500,000 - $300,000). In other words, a dollar-for-dollar reduction of $300,000 is equal to the amount by which the total purchase price exceeds the $2,000,000 threshold. In each example, the remaining basis (if any) is used to determine additional MACRS deductions based on the normal 3, 5, or 7 years.

- Remember that Section 179 is an election, and a corporation is not required to use it.
- Also, this election is generally not available on real property or intangibles.
- The cost of a heavy SUV that may be expensed is limited to $25,000.
- The cost of *off-the-shelf Computer Software* is eligible for Section 179 deduction or can be depreciated over 36 months on a Straight-Line basis with no half-year convention.
- **Qualified depreciable Real Property** may be treated as Section 179 property, up to the $500,000 Section 179 limit; the 2015 PATH Act eliminated the previous limit of $250,000 for tax years beginning after 2015. *Qualified depreciable real property* includes qualified leasehold improvement property, qualified restaurant property, and qualified retail improvement property.

Additional First-Year Depreciation (Bonus Depreciation)

For qualified NEW assets (tangible Sec. 1245 property with a MACRS life of 20 years or less) placed in service, **50-percent** bonus depreciation is available (after reduction for any Section 179 elections).

- For 2012 through 2014, bonus depreciation was limited to 50 percent of the qualified property's adjusted basis. The December 2015 PATH Act extended **50% bonus depreciation** through the 2017 tax year, phasing down to 40% and 30% in 2018 and 2019, respectively, before disappearing altogether. Note: On the CPA Exam, tax threshold amounts subject to frequent change will often be provided within the related problems.
- Bonus depreciation is claimed after the Section 179 expense deduction, but before the Regular depreciation expense deduction.

Intangibles (Section 197)

Qualifying intangibles include franchises, trademarks, customer-based intangibles, and acquired but not self-created goodwill. Certain intangibles qualify only if acquired in connection with the acquisition of a trade or business. These include covenants not to compete, patents, and copyrights. *Straight-line amortization* is used.

- 15 years – most intangibles (including goodwill)
- 15 years (180 months) ($5,000 immediately) – organization expense - must begin amortization in first year of operations.
- Life of contract – franchises
- Must begin amortization in month of acquisition.

Other Depreciable Assets

There are a handful of other assets rarely mentioned on the exam:

- 10 year – Water transportation equipment, single-purpose agricultural (constructed to house, raise and feed livestock) and horticultural structures (a greenhouse for Farmers) – Double-declining balance
- 15 year – Wastewater treatment plants & cement-producing assets – 150%-declining balance
- 20 year – Sewers and farm buildings – 150%-declining balance

Most of these assets are not eligible for the Section 179 election but can claim the additional first-year depreciation.

Depletion

Depletion is used for natural resources that are exhaustible or wasting assets, such as timber, minerals, oil and gas. There are 2 methods allowed:

> ***Cost method*** = $\underline{\text{Adjusted basis (cost-acc deplet)}} \times$ units sold = Depletion exp/yr
> $\qquad\qquad\qquad$ Estimated recoverable units

> ***Percentage method*** = a statutory percentage × gross income = Depletion exp
> $\qquad\qquad$ (Percentage generally ranges from 5% to 20%, but can never exceed 50%.)

Domestic Production Activities Deduction (DPAD) ("Manufacturers deduction" – Section 199)

In order to encourage production within the United States, a special Domestic Production Activities Deduction (DPAD) was established, providing U.S. companies a tax break to the extent that they conduct their activities domestically. The deduction is based on *qualified production activities*, which include:

- Manufacturing, producing, growing, and extracting tangible personal property, computer software, and sound recordings
- Construction and substantial renovation of real property, including infrastructure
- The production of certain films and certain engineering and architectural services

The DPAD is calculated on the basis of **Qualified Production Activities Income (QPAI)**, which is the excess of domestic production gross receipts (DPGR) over the total of cost of sales allocated to DPGR and other expenses, losses, or deductions properly allocable to DPGR.

- DPGR consists of the entity's gross receipts from qualified activities.
- In addition to cost of sales related to DPGR, expenses such as charitable contributions; research and development; selling, general, and administrative expenses; corporate stewardship; and interest are allocated between qualified and nonqualified activities.

The amount of the DPAD is generally calculated at **9% of the lesser of (1) QPAI or (2) taxable income** computed before this deduction; however, the second part of this calculation changes depending on the nature of the entity:

- For C corporations, the deduction is limited to taxable income (i.e., DPAD is 9% of the lesser of QPAI or *taxable income*).
- For sole proprietors, partnerships, S corporations, or LLCs, the deduction is limited to *AGI* (i.e., DPAD is 9% of the lesser of QPAI or AGI).

For all entities, the deduction cannot exceed 50% of W-2 wages.

Depreciation Recapture is discussed in another section.

Lecture 6.03

CLASS QUESTIONS

Please see the Class Questions and Class Solutions for this Lecture at the end of this Section.

Note: The 2016 forms are provided since the 2017 forms were unavailable at the time of publication.

Form **4562**	**Depreciation and Amortization**	OMB No. 1545-0172
Department of the Treasury Internal Revenue Service (99)	**(Including Information on Listed Property)** ▶ Attach to your tax return. ▶ Information about Form 4562 and its separate instructions is at *www.irs.gov/form4562*.	**2016** Attachment Sequence No. **179**

Name(s) shown on return	Business or activity to which this form relates	Identifying number

Part I Election To Expense Certain Property Under Section 179
Note: If you have any listed property, complete Part V before you complete Part I.

1	Maximum amount (see instructions)	**1**
2	Total cost of section 179 property placed in service (see instructions)	**2**
3	Threshold cost of section 179 property before reduction in limitation (see instructions)	**3**
4	Reduction in limitation. Subtract line 3 from line 2. If zero or less, enter -0-	**4**
5	Dollar limitation for tax year. Subtract line 4 from line 1. If zero or less, enter -0-. If married filing separately, see instructions	**5**

6	(a) Description of property	(b) Cost (business use only)	(c) Elected cost	

7	Listed property. Enter the amount from line 29	**7**	
8	Total elected cost of section 179 property. Add amounts in column (c), lines 6 and 7	**8**
9	Tentative deduction. Enter the **smaller** of line 5 or line 8	**9**
10	Carryover of disallowed deduction from line 13 of your 2015 Form 4562	**10**
11	Business income limitation. Enter the smaller of business income (not less than zero) or line 5 (see instructions)	**11**
12	Section 179 expense deduction. Add lines 9 and 10, but don't enter more than line 11	**12**
13	Carryover of disallowed deduction to 2017. Add lines 9 and 10, less line 12 ▶	**13**	

Note: Don't use Part II or Part III below for listed property. Instead, use Part V.

Part II Special Depreciation Allowance and Other Depreciation (Don't include listed property.) (See instructions.)

14	Special depreciation allowance for qualified property (other than listed property) placed in service during the tax year (see instructions)	**14**
15	Property subject to section 168(f)(1) election	**15**
16	Other depreciation (including ACRS)	**16**

Part III MACRS Depreciation (Don't include listed property.) (See instructions.)

Section A

17	MACRS deductions for assets placed in service in tax years beginning before 2016	**17**
18	If you are electing to group any assets placed in service during the tax year into one or more general asset accounts, check here . . . . ▶ ☐	

Section B—Assets Placed in Service During 2016 Tax Year Using the General Depreciation System

(a) Classification of property	(b) Month and year placed in service	(c) Basis for depreciation (business/investment use only—see instructions)	(d) Recovery period	(e) Convention	(f) Method	(g) Depreciation deduction
19a 3-year property						
b 5-year property						
c 7-year property						
d 10-year property						
e 15-year property						
f 20-year property						
g 25-year property			25 yrs.		S/L	
h Residential rental property			27.5 yrs.	MM	S/L	
			27.5 yrs.	MM	S/L	
i Nonresidential real property			39 yrs.	MM	S/L	
				MM	S/L	

Section C—Assets Placed in Service During 2016 Tax Year Using the Alternative Depreciation System

20a Class life					S/L	
b 12-year			12 yrs.		S/L	
c 40-year			40 yrs.	MM	S/L	

Part IV Summary (See instructions.)

21	Listed property. Enter amount from line 28	**21**
22	**Total.** Add amounts from line 12, lines 14 through 17, lines 19 and 20 in column (g), and line 21. Enter here and on the appropriate lines of your return. Partnerships and S corporations—see instructions .	**22**
23	For assets shown above and placed in service during the current year, enter the portion of the basis attributable to section 263A costs	**23**	

For Paperwork Reduction Act Notice, see separate instructions.   Cat. No. 12906N   Form **4562** (2016)

Form 4562 (2016)   Page **2**

Part V **Listed Property** (Include automobiles, certain other vehicles, certain aircraft, certain computers, and property used for entertainment, recreation, or amusement.)

Note: For any vehicle for which you are using the standard mileage rate or deducting lease expense, complete **only** 24a, 24b, columns (a) through (c) of Section A, all of Section B, and Section C if applicable.

Section A—Depreciation and Other Information (Caution: See the instructions for limits for passenger automobiles.**)**

24a Do you have evidence to support the business/investment use claimed? ☐ Yes ☐ No   **24b** If "Yes," is the evidence written? ☐ Yes ☐ No

(a) Type of property (list vehicles first)	(b) Date placed in service	(c) Business/ investment use percentage	(d) Cost or other basis	(e) Basis for depreciation (business/investment use only)	(f) Recovery period	(g) Method/ Convention	(h) Depreciation deduction	(i) Elected section 179 cost
25 Special depreciation allowance for qualified listed property placed in service during the tax year and used more than 50% in a qualified business use (see instructions) . **25**								
26 Property used more than 50% in a qualified business use:								
		%						
		%						
		%						
27 Property used 50% or less in a qualified business use:								
		%				S/L –		
		%				S/L –		
		%				S/L –		
28 Add amounts in column (h), lines 25 through 27. Enter here and on line 21, page 1 . **28**								
29 Add amounts in column (i), line 26. Enter here and on line 7, page 1 . . . . **29**								

Section B—Information on Use of Vehicles

Complete this section for vehicles used by a sole proprietor, partner, or other "more than 5% owner," or related person. If you provided vehicles to your employees, first answer the questions in Section C to see if you meet an exception to completing this section for those vehicles.

	(a) Vehicle 1	(b) Vehicle 2	(c) Vehicle 3	(d) Vehicle 4	(e) Vehicle 5	(f) Vehicle 6
30 Total business/investment miles driven during the year (**don't** include commuting miles) .						
31 Total commuting miles driven during the year						
32 Total other personal (noncommuting) miles driven						
33 Total miles driven during the year. Add lines 30 through 32						
34 Was the vehicle available for personal use during off-duty hours?	Yes / No	Yes / No	Yes / No	Yes / No	Yes / No	Yes / No
35 Was the vehicle used primarily by a more than 5% owner or related person? . . .						
36 Is another vehicle available for personal use?						

Section C—Questions for Employers Who Provide Vehicles for Use by Their Employees

Answer these questions to determine if you meet an exception to completing Section B for vehicles used by employees who **aren't** more than 5% owners or related persons (see instructions).

	Yes	No
37 Do you maintain a written policy statement that prohibits all personal use of vehicles, including commuting, by your employees?		
38 Do you maintain a written policy statement that prohibits personal use of vehicles, except commuting, by your employees? See the instructions for vehicles used by corporate officers, directors, or 1% or more owners . .		
39 Do you treat all use of vehicles by employees as personal use?		
40 Do you provide more than five vehicles to your employees, obtain information from your employees about the use of the vehicles, and retain the information received?		
41 Do you meet the requirements concerning qualified automobile demonstration use? (See instructions.) . . .		

Note: If your answer to 37, 38, 39, 40, or 41 is "Yes," don't complete Section B for the covered vehicles.

Part VI **Amortization**

(a) Description of costs	(b) Date amortization begins	(c) Amortizable amount	(d) Code section	(e) Amortization period or percentage	(f) Amortization for this year
42 Amortization of costs that begins during your 2016 tax year (see instructions):					
43 Amortization of costs that began before your 2016 tax year **43**					
44 **Total.** Add amounts in column (f). See the instructions for where to report **44**					

Form **4562** (2016)

CLASS QUESTIONS

Work through the below Class Questions while following along with the respective lectures. Once this is complete, you can begin independently practicing what you've learned by quizzing yourself on this course section in your Interactive Practice Questions (IPQ), which can be found in your online Student Dashboard. Your IPQ simulates the computer-based testing experience, and will also help you understand how concepts are applied to the exam. Each question includes answer explanations from expert CPAs that will help you determine why you answered a question correctly or incorrectly. This is key to your success on the CPA Exam.

Lecture 6.03

1. Data Corp., a calendar-year corporation, purchased and placed into service office equipment during October 20X7. No other equipment was placed into service during 20X7. Under the general MACRS depreciation system, what convention must Data use?

    a. Full-year
    b. Half-year
    c. Mid-quarter
    d. Mid-month

2. On August 1, Graham purchased and placed into service an office building costing $264,000, including $30,000 for the land. What was Graham's MACRS deduction for the office building in that year?

    a. $9,600
    b. $6,000
    c. $3,600
    d. $2,250

3. Which of the following conditions must be satisfied for a taxpayer to expense, in the year of purchase, under Internal Revenue Code Section 179, the cost of new or used tangible depreciable personal property?

    I. The property must be purchased for use in the taxpayer's active trade or business.
    II. The property must be purchased from an unrelated party.

    a. I only.
    b. II only.
    c. Both I and II.
    d. Neither I nor II.

4. A taxpayer purchased and placed into service a $690,000 piece of equipment in a year with a maximum allowable Section 179 amount of $500,000 and a ceiling of $2,000,000 of qualifying property. The equipment is 7-year property. The first-year depreciation for 7-year property is 14.29%. Before considering any depreciation deduction, the taxpayer had $700,000 of taxable income. The taxpayer elected out of any bonus depreciation. What amount is the maximum allowable depreciation deduction?

    a. $ 98,601
    b. $500,000
    c. $527,151
    d. $690,000

CLASS SOLUTIONS

1. (c) If more than 40% of depreciable property acquired during the tax period is acquired during the 4th quarter, the entity is required to apply the mid-quarter convention, under which each acquisition is depreciated from the middle of the fiscal quarter in which it was acquired. Answer (a) is incorrect because there is no full-year convention. Answer (b) is incorrect because the half-year convention generally applies to depreciable personal property when less than 40% is acquired during the 4th quarter. Answer (d) is incorrect because the mid-month convention generally applies to depreciable real estate.

2. (d) Under MACRS, a depreciable office building will be depreciated on a straight-line basis over 39 years. Annual depreciation will be on the building portion only, $264,000 - $30,000, or $234,000, resulting in depreciation of $6,000 per year or $500 per month. Depreciable real property is subject to the mid-month convention. As a result, the building will be depreciated from August 15 through December 31, 4 ½ months for depreciation of 4 ½ × $500 = $2,250.

3. (c) The Section 179 deduction, which allows a taxpayer to expense up to $500,000 ($510,000 for 2017) in purchases of depreciable personal property, rather than to capitalize and depreciate it. For businesses acquiring large amounts of qualified property, the deduction begins phasing out after acquisitions totaling $2,000,000 ($2,030,000 for 2017). It is reduced, dollar for dollar, for acquisitions in excess of $2,000,000 ($2,030,000 for 2017) and is eliminated completely when acquisitions are $2,500,000 ($2,540,000 for 2017) or greater. To qualify, the property must be acquired from an unrelated party and must be used in the taxpayer's trade or business.

4. (c) Since there is no indication that the taxpayer acquired more than the $690,000 in tangible depreciable personal property during the period, the entire $500,000 Section 179 deduction is allowed. This reduces the depreciable basis in the asset to $190,000. It is depreciated using the double-declining balance method over 7 years, indicating depreciation in the 1st year will be 2/7 of $190,000. The half-year convention is applied, however, making depreciation in the 1st year 2/7 × ½ × $190,000, or $190,000 × 14.29% = $27,151. Thus, the maximum allowable depreciation deduction will be $500,000 + $27,151, or $527,151.

TASK-BASED SIMULATIONS

Task-Based Simulation 1

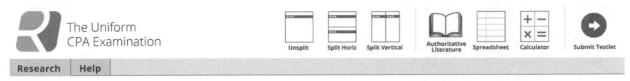

A taxpayer owns an office building and wishes to use the most aggressive depreciation method available for tax purposes.

Which code section, subsection, paragraph, and subparagraph indicates the depreciation methods available for nonresidential real property?

Task-Based Simulation 2

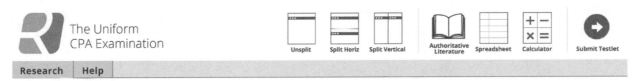

A taxpayer has purchased a delivery truck and is trying to determine if it is 5-year property.

Which code section, subsection, paragraph, and subparagraph indicates what is included in 5-year property?

Task-Based Simulation 3

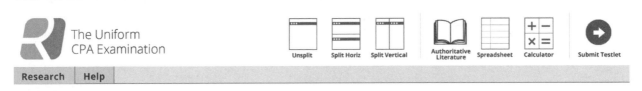

A taxpayer wishes to elect to expense certain depreciable business assets and is concerned about the dollar limitation on the amount of the deduction.

Which code section, subsection, and paragraph indicates the dollar limitation on the cost of depreciable business assets that may be treated as expense?

Task-Based Simulation 4

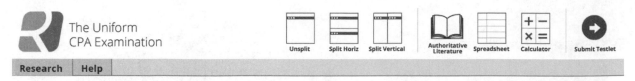

Research | Help

A company recognized goodwill that is amortizable for tax purposes as a result of a business combination and wishes to determine the minimum period over which it may be amortized.

Which code section and subsection indicates the period over which intangibles are generally to be amortized?

TASK-BASED SIMULATION SOLUTIONS

Task-Based Simulation Solution 1

168	(b)	(3)	(A)

Task-Based Simulation Solution 2

168	(e)	(3)	(B)

Task-Based Simulation Solution 3

179	(b)	(1)

Task-Based Simulation Solution 4

197	(a)

Section 7– Property & Special Property Tax Transactions

Corresponding Lectures

Watch the following course lectures with this section:

Lecture 7.01 – Property Types: Ordinary, 1231, Capital Assets
Lecture 7.02 – Depreciation Recapture (1245, 1250, Section 291)
Lecture 7.03 – UNICAP and Individual Property Transactions
Lecture 7.04 – Taxation of Property – Class Questions
Lecture 7.05 – Taxation of Property – Class Questions – TBS
Lecture 7.06 – Special Property Tax Transactions
Lecture 7.07 – Special Property Tax Transactions – Class Questions
Lecture 7.08 – Special Property Tax Transactions – Class Questions – DRS

EXAM NOTE: Please refer to the AICPA REG Blueprint in the Introduction to find a listing of the representative tasks (and their associated skill levels—i.e., Remembering and Understanding, Application, and Analysis) that the candidate should be able to perform based on the knowledge obtained in this section.

Property & Special Property Tax Transactions

PROPERTY TYPES

There are 3 types of assets that may be held by a taxpayer:

- **Ordinary income assets (current assets of a business)** – These refer to assets that were acquired or produced with the intention of being sold in the ordinary course of business, and include **inventory**, business **receivables** resulting from sales of inventory or services, and **artistic works** created by or for the taxpayer.
  - Inventory
  - Receivables arising from sales
  - Self-created artistic work
    - No special tax rules or limits

- **Section 1231 assets (non-current business assets)** – These are assets that are used in the trade or business (held longer than one year) and whose eventual sale or disposal is only incidental to the business. They include **depreciable** and **amortizable** assets, as well as **land used in the business**.
  - Depreciable and amortizable property
  - Land used in business, PP&E
  - Held over 1 year:
    - Net **loss** is ordinary income.
    - Net **gain** is Long Term Capital Gain
      - Prior depreciation is **recaptured** as ordinary income on tangible personal property.
  - If held ≤ 1 year – Ordinary

- **Capital assets (non-business assets)** – These are all assets that do not qualify as ordinary income or Section 1231 assets, and include assets held for **investment** purposes as well as the assets of an individual that are held for **personal use** by the taxpayer or the taxpayer's family or household. Also, although **goodwill** is amortizable, it is not actually used by a business in a meaningful sense, since it doesn't diminish in value as a result of usage, and so it is also treated as a capital asset.
  - Investments, personal, family, household
  - Non-business bad debts – write offs are always S/T capital losses.

  Capital assets are defined as all property held by the taxpayer, **except:**
  - Property normally included in inventory or held for sale to customers in the ordinary course of business
  - Depreciable property and real estate used in business
  - Accounts and notes receivable arising from sales or services in the taxpayer's business
  - Copyrights, literary, musical or artistic compositions
  - Treasury stock

Notice that the tax character of the item depends on the handling by the taxpayer. A *personal computer* would be an ordinary income asset to the manufacturer of the computer, a Section 1231 asset to an accounting firm which acquired the computer for use by its employees, and a capital asset to a person who bought it to run educational software for their children at home.

The tax treatment of sales of **ordinary income assets** is extremely straightforward: all gains and losses are fully included in the determination of taxable income with no special treatment or limitations (assuming an arm's-length transaction, i.e., no related parties are involved).

Capital gains and losses are combined to determine the net capital gain or loss for the year. A net capital gain is reported and included in taxable income (there is no special tax rate on long-term capital gains for corporations). A net capital loss of a corporation may **not** be deducted in the current year. Instead, it may be carried back to offset net capital gains reported in one of the **previous 3** tax years, and then carried forward to offset net capital gains in the **next 5** tax years The rules for individuals are radically different: no carryback, $3,000 per year may be deducted, and the remainder may be carried forward forever.

Sales of Section 1231 assets are the most complicated. Once the net 1231 gain or loss for the year is determined from all of the sales that took place, the amount is transferred to the forms for ordinary or capital assets as follows:
- Net 1231 **gain** – This amount is transferred to the schedule on which capital gains and losses are reported, and it is reported as a **long-term capital gain**.
- Net 1231 **loss** – This amount is transferred to the schedule on which ordinary income asset gains and losses are reported, and it will be treated as an **ordinary loss** to determine the net ordinary gain or loss for the year.

In a sense, the tax treatment of Section 1231 sales can be viewed as the **best of both worlds**. Since the gain is treated as a capital gain, it can be used to offset net capital losses that might otherwise not have been deductible in the current year. Since the loss is treated as an ordinary loss, it is fully deductible with no limits.

Holding Periods

In general, short-term capital transactions refer to sales that take place within a year of the acquisition date, and long-term transactions are those held for longer than one year. There are two exceptions:
- **Inherited assets** – Sales are always classified as long-term (**L/T**).
- **Non-business bad debts** – Write-offs are always classified as short-term capital losses (**S/T**).

When a security becomes worthless, the holding period is calculated by treating the property as if it was sold on the last day of the tax year in which it becomes worthless.

Long-term capital gains of individuals generally benefit from a special tax rate of only 15%. Individuals who are in the 15% or 10% tax bracket for ordinary income qualify for a 0% long-term capital gains tax rate. If high-income taxpayer (39.6% tax bracket), then the 15% becomes 20% for MFJ earning $450,000+ and single $400,000+ ($470,700, $418,400 – 2017). Note: No special capital gains rate for corporations.

A special long-term tax rate of 28% applies to all gains and losses on **collectibles** reported on Schedule D. Collectibles include works of art, rugs, antiques, metals (gold), gems, stamps, coins, alcoholic beverages and other certain tangible property.

Short-term capital gains and losses are combined to determine the net short-term capital gain or loss for the year. Long-term items are similarly combined to determine the net long-term capital gain or loss for the year. If one is a net gain and the other a net loss, they are combined to produce a single net capital gain or loss for the year, which will be treated as having the character of the larger of the two numbers being combined. If both are gains, they are reported separately. If both are losses, short-term losses are claimed first and then long-term losses, subject to an overall limitation of **$3,000 that can be offset against ordinary income** each year (the remainder is carried forward **indefinitely**). For individuals that file as married filing separately, the limit is $1,500. Note: A net loss in any rate group is applied to reduce the net gain in the highest rate group first (e.g., 28% collectibles gain, 25% Unrecaptured Sec. 1250 gain, then 15% capital gain).

For corporations, a *net capital loss is not deductible* against ordinary income. If capital losses exceed capital gains, the difference is **carried back 3 years and forward 5 years**.

Capital Assets Summary – Schedule D/ 8949

- o *Holding period*
  - Long term > 1 year
  - Short term ≤ 1 year

- o *How net*
  - Net L/T and L/T = $10 gain
  - Net S/T and S/T = $(3) loss....net again to L/T $7 gain
    - o A net loss in any rate group is applied to reduce the net gain in the highest rate group first (e.g., 28%, 25% then 15%).

- o *Rates*
  - **Short-Term Capital Gain**
    - o No special rates, ordinary tax rates
  - **Long-Term Capital Gain**
    - o Individuals 20% / 15% / 0% rates (Not applicable to corporations.)
    - o Collectibles @ 28%
  - **Capital losses**
    - o Corp's no **net** deduction (back 3yrs, forward 5yrs – all S/T)
    - o Individuals up to *$3,000* per year, rest carried forward *indefinitely*

- o In most cases, an individual must report capital gains and losses on **Form 8949** and then report the totals on **Schedule D**.

DEPRECIATION RECAPTURE

For **Section 1245 tangible personal property,** generally referring to the assets with MACRS recovery periods of 3, 5, or 7 years, the calculation of the Section 1231 gain may be affected by **depreciation recapture**. These assets are written off so quickly (especially when the Section 179 election to expense costs is utilized) that they often result in gains on sale. Since the depreciation deductions were ordinary deductions, the tax code requires that the **gains be reported as ordinary income to the extent of prior depreciation.** Note that Section 1245 recapture is computed the *same way* for both individuals and corporations.

For example, assume Section 1245 equipment costing $10,000 has had MACRS deductions of $4,000 to date, and then is sold. The adjusted basis of the asset on the date of sale is $6,000, and if the equipment is sold for more than $6,000, the first $4,000 of gain will be recaptured as ordinary income, with the remainder, if any, qualifying as a Section 1231 gain. If the asset is sold for less than $6,000, there is no recapture needed, since all of the depreciation was justified. Here is a schedule computing the ordinary and Section 1231 portions of the sale with different selling prices:

Original cost	10,000	10,000	10,000
MACRS deductions	4,000	4,000	4,000
Adjusted basis	6,000	6,000	6,000
Selling price	11,000	8,000	5,000
Gain (loss)	5,000	2,000	(1,000)
Depreciation recapture **(ordinary)**	4,000	2,000	
Section 1231 **(capital)**	1,000	0	0

Section 1250 Depreciation Recapture for Real Property

When depreciable real property, consisting of buildings and structural components, is sold at a gain, it is subject to Section 1250 depreciation recapture. As a result, the amount of the gain, up to *additional depreciation*, is treated as an **ordinary gain**. Any gain in excess is **Unrecaptured 1250 gain**, which is treated as Section **1231 gain**, and taxed as a **LTCG at 25%** (i.e., on an individual tax return—does not apply to corporations).

The amount of *additional depreciation*, if any, is affected by the holding period of the asset.
- If the asset was held for *1 year or less*, additional depreciation is all depreciation.
- If the asset was held for *more than 1 year*, additional depreciation is depreciation in excess of the amount that would have been taken under straight-line. Note: Since straight-line is the depreciation method required for real property, this applies in limited circumstances.

For example: Roger sells an office building for $500,000 that has an adjusted basis of $60,000, resulting in a gain of $440,000. The original cost of the building was $600,000 and $540,000 of Accelerated Depreciation has been recorded. Had Straight-line depreciation been used, the depreciation would have been $510,000. The depreciation difference between Accelerated and Straight-line is called *additional depreciation*. It is recaptured as a 1250 gain of $30,000 and is considered an *ordinary gain* ($540 − $510). The remainder of $410,000 is Unrecaptured 1250 gain and treated as a Section 1231 gain and taxed as a *LTCG at 25%*.

Section 291

When a C corporation sells Section 1250 property at a gain, a portion of the gain, in addition to the recapture of additional depreciation, is treated as ordinary income. Under Section 291, a C corporation calculates the difference between the amount of depreciation recaptured under Section 1250 (i.e., "additional depreciation" to the extent of gain) and the greater amount that would have been recaptured if the asset had been a Section 1245 asset (i.e., all depreciation to the extent of gain). Basically, the difference is the amount of Unrecaptured Section 1250 gain that would have been reported if the entity was not a C corporation; 20% of this difference is also treated as ordinary gain. The rest is Section 1231 long-term capital gain.

Assuming the same facts as the above example, $410,000 × 20% = $82,000 §291 gain + $30,000 §1250 gain = $112,000 *ordinary gain*. $440,000 total gain − $112,000 ordinary gain = $328,000, Section 1231 LTCG.

Note: Corporations do not qualify for special capital gain rates, but corporate capital losses offset corporate capital gains. Any net corporate capital gain is taxed at the ordinary corporate tax rate, while any net corporate capital loss is not deductible against ordinary income but may be carried back three years and forward five years.

Lecture 7.03

UNIFORM CAPITALIZATION RULES (UNICAP – SECTION 263A)

When a corporation, partnership or sole proprietorship has manufactured or constructed an asset for use, sale or resale, it must follow the **uniform capitalization rules (UNiCAP – Section 263A,** a subsection of 263), which require the *capitalization* into inventory of virtually all direct costs, and part of the indirect costs, associated with the manufacture or resale of the asset (this differs from GAAP so as to increase tax liability to the government). The UNICAP rules apply to costs incurred in manufacturing or constructing real or personal property, or in purchasing or holding property for sale.

Any trade or business that:
- Produces real or tangible personal property.
- Acquires property for resale with average annual gross receipts for past 3 years of more than $10 million.
    - These capitalized costs will be recovered through either depreciation/amortization, or if inventory, through cost of goods sold.
        - **Capitalized costs include:**
            - Pre-production: design, bidding exp, purchasing
            - Production costs: direct materials, labor, & production, indirect production costs (factory overhead)
            - Pre-Sale costs: storage, handling, excise tax (if levied before sale)

For inventory, the company must also *capitalize* most general, administrative, engineering, and overhead costs associated with holding the assets (such as storage costs, repackaging, warehousing) prior to sale. However, nonmanufacturing costs such as selling, advertising, marketing, research and development expenditures would be *expensed* as incurred. Also, businesses with less than **$10 million** in gross receipts for past 3 years are not required to follow these rules.

The capitalized costs are the basis for depreciation of assets used in the trade or business and also determine the gain or loss on sale for all assets subject to these rules.

CAPITALIZATION VS EXPENSE OF ACQUIRING, MAINTAINING, IMPROVING, REPAIRING AND REPLACING TANGIBLE PROPERTY (SECTION 263)

Section 263 of the Internal Revenue Code (IRC) deals with the capitalization of costs incurred in the acquisition, production, or improvement of tangible property, like buildings. Section 162 deals with deductible costs such as materials, supplies, repairs, and maintenance. These rules were established to distinguish, for example, between a repair and a renovation and also created safe harbor elections for small amounts being spent for acquisitions, materials and supplies. The regulations help to specify when a cost must be capitalized versus when it can be expensed.

Acquisition or Production Costs

As a general rule, under Section 263, an entity may deduct (expense) the cost of an item of property for each invoice or the cost of an item that is substantiated by an invoice. There is a de minimis annual **expense** election safe harbor amount of $5,000 per invoice or $5,000 per item, but an entity may be able to justify a greater amount if a higher threshold is used for financial reporting purposes (for example, if a taxpayer has a $6,500 de minimis rule in its audited financial statements, the taxpayer may use the $6,500 threshold for tax purposes).
  - To qualify for the **$5,000 per item or invoice** deduction:
    - The entity must prepare audited financial statements and must have a similar policy, effective as of the beginning of the year, for financial reporting purposes.
    - An annual election is required.
  - Taxpayers who do not prepare applicable audited financial statements are subject to a limit of **$2,500**, rather than $5,000.
  - Property with a useful life of **12 months or less** may also be deducted. This deduction also requires a comparable policy, as of the beginning of the year, for financial reporting purposes.

An entity electing to take this deduction must also apply the de minimis safe harbor limitations to expenditures for repairs and maintenance.

Deductible amounts are considered on an "all or nothing" basis. If the cost of an item exceeds the limit, no portion of the cost is deductible under the safe harbor, and must be capitalized. An entity may not divide the cost of property into components in order to keep amounts within the limitations.

Improvements (BAR)

Amounts paid to improve tangible property are required to be **capitalized** if the costs incurred result in a *Betterment* to the property, or an *Adaptation* of the property for a different use, or a *Restoration* of the property.
  - If a taxpayer disposes of property in a circumstance where no gain or loss is recognized, the cost of removal is deducted.
  - Otherwise, the cost of removal of property is capitalized to the property.

In order for a cost to result in a **Betterment**, the expenditure must be used to correct a defect that existed prior to acquisition or occurred during production; must be intended to provide an addition to the property, such as by making it larger; or intended to cause an increase in usefulness of the property, such as increased capacity, productivity, or efficiency.

An **Adaptation** of the property is considered a new or different use that is inconsistent with the taxpayer's intended, ordinary use of the property at the time it was originally placed into service. These costs are capitalized. An example would be converting a manufacturing facility into a showroom or converting part of a pharmacy into a clinic. These would qualify as adaptations.

Costs of **Restoration** (restores basis, replaces part or a major component of the property) are required to be capitalized if they would be required to be capitalized if incurred for purposes other than restoring property. Other costs of restoration are also capitalized up to the excess of the reduction in the asset's carrying value that resulted from the casualty or other event requiring the restoration over the amount paid for costs that would otherwise be required to be capitalized.

For example, assume a building was seriously damaged in an earthquake, resulting in a casualty loss of $300,000. The entity incurs $225,000 to reconstruct the 3^(rd) story and to replace the roof and an additional $275,000 for cleaning up the site and for general repairs.
- The $225,000 cost of reconstructing the 3^(rd) story and replacing the roof would be capitalized.
- Since the basis of the building was reduced by $300,000, the excess of that over capitalized costs of $225,000, or $75,000, would also be capitalized.
- The remaining $200,000 incurred for cleanup and general repairs would be deductible.

Materials and Supplies

Materials and supplies, under Section 162, are items other than inventory that are used or consumed in the entity's business operations. They may be classified as either incidental or non-incidental. **Incidental** materials and supplies that can be **expensed** immediately (in the year **paid**) include:
- Property with a cost of less than **$200**
- Tangible property with a useful life of **12 months or less**
- Spare parts or other items used to repair tangible property but that was not acquired for a specific piece of property
- Fuel, lubricants, paper, staplers and other maintenance supplies that are expected to be consumed within 12 months of acquisition
- Other items specifically identified in IRS guidance

Non-incidental materials and supplies (other than those that are incidental) are generally deductible (**expensed**) in the period **used or consumed**. There is, however, an optional alternative treatment that is available for rotable spare parts and for temporary or standby emergency spare parts. Under the alternative, costs are *capitalized and depreciated* as separate assets.
- Rotable spare parts are items, such as a stapler attachment on a photocopy machine that may be attached to one item of property, removed and either reattached to the same property, attached to another, or stored for future use.
- Standby emergency spare parts are parts acquired for a specific piece of property to make certain that delays for repairs can be minimized.

Repairs and Maintenance

Cost of routine repairs and maintenance under Section 162 are **expensed** when they are incurred to keep existing property operating efficiently and effectively.
- The taxpayer, at the time the property is placed in service, must expect the repair or maintenance activity to occur *more than once* over the life of the property.
- For buildings and structural components of buildings, the activity must be expected to occur more than once over a 10-year period.
- Qualified Small taxpayers (Average gross receipts of $10 million or less over the preceding 3 tax years) can **expense** repairs and improvements to a building up to the *lessor of*:
  - $10,000, or
  - 2% of the building cost (original cost of less than $1 million)
    - If the amount of repairs and improvements exceed $10,000, then all improvements must be *capitalized*.

A taxpayer may elect to *capitalize and depreciate* repairs and maintenance if they are treated similarly on the taxpayer's books and records. This requires an annual election.

INDIVIDUAL TAX TRANSACTIONS

Sales of business assets by an individual are identical to those by corporations. Sales of capital assets (assets held for investment purposes or personal use) have many complicated rules specific to individuals.

The basic rule is that a capital asset that is sold results in a gain or loss equal to the difference between the sales proceeds and the basis of the asset (usually its original cost). The tax basis of property normally refers to its cost, adjusted for any depreciation previously claimed. A special problem arises, however, when property is received by an individual as either a **gift** or **inheritance**.

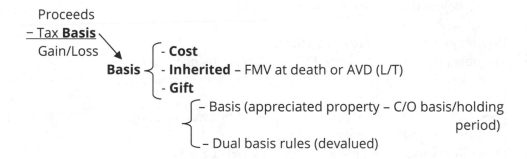

The receipt of an **inheritance** is nontaxable. The basis for inherited property is the basis used to determine estate taxes for the decedent. Usually, this is **fair market value** on the date of **death**. If, however, an election is made in the filing of the estate tax return to use the **alternate valuation date**, then the basis will be the earlier of:
- The date the property was **transferred** to the beneficiary.
- **Six months** after the date of death.

For example: Assume the decedent died on 2/1/X1 and that two different assets were distributed to the beneficiary: one on 4/24/X1 and the other on 10/25/X1. The basis of both assets would normally be the fair market value on 2/1/X1, the date of death. If, however, the executor of the estate elected the alternate valuation date, then the first asset's basis to the beneficiary is the value on 4/24/X1, and the second asset's basis to the beneficiary is the value on 8/1/X1, determined as follows:

Asset	First	Second
Date of death	2/1/X1	2/1/X1
Date of distribution	4/24/X1	10/25/X1
Six months after death	8/1/X1	8/1/X1
Earlier of last two dates	4/24/X1	8/1/X1

On a subsequent sale, the gain or loss is **always** reported as **long term**, regardless of the actual holding period. The original cost and acquisition date by the decedent are ignored in all determinations, in part because there may be no practical way to determine these items and in part because the government wants to assess estate taxes on current values instead of original purchase costs.

Gifts are excluded from gross income. Although the donor of a gift may have to report and pay gift taxes in some cases, the recipient (donee) of the gift generally does not report any taxable income on the receipt of the gift. If the gift is in the form of ***appreciated property***, the cost basis and acquisition date of the property to the donee is the same as for the donor (**Carryover basis & Carryover Holding Period**).

> **For example**: If Greta Giver purchased stock in 20X1 for $10,000, and gave it to her son Ron Recipient in 20X8 at a time the stock was worth $30,000, Ron would report no income from the receipt of the stock. If Ron sold the stock for $29,000 later in 20X8, he would have to report a long-term capital gain on the sale of $19,000. Both the gain and the long-term status result from carrying over Greta's purchase price of $10,000 in 20X1.

If the donor pays gift taxes on a gift, the portion of the tax paid attributable to the appreciation in the property's value at the date of the gift over the donor's basis, is added to the donee's basis.

> **For example**: Assume Tara gives Sam land worth $200,000 and pays $27,000 in gift taxes. Tara bought the land for $150,000. Sam's basis in the gift from Tara includes Tara's $150,000 basis in the property plus the portion of the gift taxes paid that is attributable to the increase in value at the date of the gift, calculated as follows: $200,000 FMV on date of gift – $150,000 basis = $50,000 increase in value. $50,000 increase/$200,000 FMV = 25% × $27,000 gift tax paid = $6,750 applicable portion of gift tax + Tara's $150,000 basis = $156,750 for Sam's basis.

When the value of the property on the date of the gift is lower than the donor basis (***dropped in value***), the donee must keep track of both amounts (**Dual-Basis Rules**). The higher donor basis is used to calculate a subsequent gain on sale, and the lower FMV on the gift date is used to calculate a subsequent loss on sale. If the selling price is between the two amounts, the selling price is also used as the basis, so that no gain or loss results. The effect is to not tax the donee on gains to the extent the donor suffered a non-deductible loss. The acquisition date for the donee is the date from which the amount used as basis was derived.

> **For example**: Assume Greta's stock was purchased in 20X1 for $30,000, and she gave it to Ron in 20X8 after it had declined to $10,000. The following examples assume Ron resold the stock later in 20X8 for (a) $9,000, (b) $20,000, (c) $29,000, and (d) $39,000:

20X1 Donor cost	30,000	30,000	30,000	30,000
20X8 FMV gift date	10,000	10,000	10,000	10,000
20X8 Selling price	9,000	20,000	29,000	39,000
Donee basis	10,000	20,000	29,000	30,000
Acquisition date	**Gift date**	**Sale date**	**Sale date**	**Purch date**
Gain (loss)	(1,000)	0	0	9,000
Status	Short term	Short term	Short term	Long term

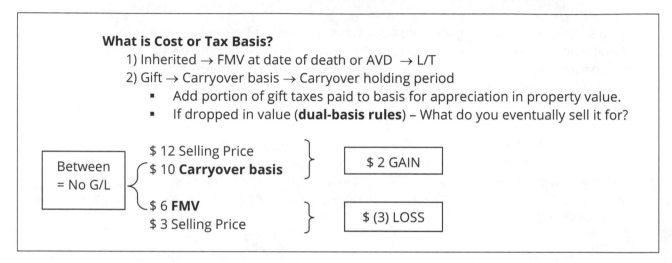

What is Cost or Tax Basis?
1) Inherited → FMV at date of death or AVD → L/T
2) Gift → Carryover basis → Carryover holding period
   - Add portion of gift taxes paid to basis for appreciation in property value.
   - If dropped in value (**dual-basis rules**) – What do you eventually sell it for?

Between = No G/L
$ 12 Selling Price
$ 10 **Carryover basis** $ 2 GAIN
$ 6 **FMV**
$ 3 Selling Price $ (3) LOSS

TYPES OF PROPERTY — SUMMARY

Property Category	Included in Category	Tax Treatment
Capital Assets	All assets **except:** • Inventory • Business receivables • Self-created artistic works • Depreciable or amortizable business assets, and land used in a business (1231) • Treasury stock	**INDIVIDUALS:** LTCG: Special rates STCG: Regular rates • Net loss: Maximum of $3,000 during the current year. • Carryforward indefinite. **CORPORATIONS:** • Net loss: Not deductible • Carryback 3 years • Carryforward 5 years • Considered S/T
Ordinary Assets	• Inventory • Business Receivables • Self-created artistic works	• Regular tax rates
Section 1231 Assets	• Depreciable or amortizable business assets • Land used in a business (parking lot and shed)	• Net gains are generally considered to be LTCG. • Net losses are generally considered to be ordinary losses.

Lecture 7.04

CLASS QUESTIONS

Please see the Class Questions and Class Solutions for this Lecture at the end of this Section.

Lecture 7.05

CLASS QUESTIONS

Please see the Class Questions and Class Solutions for this Lecture at the end of this Section.

Lecture 7.06

SPECIAL PROPERTY TAX TRANSACTIONS

Several special rules apply to transactions for **both individuals and corporations.**

1. **Wash Sales**

   Losses from wash sales are not deductible. If an asset that has been sold at a loss is repurchased within 30 days of the sale, the loss may not be deducted, but is added to the basis of the repurchased asset. This also applies to purchases of substantially identical assets in the 30 days before or after the sale.

   For example, assume the client purchased 100 shares of stock in XYZ Corporation for $300 in 20X1. On 12/20/X2, the client purchased an additional 100 shares in the company for $200. On 12/27/X2, the client sold the 100 shares acquired in 20X1 for $210. Since a purchase of substantially identical securities occurred only 7 days earlier, the loss of $90 on 12/27/X2 cannot be deducted. Instead, the basis of the shares acquired on 12/20/X2 is increased by $90 to $290.
   - **Gains** are taxable; **losses** are not deductible.

2. **Sales to a Related Party**

   Losses from related-party sales are not deductible. These are sales between:
   - Husband and wife
   - Sister and brother
   - Parent to child
   - Grandparent to grandchild
   - Ancestor and descendant
   - Majority shareholder and corporation
   - Majority partner and partnership (including a partnership interest owned directly or indirectly)
     - Not uncle, aunt, nephews, in-laws.

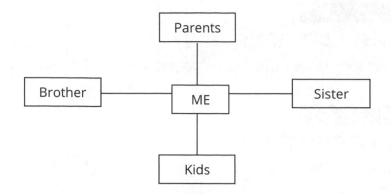

The buyer is not taxed on gains to the extent of the denial of the seller's deduction for the loss. **For example**, if a grandfather sells an asset he originally acquired for $800 to his granddaughter for $500, he cannot deduct the $300 loss, since it is a sale from ancestor to descendant. If the granddaughter later sells the asset for $900, she only reports a $100 gain.

- o **Gains** resulting from related-party sales are fully taxable.
- o **Losses** are treated in a similar manner to gift tax rules (dual-basis rules).

3. **Like-Kind Exchanges**

When tangible investment or business property (**not** intangibles, such as stock and other securities) is exchanged for similar property (i.e., Section 1031 Like-Kind Exchanges), neither a gain nor loss is reported, unless the taxpayer receives monetary consideration (boot) as part of the exchange. If boot is received, a gain for the excess of the fair value over the tax basis of the property relinquished is recognized up to a maximum of the amount of boot received. **Boot** can result from the following:

- o Cash received + unlike property
- o **Relief from debt that exceeds debt assumed**
  - ▪ **Same nature & character**, real for real, personal for personal
  - ▪ **No loss** deduction
- o **Gain** is lesser of:
  - ▪ Cash + unlike property received (FMV of boot received) or
  - ▪ Realized gain.

For example, assume that the taxpayer owned real estate with a basis of $200,000 and fair market value of $500,000, and this was exchanged for other real estate with a fair value of $400,000. In addition, the taxpayer was relieved of a mortgage on the old property of $150,000, assumed a mortgage on the new property of $80,000, and received $30,000 in cash.

Although the facts are complicated, the transaction makes financial sense, since the value given and received equal:

	Value Given	Value Received
Property	500,000	400,000
Debt Relief	80,000	150,000
Cash		30,000
Total	580,000	580,000

Since the relinquished property had a basis of $200,000 and fair market value of $500,000, the realized gain was $300,000. The recognized gain is limited to the boot received, however, which includes the cash of $30,000 and the net debt relief of $70,000 ($150,000 debt relief - $80,000 debt assumption), for a total gain reported on the tax return of $100,000.

$300 Realized Gain / Recognized Gain = $100 (for book 100/500 × 300 = $60)

The basis in the new asset will be: the basis of the old (200) + liability assumed (80) + gain recognized (100) – Liability on old (150) – cash/boot received (30) = 200 New basis. **Note:** This formula would include "+ cash/boot given" if cash/boot was given rather than received.

New - basis	**200 (plug)**	
Cash	30	
Liability old	150	
Liability new		80
Old (Basis)		200
Gain		100

It is possible to execute a like-kind exchange and defer some or all taxes in the manner just discussed even when the sale of property and acquisition of similar property are in separate transactions. In order to do this, *all of the following conditions* must be satisfied:

- The proceeds from the sale of property must not be received by the taxpayer, but must instead be paid into a separate escrow account held by a **qualified intermediary**.
- The replacement property must be identified within 45 days after the sale (the qualified intermediary must be notified in writing).
  - The taxpayer may identify more than one property as the potential replacement, as long as either of the following is satisfied:
    - No more than 3 properties are identified, or
    - The total fair value of all identified properties doesn't exceed 200% of the fair value of the property that was sold.
- The replacement property must actually be acquired *within 180 days* of the sale.

Note: The like-kind exchange provisions do not apply to exchanges of inventory, stocks, bonds, notes, convertible securities, the exchange of partnership interests, or property held for personal use. **"Like kind"** means the same class of property (real estate must be exchanged for real estate; personal property for personal property, etc.). An exchange of a personal residence for investment or business property would not qualify.

4. **Involuntary Conversions**
   When the taxpayer realizes a gain from an involuntary conversion (**Section 1033 exchange**) of property, the gain may be deferred if the property is replaced within the statutory time limit established by law. The time limit is measured from the calendar year the taxpayer received the proceeds, and equals:
   - **2 years** – Destruction or theft of property resulting in insurance recovery.
   - **3 years** – Government condemnation or eminent domain award.

- o **4 years** – Conversion in connection with a declared federal disaster.
  - ▪ Notice that the *time limit* is measured by calendar year, so the actual date for replacement is always December 31 of the year in which the *proceeds are received*.

For example, a taxpayer owns business property that is destroyed in a fire on 12/10/X1. The insurance company makes payment for the fair market value of the property (which exceeds its tax basis) on 1/20/X2. The taxpayer can defer the gain if all of the proceeds are used to replace the property by 12/31/X4. If the fire was part of a gigantic blaze that caused the president to declare the area a federal disaster area, the taxpayer has until 12/31/X6 to replace the property.

When proceeds are not fully reinvested in the new property, the gain is taxed to the extent of the unreinvested amount. Deferred gains reduce the basis of the replacement property. **Losses** are shown on Schedule A as a theft or casualty loss.

Worthless securities generally receive capital loss treatment; however, if the loss is incurred by a corporation on an investment in an affiliated corporation (80% or more ownership), the loss is treated as an ordinary loss item.

A loss resulting from a nonbusiness deposit in an insolvent financial institution is generally treated as a nonbusiness bad debt, deductible as a short-term capital loss; however, in certain circumstances, an individual can elect to treat the loss as a casualty loss or as a miscellaneous itemized deduction.

There are some special situations applicable to **individuals only**.

5. **Sale of Personal Assets**
   One involves **losses** on sales of personal assets. Sales of assets held for personal, family, or household use at prices less than original cost are not reported, since they are presumed to represent consumption. **For example**, if a refrigerator is purchased for $1,000 and then sold 15 years later for $100, the drop in value is not a loss but the result of the use of the refrigerator for all those years (**consumption loss**). The only exception is for casualty losses.
   - o Gains taxed
   - o Losses not deductible (consumption loss)

6. **Sale of Personal Residence**
   There is also special treatment for individuals for a **gain on sale of personal residences**. Under IRC Section 121, if a taxpayer sells a home that served as the taxpayer's principal residence for at least 2 of the previous 5 years, the first **$250,000** of the gain on sale is not recognized (**$500,000** for a married couple filing a joint return). Can do every 2 years.
   - o If don't meet 2-year requirement but forced to sell due to change in place of employment (50+ miles), health or other unforeseen circumstances (war, divorce, death), a pro rata amount of the exclusion applies.
   - o The exclusion of gain does not apply to periods of **nonqualified use** after 2008. Nonqualified use generally includes any use other than as a principal residence, except any use during (1) the 5 years between the sale and when the taxpayer last used the property as a personal residence, (2) a military service absence for up to 10 years, and (3) a temporary absence up to 2 years for certain unforeseen circumstances. When there is nonqualified use, the exclusion is reduced by a pro

rata amount based on the ratio of the length of nonqualified use to the total time of ownership. **For example**, if Jim owned a home for the last 5 years and used it as a personal residence for the first year, rented it out for the next 3 years, and then moved back in for the last year, the exclusion would be reduced by 3/5 for the period of nonqualified use. Thus, if Jim has a gain of $100,000 on the sale, he can exclude only 2/5 of it from his gross income, or $40,000, and must recognize the other $60,000.

7. **Stock Dividends**
The basis of stock received as a dividend depends upon whether it was included in income when received.
   o   If included in income, basis is its FMV at date of distribution.
   o   If nontaxable when received, the basis of shareholder's original stock is allocated between the dividend stock and the original stock in proportion to their relative FMVs. (e.g., own Common stock and get Preferred stock as a dividend). The holding period of the dividend stock includes the holding period of the original stock.

8. **Installment Sales**
Installment Sales Method (Form 6252) applies to gains (not losses) from the disposition of property where at least one payment is to be received after the year of sale. A portion of the gain is reported as each payment is received.
   o   A person sells property for periodic installment payments. The installment sale method is **not available** for sales of stocks or securities traded on an established market. Also not allowed for gains on property held for use in the ordinary course of business.
   o   All depreciation recaptured is reported in income in the year of sale, if applicable.
   o   A portion of the overall gain is recognized and reported on *Form 6252* and then transferred to either Schedule D or Form 4797, only as a person collects cash each year, as follows:

$$\frac{Gross\ profit}{Contract\ price} = Gross\ Profit\ \% \ \times\ Cash\ Collected = Installment\ Sale\ Income$$

Example: Steve sells property with a basis of $80,000 to Bob for a selling price of $150,000. As part of the purchase price, Bob agrees to assume a $50,000 mortgage on the property and pay the remaining $100,000 in 10 equal annual installments together with adequate interest.
   o   The contract price is $100,000 ($150,000 selling price – $50,000 mortgage).
   o   The gross profit is $70,000 ($150,000 selling price – $80,000 basis).
   o   The gross profit ratio is 70% ($70,000 gross profit ÷ $100,000 contract price). Thus, $7,000 of each $10,000 payment is reported as gain from the sale.

9. **Losses on Deposits in Insolvent Financial Institutions (Banks)**
An individual who incurs a loss as a result of maintaining deposits in a financial institution that becomes insolvent or bankrupt may deduct the loss if it can be estimated as either:
   o   A *casualty loss* on *Schedule A* (in excess of 10% AGI and $100 per event) related to personal use property, filed on Form 4864, or
   o   An ordinary loss on *Schedule A* (Miscellaneous itemized 2%)
       ▪   Not available if any part of deposit is federally insured.
       ▪   Maximum deduction is $20,000 ($10,000 MFS) and is subject to reduction by 2% of AGI.

If the actual loss exceeds the estimated amount taken as a casualty loss or ordinary loss, the *excess* is treated as a nonbusiness bad debt in the year of the actual loss. It is reported on *Schedule D* and treated as a S/T capital loss, deductible up to *$3,000 per year*.

10. **Long-Term Construction Contracts**

A contract that cannot be completed within the taxable year to manufacture, build, install or construct property is considered a long-term construction contract. Income is generally recognized under the ***Percentage-of-Completion method of accounting.*** Income is based on the cost-to-cost method and recognized during the construction period. The calculation is contract costs incurred to date/total contract costs. However, the ***Completed Contract method*** of accounting is permitted for either:

- o   Home construction contracts, or
- o   Any other construction contract that will be completed within 2 years and their average annual gross receipts for the 3 previous years is $10 million or less.
  - ▪   Under the completed contract method, gross receipts and all allocable costs incurred are recognized in the *year of completion*.

Non-Recognition Transactions

Transaction	Do Not Recognize	When it Applies
Sale of Personal Assets	Losses	A person sells personal-use property at a loss.
Wash Sale	Losses	A person acquires stock within **30 days** of selling the same stock at a loss.
Sale to Related Party	• Losses – not deductible • Gains – taxed	A person sells property at a loss to a **related party**, which includes a: • Parent, grandparent, child, grandchild, spouse or sibling • Majority-owned corporation • Majority-owned partnership
Like-Kind Exchange (1031 exchange)	• Losses • Gain is recognized only to the extent that **"boot" is received:** cash + net debt relief + unlike property	A person exchanges real estate for other real estate.

Transaction	Do Not Recognize	When it Applies
Involuntary Conversion	Gain is recognized only to the extent that a person reinvests less in a replacement property than the proceeds received from the original property.	A person who lost property due to a casualty, theft, or condemnation, if: • A similar replacement property is purchased within **2 years** from the end of the year in which the casualty or theft occurred (or within **3 years** from the year in which a condemnation occurred, or **4 years** if a federal disaster area). • An appropriate election to not report the gain is filed.
Installment Sale	A portion of the overall gain is recognized only as a person collects cash each year, as follows: *Cash Collected* × $\dfrac{Gross\ Profit}{Contract\ Price}$	A person sells property for periodic installment payments.
Sale of Principal Residence	Up to **$250,000** of reportable gain is excluded ($500,000 MFJ)	Owned and lived in the home for at least **2 of the prior 5 years**

Lecture 7.07

CLASS QUESTIONS

Please see the Class Questions and Class Solutions for this Lecture at the end of this Section.

Lecture 7.08

CLASS QUESTIONS

Please see the Class Questions and Class Solutions for this Lecture at the end of this Section.

SCHEDULE D (Form 1040)	Capital Gains and Losses	OMB No. 1545-0074
Department of the Treasury Internal Revenue Service (99)	► Attach to Form 1040 or Form 1040NR. ► Information about Schedule D and its separate instructions is at *www.irs.gov/scheduled*. ► Use Form 8949 to list your transactions for lines 1b, 2, 3, 8b, 9, and 10.	20**16** Attachment Sequence No. **12**

Name(s) shown on return	Your social security number

Part I Short-Term Capital Gains and Losses—Assets Held One Year or Less

See instructions for how to figure the amounts to enter on the lines below. This form may be easier to complete if you round off cents to whole dollars.	(d) Proceeds (sales price)	(e) Cost (or other basis)	(g) Adjustments to gain or loss from Form(s) 8949, Part I, line 2, column (g)	(h) Gain or (loss) Subtract column (e) from column (d) and combine the result with column (g)
1a Totals for all short-term transactions reported on Form 1099-B for which basis was reported to the IRS and for which you have no adjustments (see instructions). However, if you choose to report all these transactions on Form 8949, leave this line blank and go to line 1b .				
1b Totals for all transactions reported on Form(s) 8949 with **Box A** checked				
2 Totals for all transactions reported on Form(s) 8949 with **Box B** checked				
3 Totals for all transactions reported on Form(s) 8949 with **Box C** checked				

4 Short-term gain from Form 6252 and short-term gain or (loss) from Forms 4684, 6781, and 8824 .	**4**	
5 Net short-term gain or (loss) from partnerships, S corporations, estates, and trusts from Schedule(s) K-1	**5**	
6 Short-term capital loss carryover. Enter the amount, if any, from line 8 of your **Capital Loss Carryover Worksheet** in the instructions	**6**	( )
7 **Net short-term capital gain or (loss).** Combine lines 1a through 6 in column (h). If you have any long-term capital gains or losses, go to Part II below. Otherwise, go to Part III on the back	**7**	

Part II Long-Term Capital Gains and Losses—Assets Held More Than One Year

See instructions for how to figure the amounts to enter on the lines below. This form may be easier to complete if you round off cents to whole dollars.	(d) Proceeds (sales price)	(e) Cost (or other basis)	(g) Adjustments to gain or loss from Form(s) 8949, Part II, line 2, column (g)	(h) Gain or (loss) Subtract column (e) from column (d) and combine the result with column (g)
8a Totals for all long-term transactions reported on Form 1099-B for which basis was reported to the IRS and for which you have no adjustments (see instructions). However, if you choose to report all these transactions on Form 8949, leave this line blank and go to line 8b .				
8b Totals for all transactions reported on Form(s) 8949 with **Box D** checked				
9 Totals for all transactions reported on Form(s) 8949 with **Box E** checked				
10 Totals for all transactions reported on Form(s) 8949 with **Box F** checked				

11 Gain from Form 4797, Part I; long-term gain from Forms 2439 and 6252; and long-term gain or (loss) from Forms 4684, 6781, and 8824	**11**	
12 Net long-term gain or (loss) from partnerships, S corporations, estates, and trusts from Schedule(s) K-1	**12**	
13 Capital gain distributions. See the instructions	**13**	
14 Long-term capital loss carryover. Enter the amount, if any, from line 13 of your **Capital Loss Carryover Worksheet** in the instructions	**14**	( )
15 **Net long-term capital gain or (loss).** Combine lines 8a through 14 in column (h). Then go to Part III on the back	**15**	

For Paperwork Reduction Act Notice, see your tax return instructions.   Cat. No. 11338H   Schedule D (Form 1040) 2016

Part III   **Summary**

16	Combine lines 7 and 15 and enter the result	**16**

   - If line 16 is a **gain,** enter the amount from line 16 on Form 1040, line 13, or Form 1040NR, line 14. Then go to line 17 below.
   - If line 16 is a **loss,** skip lines 17 through 20 below. Then go to line 21. Also be sure to complete line 22.
   - If line 16 is **zero,** skip lines 17 through 21 below and enter -0- on Form 1040, line 13, or Form 1040NR, line 14. Then go to line 22.

17   Are lines 15 and 16 **both** gains?
   ☐ **Yes.** Go to line 18.
   ☐ **No.** Skip lines 18 through 21, and go to line 22.

18	Enter the amount, if any, from line 7 of the **28% Rate Gain Worksheet** in the instructions . . ▶	**18**

19	Enter the amount, if any, from line 18 of the **Unrecaptured Section 1250 Gain Worksheet** in the instructions . . . . ▶	**19**

20   Are lines 18 and 19 **both** zero or blank?
   ☐ **Yes.** Complete the **Qualified Dividends and Capital Gain Tax Worksheet** in the instructions for Form 1040, line 44 (or in the instructions for Form 1040NR, line 42). **Don't** complete lines 21 and 22 below.

   ☐ **No.** Complete the **Schedule D Tax Worksheet** in the instructions. **Don't** complete lines 21 and 22 below.

21   If line 16 is a loss, enter here and on Form 1040, line 13, or Form 1040NR, line 14, the **smaller** of:

   - The loss on line 16 or
   - ($3,000), or if married filing separately, ($1,500)   . . . . **21** ( )

   Note: When figuring which amount is smaller, treat both amounts as positive numbers.

22   Do you have qualified dividends on Form 1040, line 9b, or Form 1040NR, line 10b?

   ☐ **Yes.** Complete the **Qualified Dividends and Capital Gain Tax Worksheet** in the instructions for Form 1040, line 44 (or in the instructions for Form 1040NR, line 42).

   ☐ **No.** Complete the rest of Form 1040 or Form 1040NR.

Schedule D (Form 1040) 2016

Form **8949**

Department of the Treasury
Internal Revenue Service

Sales and Other Dispositions of Capital Assets

▶ Information about Form 8949 and its separate instructions is at *www.irs.gov/form8949*.
▶ File with your Schedule D to list your transactions for lines 1b, 2, 3, 8b, 9, and 10 of Schedule D.

OMB No. 1545-0074

20**16**

Attachment
Sequence No. **12A**

Name(s) shown on return

Social security number or taxpayer identification number

Before you check Box A, B, or C below, see whether you received any Form(s) 1099-B or substitute statement(s) from your broker. A substitute statement will have the same information as Form 1099-B. Either will show whether your basis (usually your cost) was reported to the IRS by your broker and may even tell you which box to check.

Part I   **Short-Term.** Transactions involving capital assets you held 1 year or less are short term. For long-term transactions, see page 2.

Note: You may aggregate all short-term transactions reported on Form(s) 1099-B showing basis was reported to the IRS and for which no adjustments or codes are required. Enter the totals directly on Schedule D, line 1a; you aren't required to report these transactions on Form 8949 (see instructions).

You *must* **check Box A, B, or C below. Check only one box.** If more than one box applies for your short-term transactions, complete a separate Form 8949, page 1, for each applicable box. If you have more short-term transactions than will fit on this page for one or more of the boxes, complete as many forms with the same box checked as you need.

- ☐ **(A)** Short-term transactions reported on Form(s) 1099-B showing basis was reported to the IRS (see **Note** above)
- ☐ **(B)** Short-term transactions reported on Form(s) 1099-B showing basis **wasn't** reported to the IRS
- ☐ **(C)** Short-term transactions not reported to you on Form 1099-B

1

(a) Description of property (Example: 100 sh. XYZ Co.)	(b) Date acquired (Mo., day, yr.)	(c) Date sold or disposed of (Mo., day, yr.)	(d) Proceeds (sales price) (see instructions)	(e) Cost or other basis. See the **Note** below and see *Column (e)* in the separate instructions	Adjustment, if any, to gain or loss. If you enter an amount in column (g), enter a code in column (f). See the separate instructions.		(h) Gain or (loss). Subtract column (e) from column (d) and combine the result with column (g)
					(f) Code(s) from instructions	(g) Amount of adjustment	
2 Totals. Add the amounts in columns (d), (e), (g), and (h) (subtract negative amounts). Enter each total here and include on your Schedule D, **line 1b** (if **Box A** above is checked), **line 2** (if **Box B** above is checked), or **line 3** (if **Box C** above is checked) ▶							

Note: If you checked Box A above but the basis reported to the IRS was incorrect, enter in column (e) the basis as reported to the IRS, and enter an adjustment in column (g) to correct the basis. See *Column (g)* in the separate instructions for how to figure the amount of the adjustment.

For Paperwork Reduction Act Notice, see your tax return instructions.   Cat. No. 37768Z   Form **8949** (2016)

Form 8949 (2016)   Attachment Sequence No. **12A**   Page **2**

Name(s) shown on return. Name and SSN or taxpayer identification no. not required if shown on other side	Social security number or taxpayer identification number

Before you check Box D, E, or F below, see whether you received any Form(s) 1099-B or substitute statement(s) from your broker. A substitute statement will have the same information as Form 1099-B. Either will show whether your basis (usually your cost) was reported to the IRS by your broker and may even tell you which box to check.

Part II   **Long-Term.** Transactions involving capital assets you held more than 1 year are long term. For short-term transactions, see page 1.

     Note: You may aggregate all long-term transactions reported on Form(s) 1099-B showing basis was reported to the IRS and for which no adjustments or codes are required. Enter the totals directly on Schedule D, line 8a; you aren't required to report these transactions on Form 8949 (see instructions).

You *must* check Box D, E, *or* F below. Check only one box. If more than one box applies for your long-term transactions, complete a separate Form 8949, page 2, for each applicable box. If you have more long-term transactions than will fit on this page for one or more of the boxes, complete as many forms with the same box checked as you need.

☐ **(D)** Long-term transactions reported on Form(s) 1099-B showing basis was reported to the IRS (see **Note** above)

☐ **(E)** Long-term transactions reported on Form(s) 1099-B showing basis **wasn't** reported to the IRS

☐ **(F)** Long-term transactions not reported to you on Form 1099-B

1 (a) Description of property (Example: 100 sh. XYZ Co.)	(b) Date acquired (Mo., day, yr.)	(c) Date sold or disposed of (Mo., day, yr.)	(d) Proceeds (sales price) (see instructions)	(e) Cost or other basis. See the **Note** below and see *Column (e)* in the separate instructions	Adjustment, if any, to gain or loss. If you enter an amount in column (g), enter a code in column (f). See the separate instructions.		(h) Gain or (loss). Subtract column (e) from column (d) and combine the result with column (g)
					(f) Code(s) from instructions	(g) Amount of adjustment	
2 Totals. Add the amounts in columns (d), (e), (g), and (h) (subtract negative amounts). Enter each total here and include on your Schedule D, **line 8b** (if **Box D** above is checked), **line 9** (if **Box E** above is checked), or **line 10** (if **Box F** above is checked) ▶							

Note: If you checked Box D above but the basis reported to the IRS was incorrect, enter in column (e) the basis as reported to the IRS, and enter an adjustment in column (g) to correct the basis. See *Column (g)* in the separate instructions for how to figure the amount of the adjustment.

Form **8949** (2016)

Form 4797

Department of the Treasury
Internal Revenue Service

Sales of Business Property
(Also Involuntary Conversions and Recapture Amounts
Under Sections 179 and 280F(b)(2))

► Attach to your tax return.
► Information about Form 4797 and its separate instructions is at *www.irs.gov/form4797.*

OMB No. 1545-0184

2016

Attachment
Sequence No. **27**

Name(s) shown on return | Identifying number

1   Enter the gross proceeds from sales or exchanges reported to you for 2016 on Form(s) 1099-B or 1099-S (or substitute statement) that you are including on line 2, 10, or 20. See instructions . . . . | **1**

Part I   **Sales or Exchanges of Property Used in a Trade or Business and Involuntary Conversions From Other Than Casualty or Theft—Most Property Held More Than 1 Year** (see instructions)

2	(a) Description of property	(b) Date acquired (mo., day, yr.)	(c) Date sold (mo., day, yr.)	(d) Gross sales price	(e) Depreciation allowed or allowable since acquisition	(f) Cost or other basis, plus improvements and expense of sale	(g) Gain or (loss) Subtract (f) from the sum of (d) and (e)

3   Gain, if any, from Form 4684, line 39 . . . . | **3**
4   Section 1231 gain from installment sales from Form 6252, line 26 or 37 . . . . | **4**
5   Section 1231 gain or (loss) from like-kind exchanges from Form 8824 . . . . | **5**
6   Gain, if any, from line 32, from other than casualty or theft . . . . | **6**
7   Combine lines 2 through 6. Enter the gain or (loss) here and on the appropriate line as follows: . . . . | **7**

Partnerships (except electing large partnerships) and S corporations. Report the gain or (loss) following the instructions for Form 1065, Schedule K, line 10, or Form 1120S, Schedule K, line 9. Skip lines 8, 9, 11, and 12 below.

Individuals, partners, S corporation shareholders, and all others. If line 7 is zero or a loss, enter the amount from line 7 on line 11 below and skip lines 8 and 9. If line 7 is a gain and you didn't have any prior year section 1231 losses, or they were recaptured in an earlier year, enter the gain from line 7 as a long-term capital gain on the Schedule D filed with your return and skip lines 8, 9, 11, and 12 below.

8   Nonrecaptured net section 1231 losses from prior years. See instructions . . . . | **8**
9   Subtract line 8 from line 7. If zero or less, enter -0-. If line 9 is zero, enter the gain from line 7 on line 12 below. If line 9 is more than zero, enter the amount from line 8 on line 12 below and enter the gain from line 9 as a long-term capital gain on the Schedule D filed with your return. See instructions . . . . | **9**

Part II   **Ordinary Gains and Losses** (see instructions)

10   Ordinary gains and losses not included on lines 11 through 16 (include property held 1 year or less):

11   Loss, if any, from line 7 . . . . | **11** (   )
12   Gain, if any, from line 7 or amount from line 8, if applicable . . . . | **12**
13   Gain, if any, from line 31 . . . . | **13**
14   Net gain or (loss) from Form 4684, lines 31 and 38a . . . . | **14**
15   Ordinary gain from installment sales from Form 6252, line 25 or 36 . . . . . . | **15**
16   Ordinary gain or (loss) from like-kind exchanges from Form 8824. . . . . . . | **16**
17   Combine lines 10 through 16 . . . . | **17**
18   For all except individual returns, enter the amount from line 17 on the appropriate line of your return and skip lines a and b below. For individual returns, complete lines a and b below:

a   If the loss on line 11 includes a loss from Form 4684, line 35, column (b)(ii), enter that part of the loss here. Enter the part of the loss from income-producing property on Schedule A (Form 1040), line 28, and the part of the loss from property used as an employee on Schedule A (Form 1040), line 23. Identify as from "Form 4797, line 18a." See instructions . . | **18a**
b   Redetermine the gain or (loss) on line 17 excluding the loss, if any, on line 18a. Enter here and on Form 1040, line 14 | **18b**

For Paperwork Reduction Act Notice, see separate instructions.   Cat. No. 13086I   Form **4797** (2016)

| **Part III** | **Gain From Disposition of Property Under Sections 1245, 1250, 1252, 1254, and 1255** (see instructions) |

19	(a) Description of section 1245, 1250, 1252, 1254, or 1255 property:	**(b)** Date acquired (mo., day, yr.)	**(c)** Date sold (mo., day, yr.)
A			
B			
C			
D			

	These columns relate to the properties on lines 19A through 19D. ▶		**Property A**	**Property B**	**Property C**	**Property D**
20	Gross sales price (**Note:** See line 1 before completing.)	20				
21	Cost or other basis plus expense of sale	21				
22	Depreciation (or depletion) allowed or allowable	22				
23	Adjusted basis. Subtract line 22 from line 21	23				
24	Total gain. Subtract line 23 from line 20	24				
25	**If section 1245 property:**					
a	Depreciation allowed or allowable from line 22	25a				
b	Enter the **smaller** of line 24 or 25a	25b				
26	**If section 1250 property:** If straight line depreciation was used, enter -0- on line 26g, except for a corporation subject to section 291.					
a	Additional depreciation after 1975. See instructions	26a				
b	Applicable percentage multiplied by the **smaller** of line 24 or line 26a. See instructions	26b				
c	Subtract line 26a from line 24. If residential rental property **or** line 24 isn't more than line 26a, skip lines 26d and 26e	26c				
d	Additional depreciation after 1969 and before 1976.	26d				
e	Enter the **smaller** of line 26c or 26d	26e				
f	Section 291 amount (corporations only)	26f				
g	Add lines 26b, 26e, and 26f.	26g				
27	**If section 1252 property:** Skip this section if you didn't dispose of farmland or if this form is being completed for a partnership (other than an electing large partnership).					
a	Soil, water, and land clearing expenses	27a				
b	Line 27a multiplied by applicable percentage. See instructions	27b				
c	Enter the **smaller** of line 24 or 27b	27c				
28	**If section 1254 property:**					
a	Intangible drilling and development costs, expenditures for development of mines and other natural deposits, mining exploration costs, and depletion. See instructions	28a				
b	Enter the **smaller** of line 24 or 28a	28b				
29	**If section 1255 property:**					
a	Applicable percentage of payments excluded from income under section 126. See instructions	29a				
b	Enter the **smaller** of line 24 or 29a. See instructions	29b				

Summary of Part III Gains. Complete property columns A through D through line 29b before going to line 30.

30	Total gains for all properties. Add property columns A through D, line 24	30	
31	Add property columns A through D, lines 25b, 26g, 27c, 28b, and 29b. Enter here and on line 13	31	
32	Subtract line 31 from line 30. Enter the portion from casualty or theft on Form 4684, line 33. Enter the portion from other than casualty or theft on Form 4797, line 6	32	

| **Part IV** | **Recapture Amounts Under Sections 179 and 280F(b)(2) When Business Use Drops to 50% or Less** (see instructions) |

			(a) Section 179	**(b)** Section 280F(b)(2)
33	Section 179 expense deduction or depreciation allowable in prior years.	33		
34	Recomputed depreciation. See instructions	34		
35	Recapture amount. Subtract line 34 from line 33. See the instructions for where to report	35		

Form **4797** (2016)

Form 6252

Department of the Treasury
Internal Revenue Service

Installment Sale Income

▶ Attach to your tax return.
▶ Use a separate form for each sale or other disposition of property on the installment method.
▶ Information about Form 6252 and its instructions is at *www.irs.gov/form6252.*

OMB No. 1545-0228

2016

Attachment
Sequence No. **79**

Name(s) shown on return

Identifying number

1	Description of property ▶
2a	Date acquired (mm/dd/yyyy) ▶ _____ **b** Date sold (mm/dd/yyyy) ▶
3	Was the property sold to a related party (see instructions) after May 14, 1980? If "No," skip line 4 . . . . . ☐ Yes ☐ No
4	Was the property you sold to a related party a marketable security? If "Yes," complete Part III. If "No," complete Part III for the year of sale and the 2 years after the year of sale . . . . ☐ Yes ☐ No

Part I **Gross Profit and Contract Price.** Complete this part for the year of sale only.

5	Selling price including mortgages and other debts. **Don't** include interest, whether stated or unstated	**5**	
6	Mortgages, debts, and other liabilities the buyer assumed or took the property subject to (see instructions)	**6**	
7	Subtract line 6 from line 5	**7**	
8	Cost or other basis of property sold	**8**	
9	Depreciation allowed or allowable	**9**	
10	Adjusted basis. Subtract line 9 from line 8	**10**	
11	Commissions and other expenses of sale	**11**	
12	Income recapture from Form 4797, Part III (see instructions) . . .	**12**	
13	Add lines 10, 11, and 12	**13**	
14	Subtract line 13 from line 5. If zero or less, **don't** complete the rest of this form (see instructions)	**14**	
15	If the property described on line 1 above was your main home, enter the amount of your excluded gain (see instructions). Otherwise, enter -0-	**15**	
16	**Gross profit.** Subtract line 15 from line 14	**16**	
17	Subtract line 13 from line 6. If zero or less, enter -0-	**17**	
18	**Contract price.** Add line 7 and line 17	**18**	

Part II **Installment Sale Income.** Complete this part for the year of sale **and** any year you receive a payment or have certain debts you must treat as a payment on installment obligations.

19	Gross profit percentage (expressed as a decimal amount). Divide line 16 by line 18. For years after the year of sale, see instructions	**19**	
20	If this is the year of sale, enter the amount from line 17. Otherwise, enter -0-	**20**	
21	Payments received during year (see instructions). **Don't** include interest, whether stated or unstated .	**21**	
22	Add lines 20 and 21	**22**	
23	Payments received in prior years (see instructions). **Don't** include interest, whether stated or unstated	**23**	
24	**Installment sale income.** Multiply line 22 by line 19	**24**	
25	Enter the part of line 24 that is ordinary income under the recapture rules (see instructions) . . .	**25**	
26	Subtract line 25 from line 24. Enter here and on Schedule D or Form 4797 (see instructions). . .	**26**	

Part III **Related Party Installment Sale Income. Don't** complete if you received the final payment this tax year.

27	Name, address, and taxpayer identifying number of related party
28	Did the related party resell or dispose of the property ("second disposition") during this tax year? . . . . . ☐ Yes ☐ No
29	**If the answer to question 28 is "Yes," complete lines 30 through 37 below unless one of the following conditions is met. Check the box that applies.**
a	☐ The second disposition was more than 2 years after the first disposition (other than dispositions of marketable securities). If this box is checked, enter the date of disposition (mm/dd/yyyy). . . ▶ _____
b	☐ The first disposition was a sale or exchange of stock to the issuing corporation.
c	☐ The second disposition was an involuntary conversion and the threat of conversion occurred after the first disposition.
d	☐ The second disposition occurred after the death of the original seller or buyer.
e	☐ It can be established to the satisfaction of the IRS that tax avoidance wasn't a principal purpose for either of the dispositions. If this box is checked, attach an explanation (see instructions).

30	Selling price of property sold by related party (see instructions)	**30**	
31	Enter contract price from line 18 for year of first sale	**31**	
32	Enter the **smaller** of line 30 or line 31	**32**	
33	Total payments received by the end of your 2016 tax year (see instructions)	**33**	
34	Subtract line 33 from line 32. If zero or less, enter -0-	**34**	
35	Multiply line 34 by the gross profit percentage on line 19 for year of first sale	**35**	
36	Enter the part of line 35 that is ordinary income under the recapture rules (see instructions) . . .	**36**	
37	Subtract line 36 from line 35. Enter here and on Schedule D or Form 4797 (see instructions). . .	**37**	

For Paperwork Reduction Act Notice, see page 4.   Cat. No. 13601R   Form **6252** (2016)

CLASS QUESTIONS

Work through the below Class Questions while following along with the respective lectures. Once this is complete, you can begin independently practicing what you've learned by quizzing yourself on this course section in your Interactive Practice Questions (IPQ), which can be found in your online Student Dashboard. Your IPQ simulates the computer-based testing experience, and will also help you understand how concepts are applied to the exam. Each question includes answer explanations from expert CPAs that will help you determine why you answered a question correctly or incorrectly. This is key to your success on the CPA Exam.

Lecture 7.04

1. Which of the following items is considered a capital asset?

    a. An automobile for personal use
    b. Depreciable business property
    c. Account receivable for inventory sold
    d. Real property used in a trade or business

2. Platt owns land that is operated as a parking lot. A shed was erected on the lot for the related transactions with customers. With regard to capital assets and Section 1231 assets, how should these assets be classified?

	Land	**Shed**
a.	Capital	Capital
b.	Section 1231	Capital
c.	Capital	Section 1231
d.	Section 1231	Section 1231

3. On January 2, 20X1, Bates Corp. purchased and placed into service seven-year MACRS tangible property costing $100,000. On July 31, 20X3, Bates sold the property for $102,000, after having taken $47,525 in MACRS depreciation deductions. What amount of the gain should Bates recapture as ordinary income?

    a. $0
    b. $2,000
    c. $47,525
    d. $49,525

4. Which of the following costs is includible in inventory under the uniform capitalization rules for merchandise manufactured by a company for sale to its customers?

    a. Advertising
    b. Marketing
    c. Engineering
    d. Selling expenses

Lecture 7.07

5. Among which of the following related parties are losses from sales and exchanges not recognized for tax purposes?

    a. Mother-in-law and daughter-in-law
    b. Uncle and nephew
    c. Brother and sister
    d. Ancestors, lineal descendants, and all in-laws

6. In 20X3, Fay sold 100 shares of Gym Co. stock to her son, Martin, for $11,000. Fay had paid $15,000 for the stock in 20X0. Subsequently in 20X3, Martin sold the stock to an unrelated third party for $16,000. What amount of gain from the sale of the stock to the third party should Martin report on his 20X3 income tax return?

    a. $0
    b. $1,000
    c. $4,000
    d. $5,000

Items 7, 8 and 9 are based on the following data:
On March 1, 20X3, Lois learned that she was bequeathed 1,000 shares of Extra Corp. common stock under the will of her uncle, Pat. Pat had paid $5,000 for the Extra Corp. stock in 20X0. Fair market value of the Extra stock on March 1, 20X3, the date of Pat's death, was $8,000 and had increased to $11,000 six months later. The executor of Pat's estate elected the alternative valuation for estate tax purposes. Lois sold the Extra stock for $9,000 on May 1, 20X3, the date that the executor distributed the stock to her.

7. How much should Lois include in her individual tax return for the inheritance of the 1,000 shares of Extra Corp's stock which she received from Pat's estate?

    a. $0
    b. $5,000
    c. $8,000
    d. $11,000

8. Lois' basis for gain or loss on sale of the 1,000 shares of Extra Corp's stock is

    a. $5,000
    b. $8,000
    c. $9,000
    d. $11,000

9. Lois should treat the 1,000 shares of Extra Corp's stock as a

    a. Short-term Section 1231 asset
    b. Long-term Section 1231 asset
    c. Short-term capital asset
    d. Long-term capital asset

Items 10 and 11 are based on the following: Conner purchased 300 shares of Zinco stock for $30,000 in 20X0. On May 23, 20X3, Conner sold all the stock to his daughter Alice for $20,000, its then fair market value. Conner realized no other gain or loss during 20X3. On July 26, 20X3, Alice sold the 300 shares of Zinco for $25,000.

10. What amount of the loss from the sale of Zinco stock can Conner deduct in 20X3?

    a. $0
    b. $3,000
    c. $5,000
    d. $10,000

11. What was Alice's recognized gain or loss on her sale?

    a. $0
    b. $5,000 long-term gain
    c. $5,000 short-term loss
    d. $5,000 long-term loss

12. An office building owned by John C was condemned by the state on January 2, 20X2. John received the condemnation award on March 1, 20X3. In order to qualify for nonrecognition of gain on this involuntary conversion, what is the last date for John to acquire qualified replacement property?

    a. August 1, 20X4
    b. January 2, 20X5
    c. March 1, 20X6
    d. December 31, 20X6

13. A taxpayer had an investment in real estate with an adjusted basis of $125,000, subject to a mortgage of $75,000. When the property had a value of $375,000, it was exchanged for another parcel of land, which the taxpayer is similarly holding for investment. The other party is assuming the $75,000 mortgage in the exchange. The land acquired has a fair value of $260,000 and is subject to a mortgage of $40,000, which the taxpayer is assuming. In addition, the taxpayer is receiving a recreational vehicle with a fair value of $30,000, and $50,000 in cash.

How much gain, if any, should the taxpayer recognize on the exchange, and what will be the basis in the new property?

	Gain recognized	Basis for real estate
a.	$250,000	$125,000
b.	$250,000	$260,000
c.	$115,000	$125,000
d.	$115,000	$260,000

14. Aviary Corp. sold a building for $600,000. Aviary received a down payment of $120,000 as well as annual principal payments of $120,000 for each of the subsequent 4 years. Aviary purchased the building for $500,000 and claimed depreciation of $80,000. What amount of gain should Aviary report in the year of sale using the installment method?

    a. $180,000
    b. $120,000
    c. $54,000
    d. $36,000

CLASS SOLUTIONS

1. (a) Capital assets are all assets that are not considered ordinary business assets, which include inventory and accounts receivable resulting from sales of inventory; depreciable personal property, or real property used in a trade or business. An automobile used for personal use would be considered a capital asset since it does not fall into any other category.

2. (d) Section 1231 assets are noncurrent assets used in a trade or business and include depreciable or amortizable personal property and land used in the business. As a result, both the land operated as a parking lot and the shed would be considered Section 1231 property.

3. (c) Sales of depreciable tangible personal property used in a trade or business are subject to Section 1245 depreciation recapture. When the asset is sold at a gain, the entire gain, up to the cumulative amount of depreciation taken, is reported as an ordinary gain since it represents a reversal of depreciation, which had been reported as an ordinary expense. As a result, $47,525 would be reported as an ordinary gain, with the remainder recognized as a 1231 gain, which will receive LTCG treatment.

4. (c) Direct materials, direct labor, and applicable indirect costs must be capitalized as a part of inventory under the uniform capitalization rules (UNICAP). Engineering expenses are considered an applicable indirect cost that must be capitalized. All the other costs are still considered expenses in the period.

5. (c) Losses from the sale or exchange of assets are not deductible when sold to certain related parties, which include husbands and wives, sisters and brothers, parents and children or grandchildren and grandparents, ancestors and descendants, and majority shareholders or partners and the related corporations or partnerships. They do not include aunts, uncles, nephews, nieces, or in-laws.

6. (b) Although the $4,000 loss incurred when Fay sold the stock to her son is not deductible, when the son subsequently sold it to an unrelated party, he reduces his gain by any unrecognized loss on the previous transfer. Martin realized a profit equal to the difference between the sales price of $16,000 and his cost of $11,000, or $5,000. It is reduced, however, by the $4,000 unrecognized loss incurred on the transfer from his mother, reducing his taxable gain to $1,000.

7. (a) Property acquired by gift or inheritance is not included in the taxable income of the recipient.

8. (c) The executor of an estate has the option of valuing assets at the date of death or an alternate valuation date (AVD), 6 months after the date of death. When the AVD is elected, as it was in this case, the basis of assets transferred will be the fair value at AVD, 6 months after the date of death, or the date on which the assets were actually transferred, if the transfer occurs during the 6-month period. Since the AVD was selected and the stock was transferred to Lois during the 6 months after death, the valuation will be its fair value on the date of transfer, $9,000, which will also be Lois's basis in the stock.

9. (d) Assets acquired by inheritance are considered to be held long-term, regardless of the actual holding period of either the donor or the recipient. Since the stock was received by inheritance, it will be treated as long-term and, since it was stock and not an asset used in a trade or business, it will be a capital asset.

10. (a) A loss cannot be deducted on a sale to a related party, which would include a sale between father and daughter. Upon subsequent sale, however, the unrecognized loss of the original seller will reduce the ultimate gain recognized by the party who had originally purchased, and subsequently sold, the asset.

11. (a) Although Alice realized a gain of $5,000 when she sold the stock purchased from her father, her gain is reduced by any unrecognized loss incurred by her father when he sold the stock to her. Conner sold the stock to his daughter at a loss of $10,000, which was not recognized on sale due to his daughter being a related party. When she subsequently sold the stock, her taxable gain is reduced by up to $10,000 and, since her gain was only $5,000, none of it will be taxable to her.

12. (d) When a taxpayer realizes a gain on an involuntary conversion, there is a certain period of time to replace that property in order to defer the gain. When the involuntary conversion results from a governmental condemnation, as occurred with John's building, the statutory period is 3 years from the end of the period in which the involuntary conversion occurred. The involuntary conversion occurred on 3/1/X3, indicating that the loss can be deferred if the property is replaced within 3 years of 12/31/X3, or by 12/31/X6.

13. (c) When property is exchanged in a like-kind exchange, the gain to be recognized will be the lower of the realized gain or the total of boot (unlike consideration) received. The taxpayer is receiving land worth $260,000, cash of $50,000, and a vehicle worth $30,000, for a total of $340,000, and is assuming a mortgage of $40,000, resulting in *net proceeds* of $300,000. The taxpayer is giving up land with a carrying value of $125,000 subject to a mortgage of $75,000, for a net of $50,000, indicating a *realized gain* of $250,000 ($300,000 net proceeds – $50,000 given). Unlike consideration includes the cash of $50,000, the vehicle of $30,000 and the $35,000 difference between the $75,000 debt that the taxpayer is being relieved of and the $40,000 debt being assumed, for a total of $115,000 boot. Since this is lower than the realized gain of $250,000, it is the amount that will be taxable.

The basis in the new property will be its fair value less any unrecognized gain. The fair value of the property received is $260,000. This will be reduced by the unrecognized gain of $135,000 ($250,000 – $115,000), making the basis in the new property equal to $125,000 ($260,000 – $135,000). The journal entry will be:

New	125	
Cash	50	
Vehicle	30	
Old mortgage	75	
Old		125
Gain		115
New mortgage		40

14. (d) With a cost of $500,000 and deprecation of $80,000, the tax basis in the property is $420,000. At a sales price of $600,000, total profit on the sale is $180,000. Aviary will be taxed on the sale using the installment method, under which profit is recognized in proportion to the portion of the sales price collected in a given year. In the year of sale, Aviary received $120,000 of the $600,000 sales price, or 20%. As a result, Aviary will be taxed on 20% of the profit, or $36,000.

Lecture 7.05

TASK-BASED SIMULATIONS

Task-Based Simulation 1

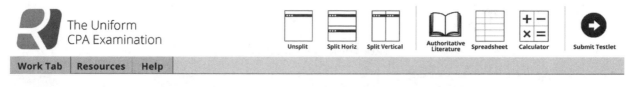

| Work Tab | Resources | Help |

Required:

Items 1 through 12 describe various types of transactions that an individual or business entity may be involved in. For each one, indicate the appropriate tax treatment. A tax treatment may be used once, more than once, or not at all.

Items to be answered:

Descriptions

A. Long-term capital gain
B. Long-term capital loss
C. Short-term capital gain
D. Short-term capital loss
E. Sec. 1231 gain or loss

F. Sec. 1245 gain
G. Sec. 1250 gain
H. Ordinary income or loss
I. Not deductible

Transaction	(A)	(B)	(C)	(D)	(E)	(F)	(G)	(H)	(I)
1. Gain from sale of stock held 10 months	O	O	O	O	O	O	O	O	O
2. Result from the sale of assets used in a trade or business, such as land, buildings, or equipment, that is not held as inventory	O	O	O	O	O	O	O	O	O
3. Portion of a gain on the sale of a machine that is taxed as ordinary income	O	O	O	O	O	O	O	O	O
4. Results from recapture of depreciation on real property	O	O	O	O	O	O	O	O	O
5. Gains are long-term capital gains, and losses are ordinary if held for more than one year	O	O	O	O	O	O	O	O	O
6. Gain on sale of personal jewelry held long term	O	O	O	O	O	O	O	O	O
7. Loss on the sale of the personal residence lived in by the taxpayer and held long term	O	O	O	O	O	O	O	O	O
8. Results from recapture of deprecation on personal property	O	O	O	O	O	O	O	O	O
9. Gambling losses in a period in which there were no gambling winnings	O	O	O	O	O	O	O	O	O
10. Difference between sales price and cost of goods held as inventory for sale in the ordinary course of business held 13 months	O	O	O	O	O	O	O	O	O
11. Gains or losses treated as ordinary if asset held for one year or less	O	O	O	O	O	O	O	O	O
12. Excess of sales price over tax basis of asset inherited 3 months prior to sale	O	O	O	O	O	O	O	O	O

Task-Based Simulation 2

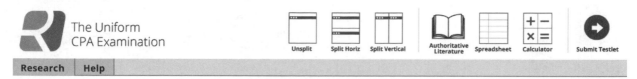

A corporation has a net capital loss in the current period. It has carried back the maximum amount allowed and is trying to determine how many of the succeeding tax years to which the remainder may be carried forward.

Which code section, subsection, paragraph, and subparagraph indicates the number of tax years that a corporation may carry forward a net capital loss?

Task-Based Simulation 3

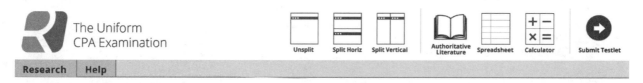

A business taxpayer has sold depreciable personal property at a gain and is trying to determine the portion that will be recognized as ordinary income.

Which code section, subsection, and paragraph indicates what portion of the gain will be taxed as ordinary income?

Task-Based Simulation 4

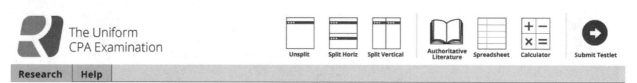

An unincorporated company sold depreciable real property at a gain. The property, which had been held for several years, was being depreciated using an accelerated method and the entity knows that additional depreciation will have to be recaptured and recognized as ordinary income, but it is not certain how to calculate additional depreciation.

Which code section, subsection, and paragraph provides a definition of additional depreciation?

Task-Based Simulation 5

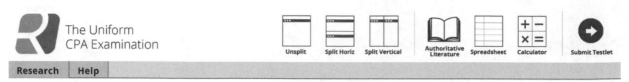

A corporation sold section 1250 property at a gain, considered a corporate preference item. As a result, a larger portion of the gain is considered ordinary income than if similar property had been sold by a noncorporate taxpayer.

Which code section, subsection, and paragraph describes how to determine the additional portion of the gain that will be treated as ordinary income?

Task-Based Simulation 6

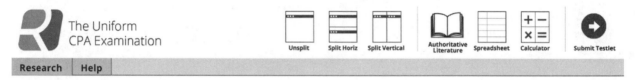

A taxpayer received property from a decedent and is trying to determine his holding period for the property.

Which code section, subsection, and paragraph indicates how to determine the holding period of property received from a decedent?

Task-Based Simulation 7

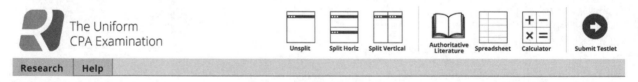

A taxpayer sold property, receiving a portion of the proceeds as a down payment with the remainder to be received in periodic payments over the next several years. As a result, the taxpayer elected to apply the installment sale method.

Which code section and subsection defines the installment method?

TASK-BASED SIMULATION SOLUTIONS

Task-Based Simulation Solution 1

Transaction	(A)	(B)	(C)	(D)	(E)	(F)	(G)	(H)	(I)
1. Gain from sale of stock held 10 months	○	○	●	○	○	○	○	○	○
2. Result from the sale of assets used in a trade or business, such as land, buildings, or equipment, that is not held as inventory	○	○	○	○	●	○	○	○	○
3. Portion of a gain on the sale of a machine that is taxed as ordinary	○	○	○	○	○	●	○	○	○
4. Results from recapture of depreciation on real property	○	○	○	○	○	○	●	○	○
5. Gains are long-term capital gains, and losses are ordinary if held for more than one year	○	○	○	○	●	○	○	○	○
6. Gain on sale of personal jewelry held long term	●	○	○	○	○	○	○	○	○
7. Loss on the sale of the personal residence lived in by the taxpayer and held long term	○	○	○	○	○	○	○	○	●
8. Results from recapture of deprecation on personal property	○	○	○	○	○	●	○	○	○
9. Gambling losses in a period in which there were no gambling winnings	○	○	○	○	○	○	○	○	●
10. Difference between sales price and cost of goods held as inventory for sale in the ordinary course of business held 13 months	○	○	○	○	○	○	○	●	○
11. Gains or losses treated as ordinary if asset held for one year or less	○	○	○	○	●	○	○	○	○
12. Excess of sales price over tax basis of asset inherited 3 months prior to sale	●	○	○	○	○	○	○	○	○

Explanation of solutions

1. (C) Capital assets that are held for one year or less are considered short-term. As a result, the gain from the sale of stock held for 10 months would be a short-term capital gain.

2. (E) Assets used in a trade or business, such as land, buildings, and equipment, are considered Section 1231 assets if they are not inventory. If they are held for one year or less, gains and losses are ordinary. If they are held for longer than one year, net gains on Section 1231 assets that exceed depreciation recaptured are taxed as long-term capital gains, and net losses on Section 1231 assets are deductible as ordinary.

3. (F) Depreciable personal property that is used in a trade or business is subject to depreciation recapture under Section 1245 to the extent of depreciation allowed on the property. The portion of the gain recaptured under Section 1245 is taxed as ordinary income. Any remaining gain on such assets held longer than one year is Section 1231 gain (i.e., treated as long-term capital gain).

4. (G) Depreciable real property that is used in a trade or business is subject to depreciation recapture under Section 1250 If accelerated depreciation methods were applied, or the property was held less than one year. For property held longer than one year, gain is recaptured as ordinary income to the extent of depreciation taken in excess of the straight-line method. For property held less than one year, gain is recaptured as ordinary income to the extent of all depreciation claimed. Any remaining gain (referred to as unrecaptured Section 1250 gain) is Section 1231 gain and is considered a long-term capital gain.

5. (E) Assets used in a trade or business, such as land, buildings, and equipment, are considered Section 1231 assets if they are not inventory. Net gains on Section 1231 assets that exceed depreciation recaptured are taxed as long-term capital gains, and net losses on Section 1231 assets are deductible as ordinary. If assets used in a trade or business are held for one year or less, gains and losses are ordinary.

6. (A) Personal assets, including personal jewelry, automobiles, and personal residences, are considered capital assets; thus, gains on the sale of personal assets are capital gains, taxed as short-term or long-term capital gains, depending on the holding period. Inherited assets, however, are always treated as long-term. In certain circumstances, some or all of the gains on personal residences are not taxable. Losses from the sale of personal assets are not deductible.

7. (I) Personal assets, including personal jewelry, automobiles, and personal residences, are considered capital assets. Gains on the sale of personal assets are capital gains, taxed as short-term or long-term capital gains, depending on the holding period. In certain circumstances, however, some or all of the gains on personal residences are not taxable. Losses from the sale of personal assets are not deductible.

8. (F) Depreciable personal property that is used in a trade or business is subject to depreciation recapture under Section 1245 to the extent of depreciation allowed on the property. The portion of the gain recaptured under Section 1245 is taxed as ordinary income. Any remaining gain on such assets held longer than one year is Section 1231 gain (i.e., treated as long-term capital gain).

9. (I) Gambling losses are deductible only to the extent of winnings from gambling. In a period in which there were no gambling winnings, gambling losses would not be deductible.

10. (H) Business assets that are held for sale in the ordinary course of business, such as inventory and receivables that result from the sale of inventory or providing services, are considered ordinary assets. Sales of ordinary business assets result in ordinary income or losses.

11. (E) Assets used in a trade or business, such as land, buildings, and equipment, are considered Section 1231 assets if they are not inventory. If they are held for one year or less, gains and losses are ordinary. If they are held for longer than one year, net gains on Section 1231 assets that exceed depreciation recaptured are taxed as long-term capital gains, and net losses on Section 1231 assets are deductible as ordinary.

12. (A) Personal assets, including personal jewelry, automobiles, and personal residences, are considered capital assets; thus, gains on the sale of personal assets are capital gains, taxed as short-term or long-term capital gains, depending on the holding period. Inherited assets, however, are always treated as long-term; therefore, this would be considered a long-term capital gain. In certain circumstances, some or all of the gains on personal residences are not taxable. Losses from the sale of personal assets are not deductible.

Task-Based Simulation Solution 2

1212	(a)	(1)	(B)

Task-Based Simulation Solution 3

1245	(a)	(1)

Task-Based Simulation Solution 4

1250	(b)	(1)

Task-Based Simulation Solution 5

291	(a)	(1)

Task-Based Simulation Solution 6

1223	(9)

Task-Based Simulation Solution 7

453	(c)

Lecture 7.08

DOCUMENT REVIEW SIMULATION

Document Review Simulation 1

The Uniform CPA Examination

Unsplit   Split Horiz   Split Vertical   Authoritative Literature   Spreadsheet   Calculator   Submit Testlet

| Work Tab | Resources | Help |

Required:

Zed Zennon is an individual client of Peat Moss, CPAs. He owns a manufacturing business as a sole proprietor, and this year he sold a number of the business assets. He also bought and sold investment assets. A staff accountant at Peat Moss, CPAs, has created a file memo draft regarding Zed Zennon's asset sales for 20X8. As the staff accountant's supervisor, please review the memo for accuracy. Supporting documents are provided for your analysis.

To revise the document, click on each segment of underlined text below and select the needed correction, if any, from the list provided. If the underlined text is already correct in the context of the document, select [Original text] from the list.

Peat Moss, CPAs

File Memo

DATE: February 22, 20X9
BY: Jordan Staff
Re: Zed Zennon's Asset Sales for 20X8

Zed Zennon sold investment assets as well as assets from his manufacturing business. 1.) The gain or loss on the investment assets should be reported on his 1040, Schedule D and the business asset transactions on Form 4797.

Zed sold investments in three stocks and one mutual fund. 2.) The recognized long-term capital losses are: Dell Weber Bank Corp, $7,700; Agro Garden Terrace, $35,250; and VNN Communications, $5,500. Ace Mutual funds gain cannot be determined due to missing data.

The business assets that Zed sold include an office building and associated land, computers, and light trucks. The office building, computers, and light trucks were subject to MACRS, while the land and the painting were not subject to cost recovery because they have unspecified lives. 3.) Since the painting was not depreciated, it appears that it is a personal capital asset and, therefore, the $35,000 gain would be a personal investment gain, subject to a maximum tax rate of 20%. The gains or losses for the other assets are categorized as follows:
- 4.) Office building—$22,821 Section 1245 recapture gain taxed as ordinary income
- 5.) Computers—$176 Section 1231 ordinary loss
- 6.) Light trucks—$65,800 Section 1245 recapture gain taxed as ordinary income

Resources

Zennon Business Asset Schedule
As of 12/31/20X8

Description	Placed in Service	Method	Life	Beginning Balance	Additions	Total Cost Recovery	Ending Balance	Disposal Date	Sales Price	Gain/ (Loss)
				Business Asset Tax Basis				Disposition		
AIRPLANE	5/6/X4	MACRS	5	250,000	70,000	264,704	55,296			
OFFICE BUILDING	1/20/X8	SL	39	500,000	50,000	12,821	537,179	12/18/X8	560,000	22,821
OFFICE LAND	03/20/X2	N/A	N/A	100,000			100,000	12/18/X8	170,000	70,000
AUTOMOBILES	8/27/X6	MACRS	5	240,000		124,800	115,200			
BARGES	11/22/X3	MACRS	15	360,000		135,648	224,352			
COMPUTERS	9/13/X5	MACRS	5	2,000		1,424	576	11/10/X8	400	(176)
COPIER	4/29/X6	MACRS	5	1,000		520	480			
DELIVERY TRUCKS	9/04/X6	MACRS	5	215,000		111,800	103,200			
EQUIPMENT	7/06/X4	MACRS	7	330,000	20,000	240,660	109,340			
LANDSCAPING	2/20/X2	MACRS	15	22,000		9,660	12,340			
LIGHT TRUCKS	2/21/X7	MACRS	5	157,000		62,800	94,200	3/03/X8	160,000	65,800
MACHINES	3/03/X4	MACRS	5	450,000		372,240	77,760			
MANUFACTURING BUILDING	1/19/X4	SL	39	675,000		68,533	606,467			
MANUFACTURE BLDG LAND	1/19/X4	N/A	N/A	150,000			150,000			
PAINTING (ART)	7/07/01	N/A	N/A	25,000			25,000	5/05/X8	60,000	35,000
SOFTWARE	10/10/X6	SL	3	10,000		10,000	0			
TOTALS				3,682,000	140,000	1,525,309	2,296,691		1,120,200	244,662

Cline & Abbot Investments   Zed Zennon Acct # 55-1212

Acquisitions and Stock Dividends from Brokered Transactions – Statement for Acquirer

Transactions which are not Reported to the IRS; Keep for Records

For Year Ending 12/31/X8

Description of property

Activity Type	Quantity Acquired	Date Acquired	Cost or Other Basis
JEWEL TOOLS LIMITED / 2325842 / JTL			
Acquisition	450	8/27/X8	45,000
DELL WEBER BANK CORP / 1519P / DWB			
Acquisition	150	2/19/X8	43,400

Cline & Abbot Investments   Zed Zennon Acct # 55-1212

Acquisitions and Stock Dividends from Brokered Transactions – Statement for Acquirer

Transactions which are not Reported to the IRS; Keep for Records

For Year Ending 12/31/X7

Description of property

Activity Type	Quantity Acquired	Date Acquired	Cost or Other Basis
ACE MUTUAL FUND			
Acquisition	200	9/13/X7	42,400
VNN COMMUNICATIONS / 9672TV9 / VNN			
Acquisition	240	5/05/X7	24,200

Xerta Investment Co

Client: Zed Zennon
Acct # 007-212121
For Year Ending 12/31/X6

Bought: 300 shares of ACE Mutual
Date: 2/20/X6
Price per share: $136
Total cost: $40,800

Cline & Abbot Investments   Zed Zennon Acct # 55-1212

Acquisitions and Stock Dividends from Brokered Transactions – Statement for Acquirer

Transactions which are not Reported to the IRS; Keep for Records

For Year Ending 12/31/X6

Description of property

Activity Type	Quantity Acquired	Date Acquired	Cost or Other Basis
DELL WEBER BANK CORP / 1494P / DWB			
Acquisition	100	3/20/X6	50,000
AGRO GARDEN TERRACE, INC / 15694J / AGT			
Acquisition	3375	5/06/X6	67,500

Cline & Abbot Investments

1099-B Proceeds From Broker and Barter Exchange Transactions – Statement for Recipient
For Year Ending 12/31/X8

Zed Zennon, Acct #55-1212
(Copy B) (OMB No. 1545-0715)

Short-Term (Box 1)
Long-Term (Box 2)
Noncovered (Box 5)

Transactions for which Basis is not Reported to the IRS; Report on From 8949, Part II, with Box E checked.

Description of property

Activity Type	Quantity sold (Box 1a)	Date Acquired (Box 1b)	Date Sold (Box 1c)	Gross Proceeds (Box 1d)	Cost or Other Basis (Box 1e)	Unadjusted Gain/(Loss)	Code, If Any (Box 1f)	Adjustment (Box 1f)	Federal Income Tax Withheld (Box 1b)
DELL WEBER BANK CORP / 1494P / DWB									
Sale	100	3/20/X6	1/28/X8	42,300	50,000	(7,700)	W	00.00	00.00
AGRO GARDEN TERRACE, INC / 15694J / AGT									
Sale	3375	5/06/X6	4/06/X8	32,250	67,500	(35,250)		00.00	00.00
VNN COMMUNICATIONS / 9672TV9 / VNN									
Sale	240	5/05/X7	5/05/X8	18,700	24,200	(5,500)		00.00	00.00
ACE MUTUAL FUND									
Sale	500	Various	6/16/X8	90,000	Not Available			00.00	5,400.00

Items for Analysis

The gain or loss on the investment assets should be reported on his 1040, Schedule D and the business asset transactions on Form 4797.

1. **Choose an option below:**

    - [Original text] The gain or loss on the investment assets should be reported on his 1040, Schedule D and the business asset transactions on Form 4797.

    - The gain or loss on the investment assets should be reported on his 1040, Schedule B and the business asset transactions on the business's tax return.

    - The gain or loss on the investment assets should be reported on his 1040, Schedule D and the business asset transactions on Schedule C.

    - The gain or loss on the investment assets should be reported on his 1040, Schedule E and the business asset transactions on the business's tax return.

    - The gain or loss on the investment assets and the business assets should be reported on the business's tax return.

The recognized long-term capital losses are: Dell Weber Bank Corp, $7,700; Agro Garden Terrace, $35,250; and VNN Communications, $5,500. Ace Mutual funds gain cannot be determined due to missing data.

2. **Choose an option below:**

    - [Original text] The recognized long-term capital losses are: Dell Weber Bank Corp, $7,700; Agro Garden Terrace, $35,250; and VNN Communications, $5,500. Ace Mutual funds gain cannot be determined due to missing data.

    - The recognized long-term capital losses are: Dell Weber Bank Corp, $7,700; Agro Garden Terrace, $35,250; and VNN Communications, $5,500. Ace Mutual funds has a recognized $47,600 short-term capital gain.

    - The recognized capital losses are: Dell Weber Bank Corp, $7,700 long-term; Agro Garden Terrace, $35,250 short-term; and VNN Communications, $5,500 short-term. Ace Mutual funds has a recognized $6,800 long-term capital gain.

    - The recognized long-term capital losses are: Dell Weber Bank Corp, $7,700; Agro Garden Terrace, $35,250; and VNN Communications, $5,500. Ace Mutual funds has recognized gains of $2,600 short-term and $4,200 long-term.

    - The recognized capital losses are: Agro Garden Terrace $35,250 long-term and VNN Communications $5,500 short-term. The Dell Weber Bank Corp loss of $7,700 is not recognized because Zed bought the stock back within 30 days, causing it to be a wash sale. Ace Mutual funds has a recognized $13,200 long-term capital gain and a $6,400 short-term capital loss.

Since the painting was not depreciated, it appears that it is a personal capital asset and, therefore, the $35,000 gain would be a personal investment gain subject to a maximum tax rate of 20%.

3. **Choose an option below:**

   - [Original text] Since the painting was not depreciated, it appears that it is a personal capital asset and, therefore, the $35,000 gain would be a personal investment gain subject to a maximum tax rate of 20%.

   - Since the painting was not depreciated, it appears to meet the definition of a collectable capital asset and the $35,000 gain will be taxed at a maximum rate of 28%.

   - Since the painting was not depreciated, Zed will need to determine what useful life should have been used and treat part of the gain as Section 1245 recapture, because the painting should have been subject to MACRS.

   - Since the painting was not depreciated, it is not a business asset. The $35,000 gain will be taxed as an unrecaptured Section 1250 gain, with a maximum rate of 25%.

   - Since the painting was not depreciated, Zed will need to determine what useful life should have been used and file amended returns to claim MACRS depreciation and then treat part of the gain as Section 1245 recapture, and any remaining gain as capital subject to a maximum rate of 20%.

Office building—$22,821 Section 1245 recapture gain taxed as ordinary income

4. **Choose an option below:**

   - [Original text] Office building—$22,821 Section 1245 recapture gain taxed as ordinary income

   - Office building—$22,821 Section 1231 gain taxed at a maximum rate of 20%

   - Office building—$22,821 unrecaptured Section 1250 gain taxed at 25%

   - Office building—$12,821 Section 1250 recapture gain taxed as ordinary income, and $10,000 short-term capital gain

   - Office building—$4,564 Section 291 recapture, $12,821 Section 1250 recapture gain, and $5,436 Section 1231 gain

Computers—$176 Section 1231 ordinary loss

5. **Choose an option below:**

   - [Original text] Computers—$176 Section 1231 ordinary loss

   - Computers—$176 Section 1245 ordinary loss

   - Computers—$176 Section 1250 ordinary loss

   - Computers—$176 Section 1231 capital loss

   - Computers—$176 Section 1245 capital loss

Light trucks—$65,800 Section 1245 recapture gain taxed as ordinary income

6. **Choose an option below:**

   - [Original text] Light trucks—$65,800 Section 1245 recapture gain taxed as ordinary income

   - Light trucks—$65,800 Section 1245 recapture gain taxed as long-term capital gain

   - Light trucks—$62,800 Section 1245 recapture gain and $3,000 Section 1231 gain taxed as long-term capital gain

   - Light trucks—$62,800 Section 1245 recapture gain and $3,000 Section 1231 gain taxed as short-term capital gain

   - Light trucks—$62,800 Section 1250 recapture gain and $3,000 Section 1231 gain taxed as long-term capital gain

DOCUMENT REVIEW SIMULATION SOLUTION
Document Review Simulation Solution 1

Peat Moss, CPAs
File Memo

DATE: February 22, 20X9
BY: Jordan Staff
Re: Zed Zennon's Asset Sales for 20X8

Zed Zennon sold investment assets as well as assets from his manufacturing business. 1.) The gain or loss on the investment assets should be reported on his 1040, Schedule D and the business asset transactions on Form 4797.

Zed sold investments in three stocks and one mutual fund. 2.) The recognized capital losses are: Agro Garden Terrace $35,250 long-term and VNN Communications $5,500 short-term. The Dell Weber Bank Corp loss of $7,700 is not recognized because Zed bought back the stock within 30 days, causing it to be a wash sale. Ace Mutual Funds has a recognized $13,200 long-term capital gain and a $6,400 short-term capital loss.

The business assets that Zed sold include an office building and associated land, computers, and light trucks. The office building, computers, and light trucks were subject to MACRS, while the land and the painting were not subject to cost recovery because they have unspecified lives. 3.) Since the painting was not depreciated, it appears to meet the definition of a collectible capital asset, and the $35,000 gain will be taxed at a maximum rate of 28%. The gains or losses for the other assets are categorized as follows:

- 4.) Office building—$12,821 Section 1250 recapture gain taxed as ordinary income, and $10,000 short-term capital gain
- 5.) Computers—$176 Section 1231 ordinary loss
- 6.) Light trucks—$62,800 Section 1245 recapture gain and $3,000 Section 1231 gain taxed as long-term capital gain

Explanation of solutions

1. **[Original text] The gain or loss on the investment assets should be reported on his 1040, Schedule D and the business asset transactions on Form 4797.**

    Form 1040, Schedule D reports an individual's capital gains and losses, and Form 4797 is for reporting sales of business property. Form 1040, Schedule B reports interest and ordinary dividends. Because Zed Zennon's manufacturing business is a sole proprietorship, his business operations are reported on his Form 1040, Schedule C. Schedule E reports supplemental income and loss from rentals, royalties, partnerships, S corps, estates, trusts, etc.

2. **The recognized capital losses are: Agro Garden Terrace $35,250 long-term and VNN Communications $5,500 short-term. The Dell Weber Bank Corp loss of $7,700 is not recognized because Zed bought back the stock within 30 days, causing it to be a wash sale. Ace Mutual Funds has a recognized $13,200 long-term capital gain and a $6,400 short-term capital loss.**

    The losses and holding periods for 3 of the 4 investments are provided on the 1099-B:

    *   Agro Garden Terrace is a long-term (held longer than 1 year, from 5/6/X6 to 4/6/X8) loss of $35,250.
    *   VNN Communications is a short-term (held for exactly 1 year, from 5/5/X7 to 5/5/X8) loss of $5,500. Note: Investments must be held *longer* than 1 year to be considered long-term.
    *   The Dell Weber Bank Corp loss of $7,700 would have been a long-term loss, but it is not recognized because Zed bought back the stock within 30 days, causing it to be a wash sale. You know this is the case by looking at the acquisition documents, where it provides that Zed purchased Dell Weber Bank Corp stock again on 2/19/X8, only 22 days after he sold the stock for a loss on 1/28/X8.

    In order to determine the capital gain/loss on the Ace Mutual Fund investments, one must compare the gross proceeds received given on 1099-B to the original cost of the investments provided on the acquisition documents. Because more than one batch of shares is sold in a single transaction, the gross proceeds must be allocated between the batches bought:

    * $90,000 proceeds/500 shares sold = $180 per share sale price.
    * $180 per share sale price - $136 per share purchase price on batch 1 = $44 gain per share × 300 shares = $13,200 long-term (held from 2/20/X6 to 6/16/X8) capital gain.
    * $180 per share sale price × 200 shares in batch 2 = $36,000 proceeds - $42,400 total acquisition cost = $6,400 short-term (held less than 1 year, from 9/13/X7 to 6/16/X8) capital loss.

3. **Since the painting was not depreciated, it appears to meet the definition of a collectible capital asset, and the $35,000 gain will be taxed at a maximum rate of 28%.**

    While long-term capital gains are generally taxed at a maximum rate of 20%, certain assets considered collectibles are taxed at a rate of 28%. Collectibles include items such as works of art, antiques, jewelry, stamps, coins, etc. Since the painting was not depreciated, it appears to meet the definition of a collectible capital asset, so the $35,000 gain will be taxed at a maximum rate of 28%. Sections 1245 and 1250 apply to depreciable property used in a business.

4. **Office building—$12,821 Section 1250 recapture gain taxed as ordinary income, and $10,000 short-term capital gain**

   Section 1250 property includes depreciable real property, such as buildings and structural components. Section 1250 recaptures gain on the sale of real property as ordinary income to the extent of "additional depreciation" taken on the property. Any depreciation taken in excess of the straight-line method is considered to be additional depreciation. Any depreciation taken on a property held for less than one year is considered to be additional depreciation for purposes of Section 1250 as well. Any gain in excess of the amount recaptured as ordinary income is treated as unrecaptured Section 1250 gain and is taxed at a special capital gain rate of 25%. However, because the building was held for less than one year (1/20/X8 to 12/18/X8), the building is not considered Section 1231 property, so none of the gain qualifies for special tax rates. Note: Section 291 does not apply to individuals, only C corporations.

5. **[Original text] Computers—$176 Section 1231 ordinary loss**

   Losses on Section 1231 property, such as computers used in a business, are treated as ordinary losses for tax purposes. Gains on Section 1231 property, on the other hand, are treated as long-term capital gains for tax purposes. However, Section 1245 applies to gains on Section 1231 personal property first to recapture any depreciation taken as ordinary income. Section 1250 applies to real property.

6. **Light trucks—$62,800 Section 1245 recapture gain and $3,000 Section 1231 gain taxed as long-term capital gain**

   While gains on Section 1231 property are generally treated as long-term capital gains for tax purposes. Section 1245 applies to gains on Section 1231 personal property first to recapture any depreciation allowed on the property. Since $62,800 of depreciation was taken on the light trucks, $62,800 of the $65,800 gain is Section 1245 recapture gain taxed as ordinary income; the remaining $3,000 is Section 1231 gain taxed as long-term capital gain. Section 1250 applies to real property.

Section 8 – Tax-Exempt Organizations

Corresponding Lecture

Watch the following course lecture with this section:

Lecture 8.01 – Tax-Exempt Organizations
Lecture 8.02 – Tax-Exempt Organizations – Class Questions

EXAM NOTE: *Please refer to the AICPA REG Blueprint in the Introduction to find a listing of the representative tasks (and their associated skill levels—i.e., Remembering and Understanding, Application, and Analysis) that the candidate should be able to perform based on the knowledge obtained in this section.*

Tax-Exempt Organizations (Form 990)

TAX-EXEMPT ORGANIZATIONS

Certain organizations are eligible to be classified as **exempt organizations** once approved by the IRS. To be considered exempt, the organization must be one of those specifically identified in the tax code and must apply for and receive an exemption. These are covered in the IRC as a 501(c). There are more than 19 different classifications under IRC Section 501(c) that are eligible for exempt status. Some examples:

- Organizations with specific charitable, educational or scientific intent
- Religious organizations
- Social and recreation clubs (fraternity or country clubs)
- Credit unions
- Condo associations
- Labor unions

Any organization that attempts to influence political legislation or support specific political candidates is denied exempt status.

An organization seeking tax-exempt status under IRC Section 501(c)(3) will complete a Form 1023. There is, however, a streamlined process for applying for tax-exempt status under this code section for applicants meeting certain requirements, including a requirement that gross receipts are NOT expected to exceed $50,000 in any of the succeeding 3 years. A qualifying organization will complete a Form 1023-EZ.

Charitable organizations are classified as **private foundations** if they receive less than 1/3 of support from the general public, and **public charities** if they receive more. An organization does **not** qualify as an exempt charity if it is merely a **feeder organization**, which is an organization operated as a business for profit but that transfers all of its net earnings to charitable organizations.

Generally, exempt status is not automatic; a written application (Form 1023) must be filed with the IRS requesting approval as an exempt organization within **27 months** from the end of the month in which they were organized. The organization generally must operate in the form of a:

- **Corporation** or
- **Trust**.

Note: Public charities with no more than $5,000 of gross receipts and religious organizations are automatically exempt if they meet the Section 501(c)(3) requirements; i.e., they need not file Form 1023.

An organization must limit its activities to those that fit the classification of exempt organization it is using as the basis for its application to the IRS. **For example**, if an organization is approved for exempt status as a private foundation and then receives the majority of its support in one year from the general public, its exempt status will terminate since it no longer operates in accordance with its category restriction. It must then reapply for exemption as a public charity.

Even though an organization is exempt, it is required to file an annual information return (**Form 990**) identifying its sources of revenue if gross receipts exceed **$50,000 in a year**. This requirement doesn't apply to **religious organizations (a church)**, however, due to the constitutional prohibition on government regulation of religious activities.

If the organization is a private foundation, it instead files a Form 990-PF, and may be subject to certain excise taxes on various investment income and transactions that occur with the person who funded the organization.

- Due date for exempt organization returns is **May 15**, with a 6-month extension available (no longer tested).

Unrelated Business Income (UBI)

Any exempt organization will have to file a business income tax return (Form 990-T) and pay income taxes if it has more than **$1,000** of **unrelated business income (UBI)**. If the organization is in the form of a corporation, it will pay at corporate tax rates, and if it is a trust, at trust tax rates. Estimated taxes are also due if it expects to owe more than $500 in taxes for the year.

Unrelated business income refers to income obtained from the operations of business activities not associated with the exempt purpose of the organization. The definition of unrelated business income specifically **excludes**:

- Legal games of chance used to raise funds, such as **bingo.**
- Activities only carried out on an intermittent basis, such as annual charity auctions.
- Business activities **related to the organization's purpose,** such as sales of educational materials to members of a professional organization established to maintain and improve the skills of its members.
- Most investment income.
- Activities that are staffed entirely by volunteers working without pay.
- The sale of merchandise that was received as a gift or contribution.
- Convenience of members, employees or students (e.g., cafeteria or bookstore).

Tax-Exempt Organizations

Form It	Filings	UBI (Unrelated Business Income)
Must fall under specific categories	**5/15** – Information Return Due- Form 990	Tattoo parlor @ church or school
Corporation OR Trust	Identify contributors	Taxed as either a corporation or trust
27 months to file paperwork when comes into existence	Identify amount contributed	**UBI** **(Expenses)** **($1,000)** = **UBTI** — Corp Rate / Trust Rate
Public/Private 1) Private = Most of funding comes from private foundation or group of people, 2) Rest are Public	Identify gross receipts/distributions	Either goods (Goodwill) or services (hospital gift shop) have to be free in order to not be taxed on UBI.
	UNLESS → No return 1) You are a CHURCH 2) Gross receipts < **$50,000**	• **Exceptions** = Campus Bookstore and Cafeteria • Related → for the benefit of the members (students)

Lecture 8.02

CLASS QUESTIONS

Please see the Class Questions and Class Solutions for this Lecture at the end of this Section.

CLASS QUESTIONS

Work through the below Class Questions while following along with the respective lectures. Once this is complete, you can begin independently practicing what you've learned by quizzing yourself on this course section in your Interactive Practice Questions (IPQ), which can be found in your online Student Dashboard. Your IPQ simulates the computer-based testing experience, and will also help you understand how concepts are applied to the exam. Each question includes answer explanations from expert CPAs that will help you determine why you answered a question correctly or incorrectly. This is key to your success on the CPA Exam.

Lecture 8.02

1. Which of the following exempt organizations must file annual information returns?

    a. Churches
    b. Internally supported auxiliaries of churches
    c. Private foundations
    d. Those with gross receipts of less than $25,000 in each taxable year

2. The filing of a return covering unrelated business income

    a. Is required of all exempt organizations having at least $1,000 of unrelated business taxable income for the year.
    b. Relieves the organization of having to file a separate annual information return.
    c. Is **not** necessary if all of the organization's income is used exclusively for charitable purposes.
    d. Must be accompanied by a minimum payment of 50% of the tax due as shown on the return, with the balance of tax payable six months later.

3. An organization that operates for the prevention of cruelty to animals will fail to meet the operational test to qualify as an exempt organization if

	The organization engages in insubstantial nonexempt activities	The organization directly participates in any political campaign
a.	Yes	Yes
b.	Yes	No
c.	No	Yes
d.	No	No

4. Which of the following statements is correct regarding the unrelated business income of exempt organizations?

    a. If an exempt organization has any unrelated business income, it may result in the loss of the organization's exempt status.

    b. Unrelated business income relates to the performance of services, but **not** to the sale of goods.

    c. An unrelated business does **not** include any activity where all the work is performed for the organization by unpaid volunteers.

    d. Unrelated business income tax will **not** be imposed if profits from the unrelated business are used to support the exempt organization's charitable activities.

5. If an exempt organization is a corporation, the tax on unrelated business taxable income is

    a. Computed at corporate income tax rates.

    b. Computed at rates applicable to trusts.

    c. Credited against the tax on recognized capital gains.

    d. Abated.

CLASS SOLUTIONS

1. (c) Private foundations are required to file an annual information return, Form 990-PF. Churches and internally supported auxiliaries of churches are not required to file due to the constitutional prohibition against regulating religious organization. Other exempt organizations are required to file information return Form 990 if they have gross receipts in excess of $50,000.

2. (a) A not-for-profit organization is required to file a business income tax return when it has unrelated business income (UBI) of $1,000 or more. Answer (b) is incorrect because if it is a private foundation or a nonreligious exempt organization with gross receipts in excess of $50,000, it is also required to file an information return. Answer (c) is incorrect because filing a return is required regardless of whether all UBI is used exclusively for charitable purposes if such income exceeds the $1,000 threshold. Answer (d) is incorrect because taxes due on UBI are payable at the time that the return is due.

3. (c) An organization that otherwise would qualify as an exempt organization, such as one operating for the prevention of cruelty to animals, will fail to qualify as an exempt organization if it has substantial, not insubstantial, activities that are unrelated to its exempt purpose or if it directly participates in any political campaign.

4. (c) Unrelated business income (UBI) excludes any activity that is staffed exclusively by volunteers working without pay. UBI is taxable to an exempt organization, but it does not disqualify the organization from exempt status. UBI relates to the performance of services or the sale of goods, unless those goods were all received by gift or donation.

5. (a) Unrelated business income (UBI) is taxable to an exempt organization. The tax is computed on the basis of how it would be computed for comparable organizations—at the corporate rate for corporate entities, and at the rate for trusts if the exempt organization is a trust. The UBI tax is not credited against tax recognized on capital gains, and the UBI tax is not abated.

TASK-BASED SIMULATIONS

Task-Based Simulation 1

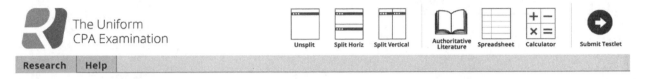

A group has decided to establish a not-for-profit organization for charitable purposes and is trying to determine if it is tax exempt.

Which code section, subsection, and paragraph indicates whether or not the organization may qualify as a tax-exempt organization?

Task-Based Simulation 2

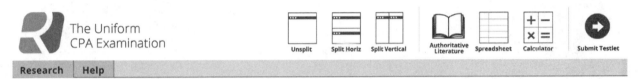

A tax-exempt organization is involved in a variety of revenue-producing activities and is trying to figure out which, if any, are considered revenues from an unrelated trade or business activity.

Which code section and subsection describe what is considered to be an unrelated trade or business?

TASK-BASED SIMULATION SOLUTIONS

Task-Based Simulation Solution 1

501	(c)	(3)

Task-Based Simulation Solution 2

513	(a)

Section 9 – Filing Requirements & Preparer Penalties

Corresponding Lectures

Watch the following course lectures with this section:

Lecture 9.01 – Filing Requirements and Preparers' Penalties
Lecture 9.02 – Multijurisdictional Tax
Lecture 9.03 – Filing Requirements and Preparers' Penalties – Class
         Questions
Lecture 9.04 – Filing Requirements and Preparer Penalties – Class
         Questions – TBS

EXAM NOTE: *Please refer to the AICPA REG Blueprint in the Introduction to find a listing of the representative tasks (and their associated skill levels—i.e., Remembering and Understanding, Application, and Analysis) that the candidate should be able to perform based on the knowledge obtained in this section.*

Filing Requirements & Preparer Penalties

CORPORATE REQUIREMENTS

A corporation is required to make quarterly **estimated tax payments** during the tax year, and is subject to a penalty for underpayment of taxes if the tax liability has not been paid in four equal installments over the course of the tax year. The quarterly estimated tax payments are due by the *15th day of the 4th, 6th, 9th and 12th* months of its taxable year (1120-ES). The penalty doesn't apply, however, if one of the following **exceptions** occurs:

- **Small balance** - The total underpayment is less than **$500.**
- **Annualized income** – The installments each quarter cover the tax on the income to date, assuming total income will, for the full 12 months, be in proportion to the income to date (e.g., the income for the first 3 months will be divided by 3/12 to estimate the full year income in determining the first quarter estimated payment).
- **Seasonal method** – The installments each quarter cover the tax on the income to date, assuming total income will, for the full 12 months, bear the same relationship to the income to date as it has, on average, in the previous 3 fiscal years (e.g., if the income during the first quarter has averaged 40% of the total annual income over the previous 3 years, the income for the first 3 months of this year will be divided by 40% to estimate the full year income in determining the first quarter estimated payment).
- **Previous year** – The payments equal at least **100% of the prior year** tax liability.

    Note: This last exception may not be used to escape a penalty, however, if either:
    - There was no tax liability in the previous year, or
    - The corporation had taxable income exceeding $1 million in any of the preceding 3 tax years.

The corporate return is due by the 15th day of the 4th month following the close of the corporation's tax year (**April 15** for calendar-year corporations). A corporation must file a return each year it is in operation, even if it has no taxable income.

For calendar year corporations, an **automatic extension** of the due date for **5 months** is available. Fiscal year corporations get a 6-month automatic extension, except corporations with a fiscal year ending June 30, which get a 7-month automatic extension. **An extension does not extend the time to pay, only the time to file.** If the entire tax liability is not paid by the original due date of the return, interest will be owed to the IRS on the unpaid balance. In addition, if the amount paid by the original due date is less than 90% of the total tax liability, a monthly delinquency penalty will be owed in addition to the interest charges.

If part of a tax underpayment is the result of fraud (i.e., the actual, deliberate or intentional misreporting of taxable income with the specific purpose of evading a tax believed to be owing), there is an additional penalty equal to 75% of the portion of the underpayment attributable to the fraud.

There is also a time limit for a **claim of refund** by means of an amended tax return by a taxpayer (**1120X**). The limit is the *later of*:
- **3 years** after original tax return was filed
    - If filed late, 3 years from date return was due (including extensions)

- **2 years** after actual tax was paid

Note: Tax return due dates, extensions, and statutes of limitation are no longer tested on the CPA exam.

INDIVIDUAL REQUIREMENTS

Individual taxpayers who have withholding on salaries and wages may not need to make estimated tax payments to the IRS during the year. If **estimated tax payments** are required, they are due by the 15th day of the *4th, 6th & 9th* months of the taxable year and by the *15th of January* (1040-ES). An individual is only subject to an underpayment penalty if the balance due on the tax return is greater than **$1,000**. Even then, there are certain exceptions to the penalty that are available:
- **Prior year tax liability** – No penalty is assessed if the withholdings and estimated payments totaled at least **100%** of the prior year tax liability, unless the taxpayer had *more than $150,000 of AGI* in the prior year. In the latter case, payments must exceed *110%* of the prior year tax liability in order to utilize this exception in the current year.
- **Annualized income method** – No penalty is assessed if the cumulative payments for each quarter cover the tax on the income to date (assuming it continues at the same rate for the remainder of the year).
- **Current tax liability** – No penalty is assessed if the payments covered at least **90%** of the current tax liability.

Any balance due must be paid by April 15, the normal due date for the individual return. An individual can obtain an automatic extension of the due date for the return until October 15 (6 months), but the extension is only for the filing, not the payment of the entire tax. Interest is charged from April 15 to the date of actual payment. In addition, there are penalties of *0.5% per month for late payment*, and *5% per month for late filing or not filing*. Both penalties have a maximum of 25% of the net tax owed. There are additional civil penalties related to negligence and substantial understatement of tax liability on the return, and civil and criminal penalties for fraud on the return. Both penalties are based on the amount of Net tax due.

An **accuracy-related penalty of 20%** of the underpayment applies if the underpayment of tax is attributable to negligence or disregard of rules and regulations, any substantial understatement of income tax, any substantial valuation overstatement, any substantial overstatement of pension liabilities, or any substantial gift or estate tax valuation understatement.

Unlike corporations, an individual is not **required to file a tax return** if the gross income during the year is clearly insufficient for any tax liability to result. This is the case if the gross income of the taxpayer for the year does not exceed the **sum of:**
- Personal exemptions for the taxpayer and spouse.
- The basic standard deduction based on filing status.
- The additional standard deductions based on age ($\geq$ 65)

For purposes of determining whether a return has to be filed, the taxpayer cannot consider dependent exemptions nor the additional standard deductions based on blindness, since these are not automatically available without supporting evidence.

Even if the taxpayer does not have gross income exceeding the calculated limit, a return must be filed if the taxpayer's income from **self-employment exceeds $400**, since self-employment taxes may be owed, even though income taxes are not.

TAX EXAMINATIONS AND PROCEDURES

While many tax returns are randomly selected for examination, tax returns also may be selected for examination for any number of reasons.

- A high score on the IRS computerized Discriminant Inventory Function System will not only cause a return to be selected for examination, but also indicates a high likelihood that the examination will result in a change in the tax liability.
- Returns are selected when information does not agree with that received from third parties in the form of W-2s or 1099s.
- Returns are examined when some source, including newspaper articles, public records, and individuals, provides information to the IRS regarding potential noncompliance.

The taxpayer is notified by letter that the return will be examined, at which time the examination begins. A taxpayer may wish to be represented in the examination proceeding, in which case a Form 2848 is completed.

If a taxpayer does not agree with a proposed adjustment that results from an examination of a return, one alternative is fast track mediation, which is often used to resolve disputes involving examinations, **offers in compromise**, trust fund recovery penalties, and other collection actions. Offers in compromise can be filed by a taxpayer to obtain a reduction in the amount of tax owed. The IRS will consider an offer in compromise if one of the following applies:

- The amount owed, or whether it is owed, is in doubt.
- The taxpayer's ability to pay the amount owed is in doubt.
- The taxpayer would suffer an economic hardship if required to pay the entire amount.
- The IRS determines that the case presents compelling reasons that are a sufficient basis for compromise.

Upon completion of an examination, there will be a closing conference with the examiner or a supervisor, after which the taxpayer will receive a **30-day letter** with a copy of the examination report. This gives the taxpayer 30 days to accept or appeal proposed changes.

If an agreement is not reached, or if the taxpayer does not respond to the 30-day letter, a **notice of deficiency**, often referred to as a **90-day letter**, is sent. This allows the taxpayer 90 days (150 days if taxpayer's address is outside the U.S.) to file a petition with the Tax Court.

As an alternative to Tax Court, a taxpayer can bring the matter to an **IRS Appeals Office**, which is the only level of appeal within the IRS. If agreement is not reached, the taxpayer may be eligible to take the matter to a court, such as the U.S. Tax Court, the U.S. Court of Federal Claims, or a U.S. District Court. The U.S. Tax Court will generally not hear a case until after it has been considered for settlement by an Appeals Office.

Tax Court hears cases related to income tax; estate tax; gift tax; or certain excise taxes of private foundations, public charities, qualified pension and other retirement plans, or real estate investment trusts. Taxes may be assessed and paid before going to Tax Court, but it is not required. In addition, if a petition is not filed on a timely basis, the taxpayer forfeits the opportunity to go to Tax Court and will be billed.

The **District Courts** and the **Court of Federal Claims** will generally not hear a case until after the tax has been paid and a claim for credit or refund has been filed. A suit may be filed any time within 2 years after a claim has been rejected and as early as 6 months after a claim has been filed if the IRS has not delivered a decision. The Court of Federal Claims will not hear a case involving a claim for a refund of a penalty related to an abusive tax shelter or to aiding and abetting the understatement of tax on someone else's return.

In court proceedings, the burden of proof is on the IRS, provided the taxpayer:
- Introduced credible evidence supporting the position being taken;
- Complied with IRS substantiation requirements;
- Maintained required records; and
- Cooperated with all reasonable requests for information.

If, however, the taxpayer is a corporation, partnership, or trust, the burden of proof will be on the IRS only if net worth did not exceed $7 million and the entity had no more than 500 employees at the time the tax liability is contested in court.

An unfavorable decision in any of the 3 courts may be brought before the U.S. Court of Appeals. Circuit courts of appeals will retry cases from lower courts. If there is a conflict between different circuit courts of appeals, the case may be taken before the U.S. Supreme Court.

TAX SHELTERS

Certain activities are listed as "reportable transactions" under the federal tax code, and must be specifically disclosed when the return is filed. These include all registered tax shelters as well as any special arrangement that changes reportable income by more than $10 million. Penalties apply for the failure to disclose such activities, even when there is no determination of an underpayment of taxes. Such activities must also meet the higher standard of "more likely than not" to succeed on its merits for the preparer to avoid penalty under IRC Section 6694 for understatement of a taxpayer's liability.

PREPARER RESPONSIBILITIES

The AICPA's *Statements on Standards for Tax Services* (SSTSs) are enforceable tax practice standards with which all AICPA members providing tax services must abide. Note, however, the SSTSs are no longer tested on the CPA exam.

There are several special obligations imposed on paid tax return preparers. Penalties for failure to comply with such obligations apply under IRC Sec. 6695. A "tax return preparer" for these purposes includes anyone who prepares *for compensation*, or who employs one or more persons to prepare, all or a substantial portion of any tax return or claim for refund. Does not include those who provide typing, reproduction, or other mechanical assistance. Also, a person who prepares a personal return for their employer (i.e., the return of an officer, partner, member, shareholder, etc.) is not considered a "tax return preparer."
- The preparer must **sign** the preparer's declaration on the tax return and provide their preparer tax identification number (i.e., **PTIN**).
- The return must be timely filed and a **copy** of the completed return must be provided to the taxpayer.
- The preparer must **retain** either **documentation** of the taxpayer's name and tax identification number or a copy of the prepared return for **3 years**.
- The preparer need not obtain from the taxpayer documentation of information provided to prepare the return, but must make *reasonable inquiries* about the existence of such support where appropriate. **For example**, the preparer should ask the client if travel and

entertainment costs are supported by a log and if charitable contributions exceeding $250 are supported by receipts from the charities.

Penalties are assessed against preparers who **knowingly** or **recklessly**:
- Understate the tax liability of a client.
- Giving erroneous advice or fail to advise a client of tax elections available.
- Endorse or negotiate a refund check for their own account.
- Adopt a frivolous position on a tax issue ($5,000 penalty).

In addition, a preparer may be held responsible for errors in the preparation of the return, but may escape liability based on exceptions for **good faith** or **reasonable cause**, when the error results from:
- Utilizing the services of a computerized tax preparation service.
- Obtaining advice from another professional on tax questions.
- Following inaccurate IRS form instructions or advice from an IRS employee.

If the preparer adopts a **non-frivolous** position (i.e., there is a reasonable basis for the position) in the tax treatment of an item that fails to meet the **substantial authority** standard, no penalty is assessed against the preparer if the position adopted is **disclosed** on the return.

A preparer is subject to a penalty equal to the greater of $1,000, or 50% of the income derived by the preparer with respect to the return or refund claim if any part of an understatement of liability is due to an *undisclosed position* on the return for which there is *not a reasonable belief* that the position is backed by **substantial authority**.
- The *substantial authority* standard requires about 40% probability of being sustained on its merits, in contrast to the *more likely than not* standard, which requires a 50% likelihood of success, and the *realistic possibility* standard, which requires a 33% likelihood of success.
- The penalty can be avoided by (1) adequate disclosure of the questionable position on the return or refund claim, and (2) showing that there was a reasonable basis for the position. The reasonable basis standard may require at least a 20% probability of being sustained on its merits.
- The penalty can also be avoided if the preparer can show there was a *reasonable cause* for the understatement and that the return preparer acted in *good faith*.

So, to put the likelihoods in order:
- *More likely than not* standard > 50% probability of success if tax position is challenged
- *Substantial authority* standard ≈ 40% probability of success (≈ approximately)
- *Realistic possibility* of success ≈ 33% (1/3) probability of success
- *Reasonable basis* standard ≈ 20% probability of success.

Any additional taxes and interest owed as a result of an error are entirely the responsibility of the taxpayer and not the preparer. The taxpayer may also be subject to negligence or fraud penalties in addition to any penalties the preparer is assessed if the taxpayer is determined to have committed a penalty offense of their own.

Information that is obtained from a client in connection with the preparation of their tax return is **confidential**, and the preparer is not permitted to use it for personal benefit or reveal this information to third parties without the consent of the taxpayer except in limited circumstances. The most important exceptions are:
- To respond to a valid government order (while discussions between CPAs and clients on federal tax matters are privileged, this does not apply to criminal matters and tax shelters).

- As part of a quality control peer review program.
- To permit the electronic preparation or submission of the taxpayer's return.
- To secure legal advice from an attorney.

A CPA is not obligated to inform the IRS or any other taxing authority of a client's failure to file a prior year return without the client's permission, although there is an obligation to promptly inform the client upon becoming aware of such a circumstance. Also, a CPA does owe a duty to inform a client if there are material errors in a previously filed tax return so that the client may file an amended return.

If a taxpayer is assessed additional taxes, the IRS will issue a 30-day letter. Upon the receipt of a 30-day letter, a taxpayer who wishes to dispute the findings has 30 days to (1) request a conference with an appeals officer or file a written protest letter, or (2) may elect to do nothing during the 30-day period and await a 90-day letter. The taxpayer would then have 90 days to file a petition with the Tax Court. A taxpayer also may choose to pay the additional taxes and file a claim for refund. When the refund claim is disallowed, the taxpayer could then commence an action in federal district court.

Income Tax Return Preparer Penalties

Penalties Imposed for	Amount of Penalty
Understatement of tax caused by: • Undisclosed position lacking substantial authority • Preparer's reckless or intentional disregard of rules or regulations	> of $1,000 or 50% of return prep fee > of $5,000 or 75% of return prep fee These amounts are **not** slated for inflation adjustment.
Failure to furnish copy of return to taxpayer	$50 per return/ up to $25,500 yr (2017)
Endorsing or negotiating taxpayer's refund check	$510 per check (2017) – unlimited
Improper disclosure of return information	$250 for each disclosure, maximum of $10,000: Criminal penalty of up to $1,000 or 1 year in prison, or both This amount is **not** slated for inflation adjustment.
Failure to sign return	$50 per return/ up to $25,500 yr (2017)
Failure to furnish identifying number of preparer on return	$50 per return/ up to $25,500 yr (2017)
Failure to retain a copy of return for 3 years or maintain a list of names and ID numbers of the taxpayers for whom the returns were prepared	$50 per return/ up to $25,500 yr (2017)
Failure to retain and make available a list of the tax return preparers employed	$50 per preparer/ up to $25,500 yr (2017)
Fraudulent or deceptive conduct, including misrepresentation of eligibility to practice before the IRS	The courts may enjoin such person from further engaging in such conduct.

MULTIJURISDICTIONAL TAX

State and Local Tax Issues

In general, an entity is allowed to do business in states other than the one in which it was formed or is physically located. **Public Law 86-272**, referred to as the *Interstate Income Act of 1959*, allows a business to go, or send a representative, into a state to solicit orders for goods without being subject to a net income tax. The law applies exclusively to orders for tangible personal property and either:

- Orders solicited by employees are approved, and shipped from, outside the state; or
- Orders solicited by independent contractors that are shipped from outside the state.

A state may impose an income tax on an entity that is doing business in that state if the entity establishes **nexus** in a state, indicating that it has a presence in that state. Although the requirements for nexus vary from state to state, nexus is generally created for income tax purposes when an entity derives income from sources within the state, has employees in the state engaged in activities other than solicitation, or has capital or property in the state.

As a result of the various nexus laws, an entity may be taxable in various jurisdictions. To avoid being taxed on the same income in multiple jurisdictions, income will be allocated among the jurisdictions in which the entity is subject to income tax. The model that is used for allocating income is the **Uniform Division of Income for Tax Purposes Act** (**UDITPA**). The allocations are dependent on the **nature of the income**:

- Net rents and royalties from real property are generally allocated to the state in which the property is located, while net rents or royalties from tangible personal property is generally allocated to the state in which the property is used.
    - If the entity is not subject to income tax in the state in which property is used, net rents and royalties are allocated to the state in which the entity is domiciled (headquartered).
    - If the property is utilized in multiple jurisdictions, income will be allocated to each on the basis of the ratio of the number of days the property earned rents or royalties in that state to the total number of days on which rents or royalties were earned from use of the property.
- The allocation of capital gains and losses is affected by the nature of the property.
    - Capital gains and losses on the sale of real estate are allocated to the state in which the real estate is located.
    - Capital gains and losses on the sale of tangible personal property are allocated to the state in which the property is located unless the entity is not subject to income tax in that state, in which case it is allocated to the state in which the entity is domiciled.
    - Capital gains and losses on the sale of intangible personal property are allocated to the state in which the entity is domiciled.
- Interest and dividends are allocated to the state in which the entity is domiciled.
- Royalties on patents and copyrights are allocated to the state in which they are used by the payer of the royalties or, when the entity is not subject to income tax in that state, it is allocated to the entity's state of domicile.
    - A patent is utilized in a state if the patented product is produced in the state.
    - A copyright is utilized in a state if printing or publication originates in it.
- Business income is multiplied by a ratio that is based on the entity's property holdings, payroll, and sales.

<u>The entity calculates 3 ratios (property, payroll, sales)</u>

1. The average value of the entity's real and tangible personal property owned, valued at its original cost, or rented, valued at 8 times net annual rent, and used by the entity in the state during the tax period is divided by the average value of all real and tangible personal property owned or rented and used by the entity for the period.
2. The total amount paid for compensation (payroll) in the state by the entity is divided by the total compensation paid everywhere.
3. Total sales by the entity in the state during the tax period are divided by the entity's total sales made everywhere.
    - The three ratios are added together and divided by 3.
    - The result is multiplied by business income to determine the amount allocated to the state.

International Tax Issues

Income Taxes - Many companies try to minimize their taxes by locating operations in foreign countries with lower tax rates, known as "*tax havens*." The United States has a few rules to combat this abusive behavior, but the method depends on the type of foreign operation:

- **Foreign Branch** – a business operation carried on by a U.S. corporation, partnership, trust, estate, or individual, outside the United States. Such an activity must be considered a permanent establishment under the terms of a treaty between the United States and the foreign country.
    - Taxed on current U.S. income and losses are deductible.

- **Foreign Subsidiary** – a company incorporated under the laws of a foreign country where it is located, but which is partially or wholly owned by a U.S. corporation.
    - U.S. income tax is generally deferred until profits are repatriated back to U.S. in the form of dividends, and losses are *not* deductible.
    - **Controlled Foreign Corporation (CFC)** is a foreign corporation where U.S. shareholders own more than 50% of the total voting power or value of all classes of the corporation's stock.
        - **Subpart F Income of a Foreign Base Company** – To prevent a taxpayer from deferring income tax on certain movable income and shifting such income to a controlled foreign entity that may be taxed at a lower tax rate, every shareholder who, on the last day of the tax year, owns, directly or indirectly, 10% or more of the voting stock in a foreign corporation that was a CFC for 30 or more continuous days during that taxable year will include the taxpayer's share of Subpart F income in gross income, regardless of whether the CFC actually makes a distribution. Subpart F income of a CFC is the sum of various factors that includes foreign base company income. There are 3 main categories of foreign base company income:
            - Foreign base company *sales* income – income received by a CFC from the purchase or sale of personal property involving a related person.
            - Foreign base company *services* income – income from the performance of services by or on behalf of a related person.
            - Foreign *personal holding company* income – investment income such as dividends, interest, rents and royalties.

Foreign base company income is essentially income earned by a CFC that results from the purchase/sale, from or on behalf of a related party, of property that is manufactured, produced, or extracted outside of the country of the CFC's organization and is sold for use, consumption, or disposition outside of the country of its organization. This might also be the case, for example, if a CFC provides services to an entity in another country as the result of a contract entered into by the CFC's parent from the United States.

Withholding taxes – Salaries, wages, etc., paid to a nonresident alien (NRA) are subject to withholding in the same way as for U.S. citizens/residents if they are effectively connected with the conduct of a U.S. trade or business. However, the following types of U.S.-sourced income paid to NRAs are generally subject to withholding at 30%, unless a tax treaty provides for a lesser rate, or exemption:

- Nonemployee compensation
- Athletes and entertainers
- Interest Income effectively connected with a U.S. trade or business
- Dividend income
- Royalties
- Pensions and annuities
- Alimony
- Taxable scholarships/fellowships
- Social Security pensions – 85% of the U.S. Social Security pension paid to an NRA is taxable at the rate of 30%, for an effective rate of tax of 25.5%. The Social Security Administration generally withholds 25.5% federal income tax on U.S. Social Security pensions paid to NRAs.

Source rules – The following rules determine whether certain types of income are considered to be U.S. or foreign-sourced:

- The country of the payor determines the source of interest Income and dividends.
- The location of property rented/used/sold determines the source of rents, royalties, and gain on the sale of real property.
- The location of services performed determines the source of payments for services.
- The location at which title to inventory passes determines the source of gain on the sale of inventory.

Foreign Tax Credit

$$\text{U.S. tax liability} \times \frac{\text{Foreign income}}{\text{Worldwide income}} = \text{Foreign tax credit (not to exceed foreign tax paid)}$$

The foreign tax credit is available for income taxes paid to foreign countries on foreign-source income that is also reported on a U.S. tax return. The credit is limited to the portion of the U.S. tax that applies to the income on which a foreign tax was also assessed.

Lecture 9.03

CLASS QUESTIONS

Please see the Class Questions and Class Solutions for this Lecture at the end of this Section.

Lecture 9.04

CLASS QUESTIONS

Please see the Class Questions and Class Solutions for this Lecture at the end of this Section.

CLASS QUESTIONS

Work through the below Class Questions while following along with the respective lectures. Once this is complete, you can begin independently practicing what you've learned by quizzing yourself on this course section in your Interactive Practice Questions (IPQ), which can be found in your online Student Dashboard. Your IPQ simulates the computer-based testing experience, and will also help you understand how concepts are applied to the exam. Each question includes answer explanations from expert CPAs that will help you determine why you answered a question correctly or incorrectly. This is key to your success on the CPA Exam.

Lecture 9.03

1. In which of the following situations will a controlled foreign corporation located in Ireland be deemed to have Subpart F income?

    a. Services are provided by an Irish company in England under a contract entered into by its U.S. parent.
    b. Property is produced in Ireland by the Irish company and sold outside its country of incorporation.
    c. Services are performed in Ireland by the Irish company under a contract entered into by its U.S. parent.
    d. Property is bought from the controlled foreign corporation's U.S. parent and is sold by an Irish company for use in an Irish manufacturing plant.

2. A tax return preparer is subject to a penalty for knowingly or recklessly disclosing corporate tax return information, if the disclosure is made

    a. To enable a third party to solicit business from the taxpayer.
    b. To enable the tax processor to electronically compute the taxpayer's liability.
    c. For peer review.
    d. Under an administrative order by a state agency that registers tax return preparers.

3. Which of the following acts constitute(s) grounds for a tax preparer penalty?

    I.   Without the taxpayer's consent, the tax preparer disclosed taxpayer income tax return information under an order from a state court.
    II. At the taxpayer's suggestion, the tax preparer deducted the expenses of the taxpayer's personal domestic help as a business expense on the taxpayer's individual tax return.

    a. I only.
    b. II only.
    c. Both I and II.
    d. Neither I nor II.

4. To avoid tax return preparer penalties for a return's understated tax liability due to an intentional disregard of the regulations, which of the following actions must a tax preparer take?

    a. Audit the taxpayer's corresponding business operations.
    b. Review the accuracy of the taxpayer's books and records.
    c. Make reasonable inquiries if the taxpayer's information is incomplete.
    d. Examine the taxpayer's supporting documents.

5. A taxpayer filed his income tax return after the due date but neglected to file an extension form. The return indicated a tax liability of $50,000 and taxes withheld of $45,000. On what amount would the penalties for late filing and late payment be computed?

    a. $0
    b. $5,000
    c. $45,000
    d. $50,000

6. Which, if any, of the following could result in penalties against an income tax return preparer?

    I.   Knowing or reckless disclosure or use of tax information obtained in preparing a return.
    II.   A willful attempt to understate any client's tax liability on a return or claim for refund.

    a. Neither I nor II.
    b. I only.
    c. II only.
    d. Both I and II.

7. In evaluating the hierarchy of authority in tax law, which of the following carries the greatest authoritative value for tax planning of transactions?

    a. Internal Revenue Code
    b. IRS Regulations
    c. Tax court decisions
    d. IRS agents' reports

CLASS SOLUTIONS

1. (a) Subpart F was enacted to prevent controlled foreign corporations (CFCs) from structuring transactions in a way to minimize or avoid U.S. taxation. Subpart F income includes income earned by a CFC that results from the purchase/sale, from or *on behalf of a related party*, of property that is manufactured, produced, or extracted *outside of the country of the CFC's organization* and is sold for use, consumption, or disposition *outside of the country of its organization*. Subpart F income also includes income earned by a CFC when providing services to an entity in another country as the result of a contract entered into by the CFC's parent from the United States. Thus, services provided by an *Irish* company in *England* under a contract entered into by its *U.S. parent* would be Subpart F income; the income in this case has been diverted from U.S. taxation and taxation in the CFC's foreign country of incorporation to a third foreign country. Answer (b) would not produce Subpart F income because the transaction was not incurred on behalf of a U.S. related party. Neither (c) nor (d) would produce Subpart F income because the transactions occurred in the CFCs' respective countries of domicile.

2. (a) Although information obtained from a tax client is confidential and its disclosure would be an illegal breach of duty, information may be provided in order to enable a tax processor to compute the taxpayer's liability, as a result of an administrative order by a state agency that registers tax return preparers, and for peer review. It would not be appropriate to provide information to a third party seeking to solicit business.

3. (b) A tax preparer may comply with an order from a state court by disclosing confidential information obtained when preparing a client's tax return. A preparer may not, however, understate a client's tax liability or take a tax position that is frivolous without incurring a penalty. Allowing a client to deduct personal domestic help as a business expense is a position that would not be sustainable and would likely be considered a frivolous position, subjecting the preparer to a penalty.

4. (c) A tax preparer is not required to verify information provided by a taxpayer for the preparation of a tax return. The preparer is, however, required to make reasonable inquiries of a taxpayer when the taxpayer's information is not complete. Answer (a) is incorrect because the tax preparer would not be required to audit the client's business and would only do so if engaged to do so. Answer (b) is incorrect because a tax preparer is not required to review a taxpayer's books and records. Answer (d) is incorrect because the tax preparer is not required to examine the taxpayer's supporting documents.

5. (b) Penalties for late filing and late payment are assessed on the basis of the net tax due. The penalties do not apply when there is no tax liability and, when there is, they are computed on the basis of the amount of the liability. Since the taxpayer had a total tax amount of $50,000 and had paid estimated taxes of $45,000, there is a net liability of $5,000, which is the amount that would be subject to a penalty for late filing and late payment.

6. (d) Information obtained from a client by a tax preparer is confidential information and the preparer will incur a penalty for disclosing it without the client's permission except in limited circumstances. Knowing or reckless disclosure would subject the preparer to a penalty. In addition, a tax preparer will be subject to penalty for willfully attempting to understate a client's tax liability or overstate a claim for refund.

7. (a) The Internal Revenue Code consists of tax law that has been passed by Congress and enacted. IRS Regulations, tax court decisions, and IRS agents' reports are all interpretations of tax law and are not as authoritative.

Lecture 9.04

TASK-BASED SIMULATIONS

Task-Based Simulation 1

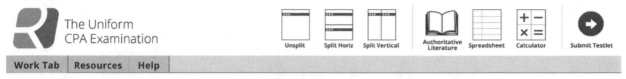

| Work Tab | Resources | Help |

A CPA sole practitioner has tax preparers' responsibilities when preparing tax returns for clients.

Items to be answered:

Items 1 through 9 each represent an independent factual situation in which a CPA sole practitioner has prepared and signed the taxpayer's income tax return. For each item, select from the following list the correct response regarding the tax preparer's responsibilities. A response may be selected once, more than once, or not at all.

Answer List

P. The tax preparer's action constitutes an act of tax preparer misconduct subject to the Internal Revenue Code penalty.

E. The Internal Revenue Service will examine the facts and circumstances to determine whether the reasonable cause exception applies; the good-faith exception applies; or both exceptions apply.

N. The tax preparer's action does **not** constitute an act of tax preparer misconduct.

	(P)	(E)	(N)
1. The tax preparer disclosed taxpayer income tax return information under an order from a state court, without the taxpayer's consent.	○	○	○
2. The tax preparer relied on the advice of an advisory preparer to calculate the taxpayer's tax liability. The tax preparer believed that the advisory preparer was competent and that the advice was reasonable. Based on the advice, the taxpayer had understated income tax liability.	○	○	○
3. The tax preparer did **not** charge a separate fee for the tax return preparation and paid the taxpayer the refund shown on the tax return less a discount. The tax preparer negotiated the actual refund check for the tax preparer's own account after receiving power of attorney from the taxpayer.	○	○	○
4. The tax preparer relied on information provided by the taxpayer regarding deductible travel expenses. The tax preparer believed that the taxpayer's information was correct but inquired about the existence of the travel expense records. The tax preparer was satisfied by the taxpayer's representations that the taxpayer had adequate records for the deduction. Based on this information, the income tax liability was understated.	○	○	○

(P) (E) (N)

5. The taxpayer provided the tax preparer with a detailed check register to compute business expenses. The tax preparer knowingly overstated the expenses on the income tax return.

    ○　○　○

6. The tax preparer disclosed taxpayer income tax return information during a quality review conducted by CPAs. The tax preparer maintained a record of the review.

    ○　○　○

7. The tax preparer relied on incorrect instructions on an IRS tax form that were contrary to the regulations. The tax preparer was **not** aware of the regulations or the IRS announcement pointing out the error. The understatement was immaterial as a result of the isolated error.

    ○　○　○

8. The tax preparer used income tax return information without the taxpayer's consent to solicit additional business.

    ○　○　○

9. The tax preparer knowingly deducted the expenses of the taxpayer's personal domestic help as wages paid in the taxpayer's business on the taxpayer's income tax return.

    ○　○　○

Task-Based Simulation 2

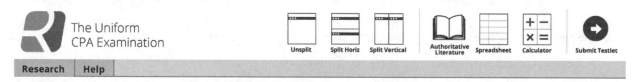

Annika, a U.S. citizen, is trying to determine whether the gain on the sale of her office building in Sweden is considered U.S. or foreign-source income for purposes of the foreign tax credit.

Which code section, subsection, and paragraph provides authority for this determination?

Task-Based Simulation 3

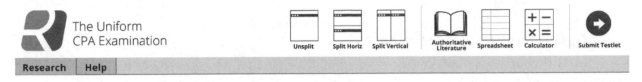

Kitri Corp., a U.S. corporation, owns 5% of a controlled foreign corporation in Spain, and would like to know if Kitri is subject to the Subpart F Income rules.

Which code section and subsection provides authority for this determination?

TASK-BASED SIMULATION SOLUTIONS

Task-Based Simulation Solution 1

For **items 1 through 9,** candidates were asked to determine for each item whether (P) the tax preparer's action constitutes an act of tax preparer misconduct subject to the Internal Revenue Code penalty; (E) the IRS will examine the facts and circumstances to determine whether the reasonable cause exception applies, the good faith exception applies, or both exceptions apply; or, (N) the tax preparer's action does not constitute an act of tax preparer misconduct.

		(P)	(E)	(N)
1.	The tax preparer disclosed taxpayer income tax return information under an order from a state court, without the taxpayer's consent.	○	○	●
2.	The tax preparer relied on the advice of an advisory preparer to calculate the taxpayer's tax liability. The tax preparer believed that the advisory preparer was competent and that the advice was reasonable. Based on the advice, the taxpayer had understated income tax liability.	○	●	○
3.	The tax preparer did **not** charge a separate fee for the tax return preparation and paid the taxpayer the refund shown on the tax return less a discount. The tax preparer negotiated the actual refund check for the tax preparer's own account after receiving power of attorney from the taxpayer.	●	○	○
4.	The tax preparer relied on information provided by the taxpayer regarding deductible travel expenses. The tax preparer believed that the taxpayer's information was correct but inquired about the existence of the travel expense records. The tax preparer was satisfied by the taxpayer's representations that the taxpayer had adequate records for the deduction. Based on this information, the income tax liability was understated.	○	○	●
5.	The taxpayer provided the tax preparer with a detailed check register to compute business expenses. The tax preparer knowingly overstated the expenses on the income tax return.	●	○	○
6.	The tax preparer disclosed taxpayer income tax return information during a quality review conducted by CPAs. The tax preparer maintained a record of the review.	○	○	●
7.	The tax preparer relied on incorrect instructions on an IRS tax form that were contrary to the regulations. The tax preparer was **not** aware of the regulations or the IRS announcement pointing out the error. The understatement was immaterial as a result of the isolated error.	○	●	○
8.	The tax preparer used income tax return information without the taxpayer's consent to solicit additional business.	●	○	○
9.	The tax preparer knowingly deducted the expenses of the taxpayer's personal domestic help as wages paid in the taxpayer's business on the taxpayer's income tax return.	●	○	○

Explanation of solutions

1. (N) Information obtained from a client by a tax preparer for the preparation of the client's tax return is confidential information that the tax preparer will incur a penalty for disclosing without the client's permission. A preparer may, however, disclose information in response to an order from a state court, for peer review, or to enable a tax processer to compute the tax liability without penalty.

2. (E) A preparer is generally responsible for errors in the preparation of a return, but a tax preparer may rely on the advice of another tax preparer if the preparer believes that the advisor is competent and that the advice is reasonable. The IRS will examine the facts to determine whether or not the reliance on the advice took into consideration the advisor's competence and the reasonableness of the advice.

3. (P) A tax preparer may not negotiate a refund check issued to a taxpayer for the preparer's own account, either directly or through an agent, and will incur a penalty for doing so.

4. (N) A tax preparer is not required to obtain documentation of information provided by a taxpayer to prepare the tax return. The preparer, however, must make reasonable inquiries about the existence of such support where appropriate. Since the IRS requires documentation to support a deduction for travel expenses, it is sufficient to inquire of the client as to whether or not the taxpayer has adequate records without being required to verify their existence.

5. (P) A tax preparer will be subject to a penalty for knowingly understating a taxpayer's tax liability, which would result from overstating a taxpayer's expenses.

6. (N) Information obtained from a client by a tax preparer for the preparation of the client's tax return is confidential information that the tax preparer will incur a penalty for disclosing without the client's permission. A preparer may, however, disclose information in response to an order from a state court, for peer or quality review, or to enable a tax processer to compute the tax liability without penalty.

7. (E) A preparer is generally responsible for errors in the preparation of a return, but will escape liability based on a good faith reliance on inaccurate IRS form instructions or advice from an IRS employee. When that appears to be the case, the IRS will evaluate the facts and circumstances to determine if it is.

8. (P) Information obtained from a client by a tax preparer for the preparation of the client's tax return is confidential information that the tax preparer will incur a penalty for disclosing without the client's permission. A preparer may, however, disclose information in response to an order from a state court, for peer review, or to enable a tax processer to compute the tax liability without penalty. The information may not, however, be used to solicit business.

9. (P) A taxpayer will be subject to penalties for knowingly and recklessly understating the tax liability of a client or adopting a frivolous position on a tax issue. By deducting personal domestic help on a client's business tax return, the preparer is taking a position that does not have a reasonable possibility of being sustained, making it a frivolous position and, as a result, is understating the client's tax liability.

Task-Based Simulation Solution 2

862	(a)	(5)

Task-Based Simulation Solution 3

951	(b)

Ethics, Professional & Legal Responsibilities

(10% - 20%)

Section 10 – Accountant Liability

Corresponding Lectures

Watch the following course lectures with this section:

Lecture 10.01 – Common Law Liability
Lecture 10.02 – Common Law Liability – Class Questions
Lecture 10.03 – Federal Security Regulations Liability
Lecture 10.04 – Federal Security Regulations Liability – Class Questions
Lecture 10.05 – Federal Security Regulations Liability – TBS

EXAM NOTE: *Please refer to the AICPA REG Blueprint in the Introduction to find a listing of the representative tasks (and their associated skill levels—i.e., Remembering and Understanding, Application, and Analysis) that the candidate should be able to perform based on the knowledge obtained in this section.*

Accountant Liability
(Part of Ethics, Professional, and Legal Responsibilities)

ACCOUNTANT LIABILITY

Accountant liability may arise out of several different areas: Common law, federal securities laws (1933/1934 Acts) or violating Accountant-client privileged information (taxes or workpapers).

Accountants face liability as a result of several different **common law principles**. Most exam testing deals with liability in connection with audits.

An audit is performed as a result of a contract between the auditor and client. For this reason, the most obvious liability facing an auditor is for **breach of contract**. Since the auditor promises to perform an audit in accordance with generally accepted auditing standards, a lawsuit charging breach of contract by the auditor must usually show violation of at least one standard. The one most often utilized is the third general standard requiring **due professional care**. As a result, the most common lawsuit against an auditor will charge **negligence**, which is an absence of due care.

COMMON LAW LIABILITY

Breach of Contract

An accountant who does not fulfill the terms of the contract or engagement will be held liable for Breach of Contract as a result of non-performance. The accountant will be liable to the client (in privity) and any intended third party beneficiaries for **compensatory damages**.

Who can sue?
- Anyone in privity → Anyone who hired you
- Intended 3rd party beneficiary (named in contract by client)

Plaintiff (Purchaser) must prove (**MILE**):
- **M**aterial misstatement or omission – The financial statements (F/S) must contain material misstatements or omissions.
- **I**nfo – was relied upon; i.e., information in the F/S was the proximate cause of the harm to the plaintiff.
- **L**oss (damages) – The plaintiff must have suffered a financial loss as a result of the above.
- **E**rror
  - Caused by breach (non-performance)

Defenses by accountant
- Didn't breach or fully performed under the contract terms.

3 DIFFERENT TORTS RESULTING FROM AUDITOR'S LIABILITY (NEGLIGENCE, GROSS NEGLIGENCE (CONSTRUCTIVE FRAUD), OR ACTUAL FRAUD)

Negligence (Foreseen User)

An accountant has a duty in the performance of an engagement to exercise due professional care expected of an ordinarily prudent CPA. The accountant will be liable to the client or an intended 3rd party beneficiary named in the engagement (privity). In the majority of states (those that follow the **Second restatement of torts)**, liability extends to anyone (3rd party) who is **known or foreseen** by the CPA.

Who can sue?

- Anyone in *privity* (client and intended 3rd party)
- Anyone *known and foreseen* by CPA (shareholder)
  - But not in the minority of states that follow the decision in ***Ultramares*** v. *Touche*

Plaintiff must prove **(MILE):**

- MIL-E
- Error
  - No due professional care / **NEG**ligent
  - **Absence of due care** – The auditor must have demonstrated carelessness in the audit.

> **N**ondisclosure of information to client (e.g., I/C weaknesses)
>
> **E**rrors previously discovered not corrected
>
> **G**AAS/GAAP not followed

- **Privity**
  The privity requirement is often the biggest obstacle in a negligence suit. The client that engaged the auditor to perform the work has privity of contract. Others normally must demonstrate the status of **intended third party beneficiary**, proving that a principal purpose of the audit was to provide them with audited financial statements in connection with a loan or investment decision.

  Parties that are not specifically cited as intended beneficiaries may attempt to prove they are **foreseen** beneficiaries, but foreseen beneficiaries do not have privity to sue for negligence in a state that conforms to the ***Ultramares*** decision. Most states, however, have now adopted the **Second Restatement of Torts**, which permits a user that is within a *class of people* known or foreseen by the auditor to be relying on the statements to sue for negligence. In all states, however, an unforeseeable third party lacks the proper standing to sue for negligence, so the auditor is never responsible for negligence to a third party that the auditor couldn't foresee would be relying on the statements. To summarize:
  - Under Restatement of Torts (majority of states), foreseen 3rd party has privity to sue.
  - Under *Ultramares* case (minority of states), foreseen 3rd party lacks privity.
  - Unforeseen 3rd party NEVER has privity to sue for negligence.
    - A **foreseen party** is a third party or a member of a limited class that the accountant *knew* would be relying on the financial statements for a limited transaction. The accountant is liable to foreseen parties for negligence.

- **Foreseeable parties** are any party the accountant could reasonably foresee would receive financial statements and use them. The accountant is NOT usually liable for negligence to foreseeable parties.

A plaintiff must prove all of the following (*CAMPS or MILE*) in order to be successful in a case based on negligence:
- **Causal Relationship** – The behavior of the accountant must be the *proximate cause* of the harm to the plaintiff.
- **Absence of due care** – The accountant must have performed the audit in a careless manner.
- **Material misstatement** – The financial statements must have contained material misstatements or omissions.
- **Privity or equivalent** – The plaintiff must show they have the proper standing to be able to sue for negligence (client, intended 3rd party, or foreseen 3rd party in state following 2nd restatement of torts).
- **Suffered loss** – The plaintiff must have suffered a financial loss.

Defenses by accountant:
- Followed GAAS (showing due professional care)
- Lack of privity (useless against client or intended 3rd party)
- Not the proximate cause of the loss

  A CPA's **duty of due care** is guided by the following standards:
  - State and federal statutes
  - Court decisions
  - Contract with the client
  - GAAS and GAAP
  - Customs of the profession

Fraud or Gross Negligence (1934 act)

A common law theory of liability that can be used by **any** party, including one who is unknown to the auditor, is **fraud**. Fraud refers to **intent to deceive**, and takes two basic forms:

- **Actual fraud** – Making false statements with **knowledge of their falsity**. For example, an auditor issues an unmodified opinion on financial statements knowing they contain material misstatements and should be receiving a qualified or adverse opinion, or recording a bribe in the financial statements as a consulting fee (**Scienter** – Knowingly made with **Intent**).

- **Constructive fraud (Gross Negligence)** – Making false statements with a *Reckless Disregard for truth*, not knowing if the statements are true or false. For example, an auditor issues an unmodified opinion on financial statements that have not been audited, and on which they should be disclaiming any opinion.

An audit meets the standards of constructive fraud if it is performed in a **grossly negligent** manner. Note that ordinary negligence does not meet this standard. It is sometimes difficult to evaluate the evidence to determine if the negligence in an audit is substantial enough to be considered gross negligence. Always assume on the CPA exam that negligence or carelessness is ordinary unless there is a clear statement in the problem that it constitutes gross or reckless behavior.

Who can sue?

- Anyone, including unforeseen parties

A plaintiff must prove all of the following in order to succeed in a case based on fraud (**RIMS** or **MILE**):

- **Reliance** – The plaintiff must have justifiably relied on the financial statements.
- **Intent to deceive** – The auditor must have had actual or constructive knowledge that their opinion was inappropriate.
- **Material misstatement** – The financial statements must have contained material misstatements or omissions.
- **Suffered loss** – The plaintiff must have suffered a financial loss as a result of the above.

Defenses by accountant:

- Not gross negligent; followed GAAS (showing due professional care)
- Not material
- Good faith and no knowledge of falsity

There is a difference between the manner in which an auditor will defend against a negligence and a fraud case. In either case, the best defense would be to prove that the audit was conducted in accordance with Generally Accepted Auditing Standards (GAAS), since this would demonstrate that the audit was conducted with due professional care.

If the auditor cannot demonstrate that GAAS was followed, negligence cases make available the privity defense, since parties unknown to the auditor, and foreseen parties in a jurisdiction following *Ultramares*, lack the standing of privity required in a negligence case. Since privity need not apply in a fraud case, the privity defense wouldn't be useful in a case based on actual or constructive fraud, including gross negligence.

Fraud cases make available the good faith defense, in which the auditor does not deny carelessness but claims a lack of knowledge of the falsity of the financial statements. This would not be sufficient to escape liability in a negligence case. Also keep in mind that the auditor must **lack** both **actual and constructive** knowledge of the falsity of the statements.

For example, an auditor may be sued by a creditor of the client who granted a loan in reliance on materially misstated financial statements. If the creditor can prove that GAAS was not carefully followed in the audit, the auditor's best defense depends on what type of suit has been filed:

- **Negligence** – The auditor may argue that the financial statements were not audited for purposes of providing statements to the creditor in connection with the loan, so that the creditor lacked the privity to sue.
- **Fraud** – The auditor may argue that the audit, while careless, was conducted in good faith, and that the carelessness was not so great as to constitute reckless disregard for the truth.

Keep in mind that the burden of proof is on the plaintiff to prove all of the elements of the case, so exam questions in which all points have not been established should be decided in favor of the auditor-defendant. Also note that Punitive Damages are not levied under Common Law.

COMMON LAW LIABILITY

Breach of Contract	Negligence Law	Gross Negligence/Fraud (1934)

Who can Sue:

Breach of Contract	Negligence Law	Gross Negligence/Fraud (1934)
Privity	Privity	Anyone
Intended 3rd party beneficiary by client	Known or Foreseen by CPA	Unforeseen
	(Ultramares act – only if in Privity)	

Plaintiff Prove:

Material Misrep/omission

Info **Caused harm**

Lost money (damages)

Error Caused Injury:
  Breach of contract
  Non-performance

M

Info **Caused harm**

L

Error

  Lack of Due diligence
  Negligence (**NEG**)
  { **N**ondisclosure of information to client (I/C weaknesses)
  Errors previously discovered not Corrected
  GAAS/GAAP not followed }

M

Info was **relied upon**

L

Error

  Reckless or Intentional misconduct
  { -<u>Actual Fraud</u>-(Intent to Deceive – *Scienter*)
  -<u>Constructive Fraud</u> (Reckless Disregard) }

Defense:

Didn't breach

Adhere to GAAS
  (not NEG) or
  Lack of Privity

Not Gross Negligent
Not material
Good faith + no knowledge of falsity

ACCOUNTANTS' LIABILITY – SUMMARY (MILE)

There are *four key elements* to an action taken against an accountant. These are:
1. There is a **M**isstatement or an omission of a **M**aterial fact.
2. The plaintiff has reasonably *relied* upon the **I**nformation.
3. The plaintiff suffered a **L**oss.
4. The accountant was in **E**rror.

	Contracts	**Negligence**	**Gross Negligence or Fraud**	**1933 Act (Section 11)**	**1934 Act (Rule 10b-5) (Fraud)**
Who may bring action	Client or an intended user	Client or a foreseen user	Anyone injured	Any purchaser	Any purchaser
Accountant's error resulting in action	Breach of contract	Carelessness	Recklessness or intentional misconduct (scienter)	Lack of due diligence	Recklessness or intentional misconduct (scienter)
Plaintiff must prove	All four elements	All four elements	All four elements	Elements 1 and 3 only	All four elements

Lecture 10.02

CLASS QUESTIONS

Please see the Class Questions and Class Solutions for this Lecture at the end of this Section.

Lecture 10.03

FEDERAL SECURITY REGULATIONS LIABILITY

Securities Act of 1933 - Section 11

Auditor liability arises from several federal statutes. The earliest law to establish such liability is the **1933 Securities Act**. This law requires that audited financial statements be included in the prospectus and registration statement required when public offers fall within the law. Section 11 makes anyone who signs a registration statement liable for all damages caused by any misstatement of material fact in the registration statement. The only elements that must be **proven by the** <u>plaintiff</u> are:

*   ***M*aterial misstatement/misrepresentation or material omission of fact** – The financial statements must have contained material misstatements or omissions. The audited financial statements must have been *included in the prospectus* provided to the plaintiff.
*   ***L*oss Suffered** – The plaintiff must have sustained a loss in connection with their purchase of the securities (they need not have purchased them directly from the issuer). The monetary damages are the difference between the amount paid and the market value or the sale proceeds, if sold.

Notice that the plaintiff has no obligation to prove reliance, since the receipt of the prospectus creates that presumption. There is no privity requirement either. Finally, and most notably, the plaintiff need not demonstrate that the auditor's work was deficient; the law presumes that the audit must have been deficient due to the material misstatements.

If the plaintiff demonstrates the above elements, the burden of proof shifts to the auditor-defendant. To escape liability, the **auditor-defendant** **must prove** one of the following:
- **Due diligence** – The audit was conducted with due diligence (demonstrating that the audit was in conformity with GAAS should be persuasive on this point, since due professional care is one of the standards).
- **Plaintiff knowledge** – The plaintiff knew of the material misstatements before making their purchase.

The suit, which can only be for damages, must be brought within 1 year after discovery and within 3 years from the offering date.

1933 Federal Security Regulations

Who can sue?
- Anyone
- No Privity needed

Plaintiff must prove (MiLe):
- **M**aterial misrepresentation or material omission of fact in prospectus
- **L**oss suffered

Defenses by accountant:
- Followed GAAS (show due diligence—NOT negligent*).
- Plaintiff knew the prospectus was inaccurate (no reliance).

*Notice that plaintiff need not prove reliance nor auditor negligence; the auditor must show he was NOT negligent.

Securities Exchange Act of 1934 - Section 10(b) and Rule 10b-5
(Anti-fraud provision)

All audits of companies involved in interstate commerce are covered by the **Securities Exchange Act of 1934**. The primary source of liability is **Section 10(b) and Rule 10b-5**, commonly known as the anti-fraud provision of the Act. The principles for auditor liability are virtually identical to common law fraud, and the **plaintiff must prove** (RIMS or MILE):
- **Reliance** – The plaintiff must have justifiably relied on the financial statements.
- **Intent to deceive** – The auditor must have had actual or constructive knowledge that their opinion was incorrect.
- **Material misstatement/misrepresentation or material omission of fact** – The financial statements must have contained Material misrepresentation or a material omission of fact.
- **Suffered loss** – The plaintiff must have suffered a financial loss as a result of the above.

Instead of fraud, the law refers to **scienter**, but this is essentially the same concept. The only significant difference between a common law fraud case and one brought under Rule 10b-5 of the 1934 Act is that the former case is heard in state court and the latter in federal court. This rule is

identical to Common Law Fraud (MILE), meaning the plaintiff must prove all 4 of the requirements, including Gross Negligence (negligence is not sufficient).

The auditor's best defense is conformity to GAAS in the audit or, if that cannot be established, lack of intent to deceive; that is, the auditor acted in good faith and didn't know the information was false or misleading. The burden of proof, however, is on the plaintiff for all elements of the case, just as in common law cases and unlike the cases brought under the 1933 Act.

Violation of Rule 10b-5 can result in civil damages and/or criminal damages, or a rescission of the transactions.

Federal Security Regulations Liability
(No Privity needed to sue)

1933 (Section 11)	**1934** (Rule 10b-5)
Misleading info in Registration stmt (IPOs)	**Any written/oral statements or omissions**

Purchaser must prove **M.L.** – 2 elements
 	
  ▪ **M**aterial Misstatement, Misrepresentation or Omission in F/S
  ▪ **L**oss (damages)
	Purchaser must prove **MILE** – all 4 elements
	
	  ▪ **M**aterial Misstatement, Misrepresentation or Omission in F/S
	  ▪ Reliance (**I**nfo relied upon)
	  ▪ **L**oss (damages)
	  ▪ **E**rror - Scienter – Gross negligence (Fraud)

Auditor is Guilty until he proves either:
 	
  ▪ Investor knew of error (Prove he did not rely) OR
  ▪ Due Diligence (Without **NEG**ligence)
	Auditor defense:
	
	  ▪ Conformity to GAAS
	  ▪ Lack of intent to deceive (i.e., good faith and no knowledge of falsity)

1995 Private Securities Litigation Reform Act

When auditing publicly traded companies that report to the SEC under the 1934 Act, a CPA must also comply with the Private Securities Litigation Reform Act of 1995. This law places into the code several responsibilities already considered part of an effective audit under GAAS, including (**RIG**):
- **Related-party transactions** – The auditor must include substantive tests designed to identify all significant/material related-party transactions.
- **Illegal acts** – The auditor should attempt to identify illegal acts with a direct and material effect on the financial statements.
- **Going concern** – The auditor should perform tests to determine if there is substantial doubt as to the ability of the client to continue in existence throughout the following fiscal year.

In addition, the law imposes reporting responsibilities on the auditor whenever illegal acts are identified. The auditor should report illegal acts to the appropriate level of management. If management fails to take appropriate action in connection with material illegal acts, the auditor must inform the board of directors as soon as it is practicable. The board is given only 1 business day to make a filing informing the SEC of these illegal acts, and must provide proof of filing to the

auditor. If the auditor does not receive this proof by the filing deadline, the auditor is then given only **1 business day** to either:
- **Resign** from the engagement
- **Notify the SEC** of the failure of the board to make the appropriate filing.

An auditor who fails to comply with the reporting provisions may be held civilly liable for a proportionate share of the damages they caused; however, an auditor who complies may not be held liable in any private action for statements filed with the SEC.

1999 Federal Privacy Disclosure Act

This law (also known as the **Gramm-Leach-Briley Act**) gives the Federal Trade Commission the power to regulate the privacy practices of many financial services professionals, including CPAs, unless they are registered investment advisers with the SEC who provide financial services to consumers.

One requirement is that the professional notify all clients of their privacy practices, including the types of non-public information they may gather from the client, circumstances under which they might disclose that information to third parties, and the procedures undertaken to protect such private information from unauthorized release to third parties.

Corporate and Criminal Fraud Accountability Act of 2002 (SOX)

The SEC has stepped up its monitoring of public companies under the Corporate and Criminal Fraud Accountability Act of 2002. This Act has significant influence on the auditor's professional environment concerning the detection of fraud. Provisions include:
- Auditors are required to maintain all audit working papers for 7 years.
- It is a felony to knowingly destroy or create documents (including audit working papers) to impede, obstruct, or influence any existing or contemplated federal investigation.
- The statute of limitations on securities fraud claims is extended to 5 years from the fraud, or 2 years after the fraud was discovered.
- Employees of CPA firms (and audit clients) are extended whistleblower protection that would prohibit the employer from taking certain actions against employees.
- Whistleblower employees are also granted a remedy of special damages and attorney's fee.
- Securities fraud by CPAs (and audit clients) is punishable by up to 10 years in prison.

Paid Tax Preparers

Paid preparers of **federal income tax returns** are subject to federal statutory liability as well. A penalty may be assessed by the IRS against a preparer who:
- Fails to sign the return and provide the appropriate federal identification number.
- Fails to provide a copy of the return to the client and retain a copy for the time specified by law.
- Negotiates or endorses a client's tax refund check.

In addition, the preparer may be held liable by the client if the preparer:
- Fails to provide the client with the completed return to allow a timely filing.
- Fails to advise the client of tax elections that would have provided the client with substantial tax savings.

Additional taxes and interest for underpayment of taxes are solely the responsibility of the tax client, even if they result from the preparer's error. The preparer is not required to verify the information provided by the client, but should make reasonable inquiries when information appears incorrect or incomplete.

Discussions between a client and CPA on federal tax issues are *privileged,* except when they involve criminal matters or communications pertaining to tax shelters.

Working Papers (Audit Documentation)

The accountant, not the client, owns the working papers that an accountant creates during an engagement. Nevertheless, the accountant must maintain **confidentiality** and cannot provide the papers or information obtained during engagements to other parties without the permission of the client (it should be noted that client confidentiality does not preclude a CPA from providing access to other members of his/her firm). There are some **exceptions** to confidentiality, including:

- **Valid subpoena** - the accountant must honor a valid court order to turn over information.
- **IRS administrative subpoena**
- **Court order** (unless rare state with privilege statute).
- **Quality control peer review** - The accountant may allow other accountants and the PCAOB to see confidential information in connection with a valid program of peer review.
- Where disclosure is in compliance with **GAAP or GAAS.**

Common law does not recognize the concept of **privilege**, which would allow the accountant to refuse to honor a court subpoena. A small number of states have enacted privilege statutes, and the federal government now recognizes working papers developed in connection with the preparation of a tax return to be privileged in certain circumstances. Nevertheless, privilege may not be used if the accountant has already provided some of the information requested in the subpoena, and the purpose of privilege is to protect the client, not the accountant, so the accountant may not assert privilege, even where privilege statutes exist, if the client waives the privilege.

Criminal Liability

Although, in general, an accountant's liability in relation to the federal securities regulations is limited to civil liability, certain provisions may subject an accountant to **criminal liability**.

- Section 24 of the Securities Act of 1933, in regard to a registration statement filed under the Act, specifies that anyone who **willfully** makes an untrue statement of a material fact or omits a material fact required to be included may be fined up to $10,000, imprisoned up to 5 years, or both.
- Section 32 of the Securities Exchange Act of 1934 makes the willful violation of any Act punishable by fines of up to $5,000,000 and imprisonment of up to 20 years. A similar penalty may result from willfully or knowingly making a false or misleading statement relative to a material fact in any application, report, or document contained in a registration statement.

Other sources of criminal liability for accountants are included in the **Internal Revenue Code** (IRC) and the **Racketeer Influenced and Corrupt Organizations** (**RICO**) Act. Although most criminal offenses indicated by the IRC are perpetrated by the taxpayer, not the tax preparer, the participation by the tax preparer would extend liability to that individual as well. **Criminal offenses**, which are defined under the IRC, include:

- Actions taken with the intention to evade or defeat taxation
- Willfully failing to file a return, provide information, or pay tax

- Willfully making false statements or declarations, assisting in preparing false tax documents, or preparing a false or fraudulent return

RICO was passed to allow prosecution of individuals and organizations involved in ongoing criminal activity. It makes it illegal to invest funds obtained through a pattern of racketeering in entities involved in interstate or foreign commerce; to use a pattern of racketeering activities to obtain an interest in, or control over, an entity involved in interstate or foreign commerce; and for an entity involved in interstate or foreign commerce to engage in a pattern of racketeering activities. **Racketeering** is an illegal activity carried out as part of an enterprise that is owned or controlled by those who are engaged in the illegal activity, for example, organized crime.

Racketeering involves such activities as extortion, loansharking, bribery, and obstruction of justice. RICO also includes "any act or threat involving murder, kidnapping, gambling, arson, robbery, bribery, extortion, dealing in obscene matter, or dealing in a controlled substance." It is chargeable under State law and subject to punishment by imprisonment for more than one year. To be prosecuted under RICO, there must be a pattern of racketeering. A pattern involves repeat offenses and requires that the party be guilty of at least 2 acts of racketeering within a 10-year period.

Violations under RICO may result in fines of up to $250,000, or double the amount of profits or losses caused by the criminal activity, and imprisonment for up to 20 years, as well as the forfeiture of any property obtained through, or used in, criminal activities. Treble damages are also allowed, which involves a statute that permits a court to triple the amount of damages awarded by a court of law.

Lecture 10.04

CLASS QUESTIONS

Please see the Class Questions and Class Solutions for this Lecture at the end of this Section.

Lecture 10.05

CLASS QUESTIONS

Please see the Class Questions and Class Solutions for this Lecture at the end of this Section.

CLASS QUESTIONS

Work through the below Class Questions while following along with the respective lectures. Once this is complete, you can begin independently practicing what you've learned by quizzing yourself on this course section in your Interactive Practice Questions (IPQ), which can be found in your online Student Dashboard. Your IPQ simulates the computer-based testing experience, and will also help you understand how concepts are applied to the exam. Each question includes answer explanations from expert CPAs that will help you determine why you answered a question correctly or incorrectly. This is key to your success on the CPA Exam.

Lecture 10.02

1. Cable Corp. orally engaged Drake & Co., CPAs, to audit its financial statements. Cable's management informed Drake that it suspected the accounts receivable were materially overstated. Though the financial statements Drake audited included a materially overstated accounts receivable balance, Drake issued an unmodified (unqualified) opinion. Cable used the financial statements to obtain a loan to expand its operations. Cable defaulted on the loan and incurred a substantial loss. If Cable sues Drake for negligence in failing to discover the overstatement, Drake's best defense would be that Drake did **not**

   a. Have privity of contract with Cable.
   b. Sign an Engagement letter.
   c. Perform the audit recklessly or with an intent to deceive.
   d. Violate generally accepted auditing standards in performing the audit.

2. Ford & Co., CPAs, issued an unmodified (unqualified) opinion on Owens Corp.'s financial statements. Relying on these financial statements, Century Bank lent Owens $750,000. Ford was unaware that Century would receive a copy of the financial statements or that Owens would use them to obtain a loan. Owens defaulted on the loan. To succeed in a common law fraud action against Ford, Century must prove, in addition to other elements that Century was

   a. Free from contributory negligence.
   b. In privity of contract with Ford.
   c. Justified in relying on the financial statements.
   d. In privity of contract with Owens.

3. When performing an audit, a CPA will most likely be considered negligent when the CPA fails to

   a. Detect all of a client's fraudulent activities.
   b. Include a negligence disclaimer in the client engagement letter.
   c. Warn a client of known internal control weaknesses.
   d. Warn a client's customers of embezzlement by the client's employees.

4. Which of the following statements is correct regarding a CPA's audit documentation (working papers)? The audit documentation must be

   a. Transferred to another accountant purchasing the CPA's practice even if the client hasn't given permission.
   b. Transferred permanently to the client if demanded.
   c. Turned over to any government agency that requests them.
   d. Turned over pursuant to a valid federal court subpoena.

5. A CPA is permitted to disclose confidential client information without the consent of the client to:

   I. Another CPA who has purchased the CPA's tax practice.
   II. Another CPA firm if the information concerns suspected tax return irregularities.
   III. A state CPA society voluntary quality control review board.

      a. I and III only.
      b. II and III only.
      c. II only.
      d. III only.

6. Which of the following elements, if present, would support a finding of constructive fraud on the part of a CPA?

   a. Gross negligence in applying generally accepted auditing standards.
   b. Ordinary negligence in applying generally accepted accounting principles.
   c. Identified third-party users.
   d. Scienter.

7. In a common law action against an accountant, lack of privity is a viable defense if the plaintiff

   a. Is the client's creditor who sues the accountant for negligence.
   b. Can prove the presence of gross negligence that amounts to a reckless disregard of the truth.
   c. Is the accountant's client.
   d. Bases the action upon fraud.

8. Quincy bought Teal Corp. common stock in an offering registered under the Securities Act of 1933. Worth & Co., CPAs, gave an unmodified (unqualified) opinion on Teal's financial statements that were included in the registration statement filed with the SEC. Quincy sued Worth under the provisions of the 1933 Act that deal with omission of facts required to be in the registration statement. Quincy must prove that

   a. There was fraudulent activity by Worth.
   b. There was a material misstatement in the financial statements.
   c. Quincy relied on Worth's opinion.
   d. Quincy was in privity with Worth.

Items 9 and 10 are based on the following:
Dart Corp. engaged Jay Associates, CPAs, to assist in a public stock offering. Jay audited Dart's financial statements and gave an unmodified (unqualified) opinion, despite knowing that the financial statements contained misstatements. Jay's opinion was included in Dart's registration statement. Larson purchased shares in the offering and suffered a loss when the stock declined in value after the misstatements became known.

9. In a suit against Jay and Dart under the Section 11 liability provisions of the Securities Act of 1933, Larson must prove that

   a. Jay knew of the misstatements.
   b. Jay was negligent.
   c. The misstatements contained in Dart's financial statements were material.
   d. The unmodified (unqualified) opinion contained in the registration statement was relied on by Larson.

10. If Larson succeeds in the Section 11 suit against Dart, Larson would be entitled to

   a. Damages of three times the original public offering price.
   b. Rescind the transaction.
   c. Monetary damages only.
   d. Damages, but only if the shares were resold before the suit was started.

11. To which of the following parties may a CPA partnership provide its working papers, without being lawfully subpoenaed or without the client's consent?

   a. The IRS.
   b. The FASB.
   c. Any surviving partner(s) on the death of a partner.
   d. A CPA before purchasing a partnership interest in the firm.

CLASS SOLUTIONS

1. (d) A suit by Cable for Drake's failure to discover the overstatement is a common law action under which Cable would have to prove (MILE) a material misstatement or omission, the misstated information was the cause of harm, that they suffered a loss, and that it was caused by breach of contract. Drake's best defense would be to demonstrate that there was no breach of contract, which would be the case if Drake could prove that the engagement was conducted in accordance with GAAS, which is Drake's obligation. Answer (a) is incorrect because Cable does have privity since Cable entered into the contract directly with Drake. Answer (b) is incorrect because although Cable did not sign an engagement letter, it would be difficult to prove that there was no contract since Drake issued a report. Answer (c) is incorrect because Drake would only be concerned about showing that the audit was not performed recklessly or with the intent to deceive if the suit were asserting that Drake acted fraudulently.

2. (c) In a common law fraud action, the plaintiff would have to prove that the financial statements were justifiably relied on, there was actual or constructive fraud, the financial statements contained a material misstatement or omission, and the plaintiff suffered a loss. In a common law negligence suit, privity or the equivalent must generally be proved, but not in a common law fraud suit. Answer (a) is incorrect because Century does not have to prove a lack of negligence on its part. Answer (b) is incorrect because Century is not in privity of contract with Ford but can show that it does have standing to file suit on the basis of reasonable reliance on the financial statements. Answer (d) is incorrect because whether Century was in privity of contract with the client, Owens, is not relevant to an action against Ford.

3. (c) A CPA will be considered negligent when the CPA fails to exercise due professional care. Failure to inform a client of a known internal control deficiency keeps the client in jeopardy of potential loss that might be otherwise avoided. This would be a breach of the CPA's duty to the client and would be considered a lack of due professional care. Answer (a) is incorrect because a CPA is not expected to find all of a client's fraudulent activities. There may be some that are not material to the financial statements, which would not be within the scope of the audit. In addition, the nature of fraud makes it particularly difficult to detect. Answer (b) is incorrect because a negligence disclaimer in an engagement letter would not relieve a CPA of liability due to the CPA's negligence. Answer (d) is incorrect because a CPA is not expected to inform a client's customer of embezzlement by the client's employee. To do so would violate the CPA's duty of confidentiality to the client. The CPA would inform the client, however, and encourage the client to take appropriate action.

4. (d) Working papers are the property of the CPA, but they contain information obtained during the engagement, which is confidential. The CPA is required to respond, however, to a valid subpoena from a federal court. Answer (a) is incorrect because due to the confidentiality of the information they contain, the CPA may not transfer the working papers to another CPA purchasing the CPA's practice without the permission of the client. Answer (b) is incorrect because the CPA is, however, required to respond to a valid subpoena from a federal court. Since they are the property of the CPA, they are not required to be transferred to the client. Answer (c) is incorrect because the working papers may not be turned over to any federal agency that requests them, although they would be required to turn them over to the IRS in response to a valid administrative subpoena.

5. (d) A CPA is permitted to disclose confidential client information without the client's permission in response to a valid court order or a valid subpoena, including an IRS administrative subpoena and to a peer reviewer as part of a PCAOB or other valid peer review program. The CPA may not disclose confidential information to another CPA without the client's permission, whether in connection with the sale of the CPA's practice or due to a suspected tax irregularity.

6. (a) Constructive fraud involves making false statements without knowing if they are true or false, indicating gross negligence in the form of a reckless disregard for the truth. Answer (b) is incorrect because ordinary negligence would support a finding of breach of contract, but not constructive fraud. Answer (c) is incorrect because the auditor is not only liable to identified third-party users, but is also liable to foreseeable users. Answer (d) is incorrect because scienter would not be present since the auditor is not aware of the fact that the statement being made is false.

7. (a) An auditor's ordinary negligence would create a liability for breach of contract. As a result, the auditor would be liable to parties that are parties to the contract or are in privity of the contract. A lack of privity would be a valid defense. Answer (b) is incorrect because in a case involving gross negligence, the CPA will be liable to those who suffer a loss relying on false information, regardless of whether they are in privity of the contract. Answer (c) is incorrect because the accountant's client is a party to the contract and would be in privity. Answer (d) is incorrect because an action based on fraud creates liability to parties who suffer a loss upon relying on the false information, regardless of whether they are in privity of the contract.

8. (b) In an action under the Securities Act of 1933, the plaintiff need only show that the financial statements in a registration statement filed with the SEC contained a material misstatement or omission of fact and that a loss was incurred. Answer (a) is incorrect because there is no requirement that the plaintiff prove that the CPA was involved in fraudulent activity. Answer (c) is incorrect because there is no requirement that the plaintiff relied on the auditor's opinion. Answer (d) is incorrect because since an action would be related to constructive fraud, not breach of contract, privity of contract is not required.

9. (c) A plaintiff in an action under the Securities Act of 1933 would be successful upon demonstrating that the financial statements in a registration statement contained a material misstatement or omission of fact and that the plaintiff suffered a loss. Answer (a) is incorrect because the plaintiff would not be required to demonstrate that the auditor knew of the misstatements. Answer (b) is incorrect because the plaintiff need not demonstrate that the CPA was negligent. Answer (d) is incorrect because the plaintiff would not be required to prove reliance on the auditor's report.

10. (c) Under Section 11 of the Securities Act of 1933, a plaintiff will be successful upon proving that the financial statements included in a registration statement included a material misstatement or omission of fact and that a loss was suffered. If successful, the plaintiff will be entitled to damages. Answer (a) is incorrect because the plaintiff will not be entitled to some multiple of the original offering price. Answer (b) is incorrect because the plaintiff will not be entitled to rescind the transaction. Answer (d) is incorrect because the plaintiff is not required to resell the shares in order to be entitled to damages.

11. (c) Working papers are the property of the CPA firm. All partners are allowed access and all have the obligation to maintain those that contain information about a client obtained in the course of an engagement as confidential. Answer (a) is incorrect because working papers may not be disclosed to the IRS without a valid administrative subpoena or client consent. Answer (b) is incorrect because working papers may not be disclosed to the FASB without client consent. Answer (d) is incorrect because working papers may not be disclosed to another CPA, even as part of a sale of the CPA's practice, without client consent.

Lecture 10.05

TASK-BASED SIMULATIONS

Task-Based Simulation 1

The Uniform CPA Examination

| Unsplit | Split Horiz | Split Vertical | Authoritative Literature | Spreadsheet | Calculator | Submit Testlet |

| Work Tab | Resources | Help |

Situation

Under Section 11 of the Securities Act of 1933 and Section 10(b), Rule 10b-5, of the Securities Exchange Act of 1934, a CPA may be sued by a purchaser of registered securities.

Items to be answered:

Items 1 through 6 relate to what a plaintiff who purchased securities must prove in a civil liability suit against a CPA. For each item determine whether the statement must be proven under Section 11 of the Securities Act of 1933, under Section 10(b), Rule 10b-5, of the Securities Exchange Act of 1934, both Acts, or neither Act.

	Only Section 11 (A)	Only Section 10(b) (B)	Both (C)	Neither (D)
The plaintiff security purchaser must allege or prove				
1. Material misstatements were included in a filed document.	○	○	○	○
2. A monetary loss occurred.	○	○	○	○
3. Lack of due diligence by the CPA.	○	○	○	○
4. Privity with the CPA.	○	○	○	○
5. Reliance on the document.	○	○	○	○
6. The CPA had scienter.	○	○	○	○

TASK-BASED SIMULATION SOLUTIONS

Task-Based Simulation Solution 1

	Only Section 11 (A)	Only Section 10(b) (B)	Both (C)	Neither (D)
The **plaintiff** security purchaser must allege or prove				
1. Material misstatements were included in a filed document.	○	○	●	○
2. A monetary loss occurred.	○	○	●	○
3. Lack of due diligence by the CPA.	○	○	○	●
4. Privity with the CPA.	○	○	○	●
5. Reliance on the document.	○	●	○	○
6. The CPA had scienter.	○	●	○	○

Explanation of solutions

1. (C) Section 11 of the Securities Act of 1933 applies to circumstances in which a plaintiff suffers a loss on an investment when financial statements included in the registration statement contain a material misstatement or omission of facts. Under Section 11, the plaintiff need only prove that the registration contained the omission or misstatement and that a loss was suffered. Section 10(b) of the Securities Exchange Act of 1934 is the antifraud provision of the act under which a CPA would be liable for the commission of fraud, which would involve issuing an unmodified report with knowledge of the material misstatement. Under Section 10(b), the plaintiff has the same burden of proof as under Section 11, but must also demonstrate reliance on the document and knowledge, or scienter, on the part of the CPA.

2. (C) Section 11 of the Securities Act of 1933 applies to circumstances in which a plaintiff suffers a loss on an investment when financial statements included in the registration statement contain a material misstatement or omission of facts. Under Section 11, the plaintiff need only prove that the registration contained the omission or misstatement and that a loss was suffered. Section 10(b) of the Securities Exchange Act of 1934 is the antifraud provision of the act under which a CPA would be liable for the commission of fraud, which would involve issuing an unmodified report with knowledge of the material misstatement. Under Section 10(b), the plaintiff has the same burden of proof as under Section 11, but must also demonstrate reliance on the document and knowledge, or scienter, on the part of the CPA.

3. (D) Section 11 of the Securities Act of 1933 applies to circumstances in which a plaintiff suffers a loss on an investment when financial statements included in the registration statement contain a material misstatement or omission of facts. Under Section 11, the plaintiff need only prove that the registration contained the omission or misstatement and that a loss was suffered. Section 10(b) of the Securities Exchange Act of 1934 is the antifraud provision of the act under which a CPA would be liable for the commission of fraud, which would involve issuing an unmodified report with knowledge of the material misstatement. Under Section 10(b), the plaintiff has the same burden of proof as under Section 11, but must also demonstrate reliance on the document and knowledge, or scienter, on the part of the CPA. There is no requirement to demonstrate a lack of due diligence by the CPA under either section.

4. (D) Section 11 of the Securities Act of 1933 applies to circumstances in which a plaintiff suffers a loss on an investment when financial statements included in the registration statement contain a material misstatement or omission of facts. Under Section 11, the plaintiff need only prove that the registration contained the omission or misstatement and that a loss was suffered. Section 10(b) of the Securities Exchange Act of 1934 is the antifraud provision of the act under which a CPA would be liable for the commission of fraud, which would involve issuing an unmodified report with knowledge of the material misstatement. Under Section 10(b), the plaintiff has the same burden of proof as under Section 11, but must also demonstrate reliance on the document and knowledge, or scienter, on the part of the CPA. Since these actions are not for breach of contract, there is no requirement to demonstrate privity under either section.

5. (B) Section 11 of the Securities Act of 1933 applies to circumstances in which a plaintiff suffers a loss on an investment when financial statements included in the registration statement contain a material misstatement or omission of facts. Under Section 11, the plaintiff need only prove that the registration contained the omission or misstatement and that a loss was suffered. Section 10(b) of the Securities Exchange Act of 1934 is the antifraud provision of the act under which a CPA would be liable for the commission of fraud, which would involve issuing an unmodified report with knowledge of the material misstatement. Under Section 10(b), the plaintiff has the same burden of proof as under Section 11, but must also demonstrate reliance on the document and knowledge, or scienter, on the part of the CPA.

6. (B) Section 11 of the Securities Act of 1933 applies to circumstances in which a plaintiff suffers a loss on an investment when financial statements included in the registration statement contain a material misstatement or omission of facts. Under Section 11, the plaintiff need only prove that the registration contained the omission or misstatement and that a loss was suffered. Section 10(b) of the Securities Exchange Act of 1934 is the antifraud provision of the act under which a CPA would be liable for the commission of fraud, which would involve issuing an unmodified report with knowledge of the material misstatement. Under Section 10(b), the plaintiff has the same burden of proof as under Section 11, but must also demonstrate reliance on the document and knowledge, or scienter, on the part of the CPA.

Section 11 – Ethics, Professional and Legal Responsibilities

Corresponding Lectures

Watch the following course lectures with this section:

Lecture 11.01 – Tax Return Preparers

Lecture 11.02 – Treasury Department Circular 230

Lecture 11.03 – Licensing and Disciplinary Systems

Lecture 11.04 – Private Securities Litigation Reform Act and Working Papers

Lecture 11.05 – Ethics, Professional and Legal Responsibilities – Class Questions

EXAM NOTE: *Please refer to the AICPA REG Blueprint in the Introduction to find a listing of the representative tasks (and their associated skill levels—i.e., Remembering and Understanding, Application, and Analysis) that the candidate should be able to perform based on the knowledge obtained in this section.*

Ethics, Professional and Legal Responsibilities

TAX RETURN PREPARERS

A "tax return preparer" includes anyone who prepares *for compensation*, or who employs one or more persons to prepare, all or a substantial portion of any tax return or claim for refund.
- Need not be enrolled to practice before the IRS.
- Considered a preparer only if compensation is received, which can be either explicit or implicit.
- Performing the following acts does NOT classify a person as a tax preparer:
  - Preparing a return for family or a friend free of charge
  - Simply typing, reproducing, or providing other mechanical assistance in preparing a return

Tax return preparers are required to register for a Preparer Tax Identification Number (**PTIN**). This nine-digit number must be used by paid tax return preparers on all returns or claims for refunds. Paid preparers must renew their PTINs annually to legally prepare tax returns.

Information that is obtained from a client in connection with the preparation of their tax return is **confidential,** and the preparer is not permitted to use it for personal benefit or reveal this information to third parties without the consent of the taxpayer, except in limited circumstance. The most important **exceptions** are:
- To respond to a valid government order (while discussions between CPAs and clients on federal tax matters are privileged, this does not apply to criminal matters and tax shelters).
- As part of a quality control peer review program.
- To permit the electronic preparation or submission of the taxpayer's return.
- To secure legal advice from an attorney.

A CPA is not obligated to inform the IRS or any other taxing authority of a client's failure to file a prior year return without the client's permission, although there is an obligation to promptly inform the client upon becoming aware of such a circumstance. Also, a CPA does owe a duty to inform a client if there are material errors in a previously filed tax return so that the client may file an amended return.

Tax Services

Statements on Standards for Tax Services (SSTS) guide a member in the performance of tax services. Although the AICPA SSTS are no longer directly tested, the following information may be useful in solving other CPA exam questions.
- The member may rely on information provided by the client without verification unless it is clearly incorrect or incomplete.
- Although the preparer is acting as a client advocate, the member should not adopt any position on the return that is frivolous or lacks substantial authority (40%).
  - A preparer is subject to a penalty equal to the greater of $1,000, or 50% of the income derived by the preparer with respect to the return or refund claim if any part of an understatement of liability is due to an *undisclosed position* on the return for which there is *not a reasonable belief* that the position is backed by **substantial authority**.

- The *substantial authority* standard requires a more than 40% probability of being sustained on its merits, in contrast to the *more likely than not* standard which requires a 50% likelihood of success, the *realistic possibility* standard which requires a 33% likelihood of success, and a *reasonable basis* which requires 20%.
- The penalty can be avoided by (1) an *adequate disclosure* of the questionable position on the return or refund claim, and (2) showing that there was a reasonable basis for the position. The reasonable basis standard may require at least a 20% probability of being sustained on its merits.
- The penalty can also be avoided if the preparer can show there was a reasonable cause for the understatement and that the return preparer acted in good faith.

- If the CPA identifies an error on a previously submitted return, the client should be advised of the error. It is the client's decision how to proceed, but the CPA should consider future dealings with the client based on the client's handling of the matter once informed.
- Need not be independent, but be client advocate.
- Prepare return based on all facts known to preparer.
- Provide client with copy of return and retain copy for 3 years.
- No fee based upon results.
- Estimates are ok.

Lecture 11.02

TREASURY DEPARTMENT CIRCULAR 230

Circular 230 is a set of U.S. Treasury *regulations that govern practice before the* IRS. It affects attorneys, CPAs, enrolled agents (EA), enrolled retirement plan agents, and others who prepare tax returns, represent taxpayers before the IRS, or provide tax advice. Circular 230 consists of 5 subparts. Within each subpart, certain sections are particularly applicable to CPAs:

- Subpart A provides rules related to the authority to practice before the IRS.
  - Section 10.3 – Who may practice
  - Section 10.8 – Return preparation and application of rules to other individuals
- Subpart B describes the duties and restrictions of those authorized to practice before the IRS.
  - Section 10.20 – Information to be furnished
  - Section 10.21 – Knowledge of client's omissions
  - Section 10.22 – Diligence as to accuracy
  - Section 10.27 – Fees
  - Section 10.28 – Return of client's records
  - Section 10.29 – Conflicting interests
  - Section 10.30 – Solicitation
  - Section 10.31 – Negotiation of taxpayer checks
  - Section 10.34 – Standards with respect to tax returns and documents, affidavits and other papers
  - Section 10.37 – Requirements for other written advice
- Subpart C indicates sanctions for violations.
  - Section 10.50 – Sanctions
  - Section 10.51 – Incompetence and disreputable conduct
- Subpart D provides rules for disciplinary proceedings.
  - Section 10.60 – Institution of proceeding
- Subpart E relates to the availability of public records.

Section 10.3 – Who May Practice

In order for a CPA to practice before the IRS, the CPA:
- Must not be currently under suspension or disbarment from practice before the IRS.
- Must file a declaration with the IRS indicating the CPA is currently qualified as a CPA and authorized to represent the party

A CPA not currently under suspension or disbarment may provide written advice without filing a written declaration.

Section 10.8 – Return Preparation and Application of Rules to Other Individuals

A preparer tax identification number (PTIN) is required in order to prepare a tax return or claim for refund in exchange for compensation. Only attorneys, CPAs, EAs, and registered tax return preparers may obtain PTINs.

Section 10.20 – Information to be Furnished

Unless the practitioner believes records or information are privileged, records properly and lawfully requested by the IRS must be promptly submitted. When records are not in the possession of the practitioner:
- The IRS should be notified; and
- Inquiry should be made of the client as to who does have custody.

Section 10.21 – Knowledge of Client's Omission

If a practitioner becomes aware of an incident of a client's noncompliance with revenues laws, or of an error or omission on a filing with the IRS, the practitioner is required to:
- Promptly advise the client of the circumstance; and
- Advise the client as to the potential consequences.

Section 10.22 – Diligence as to Accuracy

While required to exercise due diligence in preparing or assisting in the preparation of filings with the IRS, and in determining the correctness of representations made by the practitioner to the IRS and to clients. This does not preclude the practitioner from relying on another person, provided the practitioner has exercised reasonable care and due diligence in engaging, supervising, training, and evaluating the individual.

Section 10.27 – Fees

A practitioner may not charge either an unconscionable fee or a contingent fee for matters before the IRS. A **contingent fee may be charged** in relation to:
- An administrative examination or a *challenge to* an original return, an amended return, or a claim for refund (not for preparing original return);
- Services related to a claim for credit or refund in connection with statutory interest or penalties charged by the IRS; or
- Services related to a judicial proceeding under the IRC.

Section 10.28 – Return of Client's Records

A practitioner is generally required to return any and all client records needed for the client to comply with tax obligations, although *copies may be retained*. A dispute over fees does not justify retention of client records.

Some states allow the retention of client records as a result of a dispute over fees. When they are retained under such circumstances, the practitioner must:
- Return those that are required to be attached to the client's tax return; and
- Provide reasonable access to the client to review and copy records necessary to comply with the client's tax obligations.

Section 10.29 – Conflicting Interests

A practitioner may not represent a client before the IRS when there is a conflict of interest, such as when representation of one client would be adverse to another, or there is a risk that representation will be limited as a result of responsibilities to other clients or others.

A practitioner may represent a client despite a conflict of interest if:
- It is reasonable for the practitioner to believe that representation will be competent and diligent;
- Representation is not prohibited by law; and
- All clients affected waive the conflict of interest, giving a written informed consent.

Section 10.30 – Solicitation

A practitioner may not make false, fraudulent, or coercive statements or claims; or misleading or deceptive statements or claims with respect to any IRS matter in any form of public communication or private solicitation. Nor may a practitioner make an uninvited solicitation to perform services in matters related to the IRS, whether written or oral, if doing so violates federal or state laws or another applicable rule.

Any lawful solicitation by or on behalf of a practitioner before the IRS must:
- Identify that it is a solicitation
- Indicate the source of information used to choose the recipient, if applicable

A practitioner may disseminate information about fees, including fixed fees for specific routine services, hourly rates, ranges of fees for particular services, and fees charged for an initial consultation. Fee information may be communicated in a variety of ways, including professional lists, telephone directories, print media, mailings, electronic mail, facsimile, hand-delivered flyers, radio, television, and any other method.

Section 10.31 – Negotiation of Taxpayer Checks

A tax preparer may not endorse or otherwise negotiate a government check issued in relation to a federal tax liability.

Section 10.34 – Standards with Respect to Tax Returns and Documents, Affidavits and Other Papers

A **tax return** should not be filed with a tax position that *lacks a reasonable basis*; is an *unreasonable position*; or represents a *willful attempt to understate the liability* or constitutes an *intentional disregard for rules or regulations*. A practitioner may **not** willfully, recklessly, or through gross incompetence:

- Sign a tax return or claim for refund when the practitioner knows or should know that it contains such a position; or
- Advise a client to take such a position or prepare a portion of a return or claim for refund containing such a position.

A tax practitioner may not advise a client to take a frivolous tax position on a **document, affidavit, or other paper** submitted to the IRS. Nor may a tax practitioner advise a client to submit a document, affidavit, or other paper to the IRS if:

- It is intended to delay or impede administration of federal tax laws;
- It is frivolous; or
- It contains or omits information indicating an intentional disregard for a rule or regulation, unless the practitioner also advises the client to submit a document indicating a good faith challenge to the rule or regulation.

A practitioner is required to **advise clients regarding potential penalties** that are reasonably likely to be assessed, and the opportunity to avoid penalty through disclosure, when those penalties have the potential of arising from:

- A tax position taken if the practitioner either signed or prepared the return or advised the client relative to the position
- A document, affidavit, or other paper submitted to the IRS

A practitioner may, in good faith, **rely on information obtained from a client** without verification. If information furnished by the client appears incorrect, incomplete, or otherwise unsatisfactory based on information known by, or furnished to the practitioner, that fact may not be ignored by the practitioner.

Section 10.37 – Requirements for Other Written Advice

A practitioner is prohibited from giving written advice that is based on unreasonable assumptions; unreasonably relies on representations, statements, findings, or agreements of the taxpayer or another; does not consider all relevant information that is known, or should be known, by the practitioner; or considers the possibility that the position, or the return on which it is taken, will not be audited or will be resolved through settlement.

A practitioner may rely on the advice of another, provided:

- The advice is reasonable, and
- Reliance is in good faith, considering all facts and circumstances.

Section 10.50 – Sanctions

The Secretary of the Treasury has the authority to **censure**, **suspend**, or **disbar** a practitioner from practice before the IRS if the practitioner:

- Is shown to be incompetent or disreputable;
- Violates requirements either willfully or as a result of gross incompetence; or

- Willfully and knowingly misleads or threatens a client or prospective client with the intent to defraud.

The Secretary of the Treasury also has the authority to impose a *monetary penalty* on any practitioner who engages in the prohibited conduct indicated above.

Section 10.51 – Incompetence and Disreputable Conduct

Some of the actions or events that indicate incompetence or disreputable conduct include:
- Conviction of a criminal offense under federal tax laws or involving dishonesty or breach of trust, or for any felony for conduct that renders the practitioner unfit to practice before the IRS.
- Knowingly giving false or misleading information, or participating in doing so, to the Department of the Treasury
- Solicitation prohibited by Section 10.30
- Willfully failing to make a federal tax return or evading, or attempting to evade, an assessment or payment of federal tax
- Willfully assisting, counseling, or encouraging a client or prospective client to violate a tax law or evade federal taxes or their payment
- Failure to promptly remit funds received from a client for the payment of taxes
- Attempting to influence an officer or employee of the IRS
- Disbarment or suspension from practice as an attorney or CPA
- Knowingly assisting another person in practicing before the IRS when disbarred or suspended
- Contemptuous conduct, such as using abusive language, knowingly making false accusations; or circulating malicious or libelous material in connection with practice before the IRS
- Knowingly, recklessly, or as a result of gross incompetence, giving a false opinion
- Willingly failing to sign a tax return when required
- Willfully disclosing or using a tax return or tax information inappropriately
- Willfully failing to file using electronic media when required to do so
- Providing covered tax services without a valid PTIN
- Willfully representing a taxpayer before the IRS when not authorized to do so

Section 10.60 – Institution of Proceeding

Any violation of laws relative to practice before the IRS may result in reprimand or a proceeding for sanctions. Instituting a proceeding requires that the respondent be advised in writing of the law, facts, and conduct warranting such action; and is given an opportunity to dispute facts, assert additional facts, and make arguments.

Lecture 11.03

LICENSING AND DISCIPLINARY SYSTEMS

Role of State Boards of Accountancy

Each state has a State Board of Accountancy that issues CPA certificates as well as licenses to engage in the practice of public accounting. In some states, the CPA certificate is the license to practice but in others, both are required to practice. Each state has its own requirements, although there is a high degree of uniformity as many have adopted the basic requirements of the Uniform Accountancy Act.

In addition, each state establishes requirements that must be met in order to maintain the certificate and license. These include minimum requirements for *continuing professional education (CPE)* and adherence to the state's *code of professional conduct*. Most states have based their code of professional conduct on the AICPA code of conduct by adopting the major components and adding detail to some provisions, adding additional requirements that are unique to the state, or enhancing AICPA requirements. A CPA who does not adhere to the AICPA Code of Professional Conduct (ET) will not be able to maintain membership in the AICPA. In addition, a violation of the AICPA code will likely result in a violation of each state's code and, as a result, may subject the CPA to sanctions. In some cases, a practitioner's *license will be suspended and it also may be revoked*.

Requirements of Regulatory Agencies

Internal Revenue Service (IRS)

The IRS is a bureau of the Department of the Treasury. The Secretary is authorized by the Internal Revenue Code (IRC) to administer and enforce internal revenue laws and created the IRS as the agency to accomplish that purpose. The Commissioner of the IRS, appointed by the Secretary, is charged with administering and supervising the execution and application of the IRC.

The mission of the IRS is to "Provide America's taxpayers top quality service" by helping them understand and meet their tax responsibilities and enforce the law with integrity and fairness to all.

This mission statement describes our role and the public's expectation about how we should perform that role.

- In the United States, Congress passes tax laws and requires taxpayers to comply.
- The taxpayer's role is to understand and meet his/her tax obligations.
- The IRS role is to help the large majority of compliant taxpayers with the tax law, while ensuring that the minority who are unwilling to comply pay their fair share.

The domain of the IRS covers all federal taxes, including income taxes, excise taxes, payroll taxes, and gift and estate taxes. Violations may subject a taxpayer or a tax practitioner to disciplinary actions. Most infractions will result in **civil** liability, which may result in a tax practitioner losing their PTIN and a taxpayer in being fined. When fraud is involved, the result may be a **criminal** action, which could result in incarceration (Jail).

Securities and Exchange Commission (SEC)

The SEC was created by the Securities Exchange Act of 1934 in order to enforce the Securities Act of 1933. Since its formation, its jurisdiction has expanded to include enforcement of the Trust Indenture Act of 1939, the Investment Company Act of 1940, The Investment Advisers Act of 1940, and the Sarbanes-Oxley Act of 2002. "The mission of the U.S. Securities and Exchange Commission is to protect investors, maintain fair, orderly, and efficient markets, and facilitate capital formation."

The SEC designates the bodies authorized to establish standards for the performance of audits of entities that report to the SEC, and to establish accounting principles for those entities. The SEC has designated the Public Company Accounting Oversight Board (PCAOB) as having responsibility for auditing standards and the Financial Accounting Standards Board (FASB) as having responsibility for accounting principles.

Entities that do not report to the SEC basically follow the same accounting principles as those that do report. There are some accounting principles that have been designated as either not applying to nonpublic entities or applying with fewer specific requirements. In addition, the SEC staff has issued Staff Accounting Bulletins, which must also be taken into consideration by those who report to the SEC.

Auditing standards that apply to nonpublic entities are promulgated by the Auditing Standards Board (ASB) of the AICPA. Although these standards have minor differences from those of the PCAOB, the organizations cooperate with one another and differences are eliminated or reduced, when appropriate.

One significant difference between PCAOB (SEC) standards and those that apply to auditors of nonpublic entities (AICPA) relates to the area of auditor independence. Auditors of nonpublic entities are required to comply with the AICPA Code of Professional Conduct. Under this code of conduct, an auditor may perform nonattest services, such as bookkeeping or tax compliance services, for an audit client without impairing independence when certain requirements are adhered to. An auditor of a public company may not perform any nonattest services for an audit client without impairing independence. There is an exception that allows the auditor to perform certain nonattest services for an audit client, such as certain tax services, provided the client's audit committee pre-approves the nonattest service after obtaining satisfaction that the nature of the service would not impair the auditor's independence. So, as you can see, the SEC (PCAOB) rules regarding independence are a bit *more restrictive* than those of the AICPA.

Lecture 11.04

PRIVATE SECURITIES LITIGATION REFORM ACT OF 1995

When auditing publicly traded companies that report to the SEC under the 1934 Federal Securities Exchange Act, a CPA must also comply with the Private Securities Litigation Reform Act. This law places into the code several responsibilities already considered part of an effective audit under GAAS, including (**RIG**):
- **Related-party transactions** – The auditor must include substantive tests designed to identify all significant related-party transactions.
- **Illegal acts** – The auditor should attempt to identify illegal acts with a direct and material effect on the financial statements (Non-compliance with applicable laws and regulations).
- **Going concern** – The auditor should perform tests to determine if there is substantial doubt as to the ability of the client to continue in existence throughout the following fiscal year.

In addition, the law imposes reporting responsibilities on the auditor whenever illegal acts (non-compliance) are identified. The auditor should report illegal acts to the appropriate level of management. If management fails to take appropriate action in connection with material illegal acts, the auditor must inform the board of directors or audit committee as soon as it is practicable. The board is given only 1 business day to make a filing informing the SEC of these illegal acts, and must provide proof of filing to the auditor. If the auditor does not receive this proof by the filing deadline, the auditor is then given only **1 business day** to either:
- **Resign** from the engagement
- **Notify the SEC** of the failure of the board to make the appropriate filing.

An auditor who fails to comply with the reporting provisions may be held civilly liable, but an auditor who complies may not be held liable in any private action for statements filed with the SEC. Defendants' liability is generally proportionate to their degree of fault, unless they knowingly caused the harm, then they are jointly and severally liable.

WORKING PAPERS (AUDIT DOCUMENTATION)

The accountant, not the client, owns the working papers that an accountant creates during an engagement. Nevertheless, the accountant must maintain **confidentiality**, and cannot provide the papers or information obtained during engagements to other parties without the permission of the client (it should be noted that client confidentiality does not preclude a CPA from providing access to other members of his/her firm). There are some **exceptions** to confidentiality, including:
- **Valid subpoena** - the accountant must honor a valid court order to turn over information.
- **IRS administrative subpoena**
- **Court order** (unless rare state with privilege statute).
- Where **disclosure** is in compliance with GAAP or GAAS.
- **Quality control peer review** - The accountant may allow other accountants and the PCAOB to see confidential information in connection with a valid program of peer review.
  - o **Note**: The PCAOB was created out of the Sarbanes-Oxley Act (SOX) to restore investor confidence and to regulate auditors of public companies subject to SEC oversight.

Common law does not recognize the concept of **privilege**, which would allow the accountant to refuse to honor a court subpoena. A small number of states have enacted privilege statutes, and the federal government now recognizes working papers developed in connection with the preparation of a tax return to be privileged in certain circumstances. Nevertheless, privilege may not be used if the accountant has already provided some of the information requested in the subpoena, and the purpose of privilege is to protect the client, not the accountant, so the accountant may not assert privilege even where privilege statutes exist if the client waives the privilege.

Under the code of professional conduct, in order for an accountant to be considered independent, there can be no more than 1 year of audit fees outstanding.

Lecture 11.05

CLASS QUESTIONS

Please see the Class Questions and Class Solutions for this Lecture at the end of this Section.

CLASS QUESTIONS

Work through the below Class Questions while following along with the respective lectures. Once this is complete, you can begin independently practicing what you've learned by quizzing yourself on this course section in your Interactive Practice Questions (IPQ), which can be found in your online Student Dashboard. Your IPQ simulates the computer-based testing experience, and will also help you understand how concepts are applied to the exam. Each question includes answer explanations from expert CPAs that will help you determine why you answered a question correctly or incorrectly. This is key to your success on the CPA Exam.

Lecture 11.05

1. Kopel was engaged to prepare Raff's 20X9 federal income tax return. During the tax preparation interview, Raff told Kopel that he paid $3,000 in property taxes in 20X9. Actually, Raff's property taxes amounted to only $600. Based on Raff's word, Kopel deducted the $3,000 on Raff's return, resulting in an understatement of Raff's tax liability. Kopel had no reason to believe that the information was incorrect. Kopel did not request underlying documentation and was reasonably satisfied by Raff's representation that Raff had adequate records to support the deduction. Which of the following statements is correct?

   a. To avoid the preparer penalty for willful understatement of tax liability, Kopel was obligated to examine the underlying documentation for the deduction.
   b. To avoid the preparer penalty for willful understatement of tax liability, Kopel would be required to obtain Raff's representation in writing.
   c. Kopel is **not** subject to the preparer penalty for willful understatement of tax liability because the deduction that was claimed was more than 25% of the actual amount that should have been deducted.
   d. Kopel is **not** subject to the preparer penalty for willful understatement of tax liability because Kopel was justified in relying on Raff's representation.

2. With respect to any given tax return, which of the following statements is correct?

   a. More than one person may be deemed to be a preparer of a tax return.
   b. The final reviewer of a tax return is automatically considered the preparer of the return.
   c. Only one person may be deemed to be a preparer of a tax return.
   d. The two individuals who have done the most work in preparing the return will be deemed to be the only preparers.

3. Which of the following statements is correct regarding the standards a CPA should follow when recommending tax return positions and preparing tax returns?

   a. A CPA may recommend a position that the CPA concludes is frivolous as long as the position is adequately disclosed on the return.
   b. A CPA may recommend a position for which the CPA has a good faith belief there is substantial authority of being sustained if challenged.
   c. A CPA will usually **not** advise the client of the potential penalty consequences of the recommended tax return position.
   d. A CPA may sign a tax return as preparer knowing that the return takes a position that will **not** be sustained if challenged.

4. A tax preparer has advised a company to take a position on its tax return. The tax preparer believes that there is a 75% possibility that the position will be sustained if audited by the IRS. If the position is not sustained, an accuracy-related penalty and a late-payment penalty would apply. What is the tax preparer's responsibility regarding disclosure of the penalty to the company?

    a. The tax preparer is responsible for disclosing both penalties to the company.
    b. The tax preparer is responsible for disclosing only the accuracy-related penalty to the company.
    c. The tax preparer is responsible for disclosing only the late-payment penalty to the company.
    d. The tax preparer has **no** responsibility for disclosing any potential penalties to the company, because the position will probably be sustained on audit.

5. Which of the following Boards has the responsibility to regulate CPA firms that audit public companies?

    a. Auditing Standards Board.
    b. Public Oversight Board.
    c. Public Company Accounting Oversight Board.
    d. Accounting Standards Board.

6. Which of the following is an auditor **not** required to establish procedures for under the Private Securities Litigation Reform Act?

    a. To develop a comprehensive internal control system.
    b. To evaluate the ability of the firm to continue as a going concern.
    c. To detect material illegal acts.
    d. To identify material related-party transactions.

7. Which of the following statements is correct regarding an accountant's working papers?

    a. The accountant owns the working papers and generally may disclose them as the accountant sees fit.
    b. The client owns the working papers but the accountant has custody of them until the accountant's bill is paid in full.
    c. The accountant owns the working papers but generally may **not** disclose them without the client's consent or a court order.
    d. The client owns the working papers but, in the absence of the accountant's consent, may **not** disclose them without a court order.

8. Lin, CPA, is auditing the financial statements of Exchange Corporation under the Federal Securities Exchange Act of 1934. He detects what he believes are probable material illegal acts. What is his duty under the Private Securities Litigation Reform Act?

    a. He must inform the principal shareholders within ten days.
    b. He must inform the audit committee or the board of directors.
    c. He need not inform anyone, beyond requiring that the financial statements are presented fairly.
    d. He should not inform anyone since he owes a duty of confidentiality to the client.

CLASS SOLUTIONS

1. (d) A tax preparer may in good faith rely on information obtained from the taxpayer without any form of verification. The CPA is only required to make inquiries or take further action if the information provided by the taxpayer appears to the CPA to be incorrect, incomplete, or otherwise unsatisfactory. Answer (a) is incorrect because the CPA need not examine the underlying document to support the deduction that the CPA has no reason to believe was incorrect. Answer (b) is incorrect because a written representation from the taxpayer would not be required. Answer (c) is incorrect because there is no rule that exempts a claimed deduction that is at least 25% of the appropriate amount.

2. (a) Multiple individuals may be held responsible as the preparer for any one tax return. Under Regulation §301.7701-15(a), a tax return preparer is defined as "any person who prepares for compensation, or who employs one or more persons to prepare for compensation, all or a substantial portion of any return of tax or any claim for refund of tax under the Internal Revenue Code (Code)." This can include a signing preparer and any number of nonsigning preparers since Regulation §301.7701-15(b)(3) provides that a single entry on a tax return could constitute a "substantial portion" of a return depending on the size and complexity of the entry. While a final reviewer, or "signing tax return preparer," has the primary responsibility for the overall substantive accuracy of the preparation of a return or claim for refund, other nonsigning preparers may also be held responsible for the same return as a preparer.

3. (b) A CPA may recommend a tax position that the CPA believes in good faith to be sustainable and backed by substantial authority (40% likelihood of success), and may prepare and sign a return taking such a position. Answer (a) is incorrect because a CPA may not recommend a frivolous position. The CPA may sign a return taking a position with a reasonable basis (20% likelihood of success), if it is adequately disclosed on the return. Answer (c) is incorrect because a CPA is required to advise the client of the potential consequences, including penalties that may be incurred, if a position taken is not sustained upon examination. Answer (d) is incorrect because a CPA may not sign a return that takes a position that the CPA knows will not be sustainable, but may sign one that takes a position with a reasonable basis (20% likelihood of success), provided it is adequately disclosed.

4. (a) A tax preparer must always inform a client of any potential penalties that are reasonably likely to apply to the client. Even if there is a 75% possibility that the position will be sustained by the IRS, there is still a reasonable chance that the client could be penalized.

5. (c) Sarbanes-Oxley established the Public Company Accounting Oversight Board and gave it the responsibility of setting auditing standards for auditors of entities reporting to the SEC and regulating the registered CPA firms that perform the audits. Answer (a) is incorrect because the Auditing Standards Board establishes auditing standards that apply to nonpublic entities. Answer (b) is incorrect because there is no Public Oversight Board that regulates CPAs. Answer (d) is incorrect because there is no Accounting Standards Board, although the Financial Accounting Standards Board is responsible for establishing generally accepted accounting principles.

6. (a) It would not be the auditor's responsibility to develop a comprehensive system of internal control, although the auditor is required to obtain and document an understanding of the client's internal control and, in the case of publicly held entities, express an opinion on management's assessment of the effectiveness of internal control. Answer (b) is incorrect because the auditor is required to evaluate the entity's ability to continue as a going concern. Answer (c) is incorrect because the auditor is expected to detect illegal acts if they are material. Answer (d) is incorrect because the auditor is expected to identify related-party transactions.

7. (c) Working papers are the property of the CPA firm, not the client. They contain, however, information about the client obtained during the course of performing a professional engagement, which must be kept confidential. It may only be disclosed with client permission except in certain circumstances, such as in response to a valid court order.

8. (b) Under the Private Securities Litigation Reform Act, an auditor that detects a probable material illegal act is required to disclose such information to those responsible for governance, which would be the board of directors. The auditor may not inform the stockholders.

Business Law

(10% - 20%)

Section 12 – Federal Securities Regulations

Corresponding Lectures

Watch the following course lectures with this section:

Lecture 12.01 – Federal Securities Regulations
Lecture 12.02 – Securities Act of 1933
Lecture 12.03 – 1933 Exemptions
Lecture 12.04 – 1933 Exemption – Private Placement (Reg D)
Lecture 12.05 – Securities Act of 1933 – Class Questions
Lecture 12.06 – Securities Act of 1934
Lecture 12.07 – Securities Act of 1934 – Class Questions
Lecture 12.08 – Federal Securities Regulations – TBS

EXAM NOTE: Please refer to the AICPA REG Blueprint in the Introduction to find a listing of the representative tasks (and their associated skill levels—i.e., Remembering and Understanding, Application, and Analysis) that the candidate should be able to perform based on the knowledge obtained in this section.

Federal Securities Regulations

FEDERAL SECURITIES REGULATIONS – OVERVIEW

After the stock market crash of 1929, the government wanted to make sure that information was available to investors and wanted to create a governing body to administer all federal security laws.

The **1933 Federal securities act**, also called the "Truth in Securities Act," is concerned with the *original* issuance of securities intended for sale to the public. The act's intent is to ensure sufficient information is available to potential investors, not to determine the desirability of the securities.

The **1934** act created the Securities and Exchange Commission (SEC), which provides ongoing reporting requirements and focuses on *secondary offerings* of securities and regulates purchases and sales after initial issuance.

The **SEC** is responsible for
- Administering federal securities laws
- Regulating brokers
- Issuing rules on details of retaining workpapers and other relevant records connected with audits or reviews (Sarbanes-Oxley act).
- *De-listing* issuers not in compliance with Sarbanes-Oxley act.

Securities

A security is defined as an investment in an enterprise, where the investor intends to make a profit through the managerial efforts of others, rather than through his own efforts. Some **examples** include:
- Common Stock, Preferred Stock, treasury stock, bonds, debentures, options, warrants, some notes, limited but not general partnership interests (since involved in the management of the co.), all investment contracts and collateral-trust certificates (type of bond). Does not include Certificates of Deposits.

SECURITIES ACT OF 1933

One cannot sell securities unless they are registered with the SEC. A registration statement, which consists of 2 parts, must be filed, unless exempt. The 2 parts include part 1, a prospectus (a written offer to sell) and part 2, which contains detailed information about the securities being issued. The *purpose* of registering securities is to adequately and accurately disclose financial and other information upon which investors may determine the merits of securities. Once a company goes public, they have ongoing reporting requirements (1934 act) and also must then comply with, for example, SOX "say on pay" rules governing audit and compensation committees, Federal Proxy Rules, Foreign Corrupt Practices Act, and many more.
- Must file a:
  - **Prospectus – part 1** (a *written, TV or radio offer* to sell securities) must be *available* to investors before or with every sale. Summarizes the information in part 2.
    - Historical company information

- Discusses the risks involved

  o Registration statement – part 2 (disclosure document)
    - **Basic information**
      - Names and addresses and amount of securities held by directors, officers, underwriters and shareholders with at least 10% of the stock
      - *Intended use* of the proceeds
      - Company's debt
      - Company's operating history and pending litigation

    - **Financial information**
      - Audited balance sheet (not more than 90 days old)
      - Audited Profit & loss statement (for previous 5 years)

Before registration, no sales may occur. Once the SEC deems the registration statements complete, **20 days** after filed, the registration is "**effective**" and the securities may now be sold, provided investors receive a prospectus with the sale. Before the registration is effective, called the **waiting period**, the company may still:

- Make Oral offers to sell
- Issue a preliminary prospectus called a "**red herring**"
  o A prospectus that has been filed but is missing certain unavailable information (like issue price) has not yet become effective.
- After the effective date, "**tombstone ads**" can be placed announcing how to acquire a prospectus.
  o A tombstone ad announces the availability of a prospectus on a potential investment, and is not itself considered an offer to sell.
- For companies that issue securities to the public on a continuous basis, such as mutual funds, a form of registration known as a **shelf registration** is available. Such a registration requires the company to periodically update the prospectus, but allows sales and resale's to be continuous for an indefinite period of time. Not available for first-time issuers.
- Most states have adopted their own securities laws called "**Blue sky laws**," which contain antifraud and registration provisions. Compliance with the federal laws doesn't automatically imply compliance with the state laws.

A registration statement must be filed and a prospectus made available when:
- Applicable offerings are based on (**SPIN**):
  o Offer **S**ecurities (stocks, bonds, debentures, options, warrants, limited but not general partnerships, all investment contracts).
  o **P**ublic Issue (large number of people that are issuers of securities)
    - Issuing company
    - Officer, director, major shareholder >10%
    - Dealer
    - Underwriter
  o **I**nterstate Commerce (between states)
  o **N**o other **exemption** is available
    - 2 types of exemptions:
      - Exempt Securities
      - Exempt Transactions

Public offers refer to attempts to transfer shares from the issuing company or other knowledgeable insiders to outsiders who may have no special understanding about the company. It does not refer to general trading among members of the public, since this law was not intended to regulate the securities industry as a whole (the 1934 Act regulates the industry).

If an issuer sells a security and fails to meet disclosure requirements of the 1933 Act, the purchaser may request rescission of the sale.

Interstate commerce refers to offers that involve people in more than a single state. Offers that stay within a single state are generally exempt from this act.

When the law applies, those offering the securities must provide each prospective investor with a document known as a **prospectus**, containing substantial historical information about the company and a discussion of the risks involved in the securities.

The exemption may relate to the security being offered **(exempt securities)** or the way in which the security is being offered **(exempt transactions).**

Emerging Growth Companies

In 2012, the JOBS Act (Jumpstart Our Business Startups) was enacted as a means of stimulating the economy by making it easier for business, and particularly *emerging growth companies (EGCs)*, to access the public capital markets.

- An EGC is a business that had revenues of **less than $1 billion** as of the end of this most recent fiscal year. An entity is no longer an EGC at the earliest of:
    - The last day of the year in which the 5th anniversary of the IPO falls
    - The last day of the year in which annual revenues are $1 billion or more
    - The date on which an entity has issued more than $1 billion in non-convertible debt in the previous 3-year period
    - The date on which the entity is considered to be a large accelerated filer ($\geq$ $700 Million market value of securities outstanding)
    - When the company has more than 2,000 shareholders (500 if they are nonaccredited)
- EGCs are exempt from certain rules that deter companies from choosing to go public.
    - Under the Securities Act of 1933:
        - Required to provide 2 years (instead of 5 years) of audited F/S with its IPO registration statement.
        - Not required to provide selected financial info in other registration statements for periods prior to the earliest audited F/S included in their IPO registration statement.
        - May solicit qualified institutional buyers and accredited investors before or after the filing of a registration statement prior to it being made public for SEC staff to review.
        - May file a confidential IPO registration statement with the SEC that must be made public at least 21 days before it begins actively promoting the sale of its offering.
    - Under the Securities Exchange Act of 1934:
        - Not required to allow stockholders a "say on pay" vote related to executive compensation.
        - Reduced executive compensation disclosure requirements.

- o Under Sarbanes-Oxley:
  - May use the later effective date applicable to nonpublic entities for new financial accounting standards.
  - Auditor not required to attest to management's assessment of internal control over financial reporting.

1933 EXEMPTIONS (ACID-BRAINS)

Section 3 of the Securities Act of 1933 describes certain *securities* that are exempt, while Section 4 describes certain *transactions* that are exempt.

- Regulation **A** – small public offerings (≤ $50M over 12 months; 20-day notice/waiting period; offering circular; can advertise/resell)
- **C**ommercial paper (notes, bonds) mature ≤ 9mo's and used for Commercial (not investing) purposes
  - o **C**asual sales by other than issuer, underwriter, dealer
  - o **C**rowdfunding (≤ $1M over 12 months sold through online intermediary)
- **I**ntrastate offerings
  - o At least 80% of co sales are exclusive to state of incorporation and principal place of business, but buyers cannot resell outside the state for 9 months.
- Regulation **D** – Private placement offerings (Rule 504 ≤ $5M; Rule 506 = unlimited)
- **B**rokerage transactions
- **R**egulated industries (Savings and loans – e.g., cd's)
- **A**gencies of the Gov. (Railroads, Municipal bonds)
- **I**nsurance contracts/Policies
  - o But stock issued by insurance companies is not exempt.
- **N**ot for profit (charity/church)
- **S**tock dividends / **S**plits (i.e., exchanges with existing holders) as long as no commission is paid.

Regulation A – Small Public Offerings of Privately Held Corporations

Regulation A applies to offerings that raise up to **$50 million** over a period not exceeding **12 months**. Securities must be unrestricted equity securities, debt securities, and debt securities that are convertible into equity securities. The requirements are:

- The SEC must be notified within **20 days** of the first sale.
- An **offering circular** (mini-registration statement) containing key information about the company must be prepared and provided to all prospective investors (an offering circular is far less extensive than a prospectus).
- The following disclosure requirements apply depending on the total amount of offerings within a 12-month period:
  - o Tier 1—Up to **$20 million**, with up to $6 million in offers by affiliates of the issuer.
    - **Unaudited** financial statements required.
  - o Tier 2—Up to **$50 million**, with up to $15 million in offers by affiliates of the issuer.
    - **Audited** financial statements required.
    - Non-accredited investors are limited to 10% of annual income or net worth, if greater.

- Secondary sales are limited to 30% of the original offering or any other offering in the first year.

Casual sales are exempt. These refer to sales by persons not connected with the issuing company, and are available to all sellers except:
- Issuers
- Underwriters
- Dealers
- Directors
- Officers
- Owners of at least 10% of any class of shares

Regulation Crowdfunding

Allows entities to issue securities through "**crowdfunding,**" which is the obtaining of small investments from a large number of investors. This exemption makes it possible for privately owned companies to sell securities to investors over the internet through an SEC-registered intermediary—i.e., either a broker-dealer or a "funding portal."
- Up to **$1 million** may be raised in a **12-month** period ($1,070,000 as adjusted for inflation).
- Limits are set on amounts individual investors may invest per 12-month period:
    - The greater of $2,000 ($2,200 as adjusted for inflation) or 5% of annual income or net worth (if less), for those with annual income or net worth less than $100,000 ($107,000 as adjusted for inflation).
    - Up to 10% of annual income or net worth (if less) up to a maximum of $100,000 ($107,000 as adjusted for inflation), if both annual income and net worth equal or exceed $100,000 ($107,000 as adjusted for inflation).
- Securities generally cannot be resold for 1 year.
- Among *other disclosure requirements*, the following is required depending on the total amount of offerings within a 12-month period:
    - Up to $100,000
        - Federal income tax return information
        - F/S certified by principal executive officer
    - $100,000 – $500,000
        - Reviewed F/S
    - $500,000 – $1,000,000
        - Audited F/S —however, if issuing for first time under Regulation Crowdfunding, then reviewed F/S

Intrastate offers are exempt as long as:
- The company does at least 80% of its business operations in a single state.
- Securities are offered **exclusively** to residents of that state.
- The investors agree not to resell their securities to non-residents for at least *9 months.*

In addition to the exemptions already mentioned (Regulation D, Regulation A, intrastate offers, casual sales), there are several other **minor exemptions** that are occasionally mentioned on the exam, though not in any detail:
- Sales of **government securities**
- Issuances by companies that are already being **regulated by a federal agency** (such as banks regulated by the Federal Reserve System and railroads regulated by the Interstate Commerce Commission)

- **Insurance policies**
- Fund-raising by **non-profit organizations**
- Short-term loans to be **repaid within 9 months** (also known as **commercial paper**)
- Exchanges of securities with **existing shareholders at no charge**, such as stock splits and dividends

The Securities Act of 1933 imposes substantial obligations on the auditors involved in the preparation of the prospectuses. These liability issues are discussed as part of the accountant liability section.

Lecture 12.04

Regulation D Exemption – Private Placement (504, 506)

- The general purpose of Regulation D is to simplify the sale of securities to sophisticated and "accredited investors." **Accredited investors** include:
    - Banks, savings and loans, credit unions, insurance companies, broker dealers, certain trusts, partnerships, corporations, etc.
    - Wealthy individuals
        - Net worth exceeding $1,000,000 (*excluding primary residence*) or
        - Net income of $200,000 ($300,000 MFJ) for the two most recent years

- Rule **504** – Offerings up to **$5 million** to be completed within **12 months** (Seed Capital exemption).
    - SEC must be notified (Form D) within **15 days** of first sale.
        - No general advertising or solicitation is generally allowed.*
        - Generally, restricted securities – Resale is permitted after **one year**.*
        - No special info given to investors.
        - Unlimited number of investors, accredited or nonaccredited.
        - Companies *cannot use* this exemption if they are already required to report under the 1934 act or if they are an investment company.
        *Note: Solicitation and resale restrictions may not apply if securities are exempt under certain state laws (i.e., blue sky laws).

- Rule **506** – **Unlimited** as to dollar value and time.
    - SEC must be notified (Form D) within **15 days** of first sale.
    - General solicitation and advertising of the offer is allowed as long as sales are made only to *accredited investors*.
    - No resale for **one year** (investment purpose only – restricted security).
        - *The issuer needs to take reasonable steps to assure* that *the purchaser is buying for investment purposes and not for underwriting purposes.*
    - Unlimited number of accredited investors allowed.
    - Limited to 35 or fewer nonaccredited investors. Such nonaccredited investors must be sophisticated investors or be represented in their purchase by a *sophisticated investor* (i.e., an investor with the knowledge and experience in financial and business matters that enables them to evaluate the merits and risks of the investment).
    - Audited balance sheet (at a minimum) must be provided to nonaccredited investors.
    - Can use if required to report under 1934 act.

Regulation D – Private Placement

Rule 504	Rule 506
Notify SEC within **15 days** of first sale (Form D)	
No general solicitation or advertising* (generally)	General solicitation and advertising* allowed if purchasers are all accredited investors
Resale generally restricted up to 1 year	Investment purpose only – Cannot resell for 1 year
Offerings ≤ $5,000,000	Unlimited dollar amount
Offerings must occur within 12-month period	Unlimited amount of time for issuance
Unlimited number of investors	*Unlimited Accredited* Investors
	Non-accredited ≤ 35 (0 if general solicitation)
Financial information given: Nothing	Accredited = Nothing
	Nonaccredited = Audited B/S and represented by sophisticated investor

* *General solicitation/advertising* includes newspaper, magazine, TV, and radio ads, ads on public websites, as well as any seminars where participants are invited by such advertising.

Exemption under Rule 144

A purchaser of restricted securities in a private offering (REG D), who purchased them for investment purposes rather than resale, may resell the securities subject to certain restrictions, without being subject to the registration provisions. The securities must have been held for *at least 1 year*; only limited amounts of stock may be sold (i.e., they may not all be "dumped" on the market, but rather "trickled" (no more than 1% of all outstanding shares sold every 3 months); and the SEC must be notified of the intention to sell the restricted securities. Note: The holding period is 6 months for a company subject to the reporting requirements under the 1934 Act.

Lecture 12.05

CLASS QUESTIONS

Please see the Class Questions and Class Solutions for this Lecture at the end of this Section.

Lecture 12.06

SECURITIES EXCHANGE ACT OF 1934

The Securities Exchange Act of 1934 is the law that created the Securities Exchange Commission (SEC) and gave it broad powers to regulate the securities industry. The application of this law is unrelated to the Securities Act of 1933, and a company that is exempt from one is not automatically exempt from the other, nor would the applicability of one necessarily indicate the applicability of the other.

A company which violates provisions of the 1934 Act may be sanctioned by the SEC by having trading of its securities suspended, or having registration of its securities for sale to the public denied, suspended, or revoked. The SEC also has the power to regulate and sanction brokerage firms and investment advisers.

The law also imposed legal obligations on accountants in connection with audits of companies involved in interstate commerce.

Deals with the subsequent purchase and sales of securities. Says that certain size companies have registration and reporting requirements and all purchasers and sellers of securities must adhere to the **anti-fraud provisions**. Not related to the 1933 act, so if exempt under one act, not automatically exempt under the other.

Under the Liability provisions of Section 10, Rule 10b-5, it is unlawful to make any untrue statement of a material fact or to omit a material fact (e.g., writing off a material bribe as a consulting fee in a 10Q). Under Section 18, it is unlawful to make false or misleading statements with respect to a material statement unless done in "good faith" (e.g., Intentionally filing an incorrect quarterly report with the SEC).

- Registration and reporting requirements (S-1) apply if either:
  - o Listed or Traded on a **national exchange,** or
  - o At least $10 million in assets and 2,000 shareholders (500 if nonaccredited shareholders). Note: Shares held by employees who received their shares under an employee stock compensation plan are not included in nonaccredited shareholder count.
    - *Required disclosures*:
      - Names of officers and directors
      - Nature of business
      - Financial structure of firm
      - Any bonus and profit-sharing provisions
- Forms S-2 and S-3 that require less detailed information may be filed by issuers under certain circumstances.

Periodic Reports

Periodic reports to be filed by the company with the SEC:
- **Form 10K** – Annual comparative Audited financial statements certified by a CPA within:
  - o **60 days** after the end of the fiscal year covered by the report for *large* accelerated filers (companies with a market value of at least **$700 million** in equity held by nonaffiliates),
  - o **75 days** after the end of the fiscal year covered by the report for *accelerated* filers (**at least $75 million** in equity), or
  - o **90 days** after the end of the fiscal year covered by the report for *all other* registrants (**less than $75 million** in equity) (non-accelerated filer).
- **Form 10Q** - Quarterly unaudited (Reviewed) financial information for each of the first 3 fiscal quarters due within 45 days of the end of each quarter (**40 days** after the end of the fiscal quarter for accelerated and large accelerated filers).
- **Form 8K** – Current reports due shortly after certain key events (change in officers, directors, resignation of directors, change in control) must be filed within **4 days** of a major change in the company.
- **Proxy statement** – Identification and objective discussion of matters to be voted on at the upcoming shareholder meeting

	Market Value of Outstanding Securities	10-K	10-Q
Large Accelerated Filer	≥ $700 million	60 days	40 days
Accelerated Filer	$700 million ≥ $75 M.	75 days	40 days
Non-Accelerated Filer	< $75 million	90 days	45 days

Other Reporting Requirements:

- **Tender offer** (attempts to buy 5% or more of a class of stock) is a takeover bid by a prospective acquirer to all stockholders to tender their stock at a specified price. The person wishing to acquire the stock (the bidder) must file with the SEC. The target company need not file.
- Owners of 5% or more must file **Schedule 13D** showing:
    - Source of the funds used for purchase
    - Amount of stock owned
    - Price offered for the shares
    - Future plans for the company
        - Disclose to SEC, the company, and the stock exchange.
- **Insider trading**
    - Directors, officers, and 10% or greater shareholders must report every purchase and sale.
    - Profits resulting from a purchase and sale within 6 months (short-swing profits) must be returned to the corporation.
- **Proxy solicitations**
    - The right to vote someone's shares at a shareholder meeting.
    - Must be sent to each shareholder and must notify the SEC 10 days prior to mailing.
- **Regulation Fair Disclosure (FD)**
    - If an issuer **unintentionally** discloses material information to select persons (including holders of the securities and stock market professionals), the SEC requires that the info be disclosed as soon as possible to the general public through either:
        - Press release
        - Form 8K
    - If an issuer **intentionally** discloses material information to select persons, they must disclose that information **simultaneously** to the general public.
- **Liability**
    - A company not meeting the reporting requirements or violating provisions of the 1933 or 1934 Acts could have the registration of its securities suspended or revoked and be Civilly liable.
    - The CPA may be Criminally liable if they violate any provision of the acts or willfully omit a material fact required to be stated in a registration statement. Liability under the 1933 and 1934 acts is discussed in the Accountant Liability section.
- **Sarbanes-Oxley Act**
    - Each periodic report that contains financial reports of the issuer must be accompanied with written statement of *CEO or CFO that certifies* that reports comply fully with relevant securities laws and also fairly present the financial condition of the company in all material aspects:
        - Any officer who makes certification while knowing it does not comply with SEC requirements can be fined up to $1M or imprisoned for up to 10 years, or both.

                  □   Officers can be fined up to $5M or imprisoned for up to 20 years, or both, for willful violation of this certification requirement.

- o   Amends 1934 Act to make it illegal for issuer to give various types of personal loans to or for any executive officer or director.
- o   Requires executives of an issuer to forfeit any bonus or incentive-based pay or profits from the sale of stock, received in the 12 months prior to an earnings restatement when misconduct was present.
- o   Requires the auditor to promptly inform the board of directors (audit committee) of all significant problems identified during the engagement.
- o   Violation of rules of the Public Company Accounting Oversight Board (PCAOB) of the Sarbanes-Oxley Act are treated as a violation of the Securities Exchange Act of 1934 with its penalties.

Audit Reports

There are *5 basic types* of Opinions:
- Unqualified (unmodified) opinion, which is a standard "clean" Report
- Unqualified (unmodified) opinion with emphasis of a matter paragraph added to the report
  - o   Uncertainty, division of responsibility, "emphasis of a matter" or "other matter"
- Qualified opinion - "except for"
- Disagreement (Non-GAAP, Inadequate Disclosure, Inconsistency), Scope Limitation
- Adverse opinion – "do not present fairly"
- Disclaimer of opinion – "we do not express an opinion"

Lecture 12.07

CLASS QUESTIONS

Please see the Class Questions and Class Solutions for this Lecture at the end of this Section.

Lecture 12.08

CLASS QUESTIONS

Please see the Class Questions and Class Solutions for this Lecture at the end of this Section.

CLASS QUESTIONS

Work through the below Class Questions while following along with the respective lectures. Once this is complete, you can begin independently practicing what you've learned by quizzing yourself on this course section in your Interactive Practice Questions (IPQ), which can be found in your online Student Dashboard. Your IPQ simulates the computer-based testing experience, and will also help you understand how concepts are applied to the exam. Each question includes answer explanations from expert CPAs that will help you determine why you answered a question correctly or incorrectly. This is key to your success on the CPA Exam.

Lecture 12.05

1. Under the Securities Exchange Act of 1934, which of the following types of instruments is excluded from the definition of "securities"?

    a. Investment contracts.
    b. Convertible debentures.
    c. Nonconvertible debentures.
    d. Certificates of deposit.

2. Under the Securities Act of 1933, which of the following statements most accurately reflects how securities registration affects an investor?

    a. The investor is provided with information on the stockholders of the offering corporation.
    b. The investor is provided with information on the principal purposes for which the offering's proceeds will be used.
    c. The investor is guaranteed by the SEC that the facts contained in the registration statement are accurate.
    d. The investor is assured by the SEC against loss resulting from purchasing the security.

3. Which of the following securities would be regulated by the provisions of the Securities Act of 1933?

    a. Securities issued by not-for-profit, charitable organizations.
    b. Securities guaranteed by domestic governmental organizations.
    c. Securities issued by savings and loan associations.
    d. Securities issued by insurance companies.

4. Which of the following facts will result in an offering of securities being exempt from registration under the Securities Act of 1933?

    a. The securities are nonvoting preferred stock.
    b. The issuing corporation was closely held prior to the offering.
    c. The sale or offer to sell the securities is made by a person other than an issuer, underwriter, or dealer.
    d. The securities are AAA-rated debentures that are collateralized by first mortgages on property that has a market value of 200% of the offering price.

5. Regulation D of the Securities Act of 1933

    a. Restricts the number of purchasers of an offering to 35.
    b. Permits an exempt offering to be sold to both accredited and nonaccredited investors.
    c. Is limited to offers and sales of common stock that do not exceed $1.5 million.
    d. Is exclusively available to small business corporations as defined by Regulation D.

Questions 6 and 7 are based on the following:

Pix Corp. is making a $56,000,000 stock offering. Pix wants the offering exempt from registration under the Securities Act of 1933.

6. Which of the following provisions of the Act would Pix have to comply with for the offering to be exempt?

    a. Regulation A.
    b. Regulation D, Rule 504.
    c. Regulation Crowdfunding.
    d. Regulation D, Rule 506.

7. Which of the following requirements would Pix have to comply with when selling the securities?

    a. No more than 35 investors.
    b. No more than 35 Nonaccredited investors.
    c. Accredited investors only.
    d. Nonaccredited investors only.

8. Which of the following statements concerning an initial intrastate securities offering made by an issuer residing in and doing business in that state is correct?

    a. The offering would be exempt from the registration requirements of the Securities Act of 1933.
    b. The offering would be subject to the registration requirements of the Securities Exchange Act of 1934.
    c. The offering would be regulated by the SEC.
    d. The shares of the offering could **not** be resold to investors outside the state for at least one year.

Lecture 12.07

Items 9 through 11 are based on the following:
Link Corp. is subject to the reporting provisions of the Securities Exchange Act of 1934.

9. Which of the following situations would require Link to be subject to the reporting provisions of the 1934 Act?

	Shares listed on a national securities exchange	More than one class of stock
a.	Yes	Yes
b.	Yes	No
c.	No	Yes
d.	No	No

10. Which of the following documents must Link file with the SEC?

	Quarterly reports (Form 10-Q)	Proxy Statements
a.	Yes	Yes
b.	Yes	No
c.	No	Yes
d.	No	No

11. Which of the following reports must also be submitted to the SEC?

	Report by any party making a tender offer to purchase Link's stock	Report of proxy solicitations by Link stockholders
a.	Yes	Yes
b.	Yes	No
c.	No	Yes
d.	No	No

12. Adler, Inc. is a reporting company under the Securities Exchange Act of 1934. The only security it has issued is voting common stock. Which of the following statements is correct?

    a. Because Adler is a reporting company, it is **not** required to file a registration statement under the Securities Act of 1933 for any future offerings of its common stock.
    b. Adler need **not** file its proxy statements with the SEC because it has only one class of stock outstanding.
    c. Any person who owns more than 10% of Adler's common stock must file a report with the SEC.
    d. It is unnecessary for the required annual report (Form 10-K) to include audited financial statements.

CLASS SOLUTIONS

1. (d) Investment contracts and debentures, whether convertible or not, are considered securities under the Securities Exchange Act of 1934. Certificates of deposit are considered commercial paper, not a security.

2. (b) The SEC protects investors by making certain that they have all of the information they should need to make an informed investment decision. That includes the purpose for which proceeds from an offering will be used. Answer (a) is incorrect because information about shareholders is not provided. Answer (c) is incorrect because the SEC does not attest to the facts in the registration statement; it only makes certain that it is complete. Answer (d) is incorrect because the SEC does not provide any assurances against losses.

3. (d) The Securities Act of 1933 provides exemptions for certain securities, including those issued by not-for-profit charitable organizations, those guaranteed by domestic government organizations, and those issued by savings and loan associations. While insurance contracts are exempt, securities issued by insurance companies are not.

4. (c) The Securities Act of 1933 requires the registration of securities being offered by an issuer, underwriter, or dealer. Securities offered by other parties are exempt. Answer (a) is incorrect because it does not matter if the securities are voting or nonvoting. Answer (b) is incorrect because an entity that was previously closely held, which would be the case with any IPO, is not exempt. Answer (d) is incorrect because the fact that the securities are collateralized is not relevant.

5. (b) Regulation D provides 2 exemptions for private placements of securities. Although there are restrictions, both exemptions allow for the sale of exempt securities to both accredited and nonaccredited investors. Answer (a) is incorrect because the exemption under Rule 506 does limit nonaccredited investors to a maximum of 35, but not all investors. Answer (c) is incorrect because the exemptions under Rules 504 and 506 allow for offerings of up to $5 million and an unlimited amount, respectively. Answer (d) is incorrect because the exemptions are not limited to small business corporations. **Note:** Rule 505 has been repealed.

6. (d) Rule 506 of Regulation D allows an exemption for offerings that are unlimited as to amount and the length of time, provided certain requirements are met. Exemption under Regulation A is limited to offerings of up to $50 million. Rule 504 of Regulation D is limited to offerings of up to $5 million. Regulation Crowdfunding is limited to offerings up to $1,000,000, as adjusted for inflation.

7. (b) Under Rule 506 of Regulation D, there is no limit on sales to accredited investors but sales to nonaccredited investors is limited to a maximum of 35.

8. (a) The Securities Act of 1933 applies to issuances of securities in *inter*state commerce. An offering that is exclusively *intra*state by an issuer that resides and does business in that state would be exempt and would not be regulated by the SEC. Such shares are to be held for at least 9 months before being sold to investors outside the state.

9. (b) A company will be subject to the reporting requirements of the Securities Exchange Act of 1934 if its securities are listed on a national securities exchange, which makes them subject to SEC regulation. Issuing more than one class of stock does not make a company subject to the 1934 Act.

10. (a) An entity subject to the Securities Exchange Act of 1934 is required to provide various periodic reports including 10Ks, 10Qs, 8Ks, and proxy statements.

11. (a) In addition to periodic reports, the Securities Exchange Act of 1934 requires an issuer to report tender offers, insider trading, and proxy solicitations.

12. (c) Directors, officers, and owners of 10% or more of an issuers stock are required to report every purchase and sale to the SEC. Answer (a) is incorrect because under the Securities Act of 1933, a registration statement is required for every offering that does not meet one of the exemptions. Answer (b) is incorrect because the number of classes of stock an issuer has does not affect its reporting requirements. Answer (d) is incorrect because the annual report on Form 10-K is required to include audited financial statements.

Lecture 12.08

TASK-BASED SIMULATIONS

Task-Based Simulation 1

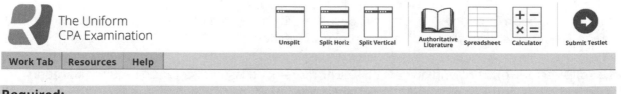

| Work Tab | Resources | Help |

Required:

You will have 15 questions based on the following information:

Butler Manufacturing Corp. planned to raise capital for a plant expansion by borrowing from banks and making several stock offerings. Butler engaged Weaver, CPA, to audit its December 31, 20X1 financial statements. Butler told Weaver that the financial statements would be given to certain named banks and included in the prospectuses for the stock offerings.

In performing the audit, Weaver did not confirm accounts receivable and, as a result, failed to discover a material overstatement of accounts receivable. Also, Weaver was aware of a pending class action product liability lawsuit that was not disclosed in Butler's financial statements. Despite being advised by Butler's legal counsel that Butler's potential liability under the lawsuit would result in material losses, Weaver issued an unmodified (unqualified) opinion on Butler's financial statements.

In May 20X2, Union Bank, one of the named banks, relied on the financial statements and Weaver's opinion in giving Butler a $500,000 loan.

Butler raised an additional $16,450,000 through the following stock offerings, which were sold completely:
- June 20X2—Butler made a $450,000 unregistered offering of Class B nonvoting common stock under Rule 504 of Regulation D of the Securities Act of 1933. This offering was sold over one year to 20 accredited investors with no general solicitation. The SEC was notified eight days after the first sale of this offering.
- September 20X2—Butler made a $10,000,000 unregistered offering of Class A voting common stock under Rule 506 of Regulation D of the Securities Act of 1933. This offering was sold over one year to 200 accredited investors and 30 non-accredited investors through a private placement. The SEC was notified 14 days after the first sale of this offering.
- November 20X2—Butler made a $6,000,000 unregistered offering of preferred stock under Rule 504 of Regulation D of the Securities Act of 1933. This offering was sold during a one-year period to 40 non-accredited investors by private placement. The SEC was notified 18 days after the first sale of this offering.

Shortly after obtaining the Union loan, Butler began experiencing financial problems but was able to stay in business because of the money raised by the offerings. Butler was found liable in the product liability suit. This resulted in a judgment Butler could not pay. Butler also defaulted on the Union loan and was involuntarily petitioned into bankruptcy. This caused Union to sustain a loss and Butler's stockholders to lose their investments. As a result

- The SEC claimed that all three of Butler's offerings were made improperly and were not exempt from registration.
- Union sued Weaver for
  - Negligence
  - Common Law Fraud
- The stockholders who purchased Butler's stock through the offerings sued Weaver, alleging fraud under Section 10(b) and Rule 10b-5 of the Securities Exchange Act of 1934.

These transactions took place in a jurisdiction providing for accountant's liability for negligence to known and intended users of financial statements.

Items to be answered:

Items 1 through 5 are questions related to the June 20X2 offering made under Rule 504 of Regulation D of the Securities Act of 1933. For each item, indicate your answer by choosing either Yes or No.

	Yes	No
1. Did the offering comply with the dollar limitation of Rule 504?	○	○
2. Did the offering comply with the method of sale restrictions?	○	○
3. Was the offering sold during the applicable time limit?	○	○
4. Was the SEC notified timely of the first sale of the securities?	○	○
5. Was the SEC correct in claiming that this offering was not exempt from registration?	○	○

Items 6 through 10 are questions related to the September 20X2 offering made under Rule 506 of Regulation D of the Securities Act of 1933. For each item, indicate your answer by choosing either Yes or No.

	Yes	No
6. Did the offering comply with the dollar limitation of Rule 506?	○	○
7. Did the offering comply with the method of sale restrictions?	○	○
8. Was the offering sold to the correct number of investors?	○	○
9. Was the SEC notified timely of the first sale of the securities?	○	○
10. Was the SEC correct in claiming that this offering was not exempt from registration?	○	○

Items 11 through 15 are questions related to the November 20X2 offering made under Rule 504 of Regulation D of the Securities Act of 1933. For each item, indicate your answer by choosing either Yes or No.

	Yes	No
11. Did the offering comply with the dollar limitation of Rule 504?	○	○
12. Was the offering sold during the applicable time limit?	○	○
13. Was the offering sold to the correct number of investors?	○	○
14. Was the SEC notified timely of the first sale of the securities?	○	○
15. Was the SEC correct in claiming that this offering was not exempt from registration?	○	○

TASK-BASED SIMULATION SOLUTIONS

Task-Based Simulation Solution 1
Items 1 through 5

		Yes	No
1.	Did the offering comply with the dollar limitation of Rule 504?	●	○
2.	Did the offering comply with the method of sale restrictions?	●	○
3.	Was the offering sold during the applicable time limit?	●	○
4.	Was the SEC notified timely of the first sale of the securities?	●	○
5.	Was the SEC correct in claiming that this offering was not exempt from registration?	○	●

Explanations

1. **(Y)** The dollar limitation for an offering under Rule 504 of Regulation D is $5 million. Since the offering was for $450,000, it complies.

2. **(Y)** Under Rule 504 of Regulation D, general solicitation is generally not allowed to (unless exempt under state law).

3. **(Y)** Rule 504 of Regulation D applies to offerings of up to $5 million that are completed within 12 months.

4. **(Y)** Under Rule 504 of Regulation D, an issuer is required to notify the SEC within 15 days of the first sale.

5. **(N)** It appears that the offering in June 20X2 met all of the requirements for exemption under Rule 504 of Regulation D, and the SEC is not correct in its assertion.

Items 6 through 10

		Yes	No
6.	Did the offering comply with the dollar limitation of Rule 506?	●	○
7.	Did the offering comply with the method of sale restrictions?	●	○
8.	Was the offering sold to the correct number of investors?	●	○
9.	Was the SEC notified timely of the first sale of the securities?	●	○
10.	Was the SEC correct in claiming that this offering was not exempt from registration?	○	●

Explanations

6. **(Y)** There is no limit on the dollar amount of an offering under Rule 506 of Regulation D.

7. **(Y)** A private placement is generally an issuance of securities to a small number of investors in a private offering, not a public offering and would qualify for exemption from registration under Rule 506 of Regulation D.

8. **(Y)** Rule 506 of Regulation D allows sales to an unlimited number of accredited investors and up to 35 non-accredited investors.

9. **(Y)** Rule 506 of Regulation D requires that the SEC be notified within 15 days of the first sale of securities.

10. **(N)** It appears that the offering in September 20X2 met all of the requirements for exemption under Rule 506 of Regulation D, and the SEC is not correct in its assertion.

Items 11 through 15

		Yes	No
11.	Did the offering comply with the dollar limitation of Rule 504?	○	●
12.	Was the offering sold during the applicable time limit?	●	○
13.	Was the offering sold to the correct number of investors?	●	○
14.	Was the SEC notified timely of the first sale of the securities?	○	●
15.	Was the SEC correct in claiming that this offering was not exempt from registration?	●	○

Explanations

11. **(N)** Rule 504 of Regulation D allows for an exemption from registration for offerings of up to $5 million.

12. **(Y)** Rule 504 of Regulation D requires offerings to be completed within 12 months.

13. **(Y)** Rule 504 of Regulation D allows sales to an unlimited number of investors of any type.

14. **(N)** Rule 504 of Regulation D requires notification of the SEC within 15 days of the first sale.

15. **(Y)** This offering violated a couple of the requirements of Rule 504 of Regulation D, including being over the $5 million limit by $1 million and not notifying the SEC until 18 days after the first sale, instead of the required 15 days.

Section 13 – Contracts

Corresponding Lectures

Watch the following course lectures with this section:

Lecture 13.01 – Common Law Contracts: Offer
Lecture 13.02 – Acceptance and Consideration
Lecture 13.03 – Common Law – Class Questions
Lecture 13.04 – Defenses
Lecture 13.05 – Parol Evidence Rule .
Lecture 13.06 – Common Law Contracts – Class Questions
Lecture 13.07 – Common Law Contracts – TBS

EXAM NOTE: *Please refer to the AICPA REG Blueprint in the Introduction to find a listing of the representative tasks (and their associated skill levels—i.e., Remembering and Understanding, Application, and Analysis) that the candidate should be able to perform based on the knowledge obtained in this section.*

Contracts

COMMON LAW CONTRACTS

An agreement between parties that may involve either a promise being exchanged for a promise, or a promise being exchanged for an act.

- **Bilateral contract** – Two promises are made, so it is basically a promise for a promise (e.g., I promise to pay you $50,000 if you promise to do my audit). A contract is formed when the promises are exchanged.
- **Unilateral contract** – One promise for an act (e.g., I'll pay anyone $100 who will find my dog). A contract is formed when performance is completed.

There are two main sources of contract law, common law derived from courts (real estate and services) and the Uniform Commercial Code (UCC), derived from Statutory Law (Sales of goods). The UCC has adopted much of common law; so most of what we cover in this section will still apply for the sale of goods section.

Formation

Formation of a valid Common Law contract requires Offer, Acceptance, Consideration and a lack of Defenses.

Offer

The offeror expresses a willingness to enter into a contract with the offeree.

- **Definite terms** - may be implied.
  - Price to be paid
  - Parties
  - Nature of the subject matter
  - Quantity involved
  - Time for performance
- **Intent** to make offer or contract – We are concerned with Objective intent (what a reasonable person believes). An advertisement does not have such intent, so it is considered a mere invitation to offer (unless we limit the scope, **for example,** "offer valid to only the first 10 people in line," is a valid offer).
- **Communicated to offeree** – constructively received when available to offeree (mail delivered to offeree's home or fax printed at offeree's business).

The terms of an offer must be definite to permit the formation of a contract, including clear agreement as to subject matter (including quantity), price, and time of performance. This is called an *express contract* as it is formed by **express** language. This does **not** mean the terms must be explicitly stated by the offeror. The terms can be **implied-in-fact**, meaning that the behavior or conduct of the two parties makes clear what the terms of the agreement are.

For example, if an individual calls up a pizza parlor and orders a medium pepperoni pizza to go, it is not necessary for the parties to discuss the price on the phone. A **reasonable person** would presume that the caller intended to pay the posted prices in the restaurant or on the takeout menus.

In rare cases, a contract can also be **implied-in-law (Quasi-contract)**. This occurs when the courts decide that parties should be treated as if they had an agreement, even though they did not, in order to avoid one party being unjustly enriched at the expense of the other.

For example, if a person who appears to be destitute asks a doctor to provide substantial medical services for free, and the doctor does so, but later discovers the individual is extremely wealthy, the courts may invoke this principle to allow the doctor to bill the patient customary charges. The court-defined arrangement is known as a **quasi-contract**.

Offers must be intentional. A statement made in jest or anger is not an offer. Also, advertisements are considered invitations to negotiate deals and not offers.

Offers must be **received** by the offeree. If the offer is made to a specific person, a different person cannot accept it. If an offer is made to the public, such as a reward for information on a crime, it can be accepted by anyone who knows of the offer. A party who provides information without knowing of the reward is not entitled to receive it.

- An offer must be accepted before it **Terminates**. The following would terminate an offer:
    - **Expiration** – expires after reasonable time if no stated date.
    - **Revocation** – may revoke even if promised not to do so (unless **option contract**, consideration paid to keep offer open). Revocation must be received to be effective.
        - Direct – phone call
        - Indirect – knowing that the lost dog has been returned and the reward paid.
    - **Rejection** – refusal by offeree, must be received by offeror.
    - **Counteroffer** – a form of rejection by offeree (an inquiry is not a counteroffer).
    - Operation of law
        - Death or insanity of either party
        - Destruction of subject matter
        - Illegality of subject matter (an offer to commit a crime for compensation)

It is not a counteroffer for the offeree to make inquiries about possible changes in the original offer, so an inquiry doesn't terminate the original offer. Offers may not be assigned, but an option contract may be assigned.

For example, assume a homeowner offers to sell their house for $200,000, and the offeree responds by asking "Would you be willing to sell for $190,000?" This is simply an inquiry, and not a counteroffer to purchase at $190,000. As a result, if the offeror indicates they will not sell at $190,000, the offeree can still accept the original offer at $200,000.

On the other hand, acceptances that add or change conditions in the original offer **are** counteroffers. **For example**, if the offeree responds to the offer at $200,000 by indicating that they accepted the price but wanted a termite inspection report and a 30-day escrow, they've actually rejected the offer and made a counteroffer with the two additional terms.

A contract is executory if certain duties still remain to be performed; however, a contract is considered executed when all contractual duties have been performed.

Lecture 13.02

Acceptance

Acceptance of an offer creates a contract. Two important rules:
- **Mirror image rule** – Must accept all terms and conditions of the offer without any alteration; otherwise, it's a counteroffer which would terminate the offer. An acceptance must be unequivocal and unqualified with respect to the precise terms specified by the offer.
- **Early acceptance rule** (mail-box rule) – Acceptance is effective when transmitted or *dispatched.*

However, the maker is the master of his offer, so if the offer specifies the means of acceptance, the acceptance must conform to those specifications in the offer to be effective.

Acceptance would be effective **when received** if:
- States "only valid upon receipt" by offeror, so mailbox rule won't apply.
- Acceptance is made by some unauthorized means.
- Offer indicates that acceptance must be received by a specific date.
  - Note: If accept/reject, the early acceptance rule doesn't apply, and whatever is received first applies.
  - An acceptance received after an offer has terminated is considered a counteroffer.

Example: Send offer on 1st, received on 4th. Offer expires on the 10th. B accepts on the 9th and is received by A on the 11th. If early acceptance rule, contract on the 9th. If A states only when received, no contract, but B has now made a counteroffer.

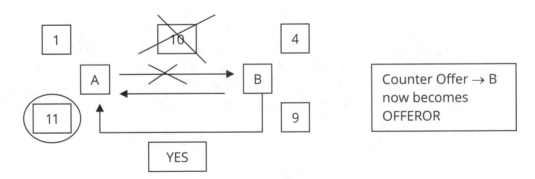

The trickiest responses are acceptances with **conditions precedent**. These are actually acceptances of the offer that cite events outside of the contract which must take place before the acceptance is effective. **For example**, if the offeree responds to the $200,000 home sale offer by indicating they accepted as long as the bank approved the offeree's loan application, this would be a valid attempt to accept. The loan from the bank to the offeree is not a change that adds to the offeror's obligations or the offeree's rights under the home sale contract. When a condition precedent is set, the offeree must make a good faith attempt to ensure the condition is satisfied. In this example, the offeree must submit a valid loan application and sincerely attempt to obtain loan approval from the bank.

In general, an acceptance must **mirror** the offer in all ways. If the offer requires the offeree to perform some action in order to accept, the offeree must perform the action and not merely promise to perform it. A contract that can be accepted by a promise is called a **bilateral contract,** and a contract that can only be accepted by actual performance is called a **unilateral contract.**

For example, if a firm partner offers to give a staff member a promotion to manager if they pass the CPA exam within a year, they've made an offer of a unilateral contract. The subordinate cannot accept merely by promising to the pass the exam, since that is an attempt to change a unilateral contract into a bilateral contract.

Of course, when an offer is in unilateral form, the offeree hasn't actually accepted until they've completed the required action, so there is the danger that the offeror will revoke the offer after the offeree has begun performance but before they've completed it. To prevent this, common law prohibits an offeror from revoking an offer if the offeree is in the process of performing such actions, although they can revoke if the offeree stops making reasonable efforts in the direction of completion.

For example, if the staff member in this example enrolls in a review course and pursues study, the partner cannot revoke the offer. If the staff member makes no efforts in the direction of study, or signs up for a course but then goes a month without studying with no special excuse, the partner may revoke the offer.

The mirror rule also requires the offeree to accept in a manner dictated by the offer. If the offeror indicated that acceptance must be by mail, any response other than by mail is a counteroffer. If the offeror sent the offer through the mail without indicating the manner of response, an acceptance by mail or any faster means is considered a valid acceptance.

Unlike offers, revocations, and rejections, which must be **received** by the other party to be effective, an acceptance is normally effective when transmitted, based on the early acceptance rule (sometimes called "the mailbox rule").

For example, assume an offer is mailed on the 1st and received on the 4th of the month. The offeror then mails a revocation on the 5th that is received on the 8th. The offeree mails a valid acceptance on the 6th that is received by the offeror on the 9th. A contract is formed in this case, since the offer is effective on the 4th, when received, the acceptance is effective on the 6th, when transmitted, but the revocation is not effective until the 8th, when received.

Action	Mailed	Received
Offer	1	4*
Revocation	5	8*
Acceptance	6*	9

* The effective date of the action

Note: **the early acceptance rule does not apply when the original offer explicitly requires acceptance to be received by the offeror in order to be effective.** The early acceptance rule does apply when the offeror indicates that the offeree must accept by a certain date, but doesn't indicate if acceptance refers to transmission or receipt. **For example**, if the offer requires the offeree to accept by mail by August 1, the acceptance only needs to be postmarked by August 1 and not received. A valid early acceptance is effective even if the offeror never receives it due to an error by the delivery service.

The offeree cannot use the early acceptance rule if they send a contradictory rejection to the offeror. **For example**, assume the offer is mailed on the 1st and received on the 4th, as before. This time, though, the offeree sends a rejection on the 5th that is received by the offeror on the 8th, and later mails an unconditional acceptance of the original offer on the 6th which is received by the offeror on the 9th. Although rejections are normally effective when received and acceptances when transmitted, this would be unjust in the current situation, since the offeror receives a rejection on the 8th and doesn't know that an acceptance is in transit. As a result, the offeror might take action based on a belief that the offeree rejected the offer. Acceptance is not considered effective in this case until the 9th, when received, which is too late to accept, since rejection occurred the day before.

Action	Mailed	Received
Offer	1	4*
Rejection	5	8*
Acceptance	6	9*

* Effective date of action

It is possible, however, for acceptance to occur after a rejection has been transmitted, since the rejection is still not effective until received. The offeree must use a fast-enough means of acceptance so that it will be received by the offeror before the rejection is received. If, in this example, the acceptance is sent by express mail on the 6th and is received on the 7th, the contract will be formed on the 7th, without needing the early acceptance rule.

Action	Mailed	Received
Offer	1	4*
Rejection	5	8*
Acceptance	6	7*

* Effective date of action

Consideration ("of value" and "bargained for")

Both parties to a contract must provide some consideration as a result of the contract. A contract in which only one side has obligations is not valid. The consideration offered must be **legally sufficient**, meaning it must represent a true value under law. It can take several different forms:
- Paying or lending money
- Transferring or lending property
- Rendering services
- Relinquishing the right to receive money, property, or services
- Waiving the right to take certain actions (forbearance to sue)

Examples of the last include:
- **Covenant not to compete** – A seller of a business agrees not to open a competing business. The agreement must be reasonable as to length of time, location, and type of business forbidden. It would be reasonable for a seller of a travel agency to agree not to start another travel agency business within 5 miles of the business being sold for the next

2 years. It would be unreasonable for the seller to be required not to open any business in the United States for the next 20 years.
- **Out-of-court settlement** – A plaintiff in a lawsuit agrees to drop all claims and refrain from any further legal action in exchange for a payment or promise from the defendant.

In order to be valid, the consideration in a contract must be the result of the contract. It *cannot be*:
- **Past consideration** – Actions taken before the contract was formed.
- **Pre-existing duty** – An obligation which the party already had before the contract was formed.

As an example of **past consideration**, assume that a corporation has a suggestion box to encourage employees to offer ideas that will benefit the company. Over the years, they've received only a handful of useful suggestions, including one that suggested they start paying for useful suggestions instead of expecting them for free! The board of directors likes this idea, and proposes to pay 10% of the benefit to any employee who makes a suggestion that increases the corporation's net income. Letters are drafted and mailed to all employees about this decision. After the letters are mailed, one employee drops a suggestion in the box in the morning, then gets the letter in the mail when they return home in the evening and finds out about the new policy. If the suggestion is helpful to the company, it does not have to pay the employee for it, since the offer was not made until it was received by the employee, and the employee had already made the suggestion before that time. Also, the company doesn't have to pay other employees who made suggestions in the past, including the one who suggested paying for suggestions.

It is **not** a case of past consideration for an offeree to respond to a unilateral contract offer by providing the consideration demanded in the offer. If the offeror promises to promote the offeree if they pass the CPA exam, the contract is not formed until the offeree passes, but the offeror cannot argue that the offeree passed the exam before the contract was formed, since that was the specific consideration required to form the present contract.

The **pre-existing duty** rule is most often applied when two parties attempt to **modify a contract.** Under common law, such modification is only binding if both parties are providing **new consideration** as a result of it.

As an **example** of pre-existing duty, assume a painter signs a contract with a homeowner on November 1 to paint the house by December 1 for $1,000. After signing the contract, the painter decides that the time estimates they gave the customer were unrealistic, and they inform the homeowner that the job cannot be completed by December 1 unless the painter hires an assistant. The painter informs the homeowner that either the job cannot be completed as promised or the homeowner will have to pay $1,300 for a December 1 completion to cover the painter's additional costs. The homeowner agrees to pay $1,300, and a new contract is signed by both parties on November 4. The painter finishes the job by December 1 with the help of the assistant. The homeowner is only obligated to pay $1,000. The additional $300 demanded by the painter was not supported by any consideration, since the facts make clear the assistant would have been needed to meet the original promise by the painter. On November 4, the painter is only offering the same consideration they were already obligated to provide to fulfill the earlier agreement.

The pre-existing duty rule also applies to legal obligations that a party had from contracts with third parties or general law. A police officer cannot be offered a reward for catching a criminal, since their employment already implied an obligation to make their best efforts in this direction. A parent cannot charge their minor child for room and board, since the law mandates they provide it.

One exception that allows a modification of a contract without apparent consideration on one side is when there is a dispute, and an adjustment is made to settle it.

For example, a client agrees to pay $2,000 to a financial planner for the development of a complete financial plan. The planner prepares a report which the client considers to be far less detailed and complete than was reasonable to expect, and refuses to pay the planner, charging that they didn't perform the work promised. The planner agrees to reduce the fee to $1,000 if the client agrees no further services are required from the planner. This is a valid modification, even though the client is receiving a fee reduction, since it settles a dispute over the level of services required of the planner.

A modification can, of course, be made when both sides have altered obligations, since the changes are mutual. A price increase offered in exchange for an increase in the services rendered, or a price decrease offered in exchange for a decrease in the services required, would be acceptable.

In all of the discussions, notice there is no evaluation of the size or fairness of the consideration offered. Under common law, it is generally assumed that the consideration is fair because it resulted from the **bargaining** of two parties. If, however, consideration is imposed without negotiation, the courts may refuse to enforce the agreement due to the absence of bargaining, unless it considers the agreement to be reasonable.

For example, if a motorist is stranded on an isolated highway, and a passerby agrees to give them a ride for a fee of $5,000, "take it or leave it," the motorist can accept the ride and the courts will not enforce the fee. The motorist clearly was not in a position to bargain and the passerby was imposing outrageous consideration without allowing negotiation.

Consideration

- **Of value** (legally sufficient)
    - Money, goods, services or the promise to perform
    - Giving up a legal right
    - No preexisting legal obligation
    - Need not be of equal value

- **Bargained for exchange**
    - What the parties intended to receive
    - A gift is not bargained for
    - Past consideration is no consideration

- **Modification** of contract requires **additional consideration** by both.
- Situations where no consideration is required to be binding
    - Promises to a charity (promissory estoppel) where a charity might rely upon that promise to its detriment.

Lecture 13.03

CLASS QUESTIONS

Please see the Class Questions and Class Solutions for this Lecture at the end of this Section.

Lecture 13.04

Defenses

There are certain **defenses** available to parties seeking to escape a contract. They may claim the contract is invalid because it may either be void, or voidable.

Voidable Contracts

One or more of the parties may escape the contract.

- **Duress** – A party enters into a contract as a result of an improper threat by the other party (**for example**, a tax preparer refuses to turn over client records needed for an IRS audit until the client agrees to sign a contract engaging the preparer to do their tax returns for the next 5 years). Coerce someone into a contract through force or threats, but the threats are economic or social in nature ("sign or I will fire you").
- **Undue influence** – Violate or abuse a relationship of trust or confidence. A party has entered into a contract because they trusted the other party as one who represented their interests (**for example**, a client enters into a business partnership with their accountant based on the accountant's financial forecasts).
- **Misrepresentation of a Material fact** – A contract is voidable if a party enters into a contract after receiving inaccurate information about relevant matters from the other party (**for example**, a home buyer was told by the seller that the plumbing was in excellent shape when it was actually on the verge of failure). To use this defense, the misinformed party must prove that the inaccurate statements were made with the expectation they'd be relied on, the information was the *proximate cause* of the harm to the plaintiff, and that this caused them some detriment or harm. This is known as **innocent misrepresentation**.

  A contract is also voidable when there is **fraud in the inducement**. This is similar to innocent misrepresentation, except that the other party had actual or constructive knowledge that they were providing inaccurate information.

  Both of these defenses permit the victim to elect to withdraw from the contract or to enforce it, as they prefer. Fraud in the inducement entitles the victim to damages as well.

  o **Innocent** misrepresentation allows contract to be rescinded – must prove **MILE**:
    - **M**aterial misrepresentation or Omission
    - **I**ntent to induce reliance by the party making the misrepresentations/Relied upon
    - **L**oss occurred (damages)
    - **E**rror caused by misrepresentation

- o **Fraudulent misrepresentation** (Fraud is an intentional Tort) allows suit for damages – must prove actual or constructive intent to deceive (scienter).
  - **MIL** & **E**rror caused by Fraud (Scienter)
    - Scienter (constructive Fraud or Gross Negligence)
      - Intent to mislead, deceive, manipulate, or defraud
        - o Reckless disregard of truth or knowledge of falsity

- **Mistake**
  - o *Mutual mistake of fact* – both parties are mistaken
    - A mutual mistake of fact typically causes a contract to be unenforceable and allows it to be *rescinded*.
  - o *Unilateral* – one person is mistaken, usually offeror.
    - If the other party knew or should have known – Material
    - An immaterial unilateral mistake generally does not permit either party to void a contract.

- **Capacity**
  One possible reason for the courts to refuse to enforce a contract is that a party to the contract lacked the **capacity** to make one. This is usually the case when a party to the contract is a minor. The age of majority varies between 18 and 21 in the various states, and will be provided in the CPA exam question if necessary.

  A contract between a minor and an adult is a valid contract, but is **voidable** by the minor, meaning the minor can withdraw from the contract if they so choose. The other party to the contract cannot withdraw, however, so the contract is enforceable if the minor wishes it to be. The minor can withdraw from the contract at any time prior to reaching the majority, even if they have obtained substantial benefits from the contract so far. **After** reaching the necessary age, they may **ratify** the contract and become bound to it. In fact, a minor who reaches the age of majority is treated as having ratified it if they do not disaffirm the contract within a reasonable period of time after reaching adulthood.
  - o **Minor** – someone under the age of 18 usually lacks capacity to enter into a contract, unless they are for necessities, such as food, shelter, or clothing.
    - May *disaffirm* the contract any time prior to or within a reasonable time of reaching the age of majority. The non-minor is required to perform under the contract, unless the minor exercises his right to disaffirm the contract in a timely fashion.
    - May ratify the contract, thereby becoming liable once they reach the age of majority.
  - o **Intoxication** – can avoid if the other party knew of your impairment.
  - o Similar capacity issues arise if a party to a contract was **legally intoxicated** at the time they made the contract. After becoming sober, they can ratify the contract if they wish to enforce it, or may withdraw from the contract once they understand what they have agreed to. Keep in mind that a person is not automatically intoxicated just because they've had a drink, and a person will have the capacity to make a contract even if they have consumed alcohol as long as they did not reach the point of being legally intoxicated.
  - o **Incompetent Persons** – Contracts entered into before adjudication of insanity, may be voidable by incompetent person, but once adjudicated insane by a court of law, they are considered void.

Void Contracts

Void contracts – Under certain circumstances, a contract is **void** and cannot be enforced by either party.

- **Extreme duress** – A party enters into a contract as a result of a physical threat of force, so great that it impairs any ability to exercise free will (**for example**, they sign the contract while a gun is being pointed at them).
- **Fraud in the Execution** – If a party enters into a contract without being aware of it, as a result of the other party getting them to sign an agreement without realizing they are signing a contract (deception), this is known as fraud in the execution.
    - As in the case of fraud in the inducement, fraud in the execution refers to actual or constructive knowledge by the perpetrator that they are acting improperly, and entitles the victim to sue for damages.
- **Illegal subject matter** – contract to kill the CPA examiners.
    - If violates licensing agreement, but it is merely for revenue generating purposes, still valid contract.
    - Covenant not to compete is binding if not "too limiting."
- **Incompetent Persons** – Contracts entered into once adjudicated insane by a court of law are considered void.

The courts will not enforce any agreement to violate the law or public policy. Such contracts are **void** and cannot be enforced by either party.

For example, assume Smith agrees to pay $20,000 to Jones in exchange for Jones' promise to steal trade secrets from Jones' employer and pass them to Smith. Smith gives Jones a $5,000 deposit at the time the contract is formed. The courts will not help Jones collect the other $15,000 if they steal the secrets and will not help Smith recover the $5,000 deposit if Jones doesn't steal them. Of course, both persons are also subject to appropriate criminal prosecution.

Statute of Frauds

Statute of Frauds – Under common law, there is no requirement that a contract be in writing. However, specific legislation known as the **statute of frauds** has been enacted to require written evidence supporting certain contracts.

- Requires written evidence signed by defendant to enforce certain contracts (**GROSS**):
    - Sale of **G**oods worth $500 or more
    - **R**eal estate sales
    - **O**ver one year required to perform contract (Bilateral contract)
    - **S**uretyship (Guarantee debt of another)
    - **S**tatements in consideration of marriage ("if you marry my daughter, I will make you VP of my co" – Marriage is the consideration, or my brother would always say, if you get married this week only, I will give you a washing machine!!).
- **Sales over the internet** – If a transaction over the internet falls under the Statute of Frauds, most states have passed laws allowing such contracts to be enforceable to facilitate commerce.

- Contract needs to be signed by person backing out (weasel).

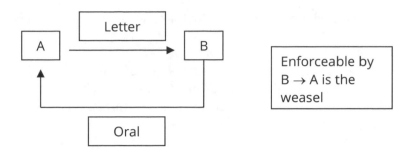

Note that a contract of **indefinite duration** does not fall within the over-one-year category, even if it is likely to take over one year to complete. **For example**, a contract hiring someone for a job may result in employment for several decades, but at the time the contract was made, it could have resulted in employment for a period shorter than a year. As a result, the statute of frauds doesn't apply, and such a contract does not have to written.

When the statute of frauds applies, the courts will generally not enforce a contract unless written evidence supporting the existence of the contract can be presented. This doesn't necessarily require a written contract, but requires some writing **signed by the defendant** that refers to the contract or otherwise indicates a contract was made. All the terms of the contract need not be in writing but, at a minimum, the subject matter of the contract must be mentioned. Must show that the contract was signed by the person trying to avoid the contract (the defendant).

For example, assume a buyer and seller orally agree on the sale of a home for $200,000. If the seller later denies in court that the contract was made, the buyer cannot enforce the sale, even if there were witnesses to the agreement willing to testify that the contract was made. If, however, the buyer can produce a letter signed by the seller and dated the day after the oral agreement, thanking the buyer for purchasing the home from them, the statute of frauds is satisfied and the contract is enforceable.

The statute of frauds provides for certain **exceptions** to the requirement of written evidence. A contract falling within the statute will still be enforced when:
- The contract has already been **performed** by both parties.

As an **example** of the latter, let's say an oral contract is made to sell a desk for $1,000. If the buyer pays the seller $1,000 and the seller delivers the desk to the buyer without any writing by either side, the courts will not allow either party to challenge the contract afterwards just because it was not written.

For contracts involving the sale of goods, there are additional **exceptions (SPAM)**:
- A contract involving goods that are being **Specifically manufactured** by the seller can be enforced by the seller.
- A contract that has been **Partially performed** will be enforced to the extent of performance.
- The defendant **Admits in court** to having made the contract.
- If a written confirmation of a contract is sent to a merchant dealing in the goods in question, the confirmation can be used against the merchant if the **Merchant does not object within 10 days** of receiving the confirmation (Merchants bound by their silence).

Parol Evidence Rule

The parol evidence rule prohibits the use of oral or written evidence that contradicts the terms of the written contract.

Even if a contract is *not* required to have written evidence under the statute of frauds, if the parties do choose to make a written contract, the **parol evidence rule** applies.
- This rule bars from court testimony any **prior or contemporaneous** oral or written contracts that contradict the written contract.

For example, if two parties make a written contract on August 20 to sell a house, and the contract includes a clause indicating that the seller makes no warranty as to the absence of termites, the buyer will not be allowed to introduce court evidence that the seller orally promised on August 15 to provide a warranty of freedom from termites in the sale. The buyer also would be prohibited from claiming in court that an oral discussion occurred at the same time the written contract was being signed, guaranteeing the absence of termites.

The parol evidence rule **does not prevent** the introduction of evidence about:
- Subsequent oral (or written) modifications of the contract.
- Fraud in the execution of the written contract.
- Oral discussions prior to the agreement that clarify ambiguous or missing terms in the written contract.

For example, if a written contract to sell a house is signed on August 20, and there are no clauses in the contract discussing the seller's responsibility for termites, the buyer is permitted in court to introduce testimony about oral promises made by the seller on August 15 regarding guarantees against termites.

A written contract sometimes includes an **entirety clause** claiming that there are no agreements other than those contained within the written contract. In this case, the absence of a promise involving termites is not considered an ambiguous or missing term, but a clear indication that there is no such promise. As a result, the buyer would not be allowed to contradict the entirety clause by claiming an oral promise had been made prior to the signing of the written contract. The entirety clause still doesn't prevent subsequent oral modifications, however, and these could be introduced.

Parol Evidence Rule

- Whenever a written contract exists, it **bars from court**:
  - Prior written or oral contracts on the same subject.
  - Concurrent oral contracts. (Contemporaneous)

- Rule **doesn't bar (still admissible):**
  - Subsequent oral modifications.
  - Evidence to prove fraud, duress, mistakes of written contract.
  - Subjects not addressed or ambiguous in written contract.

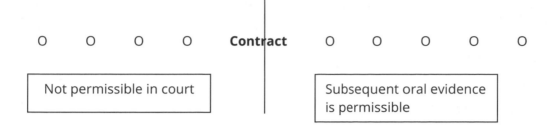

Assignment of Rights and Delegation of Duties

Any right may be assigned and any duty may be delegated **unless**:
- Contract specifically prohibits it.
- The duty is personal in nature.
- Materially alters the rights and responsibilities of the other party.
- Involves specialized personal services.
  - Once assigned or delegated, both parties are now liable on the contract (assignor and assignee). The assignor makes certain **implied warranties**:
    - Assignor will not impair the assignment.
    - The assigned right actually exists.
    - The assignor has no knowledge of information that would impair the value of the assignment.
- The assignor is still liable on the contract, unless the other party to the contract accepts the assignee in place of the assignor, which is called a **novation.**

Third Party Rights

In general, contracts cannot be enforced by persons who are not participants in the formation of the contract. This is based on the concept of **privity**, which considers a contract to be a private matter not involving outsiders. There are several exceptions to this rule, however:
- **Assignment** – If a party transfers the rights they possess in a contract to a third party, the assignee will be able to enforce the rights transferred to them. The assignor loses the ability to enforce.
- **Intended third party beneficiary** – If a contract is specifically designed to benefit an outside party, that party has privity of contract and can enforce it.

There are two types of **intended beneficiaries:**
- A **donee beneficiary** who is receiving benefits as a gift may only enforce against the party owing them benefits, and not the party arranging them. **For example**, a customer purchases a car from a dealer to be delivered to the customer's child as a birthday present. If the car is not delivered, the child can sue the dealer but not their parent. The consideration paid by the parent binds the dealer to the contract.
- A **creditor beneficiary** who is receiving benefits to settle a debt owed them can sue either party. **For example**, a customer purchases a car from a dealer to be delivered to a person whose car was totaled by the customer in an auto accident. If the car is not delivered, the beneficiary can sue both the dealer and the car buyer.

Just because someone benefits from a contract doesn't make them an intended third-party beneficiary. An **incidental third-party beneficiary** obtains benefits that didn't represent the purpose of the contract, and cannot enforce against either party. **For example**, an auto mechanic is ordered by their customer to use replacement parts made by the car's original manufacturer because the customer believes them to be higher quality. If the mechanic fails to use the parts, the manufacturer cannot sue either party, since the purpose of the requirements in the contract was not to benefit the manufacturer.

Discharge of Contracts

- **By performance**
    - If fully performed, the parties are discharged.
    - Substantial performance – may not be discharged if used substandard materials.
- **By agreement**
    - Rescission – the parties are restored to their original position.
    - Accord and satisfaction – performance of the substituted duty is the "satisfaction" that discharges the original duty.
    - Novation – One party accepts the performance of a third party in place of the party obligated under the original contract.
- **By Operation of law**
    - Impossibility – the objective of the contract becomes impossible.
    - Death or incapacity of the party obligated to perform a personal service contract
    - Discharge in bankruptcy
    - Illegality of the services to be performed
- **By Breach**
    - Violation of contract terms
    - Anticipatory breach of contract – One party lets the other party to the contract know that performance will not occur.
        - Can cancel the contract.
        - Could sue for compensatory damages.
        - Doctrine of *anticipatory repudiation* allows a party to either sue at once or wait until after performance is due when the other party indicates performance will not occur.

Remedies for Breach

- Rescind (cancel) the contract and sue for restitution
- Affirm the contract and sue for damages

Damages

When a contract is breached, the victim of breach is normally only entitled to recover **actual damages**. This includes damages directly caused by the breach and incidental to it, but not unforeseen consequential damages. The courts also do **not** award **punitive damages** that are designed specifically to punish the defendant for the act of breach. The victim also cannot usually demand **specific performance** of the contract, unless it involves unique property.

To simplify enforcement, the parties to a contract sometimes place a **liquidated damages clause** in the contract, specifying an amount that will be awarded in the event of breach. A student might, **for example**, make a 10% down payment to enroll in an upcoming course at a school, and the contract might stipulate that the student forfeits the down payment if they do not pay the balance by the start date. Such a clause will be enforceable if the forfeited amount represents a reasonable estimate of the damages to the school. The clause will not be enforced if the payment is deemed a penalty, because of the prohibition against punitive damages for breach of contract.

Breach may occur when a party fails to perform a required term of a contract, or when a party indicates in advance that they will not perform a term required in the future. The latter is known as **anticipatory breach**. The victim of breach must take reasonable action to minimize the damages, and cannot recover damages they could have reasonably avoided. **For example**, if a part needed for the functioning of a plant is not repaired when promised, the customer must attempt to obtain the necessary part as soon as possible, and cannot leave the plant idle and then attempt to collect all the lost revenues from the shutdown in production.

- **Compensatory damages** – to compensate for direct losses and lost profits.
- **Consequential damages** – Indirect costs and anticipated losses.
- **Nominal damages** – no real, provable loss.
- **Punitive damages** – to punish, usually for fraud, not for a breach of contract.
- **Specific performance** – available for *unique* property (patents), not for personal services.

Statute of Limitations

- Time period in which a lawsuit must be initiated
- Enforcement is measured from the time the contract is made.
- An action for Breach of contract begins at the **date of breach.**
- Generally, 4 to 6 years

Lecture 13.06

CLASS QUESTIONS

Please see the Class Questions and Class Solutions for this Lecture at the end of this Section.

Lecture 13.07

CLASS QUESTIONS

Please see the Class Questions and Class Solutions for this Lecture at the end of this Section.

CLASS QUESTIONS

Work through the below Class Questions while following along with the respective lectures. Once this is complete, you can begin independently practicing what you've learned by quizzing yourself on this course section in your Interactive Practice Questions (IPQ), which can be found in your online Student Dashboard. Your IPQ simulates the computer-based testing experience, and will also help you understand how concepts are applied to the exam. Each question includes answer explanations from expert CPAs that will help you determine why you answered a question correctly or incorrectly. This is key to your success on the CPA Exam.

Lecture 13.03

1. Opal offered, in writing, to sell Larkin a parcel of land for $300,000. If Opal dies, the offer will

   a. Terminate prior to Larkin's acceptance only if Larkin received notice of Opal's death.
   b. Remain open for a reasonable period of time after Opal's death.
   c. Automatically terminate despite Larkin's prior acceptance.
   d. Automatically terminate prior to Larkin's acceptance.

2. On September 27, Summers sent Fox a letter offering to sell Fox a vacation home for $150,000. On October 2, Fox replied by mail agreeing to buy the home for $145,000. Summers did not reply to Fox. Do Fox and Summers have a binding contract?

   a. No, because Fox failed to sign and return Summers' letter.
   b. No, because Fox's letter was a counteroffer.
   c. Yes, because Summers' offer was validly accepted.
   d. Yes, because Summers' silence is an implied acceptance of Fox's letter.

Lecture 13.06

3. Grove is seeking to avoid performing a promise to pay Brook $1,500. Grove is relying on lack of consideration on Brook's part. Grove will prevail if he can establish that

   a. Prior to Grove's promise, Brook had already performed the requested act.
   b. Brooks' only claim of consideration was the relinquishment of a legal right.
   c. Brook's asserted consideration is only worth $400.
   d. The consideration to be performed by Brook will be performed by a third party.

4. Rail, who was sixteen years old, purchased an $800 computer from Elco Electronics. Rail and Elco are located in a state where the age of majority is eighteen. On several occasions, Rail returned the computer to Elco for repairs. Rail was very unhappy with the computer. Two days after reaching the age of eighteen, Rail was still frustrated with the computer's reliability, and returned it to Elco, demanding an $800 refund. Elco refused, claiming that Rail no longer had a right to disaffirm the contract. Elco's refusal is

   a. Correct, because Rail's multiple requests for service acted as a ratification of the contract.
   b. Correct, because Rail could have transferred good title to a good-faith purchaser for value.
   c. Incorrect, because Rail disaffirmed the contract within a reasonable period of time after reaching the age of eighteen.
   d. Incorrect, because Rail could disaffirm the contract at any time.

5. If a person is induced to enter into a contract by another person because of the close relationship between the parties, the contract may be voidable under which of the following defenses?

     a.   Fraud in the inducement.

     b.   Unconscionability.

     c.   Undue influence.

     d.   Duress.

CLASS SOLUTIONS

1. (d) An offer is automatically terminated upon the death or insanity of the offeror or the offeree, regardless of whether notice of death was received by the other party.

2. (b) Acceptance of an offer to enter into a common law contract must mirror the offer. An acceptance that modifies a significant term of an offer is considered a rejection of the offer, terminating it, and a counteroffer. A contract will ensue only if the original offeror accepts the counteroffer. Answer (a) is incorrect because acceptance does not have to be in a signed writing to be effective. Answer (c) is incorrect because a contract will ensue only if the original offeror accepts the counteroffer. Answer (d) is incorrect because a contract will ensue only if the original offeror accepts the counteroffer.

3. (a) A contract cannot be formed without consideration, which does not include past consideration. If a party has already performed an act, agreeing to do so would be considered past consideration and insufficient to bind a contract. Answer (b) is incorrect because the relinquishment of a legal right is considered legally sufficient as consideration. Answer (c) is incorrect because in determining if a contract is valid, the amount of consideration is not considered, only if it is of value and bargained for. Answer (d) is incorrect because it is not significant if consideration will be performed by a party to the contract or a third party as long as it is legally sufficient.

4. (c) A minor may disaffirm a contract up until a reasonable time after reaching majority, in which case the contract is considered void. Although there is no legal definition of what is a reasonable period of time, it is likely that 2 days would be considered reasonable. Answer (a) is incorrect because it is not likely that requests for service would necessarily be interpreted as a ratification of a contract but, regardless, a contract can only be ratified by a minor after reaching majority and Rail's requests for service were prior to that time. Answer (b) is incorrect because although Rail could have transferred title to the computer to a good faith purchaser, it does not negate a minor's right to disaffirm a contract. Answer (d) is incorrect because a minor may not disaffirm a contract at any time, only up to a reasonable time after reaching majority.

5. (c) It is considered undue influence when a party enters into a contract as a result of reliance on another that the contracting party believed they had a valid reason to rely upon. Undue influence makes the contract voidable. Answer (a) is incorrect because fraud in the inducement results from one party to a contract deceiving the other party in order to encourage the other party. Answers (b) and (d) are incorrect because undue influence makes the contract voidable.

Lecture 13.07

TASK-BASED SIMULATIONS

Task-Based Simulation 1

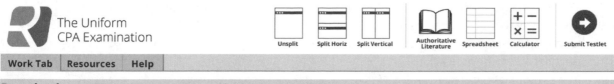

| **Work Tab** | **Resources** | **Help** |

Required:

On December 15, Blake Corp. telephoned Reach Consultants, Inc. and offered to hire Reach to design a security system for Blake's research department. The work would require two years to complete. Blake offered to pay a fee of $100,000 but stated that the offer must be accepted in writing, with the acceptance received by Blake no later than December 20.

On December 20, Reach faxed a written acceptance to Blake. Blake's offices were closed on December 20 and Reach's fax was not seen until December 21.

Reach's acceptance contained the following language:

"We accept your $1,000,000 offer. Weaver has been assigned $5,000 of the fee as payment for sums owed Weaver by Reach. Payment of this amount should be made directly to Weaver."

On December 22, Blake sent a signed memo to Reach rejecting Reach's December 20 fax but offering to hire Reach for a $75,000 fee. Reach telephoned Blake on December 23 and orally accepted Blake's December 22 offer.

Items to be answered:

Items 1 through 7 relate to whether a contractual relationship exists between Blake and Reach. For each item, determine whether the statement is True or False.

		True	**False**
1.	Blake's December 15 offer had to be in writing to be a legitimate offer.	○	○
2.	Reach's December 20 fax was an improper method of acceptance.	○	○
3.	Reach's December 20 fax was effective when sent.	○	○
4.	Reach's acceptance was invalid because it was received after December 20.	○	○
5.	Blake's receipt of Reach's acceptance created a voidable contract.	○	○
6.	If Reach had rejected the original offer by telephone on December 17, he could not validly accept the offer later.	○	○
7.	Reach's December 20 fax was a counteroffer.	○	○

Items to be answered:

Items 8 through 12 relate to the attempted assignment of part of the fee to Weaver. Assume that a valid contract exists between Blake and Reach. For each item, determine whether the statement is True or False.

		True	**False**
8.	Reach is prohibited from making an assignment of any contract right or duty.	○	○
9.	Reach may validly assign part of the fee to Weaver.	○	○
10.	Under the terms of Reach's acceptance, Weaver would be considered a third-party creditor beneficiary.	○	○
11.	In a breach of contract suit by Weaver, against Blake, Weaver would not collect any punitive damages.	○	○
12.	In a breach of contract suit by Weaver, against Reach, Weaver would be able to collect punitive damages.	○	○

Items to be answered:

Items 13 through 15 relate to Blake's December 22 signed memo. For each item, determine whether the statement is True or False.

		True	**False**
13.	Reach's oral acceptance of Blake's December 22 memo may be enforced by Blake against Reach.	○	○
14.	Blake's memo is a valid offer even though it contains no date for acceptance.	○	○
15.	Blake's memo may be enforced against Blake by Reach.	○	○

TASK-BASED SIMULATION SOLUTIONS

Task-Based Simulation Solution 1
Items 1 through 7

		True	**False**
1.	Blake's December 15 offer had to be in writing to be a legitimate offer.	○	●
2.	Reach's December 20 fax was an improper method of acceptance.	○	●
3.	Reach's December 20 fax was effective when sent.	○	●
4.	Reach's acceptance was invalid because it was received after December 20.	○	●
5.	Blake's receipt of Reach's acceptance created a voidable contract.	○	●
6.	If Reach had rejected the original offer by telephone on December 17, he could not validly accept the offer later.	●	○
7.	Reach's December 20 fax was a counteroffer.	●	○

Explanation of solutions

1. **(F)** Since this contract requires more than a year to complete, it is subject to the Statute of Frauds and must be in writing. The offer, however, is not required to be in writing.

2. **(F)** Blake's offer required that acceptance be in writing but did not specify the form of the writing. A fax of a written acceptance is considered acceptance in writing.

3. **(F)** Blake's offer specified that acceptance was required to be received by December 20. As a result, Reach's acceptance would not be effective until it was received by Blake.

4. **(F)** Although Blake's office was not open on December 20, preventing Blake from being aware of the receipt of acceptance, it was received by fax on December 20 and would not have failed on the basis of not having been received timely.

5. **(F)** Acceptance in a common law contract is required to mirror the offer. Since Reach's acceptance cites a fee of $1,000,000, compared to $100,000 in the offer, the acceptance does not mirror the offer and no contract is formed. Instead, the offer is considered rejected and the acceptance represents a counteroffer.

6. **(T)** Once an offer is rejected, it terminates the offer. Subsequent acceptance would be considered a counteroffer, not acceptance of the original offer.

7. **(T)** An acceptance that specifies terms that are different from the original offer, such as citing a fee of $1 million compared to $100,000 in the original offer, is considered a rejection of the original offer and a counteroffer.

Items 8 through 12

		True	False
8.	Reach is prohibited from making an assignment of any contract right or duty.	○	●
9.	Reach may validly assign part of the fee to Weaver.	●	○
10.	Under the **terms** of Reach's acceptance, Weaver would be considered a third-party creditor beneficiary.	●	○
11.	In a breach of **contract** suit by Weaver, against Blake, Weaver would not collect any punitive damages.	●	○
12.	In a breach of **contract** suit by Weaver, against Reach, Weaver would be able to collect punitive damages.	○	●

Explanation of solutions

8. (F) Any right in a contract may be assigned and any duty delegated, provided the contract does not prohibit it, the duty is not personal in nature, assignment or delegation does not materially alter the rights or responsibilities of the other party to the contract, and the contract does not involve specialized personal services. Since none of those exceptions apply, Reach may assign rights and duties under the contract.

9. (T) The right to receive compensation is a right that may be assigned to a third party unless it is prohibited in the contract.

10. (T) When a third party is named as a beneficiary to a contract as a result of an obligation owed to that party by one of the parties to the contract, the third party is considered a creditor beneficiary, giving Weather rights against both Blake and Reach in the case of nonperformance.

11. (T) Punitive damages are designed to punish a party for wrongdoing and not for breach of contract. In a Breach of contract suit, a prevailing party will receive compensatory damages to compensate for losses, and may receive consequential damages if there are unanticipated losses, but would not receive punitive damages. As a creditor beneficiary, Weather has rights against both Reach and Blake, but would not be entitled to punitive damages.

12. (F) Punitive damages are designed to punish a party for wrongdoing and not for breach of contract. In a Breach of contract suit, a prevailing party will receive compensatory damages to compensate for losses, and may receive consequential damages if there are unanticipated losses, but would not receive punitive damages. As a creditor beneficiary, Weather has rights against both Reach and Blake, but would not be entitled to punitive damages.

Items 13 through 15

		True	False
13.	Reach's oral acceptance of Blake's December 22 memo may be enforced by Blake against Reach.	○	●
14.	Blake's memo is a valid offer even though it contains no date for acceptance.	●	○
15.	Blake's memo may be enforced against Blake by Reach.	●	○

Explanation of solutions

13. **(F)** A contract that will require more than one year to perform, as in the case of the 2-year requirement to complete the design of the security system, is subject to the Statute of Frauds. As a result, it can only be asserted against a defendant who has signed the contract. Since Reach's acceptance was oral, there is no writing with Reach's signature and Reach would not be held liable under the contract.

14. **(T)** An offer is not required to have a date or time period during which it may be accepted. If no date or time period is specified, it is assumed that the offer will remain open for a reasonable period of time.

15. **(T)** A contract that will require more than one year to perform, as in the case of the 2-year requirement to complete the design of the security system, is subject to the Statute of Frauds. As a result, it can only be asserted against a defendant who has signed the contract. Since Blake's offer was made in a signed writing, Reach will be able to hold Blake liable.

Section 14 – Sales Contracts

Corresponding Lectures

Watch the following course lectures with this section:

Lecture 14.01 – Sales of Goods Contracts Formation
Lecture 14.02 – Sales of Goods Contracts Formation – Class Questions
Lecture 14.03 – Title and Risk of Loss Transfer
Lecture 14.04 – Sales Warranties
Lecture 14.05 – Sale of Goods Contracts – Class Questions

EXAM NOTE: *Please refer to the AICPA REG Blueprint in the Introduction to find a listing of the representative tasks (and their associated skill levels—i.e., Remembering and Understanding, Application, and Analysis) that the candidate should be able to perform based on the knowledge obtained in this section. Sales contracts are eligible to be tested under Area II.B – Contracts, even though they are not explicitly mentioned.*

Sales Contracts

CONTRACTS FOR THE SALE OF GOODS

Article 2 of the **UCC** (Uniform Commercial Code) deals with contracts for the sale of goods (**tangible personal property** that is moveable) derived from statutory law, not real property or services, which were covered in Common Law. When there are no specific provisions in the UCC, the rules of common law apply. The seller of the goods may be a *merchant or a non-merchant*.   A Merchant is a dealer in the goods involved in the transaction.

FORMATION OF THE SALES CONTRACT

To have a binding sales contract, as with common law, we still need Offer, Acceptance, and Consideration. All rules of common law apply except as modified below.

Offer (Intent & Communicated)

- Terms can be **vague**. May be based on:
  - Standard trade practice
  - Past experience
    - Need not be definite as in Common Law.

Under the UCC, only the type and quantity of goods involved needs to be explicit. Price, delivery date, and other terms can be established by prior dealings between the parties or normal practices. Even the quantity need not be identified as a number, as long as there is a reasonable way to determine what is intended. Two typical examples are:
- **Output contract** – The buyer agrees to purchase as much as the seller is able to produce for a specific period of time, and the seller agrees to sell that entire output to the buyer.
- **Requirements contract** – The seller agrees to supply all of the needs of the buyer for a specified product for a specific period of time, and the buyer agrees to purchase whatever they need entirely from that seller.

Both contracts are subject to reasonable interpretation. If the buyer in a requirements contract acquires another business immediately after making the deal, and suddenly needs 20 times as much of the product as anticipated by the seller in making the agreement, the seller will not be considered in breach of contract if they're unable to supply all of the buyer's needs. On the other hand, if the buyer in a requirements contract for heating oil needs much more of the product than expected due to a harsh winter, the seller **is** required to supply the additional amounts, since such a possible circumstance could have been reasonably anticipated when the contract was made.

Orders for specific quantities are not subject to such interpretations. If a buyer orders 3,000 gallons of heating oil for the winter, and then a very mild winter causes the buyer's needs to be much smaller, the buyer is still obligated to the contract for 3,000, since that is the clear agreement.

Under the UCC, however, there is an additional exception known as a **firm offer**, which cannot be revoked even if **no consideration** was provided by the offeree. A firm offer exists under the UCC when **all three** (*SUM*) of the following conditions are satisfied:

- **Signed** – The promise to keep the offer open must be in writing, and the offeror must specifically sign their name on the page containing the promise.
- **Up to 3 months** – The promise is enforceable for the time specified in the writing, or a reasonable period of time, up to a maximum of 3 months from the date of the writing.
- **Merchant** – The promise must be made by a merchant in the goods (remember that the UCC only applies to goods), referring to someone who deals in the goods on a regular basis or claims a special expertise in them. A merchant is one who either deals in the goods similar to the ones involved in the transaction or who, by occupation, represents that he has particular knowledge or skill relating to the practices or goods involved in the transaction. In the case of a merchant, "good faith" means honesty in fact and the observance of reasonable commercial standards of fair dealing in the trade.
  - An example would be a "*rain check*" for advertised goods.

Under **common law,** an offer can be revoked at any time prior to acceptance, even if the offeror made a promise to keep the offer open for a certain period of time. The only exception is when the offeree has provided some **consideration** to keep the offer open, such as paying an option price of $100 to keep an offer on a house open for 30 days (**Option Contract**).

Acceptance

Acceptance – (Can have *minor variations* from original offer unless prohibited in offer)
- Payment terms
- Change a warranty
  - **Major** change not ok:
    - Material Price increase
    - Quantity
    - Delivery date
- Do not need to Mirror the offer as in Common Law.
- Early acceptance rule (mail-box rule) still applies.
- An **auction** is an "invitation to offer," not an offer. A bid is an offer.
  - *With reserve* – right to withdraw the goods prior to acceptance (assumed unless otherwise stated).
  - *Without reserve* – the property will be sold to the highest bidder. Cannot be withdrawn unless no bid is made.

Another difference applicable only to the sale of goods by a merchant involves acceptance. Under common law, an acceptance must be unequivocal and unqualified with respect to the precise terms specified by the offer. The UCC allows the offeree to make minor changes in the process of acceptance, however. **For example**, a party might order goods by requesting a prompt shipment. The offeree can accept by promising to ship the goods promptly. Had the contract involved real estate or services, where common law principles apply, the acceptance would not have been valid (it would have been treated as a counteroffer), since the offer was unilateral in form, requesting action (shipment), and the response was bilateral in form, making only a promise. The UCC doesn't make these distinctions.

In a sale of goods contract, the offeree can also add or adjust **minor** terms of a contract. **For example**, the offer to buy goods could be accepted along with an indication by the seller that payment must be made by certified check at or before time of delivery. Although this identification of payment terms was not in the original offer, the offeror is assumed to have consented to the additional terms as long as the offeror is a **merchant** in the goods and **doesn't object** to the new term. Minor changes in terms often occur in sale of goods contracts between merchants because of the use of standardized purchase order and sales order forms, which may have several terms pre-printed on the forms. The discrepancies would have invalidated the contract under common law, but the UCC treats them as a **battle of forms**, and enforces the contract as long as the parties are both acting as if they believe they have a contract.

Note that the assumption that the offeror has agreed to a change in terms contained in an acceptance only applies to merchants: a non-merchant in the goods is only assumed to have consented to changes that they have explicitly agreed to make. **A merchant is bound by silence**, but a non-merchant is not.

The consideration rule is extensively modified under the UCC. Essentially, as long as there is offer and acceptance, the contract will be enforceable. This includes **modification** of sales of goods contracts when **no consideration** at all is provided by one side.

For example, assume that Randi Retailer agrees on November 1 to sell a chair to Carl Consumer at a price of $400, with a scheduled delivery to Carl's home on November 30. After the contract is signed, Carl requests that the chair be delivered by November 20, because Carl wishes to have it in time for a Thanksgiving party at the house. If Randi agrees to change the terms of the contract to a delivery date of November 20 at no additional charge, the change will be enforceable against Randi, even though Carl has provided no additional consideration for the change.

The same principle allows a seller and buyer to change the price on a bilateral contract after it is made but before it is performed. Of course, both parties must agree to the change in good faith. In the above example, if Randi notifies Carl on November 5 that, due to a price increase from Randi's supplier, the cost of the chair once delivered will be $450, and Carl agrees to pay the increased price, Carl will owe $450 for the chair (notice that a similar agreement would not have been binding in a real estate or service contract under common law due to the absence of consideration).

Once again, **merchants are bound by silence**. If Carl had been a merchant buying the chair for his business, and he received a notice from Randi of the price increase, he would have been bound to the higher price as long as he didn't specifically object to the notice (for most purposes, a merchant has 10 days to object before their silence is treated as consent).

- **Acceptance by promise to ship**
  - Under the UCC, there is no distinction between unilateral and bilateral contracts, so can accept by prompt shipment or a prompt promise to ship.
  - If ship non-conforming goods, that constitutes both an acceptance and a breach by the seller.

- If A (merchant) gives an offer to B (non-merchant) and B accepts with a minor change, A has a reasonable period of time to respond, if no response is made, A is bound to the NEW changes. Hence, a Merchant is **Bound by their silence**. If A were a non-merchant, it is just considered a proposal to change.

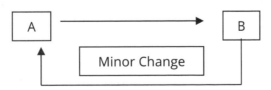

Consideration

Consideration is required in order to form a contract.
- For sale of goods, additional consideration is **NOT required** to make changes to a contract if it is a good faith price increase.
  - Common law, additional consideration is required.
- An **output or requirements contract** (I'll buy everything you produce) does satisfy the consideration requirement, even though the quantity is uncertain.

Statute of Frauds

Statute of frauds says that certain contracts need to be in writing in order to be enforceable by a court of law **(GROSS):**
- **G**oods worth $500 or more
- **R**eal estate sales
- **O**ver one year required to perform contract (Bilateral contract)
- **S**uretyship
- **S**tatements in consideration of marriage

If the contract for the sale of goods is below $500, an oral agreement is binding. If the contract is changed, additional consideration is not required; however, if the new contract is now $500 or more, it must be in writing.

Exceptions

Exceptions to written requirement includes (**SPAM**):
- **S**pecifically manufactured goods at request of buyer (e.g., Roger CPA Review shirts).
- **P**erformance of contract already has occurred (partial performance binds to the extent of performance in sale of goods).
- **A**dmitted in court by defendant.
- **M**erchant in goods not objecting to written confirmation within 10 days, is treated as if they had signed it (merchants bound by their silence).
  - All parties need not sign the contract, just the party against whom it is being enforced (the Weasel).

Parol Evidence Rule

Parol evidence rule still applies, so subsequent oral evidence is admissible in court.
- **Ex.** If written contract is orally changed from $700 to $450:
  - New contract is oral – ok since <$500.
  - No additional consideration required to make change.
  - Admissible in court since not barred by parol evidence rule.

Lecture 14.02

CLASS QUESTIONS

Please see the Class Questions and Class Solutions for this Lecture at the end of this Section.

Lecture 14.03

PASSAGE OF TITLE AND RISK OF LOSS

- **Title** to the goods means whose books the asset would be recorded in at year-end.
- **Risk** of loss deals with who will bear the risk of loss if goods are damaged or lost.
  - Neither may pass until **goods exist** and are **identified** to the contract.

Title and risk of loss transfer based upon:

1. **Contract terms** determine passage of title and risk of loss.
2. If no contract terms, then passage is determined by **shipping terms (Carrier case).**
   - Common carrier:
     - **Shipment contract** – title and risk of loss transfer when "placed with" the common carrier.
       - FAS – Free Along Side
       - CIF – Cost Insurance and Freight
       - FOB shipping point – Free On Board shipping point (seller's warehouse)
     - **Destination contract** – Title and risk of loss transfer when "Tendered" to the buyer.
       - FOB destination – Free On Board destination (buyer's warehouse)

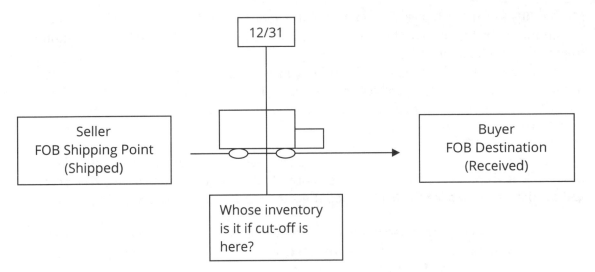

3. If no contract terms and there are no carrier terms, then:
   Not a common carrier - Buyer picks up the goods.
   - **Title** passes when contract formed.
   - **Risk** of loss
     - Merchant – Goods <u>received</u> by buyer (Sears)
     - Non-merchant – Goods <u>tendered</u> to buyer (my garage sale)

Common carrier liability based on strict liability, whereby the carrier is liable for losses to property irrespective of negligence. Also, common carriers are not liable for losses due to causes deemed natural disasters and other "acts of God."

Under both the UCC and the United Nations Convention for the International Sale of Goods, the risk of loss of the goods will generally pass to the buyer when the seller delivers goods to the "first carrier" for transmission to the buyer.

Under common law, ownership of property confers all the rights and liabilities associated with the asset. The owner of a home is entitled to use it and receive the proceeds in the event of sale, but is also liable for injuries to people that occur in the home.

Under the Uniform Commercial Code (UCC), however, the rights to goods are distinguished from the liabilities in connection with the goods. It is possible for one person to have **title** to the goods and be entitled to the benefits while another person has **risk of loss** in the event the goods are damaged or destroyed. In fact, the UCC considers title irrelevant in determining the risk of loss.

One example of this situation is a **bailment**, in which the owner of goods (bailor) entrusts them to another party (bailee) temporarily. If the goods are damaged as a result of an absence of due care on the part of the bailee, they will generally bear the loss, even though the bailor has title to the goods. In this circumstance, the risk of loss is a result of the carelessness of the bailee. In many situations, however, a party that has not been careless may still be liable on goods to which they have no title. If goods are sold as a result of the negligence of the bailee, a good faith purchaser will not be required to return the goods, and the bailor will not be able to retrieve the goods, but will be entitled to damages from the bailee.

The most common exam questions involve determining the point in time when title and risk of loss pass from the seller to the buyer in a transaction. Usually, this would be determined by the terms of the contract, but the following principles **override all other issues** in determining the time of passage:
- Neither title nor risk can pass on goods until the **goods exist**. For example, if a contract is signed for goods that have to be manufactured, the buyer cannot obtain the goods until they've actually been produced.
- Once they exist, they must also be **identified to the contract**. If, for example, the seller has a large inventory of the product being sold, the buyer cannot be provided with title or risk of loss if the seller hasn't determined which goods from the inventory will be transferred to the buyer.

Assuming these events have both occurred, the terms of the contract might still be overridden with regard to risk of loss if one of the parties commits a breach of contract. In such cases, **risk of loss is imposed on the party in breach**. This will not affect the issue of title, however.

Assuming goods exist and are identified to the contract, neither side has breached the contract, and the contract is silent as to the timing of the passage of title and risk of loss, these issues are settled by examining the terms of delivery of the goods:
- **Shipment contract** – In such contracts, the seller's rights (title) and responsibilities (risk of loss) end as soon as the goods have been properly transferred to the carrier (usually a trucking company) at the seller's location. Shipment contracts are identified by several different possible terms, including *FOB shipping point*, *FOB seller's place of business*, *FA vessel* (for items being sent by boat), *CIF* (cost, insurance, freight to be charged to the buyer), or *C & F* (cost and freight to be charged to the buyer). The references to *FOB* (free on board) and *FAS* (free alongside) are to indicate that the transfer of ownership occurs when the goods are loaded onto the truck or placed on the loading dock next to the boat, respectively.
- **Destination contract** – In such contracts, title and risk of loss pass when the goods arrive at the buyer's location and are tendered (offered) to the buyer by the carrier. Destination contracts are identified by the terms *FOB destination point* or *FOB buyer's place of business*. Notice that the transfer of ownership occurs while the goods are still on board the truck, as soon as the carrier offers the goods to the buyer.

- **Not a common carrier, "Hold for pickup"** – In such contracts, the seller doesn't deliver the goods, but simply makes them available to the buyer for pickup. **Title passes** as soon as the contract is **formed** (assuming the goods exist and are identified to the contract, of course). **Risk** of loss, however, doesn't pass at that time. If the goods are being held by a **merchant seller**, risk of loss passes once the buyer has **received** the goods from the seller and removed them from the merchant's premises. If a **non-merchant seller** is holding the goods, risk of loss passes as soon as the seller **tenders** the goods to the buyer.

Special situations often arise on the exam in determining the transfer of ownership. A common one involves **conditional sales**, in which the buyer is given the option to cancel the deal and return the goods. There are two possible situations:

- **Sale on approval** – This refers to a contract that permits the buyer to obtain the goods for use and make a decision as to whether or not to purchase them later. Normally, there is a time limit (typically 30 days) after which the buyer is presumed to have accepted the goods. In these contracts, title and risk of loss transfer to the buyer as soon as they've accepted the goods explicitly or the time period has elapsed.
- **Sale or return** – This refers to a contract in which the buyer is acquiring the goods for resale and is given the right to cancel the sale if they are unable to resell them to others. A sale or return contract is treated in the same fashion as normal sales, and the rules for passage of title and risk of loss are based on the shipping terms (shipment, destination, or pickup) discussed previously.

Also, there are times when a buyer attempts to cancel the contract. There are two different situations:

- **Buyer rejects delivery** – When the carrier arrives to tender delivery under either a shipment or destination contract, the buyer might refuse to accept delivery and order the carrier to return the goods to the buyer. Title, in such cases, immediately reverts to the seller. As for risk of loss, it depends on whether the buyer's rejection is proper. If so, then risk of loss reverts to the seller as well. If the buyer wrongfully rejects the goods, the overriding principle that holds the **party in breach** liable causes the buyer to continue to bear risk of loss.
- **Buyer revokes acceptance** – After accepting delivery of goods, the buyer might attempt to revoke acceptance. This commonly occurs when the buyer inspects goods after delivery and discovers they do not conform to the requirements of the contract. As long as the buyer's revocation is proper, title and risk of loss revert to the seller. A buyer's attempt to revoke acceptance without a valid reason has no effect, however, and the buyer retains both title and risk.

If there is a **document of title** representing goods held at a public warehouse, the transfer of the document to the buyer transfers title. Risk of loss also transfers to the buyer if the document of title is a negotiable instrument, but the warehouse must be notified of the transfer of a non-negotiable document of title before the buyer can obtain them, so risk of loss doesn't transfer on non-negotiable documents until such notice takes place.

- If buyer rejects goods
    1. **Title** reverts back to seller.
    2. **Risk** of loss
        - **Rightful rejection** (non-conforming goods – seller breaches) – this is considered an acceptance and a breach; both title and risk of loss reverts back to seller.
        - **Wrongful rejection** (conforming goods – buyer breaches) –risk of loss stays with buyer.

□ Note: Risk of loss stays with party in breach.
□ If seller breaches, buyer may accept *all, some, or none* of the goods.

The following chart summarizes the time of transfer of title and risk of loss on goods that exist and are identified to the contract:

Situation	Passage of Title	Passage of Risk
Shipment contract	Placed with carrier	Placed with carrier
Destination contract	Tendered to buyer	Tendered to buyer
Pickup from merchant	Contract formed	Received by buyer
Pickup from non-merchant	Contract formed	Tendered to buyer
Sale on approval	Accepted by buyer	Accepted by buyer
Sale or return	See normal sale rules	See normal sale rules
Buyer rejects goods	Reverts to seller	Reverts if proper
Buyer revokes acceptance	Reverts if proper	Reverts if proper
Negotiable document	Transfer of document	Transfer of document
Non-negotiable document	Transfer of document	Transfer and notice

Lecture 14.04

WARRANTIES

Warranties **are** an expectation the buyer has, that the seller is legally obligated to fulfill.

- **Implied Warranty of Title and Infringement** – Automatically exists in all sales. Seller warrants good title, transfer is rightful, no liens or encumbrances, and that transfer doesn't violate law or infringe on rights of third parties, such as patent or trademark rights.
  - o   Disclaimer must be explicit in the contract.
- **Express Warranty** – Any statements or claims that become a "basis of the bargain." This would include a description, sample, or model.
  - o   Cannot be disclaimed.
- **Implied Warranties of:**
  - o   **Merchantability (*ordinary purpose*)** – When seller is a merchant, seller warrants goods are in fair condition for their *ordinary purpose* and conform to all package claims.
    - ▪   Disclaimer may use language "as is" or "with all faults."
  - o   **Fitness for *particular or ordinary purpose*** – When buyer is relying on the seller's judgment in selecting the product, seller warrants the goods will fulfill the specific needs of the buyer.
    - ▪   Disclaimer must be in writing and use language such as "as is" or "with all faults."

When goods are sold, the seller makes certain promises to the buyer, and those that the buyer can legally enforce are known as **warranties**. Warranties come in two basic varieties:

- **Express warranties** refer to specific promises and claims about the goods made by the seller.
- **Implied warranties** refer to promises that are present without any specific statement by the seller.

During the negotiation and formation of a contract, the seller usually makes certain claims about the product, and often demonstrates its use. These might become express warranties. The principle is that a statement or demonstration is an express warranty if it becomes a **basis of the bargain**, meaning it was one of the reasons the buyer made the purchase or it affected the price or other terms of the agreement in some way.

In contrast, there are certain claims that are clearly meant as "sales talk" and are not express warranties. **For example**, if an auto dealer describes a specific car as "the sportiest car in America," this is not a warranty, since it has no specific meaning that could be claimed as a promise to the buyer. If the dealer says the car "goes from zero to 60 miles per hour in the blink of an eye," it is an obvious exaggeration. On the other hand, if the dealer says the car "goes from zero to 60 miles per hour in 8 seconds," this is a specific claim that is objective and might have been relied on by the buyer in deciding to make the purchase.

In general, claims and promises made by the seller after the contract is formed are not warranties, since the bargain has already been made. If the sale is conditional, however, and a promise is made to discourage the buyer from canceling the purchase, it may also become a basis of the bargain and an express warranty.

Express warranties made in the contract itself cannot be disclaimed, but express warranties that are created during the process of negotiation before sale can be disclaimed in the contract as long as the disclaimer is clear and understood by the buyer.

There are three possible **implied warranties** when a sale of goods takes place:

- **Title** – The seller claims to have good title to the product with no undisclosed liens or claims against it and also promises that the transfer of ownership to the buyer has been performed correctly and doesn't infringe on the rights of any other party. These rights may also include warranty against infringement, such as patent or trademark. This warranty is present in **all** sales of goods, unless specifically disclaimed by the seller in a manner that makes clear the seller is not promising clear title (general disclaimers of warranty or statements of "as is" or "with all faults" are not sufficient).
- **Merchantability** – The seller claims that the goods are fit for their normal uses and that they perform in accordance with any claims or descriptions on their packaging. This warranty is only implied when the goods are **sold by a merchant**. The merchant can disclaim this warranty by name or by selling the goods "as is" or "with all faults."
- **Fitness for particular or ordinary purpose** – The seller promises that the goods will meet the specific needs of the buyer. This warranty is only implied when the **buyer relies on the seller's judgment** and skill in the selection of the product. The seller may disclaim this warranty by name or by selling the goods "as is" or "with all faults."

For example, assume that a consumer enters a department store and asks a clerk in the tools section for a recommendation of a saw to cut down a tree in the consumer's backyard. The clerk recommends a particular power chainsaw and the consumer purchases it. Even if no promises are expressly made by the clerk, the consumer has an automatic warranty of title, a warranty of merchantability since the store selling the saw is a merchant, and a warranty of fitness for particular purpose because the consumer relied on the store employee's judgment and skill in selecting the saw.

In general, disclaimers may be either written or oral, as long as they are clearly understood by the buyer. An attempt to disclaim the fitness for particular purpose by name must be written, however.

When a user of a product suffers an injury or illness in connection with it, the UCC permits claims based on **product liability law**. In such cases, the defendant in the case is not permitted to use the **privity** defense, meaning that the plaintiff need not have purchased the product from the defendant. As a result, a manufacturer can be held liable by a consumer, even though the consumer actually purchased the product from a retail store, and the plaintiff need not have been a purchaser at all, but could have been a relative or friend of the purchaser.

Assume, **for example**, that the purchaser of the chainsaw in the previous example was buying it as a gift for a friend, and the friend suffers an injury in its use because of a defective part. The friend may be able to sue the department store, the distributor, and the saw manufacturer, and none of them can use the privity defense.

The use of **breach of warranty** as a theory of liability in such cases requires the plaintiff to demonstrate all of the following:
- An express or implied warranty that wasn't effectively disclaimed.
- An injury or illness that resulted from the breach.

A common theory of liability is **negligence** law, which holds a person responsible for careless acts causing harm to others. In a product liability case, the **plaintiff must prove** all of the following:
- An **Absence of due care** by the defendant in connection with the product.
- A **Defect** in the product caused by the carelessness.
- **Damages** to the plaintiff resulting from the defect.

Negligence cases can be difficult for plaintiffs, because they must prove the existence of a defect that is the fault of the defendant. Often, a product is dangerous, but all manufacturers produce the item in a manner that contains that danger, so it is not considered a defect. Also, the party that caused the defect can be difficult to identify. A customer in a store who is injured when clothing is caught in an escalator might sue the store, which may claim the escalator was defectively designed so that the store is not at fault. The customer then sues the manufacturer, who claims the cause of the injury was not the design but improper maintenance by the store. Even though both defendants concede the product has a defect, the difficulty of identifying the cause of the defect makes it difficult for the customer to win either case.

Additionally, a defense against negligence is **contributory negligence** on the part of the plaintiff. In some states, any evidence that the plaintiff was also careless is a total bar to recovery, and in all other states, such evidence reduces the liability based on the doctrine of comparative negligence.

The easiest cases for plaintiffs to win are based on **strict liability** law. In such cases, the plaintiff must prove:
- A **defect or unreasonable danger** in the product.
- **Damages** caused by this danger.
- The danger existed when the **product left the defendant's control**.
- The defendant is in the **business of selling** the product.

Notice that there is no need to prove that the product contained a defect in the traditional sense: any danger in the product that wasn't a necessary part of it could be sufficient. Also notice that the plaintiff doesn't need to prove that the defendant caused the danger. If a dangerously manufactured product is sold to a distributor, who sells it to a retail store, who sells it to a customer, the customer can collect for damages from any of the three parties in the chain of sale under the theory of strict liability.

Contributory negligence cannot be used as a defense in a strict liability case. Intentional misuse of the product by the plaintiff or reasonable danger may be used. **For example**, a kitchen knife must be capable of cutting easily in order to be useful, and a cook who is injured by a cut while chopping vegetables cannot sue for the injury, since a knife not capable of cutting, is not functional.

Product Liability

If a defective product injures someone, the manufacturer and seller may be liable under the theory of Strict Liability in tort (liable without fault). The Injured party must prove:
- Suffered an **injury**.
- Seller was in the business of selling that product.
- Product was sold in a **defective** condition (unreasonably dangerous condition).
- The defect made the product ***unreasonably* dangerous**.
    - **Seller is liable** regardless of:
        - Unaware of the defect and were not negligent.
        - Injured party didn't exercise due care in the use of the product.
        - *Not in privity* with the injured party.
            - Cannot disclaim product liability.
- Under the UCC, limitation of damages for personal injury in the case of consumer goods is considered to be unconscionable and, thus, not allowed.

REMEDIES FOR BREACH

When it doesn't appear that one party to the contract will perform (**anticipatory breach** of contract), reasonable and/or adequate assurance of their ability to perform can be requested. If they refuse, the wronged party can cancel the contract and be released of all obligations. *Anticipatory repudiation* occurs when a party renounces the duty to perform the contract before the party's obligation to perform arises. The seller may then resell the goods to another party and recover damages.

Both parties are expected to act in good faith; if this doesn't occur, there are remedies available to the seller and the buyer.

Seller's Remedies
- Right to resell the goods
- Right to stop the carrier from delivering the goods (Rescind contract)
- Cancel the contract
- Recover damages
    - Incidental damages
    - Consequential damages
    - Not punitive damages
- Cure – Seller has time to cure non-conforming goods before the contract due date.

The UCC provides a victim of breach of contract with several options. The victim may cancel the contract while retaining the right to sue for damages (under common law, such cancellation normally cancels the right to damages).

If the seller has not yet completed the manufacture of goods when the buyer notifies them that they intend to dishonor the contract (**anticipatory breach**), the seller may sell the uncompleted goods for scrap or complete them and attempt to sell them elsewhere, whichever seems more commercially feasible. The seller has the right to recover from the buyer whatever losses cannot be avoided by such actions. If the seller learns that the buyer is insolvent, they may stop delivery on goods or reclaim them within 10 days after delivery. The seller must honor the contract, however, if the insolvent buyer pays cash for the goods.

Buyer's Remedies (Non-Conforming Goods)

- Accept all, some or none of the goods.
- Cover – purchase substitute goods and recover the excess paid from the seller.
- Specific performance – very unique goods.
- Recover damages
  - Incidental damages
  - Consequential damages
  - Not Punitive damages
- Rescission of contract

If a buyer does not receive promised goods from the seller, they may **cover** by obtaining the goods elsewhere and charge the seller any extra price the buyer had to pay. If the goods are in the possession of the seller, the buyer may exercise the right of **replevin** and claim ownership of the goods, if the buyer has paid the seller for them. If the buyer receives nonconforming goods, they should inform the seller, who has the right to **cure** by sending conforming goods by the original contract date or within a reasonable time after learning the goods do not conform to the contract.

If goods are destroyed before risk of loss passes, the contract is voided and the seller is released from obligation to perform.

If a **strike** happens and delivery cannot occur by the agreed-upon means, if a valid substituted performance occurs, both parties are still liable.

A **liquidated damages** clause is valid as long as the amount is reasonable in light of the anticipated loss. When no provision is stated, the seller may keep the lesser of $500 or 20% of the contract price.

Statute of Limitations

There is a statute of limitations on sales contracts of 4 years, starting from the date of breach (technically, the statute starts running the day after breach). The parties can mutually agree to shorten the statute of limitations to as little as one year, but cannot agree to lengthen it. Once the statute of limitations has expired, no claims can be filed in court charging breach of contract.

Lecture 14.05

CLASS QUESTIONS

Please see the Class Questions and Class Solutions for this Lecture at the end of this Section.

CLASS QUESTIONS

Work through the below Class Questions while following along with the respective lectures. Once this is complete, you can begin independently practicing what you've learned by quizzing yourself on this course section in your Interactive Practice Questions (IPQ), which can be found in your online Student Dashboard. Your IPQ simulates the computer-based testing experience, and will also help you understand how concepts are applied to the exam. Each question includes answer explanations from expert CPAs that will help you determine why you answered a question correctly or incorrectly. This is key to your success on the CPA Exam.

Lecture 14.02

1. Under the Sales Article of the UCC, a firm offer will be created only if the

   a. Offer states the time period during which it will remain open.
   b. Offer is made by a merchant in a signed writing.
   c. Offeree gives some form of consideration.
   d. Offeree is a merchant.

2. Under the Sales Article of the UCC, in an auction announced in explicit terms to be without reserve, when may an auctioneer withdraw the goods put up for sale?

   I. At any time until the auctioneer announces completion of the sale
   II. If no bid is made within a reasonable time

   a. I only.
   b. II only.
   c. Either I or II.
   d. Neither I nor II.

3. Which of the following contracts is handled under common law rules rather than under Article 2 of the Uniform Commercial Code?

   a. Oral contract to have hair styled in which expensive products will be used on the hair.
   b. Oral contract to purchase a textbook for $100.
   c. Written contract to purchase an old handcrafted chair for $600 from a private party.
   d. Written contract to purchase a heater from a dealer to be installed by the buyer in her home.

4. On May 2, Mason orally contracted with Acme Appliances to buy for $480 a washer and dryer for household use. Mason and the Acme salesperson agreed that delivery would be made on July 2. On May 5, Mason telephoned Acme and requested that the delivery date be moved to June 2. The Acme salesperson agreed with this request. On June 2, Acme failed to deliver the washer and dryer to Mason because of an inventory shortage. Acme advised Mason that it would deliver the appliances on July 2 as originally agreed. Mason believes that Acme has breached its agreement with Mason. Acme contends that its agreement to deliver on June 2 was not binding. Acme's contention is

    a. Correct, because Mason is not a merchant and was buying the appliances for household use.
    b. Correct, because the agreement to change the delivery date was not in writing.
    c. Incorrect, because the agreement to change the delivery date was binding.
    d. Incorrect, because Acme's agreement to change the delivery date is a firm offer that cannot be withdrawn by Acme.

Lecture 14.05

5. Bond purchased a painting from Wool, who is not in the business of selling art. Wool tendered delivery of the painting after receiving payment in full from Bond. Bond informed Wool that Bond would be unable to take possession of the painting until later that day. Thieves stole the painting before Bond returned. The risk of loss

    a. Passed to Bond at Wool's tender of delivery.
    b. Passed to Bond at the time the contract was formed and payment was made.
    c. Remained with Wool, because the parties agreed on a later time of delivery.
    d. Remained with Wool, because Bond had **not** yet received the painting.

6. Under the Sales Article of the UCC, which of the following factors is most important in determining who bears the risk of loss in a sale of goods contract?

    a. The method of shipping the goods.
    b. The contract's shipping terms.
    c. Title to the goods.
    d. How the goods were lost.

7. Under the Sales Article of the UCC, in an FOB place of shipment contract, the risk of loss passes to the buyer when the goods

    a. Are identified to the contract.
    b. Are placed on the seller's loading dock.
    c. Are delivered to the carrier.
    d. Reach the buyer's loading dock.

8. Under the Sales Article of the UCC, which of the following students is correct regarding risk of loss and title to the goods under a sale or return contract?

    a. Title and risk of loss are shared equally between the buyer and the seller.
    b. Title remains with the seller until the buyer approves or accepts the goods, but risk of loss passes to the buyer immediately following delivery of the goods to the buyer.
    c. Title and risk of loss remain with the seller until the buyer pays for the goods.
    d. Title and risk of loss rest with the buyer until the goods are returned to the seller.

9. Grill deals in the repair and sale of new and used clocks. West brought a clock to Grill to be repaired. One of Grill's clerks mistakenly sold West's clock to Hone, another customer. Under the Sales Article of the UCC, will West win a suit against Hone for the return of the clock?

    a. No, because the clerk was not aware that the clock belonged to West
    b. No, because Grill is a merchant to whom goods had been entrusted
    c. Yes, because Grill could not convey good title to the clock
    d. Yes, because the clerk was negligent in selling the clock

10. Thorn purchased a used entertainment system from Sound Corp. The sales contract stated that the entertainment system was being sold "as is." Under the Sales Article of the UCC, which of the following statements is (are) correct regarding the seller's warranty of title and against infringement?

    I. Including the term "as is" in the sales contract is adequate communication that the seller is conveying the entertainment system without warranty of title and against infringement.
    II. The seller's warranty of title and against infringement may be disclaimed at any time after the contract is formed.

    a. I only.
    b. II only.
    c. Both I and II.
    d. Neither I nor II.

11. An appliance seller promised a restaurant owner that a home dishwasher would fulfill the dishwashing requirements of a large restaurant. The dishwasher was purchased but it was not powerful enough for the restaurant. Under the Sales Article of the UCC, what warranty was violated?

    a. The implied warranty of marketability
    b. The implied warranty of merchantability
    c. The express warranty that the goods conform to the seller's promise
    d. The express warranty against infringement

12. Under the Sales Article of the UCC, which of the following circumstances will relieve a buyer from the obligation of accepting a tender or delivery of goods?

    I. If the goods do not meet the buyer's needs at the time of the tender or delivery.
    II. If the goods at the time of the tender or delivery do not exactly conform to the requirements of the contract.

    a. I only.
    b. II only.
    c. Both I and II.
    d. Neither I nor II.

13. High sues the manufacturer, wholesaler, and retailer for bodily injuries caused by a power saw High purchased. Which of the following statements is correct under strict liability theory?

   a.   Contributory negligence on High's part will always be a bar to recovery.
   b.   The manufacturer will avoid liability if it can show it followed the custom of the industry.
   c.   Privity will be a bar to recovery insofar as the wholesaler is concerned if the wholesaler did **not** have a reasonable opportunity to inspect.
   d.   High may recover even if he **cannot** show any negligence was involved.

CLASS SOLUTIONS

1. (b) In order to be valid, a firm offer must be created by a merchant, it must be in a signed writing, and it must be for a reasonable period of time. Answer (a) is incorrect because if a firm offer does not state the time period during which it will remain open, it will still be valid and will remain open for a reasonable period up to 3 months. Answer (c) is incorrect because consideration is not required in order for a firm offer to enter into a sales contract to be valid but would be required if the offer is for a common law contract, making it an option contract. Answer (d) is incorrect because the offeror must be a merchant, but not the offeree.

2. (b) When goods are put up for auction, they may be withdrawn at any time until the completion of the sale if they are offered with reserve. If they are offered without reserve, however, they may not be withdrawn unless there are no bids.

3. (a) Article 2 of the UCC covers the sale of goods, not services. Even when a service requires the use of certain goods, such as hair styling, it is still a sale of a service and subject to common law, rather than the UCC. Answer (b) is incorrect because a contract to purchase a textbook is a contract involving the sale of goods. There is no minimum amount required in order for the contract to be covered by the UCC; although, since this contract is for under $500, it is not required to be in writing under the Statute of Frauds. Answer (c) is incorrect because Article 2 of the UCC indicates certain rights and obligations applicable to merchants that are not applicable to private parties but the sale of goods by a private party is covered by the Article. Answer (d) is incorrect because a purchase of a heater from a dealer is a sale of goods by a merchant and covered by Article 2 of the UCC. The fact that the contract includes installation does not change it to a sale of services.

4. (c) In a contract for the sale of goods covered under Article 2 of the UCC, a contract modification, such as a change in the delivery date, will be binding without additional consideration. Since the contract, with the modification, is for less than $500, neither it nor the modification is subject to the Statute of Frauds and both may be oral. It makes no difference that the buyer is not a merchant and the agreement to change the delivery date is a modification to the contract, not a firm offer, which would have to be in writing.

5. (a) When a seller is not a merchant, both title and risk of loss transfer to the buyer when delivery of the goods is tendered to the buyer.

6. (b) Unless a contract specifies, the shipping terms will determine the point at which the risk of loss transfers from the seller to the buyer. Answer (a) is incorrect because the method of shipping the goods is irrelevant unless they are not to be delivered by a common carrier, in which case, risk of loss transfers to the buyer when delivery is tendered. Answer (c) is incorrect because the transfer of title is separate from the transfer of the risk of loss. Answer (d) is incorrect because how goods are lost is irrelevant.

7. (c) The term FOB stands for "free on board" and indicates that risk of loss is transferred when goods are "on board" a common carrier's vessel or, in other words, when the goods are delivered to (and loaded on) the common carrier. Answer (a) is incorrect because goods must be identified to the contract in order for risk of loss to pass, but it does not pass as soon as they are identified. Answer (b) is incorrect because if terms were FAS shipping point, which stands for "free alongside," risk of loss would transfer when goods are where the common carrier is to take possession of them, typically the seller's loading dock. Answer (d) is incorrect because title would transfer when goods reached the buyer's loading dock if the terms were FOB destination, not place of shipment.

8. (d) A sale or return contract is treated like an ordinary sale, and both title and risk of loss transfer to the buyer according to the shipping terms. Upon return of the goods, they revert back to the seller.

9. (b) Entrusting goods to a merchant creates a bailment in which the bailee, the merchant taking possession, owes a duty of care to the bailor, the owner of the goods. If the goods are sold as a result of the negligence of the bailee, a good faith purchaser will not be required to return the goods. The bailor will not be able to retrieve the goods but will be entitled to damages. Answer (a) is incorrect because the fact that the clerk did not know the clock belonged to West does not relieve the bailee of its responsibilities. Answer (c) is incorrect because, as a merchant, Grill is actually conveying good title to the clock, which is why West will not be able to retrieve it.

10. (d) The warranty of title can only be disclaimed using language that makes it clear that it is being disclaimed. Warranties of fitness and merchantability can be disclaimed using general terms such as "as is" or "with all faults." A disclaimer of a warranty of title must be made before, not after, the contract is entered into.

11. (c) When a sale is made based on promises by the seller that the goods will meet the buyer's objectives, the seller is providing a warranty of fitness, which is an express warranty that the goods will work as the seller promised. Answer (a) is incorrect because there is not warranty of marketability. Answer (b) is incorrect because the implied warranty of merchantability is that the goods will perform in accordance with claims in its packaging but does not relate to specific claims by the seller. Answer (d) is incorrect because the warranty against infringement is the warranty of title that the seller has good title to the goods and has not infringed upon another's claim.

12. (b) A buyer will be relieved of the obligation to accept a tender or delivery of goods if they are nonconforming goods, such as when they do not conform to the requirements of the contract. The fact that they do not meet the buyer's needs would relieve the buyer only if the sale was predicated on their ability to do so, indicating a warranty of fitness.

13. (d) Under the theory of strict liability, all an injured party must prove to recover damages is that damages were caused by a defect or unreasonable danger associated with the product that existed when the product left the defendant's control and that the defendant is in the business of selling the product. Answer (a) is incorrect because, in the case of strict liability, the defendant will not avoid damages due to the contributory negligence of the buyer. Answer (b) is incorrect because, in the case of strict liability, the defendant cannot avoid liability by showing it followed the customs of the industry. Answer (c) is incorrect because, in the case of strict liability, privity of contract is not required on the part of the plaintiff.

Section 15 – Business Structures

Corresponding Lectures

Watch the following course lectures with this section:

Lecture 15.01 – General Partnerships
Lecture 15.02 – Fiduciary Duties of Partners
Lecture 15.03 – General Partnerships – Class Questions
Lecture 15.04 – Limited Partnerships, LLC, LLP
Lecture 15.05 – Limited Partnerships, LLC, LLP – Class Questions
Lecture 15.06 – Corporations
Lecture 15.07 – Corporations vs. Partnerships – Class Questions
Lecture 15.08 – Board of Directors
Lecture 15.09 – Shareholders' Rights
Lecture 15.10 – Corporations – Class Questions

EXAM NOTE: *Please refer to the AICPA REG Blueprint in the Introduction to find a listing of the representative tasks (and their associated skill levels—i.e., Remembering and Understanding, Application, and Analysis) that the candidate should be able to perform based on the knowledge obtained in this section.*

Business Structures

GENERAL PARTNERSHIPS

A partnership (General Partnership) is an association between two or more persons to operate a business as co-owners *for profit*. Nonprofit associations such as charitable organizations, labor unions or clubs do not qualify. **Informally created** since the partners have **Unlimited** Liability. The Partners are **agents** of the partnership. *Characteristics:*

- Limited duration.
- Transfer of ownership requires agreement.
- Under RUPA (Revised Uniform P/S Act), partnerships are *separate legal entities*.
  - May sue and be sued.
  - May own property in partnership name.
- Unlimited liability of partners for partnership debts.
- Ease of formation, can be very informal.
- Not a taxable entity, flow-through entity (1065).

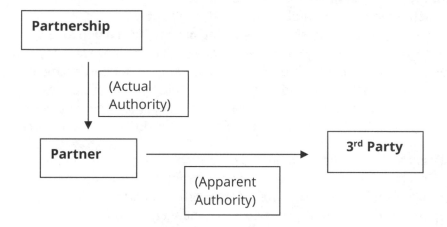

3 Basic Partner Rights

A partnership is an association between two or more persons to operate a business as co-owners for profit. **Informally created** since the partners have Unlimited Liability. The Partners are **agents** of the partnership. In such an arrangement, partners have **three basic rights**:

- **Profits (Interest)** – Each partner generally has a right to a proportionate share of (1) the profits generated by the business and (2) a return of the net assets in the partnership in the event the partnership terminates. This is known as the **partnership interest**. The right is personal and **transferable/assignable** without the need for approval by the other partners. As a result, a partner can transfer their interest in the partnership to a personal creditor, or the courts may permit a personal creditor to seize that interest to satisfy an unpaid personal debt of the partner. When that occurs, the creditor is entitled to receive that partner's share of profits and distributions.
- **Property** – All property acquired by a partnership becomes partnership property and belongs to the partnership as an entity, rather than to the individual partners. Each partner has a right to use partnership property for partnership purposes. Under RUPA, partnership property not only includes property purchased in the partnership name but also includes property purchased by a partner, who is an agent of the partnership, with

partnership funds. This right is **not transferable/assignable**, so a personal creditor of a partner cannot obtain a right to any specific partnership property as a result of an assignment of interest by that partner.

- **Participation (Management Right – vote/make contracts/debts)** – Each partner has a right to participate in the management of the business, including a right to inspect the books and records of the business at any time, make contracts, and vote on partnership actions. This right is also **not transferable/assignable**.

Formation (Informal)

The establishment of a partnership can result from an agreement that is:
- **Written** – This is required only when the *statute of frauds* applies, such as a partnership with a specific term exceeding one year. Requires written evidence signed by defendant to enforce certain contracts (**GROSS**):
    - Sale of **G**oods worth $500 or more
    - **R**eal estate sales
    - **O**ver one year required to perform contract (Bilateral contract)
    - **S**uretyship (Guarantee debt of another)
    - **S**tatements in consideration of marriage ("if you marry my daughter, I will make you VP of my co" - Marriage is the consideration).
- **Oral** – This is acceptable when the statute of frauds doesn't apply.
- **Implied** – Whenever two or more persons are **sharing profits from a venture**, they are presumed to be partners, unless they can prove otherwise (a person proves they're not a partner by showing they do not use partnership property and do not participate in the management of the business). This is known as a partnership by rebuttable presumption.
    - Partners' capital may not only be in cash, property, or services already performed, but also may be in the form of promises to give or perform these at a future date.

No government approval is needed for the creation of a partnership (**informal**), and there are no special filings required. A partnership may use the names of current or former partners without approval. A partnership that wishes to have a business name with other information may need to file a fictitious name statement with the appropriate government agency.

Types of Authority
- **Actual** – Partnership intends to give the partner power to contract.
    - **Express** – Partnership explicitly states partner has authority.
    - **Implied** – Partnership assigns task, which requires authority to carry out duties. Reasonable and necessary to get job done.
- **Apparent** – Partnership creates impression that partner has authority.
    - **Good faith 3rd party** reasonably assumes you have.
- **Unauthorized action** – not liable unless ratify.
    - **Ratification** – Partnership gives partner authority after contract is made.
        - Principal (Partnership) must be fully or partially disclosed.
        - Must know details of contract made by partner on behalf of Partnership.
        - Must ratify before 3rd party withdraws.

The right of a partner to participate in management includes broad agency authority: the partners are, in effect, mutual agents and principals with the power to make contracts binding each other. The actual authority of a partner is based on agreement, but a partner has the **apparent**

authority to make virtually any contract that involves the business of the partnership, with the following exceptions:

- **Admitting a new partner** – No partner may admit a new partner to the business without the unanimous consent of all partners. This is because each new partner has agency power and is entitled to a share of the profits, and such rights must be clearly agreed to by all affected parties.
- **Selling or pledging property (Can't sell Goodwill of P/S)** –The sale of property or pledging as collateral for a loan requires consent of all partners; although, partners have the right to use partnership property. A partner *does*, however, have the apparent authority to sell *inventory* in the ordinary course of business.
- **Admitting or submitting a legal claim** – No partner may waive the legal rights of the other partners by admitting responsibility in *court* or by agreeing to submit disputes with others to binding *arbitration* without all partners consenting to the arrangement.
- **Promising to pay the debts of another** – No partner can make the partnership a surety or guarantor of the debts of another party. Furthermore, surety arrangements fall within the statute of frauds, so each partner who is to act as a *surety* must individually sign the agreement.

In addition to these four limits on the apparent authority of a partner, the doctrine of apparent authority does not apply when the partners **agree to limits on the actual authority** of a partner **and notify third parties of the limits**. For example, assume the partners are negotiating the purchase of machinery, a transaction that normally can be approved by any one of them and be binding on the entire partnership. If the partners privately agree that the purchase decision will require the unanimous consent of the partners, this will not change the apparent authority of a partner to make the deal *without* such consent. If, however, the owner of the machinery is informed of the private agreement, apparent authority is eliminated, and the deal *will* require unanimous consent.

- Unanimous consent required for the following (**AGAST**):
  - **A**dmitting a new partner.
  - **G**uaranteeing the debts of a third party (suretyship).
  - **A**dmitting or submitting a legal claim in court or to arbitration.
  - **S**ale or pledge of partnership property (sell goodwill).
  - **T**hird parties are notified (aware) of a limit to the partner's actual authority.

Lecture 15.02

Fiduciary Duties of Partners

- Duty of *loyalty*
- Duty of *care* – Partners must refrain from engaging in grossly negligent or reckless conduct, intentional misconduct, or knowingly violate the law.
- Partners must *refrain from competing* with the partnership.
- Partners also have a duty of *good faith and fair dealing* in the discharge of all their duties.

Liability

Partners have **joint & several** liability on the **contracts & debts** (voluntary) made by the partnership with third parties. If the partnership breaches a contract, the third party must attempt to recover damages out of partnership assets first, then may access the personal assets of the partners for remaining amounts owed. If one partner is personally bankrupt, the third party may access sufficient assets of the solvent partners to satisfy the claim.

Partners are **jointly and severally** liable on the **torts** (involuntary) committed by any of the partners within the scope of the partnership. Third parties may access partnership and personal assets of the partners in any order. A tort is a wrongful act, whether intentional or negligent, not arising out of contractual obligations, which causes an injury and can be remedied at civil law, usually through awarding damages.

Partners are normally not liable for **crimes** committed by other partners, but recent legislation has expanded liability in some cases, and the CPA exam generally avoids areas of law that are not consistent on a nationwide basis.

- RUPA requires creditors to first attempt collection from the partnership before partners, unless the partnership is bankrupt.

A *silent partner* in a general partnership does not participate in the management of the partnership, but nonetheless has unlimited liability.

Admitting or Retiring a Partner

When a new partner enters a partnership, the partner will be liable for contracts and torts that arise after the date of admission in accordance with the principles just discussed.

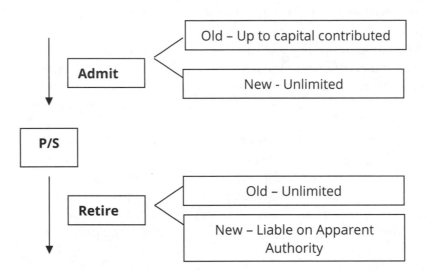

Unless they make a specific agreement to become so, a new partner is **not personally liable** for actions taken **before admission**. Any capital contributions made by the partner, however, can be accessed by partnership creditors with claims arising before that partner's admission.

When an existing partner retires from the partnership, the partner will continue to be liable for debts created before retirement, unless the **creditors** agree to perform a **novation** to release the retiree. An agreement by the **other partners** to hold the retiring partner harmless for all debts will **not** release them, since the debts are not owed to the other partners. Such an agreement will, however, serve as an indemnification agreement requiring the remaining partners to reimburse the retiree for any amounts they are forced to pay creditors.

A retiree may continue to be held **liable** for debts created **after retirement** if proper notice of retirement isn't given. Parties that dealt with the retiree in the past must be given **actual notice**, while others who might have become aware of the partner are considered notified if the partnership provides **constructive notice** of the retirement through the publication of an announcement of the change. Notice is not required upon the death of a partner, since the termination of that partner's participation is by operation of law. Note that a retiring partner also has the ability to make contracts that are binding on the remaining partners if proper notice of retirement hasn't been made.

- **Actual notice** – Third parties are directly informed (personal notice).
- **Constructive notice** – An announcement of the termination is made in publications that third parties are likely to read (public notice).

The allocation of losses to the partners is based on their agreement. In the absence of an explicit agreement, partners share losses in the same proportion that they share profits. If there is no agreement on the sharing of profits either, then profits and losses are **shared equally based on the number of partners,** except in unusual circumstances.

If a partner's losses reduce the partner's capital account below zero, the partner is personally liable for the deficit.

When a partner **transfers their interest** in the partnership to another party (such as a personal creditor in settlement of a claim), the transferor remains the partner and continues to have liability for losses and claims against the partnership. The transferee is entitled to that partner's share of profits and surplus, but has no other rights or obligations in connection with the partnership, and is **not** considered a partner.

Dissolution and Termination

Dissolution is the result of the change in the relation of the partners when a partner ceases to be associated with the carrying on of the business. The partnership does not terminate on dissolution, but continues until the winding up of the partnership is complete. Dissolution may be accomplished either without violation of the partnership agreement or in violation of the partnership agreement. The **entity theory** of partnership provides a conceptual basis for continuing the firm itself, despite a partner's withdrawal from the firm.

Under RUPA, a **change in the makeup of the partnership does not dissolve** it, unless the partners agree to do so (a withdrawal that reduces the number of partners to one, however, does cause dissolution, since one person alone cannot be considered a partnership). Dissolution does not mean that the partnership must liquidate all assets and cease business, but simply that the legal entity that exists after the change in partners is not considered a continuation of the previous partnership. As a result, various legal arrangements and claims may need to be modified or refiled in court. Because of the inconvenience dissolution causes, partners normally will make an agreement not to dissolve upon a change in partners. A "**partnership at will**" is used to describe a partnership without a specified duration.

Tax law treats a partnership as a separate legal entity for the purpose of collection and payment of payroll taxes. A partnership is not obligated to pay income taxes, but must file annual information returns (Form 1065), allocating the income of the partnership to the partners, who are personally responsible for all income tax obligations.

Dissolution of a partnership is generally the first step in terminating it. A partnership may be dissolved without being terminated but, if it is to be terminated, dissolution will be followed by a winding up of partnership affairs and the distribution of partnership property. During the period of dissolution and winding up, the partners continue to have the authority to bind the partnership, which continues until such time as the partnership is terminated.

A partnership agreement may specify the length of time it is intended to remain in operation and dissolution will occur when its term expires. When a term is specified, a partner may dissolve the partnership only with the consent of the other partners. If there is no term specified, however, any partner may dissolve the partnership at any time. A partnership may also be dissolved as a result of:

- *A court decree*, which will likely be granted if a partner becomes insane or incapacitated
- A *violation* of the partnership agreement

Since RUPA considers a partnership to be a legal entity, it is **not automatically dissolved** as a result of the **withdrawal, death, or bankruptcy** of a partner. When one of those circumstances does occur, remaining partners with a majority share of the partnership may continue the partnership.

- A partnership may NOT continue if only one partner remains, since a partnership requires two or more partners.
- Any partner has the power to withdraw from the partnership.
- A withdrawing partner who had agreed not to withdraw may be in breach of contract.

When a partnership is terminated, there is a **winding up** of the partnership's affairs. All assets will be sold, liabilities will be paid, and any surplus will be distributed to the partners. Gains or losses will be allocated among the partners according to their profit and loss percentages.

A partner with a **deficit balance** is generally required to make a contribution to the partnership to eliminate the deficit. If the partner is bankrupt, however, the partner's deficit balance will be allocated among the remaining partners according to their profit and loss percentages.

In determining the amount that will be distributed to a partner upon **termination** of the partnership:

- First, upon the sale of assets, allocate all gains and losses to the partners in accordance with their profit and loss percentages.
- If any partner has a deficit balance and is bankrupt and unable to contribute the amount of the deficit, any remaining deficit, after what contributions the partner does make, is allocated to the remaining partners in accordance with their profit and loss percentages.
- When all assets are sold, profits and losses are allocated, and liabilities are paid, the remaining cash will be equal to the total of the partners' capital balances.
- The cash will then be distributed to the partners.

Distributions to partners will be made in the following order:

- Amounts owed to partners for loans to the partnership
- Partners' capital accounts
- Amounts owed to partners for profits

Lecture 15.03

CLASS QUESTIONS

Please see the Class Questions and Class Solutions for this Lecture at the end of this Section.

LIMITED PARTNERSHIPS (LP) (FORMAL)

In some circumstances, individuals will want to achieve the benefits of the corporate structure—limited liability in particular—with the benefits of a partnership that include the ease of formation and being treated as a pass-through entity for tax purposes. The solution is the limited partnership (LP), which has many of the characteristics of a partnership, while providing limited liability to some of its partners.

Formation

Not all states allow the formation of an LP and one cannot be formed in a state without an enabling statute. Most states that allow LPs have adopted the Revised Uniform Limited Partnership Act (RULPA), although a few states have adopted the newer Uniform Limited Partnership Act (New ULPA).

In order to be formed, an LP requires at least one general partner and at least one limited partner. As a general rule, the **general partner** is responsible for the management and operations of the partnership and has unlimited liability while a **limited partner** is a passive investor with limited authority and liability that, in most cases, is limited to the amount invested. A limited partner generally has no personal liability for the obligations of the partnership, including those resulting from contracts or torts.

Because of the limited liability provided to some partners, forming a limited partnership requires a more formal process than forming a partnership, including the filing of **a certificate of limited partnership** (**Formal**) with the Secretary of State, which generally includes:
- The names and signatures of all general partners
- The name and address of the LP, which may not include the name of a limited partner who is not also a general partner and must include the words "limited partnership" or the abbreviation
- The name and address of its agent
- The latest date on which the LP is expected to terminate

The certificate, which does not require the names of the limited partners, must be amended for the addition or deletion of general partners. If the certificate is not properly filed, the LP will be treated as a general partnership.

Both general and limited partners may obtain their partnership interests in exchange for cash or other monetary or nonmonetary assets, the performance of services, or the promises to deliver cash or other assets or perform services.

Rights and Obligations

General partners, as indicated, are responsible for the management of the entity, have a fiduciary responsibility to the LP and its partners, and have unlimited personal liability for the obligations of the partnership. A general partner may, however, be a corporation providing its limited liability protections.

A person can become a **general partner** by being so indicated in the limited partnership agreement, as a replacement for a general partner that is dissociated from the partnership, as a result of a conversion or merger, or with the consent of all partners.

- A general partner is an **_agent_** of the limited partnership with all the rights and obligations associated with agency.
- A limited partnership is liable for the actions of the general partner that are in the ordinary course of the partnership's business or are with the authority of the partnership.
- All general partners are _jointly and severally liable_ for the _obligations_ of the limited partnership.
  - A person becoming a general partner is not liable for partnership obligations _before_ they became a general partner.
  - Obligations incurred by a limited partnership during a time that it is an LLLP are solely the obligation of the limited partnership, not the general partners.
- General partners have equal _rights of management._
- General partners have a _fiduciary duty_ to the limited partnership and the partners that is limited to the duties of loyalty and care.
  - Refrain from dealing with parties whose interests are adverse to the partnership
  - Refrain from competing with the partnership
  - Refrain from grossly negligent or reckless conduct, intentional misconduct, or knowingly violating the law

A **general partner** may **withdraw** from the partnership upon:
- Providing notice of an express will to withdraw to the partnership.
- Occurrence of an event specified in the partnership agreement.
- Expulsion either in accordance with the terms of the partnership agreement, or by the unanimous consent of the other partners.

Limited partners also may be general partners, in which case they will have the same liability as general partners. One that is not, however, may not participate in management, and doing so will generally eliminate that partner's limited liability protection.

A limited partner does _not have a fiduciary duty_ to the LP, or to the other partners, and may conduct business with the LP in the same manner as a third party, and may have a competing interest. A limited partner may act as an agent or surety for the LP, may be a creditor (secured or unsecured), or act as a consultant to the LP without impairing the protection of limited liability.

In addition, a limited partner may bring a **derivative suit** on behalf of the LP and may participate in (i.e., **vote on**) decisions related to:
- Amendments the LP agreement
- Dissolution or winding up
- Changes to the nature of the LP's business
- Loans
- General partner changes

Profits and losses of an LP are distributed in accordance with the provisions of the LP agreement. When there is no agreement, unlike a general partnership, which calls for the equal distribution of profits and losses, profits and losses in an LP are distributed in proportion to LPs' capital investments.

A limited partner has certain **rights** that include the right to inspect the partnership's books and records. Although the admission of a new partner requires the approval in writing of all partners, unless otherwise specified in the LP agreement, an LP interest may be assigned without the approval of other partners. The acquirer, however, obtains only the limited partner's rights to profits and is considered a creditor of the LP.

A **limited partner** does not have the **right to withdraw** from the limited partnership but may do so:
- By giving notice to the limited partnership of the express will to withdraw
- Upon occurrence of an event or condition cited in the partnership agreement
- Upon expulsion either in accordance with the partnership agreement or by the unanimous vote of the other partners

Distributions by a limited partnership are required to be made to all partners in proportion to the value of contributions the partner has made to the limited partnership. The value is required to be stated in the records of the limited partnership. A distribution *may not be made*:
- In violation of the partnership agreement.
- Such that the limited partnership will be unable to pay its debts as they come due.

Dissolution and Termination

An LP agreement will generally specify the term of the partnership, or the date on which it is to be dissolved, or the event or transaction that the LP was formed to enter into, after which the LP would terminate. In addition, an LP may be **dissolved** as a result of:
- The written consent of all partners
- Court decree
- The illegality of the LP's business

In addition, the **withdrawal of the general partner**, other than as a result of insolvency, will generally dissolve an LP. It will continue, however, if allowed to by the LP agreement or all remaining partners agree to do so in writing. The death or withdrawal of a limited partner does not result in dissolution.

When an LP will not continue, **distributions upon winding up** will first be made to creditors, followed by unpaid distributions to partners and ex-partners. All partners will next receive a return of capital, after which any remaining partnership assets will be distributed in proportion to the partners' profit percentages (unless otherwise agreed-upon).

OTHER BUSINESS STRUCTURES

There are a variety of business structures that may be used in addition to partnerships, each of which has different characteristics and each of which would be used for a different purpose. These include limited partnerships (LPs), limited liability partnerships (LLPs), limited liability companies (LLCs), and limited liability limited partnerships (LLLPs).
- **LPs** (just discussed) are most applicable in arrangements like real estate deals where one group of partners, the limited partners, provide most of the capital and benefit from limited liability; and another group, the general partners, do the work and make the decisions and do not have limited liability.
- **LLPs** are popular among professionals, such as accountants, and many states allow LLPs only for such groups. They are designed to provide protection to innocent partners against the actions of other partners.
- **LLCs** are used by other entities to provide characteristics of a corporation in the form of limited liability to its owners with the tax characteristics of a sole proprietorship, in the case of a single member LLC (Schedule C), or a partnership (Schedule E), in a multi-member LLC. In many cases, an LLC is the general partner in an LP for the purpose of providing the general partners with the same limited liability as limited partners.

As indicated above, some states have adopted a newer version of the **ULPA,** which is designed to *replace* the **Revised Uniform Limited Partnership Act (RULPA).** Under the new ULPA, the basic structure of a limited partnership remains the same. The ULPA, however, allows for the formation of a **limited liability limited partnership (LLLP)** under which neither general partners nor limited partners are personally liable for the obligations of the partnership.

In an LLLP, both limited partners and general partners are free of liability for the limited partnership's obligations similarly to corporate shareholders, members of an LLC, or partners in an LLP. A general partner is only responsible for the debts incurred by the LLLP by agreeing to be held liable. A limited partnership does not obtain LLLP status automatically, but does so by including a statement to that effect in the **certificate of limited partnership**.

Some of the **additional differences between the RULPA and the ULPA** include:
- **Term**
  - RULPA – specific term identified in certificate of limited partnership
  - ULPA – perpetual
- **Inclusion of name** of limited partner in partnership name
  - RULPA – prohibited
  - ULPA – permitted
- Personal liability of **limited partners** for **debts and obligations** of limited partnership
  - RULPA – none, unless limited partner participates in management
  - ULPA – none, even if limited partner participates in management
- Personal liability of **general partners** for **debts and obligations** of limited partnership
  - RULPA – unlimited liability, subject to its own protection, such as if the general partner is a corporation
  - ULPA – may be avoided through LLLP status by including a statement to that effect in the certificate of limited partnership
- **Withdrawal** of limited partner
  - RULPA - May withdraw with 6 months' notice unless otherwise specified in limited partnership agreement
  - ULPA – no right to withdraw from the partnership before termination of limited partner

Limited Liability Companies (LLC)

Some states, most of which follow the Revised Uniform Limited Liability Company Act (RULLCA), have an enabling statute that allows for the formation of **Limited Liability Companies** (**LLC**s). LLCs have characteristics of both partnerships and corporations; they are pass-through entities from a tax standpoint, while they provide their owners, referred to as members, with the limited liability protection of a corporation. Also, like a corporation, members have no interest in the LLC's assets but only in the LLC itself.

For **tax purposes**, a single-member LLC is generally referred to as a "disregarded entity." It is treated like a sole proprietorship, and its information is reported to the IRS on a Schedule C, accompanying the single owner's tax return. An LLC with multiple owners is generally treated as a partnership for tax purposes. The LLC files a Form 1065 information return and each member of the LLC will receive a Schedule K-1 that flows to their Schedule E (similar to an S corporation).

An LLC is a legal entity that can only be formed in a state that allows their formation and, as a result, can be sued or file suit in its own name. Like limited partnerships, they file a **certificate**

with the Secretary of State. The certificate must include the entity's name, which must include the words limited liability company, limited company, or appropriate abbreviations.

Members may participate in management (agents) without restriction and owe the same duties of loyalty and care to the LLC as owed to a limited partnership by the general partner. Also, similar to a general partner in a limited partnership, a member cannot freely transfer an interest, and a new member must be admitted upon the consent of the other members.

An LLC may be member-managed or manager-managed. A member-managed LLC will be bound by the actions of any of its members, who are considered agents of the LLC. A manager-managed LLC is only bound by the actions of the manager that are either authorized or in the ordinary course of business. In either case, a member or manager able to bind the LLC owes it both a duty of loyalty and of care. A member of a manager-managed LLC, however, owes no fiduciary duty to the LLC.

Allocations of profits and losses of an LLC will generally be made in accordance with the LLC agreement. In its absence, profits and losses in states that have adopted the RULLCA will be allocated to the members equally. In those states that have not adopted the RULLCA, allocations are generally in proportion to members' capital contributions.

Like an LP, many LLCs will terminate upon expiration of the term specified in the LLC agreement or upon the occurrence of an event or transaction. It may also be **dissolved** as a result of:
- The written agreement of all members
- Withdrawal, death, bankruptcy, or incompetency of a member
- Court order

Upon dissolution, after settlement with creditors, including amounts owed to members for loans but not for profits, distributions are made first for unpaid distributions and then capital contributions. Remaining distributions are allocated similarly to profits.

Businesses such as doctors' offices and CPA firms that are required to obtain a license in order to perform services are not allowed to form LLCs in many states and may instead form Professional Limited Liability Companies.

Limited Liability Partnership (LLP)

Another form of entity that is allowed by most states and that provides some or all of its owners limited liability is the **Limited Liability Partnership** (**LLP**). In most circumstances, a partnership will qualify as an LLP by registering with the Secretary of State. Some require proof of adequate insurance or proof that assets are adequate to satisfy claims against the LLP.

Most states require an LLP to file articles with the Secretary of State and have a name that includes the words limited liability partnership or registered limited liability partnership, or appropriate initials.

Like an LLC, an LLP has characteristics of partnerships and of corporations. For tax purposes, LLPs are pass-through entities but, as indicated, both general and limited partners may be afforded limited liability. Partners are personally liable for their own torts and, in many cases, the torts of those under their supervision.

The degree of protection (from **Liability**) available to partners in an LLP depends largely on the jurisdiction in which it is formed. In general:

- Partners are not liable for the actions of other partners, including negligence, incompetence, error, omission, or malfeasance.
- Some jurisdictions provide very broad protection, but many hold partners liable for their own negligence or misconduct.
- Others hold partners personally liable for the contracts and debts of the LLP without limit.
- LLPs are taxed as a partnership, so the income is passed through to the individual taxpayer's tax return on Schedule E.

Similarities and Differences between LLPs and LLCs

Formation

- Both require an enabling statute in the state of formation.
- Both are easier to form than a corporation.
- Both require filing a certificate with an appropriate state authority, such as the Secretary of State.
- An LLC may be formed with one or more owners, referred to as members, while an LLP requires 2 or more partners.

Taxation

- Both are pass-through entities.
- Both may report their operations by filing Form 1065 and distributing K-1s to its members or partners.
  - An LLP is always treated as a partnership.
  - An LLC with more than one member is treated as a partnership, and those with one member are treated as sole proprietorships (Schedule C). **Note:** These are the default tax classifications; an LLC can also elect to be treated as a corporation by filing Form 8832, *Entity Classification Election*.

Liability

- Both provide owners with some degree of protection.
  - LLCs generally limit the liability of members to their investments, plus the costs resulting from their own negligence or malpractice.
  - Partners of LLPs are generally not liable for the actions of copartners, but are generally liable for the obligations and debts of the LLP.

Joint Venture

A *joint venture* is an informal arrangement between 2 or more parties to conduct business with one another. A joint venture is not a legal entity, although it has *many characteristics of a partnership*. It generally has a finite life and is established for a specific period of time, or to accomplish a particular objective. All joint venturers have access to the property that is the subject to the joint venture, have the right to participate in management, are jointly and severally liable for the obligations of the joint venture, and owe a fiduciary duty to the other venturers. The death of a joint venturer does NOT dissolve the joint venture.

Sole Proprietorships

A sole proprietorship is the most common form of business in the U.S. and is not a legal entity that is separated from its owner. One can be established by an individual (one owner), who will have exclusive right to manage the business, will have access to all assets, and will have *unlimited personal liability* for all obligations of the sole proprietorship. A fictitious name statement must be filed with the government if operating under a name other than that of the sole proprietor.

A sole proprietorship is *not a taxable entity*. The single owner includes its operations on a Schedule C, filed with the owner's individual tax return, and the income is taxable directly to the owner.

LLC	LLP (Accounting Firms)	LLLP
Formal creation	Formal	Formal
1 Person	2+ people	2+ people
• <u>Limited Liability</u> for Contracts and debts • <u>Unlimited Liability</u> for Malpractice or Negligence	• <u>Limited Liability</u> for Malpractice or Negligence • <u>Unlimited Liability</u> for Contracts/Debts	• <u>Limited Liability</u> for ALL Partners (General and Limited)
Agents/Member	Agents	Agents
Taxed as a P/S	Taxed as a P/S	Taxed as a P/S

Partnership	Limited Partnership		C Corporation
Informal creation	Formal		Formal
Unlimited liability	**(General)** Unlimited	**(Limited)** Limited	Limited Liability
Partnership **Interest** (Profit/Losses)	→	Interest ————→	
Partnership **Property**	→	NO Property ————→	
Partnership **Management**	→	NO Management – EXCEPT can look at the **books** and **vote** ————→	
Agents ————→		NOT automatically Agent ————→	

Survivorship

Comparison of Business Structures

	General Partnership	Limited P/S	Limited Liability P/S (LLP)	Limited Liability Company (LLC)	Limited Liability Limited Partnership (LLLP)	Corporation
Governed by:	RUPA	RULPA	Individual Secretary of State LLP Act	RULLCA	ULPA	MBCA
Required to Formally File with State?	No	Yes	Yes	Yes	Yes	Yes
Owners referred to as:	Partners	General Partners and Limited Partners	Partners	Members	Partners	Shareholders
Authority to Bind to Contracts	Partners	General Partners	Partners	Managers	Partners	Officers/Directors
Formal Creation?	Partnership Agreement	Certificate and Partnership Agreement	Partnership Agreement and Application for LLP	Articles of Organization and Operating Agreement	Certificate of Limited Partnership	Articles of Incorporation and Bylaws, Shareholder Agreements
Limited Liability	No	**No** for general Partners, **Yes** for Limited Partners	Yes, if election made	Yes	Yes	Yes
Ownership Interest Considered a Security under 1933 Fed Sec Reg's	Generally No	*General* Partnership interests – NO *Limited* Partnership Interests - **Yes**	Generally No	Generally No	Generally No	Generally **Yes**
Taxation	Income passed through to partners on K-1 then to Sch. E	Income passed through to partners on K-1 then to Sch. E	Income passed through to partners on K-1 then to Sch. E	Income passed through to members. If single member Sch. C, if multiple, Sch. E	Income passed through to partners on K-1 then to Sch. Sch. E	**S Corp** – Income passed through to shareholders on K-1 then Sch. E. **C Corp**- Taxed directly on 1120 and distributions taxed to shareholders on Sch. B

CLASS QUESTIONS

Please see the Class Questions and Class Solutions for this Lecture at the end of this Section.

CORPORATIONS

C Corporation

A C corporation is an artificial person created by statute and governed by the Model Business Corporation Act (MBCA). It is considered to be separate from the owners (i.e., shareholders), giving it several characteristics not present in other forms of business organization (such as partnerships and proprietorships). Under the federal Subchapter S Revision Act, all corporations are designated as either a Subchapter S corporation or a Subchapter C corporation, and any corporation that does not meet all the criteria of a Subchapter S corporation is categorized as a Subchapter C corporation. Among the *characteristics* (with certain minor exceptions) that distinguish C corporations are:

- **Limited liability** – Shareholders are not responsible for the debts of the corporation.
- **Independent life** – The death of a shareholder doesn't cause the corporation to dissolve (Perpetuity).
- **Ease of transfer** – Changes in ownership are effected simply by a transfer of shares (intangible personal property) and require no approval from others in the business or novations by creditors of business.
- **Taxation** – The corporation must file and pay its own income taxes (Form 1120). Since dividends paid to shareholders by C corporations are not deductible for tax purposes, the earnings of such corporations are said to be subject to double taxation to the extent that they are paid out as dividends.
- **Centralized management** – The corporation is effectively controlled by an internal group known as the board of directors, and not by the shareholders.

S Corporation

An S corporation is a special type of corporation that avoids taxes at the corporate level since they flow through to the individual shareholder's tax return (**K-1**). The requirements that must be met to qualify are: (**Simple & Small**)

- **Formal creation** as shareholders generally have **limited liability.**
- There can be no more than **100 shareholders** (family members with a common ancestor no more than six generations above and their spouses may be treated as a single shareholder for purposes of this rule).
- All shareholders must be **individuals** (or certain estates or trusts for the benefit of individuals).
    - Husband and wife count as one until divorce is final.
    - No corporations, partnerships or big trusts.
- All shareholders must be either **residents or citizens** of the United States.
- The corporation must be a **domestic** corporation.
- There can be only **one class** of stock. No preferred stock.
- Once an S corporation's status has been revoked, it cannot reelect such status for **5 years**.

Closely Held Corporation

Closely held corporation (also called "close corporation" or "closed corporation") is one whose stock is NOT offered to the public on a securities exchange and is owned by a limited number of persons (< 50 shareholders) usually with restrictions on the transfer of stock to keep it out of the hands of outsiders. Many of the shareholders participate in the management of the business.

A corporation receives its charter from the state in which it incorporates, and is considered a **domestic** corporation in that state. A corporation that attempts to operate in a state other than the state that provided the charter is considered a **foreign** corporation, and must meet the operating requirements (file a certificate of Authority) of that state if it wishes court protection.

For example, let's say a company with a charter in California starts doing business in Texas, but fails to obtain regulatory licenses required by the Texas government to protect the public. If it is a victim of breach of contract in Texas, the corporation will not be able to sue in Texas court and cannot recover its loss. This prohibition doesn't apply if the company has violated non-substantive rules, such as licenses that are only for the purpose of raising revenue for the state.

Prior to the formation of a corporation, **promoters** might enter into contracts on its behalf. A promoter is not an agent of the corporation, since the promoter performs work before the corporation itself exists. As a result, a contract by a promoter is not binding on the corporation unless the board of directors elects to **adopt** the contract. The promoter is personally liable on the contract prior to adoption, and remains liable afterwards unless the other party to the contract releases the promoter and gives them a **novation** (substitution of promoter for the new corporation). The board cannot ratify the contract (giving it retroactive authority to the date it was made), since it cannot go back to a time prior to the corporation's birth. Promoters have a **fiduciary duty** to act loyally toward the future corporation, but aren't entitled to compensation. The board also adopts the corporation's initial bylaws.

The corporation is **formed (formal)** once the state receives and accepts the **articles of incorporation** filed on its behalf. The Articles can subsequently be amended by a shareholder vote. Some of the items that are included in the articles are:
- **Name** – The proposed name of the corporation.
- **Nature & Purpose** – An indication of the powers sought and restrictions on the charter. For example, a corporation may be established for strictly charitable purposes as a non-profit organization, or as a business with broad powers to enter into any types of for-profit ventures.
- **Term** – The life of the corporation. Most articles request an indefinite duration (Perpetuity).
- **Name and address** – of each Incorporator.
- **Capitalization** – The amount and types of shares of stock that the corporation wants to be authorized to issue. It is no longer necessary for the corporation to assign a par value to shares.
- **Initial Board** – The names of the people who will serve as the members of the board of directors until the first shareholder meeting.
- **Registered Agent** – The place where the state may serve a court order if the corporation is being sued or needs to be legally notified of actions involving it. The registered agent is often an attorney. The corporation need not identify the places of business, and may not even do business within the state of incorporation, but the registered agent must be located within the state.
  - When complete, the articles of incorporation are filed with the state which issues a certificate of incorporation or corporate **Charter**.

By-Laws – Rules and regulations that govern and help to guide the internal management in performing its duties. Either the incorporators or the board adopts them.

Lecture 15.07

CLASS QUESTIONS

Please see the Class Questions and Class Solutions for this Lecture at the end of this Section.

Lecture 15.08

BOARD OF DIRECTORS

The principal agent of the corporation is the board of directors, a small group that meets 1 to 12 times per year to set policy and make broad decisions. They are in charge of the *general operations* of the corporation. Some of the important principles associated with the board are:

Board of Directors
- Act as a board (act as a group)
- Not agents
- In charge of general operations
- Adopt the bylaws
  1. Select the **officers** (e.g., president)
     - In charge of day-to-day operations
     - Agents of Corporation
     - Right to be Indemnified (right to get reimbursement)
  2. **Reacquire** treasury stock unless insolvent or makes them insolvent (stock that is authorized, issued but not outstanding)
  3. **Declare** dividends

Board of Directors

The role of the board of directors, including some of its operating characteristics, its areas of authority, and its responsibilities include the following:
- **Collective** – The power rests with the board, and not individual directors. A director has a vote at official board meetings the director attends. Directors may not enter into contracts on behalf of the corporation individually (**Not agents of corporation**), and *must be present* at board meetings in order to vote (they cannot vote by proxy).
- **Issuing Stock** – The board is the authority that issues stock. It may issue stock at any price that is mutually agreeable to the board and the purchaser, but some real consideration, in the form of cash, property, or services, must be provided. Valid consideration for the purchase of stock can be any benefit to the corporation, including any services contracted for that are yet to be performed.
- **Repurchasing Stock** – The board has the implied authority to reverse issuances by repurchasing stock on the open market or in a private arrangement with specific shareholders, at any mutually agreeable price. Once repurchased, the stock is either retired (canceled) or held as **treasury stock.** Treasury stock cannot be voted or receive a cash dividend, since it has no formal owner. The Board can resell it below par. *Treasury stock is stock that is authorized, issued, but no longer outstanding. Canceled stock is stock that is no longer issued nor outstanding.*

- **Officers** – The board hires, fires, and sets salaries of officers, who are responsible for the *day-to-day management* of the business. The authority of an officer is based on the delegation of the board's authority, so the board may adjust it as it chooses. The board has the right to fire an officer, even in breach of contract, if it believes this is in the best interests of the corporation and its shareholders. Officers are considered **agents** of the corporation. Officers and managers of the corporation may be, but need not be, shareholders of the corporation. Officers have the rights of Participation and inspection, may be compensated and indemnified (Reimbursement).

- **Borrowing** – As part of their responsibility for the day-to-day management of the businesses, officers may issue corporate debt securities as permitted by the corporate bylaws. Such securities include registered bonds, bearer bonds, debenture bonds, mortgage bonds, redeemable bonds, convertible bonds, etc. A warrant is not a corporate debt security, but rather written evidence of a stock option which grants its owner the right to purchase a specified number of shares of stock at a fixed price within a specified period of time.

- **Dividend Policy** – The board determines if and when dividends will be declared and paid to common and preferred shareholders. Until declaration, the corporation has no liability to the shareholders. The board may not declare a dividend if the company is insolvent or the dividend will render it insolvent, since creditors have priority over shareholders. If the corporation is solvent, the board may declare any dividend amount up to the higher of the company's retained earnings or current period earnings. If the board wishes to declare a dividend that exceeds these amounts, the shareholders must approve the portion that is a return of capital (liquidating dividend). If a corporation improperly pays a dividend, the shareholder may keep it as long as the shareholder was unaware that it was illegal and the corporation was solvent. Shareholders must repay illegal distributions that they receive when the corporation is insolvent.

Common Stock – A corporation begins operations by issuing stock in order to raise funds. It will obtain the authority to issue shares from the state of incorporation. All corporations will issue some form of common stock, which normally has a **par value (Certificate of Incorporation)** or **stated value (board of directors)** assigned to it. Common shareholders vote in the board of directors.

Preferred stock refers to stock similar to debt instruments, with two advantages over common stock:
- ○ **Dividends** – Preferred shareholders must be paid a dividend before the company is allowed to pay the common shareholders a dividend.
- ○ **Liquidation** – If the corporation liquidates, preferred shareholders must be paid before the common shareholders.

Along with the stated annual preference, preferred shareholders may be paid additional amounts if the shares are:
- ○ **Cumulative** – Dividends missed in earlier years also must be paid before the common shareholders receive anything (*arrears*).
- ○ **Participating** – If the common shareholders get a dividend that is a higher rate on its par value than the stated rate on the preferred shares, the preferred shareholders must get the same higher rate.

3 Important dates for Dividends

o **Declaration** = Not a liability until declared

Retained Earnings	XXX	
Dividend Payable		XXX

o **Date of Record** = No journal entry → who gets the money (determined as of the *ex-dividend date*, which is generally two days prior to the date of record)

o **Date of Distribution**

Dividend Payable	XXX	
Cash		XXX

o **Types of Dividends** (Board of Directors – **declares**)
- Cash
- Property (FMV @ date of declaration)
- Scrip
- Liquidating
- Stock – Small (FMV) / Large (Par)
- Stock split

Cash Dividend	**Scrip** – Give dividend but no money	**Stock Dividend**

RE 25
  Cash 25
	RE 25
	  Note Payable 25
		Small < 20 – 25% - FMV
		RE 25
		  CS 20
		  APIC 5

	Partial Liquidating Dividend
	RE 15
	APIC 10
	  Cash 25
		Large > 20 – 25% - Par
		RE 20
		  CS 20

Property (FMV)	**Person receiving Liq Div**	**Stock Splits** – Double shares, Half par

RE 25
  Asset 20
  Gain 5
	Cash 25
	  Div income 15
	  Investment 10
		CS (10(10)) 100
		  CS (20(5)) 100

Net effect on Stkhldrs equity = 20

- **Note**: All dividends reduce Stockholders' Equity except for Stock dividends and Stock splits.

The members of the board of directors are bound by a **fiduciary duty** to act loyally in the best interests of the corporation and its shareholders. The directors are not liable for honest errors of judgment, but can be held **individually** liable for acts of bad faith or negligence. **For example**, if the board or its management takes an action that exceeds the powers granted to it under the corporate charter (this is known as an ***ultra vires*** act, e.g., making the corporation a Surety, when the Articles do not allow it), the directors who voted to take the action can be sued individually. The directors who voted not to take the action aren't held liable for the misbehavior of the majority. The doctrine of ***respondeat superior*** provides that an employer is responsible for the torts committed by employees in the normal scope of duties.

Officers

Officers of a corporation also have a **fiduciary duty** to the corporation and shareholders. The board, however, may vote to *indemnify* the officers against personal liability for negligent or illegal acts if the board believes this is in the best interests of the corporation and the court does not hold such a reimbursement agreement to be a violation of public policy. The doctrine of *respondeat superior* provides that an employer (the corporation) is responsible for the torts committed by its employees in the normal scope of their duties.

Directors and Officers must act with a duty of care (honestly and prudently) and with a duty of loyalty. They **may NOT:**
- Compete with the corporation
- Take advantage of a corporate opportunity for personal gain
- Have an interest that is in conflict with the interests of the corporation
- Engage in insider trading
- Authorize transactions that are detrimental to minority shareholders
- Sell control over the corporation

The **"Business Judgment Rule"** is a principle that protects directors, officers, and managers from personal liability for acts performed in good faith (not liable for *errors of judgment*) on behalf of a corporation that are within the scope of their authority. They are still liable for their own negligence.

Lecture 15.09

SHAREHOLDERS' RIGHTS

The shareholders of a corporation have various rights that are discussed on the exam. Shareholders with common stock normally have a **right to vote** at shareholder meetings on certain significant matters affecting the company. A shareholder need not attend the meeting in order to vote, but may sign a proxy, authorizing others to vote their shares on their behalf at the meeting.

Shareholders' Rights
- Right to *vote* for the following:
    1) Board of Directors
    2) Liquidating dividends
    3) Dissolve Corporation
    4) Mergers/Consolidations
    5) Amend the Articles of Incorporation
    6) Loans to Directors
- They are Not considered an *Agent.*
- *Transfer shares* without approval (freely transferable)
- Right to declared dividends (unsecured creditor)
- Right to inspect books and records (*Inspection Rights*)
- **Appraisal Right** – Right to get stock appraised if disagree with merger
- Right to bring a **derivative lawsuit** → sue in name of corporation (on behalf of the corporate name)
- **Preemptive right** – prevent dilution of ownership with newly authorized stock only
- Limited liability unless **pierce the corporate veil** (do something illegal) → will do if fraudulent corporation, commingled funds, undercapitalized

---

Voting Rights

Examples of matters that may be voted on at shareholder meetings include:

- **Board of directors** – At least once a year, the shareholders must vote on the members who will constitute the board of directors. The shareholder has one vote for each available position on the board. Thus, if there are nine directors on the board, each shareholder is given nine votes. In some states, voting for directors is **cumulative**, which allows a shareholder to place all the votes available for the same person. This prevents significant minority shareholders from being locked out of representation on the board by a majority block of shareholders that all vote for the same slate of people and would be able to get unanimous control of the board without cumulative voting.
- **Liquidating dividends** – The board of directors may declare dividends out of the earnings of the company without shareholder approval, but dividends that are to come out of contributed capital must be declared by the board and then approved by the shareholders.
- **Changes in the corporate structure** – Amendments to the bylaws, Articles of Incorporation and changes in the charter of the corporation require shareholder approval.
- **Business combinations** – Mergers (one company absorbing another and becoming liable for all obligations of the acquired corporation) and consolidations (two companies forming a new entity) require support of a majority of both boards and both sets of shareholders (unless the change in ownership isn't significant, such as the merger of a subsidiary that is already 90%-owned by the parent). Any shareholder that dissents from the combination is entitled to make a written demand for **appraisal** of their shares, which the board must then repurchase at the appraised amount.
- **Dissolution** – A corporation may be dissolved:
  - *Voluntary* – by a board resolution to dissolve that is approved by a majority of shareholders.
  - *Involuntary* – by shareholder action (if board has committed fraud or is deadlocked), by state action if corp. exceeds its authority, by merger, consolidation or expiration of time period set out in the charter.

Although shareholders have the right to dividends out of available profits and surplus of the corporations, the decision to declare them must be made by the board of directors. Once a dividend is declared, the shareholders are considered **unsecured creditors** for that amount. Preferred shareholders with a dividend preference are entitled to be paid prior to common shareholders, but have no creditor claim for dividends until they are declared, even on cumulative stock.

Shareholders have the right to **inspect the books and records** (Inspection Rights) of the corporation at a reasonable time and place for a reasonable purpose. Examples of reasonable purposes are inspection of books to determine that they agree with financial reports and obtaining shareholder lists to send proxy solicitations to replace the existing board of directors. Generally, a shareholder is presumed to have a reasonable purpose if they own at least 5% of the stock or have owned stock for at least 6 months. Otherwise, they may be required to prove a reasonable purpose before being allowed to inspect.

Any misuse of information by a shareholder bars them for **2 years** from access to records. Examples of misuse include inspection of books to help establish a competing firm and obtaining shareholder lists in order to send them advertising literature for a personal business of the shareholder.

Various other **Shareholder rights** that are occasionally tested on the exam include:
- **Transfer of shares** – A shareholder can transfer ownership of shares without requiring the approval of the board or other shareholders. Limited restrictions are permitted for *closely held corporations* (in which shareholders wishing to sell are expected to offer their stock to the other existing shareholders before selling to outsiders), but must be printed directly on the certificates to be enforceable.
- **Preemptive rights** – Existing shareholders have the right to subscribe to new issuances of shares up to the percentage they own of existing shares, to prevent dilution of their interests.
- **Derivative lawsuits** – A shareholder may sue on behalf of the corporation if harmful actions against the company are not countered by the board (or if the board itself has committed the acts). The corporation, not the shareholder, receives the damages awarded if the action is successful.
- **Loans to directors** – Generally, shareholder approval is required for corporate loans to directors; however, shareholder approval is not generally required for charitable contributions made by the corporation.

Shareholder liability is not always limited to the amount of their investment. If stock is issued for less than its par value, it is considered **watered stock**, and the shareholder acquiring such shares (as well as a subsequent shareholder who knew the stock was watered when they acquired it) has a contingent liability for the difference between the issue price and par value. The watered stock rule doesn't apply to treasury shares or to subsequent resale by a shareholder at below par value.

For example, if 1,000 shares of $10 par value common stock are issued for $8 per share to Fred. First, Fred is liable for an additional $2,000 if the corporation becomes insolvent and creditors of the corporation demand these funds be contributed to the corporation. Let's say Fred sells 500 shares to Irv Ignorant, who doesn't know the shares were originally issued below par value, and the other 500 shares to Alice Aware, who knows Fred originally paid only $8 when the shares were issued. The creditors of the corporation cannot demand payment from Irv, but Alice is liable for $1,000 as well (unless Fred pays the full $2,000 into the corporation). The prices paid by Irv and Alice to Fred are irrelevant, since those amounts did not benefit the corporation.

Sometimes, the courts will **pierce the corporate veil** and hold shareholders personally liable for all the corporation's debts. Circumstances that may cause the court to act in this manner include:
- **Undercapitalized** – The courts examine the amount of capital present at the formation of the corporation. If that amount is inadequate to meet the reasonable foreseeable financial needs, it is undercapitalized and shareholders may be held personally liable upon the insolvency of the corporation.
- **Shareholder fraud** – The shareholders are intentionally using the corporation for illegal activities (do not confuse this with ultra vires acts by directors or officers, which do not result in shareholder liability).
- **Direct action** – The shareholders are running the business directly, without electing a board of directors, or without the board meeting at least once a year.
- **Commingling assets** – The shareholders are treating corporate assets as if they were personal assets, regularly using them for personal purposes, such as home mortgage payments or grocery purchases for their family.

Concentrations of Voting Power

Certain devices enable groups of shareholders to combine their voting power for purposes such as obtaining or maintaining control or maximizing the impact of cumulative voting. The most important methods of concentrating voting power are proxies, voting trusts and shareholder agreements.

- **Proxies** – A proxy is the authorization by a shareholder to an agent to vote his shares at a particular meeting. Proxies must be in writing to be effective and are revocable. The duration is limited by statute to no more than 11 months, unless the proxy specifically provides otherwise. The solicitation of proxies by publicly held corporations is also regulated by the Securities Exchange Act of 1934.
- **Voting Trusts** – A device by which one or more shareholders separate the voting rights of their shares from the ownership of them. Under a voting trust, all or part of the stock of a corporation may, by written agreement among the shareholders, be issued to a trustee who then holds legal title to the stock and has all of the voting rights possessed by the stock. They are usually limited in duration to 10 years.
- **Shareholder Agreements** – Shareholders may agree in advance to vote in a specified manner for the election or removal of directors or any matter subject to shareholder approval. Unlike voting trusts, shareholder agreements are NOT limited in duration. They are frequently used in closely held corporations, especially in conjunction with restriction on the transfer of shares.

Other circumstances occasionally tested that may result in shareholder liability include:
- **Majority ownership** – A shareholder holding a majority of the voting stock of a company is in a position to effectively control the activities of the corporation. As a result, the law imposes a *fiduciary obligation* on the majority shareholder to act loyally to protect the interests of the minority shareholders.
- **Subscriptions** – If a person signs a contract agreeing to purchase shares of a corporation once they become available, they are bound to this contract and cannot revoke it under the Model Business Corporation Act if the shares are made available to them within 6 months of the subscription.
- **Professional corporation** – The shareholders in a professional corporation are licensed members of the specified profession, and are held personally liable for acts of malpractice in accordance with the licensing laws. Normally, only licensed professionals can be shareholders in such corporations. They still have normal protection for corporate debts not associated with the practice of their professional responsibilities.

Partnership	Limited Partnership		C Corporation
Informal creation	Formal		Formal
Unlimited liability	Unlimited (**General**)	Limited (**Limited**)	Limited Liability
Partnership **Interest** (Profit/Losses)	⟶	Interest ⟶	
Partnership **Property**	⟶	NO Property ⟶	
Partnership **Management**	⟶	NO Management – EXCEPT can look at the **books** and **vote** ⟶	
Agents ⟶		NOT an Agent ⟶	

Survivorship

Lecture 15.10

CLASS QUESTIONS

Please see the Class Questions and Class Solutions for this Lecture at the end of this Section.

CLASS QUESTIONS

Work through the below Class Questions while following along with the respective lectures. Once this is complete, you can begin independently practicing what you've learned by quizzing yourself on this course section in your Interactive Practice Questions (IPQ), which can be found in your online Student Dashboard. Your IPQ simulates the computer-based testing experience, and will also help you understand how concepts are applied to the exam. Each question includes answer explanations from expert CPAs that will help you determine why you answered a question correctly or incorrectly. This is key to your success on the CPA Exam.

Lecture 15.03

1. A general partnership must

    a. Pay federal income tax.
    b. Have two or more partners.
    c. Have written articles of partnership.
    d. Provide for apportionment of liability for partnership debts.

2. Cobb, Inc., a partner in TLC Partnership, transfers its partnership interest to Bean, who is not made a partner. After the transfer, Bean asserts the rights to

    I. Participate in the management of TLC.
    II. Cobb's share of TLC's partnership profits.

Bean is correct as to which of these rights?

    a. I only.
    b. II only.
    c. I and II.
    d. Neither I nor II.

3. Which of the following statements best describes the effect of the transfer/assignment of an interest in a general partnership?

    a. The transferee/assignee becomes a partner.
    b. The transferee/assignee is responsible for a proportionate share of past and future partnership debts.
    c. The transfer/assignment automatically dissolves the partnership.
    d. The transfer/assignment transfers the assignor's interest in partnership profits and surplus.

4. Lark, a partner in DSJ, a general partnership, wishes to withdraw from the partnership and sell Lark's interest to Ward. All of the other partners in DSJ have agreed to admit Ward as a partner and to hold Lark harmless for the past, present, and future liabilities of DSJ. As a result of Lark's withdrawal and Ward's admission to the partnership, Ward

    a. Acquired only the right to receive Ward's share of DSJ profits.
    b. Has the right to participate in DSJ's management.
    c. Is personally liable for partnership liabilities arising before and after being admitted as a partner.
    d. Must contribute cash or property to DSJ to be admitted with the same rights as the other partners.

5. The apparent authority of a partner to bind the partnership in dealing with third parties

    a. Will be effectively limited by a formal resolution of the partners of which third parties are aware.
    b. Will be effectively limited by a formal resolution of the partners of which third parties are unaware.
    c. Would permit a partner to submit a claim against the partnership to arbitration.
    d. Must be derived from the express powers and purposes contained in the partnership agreement.

6. Dowd, Elgar, Frost, and Grant formed a general partnership. Their written partnership agreement provided that the profits would be divided so that Dowd would receive 40%; Elgar, 30%; Frost, 20%; and Grant, 10%. There was no provision for allocating losses. At the end of its first year, the partnership had losses of $200,000. Before allocating losses, the partners' capital account balances were: Dowd, $120,000; Elgar, $100,000; Frost, $75,000; and Grant, $11,000. Grant refuses to make any further contributions to the partnership. Ignore the effects of federal partnership tax law.

    After losses were allocated to the partners' capital accounts and all liabilities were paid, the partnership's sole asset was $106,000 in cash. How much would Elgar receive on dissolution of the partnership?

    a. $37,000
    b. $40,000
    c. $47,500
    d. $50,000

Lecture 15.05

7. Owners and managers of a limited liability company (LLC) owe

    a. A duty of due care.
    b. A duty of loyalty.
    c. Both a duty of due care and a duty of loyalty.
    d. None of the above.

8. Which of the following is (are) true of a limited partnership?

    I. Limited partnerships must have at least one general partner.
    II. The death of a limited partner terminates the partnership.

    a. I only.
    b. II only.
    c. Neither I nor II.
    d. Both I and II.

9. Which of the following partners of a limited liability partnership (LLP) may avoid personal liability when a partner commits a negligent act?

    a. All the partners
    b. The supervisor of the negligent partner
    c. All the partners other than the negligent partner
    d. All the partners other than the supervisor of, and the negligent partner

10. In which type of business entity is the entire ownership most freely transferable?

    a.   General partnership.
    b.   Limited partnership.
    c.   Corporation.
    d.   Limited liability company.

Lecture 15.07

11. The main difference between Subchapter S corporations and Subchapter C corporations is

    a.   Their tax treatment.
    b.   That the federal Subchapter S Revision Act covers Subchapter S corporations but does not cover Subchapter C corporations.
    c.   Their limited liability of their shareholders.
    d.   Their structure of their corporate management.

12. Which of the following facts is (are) generally included in a corporation's articles of incorporation?

	Name of registered agent	Number of authorized shares
a.	Yes	Yes
b.	Yes	No
c.	No	Yes
d.	No	No

13. Which of the following statements is correct concerning the similarities between a limited partnership and a corporation?

    a.   Each is created under a statute and must file a copy of its certificate with the proper state authorities.
    b.   All corporate stockholders and all partners in a limited partnership have limited liability.
    c.   Both are recognized for federal income tax purposes as taxable entities.
    d.   Both are allowed statutorily to have perpetual existence.

Lecture 15.10

14. Which of the following statements best describes an advantage of the corporate form of doing business?

    a.   Day-to-day management is strictly the responsibility of the directors.
    b.   Ownership is contractually restricted and is **not** transferable.
    c.   The operation of the business may continue indefinitely.
    d.   The business is free from state regulation.

15. Price owns 2,000 shares of Universal Corp.'s $10 cumulative preferred stock. During its first year of operations, cash dividends of $5 per share were declared on the preferred stock but were never paid. In the second year, dividends on the preferred stock were neither declared nor paid.

If Universal is dissolved, which of the following statements is correct?

    a.   Universal will be liable to Price as an unsecured creditor for $10,000.
    b.   Universal will be liable to Price as a secured creditor for $20,000.
    c.   Price will have priority over the claims of Universal's bond owners.
    d.   Price will have priority over the claims of Universal's unsecured judgment creditors.

16. The corporate veil is most likely to be pierced and the shareholders held personally liable if

    a.   The corporation has elected S corporation status under the Internal Revenue Code.
    b.   The shareholders have commingled their personal funds with those of the corporation.
    c.   An ultra vires act has been committed.
    d.   A partnership incorporates its business solely to limit the liability of its partners.

17. A corporate stockholder is entitled to which of the following rights?

    a.   Elect officers.
    b.   Receive annual dividends.
    c.   Approve dissolution.
    d.   Prevent corporate borrowing.

18. Under the Revised Model Business Corporation Act, which of the following statements is correct regarding corporate officers of a public corporation?

    a.   An officer may **not** simultaneously serve as a director.
    b.   A corporation may be authorized to indemnify its officers for liability incurred in a suit by stockholders.
    c.   Stockholders always have the right to elect a corporation's officers.
    d.   An officer of a corporation is required to own at least one share of the corporation's stock.

19. Which of the following rights is a holder of a public corporation's cumulative preferred stock always entitled to?

    a.   Conversion of the preferred stock into common stock.
    b.   Voting rights.
    c.   Dividend carryovers from years in which dividends were **not** paid, to future years.
    d.   Guaranteed dividends.

CLASS SOLUTIONS

1. (b) A partnership is an association of two or more persons to operate a business as co-owners for profit. It must have two or more partners or, otherwise, it would be a sole proprietorship. Answer (a) is incorrect because a partnership is a pass-through entity that does not pay federal income taxes. It files an information return and its partners are subject to tax on its income. Answer (c) is incorrect because a partnership may be formal or informal and may or may not have a written partnership agreement or written articles. Answer (d) is incorrect because a partnership is not required to provide for apportionment of partnership liabilities, in which case they well be allocated in accordance with partnership percentages.

2. (b) A partner's interest, which includes the right to receive a portion of partnership profits and losses, may be assigned by a partner without the consent of other partners. The assignee is not, however, a partner and does not have the rights associated with partnership, including the right to participate in management.

3. (d) A partner's interest, which includes the right to receive a portion of partnership profits and losses, may be assigned by a partner without the consent of other partners. The assignee is not, however, a partner and does not have the rights associated with partnership, including the right to participate in management. A transfer or assignment of a partner's interest does not cause a dissolution of the partnership.

4. (b) When a partner sells a partnership interest to another party who the existing partners admit into the partnership, the new partner takes on all the rights and responsibilities of a partner, including the right to participate in management. The new partner is not liable for liabilities occurring before being admitted to the partnership, unless that is agreed to as part of the purchase. When a sale of a partnership interest occurs outside of the partnership, the new partner is not required to make a contribution to the partnership.

5. (a) Apparent authority is the authority a partner has to bind a partnership resulting from the innocent and appropriate belief of others that the partner has the authority to do so. When third parties are aware of a limitation on a partner's authority, the partner does not have apparent authority. Third parties who are not aware of a limitation on a partner's authority, may innocently believe that the partner does have the authority, resulting in apparent authority. Apparent authority relates to the ability of a partner to bind the partnership in a transaction with third parties and does not give the partner authority in an action against the partnership. Authority derived from the partnership agreement is express authority, not apparent authority.

6. (a) The first step would be to allocate the $200,000, which will be allocated using the profit percentages since there is no specific provision for allocating losses. As a result, the partners' balances will be $40,000 for Dowd (D) ($120,000 - $80,000 loss), $40,000 for Edgar (E) ($100,000 - $60,000 loss), $35,000 for Frost (F) ($75,000 - $40,000 loss) and $(9,000) for Grant (G) ($11,000 - $20,000 loss). Since G will not make an additional contribution to the partnership, the $9,000 deficit must be allocated to the remaining partners using their remaining percentages with D getting 40%/90% or $4,000, E getting 30%/90% or $3,000, and F getting 20%/90% or $2,000. As a result, the balances will be $36,000 ($40,000 - $4,000) for D, $37,000 ($40,000 - $3,000) for E, $33,000 ($35,000 - $2,000) for F, and $0 for G. Thus, E will receive $37,000.

7. (c) Owners and managers of an LLC owe both a duty of due care (requiring that they act without gross negligence) and a duty of loyalty to the LLC.

8. (a) A limited partnership requires at least one general partner and at least one limited partner. The general partner has unlimited liability for the obligations of the partnership. A limited partnership interest is readily transferable, similar to a share of stock, and passes along to the limited partner's estate when the limited partner dies without causing a termination of the partnership.

9. (d) The nature of a limited liability partnership is to protect the partners from personal liability. Liability resulting from a partner's negligence will be attributed to that partner and the partner's supervisor, but not to the other partners.

10. (c) Of the different types of entities, an ownership interest in a corporation is generally easiest to transfer since it is represented by shares of stock, which are securities that may be sold or traded without the permission of other owners.

11. (a) From a legal standpoint, there is no significant difference between a C corporation and an S corporation. The most significant difference is that a C corporation is a taxable entity and an S corporation is a pass-through entity for federal income tax purposes. Answer (b) is incorrect because the Subchapter S Revision Act changed rules so that a difference in voting rights would not create a second class of stock, precluding a Subchapter S election. Answer (c) is incorrect because both offer limited liability to shareholders. Answer (d) is incorrect because both may be structured similarly.

12. (a) Articles of incorporation will generally include the corporation's name, its nature and purpose, its term, the name and address of each incorporator, the amount and types of shares it is authorized to issue, the names of members of its initial board, and its registered agent.

13. (a) Both corporations and limited partnerships obtain their right to existence as a result of an enabling statute in their state of domicile and both must file a certificate with the proper state authorities. Answer (b) is incorrect because while all stockholders of a corporation have limited liability, only the limited partners, and not the general partners of a limited partnership have limited liability. Answer (c) is incorrect because a corporation is a taxable entity for federal income tax purposes, but a limited partnership is a pass-through entity that does not pay federal income tax. Answer (d) is incorrect because a corporation has statutory perpetual existence, but a limited partnership does not.

14. (c) One advantage of the corporate structure is that it has statutory perpetual existence and its life is not limited by the lives of its owners. Answer (a) is incorrect because the directors are responsible for strategic planning and oversight of management, but management is responsible for day-to-day operations. Answer (b) is incorrect because ownership, in the form of shares of stock, is readily transferrable. Answer (d) is incorrect because corporations like other entities, are subject to state regulation.

15. (a) When dividends are declared, they become a legal obligation of the corporation and must be paid upon liquidation. The preferred stockholders will be considered unsecured creditors to the extent of 2,000 shares at $5 per share, or $10,000, and will have priority over the claims of common stockholders, but not other creditors. There is no liability for the dividends that were not declared for the following year.

16. (b) The courts will pierce the corporate veil and hold stockholders personally liable for debts of the corporation when shareholders are using the corporation specifically to avoid liability, rather than for some legitimate purpose. Indications would include undercapitalization, shareholder fraud, shareholders running the business without the oversight of a board, and commingling shareholder and corporate assets. Answer (a) is incorrect because electing S corporation status is a decision as to how the entity will be taxed and would not cause the courts to pierce the corporate veil. Answer (c) is incorrect because an ultra vires act is one committed by management or the board that exceeds their authority. It may cause those directors who approved the decision to be liable, but would not extend general liability to shareholders. Answer (d) is incorrect because limiting the liability of partners is a legitimate reason to incorporate a partnership.

17. (c) A corporation may not be dissolved without the approval of shareholders. Answer (a) is incorrect because the directors, not the shareholders, elect officers. Answer (b) is incorrect because the declaration of dividends is at the discretion of the board of directors, not the shareholders. Answer (d) is incorrect because it is up to management, within the authority granted by the board of directors, to make borrowing decisions. Shareholders would not have the ability to prevent corporate borrowing.

18. (b) The Revised Model Business Corporations Act authorizes a corporation to indemnify officers for liability, including expenses, attorney fees, fines, and judgments, that result from a suit by shareholders. Answer (a) is incorrect because an officer may serve as a director and, in fact, it is not uncommon for the chief executive officer to also serve as the chair of the board of directors. Answer (c) is incorrect because directors, not shareholders, elect corporate officers. Answer (d) is incorrect because an officer is not required to own stock in the corporation in which they serve as part of management.

19. (c) When preferred stock is cumulative, preferred dividends that are not paid in a given year carry over to subsequent periods, referred to as *dividends in arrears*. These must be paid to preferred stockholders before a dividend can be paid to common stockholders. Answer (a) is incorrect because some preferred shares may be convertible, but they would be specified as convertible shares. Answer (b) is incorrect because preferred shareholders do not ordinarily receive voting rights. Answer (d) is incorrect because dividends are not guaranteed, but must be paid before dividends can be paid to common stockholders.

Section 16 – Regulation of Business Employment, Environment & Antitrust

Corresponding Lectures

Watch the following course lectures with this section:

Lecture 16.01 – Reg. of Business Employment, Environment & Antitrust
Lecture 16.02 – Reg. of Business Employment, Environment & Antitrust
– Class Questions

EXAM NOTE: *Please refer to the AICPA REG Blueprint in the Introduction to find a listing of the representative tasks (and their associated skill levels—i.e., Remembering and Understanding, Application, and Analysis) that the candidate should be able to perform based on the knowledge obtained in this section.*

Regulation of Business Employment, Environment & Antitrust

REGULATION OF BUSINESS EMPLOYMENT, ENVIRONMENT & ANTITRUST

Employee Benefits

There are two federal taxes assessed on employers. The **Federal Unemployment Tax Act (FUTA)** imposes a tax *paid entirely by employers* on applicable wages of employees. There are a few categories of employment exempt from FUTA, and an employer is not required to pay these taxes unless at least one person is employed in each of 20 different weeks of the year (or total wages in a calendar quarter exceed $1,500). The law permits a credit against the federal tax for employers that are subject to state unemployment taxes for an amount equal to the standard tax rate imposed by the state.

- **Unemployment benefits** are fully taxable to former employees. Benefits are **not paid** if the person:
  - Left employment voluntarily (business reversals – ok)
  - Refuses to accept equivalent work that has been offered
  - Was dismissed by the employer for illegal activity

The **Federal Insurance Contributions Act (FICA)** (7.65%) imposes a tax *paid equally by employer and employee* based on the gross wages of the employee (self-employed persons pay a combined employer-employee rate of 15.3% on net self-employment income). The employer withholds the employee's share from gross pay and remits it along with the employer's share. An employer who fails to withhold is liable for both shares, and the employee is considered to have received additional compensation if they do not reimburse the employer. The employer may be assessed penalties for failing to make timely deposits of amounts owed to the IRS or for failing to provide the tax identification number of the employee. All compensation for services is subject to FICA taxes, including awards for productivity and fees paid to directors.

- **Benefits** are paid by the Social Security Administration for old age, survivors, spouses (including divorced spouses), disability, and Medicare (1.45%). Benefits for old age may be reduced or eliminated prior to a certain age (typically 70) if the person continues to receive compensation for services, but investment income will not affect the amount of benefits. Cash benefits may be non-taxable or partially taxable, depending on the overall adjusted gross income of the recipient.
  - Old age or retirement benefits
  - Benefits to survivors and divorced spouses
  - Payments for disability and to disabled children
  - Medicare benefits

Several laws regulate benefits provided to employees by their employer. The **Employment Retirement Income Security Act (ERISA)** applies to employers who have chosen to provide private *pension benefits* to employees (the law doesn't require such benefits). There are requirements related to:

- **Participation** – The plan must cover all employees that fall within the same class.

- **Vesting** – Amounts paid into plans by employees (these are known as contributory plans) must be vested immediately. Amounts paid into plans by employers must vest within a reasonable period of time (usually within 5 years).
- **Funding** – The employer must remit amounts collected from employees and amounts owed by the employer to an independent trustee within a reasonable period of time.

The **Comprehensive Omnibus Budget Reconciliation Act (COBRA)** allows employees to continue medical, dental, and optical coverage provided by their employer after termination of employment for up to *18 months* (longer in the case of disability) by remitting to the employer the cost of such coverage. Coverage may be continued for the employee and other family members who were included under the plan during employment.

The **Family Medical Leave Act (FMLA)** requires companies with 50 or more employees to permit them up to 12 weeks in any 12-month period of unpaid leave for family or medical reasons. The employer must continue health coverage during this time and offer the employee a return to their previous position or comparable work.

With regard to hiring and pay arrangements, employers are subject to several laws. The **Fair Labor Standards Act (FLSA)** requires a **minimum wage** (the amount is periodically revised) that must be paid to all employees without exception, including hourly and salaried employees.   Payment on the basis of piecework is allowed, provided workers receive at least the equivalent of the minimum hourly wage. It prohibits **child labor** in certain occupations or for more than a certain number of hours. It also establishes a workweek of 40 hours, and requires **overtime compensation** at the rate of 1 ½ times normal pay for any work exceeding 40 hours in any calendar week, but this provision doesn't apply to executives, professional employees, and outside salespersons.

Telephone Consumer Protection Act - TCPA (Do Not Call List)

The Telephone Consumer Protection Act (TCPA) was enacted to restrict telephone solicitations and the use of automated telephone equipment. The Act:
- Prohibits solicitors from calling residences before 8 am or after 9 pm
- Requires them to maintain and honor a "do not call" (DNC) list
- Requires solicitors to identify themselves
- Prohibits solicitors from using an artificial voice or recording
- Prohibits the use of automated calling equipment to call emergency numbers, hospitals, doctors' offices, and any recipient required to pay for the call
- Prohibits the sending of unsolicited faxes

Violations of the act are punishable by a fine or up to one year of imprisonment, or both. A second conviction is punishable by a fine and imprisonment of up to 2 years. Alternatively, violators may be subject to a criminal fine for each violation or 3 times that amount for a continuing violation.

In addition, a violator may be subject to a forfeiture penalty for each violation or 3 times that for each day in the case of a continuing violation, with a maximum penalty of $1,000,000 for a single continuing violation.

A call is exempt from the TCPA if the call:
- Is made on behalf of a tax-exempt nonprofit organization.
- Is not made for a commercial purpose.
- Does not include an unsolicited advertisement, even if it is made for a commercial purpose.

- Is made to a consumer with whom the calling company has an established business relationship.

As of October 2013, prior express written consent is required for all autodialed and/or pre-recorded calls/texts sent/made to cell phone and pre-recorded calls made to residential land lines for marketing purposes.

The **National Labor Relations Act (NLRA)** guarantees employees the right to **form unions** and demands good faith collective bargaining by both sides in disputes. The law applies to bargaining involving wages as well as vacation and sick pay.

The Labor-Management Relations Act, also known as the **Taft-Hartley Act,** prohibits an employer from requiring union membership of all employees.

Other Employment Regulations

The **Occupational Safety and Health Act (OSHA)** was enacted to provide safe and healthful workplaces for employees. The Department of Labor has responsibility for setting standards, making inspections, and enforcing the provisions of the act. When employees are injured:
- The company must maintain records of injury and illness for each employee if 11 or more are employed.
- Each record must be available for inspection by an OSHA inspector.

Employers are subject to a large number of federal and state laws governing their relations with employees. Perhaps the earliest involvement of legislation on the relationship was in the area of **workers' compensation laws**. These statutes guarantee an employee compensation for a job-related injury or illness (or an existing injury or illness that is exacerbated by the job), but at the same time prohibits the employee from suing their employer in an attempt to collect additional sums (they can still sue third parties other than the employer that are responsible for their injury or illness). Workers' compensation laws apply to employees (whose time and performance of work are controlled by their employer), but do not apply to independent contractors.
- The effect of workers' compensation laws was to eliminate many of the defenses against payment available to an employer under common law (a form of **Strict Liability**). A worker is entitled to collect benefits under these laws, even if one or more of the following conditions is applicable:
  - **Contributory negligence** – The employee's own carelessness (or even recklessness) in violating workplace rules was a contributing factor in causing the injury or illness.
  - **Assumption of risk** – The employee was aware of the dangers of the occupation and signed a waiver of liability.
  - **Negligence of fellow employee** – The injury or illness resulted from the careless or reckless violation of employer rules by another employee.
- On the other hand, there are still some **defenses available** against payment. A worker will not be able to collect under workers' compensation if one of the following conditions is applicable (**BIND**):
  - **Brawling** – The employee is injured while fighting on the job.
  - **Intoxication** – The injury or illness resulted from the employee's intoxication from alcohol or other drugs.
  - **Not job-related** – The employee is injured while commuting to or from work or at some other time when they weren't on the job.

- o **Deliberate self-infliction** – The employee intentionally attempts to become injured or ill.
- **Benefits** may include:
  - o Burial expenses
  - o The cost of prosthetic devices
  - o Monthly payments to surviving dependent(s)

There are several laws dealing with **discrimination in employment** and in treatment of customers:

- Title VII of the Civil Rights Act (CRA) of 1964 prohibits discrimination on the basis of **race, color, national origin, religion, or gender.**
- The Age Discrimination in Employment Act (**ADEA**) prohibits discrimination against workers who are at least 40 years old and generally prohibits mandatory retirement under age 70.
- The **Equal Pay Act** prohibits unequal pay on the basis of gender.
  - o Differences may be based on merit, quality of work, or seniority.
- The Americans with Disabilities Act (**ADA**) prohibits discrimination against disabled employees and requires that reasonable accommodation be made to the needs of disabled workers and customers.
- The **Pregnancy Discrimination Act** requires that pregnant workers be categorized as disabled, and receive the same protections.
- **Whistleblower Protection Act** protects employees from retaliation by employers for blowing the whistle on employers.
- **Federal Employee Polygraph Protection Act** says that private employers may not require employees or prospective employees to take lie detector test or make adverse employment decisions based on such tests or refusal to take them.
  - o Government employees are exempted.
  - o Private employer may use the test as part of investigation of economic loss when employer has reason to suspect individual.

An employer is liable for actions that are intended to discriminate, as well as actions that have the unintended effect of discriminating against a protected group.

All discrimination laws allow an employer to dismiss an employee for misconduct, and to engage in discrimination that has a business necessity, is a clear occupational qualification, or results from a fair seniority system. **For example**, a studio can limit the auditions for the part of *Queen Victoria* in a movie to women.

Antitrust

To prevent large corporations from taking actions that may be in restraint of trade, several antitrust laws have been passed to promote fair competition. The most significant of these are the Sherman Antitrust Act, the Clayton Antitrust Act, the Federal Trade Commission Act, the Robinson-Patman Act, and the Celler-Kefauver Act.

The **Sherman Antitrust Act**, enacted in 1890, the purpose of which was, according to Senator John Sherman of Ohio, "To protect the consumers by preventing arrangements designed, or which tend, to advance the cost of goods to the consumer." One of the two main provisions of the act makes contracts, combinations, or conspiracies that are in restraint of trade illegal. The other makes it a felony to monopolize, *attempt to monopolize*, or combine or conspire to monopolize any part of trade or commerce.

The **Clayton Antitrust Act**, enacted in 1914, was intended to enhance the Sherman Antitrust Act by prohibiting specific types of conduct that are not considered to be in the best interests of a competitive market. These include:

- Price discrimination between different purchasers;
- Tying products by making the purchase of a product a requirement in order to be able to purchase the desired product;
- Mergers and acquisitions that will lessen competition; and
- A director serving on the boards of competing entities.

The **Federal Trade Commission Act**, also enacted in 1914, created the Federal Trade Commission, which issues "cease and desist" orders to large corporations that are involved in *unfair trade practices*.

The **Robinson-Patman Act** (also referred to as the Anti-Price Discrimination Act) was enacted in 1936 as an amendment to the Clayton Act; it prohibits price discrimination when selling goods to different distributors such that it causes a decrease in competition, such as by selling goods at a lower price to a chain store than to a locally owned store that is in competition with the chain store.

The **Celler-Kefauver Act**, enacted in 1950, enhanced the Clayton Antitrust Act by making acquisitions of assets and of entities *that are not direct competitors* subject to comparable scrutiny, restrictions, and sanctions as provided for in the Clayton Antitrust Act.

Environmental Regulation

Businesses are affected by several laws designed to **protect the environment**. Among these are:

- **Environmental Protection Act** – This law created the Environmental Protection Agency (**EPA**), empowering it to establish regulations and pursue civil and criminal actions against companies and responsible corporate officers for damage to the environment. Suits may also be filed by private citizens and the various states against polluters or the EPA.
- **Comprehensive Environmental Response, Compensation, and Liability Act (CERCLA)** – Also known as the **Superfund law,** it authorizes the government to clean up dangerous toxic sites and attempt to recover the costs from current or former owners and operators of the site and persons transporting wastes to the site. All parties are jointly and severally liable for the costs of cleanup, allowing the government to recover the entire cost from a party who is responsible for only a small part of the pollution.
- Various federal laws **governing the use of toxic substances** exist, including the Toxic Substances Control Act, the Federal Insecticide, Fungicide, and Rodenticide Act, the Nuclear Waste Policy Act, and the Federal Environmental Pesticide Control Act.
- **Federal Water Pollution Control Act** – Also known as the Clean Water Act, it allows the EPA to regulate any actions that may harm public waters.
- **Clean Air and Noise Pollution Acts** –Requires use of the best available technology by companies to reduce harmful emissions and excessive noise. Emissions from nuclear power plants are governed by this act, and not the Nuclear Waste Policy Act.
- **National Environmental Policy Act (NEPA)** - This 1969 act established the Council on Environmental Quality (CEQ), which helps ensure that various environmental laws are followed. NEPA also requires an environmental impact statement before any federal laws can be adopted or activities undertaken that might affect the environment.

Lecture 16.02

CLASS QUESTIONS

Please see the Class Questions and Class Solutions for this Lecture at the end of this Section.

CLASS QUESTIONS

Work through the below Class Questions while following along with the respective lectures. Once this is complete, you can begin independently practicing what you've learned by quizzing yourself on this course section in your Interactive Practice Questions (IPQ), which can be found in your online Student Dashboard. Your IPQ simulates the computer-based testing experience, and will also help you understand how concepts are applied to the exam. Each question includes answer explanations from expert CPAs that will help you determine why you answered a question correctly or incorrectly. This is key to your success on the CPA Exam.

Lecture 16.02

1. An unemployed CPA generally would receive unemployment compensation benefits if the CPA

   a. Was fired as a result of the employer's business reversals.
   b. Refused to accept a job as an accountant while receiving extended benefits.
   c. Was fired for embezzling from a client.
   d. Left work voluntarily without good cause.

2. Which of the following payments are deducted from an employee's salary?

	Unemployment compensation insurance	Workers' compensation insurance
a.	Yes	Yes
b.	Yes	No
c.	No	Yes
d.	No	No

3. Kroll, an employee of Acorn, Inc., was injured in the course of employment while operating a forklift manufactured and sold to Acorn by Trell Corp. The forklift was defectively designed by Trell. Under the state's mandatory workers' compensation statute, Kroll will be successful in

	Obtaining workers' compensation benefits	A negligence action against Acorn
a.	Yes	Yes
b.	Yes	No
c.	No	No
d.	No	No

4. Generally, which of the following statements concerning workers' compensation laws is correct?

   a. The amount of damages recoverable is based on comparative negligence.
   b. Employers are strictly liable without regard to whether or **not** they are at fault.
   c. Workers' compensation benefits are **not** available if the employee is negligent.
   d. Workers' compensation awards are payable for life.

5. Under the Fair Labor Standards Act, which of the following pay bases may be used to pay covered, nonexempt employees who earn, on average, the minimum hourly wage?

	Hourly	**Weekly**	**Monthly**
a.	Yes	Yes	Yes
b.	Yes	Yes	No
c.	Yes	No	Yes
d.	No	Yes	Yes

6. Under the Employee Retirement Income Security Act of 1974 (ERISA), which of the following areas of private employer pension plans is (are) regulated?

	Employee vesting	**Plan funding**
a.	Yes	Yes
b.	Yes	No
c.	No	Yes
d.	No	No

CLASS SOLUTIONS

1. (a) Unemployment benefits will be denied to an individual who left employment voluntarily without good cause, refused to accept equivalent work that had been offered, or was dismissed from employment for illegal activity. Benefits will be paid to an individual who loses their job due to no fault of their own, such as being laid off due to an employer's business reversals.

2. (d) Both unemployment tax and workers' compensation insurance premiums are paid for in their entirety by the employer. The employee pays no portion.

3. (b) Workers' compensation insurance is designed to compensate employees for injuries incurred on the job without assigning fault. Although Kroll may have recourse against Acorn in a negligence action, it will not fall under the mandatory workers' compensation statute.

4. (b) Workers' compensation insurance is designed to compensate employees for injuries incurred on the job without assigning fault. Answer (b) is incorrect because comparative negligence is irrelevant. Answer (c) is incorrect because benefits are available despite the employee's negligence. Answer (d) is incorrect because awards may or may not be payable for life, depending on the nature of the injury suffered.

5. (a) Although the Fair Labor Standards Act requires that employees be paid at least the equivalent of the minimum hourly wage, the basis on which it is to be paid may be piecemeal or on some other basis such as hourly, weekly, or monthly.

6. (a) The Employee Retirement Income Security Act (ERISA) establishes requirements regarding employee participation in retirement plans, vesting, and funding.

Section 17 – Property Law & Intellectual Property Rights

Corresponding Lectures

Watch the following course lectures with this section:

Lecture 17.01 – Property Law
Lecture 17.02 – Property Law – Class Questions
Lecture 17.03 – Different Forms of Concurrent Ownership
Lecture 17.04 – Intellectual Property and Computer Technology Rights
Lecture 17.05 – Property Law & Intellectual Property – Class Questions

EXAM NOTE: *Please refer to the AICPA REG Blueprint in the Introduction to find a listing of the representative tasks (and their associated skill levels—i.e., Remembering and Understanding, Application, and Analysis) that the candidate should be able to perform based on the knowledge obtained in this section. The following material is relevant to multiple topics under Area II—Business Law, even though it is not explicitly mentioned in the Blueprint. For example, U.S. copyright law would fall under Area II.D.2.a—Other federal laws and regulations.*

Property Law & Intellectual Property Rights

PROPERTY LAW

Ownership of Property

Property is classified in one of two categories:

- **Real** – Property that is fixed to one specific location. Examples include land and buildings that are permanently attached to the land.
- **Personal** – All other property. Examples include tangible property that is movable, such as furniture, equipment, and automobiles, and intangible assets such as patents, receivables, stock, and royalty rights.

Fixtures are assets that start out as personal property but are attached (**affixed**) to real property. Sometimes, personal property is attached in a manner that makes it become a part of the real property (e.g., cementing a chalkboard to a wall), and at other times it remains personal property (e.g., the same chalkboard attached to the wall using screws instead of cement).

Personal property is subject to many of the legal sections of the Uniform Commercial Code, including the sales, secured transactions, and negotiables sections. Real estate is specifically exempt from the UCC. As a result, the determination as to whether property is real or personal affects the methods of transfer, rights of creditors, and negotiability of documents of ownership to the property.

Crops under cultivation are part of the land and are generally considered real property. Since crops can be sold separately from land, however, they can be considered personal property under the UCC.

Determining whether a fixture has become part of the real estate can be especially important in the case of leased property, since it may determine what the lessee is permitted to remove from the property at termination of the lease. In general, the determination is based on the **intentions of the parties**, but in the absence of an explicit contractual agreement, the courts can evaluate the intentions of the parties by the manner of attachment and the damage that would be caused by removal of the fixture.

Based upon:
- **Use**
- **Intention of parties**
- **How attached**
    - **Not –** price or depreciable life.

Transfer of Ownership

There are a variety of ways in which property can be transferred from one party to another. The rights of the party obtaining ownership, and any rights retained by the party transferring the property will depend on the how the transfer of ownership is accomplished.

Different methods of transferring ownership are used for personal property and real property.

Ownership of Personal Property

Ownership of personal property can be acquired in numerous ways. When personal property is not acquired by purchase, ownership may be acquired by:
- Taking **possession** of property that is not owned by another party, such as the capture of a wild animal
- **Production** of property through the use of the party's own efforts
- Receiving the property as a **gift**
- Obtaining the property through a **will** or by **inheritance**
- **Accession**, where property is improved or added to, generally making the owner of the original property the owner of the addition
- **Confusion**, such as when identical goods are commingled

A party finding personal property may take title to it, depending on the circumstances. When property is **mislaid**, such as someone leaving his or her glasses at the theater, the finder does not obtain title but becomes the caretaker of the property. When property is **lost**, the finder takes title to the property that is effective against anyone but the true owner of the property. When property is **abandoned** (discarded), the finder takes title to it that is effective against all parties, including the original owner.

Adverse possession: A possessor of land who is not the lawful owner may acquire title if he or she holds it for the statutory period, which varies by state. The true owner must begin legal action before statute runs or the adverse possessor obtains title. The necessary elements for adverse possession are as follows:
- Open possession, such that the lawful owner is deemed to have reasonable notice.
- Hostile possession - the possessor must indicate intention of ownership.
- Actual possession - possession consistent with normal use (cultivation of farm land, use of a warehouse, etc.)
- Continuous and exclusive possession.

Easements (such as a right-of-way) are established in the same fashion as adverse possession.

Ownership of Real Property

Transferring the ownership of real estate is accomplished through the use of a document of title, known as a deed. The deed must identify the property and be signed by the transferor of the property. It does not need to be recorded in order to be valid between the transferor and transferee.

Deed – To transfer ownership (to be **effective**) / (**Statute of frauds**)
- Names of Grantor (transferor) and Grantee (transferee)
- Intent
- Description
- The deed must be delivered to the purchaser.
- Grantor's signature
  - Not price or depreciable life / Need not be recorded to be effective between Grantor and Grantee.

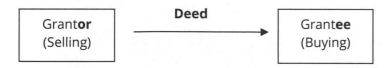

There are **three types of deeds:**
- **Quitclaim deed** – ("As is") The transferor makes no warranties whatsoever. Such deeds are rarely used in sales, but are the primary means for transferring property by gift or inheritance.
- **Grant deed** – The transferor warrants that they have done nothing to create any impairments of title during their period of ownership. This warranty does not, however, protect the transferee against defects in title that arose prior to the transferor's period of ownership. This deed is sometimes known as a **bargain and sale** deed or **special warranty** deed.
- **Warranty deed** – The transferee is guaranteed full rights of use and enjoyment of the property, including a promise that there are no undisclosed claims against the property by any other party from the time the property was first used to the date of transfer. This deed is sometimes known as a **general warranty** deed.

For example, assume a house is built during 20X1 and the original owner lives there until 3/18/X5 before selling it, then the second owner lives there until 8/13/X7. If, in the 20X7 sale, the buyer (third owner) receives a warranty deed, the seller (second owner) is promising the buyer that there are no defects in title from any events prior to 8/13/X7. If the buyer receives a grant deed, the promise is only that no defects in title resulted from events between 3/18/X5 and 8/13/X7. If the buyer receives a quitclaim deed, the seller is making no promises about title, but is only transferring the title they possess.

Interests in Real Property: Any claim in, to or on real property, including title, security or lease. Types of present interest:
- *Fee simple absolute* – highest estate in law (has most rights). May be transferred *inter vivos* (while living), or upon death. May be subject to mortgage or other lien.
- *Fee simple defeasible* – subject to a condition or subsequent event.
- *Life interest* – an interest whose term is usually the life of the holder, but may be measured by the life of others.
- *Leaseholds* – Lessor-Lessee, pursuant to a lease agreement.

A transferee may obtain **title insurance** to protect their deed. Such a policy compensates the insured if a defect existed at the date the transferee acquired the property. The insurance company will perform a title search prior to issuing such a policy, and any defects they identify will be listed as **exceptions** to the policy, meaning the company is not liable for these defects. An *easement* would be an example of an exception. The policy is personal to the insured and cannot be transferred to another party. Also, it does not cover defects that arise after the date of acquisition by the insured.

In order for a deed to be valid against third parties, it must be recorded at the appropriate government office. If a deed is recorded prior to any other claims being made against the property, the recorder will have priority over all later parties.

Marketable title means that the title to real estate is free from encumbrances, such as mortgages, easements, liens and defects. It does not mean free from recorded zoning restrictions, public rights-of-way, or recorded easements.

If, however, a later claimant arises before the deed is recorded, the priority of the two claims will depend on the jurisdiction in which the real estate is located and the circumstances surrounding the two claims. The overwhelming number of states are **notice-race** jurisdictions, and in such cases the earlier claim will win if either of the following circumstances applies:

- The later claimant knew about the earlier claim when they obtained theirs.
- The earlier claimant eventually records the deed before the later claimant.

As a result, the only time the later claim prevails in a notice-race jurisdiction is when the later claimant records first **and** did not know about the earlier claim when they acquired their rights.

For example, assume that Roger originally sells his home to Frieda First, giving her a valid deed, which Frieda does not immediately record. Roger then sells the same home to Sidney Second, providing an identical deed. Both Frieda and Sidney later record their deeds. The party with priority in a notice-race jurisdiction depends on (1) Sidney's knowledge of Frieda's earlier claim at the time of his purchase and (2) who recorded first.

PRIORITY IF:	Sidney knew	Sidney didn't know
Frieda recorded first	Frieda	Frieda
Sidney recorded first	Frieda	Sidney

Lecture 17.02

CLASS QUESTIONS

Please see the Class Questions and Class Solutions for this Lecture at the end of this Section.

Lecture 17.03

Concurrent Ownership

Property can be concurrently owned by more than one person. **Different forms of concurrent ownership** available in all states are:
- **Tenancy in common** (no "right of survivorship")
- **Joint tenancy** ("right of survivorship")
- **Tenancy by the entirety**

Tenancy in common refers to two or more persons with separate interests in the same property. This is the simplest form of concurrent ownership, and the following principles apply:
- The interests can be of different percentages of the property.
- Upon death of one of the co-owners, their interest will be distributed to their beneficiaries based on their will (or state intestate succession laws if they died without a will).
- Each person may transfer their interest without the consent of the others and with no impact on the rights of the others.

A joint tenancy is a more restrictive arrangement that includes a **right of survivorship**, and the following principles apply:

- The interests must be equal as to **T**ime, **T**itle, **I**nterest, and **P**ossession. **(TTIP)**
- Upon death of one of the co-owners, their interest will be automatically transferred to the other joint tenants in equal shares, regardless of the provisions of any will of the decedent.
- Each person may transfer their interest without the consent of the others, but the right of survivorship will no longer apply between the transferee and other joint owners.

Tenancy by the entirety
- Joint interest held by a husband and wife
- Each spouse has a right of survivorship
- Divorce, death, or mutual agreement severs right of survivorship

For example, if A, B, and C are each 1/3 joint tenants in property, and A sells their interest to X, X will now have a 1/3 tenancy in common, and not share right of survivorship. If B subsequently dies, C will become a 2/3 owner (and a tenant in common, since there is no remaining party with whom C shares the right of survivorship). If X subsequently dies, X's heirs will receive X's 1/3 tenancy in common.

Mortgages – A Security Interest in Real Property

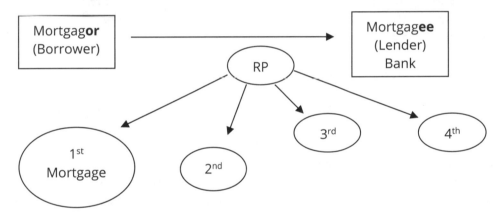

Mortgages are security interests in real estate. The UCC rules on secured transactions do not apply to mortgages, but many of the principles are similar.

There must be a written mortgage signed by the debtor in order to **attach** the mortgage to the property and make it effective between the debtor (mortgagor) and creditor (mortgagee). In order to make the mortgage effective against later parties that may obtain mortgages or deeds on the property, the creditor must **perfect** the mortgage by recording it. If they fail to record the mortgage quickly, they may lose priority to a later party in a notice-race jurisdiction as long as the later party records first and doesn't know about the earlier claim at time of recording.

Mortgage – A security interest in Real Property (to be **effective**):
- Written
- Description
- Signed by mortgagor and delivered to mortgagee
  - Same rule as for deeds...**Notice-race**
  - Upon default by the mortgagor, the mortgagee may **Foreclose** on the property.

For example, assume that Denny Debtor purchases a home in January, financing 75% of it through First Bank, and giving First a mortgage on the home, which the bank immediately records. In February, Denny takes out a home improvement loan with Second Bank, giving them a mortgage on the same property. Second fails to record the mortgage until April. In March, Denny borrows money from Third Bank to consolidate personal debts, and gives Third a mortgage, which Third records immediately. First has highest priority by having the earliest mortgage and recording before the others. Second failed to record in a timely fashion, so Third will have the next priority in a notice-race jurisdiction **as long as Third Bank didn't know about the mortgage given to Second Bank** at the time Third recorded. Second's claim will be the last of the three. If Third knew about Second's earlier claim, then Second will have priority over Third.

If the debtor defaults on a loan secured by a mortgage, the court may **foreclose** on the property and sell it at auction on behalf of the secured creditor or creditors.

The proceeds are paid in the exact order of priority established for the creditors, and the debtor receives any remaining available funds once all secured claims are repaid. If there is not a sufficient amount to pay all secured creditors, the debtor remains personally liable for the unpaid amounts. Prior to the court-ordered sale, the buyer may redeem the property by paying all amounts owed, but cannot do so after the sale.

If property is sold at a time a recorded mortgage is still outstanding, the mortgagee will retain the right to foreclose on the property and have priority over the buyer with respect to the proceeds from foreclosure. If, however, the proceeds are not sufficient to satisfy the unpaid debt, a question arises as to the liabilities of the seller and buyer for the deficiency.

There are three possible situations, depending on the buyer's actions at the time of purchase:

1. If the buyer **assumes** the mortgage, then the buyer is accepting personal liability for the deficiency. The seller remains liable as well, since they borrowed from the mortgagee originally.
2. If the buyer takes the property **subject to** the mortgage, without assuming it, then the buyer is merely acknowledging the priority of the mortgagee on the property for the unpaid balance of the loan, but is not accepting personal liability for the debt itself. The seller remains liable to the mortgagee for the entire unpaid debt.
3. If the buyer and the mortgagee agree to a **novation** on the debt, then the buyer is accepting personal liability on it in exchange for the mortgagee's agreement to completely release the seller from liability.

Mortgage lenders are regulated by the Real Estate Settlement Procedures Act (RESPA) of 1974, whereby home buyers must be provided with adequate disclosures and explanations of the closing procedures followed and fees charged.

Leases

When property is leased by the owner to another party, the lessee obtains the rights identified in the contract to use the property for a certain time period. Unless these are **specifically** and **individually** prohibited in the agreement, the lessee also has the right to:

- **Assign** – This is a transfer of the balance of the lease to another person, giving the assignee both the right to use the premises and the obligation to pay the owner. The assignor loses the right to the use the premises (since they've been assigned to another) but retains the obligation to the owner as a guarantee of performance by the assignee.
- **Sublet** – This is a separate contract made by the lessee to transfer a portion of the rights under the contract to a sub-lessee for a payment to the lessee. The sub-lessee has the rights under the sub-lease and the obligation to pay the lessee, but no obligation to the owner. The lessee retains the obligations to the owner, and must honor whatever promises they've made to the sub-lessee as far as transferred rights.
  - If lease expires and person will not move, it is called "tenancy at sufferance."
  - If it is ok for the tenant to stay, called "tenancy from period to period."
  - A landlord implies 3 different Warranties:
    - The right of Possession
    - The warranty of Quiet Enjoyment
    - The warranty of Habitability (up to code)

  A residential lease agreement must contain the following:
  1. The parties involved
  2. Lease payment amount
  3. Lease term
  4. Description of the leased property

If receive money to cancel a lease (money to move out early), this is considered a capital gain and is L/T or S/T based on the length of the lease.

For example, assume a lessee signs a rental agreement on a house, giving them the right to live there for the entire calendar year 20X1, with rental payments of $1,000 per month. In June, the lessee rents the property out to another family for a month for $800, to live there while the lessee is on vacation. This is a sublet: the sub-lessee is obligated to pay the lessee $800, and the lessee is responsible to pay the owner of the house the regular $1,000. At the beginning of September, the lessee buys their own home, and transfers the remaining 4 months of the lease to another family that agrees to move in and take over the $1,000 monthly payments to the owner. This is an assignment: the assignee is obligated to pay the owner $1,000 per month, and the assignor is liable for the $1,000 as well in the event the assignee doesn't honor the promise.

Lecture 17.04

INTELLECTUAL PROPERTY AND COMPUTER TECHNOLOGY RIGHTS

Entities and individuals use a wide variety of means by which to protect intellectual property. Various laws have been enacted to take into account the unique characteristics of intellectual property. Some of the means of protection are:
- Copyright
- Patent
- Trademark

Copyrights (©)

Copyrights are designed to protect the creators of original works by giving them the exclusive rights to it. Prior to the application of electronic media, most original works were in written form and a copyright is, literally, **an exclusive right to reproduce and distribute a creative work**. The copyright holder also has the exclusive right to:
- Create work that is derived from the original work, referred to as derivative work
- Perform, display, or otherwise transmit the work
- Sell, assign, license, or otherwise transfer the legal rights to the work

A copyright is valid for the life of the creator plus 70 years. Once the creator has been deceased for 70 years, the work is considered part of the public domain. Copyrights of works by corporations or businesses expire at the earlier of 100 years from the date of creation or 75 years from the date of publication.

A copyright may be registered with the U.S. Copyright office, but the rights also may be obtained by indicating that the item is copyrighted on its face with the date, generally using the copyright symbol, such as © 2018 by John Johnson, CPA. Copyright of a sound recording protected under the copyright laws is denoted with a similar symbol that has a letter "p" in a circle ℗ instead of the letter "c."

The creator of an original work is presumably entitled to the rights afforded by copyright protection. When the identity of the creator is in question, however, the first party to obtain a copyright will generally prevail.

One of the limitations on the rights of a copyright holder is referred to as the **fair use doctrine**, which allows the reproduction of a work that has been copyrighted if it is for a purpose that is considered fair, such as for criticism or comment, news reporting, or teaching or research.

The Computer Software Copyright Act of 1989 was enacted to extend copyright protection to computer programs, which are defined as sets of instructions, whether written or in machine-readable form, used directly or indirectly by a computer to achieve a particular objective. It does allow an owner of a copy to make copies or adaptations in order to be able to use the software for its intended purpose.

The **No Electronic Theft** (**NET**) **Act** was enacted in 1997 to make it a crime to infringe a copyright over the Internet. Infringement is punishable by up to 3 years in prison and a fine of up to $250,000.

The **Digital Millennium Copyright Act of 1998** is an attempt to protect copyright holders against infringement (pirating) and, at the same time, protect internet service providers (ISPs) from liability from the actions of their users. It prohibits unauthorized access to copyrighted digital works and the circumvention of access controls, whether access is obtained or not. It also protects ISPs from liability if they take reasonable steps to prevent or properly react to infringements.

Patents

Patents are designed to protect inventors similarly to how copyrights protect creators of original works. *They prevent someone other than the patent holder from making, using, or offering the patented item for sale.* The three types of patents are:
- **Utility** (usefulness) patents are granted to one who invents or discovers a "new and useful" process, machine, or item to be manufactured or an improvement to one.

- **Design** patents are granted to one who invents a "new, original, and ornamental design" for an item to be manufactured.
- **Plant** patents are granted to one who discovers and reproduces a distinct new plant variety.
    - Utility and plant patents are valid for 20 years and design patents are valid for 14 years from the date of filing.

Trademarks (® and TM)

Trademark protection is given to a *distinctive sign*, which may be a *word, name, symbol, shape, or other format that will be recognizable.* It is used to distinguish goods as being identified with a particular entity, such as a merchant or manufacturer. Companies may use a symbol, like Nike's "Swoosh," which makes a garment or other sports-related product immediately recognizable as a Nike product, even if the name is not displayed.

Trademark protection is generally provided for 10 years.
- During the 6th year of a 10-year term, the holder is required to indicate that the trademark is still in use.
- Trademarks that remain in use can be renewed in 10 year incremental periods indefinitely.
- Trademarks for which an affidavit of use is not filed expire.

Trade Secrets

The **Uniform Trade Secrets Act** was enacted to provide entities with enhanced protection for their trade secrets, which are *formulae, patterns, processes, and other techniques* that have actual or potential economic value and are the subject to reasonable efforts to maintain their secrecy. Protection is for an indefinite period of time and remains in effect as long as the trade secret is relevant.

Semiconductor Chip Protection Act

The **Semiconductor Chip Protection Act of 1984** provides layouts of printed circuits with protections similar to copyrights or patents. It also protects "mask works," which are "a series of related images, however fixed or encoded (1) having or representing the predetermined three-dimensional pattern of metallic, insulating, or semiconductor material present or removed from the layers of a semiconductor chip product...." This protects the creator of a semiconductor chip from another party "reverse engineering" the chip by taking it apart and copying it.

Protection is given for 10 years, expiring at the end of the 10th calendar year after the protection began.

Money Laundering Control Act (MLCA)

The **Money Laundering Control Act of 1986** makes money laundering a federal crime. Money laundering is the process of changing large sums of money that have been gained through illegitimate means to make it appear as if it came from a legitimate source. Under the law, transactions involving transfers of money in excess of $10,000 must be disclosed.

Lecture 17.05

CLASS QUESTIONS

Please see the Class Questions and Class Solutions for this Lecture at the end of this Section.

CLASS QUESTIONS

Work through the below Class Questions while following along with the respective lectures. Once this is complete, you can begin independently practicing what you've learned by quizzing yourself on this course section in your Interactive Practice Questions (IPQ), which can be found in your online Student Dashboard. Your IPQ simulates the computer-based testing experience, and will also help you understand how concepts are applied to the exam. Each question includes answer explanations from expert CPAs that will help you determine why you answered a question correctly or incorrectly. This is key to your success on the CPA Exam.

Lecture 17.02

1. What is an example of property that can be considered either personal property or real property?

    a. Air rights.
    b. Mineral rights.
    c. Harvested crops.
    d. Growing crops.

2. Which of the following factors help determine whether an item of personal property is a fixture?

    I. Degree of the item's attachment to the property.
    II. Intent of the person who had the item installed.

    a. I only.
    b. II only.
    c. Both I and II.
    d. Neither I nor II.

3. Which of the following elements must be contained in a valid deed?

	Purchase price	Description of the land
a.	Yes	Yes
b.	Yes	No
c.	No	Yes
d.	No	No

4. For a deed to be effective between the purchaser and seller of real estate, one of the conditions is that the deed must

    a. Contain the signatures of the seller and purchaser.
    b. Contain the actual sales price.
    c. Be delivered by the seller with an intent to transfer title.
    d. Be recorded within the permissible statutory time limits.

5. A purchaser who obtains real estate title insurance will

    a. Have coverage for the title exceptions listed in the policy.
    b. Be insured against all defects of record other than those excepted in the policy.
    c. Have coverage for title defects that result from events that happen after the effective date of the policy.
    d. Be entitled to transfer the policy to subsequent owners.

6. Which of the following is a defect in marketable title to real property?

    a. Recorded zoning restrictions.
    b. Recorded easements referred to in the contract of sale.
    c. Unrecorded lawsuit for negligence against the seller.
    d. Unrecorded easement.

Lecture 17.05

7. Long, Fall, and Pear own a building as joint tenants with the right of survivorship. Long gave Long's interest in the building to Green by executing and delivering a deed to Green. Neither Fall nor Pear consented to this transfer. Fall and Pear subsequently died. After their deaths, Green's interest in the building would consist of

    a. A 1/3 interest as a joint tenant.
    b. A 1/3 interest as a tenant in common.
    c. No interest because Fall and Pear did **not** consent to the transfer.
    d. Total ownership due to the deaths of Fall and Pear.

8. Which of the following unities (elements) are required to establish a joint tenancy?

	Time	**Title**	**Interest**	**Possession**
a.	Yes	Yes	Yes	Yes
b.	Yes	Yes	No	No
c.	No	No	Yes	Yes
d.	Yes	No	Yes	No

9. Which of the following conditions must be met to have an enforceable mortgage?

    a. An accurate description of the property must be included in the mortgage.
    b. A negotiable promissory note must accompany the mortgage.
    c. Present consideration must be given in exchange for the mortgage.
    d. The amount of the debt and the interest rate must be stated in the mortgage.

10. Rich purchased property from Sklar for $200,000. Rich obtained a $150,000 loan from Marsh Bank to finance the purchase, executing a promissory note and a mortgage. By recording the mortgage, Marsh protects its

    a. Rights against Rich under the promissory note.
    b. Rights against the claims of subsequent bona fide purchasers for value.
    c. Priority against a previously filed real estate tax lien on the property.
    d. Priority against all parties having earlier claims to the property.

11. Kemp created and patented a new process to convert liquid gas to powder. Two years later, Mill independently, and without knowledge of the Kemp patent, developed the identical process. Mill only wanted to use the process for Mill's own business and did not attempt to patent the process. Kemp learned about Mill's process and sued for patent infringement. Will Kemp prevail?

   a.   Yes, because Kemp was the first to patent the process.
   b.   Yes, because Mill should have known about Kemp's patent.
   c.   No, because Mill came up with the process independently.
   d.   No, because Mill only used the process for Mill's own business.

CLASS SOLUTIONS

1. (d) Growing crops are considered real property because, when they are growing, they are attached to the land. They can be sold separately from the land, however, and can also be considered personal property. Answer (a) is incorrect because air rights cannot be separated from the real estate that they are associated with and are considered real property. Answer (b) is incorrect because mineral rights, the right to extract minerals from property, cannot be separated from the real property that it is associated with and are considered real property. Answer (c) is incorrect because harvested crops are separate from the land and are considered personal property.

2. (c) Real property is land and anything that is permanently affixed to it. As a result, the degree to which an item is attached to the land is relevant as is the intent of the person that had the item installed.

3. (c) In order to be valid, a deed must describe the property to which it relates so the property can be properly identified. The purchase price, which may not even be determinable in the case of a gift or an exchange, is not necessary information.

4. (c) In order to be effective, a deed must indicate that it conveys some rights to the property and must be delivered by the grantor. Answer (a) is incorrect because it requires the signature of the grantor, or seller, but not the grantee, or buyer. Answer (b) is incorrect because a deed need not indicate the price, which may not be determinable in the case of a gift or exchange. Answer (d) is incorrect because recording a deed gives notice of its existence to individuals not part of the transaction but does not affect the validity of it.

5. (b) A title insurance policy provides a buyer of property protection against defects in the property's title. It is issued after the title insurance policy researches the title and applies to defects in existence as of the date of the policy. A title insurance policy will generally list exceptions, which are types of defects against which it will not provide protection. A title insurance policy provides no protection from actions of the buyers and does not cover defects to the title that occur after the date of the policy. Since the policy is as of a particular date, it cannot be transferred to a subsequent purchaser.

6. (d) A defect in the marketable title of property is a claim against that property that the buyer is not aware of. Those that are recorded are presumed known to the buyer since they are a matter of public record. An unrecorded claim, such as an unrecorded easement, is a claim that the buyer would not be aware of. An unrecorded lawsuit for negligence against the seller may result in monetary damages, but would not give the plaintiff a claim to the property.

7. (b) In general, a joint tenancy arrangement provides surviving joint tenants with a proportionate share of a deceased joint tenant's share. When a joint tenant transfers their interest without the consent of the remaining joint tenants, the acquirer does not obtain the right of survivorship and will be entitled to the transferor's proportionate share. In this case, Green would not have a right of survivorship and would have a 1/3 interest as a tenant in common.

8. (a) A joint tenancy provides each joint tenant with an undivided interest in the entire property and each has the right of survivorship when a joint tenant dies. As a result, all joint tenants must have equal rights to the property, including time, the duration of ownership; title; interest; and possession.

9. (a) A mortgage is a security interest in real property that remains in effect until the underlying obligation is satisfied or the property is obtained by the mortgage holder through repossession. It must include an accurate description of the property so that the property to which it applies can be identified. Although a mortgage is security for a loan against real estate, there is no requirement that it be in the form of a negotiable promissory note. The mortgage may be given in exchange for present or past consideration. The amount of the debt will change over time and neither it nor the interest rate is required to be stated in the mortgage.

10. (b) Recording a security interest, including a mortgage, is a means of making the public aware of it. It is assumed that anyone subsequently obtaining a claim against property will be aware of it and will take the property subject to it. By recording the mortgage, Marsh is protected from claims of future purchasers. The note itself, with the terms of the debt, is all that is necessary to obtain rights against the debtor. It does not provide protection against claims occurring before the recording date.

11. (a) The first person to invent and patent a process has the exclusive right to use that process for the duration of the patent. A lack of knowledge of the patent by third parties does not reduce the patent holder's rights and does not allow the third party to infringe upon them. It does not matter whether Mill should have known about Kemp's patent. The first person to invent and patent a process has the exclusive right to use that process for the duration of the patent, even if others do not know of the patent. Even if Mill came up with the process independently or only used the process for Mill's own business, the first person to invent and patent a process has the exclusive right to use that process for the duration of the patent. Kemp will prevail. Any party benefiting from the patent must do so with the permission of the patent holder.

Section 18 – Agency

Corresponding Lectures

Watch the following course lectures with this section:

Lecture 18.01 – Agency Law
Lecture 18.02 – Agency Law – Class Questions

__EXAM NOTE:__ Please refer to the AICPA REG Blueprint in the Introduction to find a listing of the representative tasks (and their associated skill levels—i.e., Remembering and Understanding, Application, and Analysis) that the candidate should be able to perform based on the knowledge obtained in this section.

Agency

AGENCY LAW

An agency relationship exists when one party acts on behalf of another for contractual obligations. The **Principal needs capacity**, but the agent does not. An agent must have authority from the principal in order to act on the principal's behalf. The agent must merely have sufficient mental and physical ability to carry out instructions of his/her principal.

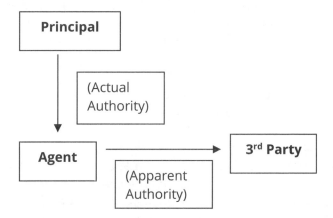

An agency does not require a contract and no consideration need be offered, but there must be consent ("a meeting of the minds"). The agency agreement itself need **not be in writing**, except under circumstances when the **Statute of Frauds** (GROSS) applies. Examples where the statute applies include:

- An agency to sell real estate (**Real estate**).
- An agency to run for a period exceeding one year (**Over 1 year**).

An agent has a **fiduciary duty** to act loyally on behalf of the principal. The agent must always act in the best interest of the principal. This includes a duty to account for any property of the principal the agent handles, and a prohibition against commingling the funds of the principal with other funds held or owned by the agent. Also, an agent is liable to the principal if the agent binds the principal to a contract based on apparent authority when the agent knew they did not have the actual authority to enter into the contract. The principal, however, does not owe a fiduciary duty to the agent.

Businesses may engage in relationships with **two special types of agents**: employees and independent contractors. In determining whether one is an employee or an independent contractor, the most significant factors to consider are who controls the behavior of the individual, who controls the financial aspects of the individual's efforts, and how the parties perceive their relationship.

An **employee** is under the control of the employer. The employer (a type of principal) determines what behavior on the part of the employee (the agent) is appropriate or inappropriate. The employer not only determines the objective of the relationship, but also the means by which the objective is met as well as when the employee will perform the functions necessary to achieve it (i.e., employer controls the *time and manner* of performance). The employer is also responsible for the financial risks associated with the relationship. The employee may be paid on a piecemeal basis or by the hour, week, month, or some other basis and is entitled to payment for hours worked, regardless of effectiveness, and will receive a **W-2** from the employer, indicating amounts earned and taxes withheld.

Since an employer has control over the actions of the employee while engaged in employment-related activities, the employer will be liable for the employee's *torts* committed during the *course* of employment and within the parameters (*scope*) of the employment relationship.

An **independent contractor** (the agent) is not subject to the control of the principal. Although the principal will determine what constitutes acceptable results, the independent contractor is responsible for determining the means by which objectives will be achieved, as well as when and how the functions necessary to achieve it will be performed. The independent contractor bears financial risk in that efficiencies and inefficiencies are their own responsibility. The independent contractor is normally paid an agreed-upon amount, is responsible for paying their own taxes without having taxes withheld, and receives a **1099,** indicating the gross amount received, against which expenses may be deducted.

Since the principal is not in control of the actions of the independent contractors, the principal is *generally not responsible for their torts*; however, there are always exceptions to the general rule.

There are three ways the agent may obtain this authority:
- **Actual authority** – The principal intends to give the agent the authority. This includes *express authority*, in which the principal explicitly states that the agent has authority, and *implied authority*, in which the principal assigns the agent a task which cannot be carried out without having certain authority to act on the principal's behalf. For example, hiring someone as a bartender gives them the actual authority to sell drinks at the bar.
- **Apparent authority** – The principal takes an action that creates the appearance to third parties that the agent has certain authority. This could result from hiring someone to a position that normally has great authority, or where the customs of the profession provide certain authority. (Note that the principal must take an action that creates the appearance the agent has authority. This doctrine doesn't bind a person simply because another person is claiming to be their agent). For example, giving someone a title of vice-president in the company gives them apparent authority for a broad range of contracts on the company's behalf, even if the private agreement among the principal and agent is that the new title is simply for prestige.
- **Ratification** – The agent acts without authority, but the principal decides after the contract is made to honor it anyway. To ratify, the principal must have been *fully or partially disclosed, understand the contract made on their behalf by the agent, and act to ratify before the third party discovers that the agent acted without authority*. The principal can ratify by explicitly stating their intention to honor the contract, or by accepting the benefits of the contract. For example, if the friend of someone trying to sell their car finds out about an interested party and contracts on behalf of the owner to sell the car without their knowledge or consent, the contract is without authority. If, however, the friend gives the owner a check from that party, indicating that it is the agreed payment for the car, the deposit of the check by the owner is a ratification of the deal and makes it valid and binding on all parties.

One important point to note is that a principal who has accepted contracts made by the agent in the past creates the appearance that the agent has the authority to make similar contracts in the future.

A common form of agency is a **power of attorney**, which is a written authorization for the agent to act on behalf of the principal for a specific or indefinite period of time. It may be a limited power of attorney that only grants the authority to act in certain matters, or a general power of attorney allowing the agent to act on behalf of the principal on all matters affecting them. A power of attorney is often written with a specific provision keeping it enforceable in the event of the insanity or incapacity of the principal, since it may be created in anticipation of possible mental deterioration of the principal. A power of attorney always terminates upon the death of the principal, however.

Types of Authority
- **Actual** – Principal intends to give agent power to contract.
  - **Express** – Principal explicitly states agent has authority.
  - **Implied** – Principal assigns task, which requires authority to carry out duties. Reasonable and necessary to get job done.

- **Apparent** – Principal creates impression that agent has authority.
  - **Good faith 3rd party** reasonably assumes you have.
    - Hires agent to position that customarily has authority.
    - Has acquiesced to contracts made in past by agent on principal's behalf.

- **Unauthorized action** – not liable unless ratify.
  - **Ratification** – Principal gives agent authority after contract is made.
    - Principal must be fully or partially disclosed.
    - Must know details of contract made by agent on behalf.
    - Must ratify before 3rd party withdraws.

Types of Principals
- **Fully disclosed**
  - 3rd party knows identity of principal.
  - Principal liable – Agent not liable to 3rd party.
- **Partially disclosed**
  - 3rd party knows agent is acting for another, but not identity.
  - Principal and agent jointly and severally liable.
- **Undisclosed**
  - 3rd party believes agent is acting for themselves only.
  - 3rd party may hold either principal or agent liable.
  - Agent required to perform under the contract.
  - When principal is undisclosed, the agent *cannot have apparent authority*.
  - 3rd party not entitled to disclosure of principal.

Types of Agents
- **General Agent** – Has broad authority to act for the principal in a variety of transactions.
- **Special Agent** – Has authority that is limited to a single transaction or series of transactions.
- **Sub-Agent** – An agent appointed by another agent who is authorized to appoint sub-agents in connection with his performance of the principal's business. A sub-agent has a fiduciary duty and a duty of loyalty to both the principal and agent.

Once an agent has authority, it can be **terminated** in the following ways:
- **Agreement** – The parties originally contracted for the agency to last a period of time that has elapsed, or the parties mutually agree to terminate an agency of indefinite duration.
- **Unilateral** – The principal dismisses the agent, or the agent resigns. Normally, either party has the power to terminate the agency at any time, even in breach of contract.
- **Operation of law** – The agency terminates due to a provision of the law. These include death, insanity, illegality and destruction of the subject matter. The death or insanity of a party will not affect the enforceability of contracts made before such an event. An illegal contract will, however, be unenforceable, even if the provisions were agreed to before the law declared them illegal.
  - **Operation of law** – Authority terminates without notice.
    - Death of principal or agent (contracts already made, stand).
    - Insanity of principal.
    - The subject of the agreement becomes Illegal or impossible (destroyed).
    - Principal bankrupt.

Occasionally, the agent will obtain an **agency coupled with an interest**. This results from an arrangement in which the agent has some legal rights to the subject matter of the agency, and such an agency **cannot be terminated unilaterally by the principal**. For example, a secured creditor who has seized the debtor's collateral as a result of default is an agent with the right to sell the debtor's property. Since the creditor is entitled to some of the sales proceeds, their agency is coupled with an interest in the property, and cannot be terminated by the debtor unilaterally (it can still be terminated by the creditor unilaterally or by mutual agreement of the creditor and debtor).

The **termination** of an agency by operation of law applies to both actual and apparent authority. Other terminations, however, only apply to actual authority, and it is necessary to give **notice to third parties** to terminate apparent authority. Two kinds of notice are needed:
- **Actual notice** – Third parties are directly informed that the agency has terminated (Personal Notice).
- **Constructive notice** – An announcement of the termination is made in publications that third parties are likely to read (Public Notice).

Actual notice must be given to each third party that dealt with the agent in the past. Constructive notice must be given so as to eliminate apparent authority with third parties who haven't dealt with the agent, but who might have been aware of the agency relationship.

For example, assume Sal Salesperson has been working for Western Widgets for 5 years. If Western fires Sal, that terminates Sal's actual authority to make contracts, but if none of the customers know about this, apparent authority remains. Western must notify the customers that previously made purchases of Western products through Sal of the termination. Nevertheless, there is a danger that Sal will go to a person who hasn't made previous purchases, but who is aware that Sal worked for Western as a salesperson through various business contacts. Western, to protect itself, must place ads indicating that Sal is no longer an employee of Western.

A principal and agent have responsibilities toward one another. If an agent has acted without actual authority, binding the principal due to the agent's apparent authority, the agent is liable to the principal for losses or damages incurred. Similarly, if an agent acts with actual authority, the principal is obligated to reimburse or indemnify the agent for payments made that were either expressly authorized or necessary in promoting the principal's business.

In the case of a *breach by the principal*, the courts are reluctant to require parties to interact and specific performance would not be available. The agent may, however, be entitled to:
- Recovery for past services
- Recovery for future damages
- The authority to withhold further performance for the principal

A **tort** is an action that causes injury to another person or their property, whether intentional or caused by negligence, which may result in a *civil trial*. Generally, when there is criminal intent and a criminal act, the action may also constitute a **crime**, which would result in a *criminal trial*; however, not all crimes require criminal intent (e.g., selling alcohol to a minor without knowing he or she is, in fact, a minor). An individual is always responsible for their own torts and crimes. A principal is responsible for torts committed by an agent when committed in the course and scope of the agency relationship. A principal, however, is not responsible for crimes committed by an agent, although some states are expanding a principal's liability for actions of their agents.

Lecture 18.02

CLASS QUESTIONS

Please see the Class Questions and Class Solutions for this Lecture at the end of this Section.

CLASS QUESTIONS

Work through the below Class Questions while following along with the respective lectures. Once this is complete, you can begin independently practicing what you've learned by quizzing yourself on this course section in your Interactive Practice Questions (IPQ), which can be found in your online Student Dashboard. Your IPQ simulates the computer-based testing experience, and will also help you understand how concepts are applied to the exam. Each question includes answer explanations from expert CPAs that will help you determine why you answered a question correctly or incorrectly. This is key to your success on the CPA Exam.

Lecture 18.02

1. Which of the following actions requires an agent for a corporation to have a written agency agreement?

    a. Purchasing office supplies for the principal's business.
    b. Purchasing an interest in undeveloped land for the principal.
    c. Hiring an independent general contractor to renovate the principal's office building.
    d. Retaining an attorney to collect a business debt owed the principal.

2. Young Corp. hired Wilson as a sales representative for six months at a salary of $5,000 per month plus 6% of sales. Which of the following statements is correct?

    a. Young does **not** have the power to dismiss Wilson during the six-month period without cause.
    b. Wilson is obligated to act solely in Young's interest in matters concerning Young's business.
    c. The agreement between Young and Wilson is **not** enforceable unless it is in writing and signed by Wilson.
    d. The agreement between Young and Wilson formed an agency coupled with an interest.

3. An agent will usually be liable under a contract made with a third party when the agent is acting on behalf of a(n)

	Disclosed principal	**Undisclosed principal**
a.	Yes	Yes
b.	Yes	No
c.	No	Yes
d.	No	No

4. When a valid contract is entered into by an agent on the principal's behalf, in a nondisclosed principal situation, which of the following statements concerning the principal's liability is correct?

	The principal may be held liable once disclosed	**The principal must ratify the contract to be held liable**
a.	Yes	Yes
b.	Yes	No
c.	No	Yes
d.	No	No

5. When an agent acts for an undisclosed principal, the principal will **not** be liable to third parties if the

    a. Principal ratifies a contract entered into by the agent.
    b. Agent acts within an implied grant of authority.
    c. Agent acts outside the grant of actual authority.
    d. Principal seeks to conceal the agency relationship.

6. Bolt Corp. dismissed Ace as its general sales agent and notified all of Ace's known customers by letter. Young Corp., a retail outlet located outside of Ace's previously assigned sales territory, had never dealt with Ace. Young knew of Ace as a result of various business contacts. After his dismissal, Ace sold Young goods, to be delivered by Bolt, and received from Young a cash deposit for 20% of the purchase price. It was not unusual for an agent in Ace's previous position to receive cash deposits. In an action by Young against Bolt on the sales contract, Young will

    a. Lose, because Ace lacked any implied authority to make the contract.
    b. Lose, because Ace lacked any express authority to make the contract.
    c. Win, because Bolt's notice was inadequate to terminate Ace's apparent authority.
    d. Win, because a principal is an insurer of an agent's acts.

CLASS SOLUTIONS

1. (b) In general, an agency relationship is not required to be in writing. The Statute of Frauds, however, does require certain contracts to be in writing to be enforceable and when an agency contract is established to enter into a contract that is subject to the Statute of Frauds, the agency relationship is required to be in writing. This includes when the objective of the agency cannot be accomplished within one year and when the subject is the purchase or sale of real estate.

2. (b) An agent has a fiduciary responsibility to the principal and, in matters concerning the principal's business, is required to act in the principal's best interest. Answer (a) is incorrect because a principal has the authority to dismiss an agent, provided the agent is not an agent coupled with an interest. Answer (c) is incorrect because an agency relationship is not required to be in writing to be enforceable, unless it is established to deal with a contract that is required to be in writing under the Statute of Frauds. Answer (d) is incorrect because Wilson is not an agent coupled with an interest, which is an agent that has an interest in the subject matter of the agency relationship, which is not the case.

3. (c) When an agent is acting on behalf of a disclosed principal, the third party knows that the agent is dealing on behalf of the principal and only the principal is liable. When an agent is acting on behalf of an undisclosed principal, the third party is not aware of the agency relationship and believes the relationship is with the agent. As a result, the agent will be liable to the third party but will have recourse against the principal.

4. (b) When an agent is acting on behalf of an undisclosed principal, the third party is not aware of the agency relationship and believes the relationship is with the agent. As a result, the agent will be liable to the third party but will have recourse against the principal. The principal will be liable to the agent as long as the agent's actions were authorized without requiring ratification.

5. (c) When an agent is acting on behalf of an undisclosed principal, the third party is not aware of the agency relationship and believes the relationship is with the agent. As a result, the agent will be liable to the third party but will have recourse against the principal. The principal will be liable to the agent as long as the agent's actions were authorized. Answer (a) is incorrect because a principal would also be liable for an agent's unauthorized actions if the principal ratifies the action. Ratification does not reduce liability. Answer (b) is incorrect because actions are authorized whether the authority is explicit or implied. Answer (d) is incorrect because the purpose of an undisclosed principal relationship is to allow the principal to hide the agency.

6. (c) Actual notice in the form of a letter to customers who have dealt with the agent is sufficient to prevent further liability to those parties. The principal, however, must also provide constructive notice, such as an ad in a newspaper, to inform those who have not dealt with the agent that the agent lacks authority. Bolt's letter would not prevent liability to third parties who have not previously dealt with Ace. Answer (a) is incorrect because they would justifiably assume that Ace still had authority, referred to as ostensible, or implied, authority. Answer (b) is incorrect because although Ace does lack express authority, the lack of proper notice may lead third parties to believe Ace had authority, referred to as implied authority. Answer (d) is incorrect because a principal is liable for the authorized commitments made by an agent but is not an insurer.

Section 19 – Secured Transactions

Corresponding Lectures

Watch the following course lectures with this section:

Lecture 19.01 – Secured Transaction
Lecture 19.02 – Attachment and Perfection
Lecture 19.03 – Inventory Rule
Lecture 19.04 – Secured Transactions – Class Questions

EXAM NOTE: *Please refer to the AICPA REG Blueprint in the Introduction to find a listing of the representative tasks (and their associated skill levels—i.e., Remembering and Understanding, Application, and Analysis) that the candidate should be able to perform based on the knowledge obtained in this section.*

Secured Transactions

Lecture 19.01

SECURED TRANSACTIONS

A transaction where a Creditor either lends money or extends credit to the Debtor and, in exchange, obtains a security interest in the Debtor's property, called Collateral (**UCC Article 9**). The property is usually either Personal property or Fixtures, not Real property.

Types of Collateral

- **Tangibles**
    - *Inventory* – goods held for sale or lease in the normal course of business, raw materials used in manufacturing (TV a store will sell)
    - *Equipment* – goods that will be used in a trade or business (TV located in a Gym)
    - *Consumer goods* – goods used for personal or household purposes (TV in your home)
    - *Chattel paper* – Writings that evidence both a monetary obligation (buy equipment on credit, the loan agreement then becomes the collateral for another loan by the previous creditor) and security interest in specific goods or equipment
- **Intangibles**
    - *Accounts* – Any right to payment for goods or services that is not evidenced by an instrument
    - *Negotiable instruments*, warehouse receipts, bills of lading

    Note: Items may change from one category to another, depending on who has possession.

The character of the collateral depends on the debtor's intended use. A personal computer is inventory to a computer store, consumer goods to a family that is using it to play video games, and equipment to a business that is using it to maintain accounting records.

Purchase Money Security Interest (PMSI)

- When the Creditor gives the Debtor the purchase money or the credit to acquire the collateral. This gives the creditor priority over all other types of security interests in the same collateral.
    - **PMSI** – an interest in personal property or fixtures that secures payment of an obligation that is:
        - Taken by the seller of the collateral to secure all or part of its price, OR
        - Taken by a person who loans money or extends credit to enable the debtor to acquire the collateral.

The Creditor would like to protect their interest from several different parties: (**DOTS**)

- **D**ebtor – (Only needs Attachment)

Attach & Perfection
- **O**ther creditor claiming an interest in the same collateral
- **T**rustee in Bankruptcy
- **S**ubsequent purchaser from the debtor without knowledge of perfection

Note: For the creditor to protect themselves from the debtor (D), they must only attach; to protect themselves from the other parties (OTS), they must first Attach and then Perfect.

Lecture 19.02

Attachment

If the debtor does not pay the debt as promised, the creditor will be able to enforce the security agreement, seizing the asset and selling it to raise funds, then returning to the debtor any value exceeding the debt owed, as long as the security interest has attached to the collateral.

Attachment gives a secured party the right to repossess collateral, when the debtor doesn't pay the secured debt. This gives the creditor legally enforceable rights against only the debtor. In order to attach, **all 3** must occur. When the last of the 3 occurs, the interest is considered to have attached.

- **Property owned** by the debtor ("**rights**") (this may involve ownership of the collateral or other claims, such as royalty rights).
- **Interest is created** (one of 2 ways).
  - *Signed security agreement*
    - A reasonable description of the collateral
    - Signed by the debtor
  - *Take possession* (pledge as collateral)
- **Give value** to the debtor (a promise to give value in the future is not sufficient).
  - Line of credit is value when given authority, not when money is distributed.

Attachment also covers the following:

- Can attach to the **proceeds** from the sale of the collateral, if debtor sells the property.
- A security agreement also may apply to **after-acquired property.** If the debtor were to purchase inventory or equipment after the attachment occurred, the creditor may attach to these items.

Once all three conditions are satisfied, the creditor has a security interest that can be enforced against the debtor. In some cases, the creditor was the one who provided the debtor with the financing that allowed the debtor to purchase the collateral. In such cases, the creditor has a **purchase money security interest (PMSI)**. In certain cases, a PMSI has advantages over other security interests.

Assume that D purchases a television for personal use (consumer goods) for cash on November 1. On December 10, D arranges to borrow $300 from C, signing and delivering to C a security agreement giving C the right to use the television as collateral for the loan. On December 15, C lends D the money. Attachment takes place on December 15, based on the application of the rules of attachment:

- November 1 – The debtor obtained rights in the collateral.
- December 10 – The debtor provided the creditor with a signed security agreement.
- December 15 – The creditor gave value to the debtor.

As of December 15, all three events required for attachment have occurred, and C obtains a security interest. It is not a purchase money security interest, since C did not provide D with the financing to purchase the television.

As a second example, assume D goes to C on April 24 and asks to borrow $1,000 to purchase a video surveillance camera for D's business (equipment). D signs a security agreement and C loans the money. On May 12, D purchases the camera from a video supplier for $1,500, using the funds obtained from C earlier and an additional $500 of D's own money. Attachment takes place on May 12, based on the application of the rules:
- April 24 – The creditor gave value, and the debtor provided a signed security agreement.
- May 12 – The debtor obtained rights in the collateral.

As of May 12, all three events have occurred, and C obtains a security interest. It is a purchase money security interest, since C did provide D with the financing to purchase the camera.

Once attachment has occurred, the creditor has a non-possessory right in the debtor's collateral. This means the creditor has rights but not ownership. In the event the debtor defaults on the debt, the creditor may demand the asset, and then may sell it in either a public or private sale. The creditor may even retain the asset in some cases to satisfy the debt, but may not do so if the collateral is consumer goods and the debtor has paid at least 60% of the purchase price of the collateral before default. The creditor is entitled to keep only the amount owed to them, and the remaining value must be returned to the debtor. Furthermore, the debtor may redeem the property (demand its return) after the creditor has seized it, but prior to sale to a third party by paying the amount owed to the creditor and any reasonable expenses incurred by the creditor. Once a sale has taken place to a third party, though, the debtor will no longer be able to redeem it. The third party is not liable for any of the claims against the property by the creditors of the debtor as long as they purchased it without knowledge of any defects in title.

The law provides creditors with rights *similar to attachment* in various circumstances:
- **Judicial lien** – A court orders certain property to be made available to the plaintiff to satisfy a claim against the defendant in a case. Under Article 9 of the UCC, security interests in tort claims already assessed by a court of law are available to satisfy plaintiff's judgments.
- **Statutory lien** – A service person who repairs *personal property* is given rights by legal statute in the property in the form of an **artisan's lien** until the owner pays for the repairs (this is called a **mechanic's lien** when work is done in connection with *real property*).
- **Garnishment** – A creditor obtains a judicial order allowing them to be paid a portion of the debtor's wages out of each paycheck directly from the debtor's employer.

In general, these types of claims have priority over creditors who have attached the same property, unless the creditors perfected their interests before these claims arose. A statutory lien has priority over all other claims, including prior perfected claims, unless the statute expressly denies this.

Perfection

Perfection gives the creditor legally enforceable rights against the debtor (D) and all other parties (OTS) claiming an interest in the same collateral. To perfect, must satisfy **any 1** of the following:
- **File a financing statement** in the appropriate public office
  - A listing or description of the types of collateral
  - Signature and address of debtor (jurisdiction for filing)
  - Name and address of creditor

- Must be done for accounts (A/R, copyrights, trademarks, goodwill)
- The filing lasts for 5 years and can be continued indefinitely if refiled within 6 months of expiring for another 5 years.
  - **Automatic Perfection**
    - A PMSI in **consumer goods** is automatically perfected without filing or taking possession as soon as it attaches.
      - *Loophole* – if the debtor sells the consumer goods to another good faith consumer, the new purchaser takes the property free of the automatic perfection ("garage sale" rule).
      - To close the loophole, the creditor must file a financing statement within **20 days of attachment**. (Retroactive to date of attachment if within 20 days)
        - The 20-day rule also applies to equipment, but not to inventory.
  - **Take possession** of the collateral
    - Must be done for negotiable and nonnegotiable instruments, investment securities (stock certificates or promissory notes) and money. Example: a pawnbroker lending money.

Of course, a security interest can be perfected only if it has been attached. If a creditor files a financing statement prior to the 3 requirements of attachment being satisfied, the perfection will occur once attachment occurs.

Filing a financing statement is a way of informing other potential claimants against the property of the creditor's claim. The statement is filed in the jurisdiction of the debtor. If the property was acquired by the debtor for personal use (consumer goods), the jurisdiction is based on the debtor's principal residence. If the property was acquired by the debtor for resale (inventory) or use in their trade or business (equipment), the jurisdiction is based on the debtor's principal place of business. If the jurisdiction of the debtor changes, the financing statement remains valid for **120 days** before the creditor must refile in the new jurisdiction. To summarize, the jurisdiction for almost all Filings is determined by the *Debtor's location*, rather than the collateral's location.

Normally, perfection occurs at the time the financing statement is filed. If, however, a creditor with a **PMSI files within 20 days** of the debtor's acquisition of the collateral, the perfection will become effective retroactively to the date of attachment, unless the collateral is inventory.

If a creditor lends money and obtains a security agreement in previously purchased equipment of a debtor on February 1, and files a financing statement on February 11, perfection occurs on February 11. If, on the other hand, the creditor lends the debtor the money to buy the equipment currently on February 1, and files a financing statement on February 11, perfection occurs on February 1, because the creditor has a PMSI. If the PMSI creditor doesn't file until February 22, the perfection occurs on February 22, since it doesn't satisfy the 20-day rule.

Perfections against **inventory** are not as complete as those against other types of property (**Inventory Rule**). Since inventory is acquired by the debtor for the specific purpose of being sold, a perfection against inventory will not protect the creditor after the debtor sells the inventory in the ordinary course of business, even if the buyer knows of the security interest and even if the buyer is not a consumer. However, the creditor will have rights against the proceeds from sale, and the perfection against inventory will give the creditor priority over other creditors and the trustee-in-bankruptcy.

There is one method of perfection that requires no further action by the creditor beyond the requirements of attachment. The creditor's claim is perfected automatically when they attach a purchase money security interest **in consumer goods** acquired from a dealer.

For example, if a consumer purchases goods from a store and the transaction is financed by the store directly, the store will obtain an automatic perfection at the time of the sale. Similarly, if the consumer purchases goods from a store and finances the transaction with a loan from the bank, the bank will obtain an automatic perfection at the time of the sale. The automatic perfection does not apply to goods the debtor is buying for business purposes, nor to purchases of consumer goods from other consumers, but to regular dealers in the goods. In other words, the goods must have been inventory to the seller and must be consumer goods to the buyer (debtor).

Although the creditor obtains a perfection in these consumer goods without having to file a financing statement, there is a **loophole** in the perfection which may cause the creditor to decide to file anyway. This loophole allows another consumer who purchases the goods from the consumer-debtor to be free of the perfection as long as they didn't know about it.

If a consumer purchases a home exercise machine from a department store on credit from the store, the store obtains an automatic perfection since they financed the purchase of the collateral. If the debtor sells the machine to a friend without telling them the store has a claim against it, the friend will acquire the machine free of the store's security interest if the store relied on the automatic perfection. If the store filed a financing statement before the sale, however, they will have an enforceable perfection against the friend.

In rare cases, the creditor will perfect their interest by **taking possession** of the collateral. This is usually impractical because it prevents the debtor from using the property. In the case of automobiles, however, the creditor may take possession of the document of title (pink slip) to the vehicle. There are no loopholes to a perfection by possession (assuming there are no creditors who have already perfected their security interest by filing a financing statement).

To summarize the different methods of perfection and related issues:

Method	Loophole	Comment
Filing a financing statement	Sale of inventory	Filing of PMSI within 20 days retroactive to attachment.
Attaching PMSI in consumer good purchase from dealer	Sale by debtor to another good faith consumer	Loophole can be closed if the creditor files a financing statement.
Take possession of collateral	No loophole	May take possession of document of title.

Special Rules for Perfection

When collateral is taken from one state to another, the creditor must perfect in the new state within **4 months**, or lose their priority.

A security interest in instruments and negotiable documents of title is automatically perfected upon attachment without filing or possession for a period of **20 days,** to allow the creditor to gain possession of the collateral. (For example, if you loan me money in exchange for my bank CD, you will have 20 days to take possession of the CD.)

Lecture 19.03

INVENTORY RULE

If acquiring goods in the ordinary course of business (inventory to seller), buyer's claim is superior to all other claims. So, if the goods are purchased from a retailer, the inventory is acquired free of all other claims, even if the purchaser is aware of the claims (I – Inventory, C – Consumer Goods, E-Equipment).

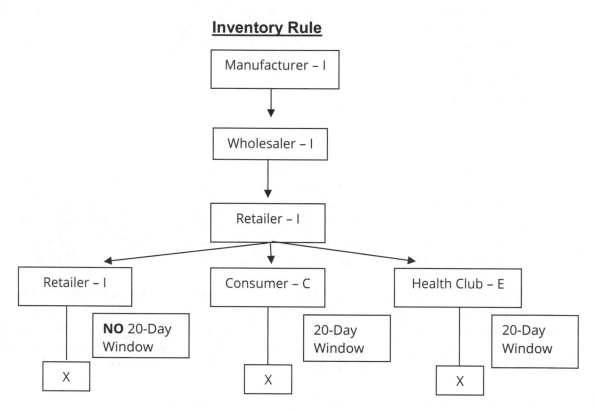

Filings – The jurisdiction for almost all Filings is determined by the **debtor's location**, rather than the collateral's location.

Priority among Creditors

1. Inventory rule – buyer in the ordinary course of business.
2. Holder of a statutory lien (mechanic's lien), depending on state statute.
3. PMSI when attached and perfected simultaneously.
4. Among other perfections by filing, order of filing (even if not yet perfected).
5. Other Perfected interests or judicial liens (court order/garnish wages) in order of perfection.
6. Order of attachment, if no one perfected.

If more than one creditor has perfected their interest in the same collateral, the **priority** among the creditors is as follows:
- A PMSI has priority over all other interests if the creditor perfected at the same time as attachment. This is always the case for consumer goods bought from a dealer.
    - Would apply to perfection by filing within 20 days for other consumer goods and equipment.

- o Would not usually apply to inventory, unless filing took place before the debtor acquired the inventory.
- Among other perfections by filing, priority is based on the **order of filing.**
- If one creditor has a perfection by filing, and another has perfection by possession, the one who has **perfected first** in their own way has priority over the other.

For example, assume that 3 different creditors have perfected interests by filing against a debtor's equipment. Creditor A financed the purchase of the equipment by the debtor on April 1, and filed a financing statement on April 10. Creditor B made a loan to the debtor on April 3, and filed on April 6. Creditor C made a loan to the debtor on April 7, but filed against the equipment on April 2 during the negotiations over the loan.

The highest priority goes to A, since they have a PMSI and filed within 20 days of the debtor's purchase of the collateral, so perfection occurred at the same time as attachment. Creditor C is second in line, since they filed on April 2, earlier than the April 6 filing of Creditor B. Notice that C has priority over B, even though C's perfection didn't occur until April 7; priority among filers is based on the order of filing and not the order of perfection.

If the facts in the above are changed so that the collateral in question is inventory, C is first, B is second, and A is last, because there is no 20-day rule for inventory, and A's perfection did not occur as of the date of attachment. In this case, the order of filing is used for all. Similarly, even if the collateral is equipment, if A filed on April 22, they would be last, since they filed more than 20 days after the debtor acquired the collateral.

Creditor Responsibilities

A secured creditor has certain responsibilities to the debtor in connection with the security agreement. They must:
- Use reasonable care to preserve any collateral in their possession.
- Confirm the unpaid amount of the debt when requested by the debtor.
- File or send the debtor a termination statement, releasing the collateral once the debt has been repaid.

Procedures on Default of the Debtor

When a debtor fails to meet its obligations, it is in default and the secured creditor has a claim to the property that was used as security for the obligation. The creditor may obtain a general judgment against the debtor without foreclosing upon the property. Otherwise, the creditor will foreclose on the property, which is a legal means by which the lender attempts to recover amounts owed. The debtor's **right of redemption** is terminated, and the creditor repossesses the property and forces a sale.

Before the creditor may repossess and sell property pledged as collateral, the debtor's right of redemption must be terminated. The debtor's right of redemption allows the debtor to repay the loan, along with any penalties that may have arisen due to missed payments, and any costs incurred by the creditor.

If the debtor fails to redeem the property, the creditor will take possession of the property and force its sale in either a public or a private sale. When there is more than one creditor, the creditor with the highest priority has the right to repossess the property.

Upon sale, the proceeds will first be used to *pay any reasonable expenses* associated with the sale. Excess proceeds will be applied against the claim of the secured creditor with the highest priority.

If the proceeds are not sufficient:
- If the loan is "without recourse," the lender has no further claim against the debtor.
- If the loan is "with recourse," the debtor will be personally responsible for any unpaid portion, referred to as a **deficiency judgment**.

If the proceeds exceed the claims of the secured creditor with the highest priority:
- Any excess is first applied to the claims of other secured creditors, beginning with the secured creditor with the highest priority, followed by those with lower priorities.
- The debtor will be entitled to any remaining proceeds.

Some jurisdictions allow for "strict foreclosure." In a strict foreclosure, the creditor brings a suit against the debtor and, upon being successful, a court order is issued to the debtor to satisfy the obligation within a specific period of time. If the obligation is not paid off, the creditor obtains title to the property and has no obligation to sell it. If a court order is not obtained and the creditor decides to keep the property:
- The creditor must provide notice to the debtor and all other secured creditors.
- An objection within 21 days will require the creditor to sell the property.

In the case of consumer goods, a creditor may not retain the property and is required to dispose of it within **90 days** if the debtor has paid **at least 60%** of the obligation.

Lecture 19.04

CLASS QUESTIONS

Please see the Class Questions and Class Solutions for this Lecture at the end of this Section.

CLASS QUESTIONS

Work through the below Class Questions while following along with the respective lectures. Once this is complete, you can begin independently practicing what you've learned by quizzing yourself on this course section in your Interactive Practice Questions (IPQ), which can be found in your online Student Dashboard. Your IPQ simulates the computer-based testing experience, and will also help you understand how concepts are applied to the exam. Each question includes answer explanations from expert CPAs that will help you determine why you answered a question correctly or incorrectly. This is key to your success on the CPA Exam.

Lecture 19.04

1. Under the Revised UCC Secured Transaction Article, which of the following events will always prevent a security interest from attaching?

    a. Failure to have a written security agreement.
    b. Failure of the creditor to have possession of the collateral.
    c. Failure of the debtor to have rights in the collateral.
    d. Failure of the creditor to give present consideration for the security interest.

2. Under the Secured Transaction Article of the UCC, which of the following statements is (are) correct regarding the filing of a financing statement?

    I. A financing statement must be filed before attachment of the security interest can occur.
    II. Once filed, a financing statement is effective for an indefinite period of time provided continuation statements are timely filed.

    a. I only.
    b. II only.
    c. Both I and II.
    d. Neither I nor II.

3. Grey Corp. sells computers to the public. Grey sold and delivered a computer to West on credit. West executed and delivered to Grey a promissory note for the purchase price and a security agreement covering the computer. West purchased the computer for personal use. Grey did not file a financing statement. Is Grey's security interest perfected?

    a. Yes, because Grey retained ownership of the computer.
    b. Yes, because it was perfected at the time of attachment.
    c. No, because the computer was a consumer good.
    d. No, because Grey failed to file a financing statement.

4. Mars, Inc. manufactures and sells DVRs on credit directly to wholesalers, retailers, and consumers. Mars can perfect its security interest in the DVRs it sells without having to file a financing statement or take possession of the DVRs if the sale is made to

    a. Retailers.
    b. Wholesalers that sell to distributors for resale.
    c. Consumers.
    d. Wholesalers that sell to buyers in the ordinary course of business.

5. On June 15, Harper purchased equipment for $100,000 from Imperial Corp. for use in its manufacturing process. Harper paid for the equipment with funds borrowed from Eastern Bank. Harper gave Eastern a security agreement and financing statement covering Harper's existing and after-acquired equipment. On June 21, Harper was petitioned involuntarily into bankruptcy under Chapter 7 of the Federal Bankruptcy Code. A bankruptcy trustee was appointed. On June 23, Eastern filed the financing statement. Which of the parties will have a superior security interest in the equipment?

   a. The trustee in bankruptcy, because the filing of the financing statement after the commencement of the bankruptcy case would be deemed a preferential transfer.
   b. The trustee in bankruptcy, because the trustee became a lien creditor before Eastern perfected its security interest.
   c. Eastern, because it had a perfected purchase money security interest without having to file a financing statement.
   d. Eastern, because it perfected its security interest within the permissible time limits.

6. Under the Secured Transactions Article of the UCC, for which of the following types of collateral must a financing statement be filed in order to perfect a purchase money security interest?

   a. Stock certificates
   b. Promissory notes
   c. Personal jewelry
   d. Inventory

7. Under the Revised Secured Transaction Article of the UCC, what would be the order of priority for the following security interests in consumer goods?

   I. Financing statement filed on April 1.
   II. Possession of the collateral by a creditor on April 10.
   III. Financing statement perfected on April 15.

   a. I, II, III.
   b. II, I, III.
   c. II, III, I.
   d. III, II, I.

CLASS SOLUTIONS

1. (c) For a security interest to attach, the debtor must have rights to the property; the creditor must have an interest in the property, which may be in the form of a signed security agreement or possession; and the creditor must have given value. If the debtor does not have rights to the property, a secured interest cannot attach. Answer (a) is incorrect because a written security agreement is not required if the creditor takes possession of the property. Answer (b) is incorrect because possession of the property is not required if the creditor obtains a signed security agreement. Answer (d) is incorrect because value given by the creditor may be present or past consideration. If, for example, a debtor defaults on an unsecured loan, the creditor may take a secured interest in property of the debtor in lieu of some other action.

2. (b) A financing statement is one means of perfecting a security interest while attachment requires debtor rights to the property, a creditor's interest in the property, and the giving of value by the creditor. Once perfected by filing a financing statement, perfection remains in effect for a period of 5 years. The period may be extended indefinitely by the filing of continuation statements by the creditor.

3. (b) Since Grey sells computers to the public and West purchased it for personal use, the computer is consumer goods. Since West's promissory note was executed for the purchase, Grey has a purchase money security interest (PMSI) in consumer goods. A PMSI in consumer goods is perfected automatically when the security interest attaches. Attachment has occurred because the debtor has rights to the property, the debtor has an interest in the property, and the debtor has given value. Grey has a security interest in the computer, but did not retain ownership. Filing a financing statement is not required to perfect a PMSI in consumer goods.

4. (c) A purchase money security interest (PMSI) in consumer goods is perfected automatically upon attachment without the filing of a financing statement and without taking possession of the goods. Goods sold to retailers and wholesalers are not considered consumer goods.

5. (d) A purchase money security interest (PMSI) in goods that are not consumer goods, such as equipment to be used by a manufacturer, is perfected either by the filing of a financing statement or by taking possession of the property. When perfected by filing a financing statement, it is perfected retroactively to the date of attachment when it is filed within 20 days. Since Eastern has a PMSI in nonconsumer goods and has filed a financing statement within 20 days of attachment, Eastern's interest is perfected as of the date of the sale, June 15. Since this is before the petition in bankruptcy, filed on June 21, Eastern's claim will have priority. Answer (a) is incorrect because the filing of a financing statement is not a preferential transfer, which would be a transfer that puts a creditor into a more favorable position than they would be under the bankruptcy proceedings. Answer (b) is incorrect because although the trustee did become a lien creditor before Eastern filed its financing statement, it was not before Eastern's interest was perfected, which occurred upon attachment. Answer (c) is incorrect because only if the PMSI had been in consumer goods could it have been perfected with neither the filing of a financing statement or taking possession.

6. (d) A purchase money security interest (PMSI) in nonconsumer goods, such as inventory, may be perfected either by the filing of a financing statement or by taking possession of the property. Answer (a) is incorrect because a security interest in stock certificates and promissory notes can only be perfected by taking possession. Answer (b) is incorrect because a security interest in stock certificates and promissory notes can only be perfected by taking possession. Answer (c) is incorrect because personal jewelry is a consumer good and perfection can be achieved automatically since they are a PMSI in consumer goods.

7. (a) Perfected security interests take priority on the basis of when they were perfected. Although these are consumer goods, the interests are not indicated as purchase money security interests and, as a result, perfection requires either the filing of a financing statement or taking possession of the property. Interest I was perfected first by the filing of a financing statement on April 1. Interest II was perfected second by taking possession of the property on April 10. Interest III was perfected last with the filing of a financing statement on April 15.

TASK-BASED SIMULATIONS

Task-Based Simulation 1

The Uniform
CPA Examination

Unsplit   Split Horiz   Split Vertical   Authoritative   Spreadsheet   Calculator   Submit Testlet
                                           Literature

| Work Tab | Resources | Help |

Required:

On January 2, 20X4, Ruiz Interiors Corp., a retailer of sofas, contracted with Alexes Furniture Co. to purchase 150 sofas for its inventory. The purchase price was $250,000. Ruiz paid $50,000 cash and gave Alexes a note and security agreement for the balance. On March 1, 20X4, the sofas were delivered. On March 10, 20X4, Alexes filed a financing statement.

On February 1, 20X4, Ruiz negotiated a $1,000,000 line of credit with Cecilia Bank, pledged its present and future inventory as security, and gave Cecilia a security agreement. On February 20, 20X4, Ruiz borrowed $100,000 from the line of credit. On March 5, 20X4, Cecilia filed a financing statement.

On April 1, 20X4, Guillermo, a consumer purchaser in the ordinary course of business, purchased a sofa from Ruiz. Guillermo was aware of both security interests.

Items to be answered:

Items 1 through 6 refer to the above fact pattern. For each item, determine whether **A**, **B**, or **C** is correct.

    1. Alexes's security interest in the sofas attached on

        A. January 2, 20X4.

        B. March 1, 20X4.

        C. March 10, 20X4.

    2. Alexes's security interest in the sofas was perfected on

        A. January 2, 20X4.

        B. March 1, 20X4.

        C. March 10, 20X4.

    3. Cecilia's security interest in Ruiz's inventory attached on

        A. February 1, 20X4.

        B. March 1, 20X4.

        C. March 5, 20X4.

4. Cecilia's security interest in Ruiz's inventory was perfected on

    A. February 1, 20X4.

    B. February 20, 20X4.

    C. March 5, 20X4.

5.   A. Alexes's security interest has priority because it was a purchase money security interest.

    B. Cecilia's security interest has priority because Cecilia's financing statement was filed before Alexes's.

    C. Cecilia's security interest has priority because Cecilia's interest attached before Alexes's.

6.   A. Guillermo purchased the sofa subject to Alexes's security interest.

    B. Guillermo purchased the sofa subject to both the Alexes and Cecilia security interests.

    C. Guillermo purchased the sofa free of either the Alexes or Cecilia security interests.

TASK-BASED SIMULATION SOLUTIONS

Task-Based Simulation Solution 1

1. (B) A security interest attaches when the debtor has an interest in the property, the creditor obtains an interest in the property, and the creditor has given value. Since the sofas were delivered on March 1, Ruiz, the debtor, obtained an interest in the property on that date and Alexes' security interest would attach.

2. (C) A purchase money security interest (PMSI) in nonconsumer goods must be perfected by either the filing of a financing statement or taking possession of the goods. Since Alexes filed a financing statement on March 10, its security interest would be perfected on that date. If the sofas had been consumer goods, filing of the financing statement within 20 days of attachment would have made it retroactive, but that is not the case with inventory. The sofas, however, are inventory, not consumer goods, to Ruiz.

3. (A) A security interest attaches when the debtor has an interest in the property, the creditor obtains an interest in the property, and the creditor has given value. Cecilia obtained an interest in Ruiz's inventory on February 1 when it received a security agreement. Ruiz already had an interest in the inventory, although it did not include the sofas, and gave value in the form of making the credit available on February 1, which is when Cecilia's security interest in the inventory attached.

4. (C) Cecilia's security interest in Ruiz's inventory was perfected upon the filing of a financing statement on March 5.

5. (B) When there are multiple creditors with security interests in the property of a debtor, perfected security interests have priority over those that are not perfected. Those that are perfected are given priority in the order perfected, followed by those who are not perfected, in the order of attachment. Since both Alexes and Cecilia had perfected security interests, Cecilia's would have priority because it was perfected on March 5, before Alexes' was on March 10.

6. (C) A purchaser of consumer goods from someone who is in the business of selling those goods takes them free of any security interest, perfected or not, even if the purchaser is aware of them.

Section 20 – Bankruptcy

Corresponding Lectures

Watch the following course lectures with this section:

Lecture 20.01 – Chapter 7 Bankruptcy
Lecture 20.02 – Chapter 7 Bankruptcy – Class Questions
Lecture 20.03 – Avoiding Powers of Trustee
Lecture 20.04 – Distribution of Assets Among Creditors
Lecture 20.05 – Chapter 11 and Chapter 13
Lecture 20.06 – Bankruptcy – Class Questions

EXAM NOTE: *Please refer to the AICPA REG Blueprint in the Introduction to find a listing of the representative tasks (and their associated skill levels—i.e., Remembering and Understanding, Application, and Analysis) that the candidate should be able to perform based on the knowledge obtained in this section.*

Bankruptcy

BANKRUPTCY

Legal process whereby the debtor is relieved of his debts, and the debtor's creditors are given satisfaction in the fairest way possible. In general, any debts that are forgiven, in bankruptcy or otherwise, result in taxable income to the debtor. This is not the case, however, when the debtor is insolvent, which would be the case when the debtor's liabilities exceed the fair value of the debtor's assets, including retirement assets.

Chapters of Federal Bankruptcy Code

- **Chapter 7 (Title 7) – Liquidation** – The assets of the debtor are turned over to a trustee, who sells them and tries to satisfy creditor claims, with remaining claims discharged.
- **Chapter 11 – Business Reorganization** – The debtor continues to operate the business while the creditors meet to restructure the debts. No trustee is usually involved.
- **Chapter 13 – Debt Adjustment Plan** – The debtor and a trustee work out a plan to restructure the debts without the involvement of the creditors. This is only available to individual debtors and small businesses.

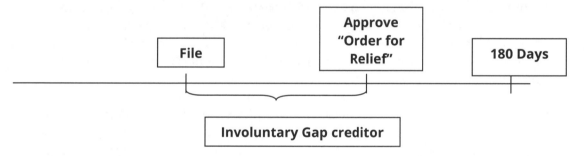

Petitions to Enter Bankruptcy

- **Voluntary – (7,11,13)**
  - The debtor files the petition for relief and the court enters immediate "order for relief" to stop individual collection efforts by creditors. Need **not be insolvent** in the "equity sense" (unable to pay debts as they come due) and spouses may file jointly to avoid duplicative fees.
  - Any person, partnership or corporation may file a voluntary bankruptcy petition. However, certain entities may **not** file a voluntary petition, such as insurance companies, savings and loans, banks, credit unions and railroads.
- **Involuntary – (7,11)**
  - The creditors are not being paid so they force the debtor into involuntary bankruptcy. A hearing is scheduled to determine if conditions have been satisfied. The courts appoint a temporary trustee. Within 20 – 40 days after the *order for relief*, a creditors meeting is held (Section 341 meeting) so the creditors can question the debtor about related issues, and the creditors can also vote to replace the trustee selected by the courts. The creditors have about 6 months to prove their claims by filing a "proof of claim" form.

- o   Certain entities may **not** be petitioned involuntarily into bankruptcy, such as farmers and nonprofit or charitable organizations.

   For an **Involuntary Bankruptcy:**
   - ▪ **12 or more creditors**
     - □ 3 signatures and unsecured claims of **$15,775** or more in the aggregate (amounts are cost adjusted every 3 years; last changed 4/16).
   - ▪ **Fewer than 12 creditors**
     - □ 1 signature and unsecured claims of **$15,775** or more in the aggregate.

   Note: If debtor **contests** the petition, just show debtor is not paying debts as they become due (cash flow approach to insolvency), and courts will approve the petition.

- • In both cases, an **"Automatic Stay"** becomes effective against most creditors of the debtor. This is to freeze the debtor's assets so the courts can take an accounting. Certain actions are exempt, like criminal proceedings, eviction proceedings, alimony and child support. Secured creditors' interests must be protected, or the courts will grant a relief from the automatic stay.

For example, assume a debtor has 4 debts outstanding, all unsecured, which they are unable to pay as they come due. Creditors A, B, and C are each owed $3,000, while Creditor D is owed $16,500. In this case, Creditor D can satisfy all of the requirements for filing without any cooperation from the others, since D is owed more than the required amount and there are fewer than 12 unsecured creditors. A joint filing by A, B, and C, on the other hand, would be dismissed, since the claims total only $9,000.

If, in addition to these claims, the debtor owed $100 each to 8 other unsecured creditors, then D couldn't file alone, since the 12 unsecured creditors in total require 3 signatures on the petition. D may, however, file jointly if any two other creditors join the petition (the sizes of their claims are irrelevant, since the minimum required claims of the filing creditors is satisfied by D's claim alone). Notice, though, that a joint filing by all 11 of the creditors other than D would still fail, since their claims total only $9,800.

Creditors who file against a debtor **without meeting the requirements** will have their petition dismissed by the court and may be liable to the debtor for **damages**, including:
- • Court costs
- • Compensatory damages
- • Punitive damages

When a petition is filed voluntarily by a debtor, the court automatically enters an **order of relief**, which stops all creditors from pursuing claims directly and begins the orderly procedures of the bankruptcy. When a petition is filed involuntarily by the creditors, a court hearing date must be set before the petition is effective, so the order of relief occurs later. The time period between the filing of the petition and the order of relief is known as the **involuntary gap**, since it only arises in an involuntary bankruptcy.

The acceptance of a bankruptcy petition and order of relief does not terminate security interests that were perfected before the petition date, nor judicial or statutory liens created earlier. Nevertheless, the stay against collection efforts applies to all claims, including these. Creditors with perfected security interests or liens must prove these to the bankruptcy court in order to enforce their claims against the collateral.

After the bankruptcy petition is filed, the debtor must submit a list of creditors, a schedule of assets & liabilities, income & expenditures, copies of tax returns, payroll stubs, a list of amounts in a QTIP and educational IRA, and a certificate from the credit counseling agency.

Once a Chapter 7 bankruptcy petition is approved by the court, a trustee is appointed to take control of the debtor's property. The trustee will obtain all the **non-exempt** interests of the debtor as of the **filing date** of the bankruptcy petition. The debtor's exemptions will depend on whether the debtor has elected to take the federal or the state exemptions applicable to their specific state. Testing has been extremely light on exemptions as they can be state-related and the CPA exam is a uniform national exam, but there are a few useful **Exemption Rules** to keep in mind:
- Limited equity in a home ($23,675) (Homestead exemption)
- Limited equity in a motor vehicle ($3,775)
- The right to reasonable alimony and child support payments
- Household goods, furnishings, clothing, appliances, books not to exceed $600 per item
- Jewelry up to $1,600
- Books and Tools of trade ($2,375)
- Social security, veteran's, and disability benefits and unemployment compensation
- Payments from pension, profit-sharing and annuity plans, up to $1,283,025 in tax-exempt retirement accounts (IRAs).
- Educational IRAs (529 plans) exempt, unless deposited between 120 and 365 days prior to filing, then exempt only up to $6,425.

The trustee will also maintain control over the earnings generated from non-exempt property, and the proceeds from sale. In general, the trustee does not have a claim on property the debtor becomes entitled to receive after the date of filing of the petition, but exceptions are made if the debtor gains the right to receive property **within 180 days** from:
- Inheritances
- Life insurance proceeds
- Divorce property settlements

The calculation is based on the date the debtor gains the right, not the date the property is actually received. **For example**, if a debtor files for bankruptcy on January 1, the debtor's father dies on June 1, and the debtor receives the proceeds from a life insurance policy on the father's life on August 1, these proceeds will be added to the bankruptcy estate. The right to receive the life insurance arose on the June 1 date of death, within 180 days of the petition date.

A trustee must determine how to deal with the **outstanding contracts** of the debtor at the time of the petition. The trustee has **three options** with respect to each contract:
- **Assume** the contract and perform the duties on behalf of the bankruptcy estate.
- **Assume** the contract and assign the benefits to a third party in exchange for a payment to the estate.
- **Reject (breach)** the contract.

The trustee should select the approach that is most beneficial to the estate. If the trustee does not assume the contract within *60 days* of the order of relief, it will be automatically rejected.

A trustee may employ court-approved professionals, such as accountants and attorneys, to handle estate matters which require professional expertise.

Lecture 20.02

CLASS QUESTIONS

Please see the Class Questions and Class Solutions for this Lecture at the end of this Section.

Lecture 20.03

AVOIDING POWERS OF TRUSTEE

The trustee is given the power to maximize the property included in the debtor's estate. There are certain transfers the trustee can avoid or set aside to maximize the corpus available to the creditors. (**FLAP**)

- **F**raudulent transfers by the debtor within *2 years* of the filing of the petition.
- **L**iens by statute (not liens that were effective before the bankruptcy petition was filed).
- **A**fter filing the petition, a transfer was made by the debtor.
- **P**referential transfer of property: (**I-WAIT**)
  - o Debtor was **I**nsolvent when the transfer was made.
  - o **W**ithin 90 days of the filing of the petition.
  - o For an **A**ntecedent debt (pre-existing debt); new value is ok.
  - o **I**mproves the creditors position (creditor gets more money than would have gotten in bankruptcy).
  - o **T**ime is increased from 90 days to 1 year for an insider (officer or close relative of Debtor.)
    - ▪ **Not preferential transfers (C-CONAC)**
      - □ **C**harity
      - □ **C**onsumer debt <$675
      - □ **O**rdinary course of business (current utility bill, lease payment)
      - □ **N**ew Value
      - □ **A**limony and child support
      - □ **C**ontinuation of installment payments

Fraudulent transfers refer to transfers made **within 2 years** before the filing of the petition that were made with the intent to hinder, delay, or defraud creditors; or a transfer made to prevent creditors from gaining access to property that would have been included in the bankruptcy estate, when the transfer was secret, or the debtor retained possession or beneficial rights in the property after its conveyance to a third party.

Statutory **liens** include claims by repair services against property that would allow them to keep the asset under normal circumstances, but which would deny other creditors a fair share of the property's value for bankruptcy distribution purposes. A trustee may set aside statutory liens that become effective when the bankruptcy petition is filed, but may not set aside those that were effective before the bankruptcy petition was filed.

Transfers made **after the filing** of the petition can be avoided because the ownership of the debtor's property was supposed to transfer to the trustee-in-bankruptcy as of the filing date.

Preferential transfers are the most common that may be avoided by a trustee. These refer to excessive payments made to one creditor at the expense of the others.

An **insider** refers to a creditor with a special relationship to the debtor that would enable them to know about the debtor's insolvency before others found out about it.

An **antecedent debt** refers to a debt created previously, and excludes from preferential transfers payments in exchange for value received at the same time and charitable contributions.

An **insolvent** debtor, according to federal bankruptcy law, is one whose liabilities exceed their assets (balance sheet approach to insolvency). The debtor is presumed to be insolvent in the 90 days prior to the date of the petition.

Payments on perfected secured debts are not preferential transfers, since the creditor is only receiving amounts that would have been paid in the bankruptcy from the collateral. Also, there are other priority claims that are paid before ordinary claims, and payments to these priority creditors are not preferential if there were enough assets in the bankruptcy estate to pay these claims. Priority claims are discussed in another module.

While making a payment on a secured loan is not a voidable preference, it **is** deemed a preferential transfer if a debtor gives a creditor a security interest on a debt that was previously unsecured. A PMSI is not a voidable preference if it is perfected within 30 days after the debtor receives possession of the collateral.

For example, if the debtor takes out a loan in 20X1, giving the creditor a mortgage on the debtor's personal residence at the same time, subsequent payments on the loan are not preferential. If, however, a loan is taken out in 20X1, but the debtor does not give the creditor a mortgage on their home until 20X3, the granting of the mortgage may be considered a preferential transfer. In the former case, an exchange of value occurred at the same time. In the latter case, the debtor is providing the creditor with collateral they didn't previously have on an antecedent debt (since the loan was made two years before the collateral was offered)

DISTRIBUTION OF ASSETS AMONG CREDITORS

Amounts get paid out 1 level at a time. If run out of money, give that one level a proportionate share of the cash available.

Order of Distribution of assets among creditors

- **Secured** creditors
    - o **Fully** secured – The collateral is worth the amount of the debt or more. Any excess is returned to the trustee.
    - o **Partially** secured – The collateral is worth less than the debt. The creditor gets the collateral, but is a general/unsecured creditor for the remainder.

- **Priority** claims (**STOP-IT – Drunk driver**)
    - o **S**upport and Alimony payments.
    - o **T**rustee, attorney, accountant, and administrative expenses.
    - o **O**wed after petition date in involuntary gap between filing and approval date (involuntary gap creditor).
    - o **P**ayroll (90 days) and Employee benefit plans (180 days) up to $12,850 per employee. Farmers and Fishermen up to $6,325.
    - o **I**ndividual Consumer deposits up to $2,850.
    - o **T**ax claims arising within 3 years of the petition.
    - o **Drunk Driver** injury claims.

- **General/unsecured creditors**
    - o This includes all remaining non-priority timely filed claims or claims exceeding amounts above (employees/consumers). If any assets are remaining after paying the general creditors, they go to the debtor.

Creditors submit their claims to the court in a Chapter 7 bankruptcy, and available assets are used to satisfy these claims as best as possible. Payments are **not**, however, equal to each creditor. Certain creditors have special priority over the others.

The highest priority for distribution is secured creditors up to the value of their collateral, as long as their interests were perfected prior to the filing of the bankruptcy petition. Secured creditors with claims that can be **fully satisfied** out of the value of the collateral are paid in full. **Partially secured creditors** with claims that exceed the value of their collateral will be paid the collateral amount, with the remaining amounts treated as non-priority claims.

The distribution of free assets (those not subject to security interests) follows a strict order of priority (**Priority Claims**). The major categories are paid in the following order:
1. **S**upport and Alimony payments
2. **T**rustee expenses – Administrative costs incurred by the trustee, Attorneys, Accountants (including their own compensation).
3. **O**wed after filing date – In an involuntary bankruptcy, creditors with claims arising after the petition date but prior to the order of relief are given special priority to make it possible for a debtor to do business while challenging an involuntary petition.

---

4. **P**ayroll costs up to $12,850 – Claims by employees for payroll and related benefits costs within 180 days have priority up to a dollar limit. Remaining amounts are non-priority claims. Grain *Farmers and Fishermen* up to $6,325 against a debtor who operates a grain storage facility.
5. **I**ndividual consumer deposits up to $2,850 – Claims by customers of the debtor on consumer goods not delivered. Business deposits are not entitled to priority, and consumer deposits exceeding the limit are non-priority claims.
6. **T**ax claims – Within 3 years. Taxes on which the statute of limitations has expired are not included.
7. **Drunk Driver** injury claims - Claims for death or personal injury arising from the operation of a motor vehicle or vessel by the debtor while he was legally intoxicated.

The order of priority must be memorized for the exam. Notice that the first letter of each claim spells **STOP-IT Drunk Driver**, and this mnemonic may be helpful in remembering the list.

After all priority claims have been paid, *non-priority claims* are considered. These will include:
- Secured claims to the extent they exceeded the value of collateral.
- Payroll and benefits exceeding $12,850.
- Consumer deposits exceeding $2,850.
- All other **General Unsecured** claims filed on a timely basis.

Creditors who fail to notify the bankruptcy court on a timely basis of their claims will be paid after all other creditors.

At some point in the distribution process, it is likely that the estate will not have sufficient funds to pay remaining claims. At the level where this occurs, all claims will be paid an equal percentage of the amount owed. Claims at lower levels will receive nothing in such cases.

For example, assume that $14,000 was available to pay the following claims outstanding in a bankruptcy:

Trustee expenses	$10,000
Wages owed to Pat Day	$3,000
Wages owed to Nat Night	$2,000
Tax claims	$5,000
Electric bill owed to power company	$1,000

After paying the highest priority trustee expenses of $10,000, only $4,000 remains to pay the next applicable priority, payroll owed to Pat and Nat totaling $5,000. There is enough to pay $4,000 / $5,000 = 80% of these claims, so Pat Day receives $3,000 × 80% = $2,400 and Nat Night receives $2,000 × 80% = $1,600. The lower priority claim for taxes and the non-priority electric bill are not paid.

Exceptions versus Denial of Discharge

Exceptions (Debtor doesn't owe anyone EXCEPT these people)

Assuming a general discharge is granted, a debtor may still not be discharged from certain specific types of debts, including:
- **A**limony or child support (maintenance)

- *Credit Card* purchases for luxury goods of $675 or more within 90 days of filing and *cash advances* of $950 or more within 70 days of filing. *Auto loans* within 3 years of filing.
- **S**tudent loans - During the period that payments are not yet owed.
- **L**oans obtained by fraud or false representations.
- **U**nscheduled/unlisted debt- Amounts owed which the debtor fails to list on the schedule of debts they must submit to the court.
- **T**ax claims within 3 years of the filing of the petition - The same debts qualifying as priority claims in distribution of assets.
    - Other items (**STD**)
        - Any debt from a securities law violation under the **S**arbanes-Oxley Act
        - Debts incurred to pay **T**axes
        - **D**runk Driver injuries or death judgments

Denial (Debtor is denied and owes EVERYONE)

In general, unpaid claims in a Chapter 7 liquidation are discharged by the bankruptcy court at the end of the case. There are certain cases in which discharge is denied, however:
- Inadequate books and records / Intentionally destroys records
- Refusing to explain a loss of assets (why missing)
- Bankruptcy offense
    - Withholding records
    - Refusing to obey a court order
- Being discharged *within 8 years*. 8 years must elapse before another discharge can be granted.
- Fraudulent transfer of property within 1 year of filing with the intent to hinder, delay or defraud creditors (concealing property).
- Debtor must be an individual.
    - A Corporation or Partnership doesn't receive a discharge under Chapter 7; instead, the entity is dissolved. Once all assets have been fully used, the case is closed. Only an individual can receive a discharge under Chapter 7.

Generally, court judgments against the debtor resulting from breach of contract and torts (negligence) may be discharged, but judgments resulting from criminal action are not.

Once discharge has occurred, a debt generally cannot be reinstated. The discharge on a debt may be revoked within one year of discharge, however, if a creditor can prove that the debtor committed fraud to conceal assets or otherwise reduce payments in the bankruptcy case.

A debtor's attempt to **reaffirm a discharged debt** after it has been discharged will not be valid. A debtor may reaffirm a debt prior to discharge, but:
- Reaffirmation must take place before the discharge is granted and be approved by the bankruptcy court.
- The debtor must be informed by the court of the consequences of reaffirming the debt.
- The debtor has 60 days to rescind the reaffirmation.

Even in these circumstances, the court may prevent the action if it feels it imposes an undue hardship on the debtor.

Chapter 11 – Reorganization Plan

The debtor and creditors formulate a plan under which the debtor repays a portion of the debts owed and the remainder is discharged. Not available to banks, savings and loans, insurance companies, and stockbrokers. Chapter 11 is typically for corporations or partnerships. Individuals, especially those whose debts exceed the limits of Chapter 13, may file Chapter 11.

- Voluntary or Involuntary (if involuntary, must meet the same requirements as Chapter 7).
- Creditors committee of unsecured creditors.
- Usually no trustee, but the debtor remains in control of the company and submits a plan for reorganization to each class of creditors.
  - Requires approval by 2/3 of the dollar ($) amount of all claims and ½ the number of claims in that class.
- Courts need to confirm the plan, but will not unless it provides payment for:
  - Trustee expenses
  - Owed to Involuntary Gap creditors
  - Payroll and employee benefits
  - Consumer advances

Under Chapter 11 (Business Reorganizations), a committee of creditors is formed. Only unsecured creditors may be included. The debtor will continue to operate the business and be advised by the committee.

Creditors (and shareholders for a corporate debtor) with similar types of claims will then form smaller committees to develop a plan of reorganization. In each creditor committee, creditors making up a majority of the total number of creditors and 2/3 of the total amount owed must approve the plan. In the shareholder committee, shareholders owning at least 2/3 of the stock must approve the plan.

After approval by the creditors and shareholders, the plan is submitted to the court, but the court may confirm a plan it deems fair, **even if some committees do not approve it**. Once the court has confirmed it, the plan is approved and requires no confirmation from the committees. The purpose of Chapter 11 is to restructure a business's finances so that it may continue to operate.

Chapter 13 – Debt Adjustment Plan

Enables a debtor who is an individual with regular income to formulate and perform a plan for the repayment of creditors over an extended period. The benefit is that the debtor gets to retain non-exempt property.

- Voluntary only.
- A trustee is appointed by the courts.
- The courts confirm or deny the plan without approval of unsecured creditors.

In a Chapter 13 (Debt Adjustment Plan) bankruptcy case, the debtor submits a repayment plan to a trustee appointed by the court. The plan must involve repayment of at least as much of the debts as would have been repaid under Chapter 7 liquidation, and may or may not involve discharge of some of the unpaid debts. The trustee may approve extensions of the due dates for loan payments for up to 3 years without court permission, or 5 years with it. The benefit of Chapter 13 is that it allows the debtor to retain their property, even that which is nonexempt.

Creditors do not participate in the administration of the case and, as mentioned earlier, cannot even file the petition to begin Chapter 13 proceedings. Chapter 13 is typically for individuals who have regular income, owe less than $394,725 of unsecured debts and less than $1,184,200 of secured debts.

Chapter 9 – Municipalities

Chapter 9 provides a procedure so that a municipality that has encountered financial difficulty and is insolvent may work with its creditors to adjust its debts. This provision is reserved for municipalities only.

Chapter 12 – Family Farmers and Fishermen

Family Farmers and Fishermen may qualify for a specialized form of bankruptcy. Family farmers can take advantage of this simplified reorganization. Modeled after Chapter 13, Chapter 12 allows the debtor to retain all property and pay creditors out of future income. However, farmers can still file using Chapters 7, 11 or 13 as well.

Chapter 15 – Cross-Border Insolvency Cases

Created by the Bankruptcy Abuse Prevention and Consumer Protection Act of 2005, Chapter 15 deals with *cross-border insolvency cases.*
- Meant to make bankruptcy proceedings across international borders more functional.
  - Favors and promotes cooperation and communication with both foreign courts and foreign representatives.

The Bankruptcy Abuse Prevention & Consumer Protection Act of 2005

This act contains many provisions that make it more difficult for an individual or a business to file for bankruptcy. When debtors consist of individuals or married couples with debt that is primarily consumer debt, the court could convert a Chapter 7 case to a Chapter 11 or Chapter 13 case, or could dismiss the petition entirely, if the courts feel that granting relief under Chapter 7 would constitute abuse. A *"means test"* has been established to determine whether *abuse* has occurred.

A debtor will first complete a median income test in which the debtor's current monthly income, excluding Social Security benefits, is compared to the median income in the debtor's state. If the debtor's income is lower than the median amount, there is no presumption of abuse and the debtor is not required to complete the means test.

The financial **"means test"** that reduces or completely eliminates the debts that would be discharged under Chapter 7 for high-income bankruptcy petitioners, is the most significant provision of the rules. If *income minus allowable living expenses* exceeds certain levels, a Chapter 7 filing will be dismissed or, with the debtor's permission, converted to a Chapter 13 filing.

Monthly Income – Living Expenses = **Net Disposable Monthly Income**
- Living Expenses include food, clothing, housing, utilities, transportation, personal care, entertainment, health and disability insurance, primary and secondary education costs, child support & alimony, for example.

- Adjusted income under this formula is multiplied by 60 to give what is called disposable income (DI). If DI is less than $7,770, the Chapter 7 filing will be allowed as no presumption of abuse exists (less than $124 of net monthly income).
- If DI is less than $12,850, a determination will be made as to whether DI is sufficient to pay at least 25% of the debtor's unsecured debt. If not, the Chapter 7 filing will be allowed as there is no assumption of abuse.
  - **For example**, if net monthly income = $150 × 60 months = $9,000. If total debt was less than $36,000, the Chapter 7 petition would be disallowed because the means test was passed. If the debt was ≥ $36,000, the Chapter 7 filing would be allowed.
- If DI is sufficient to pay at least 25% of the debtor's unsecured debt, or if the amount exceeds $12,850, the Chapter 7 filing will be disallowed as abuse is assumed (cannot go bankrupt).

The debtor may **rebut the presumption of *abuse*** by showing special circumstances (e.g., serious illness or call to active military duty) that create additional expenses or a need to adjust current monthly income. To rebut the presumption, the additional expenses and/or income adjustments must place the current monthly income after expenses below the dollar amounts that trigger the presumption.

The time allowed between Chapter 7 or 11 discharges is **eight years**. Furthermore, a Chapter 13 discharge is given to any debtor who received a discharge in a Chapter 7, 11, or 12 case within the preceding four years, or in another Chapter 13 case within the preceding two years.

An individual debtor is prohibited from filing a bankruptcy petition under Chapter 7 or 11 until the debtor receives a briefing from an approved nonprofit budget and credit counseling service. The briefing must be within 180 days of filing the bankruptcy petition.

Under the federal fair debt collection practices act, it is illegal for a debt collector to attempt to communicate with a debtor who is currently being represented by an attorney. This is to help minimize the harassment that was occurring by debt collectors.

Lecture 20.06

CLASS QUESTIONS

Please see the Class Questions and Class Solutions for this Lecture at the end of this Section.

CLASS QUESTIONS

Work through the below Class Questions while following along with the respective lectures. Once this is complete, you can begin independently practicing what you've learned by quizzing yourself on this course section in your Interactive Practice Questions (IPQ), which can be found in your online Student Dashboard. Your IPQ simulates the computer-based testing experience, and will also help you understand how concepts are applied to the exam. Each question includes answer explanations from expert CPAs that will help you determine why you answered a question correctly or incorrectly. This is key to your success on the CPA Exam.

Lecture 20.02

1. Which of the following statements is correct concerning the voluntary filing of a petition in bankruptcy?

   a. If the debtor has twelve or more creditors, the unsecured claims must total at least $15,775.
   b. The debtor must be insolvent.
   c. If the debtor has less than twelve creditors, the unsecured claims must total at least $15,775.
   d. The petition may be filed jointly by spouses.

2. Which of the following conditions, if any, must a debtor meet to file a voluntary bankruptcy petition under Chapter 7 of the Federal Bankruptcy Code?

	Insolvency	**Three or more creditors**
a.	Yes	Yes
b.	Yes	No
c.	No	Yes
d.	No	No

Lecture 20.06

3. Under the federal bankruptcy code, which of the following rights or powers does a trustee in bankruptcy not have?

   a. The power to prevail against a creditor with an unperfected security interest.
   b. The power to require persons holding the debtor's property at the time the bankruptcy petition is filed to deliver the property to the trustee.
   c. The right to use any grounds available to the debtor to obtain the return of the debtor's property.
   d. The right to avoid any statutory liens against the debtor's property that were effective before the bankruptcy petition was filed.

Items 4 through 8 are based on the following:

Dart Inc., a closely held corporation, was petitioned involuntarily into bankruptcy under the liquidation provisions of Chapter 7 of the Federal Bankruptcy Code. Dart contested the petition.

Dart has not been paying its business debts as they became due, has defaulted on its mortgage loan payments, and owes back taxes to the IRS. The total cash value of Dart's bankruptcy estate after the sale of all assets and payment of administration expenses is $100,000.

Dart has the following creditors:
- Fracon Bank is owed $75,000 principal and accrued interest on a mortgage loan secured by Dart's real property. The property was valued at and sold, in bankruptcy, for $70,000.
- The IRS has a $12,000 recorded judgment for unpaid corporate income tax.
- JOG Office Supplies has an unsecured claim of $500 that was timely filed.
- Nanstar Electric Co. has an unsecured claim of $1,200 that was not timely filed.
- Decoy Publications has a claim of $16,500, of which $2,000 is secured by Dart's inventory that was valued and sold, in bankruptcy, for $2,000. The claim was timely filed.

4. Which of the following statements would correctly describe the result of Dart's opposing the petition?

    a. Dart will win because the petition should have been filed under Chapter 11.
    b. Dart will win because there are **not** more than 12 creditors.
    c. Dart will lose because it is **not** paying its debts as they become due.
    d. Dart will lose because of its debt to the IRS.

5. Which of the following events will follow the filing of the Chapter 7 involuntary petition?

	A trustee will be appointed	**A stay against creditor collection proceedings will go into effect**
a.	Yes	Yes
b.	Yes	No
c.	No	Yes
d.	No	No

For **items 6 through 8,** assume that the bankruptcy estate was distributed.

6. What dollar amount would Nanstar Electric Co. receive?

    a. $0
    b. $800
    c. $1,000
    d. $1,200

7. What total dollar amount would Fracon Bank receive on its secured and unsecured claims?

    a. $70,000
    b. $72,000
    c. $74,000
    d. $75,000

8. What dollar amount would the IRS receive?

    a. $0
    b. $8,000
    c. $10,000
    d. $12,000

9. Hall CPA, is an unsecured creditor of Tree Co. for $18,000. Tree has a total of 10 creditors, all of whom are unsecured. Tree has not paid any of the creditors for 3 months. Under Chapter 11 of the federal bankruptcy code, which of the following statements is correct?

    a. Hall and two other unsecured creditors must join in the involuntary petition in bankruptcy.
    b. Hall may file an involuntary petition in bankruptcy against Tree.
    c. Tree may not be petitioned involuntarily into bankruptcy under the provisions of Chapter 11.
    d. Tree may not be petitioned involuntarily into bankruptcy because there are less than 12 unsecured creditors.

CLASS SOLUTIONS

1. (d) A voluntary petition in bankruptcy may be filed jointly by spouses, provided the filing is not considered an abuse. Insolvency and thresholds for minimum amounts of unsecured debt apply to involuntary petitions.

2. (d) A voluntary petition in bankruptcy may be filed by any debtor, whether solvent or not and regardless of the number of creditors or amounts of unsecured debt apply, provided it is not considered an abuse.

3. (d) Statutory liens against a debtor's property are comparable to perfected security interests. Those that were perfected prior to the filing of the bankruptcy petition would have priority to the property over the bankruptcy estate and the trustee will not be able to avoid them. Answer (a) is incorrect because an unperfected security interest has a lower priority than perfected security interests in the property, lien creditors, and a trustee in bankruptcy. Answers (b) and (c) are incorrect because the trustee has the right to take possession of the bankrupt's property for purposes of administering the bankruptcy estate and may use whatever means that are available to the debtor to obtain it and may demand that those in possession deliver it to the trustee.

4. (c) A debtor may be involuntarily petitioned into bankruptcy if, in general, the debtor is not making debt payments as they come due. Answer (a) is incorrect because the petition may be filed under either Chapter 7 or Chapter 11. Answer (b) is incorrect because a debtor is not required to have more than 12 creditors to be involuntarily petitioned into bankruptcy, but the number of debtors required to sign the petition is reduced from 3 to 1. Answer (d) is incorrect because there is no special exception to the bankruptcy rules due to a debt to the IRS.

5. (a) Once a valid petition in bankruptcy has been filed, a trustee will be appointed to administer the estate. In addition, a stay against creditor collection procedures will go into effect. Since bankruptcy law determines the amount each creditor will be entitled to, collection procedures become irrelevant.

6. (a) Unsecured creditors who do not file their claims on a timely basis, such as Nanstar, are the lowest priority in bankruptcy. Since the estate has only $100,000 and the total debts are $105,200 ($75,000 + $12,000 + $500 + $1,200 + $16,500), there will not be enough to pay Nanstar anything.

7. (c) Fracon Bank will receive $70,000, the amount received from the sale of the property on which the Bank had a secured interest. The remaining $5,000 of the Bank's claim is an unsecured debt. In addition to the $70,000, the IRS will receive the $12,000 owed as a priority claim, and Decoy will receive $2,000, which represents the secured portion of its claim. Unsecured claims that were filed timely will share in the next distribution. The amount remaining is $16,000 ($100,000 - $70,000 - $12,000 - $2,000), and unsecured claims that were filed timely include Fracon's remaining $5,000, JOG's unsecured claim of $500, and Decoy's remainder of $14,500, or $20,000 in total. Since the remainder represents 80% of the unsecured claims ($16,000/$20,000), each unsecured creditor will receive 80% of their claim. Thus, Fracon will receive an additional $4,000 (80% × $5,000) for a total of $74,000.

8. (d) Amounts owed to the IRS for taxes are considered priority claims and are paid after secured claims are settled. The secured claims include $70,000 of Fracon Bank's claim and $2,000 of Decoy's claim for a total of $72,000. This leaves $28,000 ($100,000 - $72,000) with which to pay remaining claims. Since the amount owed to the IRS is $12,000, it will be paid in full.

9. (b) A debtor may be involuntarily petitioned into bankruptcy if they are unable to pay their debts as they come due. If the debtor has 12 or more unsecured creditors, the petition requires the signature of at least 3. If the debtor has fewer than 12, however, only one signature is required so long as unsecured claims are greater than $15,775. Thus, Hall can file the involuntary petition alone, since his $18,000 claim is greater than the $15,775 required threshold.

TASK-BASED SIMULATIONS

Task-Based Simulation 1

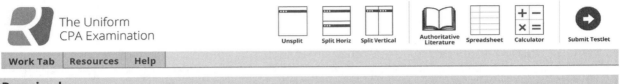

Required:

This question consists of 15 items. Select the best answer for each item.

On April 15, 20X2, Vivi Corp., an appliance wholesaler, was petitioned involuntarily into bankruptcy under the liquidation provisions of Chapter 7 of the Federal Bankruptcy Code.

When the petition was filed, Vivi's creditors included:

Secured creditors	Amount owed
Fifth Bank — 1st mortgage on warehouse owned by Vivi	$50,000
Hart Manufacturing Corp. — perfected purchase money security interest in inventory	30,000
TVN Computers, Inc. — perfected security interest in office computers	15,000

Unsecured creditors	Amount owed
IRS — 20X0 federal income taxes	$20,000
Acme Office Cleaners — services for January, February, and March 20X2	750
Ted Smith (employee) — February and March 20X2 wages	13,000
Joan Sims (employee) — March 20X2 commissions	1,500
Power Electric Co. — electricity charges for January, February, and March 20X2	600
Soft Office Supplies — supplies purchased in 20X1	2,000

The following transactions occurred before the bankruptcy petition was filed:
- On December 31, 20X1, Vivi paid off a $5,000 loan from Mary Lake, the sister of one of Vivi's directors.
- On January 30, 20X2, Vivi donated $2,000 to Universal Charities.
- On February 1, 20X2, Vivi gave Young Finance Co. a security agreement covering Vivi's office fixtures to secure a loan previously made by Young.
- On March 1, 20X2, Vivi made the final $1,000 monthly payment to Integral Appliance Corp. on a two-year note.
- On April 1, 20X2, Vivi purchased from Safety Co., a new burglar alarm system for its factory, for $5,000 cash.

All of Vivi's assets were liquidated. The warehouse was sold for $75,000, the computers were sold for $12,000, and the inventory was sold for $25,000. After paying the bankruptcy administration expenses of $8,000, secured creditors, and priority general creditors, there was enough cash to pay each non-priority general creditor 50 cents on the dollar.

Items to be answered:

a. Items 1 through 5 represent the transactions that occurred before the filing of the bankruptcy petition. For each transaction, determine if the transaction would be set aside as a preferential transfer by the bankruptcy court. Answer Y if the transaction would be set aside or N if the transaction would not be set aside.

1.	Payment to Mary Lake
2.	Donation to Universal Charities
3.	Security agreement to Young Finance Co.
4.	Payment to Integral Appliance Corp.
5.	Purchase from Safety Co.

Items to be answered:

b. Items 6 through 10 represent creditor claims against the bankruptcy estate. Select from List I each creditor's order of payment in relation to the other creditors named in items 6 through 10.

		List I
6.	Bankruptcy administration expense	A. First
7.	Acme Office Cleaners	B. Second
8.	Fifth Bank	C. Third
9.	IRS	D. Fourth
10.	Joan Sims	E. Fifth

Items to be answered:

c. Items 11 through 15 also represent creditor claims against the bankruptcy estate. For each of the creditors listed in Items 11 through 15, select from List II the amount that creditor will receive.

		List II	
11.	TVN Computers, Inc.	A.	$0
12.	Hart Manufacturing Corp.	B.	$300
13.	Ted Smith	C.	$600
14.	Power Electric Co.	D.	$1,000
15.	Soft Office Supplies	E.	$1,200
		F.	$2,400
		G.	$4,925
		H.	$12,850
		I.	$12,925
		J.	$13,500
		K.	$15,000
		L.	$25,000
		M.	$27,500
		N.	$30,000

Task-Based Simulation 2

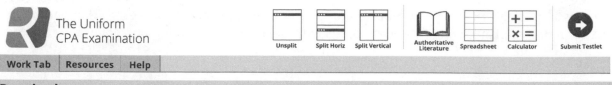

| Work Tab | Resources | Help |

Required:

On May 1, 20X1, Able Corp. was petitioned involuntarily into bankruptcy under the provisions of Chapter 7 of the Federal Bankruptcy Code.

When the petition was filed, Able had the following unsecured creditors:

Creditor	Amount owed
Cole	$18,000
Lake	2,000
Young	1,500
Thorn	1,000

The following transactions occurred before the bankruptcy petition was filed:
- On February 15, 20X1, Able paid Vista Bank the $1,000 balance due on an unsecured business loan.
- On February 28, 20X1, Able paid $1,000 to Owen, an officer of Able, who had lent Able money.
- On March 1, 20X1, Able bought a computer for use in its business from Core Computer Co. for $2,000 cash.

Items to be answered:

Items 1 through 3 refer to the bankruptcy filing. For each item, determine whether the statement is True or False.

	True	False
1. Able can file a voluntary petition for bankruptcy if it is solvent.	○	○
2. Lake, Young, and Thorn can file a valid involuntary petition.	○	○
3. Cole alone can file a valid involuntary petition.	○	○

Items 4 through 6 refer to the transactions that occurred before the filing of the involuntary bankruptcy petition. Assuming the bankruptcy petition was validly filed, for each item determine whether the statement is True or False.

	True	False
4. The payment to Vista Bank would be set aside as a preferential transfer.	○	○
5. The payment to Owen would be set aside as a preferential transfer.	○	○
6. The purchase from Core Computer Co. would be set aside as a preferential transfer.	○	○

TASK-BASED SIMULATION SOLUTIONS

Task-Based Simulation Solution 1

1. (Y)   A preferential transfer is one made when the debtor was insolvent, made within 90 days of the filing of the petition, made for an antecedent debt, and which improves the creditor's position in the distribution of assets. If the recipient is an insider, however, it is a preferential transfer if made within 1 year of the filing of the petition. Mary Lake is the sister of one of Vivi's directors, making her an insider and, since the payment was made within 1 year of the filing, it would be a preferential transfer.

2. (N)   A preferential transfer is one made when the debtor was insolvent, made within 90 days of the filing of the petition, made for an antecedent debt, and which improves the creditor's position in the distribution of assets. Contributions to charitable organizations are not considered preferential transfers.

3. (Y)   A preferential transfer is one made when the debtor was insolvent, made within 90 days of the filing of the petition, made for an antecedent debt, and which improves the creditor's position in the distribution of assets. Giving Young a security interest in the office furniture converts Young from an unsecured creditor to a secured creditor, improving Young's position in the distribution of the bankruptcy estate. Since it was done within 90 days of the filing of the petition, it is a preferential transfer.

4. (N)   A debtor is permitted to continue making payments on an installment loan as they come due. The payments would not be considered preferential transfers.

5. (N)   A payment for new value is not considered a preferential transfer. Since the alarm system provides new value, it is not a preferential transfer.

6. (B)   The first claims to be paid are those of secured creditors, which will be paid from the proceeds from the sale of the security. Any deficiency is treated as an unsecured claim. Priority claims will be paid next, with support and alimony first, followed by trustee expenses, post-petition claims, salaries, consumer deposits, taxes, and drunk driver injury claims. Next, unsecured creditors who filed on a timely basis will be paid and, if there are any funds remaining, unsecured creditors who did not file on a timely basis will receive the remainder. In this case, Fifth Bank will be paid first, as a secured creditor, bankruptcy administrative expenses second as the highest priority claim, Joan Simmons third as an employee, the IRS fourth for taxes, and Acme office cleaners fifth as an unsecured creditor.

7. (E)   The first claims to be paid are those of secured creditors, which will be paid from the proceeds from the sale of the security. Any deficiency is treated as an unsecured claim. Priority claims will be paid next, with support and alimony first, followed by trustee expenses, post-petition claims, salaries, consumer deposits, taxes, and drunk driver injury claims. Next, unsecured creditors who filed on a timely basis will be paid and, if there are any funds remaining, unsecured creditors who did not file on a timely basis will receive the remainder. In this case, Fifth Bank will be paid first, as a secured creditor, bankruptcy administrative expenses second as the highest priority claim, Joan Simmons third as an employee, the IRS fourth for taxes, and Acme office cleaners fifth as an unsecured creditor.

8. (A) The first claims to be paid are those of secured creditors, which will be paid from the proceeds from the sale of the security. Any deficiency is treated as an unsecured claim. Priority claims will be paid next, with support and alimony first, followed by trustee expenses, post-petition claims, salaries, consumer deposits, taxes, and drunk driver injury claims. Next, unsecured creditors who filed on a timely basis will be paid and, if there are any funds remaining, unsecured creditors who did not file on a timely basis will receive the remainder. In this case, Fifth Bank will be paid first, as a secured creditor, bankruptcy administrative expenses second as the highest priority claim, Joan Simmons third as an employee, the IRS fourth for taxes, and Acme office cleaners fifth as an unsecured creditor.

9. (D) The first claims to be paid are those of secured creditors, which will be paid from the proceeds from the sale of the security. Any deficiency is treated as an unsecured claim. Priority claims will be paid next, with support and alimony first, followed by trustee expenses, post-petition claims, salaries, consumer deposits, taxes, and drunk driver injury claims. Next, unsecured creditors who filed on a timely basis will be paid and, if there are any funds remaining, unsecured creditors who did not file on a timely basis will receive the remainder. In this case, Fifth Bank will be paid first, as a secured creditor, bankruptcy administrative expenses second as the highest priority claim, Joan Simmons third as an employee, the IRS fourth for taxes, and Acme office cleaners fifth as an unsecured creditor.

10. (C) The first claims to be paid are those of secured creditors, which will be paid from the proceeds from the sale of the security. Any deficiency is treated as an unsecured claim. Priority claims will be paid next, with support and alimony first, followed by trustee expenses, post-petition claims, salaries, consumer deposits, taxes, and drunk driver injury claims. Next, unsecured creditors who filed on a timely basis will be paid and, if there are any funds remaining, unsecured creditors who did not file on a timely basis will receive the remainder. In this case, Fifth Bank will be paid first, as a secured creditor, bankruptcy administrative expenses second as the highest priority claim, Joan Simmons third as an employee, the IRS fourth for taxes, and Acme office cleaners fifth as an unsecured creditor.

11. (J) Since TVN has a secured interest in the computers, the $12,000 in proceeds will go to TVN. The remaining $3,000 is unsecured and TVN will receive 50 cents on the dollar, or $1,500, for a total of $13,500.

12. (M) Hart has a secured interest in the inventory and will receive the proceeds of $25,000. The remaining $5,000 is unsecured and Hart will receive 50 cents on the dollar, or $2,500, for a total of $27,500.

13. (I) Ted Smith is an employee and his claim is a priority claim. There is a limit of $12,850, however, resulting in an unsecured claim of the difference of $150. Smith will receive the priority amount of $12,850 plus 50 cents on the dollar for the remainder, or $75, for a total of $12,925.

14. (B) Power Electric is an unsecured creditor and will receive 50 cents on the dollar, for a total of $300.

15. (D) Soft Office Supplies is an unsecured creditor and will receive 50 cents on the dollar, for a total of $1,000.

Task-Based Simulation Solution 2

Items 1 through 3

		True	False
1.	Able can file a voluntary petition for bankruptcy if it is solvent.	●	○
2.	Lake, Young, and Thorn can file a valid involuntary petition.	○	●
3.	Cole alone can file a valid involuntary petition.	●	○

Explanation of solutions

1. (T) A debtor may file a voluntary petition in bankruptcy, provided it is not considered an abuse. There is no requirement that the debtor be insolvent, although there are income limitations that may prevent the voluntary petition.

2. (F) When there are fewer than 12 creditors, it only requires 1 creditor to involuntarily petition a debtor into bankruptcy. The debt represented by those filing the petition, however, must equal at least $15,775 of unsecured debt at the time of the petition. Since the amount owed to Lake, Young, and Thorn totals only $4,500, it is not sufficient.

3. (T) When there are fewer than 12 creditors, it only requires 1 creditor to involuntarily petition a debtor into bankruptcy. The debt represented by those filing the petition, however, must equal at least $15,775 of unsecured debt at the time of the petition. Since the amount owed to Cole is $18,000, it is sufficient.

Items 4 through 6

	True	False
4. The payment to Vista Bank would be set aside as a preferential transfer.	●	○
5. The payment to Owen would be set aside as a preferential transfer.	●	○
6. The purchase from Core Computer Co. would be set aside as a preferential transfer.	○	●

Explanation of solutions

4. (T) A preferential transfer is one made within 90 days of the filing of the petition, when the debtor was insolvent, is for an antecedent debt, and puts the creditor in a better position in the distribution of the estate. The payment to Vista Bank improves its position by putting the Bank, an unsecured creditor, before secured creditors and priority claims. Since it was made within 90 days of the filing, it would be a preferential transfer.

5. (T) A preferential transfer is one made within 90 days of the filing of the petition, or 1 year in the case of an insider; when the debtor was insolvent; for an antecedent debt; and puts the creditor in a better position in the distribution of the estate. The payment to Owen improves Owen's position by putting him, an unsecured creditor, before secured creditors and priority claims. Owen is an insider so, since it was made within 1 year of the filing, it would be a preferential transfer.

6. (F) A payment in exchange for new value is not considered a preferential transfer. Since the payment to Core was for a new computer, there is new value and it is not a preferential transfer.

Section 21 – Debtor & Creditor Relationships (Suretyship)

Corresponding Lectures

Watch the following course lectures with this section:

Lecture 21.01 – Suretyship
Lecture 21.02 – Suretyship – Class Questions

__EXAM NOTE:__ Please refer to the AICPA REG Blueprint in the Introduction to find a listing of the representative tasks (and their associated skill levels—i.e., Remembering and Understanding, Application, and Analysis) that the candidate should be able to perform based on the knowledge obtained in this section.

Debtor & Creditor Relationships (Suretyship)

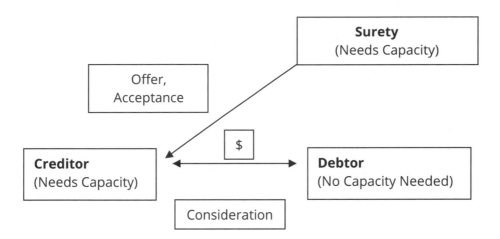

Lecture 21.01

SURETYSHIP

A suretyship is an arrangement in which a person agrees to be answerable to a creditor for a claim against another person. There are several possible varieties of agreements:

- **Primary** – When a person agrees to be a **surety accommodation party** or **cosigner**, the creditor is permitted to treat them as the debtor and demand payment without any proof of default by the principal debtor.
- **Secondary** – When a person agrees to be a **guarantor** or **endorser** of a check or negotiable instrument, the creditor may only demand payment if the principal debtor defaults on the agreement.
  - o In order to transfer a check or note, transferor may be required to obtain a surety (accommodation endorser) to guarantee payment.
  - o Official bonds, whereby a surety insures the performance of the issuer in compliance with laws and regulations.
- **Last Resort** – When a person agrees to be a **conditional surety** or **guarantor of collection**, the creditor may not demand payment from them until all available means of collection from the principal debtor are exhausted, including seizing collateral, obtaining court judgments, and filing a bankruptcy petition, as appropriate. This is a special form of secondary liability.

The behavior of the debtor is irrelevant in determining the liability of a surety (or equivalent). A **surety is obligated to pay** once the creditor has met the requirements for demanding payment, even if the debtor:

- Lacks the capacity to make contracts.
- Is discharged in bankruptcy from all debts.
- Used fraud to induce the surety to make their promise to the creditor.

The surety may assert defenses of incapacity or bankruptcy to limit liability, but may not assume the debtor's personal defenses.

Suretyships fall within the **statute of frauds** and require that the promise be in writing and signed by the surety. The creditor must provide consideration to bind the surety. Usually, this is done by obtaining the surety's promise at the time the debt is created, so that the loan itself is the consideration. If the surety is obtained later, the loan is **past consideration and cannot be used to bind.** In that case, the creditor may pay the surety for their promise, and the compensation to the surety serves as consideration.

A compensated surety (bonding company) is generally liable on the debt, unless the surety's risk of loss is increased due to a material change in the contract. An uncompensated surety (Gratuitous Surety) (e.g., co-signing a loan for your child) is relieved anytime the creditor makes a change to the agreement.

A surety has certain rights that may be exercised **upon a demand for payment** from the creditor without the surety actually having to pay. These include:
- **Offset** – The surety may offset amounts the creditor owes the surety against the amount the creditor is demanding.
- **Exoneration** – The surety may sue the principal debtor to compel them to make payment to the creditor.

If the surety makes payment to the creditor, the surety gains certain additional rights. These include:
- **Indemnification** – The surety has the right to demand reimbursement from the principal debtor for amounts paid to the creditor.
- **Subrogation** – The surety obtains all creditor claims against the debtor, including the right to **collateral pledged** by the debtor to the creditor to secure the loan.

Because the obligation of the surety is to the creditor, the creditor owes the surety a fiduciary duty to act in their best interests. A surety is released from their obligation if the creditor:
- Fails to disclose negative information the creditor has about the principal debtor.
- Makes any agreement with the debtor that increases the surety's risk of loss.
- Releases collateral that had secured the debt (this releases the surety for the value of the collateral).
- Extends the due date for repayment by the principal debtor (a compensated surety is not released unless the extension materially increases their risk).
- Refuses a tender of payment from the principal debtor.
- Releases the principal debtor from the obligation.

A special exception allows the creditor to release the debtor but **reserve rights against the surety**. In such cases, the surety still has the right to pursue the debtor for reimbursement, and is not harmed by the release, so the creditor is still entitled to seek collection from the surety. The creditor can reserve rights against the surety in connection with other actions as well.

Co-Sureties

A creditor may obtain more than one surety on a debt. When there are two or more cosureties, each is *jointly and severally liable* to the creditor, but a cosurety who pays has a **right of contribution** from the others.

For example, if Daryl Debtor borrows $10,000 from Chris Creditor, and Chris obtains written promises from Gary Guarantor and Eve Endorser on the full debt, a later default by Daryl when the remaining balance on the loan is $6,000 allows Chris to recover the entire $6,000 from either Gary or Eve. If Gary pays the entire $6,000, he has the right to obtain a contribution of $6,000 × 1/2 = $3,000 from Eve (the cosureties have the right to obtain full reimbursement from Daryl for amounts they each pay).

If cosureties have unequal limits on liability, they are expected to contribute in proportion to their limits. **For example**, if Gary agreed to be liable for the entire $10,000 debt, while Eve's agreement with Chris limited her obligation to $5,000, then Gary's relative responsibility is $10,000 / ($10,000 + $5,000) = 2/3 and Eve's is $5,000 / ($10,000 + $5,000) = 1/3. If Daryl defaults when the balance is $6,000, and Gary pays the entire amount to Chris, he can expect a contribution of $6,000 × 1/3 = $2,000 from Eve.

If the creditor releases a cosurety, that will release the other cosureties to the extent they lose the right of contribution from the released one. In the last example, a release by Chris of Eve's liability will reduce the amount Chris can obtain from Gary after the default from $6,000 to only $4,000, since Gary can no longer obtain Eve's 1/3 contribution as a result of the release. Once again, though, if Chris releases Eve but **reserves rights** against Gary, then the full $6,000 can be recovered, since Gary will be permitted to pursue a contribution from Eve.

The bankruptcy of a cosurety doesn't release the others, and they will be liable as if the bankrupt party had never been involved.

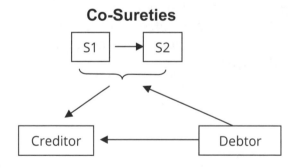

Co-Sureties

Creditors' Rights

When a debtor owes money, there are several options available to the debtor in order to satisfy the debt.

- **Composition of creditors** – An agreement in which creditors accept a proportionate amount as full settlement for their debts.
- **Assignment for the benefit of creditors** – The Debtor voluntarily transfers assets to the trustee for the benefit of creditors, but the debtor still owes the debt.
- **Writ of Attachment** – Prejudicial remedy in which a creditor is allowed to take possession of personal property of the debtor prior to getting a judgment for the past-due debt.
- **Garnishment** – Permits the creditor to seize property of the debtor that is being held by a third party.
  - Could include wages or money held in a bank account.
  - Federal social security benefits are exempt from garnishment.
- **Lien** – A claim against a debtor's property that must be satisfied before the property is available to satisfy the claims of other creditors.
  - **Consensual** – Mortgages or secured transactions
  - **Nonconsensual** – Judicial proceeding, mechanics' liens (real property – home), tax liens, artisans' liens (personal property – auto)
    - Must give notice before you sell the debtor's property.
- **Credit Card Fraud Act (CCFA)** – A credit card holder is protected from losses in excess of $50 due to unauthorized use of the holder's credit card.
- **Homestead exemption** – When going bankrupt, one can claim a certain amount of equity in one's home as exempt property; however, this doesn't prevent one from being liable if there is an IRS tax lien or a valid home mortgage lien.
- **Debt collectors** – The Fair Debt Collection Practices Act prohibits a debt collector from harassing the debtor. They are permitted to take reasonable measures to ascertain the debtor's location and collect the debt, and may commence a lawsuit to obtain collection. A debt collector may contact the debtor, but may not do so at inconvenient times and places or at the debtor's workplace if the employer objects. They must provide written notice of the amount and payee of the debt within 5 days of their first communication with the debtor, and must send verification of the validity of the debt if contested by the debtor. If the debtor is represented by an attorney, the debt collector may not communicate directly with the debtor, but must do so only through the attorney.

Lecture 21.02

CLASS QUESTIONS

Please see the Class Questions and Class Solutions for this Lecture at the end of this Section.

CLASS QUESTIONS

Work through the below Class Questions while following along with the respective lectures. Once this is complete, you can begin independently practicing what you've learned by quizzing yourself on this course section in your Interactive Practice Questions (IPQ), which can be found in your online Student Dashboard. Your IPQ simulates the computer-based testing experience, and will also help you understand how concepts are applied to the exam. Each question includes answer explanations from expert CPAs that will help you determine why you answered a question correctly or incorrectly. This is key to your success on the CPA Exam.

Lecture 21.02

1. Which of the following defenses would a surety be able to assert successfully to limit the surety's liability to a creditor?

   a. A discharge in bankruptcy of the principal debtor.
   b. A personal defense the principal debtor has against the creditor.
   c. The incapacity of the surety.
   d. The incapacity of the principal debtor.

2. Which of the following events will release a noncompensated surety from liability?

   a. Release of the principal debtor's obligation by the creditor but, with the reservation of the creditor's rights against the surety.
   b. Modification by the principal debtor and creditor of their contract that materially increases the surety's risk of loss.
   c. Filing of an involuntary petition in bankruptcy against the principal debtor.
   d. Insanity of the principal debtor at the time the contract was entered into with the creditor.

3. Which of the following rights does one cosurety generally have against another cosurety?

   a. Exoneration.
   b. Subrogation.
   c. Reimbursement.
   d. Contribution.

4. Teller, Kerr, and Ace are cosureties on a $120,000 loan with maximum liabilities of $20,000, $40,000 and $60,000 respectively. The debtor defaulted on the loan when the loan balance was $60,000. Ace paid the lender $48,000 in full settlement of all claims against Teller, Kerr and Ace. What amount may Ace collect from Kerr?

   a. $ 0
   b. $16,000
   c. $20,000
   d. $28,000

CLASS SOLUTIONS

1. (c) A surety has certain defenses that may be applied to minimize liability in the case of default by the primary debtor. These include defenses that the surety would be able to assert against one of its creditors, such as incapacity of the surety, which would be the case, for example, if the surety were a minor. Answer (a) is incorrect because a defense that would be available to the primary debtor, such as a discharge in bankruptcy of the primary debtor, is not available to the surety. Answer (b) is incorrect because a defense that would be available to the primary debtor, such as a personal defense of the primary debtor against the creditor, is not available to the surety. Answer (d) is incorrect because a defense that would be available to the primary debtor, such as the incapacity of the primary debtor, is not available to the surety.

2. (b) A surety's obligation cannot be increased without the surety's assent. As a result, a modification of the contract between the principal debtor and the creditor that materially increases the surety's risk of loss would release the surety. Answer (a) is incorrect because while the release of the principal debtor would ordinarily release the surety, if rights against the surety are reserved by the creditor, the surety will not be released. Answer (c) is incorrect because the surety cannot avoid liability by asserting defenses that are available to the primary debtor, such as the discharge in bankruptcy of the primary debtor. Answer (d) is incorrect because the surety cannot avoid liability by asserting defenses that are available to the primary debtor, such as the incapacity of the primary debtor, which would be the case if the primary debtor were insane at the time of entering into the contract.

3. (d) Cosureties share in losses that are incurred when a principal debtor defaults. The creditor, however, is not required to pursue all cosureties when there are more than one. As a result, when one cosurety pays a larger portion of the default than its proportionate share, the other cosureties would be required to contribute their proportionate shares. Answer (a) is incorrect because the right of exoneration enables a surety to require the principal debtor to make payment and is not a right asserted against cosureties. Answer (b) is incorrect because subrogation is the right of a surety to assert the rights of the creditor against the principal debtor, including taking possession of assets securing the obligation, upon satisfying the obligations of the principal debtor. It is not a right that is asserted against cosureties. Answer (c) is incorrect because the right of reimbursement is the right to be repaid by the principal debtor and is not a right that is asserted against cosureties.

4. (b) When cosureties are obligated for the same debts, they share losses in proportion to the amounts that they are guaranteeing. In this case, the total of the guarantees of the cosureties is $120,000 and Kerr's share is $40,000 of the $120,000, or 1/3. As a result, Kerr will be responsible for 1/3 of the total loss of $48,000, or $16,000.

Section 22 – REG Final Review

Corresponding Lecture

Watch the following course lecture with this section:

Lecture 22.01 – REG Final Review

Lecture 22.01

YOU FINISHED YOUR REG COURSE...NOW WHAT?

A quick guide to the final days leading up to, and following, the exam

I. FINAL REVIEW

Now is the time to make connections and solidify your understanding of the topics you found most challenging, and to review the most heavily tested topics on the exam.

❏ Reread your course notes and review bookmarked lectures.

❏ Review your Course Overview page in the Interactive Practice Questions (IPQ) software. Make sure to go through any unanswered questions and review any questions you have answered incorrectly or bookmarked for final review.

❏ A great way to gear up for the upcoming exam is by adding a Roger CPA Review Cram Course to your studies. The Cram Course works very well as a final review, as it is designed to reinforce your understanding of the most heavily tested CPA Exam topics.

❏ Take at least one full practice exam using the CPA Exam Simulator in your IPQ. This will help you hone your test-taking strategy, time management and self-discipline under exam-like conditions, while continuing to expose you to the material.

II. DAY OF THE EXAM

❏ Get a good night's rest before heading into your exam.

❏ Arrive to the Prometric testing center at least 60 minutes before your appointment so you have time to park, check-in, and use the restroom before your exam begins.

❏ Bring your Notice to Schedule (NTS) and two forms of acceptable identification (see Intro for more details).

❏ Proceed through check-in: store belongings, get fingerprinted, have photo taken, sign log book, get seated, write your Launch Code (from your NTS) on your noteboard.

❏ Don't stress. You've prepared for this; now, just breathe and power through!

III. DURING THE EXAM

❏ Remember your REG Exam time strategy, and jot down the times at which you want to be at your benchmarks:

   o   Allocate 75 seconds per multiple choice question
   o   Allocate 15-25 minutes per simulation, depending on complexity
   o   Plan to use no more than 10 minutes per research question
   o   Take the standard 15-minute break after the 3rd testlet – it does not count against your time
   o   (Remember that any other break will count against your time)

REG: 4 Hour Exam					
Testlet 1	**Testlet 2**	**Testlet 3**		**Testlet 4**	**Testlet 5**
38 MCQs	**38 MCQs**	**2 TBSs**	Break	**3 TBSs**	**3 TBSs**
48 min	**48 min**	**30 min**		**57 min**	**57 min**

❑ You will be given 10 minutes to review the welcome screens and exam instructions. You should already be familiar with these screens after taking the AICPA Sample Test, and can bypass them during your exam.

❑ Once you begin testing, make sure to read each question carefully, paying close attention to the keywords that dictate the question's intention (e.g., *except, is greater than, never, always*).

❑ Take note if your questions are getting more difficult. That's a good sign! A progressively harder exam indicates that you are performing well.

IV. AFTER THE EXAM

❑ Remember, it is normal to not feel great after you're done with your exam. It's a tough exam and designed to challenge your confidence and competencies.

❑ Relax and celebrate! You've earned it.

❑ Your scores will be released within a couple of weeks (see Intro for table).

❑ GOOD LUCK!!!

Section 23 – Document Review Simulations (DRS) Appendix

Corresponding Lectures

Watch the following course lecture with this section:

Lecture 23.01 – DRS Introduction

Document Review Simulations (DRS) Appendix

DOCUMENT REVIEW SIMULATIONS OVERVIEW

In July of 2016, the CPA Exam introduced a new type of Task-based simulation known as Document Review Simulations (DRS). These problems have been added to the AUD, FAR and REG exams, and were added to the BEC exam in conjunction with the overarching 2017 CPA Exam changes that went into effect April 1, 2017.

What is a DRS?

DRS are designed to simulate tasks that the candidate will be required to perform as a newly licensed CPA (based on up to two years' experience as a CPA). Each DRS presents a document that has a series of highlighted phrases or sentences that the candidate will need to determine are correct or incorrect. To help make these conclusions, numerous supporting documents, or resources, such as legal letters, phone transcripts, financial statements, trial balances and authoritative literature will be included. The candidate will need to sort through these documents to determine what is, and what is not important to solving the problem.

Why is this happening?

The AICPA conducted a Practice Analysis from 2014-2015 in which one main finding was clear: firms are expecting newly licensed CPAs on their staff to perform at a higher level—and they aren't. So the AICPA is raising the bar with a revamped CPA Exam that more authentically tests candidates on the tasks and skill level that will be required of them as newly licensed CPAs. The introduction of DRS in July of 2016 was the first step in this larger initiative, with the overarching changes following in 2017.

What will DRS be testing?

Up until recently, the CPA Exam has only tested candidates on the skill levels *Remembering & Understanding* and *Application* (skill levels based on Bloom's Taxonomy of Educational Objectives). To meet industry demands for the CPA Exam to test at a higher skill level, the CPA Exam is pivoting to test the higher order skills *Analysis* and *Evaluation* (Evaluation in AUD only). As a direct correlation to this exam evolution, DRS problems are designed to test these higher order skills by requiring candidates to actually analyze and evaluate documents they would see in the work force.

HOW A DRS WORKS

As shown below, the DRS will present several tabs:

- **Document Review**: The main document for the candidate to review
- **Exhibits/Resources/Financial Statements**: A series of supporting documents which may, or may not help candidates complete the problem
- **Help**: Explanation of how to answer the problem

Notice the highlighted items within the main document. These represent the specific sentences or phrases that the candidate is required to analyze.

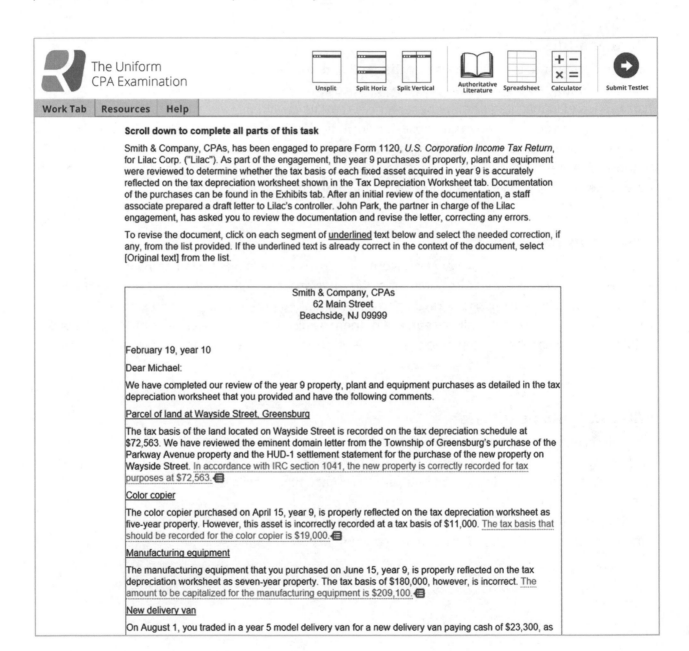

To address each item within the problem, click on the highlighted phrase to see answer options. Each item will include the option to leave original text, delete text, or edit the text using the provided edit choices.

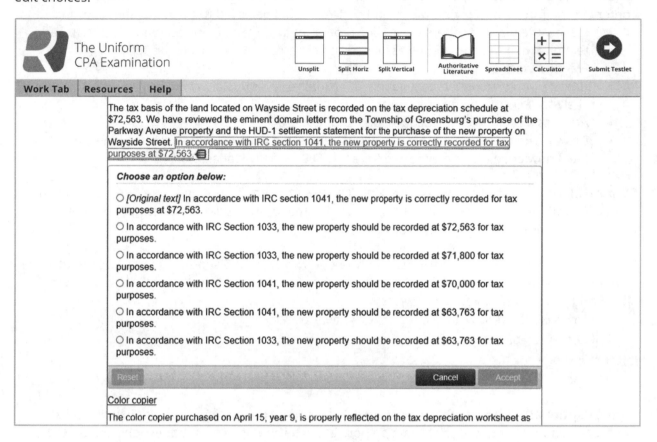

Once an item has been answered, a checkmark icon will appear next to the item in the document.

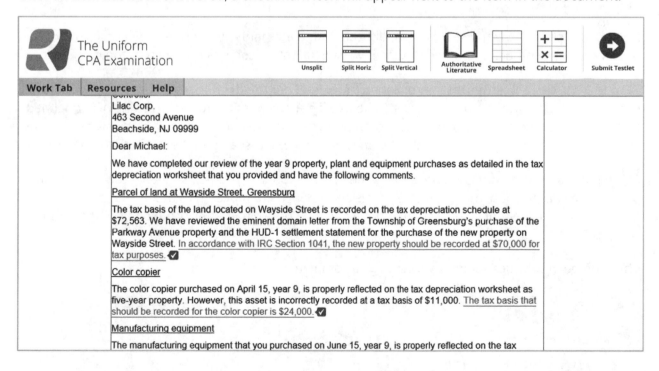

Approaching a REG DRS

Step 1 – Get the lay of the land. YOU are the CPA – what is being asked of you? Skim over all the content in the Document Review tab to find out. You could be asked to do any of the following:
- Review the work of others – use your professional judgment, professional skepticism, and technical expertise to identify issues or correct errors. ←Very likely for REG!
- Plan the work of others.
- Analyze and choose the best course of action from various alternatives presented. ←Very likely for REG tax-planning problems!
- Address a client's technical questions and requests.
- Draw on knowledge that is more extensively tested in a different exam section – detailed FAR knowledge may be expected for an AUD DRS, for instance.

Step 2 – Mentally note the gist of the DRS. "OK, this problem is about me, the CPA, reviewing the work of a staff member. Specifically, I must compare the tax depreciation worksheet he prepared and make sure it fits with the supporting evidence."

Step 3 – Note the DRS subquestions. Briefly note down each DRS subquestion on your scratch whiteboard – you bought a handheld whiteboard just for CPA Exam study, right? Use your own shorthand. For instance, you might write:
1. Tax basis, land, wayside st, replac for prkway ave?
2. Copier tax basis
3. Equipment
4. Van

Step 4 (Optional) – Choose an order of attack. Consider customizing the order in which you approach subquestions. It won't always be possible to tell, but if a few subquestions appear to be more time-consuming than others, consider moving them to the back of the queue. There probably aren't any bonus points for getting the most time-consuming subquestions right. Therefore, do the easiest ones first.

Here, subquestion 1 clearly seems more difficult than the others – it's wordier, references multiple documents right off the bat, and seems to involve involuntary conversions, a tricky topic.

Step 5 – Attack each subquestion one at a time. In either the default or custom order, work on each subquestion one at a time in order to be as efficient as possible to avoid getting overwhelmed. Remember that the necessary information for any one subquestion will almost certainly be contained across multiple documents. You may also need to research in the Authoritative Literature.

Try to focus strictly on one subquestion at a time, but if you find yourself spending too much time on any one subquestion, make a tactical decision to skip it and move on to the next one. You may even decide to leave that subquestion undone and only return to it after completing other TBSs in your TBS testlet.

Check off each subquestion on your list as you complete it.

Step 6 – Go through a process of elimination for each subquestion.

Each DRS subquestion is similar to a multiple-choice question. Process of elimination, therefore, is a great tactic to employ. You can first eliminate **documents** and then **answer choices**.

Read the subquestion and all its answer choices first. For instance, answering the subquestion with default text "The tax basis that should be recorded for the color copier is $19,000." is obviously about a copier. In the Resources tab, briefly skim over each document. Note any documents that clearly have no information about a copier, and **ignore them**. Then hone in on the documents that do appear relevant.

Next, as you focus on the relevant document(s), eliminate answer choices one by one. Here, we can immediately eliminate one answer choice because we know an item does not have be paid for in full to get depreciated:
- [Original text] The tax basis that should be recorded for the color copier is $19,000.
- The tax basis that should be recorded for the color copier is $24,000.
- The tax basis that should be recorded for the color copier is $32,407.
- The tax basis that should be recorded for the color copier is $35,000.
- ~~There should not be any amount reflected as tax basis subject to depreciation until the copier has been paid for in full.~~

The clear winner from the four remaining is "The tax basis that should be recorded for the color copier is $35,000." because that was the cost of the copier, in a simple transaction only complicated by an unusual financing arrangement which has no bearing on the depreciable base of the asset.

Follow this process of elimination for each subquestion, first eliminating documents, then answer choices. Even in cases where you're not sure there is a clear "winner" answer choice, you will at least have eliminated some clear losers and given yourself a fighting chance.

SAMPLE REG DRS
Document Review

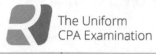 The Uniform CPA Examination

 Unsplit   Split Horiz   Split Vertical   Authoritative Literature   Spreadsheet   Calculator   Submit Testlet

| Work Tab | Resources | Help |

Scroll down to complete all parts of this task.

Smith & Company, CPAs, has been engaged to prepare Form 1120, *U.S. Corporation Income Tax Return*, for Lilac Corp. ("Lilac"). As part of the engagement, the year 9 purchases of property, plant and equipment were reviewed to determine whether the tax basis of each fixed asset acquired in year 9 is accurately reflected on the tax depreciation worksheet shown in the Tax Depreciation Worksheet tab. Documentation of the purchases can be found in the Exhibits/Resources tab. After an initial review of the documentation, a staff associate prepared a draft letter to Lilac's controller. John Park, the partner in charge of the Lilac engagement, has asked you to review the documentation and revise the letter, correcting any errors.

To revise the document, click on each segment of <u>underlined</u> text below and select the needed correction, if any, from the list provided. If the underlined text is already correct in the context of the document, select [Original text] from the list.

Smith & Company, CPAs
62 Main Street
Beachside, NJ 09999

February 19, year 10

Michael West
Controller
Lilac Corp.
463 Second Avenue
Beachside, NJ 09999

Dear Michael:

We have completed our review of the year 9 property, plant and equipment purchases as detailed in the tax depreciation worksheet that you provided and have the following comments.

<u>Parcel of land at Wayside Street, Greensburg</u>
The tax basis of the land located on Wayside Street is recorded on the tax depreciation schedule at $72,563. We have reviewed the eminent domain letter from the Township of Greensburg's purchase of the Parkway Avenue property and the HUD-1 settlement statement for the purchase of the new property on Wayside Street. 1.) <u>In accordance with IRC section 1041, the new property is correctly recorded for tax purposes at $72,563.</u>

<u>Color copier</u>
The color copier purchased on April 15, year 9, is properly reflected on the tax depreciation worksheet as five-year property. However, this asset is incorrectly recorded at a tax basis of $11,000. 2.) <u>The tax basis that should be recorded for the color copier is $19,000.</u>

Manufacturing equipment
The manufacturing equipment that you purchased on June 15, year 9, is properly reflected on the tax depreciation worksheet as seven-year property. The tax basis of $180,000, however, is incorrect.
3.) The amount to be capitalized for the manufacturing equipment is $209,100.

New delivery van
On August 1, you traded in a year 5 model delivery van for a new delivery van paying cash of $23,300, as indicated on the invoice from Beachside Car and Truck Sales. The year 9 delivery van tax basis reflected in the tax depreciation worksheet is $23,300.
4.) This tax basis is correct.

Please send a corrected copy of the tax depreciation worksheet to my attention once the revisions have been made.

Please contact us with any questions or concerns.

Sincerely,

John Park

John Park, CPA
Smith & Company, CPAs

Exhibits/Resources

Letter from Greensburg Government

Township of Greensburg
862 North Main Street
Greensburg, NJ 08999

April 1, year 9

Property Location: 462 Parkway Avenue

Lilac Corp.
463 Second Avenue
Beachside, NJ 09999

Dear Lilac Corp.:

As you know, it is necessary for the Township of Greenburg to construct a highway that requires the purchase of the property referred to above. Inasmuch as negotiations to purchase this property which stated on April 1, year 8, have not been successful to date, a final offer is hereby submitted to you. According to authorization by the Greensburg Transportation Commission, a total sum of $71,800 is offered for the required property rights, subject to clear title being delivered. Any compensation that may be due to you from this Department's Relocation Assistance Program is not included in this offer because such funds are paid to eligible persons separately.

If you choose to accept this offer, please contact Carmen North at (609) 555-1234 as soon as possible. If this offer is not accepted within fourteen (14) days from the date of delivery of this letter, it will be considered as having been rejected. We enclose herein a copy of the proposed instrument by which the property or property interest would be conveyed to the Township.

Sincerely,

_____

Right of Way Manager
Township of Greensburg

We decided to accept this offer from the Township of Greensburg for the vacant property located at 462 Parkway Avenue, Greenburg, NJ. Replacement vacant property was located on Wayside Street in Greenburg, NJ. Please note that we elected to capitalize the real estate taxes for tax purposes. We have attached the HUD-1 settlement statement showing the purchase of the Wayside Street land.

HUD-1 Settlement Statement

Buyer's and Seller's Combined Closing Statement

HUD-1 Settlement Statement

Beachside Title Corporation

Note: This form is furnished to give you a statement of actual settlement costs. Amount paid to and by the settlement agent are shown.

NAME OF BUYER: Lilac Corp.
ADDRESS OF BUYER: 463 Second Avenue, Beachside, NJ 09999

NAME OF SELLER: Specific Manufacturers, Inc.
ADDRESS OF SELLER: 243 Front Street, Greensburg, NJ 08999

PROPERTY LOCATION: 532 Wayside Street, Greenburg, NJ 08999

SETTLEMENT DATE: June 15, year 9

SUMMARY OF BUYER'S TRANSACTION		SUMMARY OF SELLER'S TRANSACTION	
100. GROSS AMOUNT DUE FROM BUYER		400. GROSS AMONT DUE TO SELLER	
101. Contract sales price	70,000.00	401. Contract sales price	70,000.00
102. Personal property		402. Personal property	
103.		403.	
Adjustment for items paid by seller in advance		Adjustment for items paid by seller in advance	
104. City/town taxes	2,563.00	404. City/town taxes	2,563.00
105. County taxes		405. County taxes	
106. Assessments		406. Assessments	
107.		407.	
120. **GROSS AMOUNT DUE FROM BUYER**	**72,563.00**	420. **GROSS AMOUN DUE TO SELLER**	**72,563.00**
200. AMOUNTS PAID BY OR IN BEHALF OF BUYER		500. REDUCTIONS IN AMOUNT DUE TO SELLER	
201. Deposit or earnest money	6,800.00	501. Excess deposit	
202. Principal amount of new loan		502. Settlement charges to seller	
203. Existing loan taken subject to		503. Existing loan taken subject to	
204.		504. Payoff of first mortgage loan	35,620.23
205.		505. Payoff of second mortgage loan	
206.		506.	
Adjustment for items unpaid by seller		Adjustment for items unpaid by seller	
207. City/town taxes		507. City/town taxes	
208. County taxes		508. County taxes	
209. Assessments		509. Assessments	
210.		510.	
220. TOTAL AMOUNTS PAID BY OR IN BEHALF OF BUYER	**6,800.00**	520. TOTAL REDUCTIONS IN AMOUNT DUE SELLER	**35,620.23**

Invoice for Purchase of Color Copier

Elmer Office Equipment   **Invoice 623**
8657 Maplewood Avenue   April 15, year 9
Elmer, NY 12354

Color copier	$32,407
Sales tax at 8%	2,593
Total billed	$35,000
Deposit due upon ordering	(11,000)
Amount financed by Elmer Office Finance USA	$24,000

Thank you for your business!

John - - - We decided to finance the purchase of the color copier over a two-year period with a promotional loan offered by Elmer Office Equipment. We paid an initial deposit of $11,000 and began making monthly principal payments of $1,000 on May 1, year 9.

Invoice for Purchase of Manufacturing Equipment

Uplift Company, LLC   Invoice 34089
32 Elmford Avenue   June 15, year 9
Smithville, WI 59999

Manufacturing machinery, including all parts and a limited five-year warranty	$180,000
Installment charge for machinery at 2305 Tenth Street, Beachside, NJ	4,300
Shipping costs (Smithville to Beachside)	9,200
Transit insurance	3,100
Extended two-year warranty	3,500
Subtotal	$200,100
Sales tax (5%) - charged on machinery only	9,000
Total billed	$209,100

THANK YOU FOR YOUR BUSINESS!

The manufacturing equipment was placed in service on July 1, year 9.

Invoice for Delivery Van Purchase

Beachside Car and Truck Sales, Inc.
123 Main Street
Beachside, NJ 09999

Purchase Agreement

This is a purchase agreement between Beachside Car and Truck Sales, Inc., and Lilac Corp. for the purchase of a year 9 delivery van on August 1, year 9.

Cost of delivery van	$30,400.00
Cost includes all accessories	
Destination charge	790.48
Less trade-in of year 5 delivery van	($9,000.00)
Subtotal	22,190.48
Sales tax at 5%	1,109.52
Total due	$23,300.00

_____

Seller

_____

Buyer

Payment received on August 1, year 9.
Lilac Corp. check number 25678

Tax Depreciation Worksheet

Lilac Corp.
Tax depreciation worksheet
(Year 9 Sec. 179 limitation $250,000)
For the year ended December 31, year 9

Description	Date placed in service	Method	Life	Property, Plant and Equipment - Tax Basis				Accumulated Tax Depreciation			
				Beginning Balance	Current year additions	Current year disposals	Ending Balance	Beginning Balance	Current year depreciation	Current year disposals	Ending balance
Buildings											
Manufacturing facility (2nd Ave., Beachside)	01/01/year 1	MACRS	39	1,500,000	-	-	1,500,000	306,135	38,460	-	344,595
Land											
Land (2nd Ave., Beachside)	01/01/year 1	N/A	N/A	75,000	-	-	75,000	-	-	-	-
Land (Parkway Avenue, Greensburg)	08/01/year 4	N/A	N/A	63,000	-	(63,000)	-	-	-	-	-
Land (Wayside Street, Greensburg)	06/15/year 9	N/A	N/A	-	72,563	-	72,563	-	-	-	-
Office furniture & equipment											
Office furniture	02/01/year 1	MACRS	7	4,083	-		4,083	4,083	-	-	4,083
Computers	02/01/year 1	MACRS	5	9,375	-		9,375	9,375	-	-	9,375
Color copier	04/15/year 9	MACRS	5	-	11,000		11,000	-	2,200	-	2,200
Manufacturing equipment											
Manufacturing equipment	01/01/year 1	MACRS	7	257,893	-		257,893	257,893	-	-	257,893
Manufacturing equipment	07/01/year 9	MACRS	7	-	180,000		180,000	-	25,722	-	25,722
Vehicles											
Year 5 delivery van	07/01/year 5	MACRS	5	18,125	-	(18,125)	-	14,993	1,044	(16,037)	-
Year 9 delivery van	08/01/year 9	MACRS	5	-	23,300	-	23,300	-	4,660	-	4,660
				1,927,476	286,863	(81,125)	2,133,214	592,479	72,086	(16,037)	648,528

Items for Analysis

In accordance with IRC section 1041, the new property is correctly recorded for tax purposes at $72,563.

1. Choose an option below:

   - [Original text] In accordance with IRC section 1041, the new property is correctly recorded for tax purposes at $72,563.

   - In accordance with IRC Section 1033, the new property should be recorded at $72,563 for tax purposes.

   - In accordance with IRC Section 1033, the new property should be recorded at $71,800 for tax purposes.

   - In accordance with IRC Section 1041, the new property should be recorded at $70,000 for tax purposes.

   - In accordance with IRC Section 1041, the new property should be recorded at $63,763 for tax purposes.

   - In accordance with IRC Section 1033, the new property should be recorded at $63,763 for tax purposes.

The tax basis that should be recorded for the color copier is $19,000.

2. Choose an option below:

   - [Original text] The tax basis that should be recorded for the color copier is $19,000.

   - The tax basis that should be recorded for the color copier is $24,000.

   - The tax basis that should be recorded for the color copier is $32,407.

   - The tax basis that should be recorded for the color copier is $35,000.

   - There should not be any amount reflected as tax basis subject to depreciation until the copier has been paid for in full.

The amount to be capitalized for the manufacturing equipment is $209,100.

3. Choose an option below:

   - [Original text] The amount to be capitalized for the manufacturing equipment is $209,100.

   - The amount to be capitalized for the manufacturing equipment is $205,600.

   - The amount to be capitalized for the manufacturing equipment is $202,500.

   - The amount to be capitalized for the manufacturing equipment is $201,300.

   - The amount to be capitalized for the manufacturing equipment is $193,300.

   - The amount to be capitalized for the manufacturing equipment is $189,000.

This tax basis is correct.

4.   Choose an option below:

- [Original text] This tax basis is correct.

- The delivery van should have a tax basis of $39,212.

- The delivery van should have a tax basis of $32,300.

- The delivery van should have a tax basis of $31,510.

- The delivery van should have a tax basis of $30,400.

- The delivery van should have a tax basis of $25,388.

Solution to DRS REG Simulation

The question is asking the candidate to review the draft letter prepared by a staff member and make corrections as necessary. The draft letter, which is addressed to the corporate tax engagement client, discusses the tax basis of several fixed assets as per the accompanying documents.

To approach this type of problem, the candidate will generally find it most appropriate to deal with each issue in the order in which it is presented.

1. The first underlined item states "In accordance with IRC section 1041, the new property is correctly recorded for tax purposes at $72,563." and, when clicked upon, the following choices appear:

    - [Original text] In accordance with IRC section 1041, the new property is correctly recorded for tax purposes at $72,563.
    - In accordance with IRC Section 1033, the new property should be recorded at $72,563 for tax purposes.
    - In accordance with IRC Section 1033, the new property should be recorded at $71,800 for tax purposes.
    - In accordance with IRC Section 1041, the new property should be recorded at $70,000 for tax purposes.
    - In accordance with IRC Section 1041, the new property should be recorded at $63,763 for tax purposes.
    - In accordance with IRC Section 1033, the new property should be recorded at $63,763 for tax purposes.

We can easily eliminate half the answer choices by first determining which IRC section is applicable.

The subquestion concerns a parcel of land at Wayside Street, Greensburg. The draft letter refers to an eminent domain document, indicating an **involuntary conversion** occurred. Searching on this term in the Authoritative Literature provided does not bring you immediately to either Section 1033 or 1041, but clicking **Next Match** several times **within** the first search result does yield a link to Section 1033.

Section 1033 is clearly the applicable section—it is all about involuntary conversions. That means we can ignore the Section 1041 answer choices.

Upon reviewing Section 1033 and the documents provided, it becomes clear that the correct answer choice is:
  - ***In accordance with IRC Section 1033, the new property should be recorded at $63,763 for tax purposes.***

Here is why:

  - The realized gain on the involuntary conversion is $8,800 [$71,800 proceeds (per letter from city) $63,000 adjusted basis of land given up (per depreciation schedule)].

  - The $8,800 gain is recognized only to the extent the $71,800 cash proceeds are not "reinvested" in like-kind replacement property. Although the contract price of the replacement property is only $70,000 (per HUD settlement statement), the company has elected under § 266 to capitalize the normally expensed real estate taxes (per memo). Therefore, the cost of the replacement property is considered to be $72,563 ($70,000 + $2,563), which exceeds the proceeds of $71,800 received. As a result, **no** gain is recognized.

- However, since the gain is postponed, a basis adjustment is required for the replacement property. To determine the basis of the new property, its cost is reduced by any gain **not** recognized. Therefore, the correct cost of the replacement land is **$63,763** ($72,563 - $8,800).

> **Conversions described in Section 1033(b)(1)(B)(2):**
> In the case of property purchased by the taxpayer in a transaction described in subsection (a)(2) which resulted in the nonrecognition of any part of the gain realized as the result of a compulsory or involuntary conversion, **the basis shall be the cost of such property decreased in the amount of the gain not so recognized;** and if the property purchased consists of more than 1 piece of property, the basis determined under this sentence shall be allocated to the purchased properties in proportion to their respective costs.

Section 1041, by the way, is irrelevant as it concerns property transfers between spouses or incident to divorce.

2. The next subquestion concerns the tax basis of a color copier purchased during the year. The default answer is "The tax basis that should be recorded for the color copier is $19,000." The choices are:

- [Original text] The tax basis that should be recorded for the color copier is $19,000.
- The tax basis that should be recorded for the color copier is $24,000.
- The tax basis that should be recorded for the color copier is $32,407.
- The tax basis that should be recorded for the color copier is $35,000.
- There should not be any amount reflected as tax basis subject to depreciation until the copier has been paid for in full.

We know we can eliminate the last answer choice because the copier is a depreciable asset regardless of whether or not it has been paid for in full.

Upon reviewing the documents provided, the correct answer choice is clearly the following:
- ***The tax basis that should be recorded for the color copier is $35,000.***

Here is why:

Sales tax is capitalized as part of the purchase price. Therefore, the cost of the copier is the purchase price plus sales tax ($32,407 + $2,593). Although financed purchases are normally recorded at the net present value, this special arraignment with the seller does not bear interest and no interest is required to be imputed for tax purposes. Principal only payments of $1,000 will be paid monthly for 24 months.

The journal entry to record purchase of the copier is as follows:

Copier	$35,000	
Cash		$11,000
Note Payable-Elmer		$24,000

3. The next subquestion concerns the tax basis of manufacturing equipment purchased during the year. The default answer is "The amount to be capitalized for the manufacturing equipment is $209,100." The choices are:

- [Original text] The amount to be capitalized for the manufacturing equipment is $209,100.
- The amount to be capitalized for the manufacturing equipment is $205,600.

- The amount to be capitalized for the manufacturing equipment is $202,500.
- The amount to be capitalized for the manufacturing equipment is $201,300.
- The amount to be capitalized for the manufacturing equipment is $193,300.
- The amount to be capitalized for the manufacturing equipment is $189,000.

In this case, we cannot eliminate any answer choices without first reviewing the documents. We can, however, quickly eliminate the irrelevant documents concerning the real estate, copier, and van transactions. Surprisingly, we can also eliminate the Tax Depreciation Worksheet after noticing that the equipment was booked for $180,000 on this worksheet.

On the invoice for purchase of manufacturing equipment, the grand total is $209,100. The $180,000 figure from the Tax Depreciation Worksheet is the cost of the machinery alone, the first line item on the invoice. Neither of these choices is correct because all costs necessary to purchase the asset and prepare it for its intended use must be capitalized, which includes sales tax, all transit costs, and installation costs. The extended warranty of $3,500 was not a cost necessary to acquire the asset and prepare it for its intended use. The correct answer, then, is:

- ***The amount to be capitalized for the manufacturing equipment is $205,600.***

This amount is the sum of the $180,000 price, $4,300 installation cost, $9,200 shipping costs, $3,100 transit insurance, and $9,000 sales tax. The cost of the 2-year extended warranty will be prorated over 24 months and treated as expense in the relevant period.

4. The final subquestion concerns the tax basis of a delivery van purchased as part of a trade-in transaction during the year. The default answer is "This tax basis is correct," referring to a tax basis of $23,300. The choices are:

- [Original text] This tax basis is correct.
- The delivery van should have a tax basis of $39,212.
- The delivery van should have a tax basis of $32,300.
- The delivery van should have a tax basis of $31,510.
- The delivery van should have a tax basis of $30,400.
- The delivery van should have a tax basis of $25,388.

Studying the Tax Depreciation Worksheet, we see that an old van with an original basis of $18,125 and accumulated depreciation of $16,037 was exchanged for a new van given a basis on the worksheet of $23,300. Turning to the delivery van invoice, we see the bottom-line amount was the $23,300 recorded in the depreciation worksheet. Should that be the basis?

Reconstructing the summarizing journal entry for acquiring the new van and taking the old van off the books should help us reach the answer:

New Van	Basis in new asset acquired?	
Accumulated Depreciation	16,037	
Old Van		18,125
Cash		23,300

The balancing journal entry for the new asset is $25,388. Another way to calculate the answer is to reduce the fair market value (FMV) of the new asset acquired, $32,300 as per the invoice, by the deferred gain of $6,912 that is part of this Section 1031 like-kind exchange. The deferred gain is the difference between the $32,300 in like-kind property received and the $25,388 in total consideration given up, which consists of the old van with an adjusted basis of $2,088 ($18,125 cost - $16,037 accumulated depreciation) plus the $23,300 in cash paid.

The correct answer, then, is:
The delivery van should have a tax basis of $25,388.